D0206123

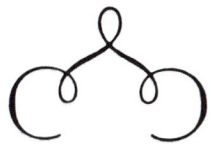

READINGS IN THE PHILOSOPHY OF RELIGION

An Analytic Approach

Second Edition

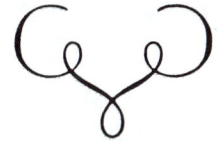

Edited by

BARUCH A. BRODY
Rice University
and
Baylor College of Medicine

Prentice Hall, Englewood Cliffs, New Jersey 07632

Library of Congress Cataloging-in-Publication Data

Readings in the philosophy of religion : an analytic approach / edited by Baruch A. Brody. —
  2nd ed.
      p.   cm.
  Includes bibliographical references.
  ISBN 0-13-756206-3
      1. Religion—Philosophy.   I. Brody, Baruch A.
  BL51.B758   1992   91-12474
  200'.1—dc200   CIP

Editorial/production supervision, interior design,
  and page makeup: *June Sanns*
Acquisitions editor: *Ted L. Bolen*
Editorial assistant: *Diane Schaible*
Copy editor: *Sally Ann Bailey*
Cover designer: *Marianne Frasco*
Prepress buyer: *Herb Klein*
Manufacturing buyer: *Patrice Fraccio*

© 1992, 1974 by Prentice-Hall, Inc.
A Simon & Schuster Company
Englewood Cliffs, New Jersey 07632

Printed in the United States of America

10 9 8 7 6 5 4 3 2 1

ISBN 0-13-756206-3

PRENTICE-HALL INTERNATIONAL (UK) LIMITED, *London*
PRENTICE-HALL OF AUSTRALIA PTY. LIMITED, *Sydney*
PRENTICE-HALL CANADA INC., *Toronto*
PRENTICE-HALL HISPANOAMERICANA, S.A., *Mexico*
PRENTICE-HALL OF INDIA PRIVATE LIMITED, *New Delhi*
PRENTICE-HALL OF JAPAN, INC., *Tokyo*
SIMON & SCHUSTER ASIA PTE. LTD., *Singapore*
EDITORA PRENTICE-HALL DO BRASIL LTDA., *Rio de Janeiro*

TO MY IN-LAWS

In Appreciation for
Twenty-five Years of Love

CONTENTS

THE ONTOLOGICAL ARGUMENT

THE COSMOLOGICAL ARGUMENT

THE TELEOLOGICAL ARGUMENT

MIRACLES AND MYSTICAL EXPERIENCE

THE PROBLEM OF EVIL

PART FOUR *RELIGIOUS MORALITY AND THE MEANING OF LIFE* **471**

PART INTRODUCTION AND BIBLIOGRAPHICAL NOTES **472**

RELIGIOUS MORALITY

DEATH, SURVIVAL, AND THE MEANING OF LIFE

PREFACE
TO THE SECOND EDITION

It is now more than fifteen years since the appearance of the first edition of this anthology. Its adoption at a wide variety of universities and colleges is testimony both to the revival of interest in the philosophy of religion done in an analytical fashion and to the felt need by many for an anthology collecting such material. The appearance of other anthologies with a similar approach is further evidence of these trends.

A great deal of important work has been done in recent years. A lot of this new work appears in this second edition. Authors such as Robert Adams, William Alston, Alvin Plantinga, and R. G. Swinburne (and their colleagues and students) have done much important work, and this edition contains many of their seminal essays. The approach is the same as in the first edition, but the level of sophistication is much higher as the current discussion has deepened our understanding of many traditional issues.

This edition incorporates most of the topics of the first edition, but there has been some reorganization of the material. This edition contains significantly increased attention to the issue of faith and reason because of the extensive recent literature devoted to it. The section on prayer and ritual has been eliminated because, despite their importance in religious life, they have not attracted sufficient philosophical attention. Perhaps a third edition will reflect an improvement in the literature on these topics. Finally, the issue of verificationism, which still exercised some influence on the first edition, is now completely and thankfully dropped.

Let me express my appreciation not only to the many faculty members who have sent me their reactions to the first edition in light of their experience with it in the classroom but also to those who contributed to the review of the current edition: Judith Barad, Indiana State University; Felmon John Davis, State University of New York, Albany; John Donnelly, University of San Diego; Richard M. Gale, University of Pittsburgh; Thomas V. Morris, University of Notre Dame; and Wesley Morriston, University of Colorado, Boulder. I would certainly appreciate receiving such comments from users of this edition as well. Finally, let me express special appreciation to Sarah V. Brakman for her special help in all aspects of the preparation of this edition.

PREFACE
TO THE FIRST EDITION

Traditionally, the philosophy of religion has been one of the central areas of philosophy. This is not surprizing. For throughout history people turned to the study of philosophy with the hope that it would shed light upon some fundamental problems encountered in connection with their religious beliefs. In the twentieth century, however, philosophy of religion lost its traditional centrality within Anglo-American philosophy.

What brought about this change? I think it can be attributed to several factors: (1) For centuries, a principal issue in traditional religious philosophy had been whether one could prove the truth or falsity of a variety of fundamental doctrines (the existence of God, the immortality of the soul, etc.). During the forties and fifties, the verifiability theory of meaning convinced many philosophers that such religious claims are cognitively meaningless and therefore neither true or false. There remained, of course, conjectures as to what type of meaning these religious statements do have, but this question did not arouse much interest. And even when the verifiability theory of meaning was abandoned, many continued to neglect the philosophy of religion. (2) Another factor is that very few working philosophers in the analytic school have had a personal religious commitment. Consequently, with the exception of those fervent nonbelievers who were concerned with proselytizing for their cause (the most notable example being Bertrand Russell), the philosophy of religion was neglected because analytical philosophers simply took no interest in religious matters.

All of this has changed in recent years. With the complete rejection of verificationism, the question of the truth and falsity of religious doctrines is now once more recognized as a legitimate question, and there is a growing number of analytical philosophers who have a real personal interest in theological issues and would like to apply to those issues the methods of the analytic school. Consequently, some very fine work in the philosophy of religion has been published in recent years.

As one scans this literature, two things emerge very clearly. The first is that there is a real affinity between recent analytic work and much of the writings of medieval theologians and rationalist and empiricist philosophers of the seventeenth and eighteenth centuries: both groups are keenly concerned with the careful analysis of the meaning and implications of religious doctrines, and with the question of whether or not different doctrines are consistent with each other; both groups are very much involved in the careful elaboration and critical analysis of proofs of the truth and falsity of religious doctrines. The second is that it is impossible to do good work in the philosophy of religion without taking into account the important advances of recent years in metaphysical analysis, in the philosophy of logic, and in philosophical psychology. Issues in the philosophy of religion tend to be intertwined with issues in all of these areas.

There have been several recent attempts to collect the new analytic material in the philosophy of religion, but they all suffer from two main defects that make them unsuitable for classroom use. First, they fail to cover systematically the major issues in the philosophy of religion, but offer merely a series of unrelated, unintegrated articles. Second, they fail to include some of the traditional writings that serve as background for the recent analytic discussions. This anthology, by the careful organization of materials and by the juxtaposition of classical and contemporary discussions, tries to show the student the continuity of philosophical thinking that he may fail to perceive in other texts.

PART ONE

*FAITH
AND
REASON*

PART INTRODUCTION AND BIBLIOGRAPHICAL NOTES

Ever since religious faith has confronted philosophical reasoning, believers and nonbelievers have struggled with the question of what ought to be the relation between them. Reactions have ranged from total indifference toward one or the other (toward faith by some nonbelievers and toward reason by some believers) to a desire to bring the two into some constructive relation with each other. This first part of our book will explore these varying reactions.

One classical answer is presented in the first of our selections, drawn from the writings of St. Thomas Aquinas. Aquinas lived in a world of Christian believers who were divided on their attitude toward the use of reason to study questions about God. His own view was that there were two sorts of truths about God, those that are discoverable by human reason and those that are not. He goes on to explain why it was important for God to reveal to those of faith both sets of truths, even though the former are also discoverable by reason, and why it is reasonable to believe in both sets of truths, even though only the former are discoverable by reason.

At first glance, it would seem that a very similar approach was adopted by John Locke many centuries later in another classical discussion of this issue. He too distinguishes religious beliefs that are discoverable by reason and religious beliefs that are not. But his attitude toward the former is very different than Aquinas's attitude toward them. For Locke, faith and revelation have nothing to contribute when reason has spoken clearly on a given issue, since we are always more certain of the reasoned conclusion than of any supposition that a true revelation has said otherwise. Aquinas, for reasons he explains, would surely disagree on this point.

This difference between Aquinas and Locke, while of great significance, is overshadowed by their joint belief that the fundamental claims of western religion about God are establishable by reasoned proofs. We shall be examining the validity of these proofs in the next part of this book, but as a matter of historical fact, those proofs on which Aquinas and Locke relied have been viewed with much greater skepticism by other authors, especially in the last two centuries. This has transformed the whole discussion, since the issue for many has now become the question of whether it is rational to believe in God when reason can no longer establish his existence.

Already in the seventeenth century, Pascal had tried to argue that it was still reasonable to hold to religious faith because, if you do anything else, you run the risk of losing everything if you are wrong. The third selection, by R. G. Swinburne, critically evaluates Pascal's approach, arguing that the approach is appropriate but that Pascal's conclusion does not follow because (1) Pascal failed to take into account the possibility that one might lose eternal life by holding the wrong religious beliefs and (2) Pascal failed to consider other ways of evaluating the consequences.

At the end of his article, Professor Swinburne raises the issue of the morality of holding religious beliefs without adequate evidence. This theme played a central role in the nineteenth-century debate between William Clifford and William James about the morality of holding religious beliefs if reasoned arguments could not prove whether or not God existed. Clifford argued that holding such beliefs (either in the existence or nonexistence of God) is immoral because it contributes to credulity, the great enemy of human progress, and that only agnosticism is appropriate in that setting. James claimed that there are at least some circumstances (circumstances in which we face what he called living, forced, and momentous options) in which we are entitled to form theistic or atheistic beliefs even though adequate evidence for such beliefs is not available.

The twentieth century has seen major attempts to defend theistic faith against the challenge of the lack of reasoned proofs for the existence of God. One of these derives from Kierkegaard's arguments against objective reasoning in religion, one derives from Wittgenstein's views about groundless beliefs and ways of life, and one derives from objections of reformed theologians to natural theology. The last three selections in this part of the book present and/or evaluate these challenges.

In his essay, Robert Adams distinguishes and critically evaluates three arguments (which he attributes to Søren Kierkegaard) against the desirability of reasoning objectively in support of religious faith. Professor Adams rejects one of the arguments. He feels that the other two might indeed work if one accepts certain conceptions of religiousness, but that those conceptions of religiousness, although appealing, are not ones which he is prepared to accept. In a tantalizing footnote at the end of the paper, he raises the possibility that these arguments might be modified to employ less extreme conceptions of religiousness.

Kierkegaard's point of departure, according to Adams, is his conception of the nature of religious faith. Wittengstein's point of departure, according to Norman Malcolm, is his reflections on the need for framework principles which form a system in which questions of justification and proof can be raised. Framework principles cannot themselves be justified, and their acceptance constitutes growing into a way of living, thinking, and talking. Malcolm suggests that religion should be viewed as one such form of life, that belief in God is part of its framework principles, and that attempts to justify that belief rationally are therefore inappropriate.

In his essay, Alvin Plantinga calls attention to the fact that ever since John Calvin, Reformed theologians have argued against the appropriateness of natural theology as an attempt to prove the existence of God. Plantinga interprets them to be asserting that rational belief systems should include as part of their basic beliefs a belief in God which is just as properly basic as self-evident beliefs or beliefs which are evident to the senses. In this way, says Plantinga, the Reformed theologian can still see his belief in the existence of God as a belief supported by reason.

There are naturally many issues raised by these last essays. They call upon us to assess the relation between the desire that certain beliefs are true and the reasonableness of believing them to be true and to reexamine our understanding of the very nature of reason. There is no doubt, however, that they have greatly added to the discussion of the relation between reason and belief.

Students interested in pursuing these issues further will find a great deal of literature devoted to these questions. Anthony Kenny's *Faith and Reason* (Columbia University Press, 1983) and Richard Swinburne's *Faith and Reason* (Oxford University Press, 1981) are good discussions of the classical and contemporary issues, while the first part of Robert Audi and William Wainright's *Rationality, Religious Belief, and Moral Commitment* (Cornell University Press, 1986) and the whole of Alvin Plantinga and Nicholas Wolterstorff's *Faith and Rationality* (University of Notre Dame Press, 1983) are devoted to contributions to the contemporary debate. Those books, and the material cited in them, will enable students to continue their study of these important issues.

ST. THOMAS AQUINAS

Different Ways of Knowing About God

CHAPTER III. ON THE WAY IN WHICH DIVINE TRUTH IS TO BE MADE KNOWN

(1) The way of making truth known is not always the same, and, as the Philosopher has very well said, "it belongs to an educated man to seek such certitude in each thing as the nature of that thing allows."[1] The remark is also introduced by Boethius.[2] But, since such is the case, we must first show what way is open to us in order that we may make known the truth which is our object.

(2) There is a twofold mode of truth in what we profess about God. Some truths about God exceed all the ability of the human reason. Such is the truth that God is triune. But there are some truths which the natural reason also is able to reach. Such are that God exists, that He is one, and the like. In fact, such truths about God have been proved demonstratively by the philosophers, guided by the light of the natural reason.

(3) That there are certain truths about God that totally surpass man's ability appears with the greatest evidence. Since, indeed, the principle of all knowledge that the reason perceives about some thing is the understanding of the very substance of that being (for according to Aristotle "what a thing is" is the principle of demonstration),[3] it is necessary that the way in which we understand the substance of a thing determines the way in which we know what belongs to it. Hence, if the human intellect comprehends the substance of some thing, for example, that of a stone or of a triangle, no intelligible characteristic belonging to that thing surpasses the grasp of the human reason. But this does not happen to us in the case of God. For the human intellect is not able to reach a comprehension of the divine substance through its natural power. For, according to its manner of knowing in the present life, the intellect depends on the senses for the origin of knowledge;

[1]Aristotle, *Nicomachean Ethics*, I, 3 (1094b 24).

[2]Boethius, *De Trinitate*, II, (PL, 64, col. 1250).

[3]Aristotle, *Posterior Analytics*, II, 3 (90b 31).

and so those things that do not fall under the senses cannot be grasped by the human intellect except in so far as the knowledge of them is gathered from sensible things. Now, sensible things cannot lead the human intellect to the point of seeing in them the nature of the divine substance; for sensible things are effects that fall short of the power of their cause. Yet, beginning with sensible things, our intellect is led to the point of knowing about God that He exists, and other such characteristics that must be attributed to the First Principle. There are, consequently, some intelligible truths about God that are open to the human reason; but there are others that absolutely surpass its power.

(4) We may easily see the same point from the gradation of intellects. Consider the case of two persons of whom one has a more penetrating grasp of a thing by his intellect than does the other. He who has the superior intellect understands many things that the other cannot grasp at all. Such is the case with a very simple person who cannot at all grasp the subtle speculations of philosophy. But the intellect of an angel surpasses the human intellect much more than the intellect of the greatest philosopher surpasses the intellect of the most uncultivated simple person; for the distance between the best philosopher and a simple person is contained within the limits of the human species, which the angelic intellect surpasses. For the angel knows God on the basis of a more noble effect than does man; and this by as much as the substance of an angel, through which the angel in his natural knowledge is led to the knowledge of God, is nobler than sensible things and even than the soul itself, through which the human intellect mounts to the knowledge of God. The divine intellect surpasses the angelic intellect much more than the angelic surpasses the human. For the divine intellect is in its capacity equal to its substance, and therefore it understands fully what it is, including all its intelligible attributes. But by his natural knowledge the angel does not know what God is, since the substance itself of the angel, through which he is led to the knowledge of God, is an effect that is not equal to the power of its cause. Hence, the angel is not able, by means of his natural knowledge, to grasp all the things that God understands in Himself; nor is the human reason sufficient to grasp all the things that the angel understands through his own natural power. Just as, therefore, it would be the height of folly for a simple person to assert that what a philosopher proposes is false on the ground that he himself cannot understand it, so (and even more so) it is the acme of stupidity for a man to suspect as false what is divinely revealed through the ministry of the angels simply because it cannot be investigated by reason.

(5) The same thing, moreover, appears quite clearly from the defect that we experience every day in our knowledge of things. We do not know a great many of the properties of sensible things, and in most cases we are not able to discover fully the natures of those properties that we apprehend by the sense. Much more is it the case, therefore, that the human reason is not equal to the task of investigating all the intelligible characteristics of that most excellent substance.

(6) The remark of Aristotle likewise agrees with this conclusion. He says that "our intellect is related to the prime beings, which are most evident in their nature, as the eye of an owl is related to the sun."[4]

(7) Sacred Scripture also gives testimony to this truth. We read in Job: "Peradventure thou wilt comprehend the steps of God, and wilt find out the Almighty perfectly?" (11:7). And again: "Behold, God is great, exceeding our knowledge" (Job 36:26). And St. Paul: "We know in part" (I Cor. 13:9).

(8) We should not, therefore, immediately reject as false, following the opinion of the Manicheans and many unbelievers, everything that is said about God even though it cannot be investigated by reason.

CHAPTER IV. THAT THE TRUTH ABOUT GOD TO WHICH THE NATURAL REASON REACHES IS FITTINGLY PROPOSED TO MEN FOR BELIEF

(1) Since, therefore, there exists a twofold truth concerning the divine being, one to which the inquiry of the reason can reach, the other which surpasses the whole ability of the human reason, it is fitting that both of these truths be proposed to man divinely for belief. This point must first be shown concerning the truth that is open to the inquiry of the reason; otherwise, it might perhaps seem to someone that, since such a truth can be known by the reason, it was uselessly given to men through a supernatural inspiration as an object of belief.

(2) Yet, if this truth were left solely as a matter of inquiry for the human reason, three awkward consequences would follow.

(3) The first is that few men would possess the knowledge of God. For there are three reasons why most men are cut off from the fruit of diligent inquiry which is the discovery of truth. Some do not have the physical disposition for such work. As a result, there are many who are naturally not fitted to pursue knowledge; and so, however much they tried, they would be unable to reach the highest level of human knowledge which consists in knowing God. Others are cut off from pursuing this truth by the necessities imposed upon them by their daily lives. For some men must devote themselves to taking care of temporal matters. Such men would not be able to give so much time to the leisure of contemplative inquiry as to reach the highest peak at which human investigation can arrive, namely, the knowledge of God. Finally, there are some who are cut off by indolence. In order to know the things that the reason can investigate concerning God, a knowledge of many things must already be possessed. For almost all of philosophy is directed towards the knowledge of God, and that is why metaphysics, which deals with divine things, is the last part of philosophy to be learned. This means that we are able to arrive at the inquiry concerning the aforementioned truth only on the basis of a great deal of labor spent in study.

---

[4]Aristotle, *Metaphysics*, Ia, 1 (993b 9).

Now, those who wish to undergo such a labor for the mere love of knowledge are few, even though God has inserted into the minds of men a natural appetite for knowledge.

(4) The second awkward effect is that those who would come to discover the above mentioned truth would barely reach it after a great deal of time. The reasons are several. There is the profundity of this truth, which the human intellect is made capable of grasping by natural inquiry only after a long training. Then, there are many things that must be presupposed, as we have said. There is also the fact that, in youth, when the soul is swayed by the various movements of the passions, it is not in a suitable state for the knowledge of such lofty truth. On the contrary, "one becomes wise and knowing in repose," as it is said in the *Physics*.[5] The result is this. If the only way open to us for the knowledge of God were solely that of the reason, the human race would remain in the blackest shadows of ignorance. For then the knowledge of God, which especially renders men perfect and good, would come to be possessed only by a few, and these few would require a great deal of time in order to reach it.

(5) The third awkward effect is this. The investigation of the human reason for the most part has falsity present within it, and this is due partly to the weakness of our intellect in judgment, and partly to the admixture of images. The result is that many, remaining ignorant of the power of demonstration, would hold in doubt those things that have been most truly demonstrated. This would be particularly the case since they see that, among those who are reputed to be wise men, each one teaches his own brand of doctrine. Furthermore, with the many truths that are demonstrated, there sometimes is mingled something that is false, which is not demonstrated but rather asserted on the basis of some probable or sophistical argument, which yet has the credit of being a demonstration. That is why it was necessary that the unshakeable certitude and pure truth concerning divine things should be presented to men by way of faith.[6]

(6) Beneficially, therefore, did the divine Mercy provide that it should instruct us to hold by faith even those truths that the human reason is able to investigate. In this way, all men would easily be able to have a share in the knowledge of God, and this without uncertainty and error.

(7) Hence it is written: "Henceforward you walk not as also the Gentiles walk in the vanity of their mind, having their understanding darkened" (Eph. 4:17–18). And again: "All thy children shall be taught of the Lord" (Isa. 54:13).

---

[5] Aristotle, *Physics*, VII, 3 (247b 9).

[6] Although St. Thomas does not name Maimonides or his *Guide for the Perplexed* (*Dux neutrorum*), there are evident points of contact between the Catholic and the Jewish theologian. On the reasons for revelation given here, on our knowledge of God, on creation and the eternity of the world, and on Aristotelianism in general, St. Thomas has Maimonides in mind both to agree and to disagree with him. By way of background for SCG, I, the reader can usefully consult the references to Maimonides in E. Gilson, *History of Christian Philosophy in the Middle Ages* (New York, 1955), pp. 649–651.

CHAPTER V. THAT THE TRUTHS THE HUMAN REASON IS NOT ABLE TO INVESTIGATE ARE FITTINGLY PROPOSED TO MEN FOR BELIEF

(1) Now, perhaps some will think that men should not be asked to believe what the reason is not adequate to investigate, since the divine Wisdom provides in the case of each thing according to the mode of its nature. We must therefore prove that it is necessary for man to receive from God as objects of belief even those truths that are above the human reason.

(2) No one tends with desire and zeal towards something that is not already known to him. But, as we shall examine later on in this work, men are ordained by the divine Providence towards a higher good than human fragility can experience in the present life.[7] That is why it was necessary for the human mind to be called to something higher than the human reason here and now can reach, so that it would thus learn to desire something and with zeal tend towards something that surpasses the whole state of the present life. This belongs especially to the Christian religion, which in a unique way promises spiritual and eternal goods. And so there are many things proposed to men in it that transcend human sense. The Old Law, on the other hand, whose promises were of a temporal character, contained very few proposals that transcended the inquiry of the human reason. Following this same direction, the philosophers themselves, in order that they might lead men from the pleasure of sensible things to virtue, were concerned to show that there were in existence other goods of a higher nature than these things of sense, and that those who gave themselves to the active or contemplative virtues would find much sweeter enjoyment in the taste of these higher goods.

(3) It is also necessary that such truth be proposed to men for belief so that they may have a truer knowledge of God. For then only do we know God truly when we believe Him to be above everything that it is possible for man to think about Him; for, as we have shown,[8] the divine substance surpasses the natural knowledge of which man is capable. Hence, by the fact that some things about God are proposed to man that surpass his reason, there is strengthened in man the view that God is something above what he can think.

(4) Another benefit that comes from the revelation to men of truths that exceed the reason is the curbing of presumption, which is the mother of error. For there are some who have such a presumptuous opinion of their own ability that they deem themselves able to measure the nature of everything; I mean to say that, in their estimation, everything is true that seems to them so, and everything is false that does not. So that the human mind, therefore, might be freed from this presumption and come to a humble inquiry after

---

[7]SCG, III, ch. 48.

[8]See above, ch. 3.

truth, it was necessary that some things should be proposed to man by God that would completely surpass his intellect.

(5) A still further benefit may also be seen in what Aristotle says in the *Ethics*.[9] There was a certain Simonides who exhorted people to put aside the knowledge of divine things and to apply their talents to human occupations. He said that "he who is a man should know human things, and he who is mortal, things that are mortal." Against Simonides Aristotle says that "man should draw himself towards what is immortal and divine as much as he can." And so he says in the *De animalibus* that, although what we know of the higher substances is very little, yet that little is loved and desired more than all the knowledge that we have about less noble substances.[10] He also says in the *De caelo et mundo* that when questions about the heavenly bodies can be given even a modest and merely plausible solution, he who hears this experiences intense joy.[11] From all these considerations it is clear that even the most imperfect knowledge about the most noble realities brings the greatest perfection to the soul. Therefore, although the human reason cannot grasp fully the truths that are above it, yet, if it somehow holds these truths at least by faith, it acquires great perfection for itself.

(6) Therefore it is written: "For many things are shown to thee above the understanding of men" (Ecclus. 3:25). Again, "So the things that are of God no man knoweth but the Spirit of God. But to us God hath revealed them by His Spirit" (I Cor. 2:11, 10).

CHAPTER VI. THAT TO GIVE ASSENT TO THE TRUTHS OF FAITH IS NOT FOOLISHNESS EVEN THOUGH THEY ARE ABOVE REASON

(1) Those who place their faith in this truth, however, "for which the human reason offers no experimental evidence,"[12] do not believe foolishly, as though "following artificial fables" (II Peter 1:16). For these "secrets of divine Wisdom" (Job 11:6) the divine Wisdom itself, which knows all things to the full, has deigned to reveal to men. It reveals its own presence, as well as the truth of its teaching and inspiration, by fitting arguments; and in order to confirm those truths that exceed natural knowledge, it gives visible manifestation to works that surpass the ability of all nature. Thus, there are the wonderful cures of illnesses, there is the raising of the dead, and the wonderful immutation in the heavenly bodies; and what is more wonderful, there is the

---

[9] Aristotle, *Nicomachean Ethics*, X, 7 (1177b 31).

[10] Aristotle, *De partibus animalium*, I, 5 (644b 32).

[11] Aristotle, *De caelo et mundo*, II, 12 (291b 26).

[12] St. Gregory, *Homiliae in evangelia*, II, hom. 26, i (*PL*, 76, col. 1197).

inspiration given to human minds, so that simple and untutored persons, filled with the gift of the Holy Spirit, come to possess instantaneously the highest wisdom and the readiest eloquence. When these arguments were examined, through the efficacy of the above-mentioned proof, and not the violent assault of arms or the promise of pleasures, and (what is most wonderful of all) in the midst of the tyranny of the persecutors, an innumerable throng of people, both simple and most learned, flocked to the Christian faith. In this faith there are truths preached that surpass every human intellect; the pleasures of the flesh are curbed; it is taught that the things of the world should be spurned. Now, for the minds of mortal men to assent to these things is the greatest of miracles, just as it is a manifest work of divine inspiration that, spurning visible things, men should seek only what is invisible. Now, that this has happened neither without preparation nor by chance, but as a result of the disposition of God, is clear from the fact that through many pronouncements of the ancient prophets God had foretold that He would do this. The books of these prophets are held in veneration among us Christians, since they give witness to our faith.

(2) The manner of this confirmation is touched on by St. Paul: "Which," that is, human salvation, "having begun to be declared by the Lord, was confirmed unto us by them that hear Him: God also bearing them witness of signs, and wonders, and divers miracles, and distributions of the Holy Ghost" (Heb. 2:3–4).

(3) This wonderful conversion of the world to the Christian faith is the clearest witness of the signs given in the past; so that it is not necessary that they should be further repeated, since they appear most clearly in their effect. For it would be truly more wonderful than all signs if the world had been led by simple and humble men to believe such lofty truths, to accomplish such difficult actions, and to have such high hopes. Yet it is also a fact that, even in our own time, God does not cease to work miracles through His saints for the confirmation of the faith.

(4) On the other hand, those who founded sects committed to erroneous doctrines proceeded in a way that is opposite to this. The point is clear in the case of Mohammed. He seduced the people by promises of carnal pleasure to which the concupiscence of the flesh goads us. His teaching also contained precepts that were in conformity with his promises, and he gave free rein to carnal pleasure. In all this, as is not unexpected, he was obeyed by carnal men. As for proofs of the truth of his doctrine, he brought forward only such as could be grasped by the natural ability of anyone with a very modest wisdom. Indeed, the truths that he taught he mingled with many fables and with doctrines of the greatest falsity. He did not bring forth any signs produced in a supernatural way, which alone fittingly gives witness to divine inspiration; for a visible action that can be only divine reveals an invisibly inspired teacher of truth. On the contrary, Mohammed said that he was sent in the power of his arms—which are signs not lacking even to robbers and

tyrants. What is more, no wise men, men trained in things divine and human, believed in him from the beginning. Those who believed in him were brutal men and desert wanderers, utterly ignorant of all divine teaching, through whose numbers Mohammed forced others to become his followers by the violence of his arms. Nor do divine pronouncements on the part of preceding prophets offer him any witness. On the contrary, he perverts almost all the testimonies of the Old and New Testaments by making them into fabrications of his own, as can be seen by anyone who examines his law. It was, therefore, a shrewd decision on his part to forbid his followers to read the Old and New Testaments, lest these books convict him of falsity. It is thus clear that those who place any faith in his words believe foolishly.

JOHN LOCKE

Faith and Reason

1. It has been above shown, 1. That we are of necessity ignorant, and want knowledge of all sorts, where we want ideas. 2. That we are ignorant, and want rational knowledge, where we want proofs. 3. That we want certain knowledge and certainty, as far as we want clear and determined specific ideas. 4. That we want probability to direct our assent in matters where we have neither knowledge of our own, nor testimony of other men, to bottom our reason upon.

From these things thus premised, I think we may come to lay down the measures and boundaries between faith and reason; the want whereof many possibly have been the cause, if not of great disorders, yet at least of great disputes, and perhaps mistakes in the world. For till it be resolved how far we are to be guided by reason, and how far by faith, we shall in vain dispute, and endeavour to convince one another in matters of religion.

2. I find every sect, as far as reason will help them, make use of it gladly: and where it fails them they cry out, it is matter of faith, and above reason. And I do not see how they can argue with any one, or ever convince a gainsayer who makes use of the same plea, without setting down strict boundaries between faith and reason; which ought to be the first point established in all questions where faith has any thing to do.

Reason therefore here, as contradistinguished to faith, I take to be the discovery of the certainty or probability of such propositions or truths, which the mind arrives at by deduction made from such ideas which it has got by the use of its natural faculties, viz. by sensation or reflection.

From John Locke, *An Essay Concerning Understanding*, Bk. IV, Ch. XVIII.

Faith, on the other side, is the assent to any proposition, not thus made out by the deductions of reason; but upon the credit of the proposer, as coming from God, in some extraordinary way of communication. This way of discovering truths to men we call revelation.

3. First then I say, that no man inspired by God can by any revelation communicate to others any new simple ideas, which they had not before from sensation or reflection. For whatsoever impressions he himself may have from the immediate hand of God, this revelation, if it be of new simple ideas, cannot be conveyed to another, either by words or any other signs. Because words, by their immediate operation on us, cause no other ideas but of their natural sounds; and it is by the custom of using them for signs, that they excite and revive in our minds latent ideas; but yet only such ideas as were there before. For words seen or heard recall to our thoughts those ideas only which to us they have been wont to be signs of; but cannot introduce any perfectly new, and formerly unknown simple ideas. The same holds in all other signs, which cannot signify to us things of which we have before never had any idea at all.

Thus whatever things were discovered to St. Paul, when he was rapt up into the third heaven, whatever new ideas his mind there received, all the description he can make to others of that place is only this, that there are such things, "as eye hath not seen, nor ear heard, nor hath it entered into the heart of man to conceive." And supposing God should discover to any one, supernaturally, a species of creatures inhabiting, for example, Jupiter or Saturn, (for that it is possible there may be such nobody can deny) which had six senses; and imprint on his mind the ideas conveyed to theirs by that sixth sense; he could no more, by words, produce in the minds of other men those ideas, imprinted by that sixth sense, than one of us could convey the idea of any colour by the sounds of words into a man, who, having the other four senses perfect, had always totally wanted the fifth of seeing. For our simple ideas then, which are the foundation and sole matter of all our notions and knowledge, we must depend wholly on our reason, I mean our natural faculties; and can by no means receive them, or any of them, from traditional revelation; I say, traditional revelation, in distinction to original revelation. By the one, I mean that first impression, which is made immediately by God, on the mind of any man, to which we cannot set any bounds; and by the other, those impressions delivered over to others in words, and the ordinary ways of conveying our conceptions one to another.

4. Secondly, I say, that the same truths may be discovered, and conveyed down from revelation, which are discoverable to us by reason, and by those ideas we naturally may have. So God might, by revelation, discover the truth of any proposition in Euclid; as well as men, by the natural use of their faculties, come to make the discovery themselves. In all things of this kind, there is little need or use of revelation, God having furnished us with natural and surer means to arrive at the knowledge of them. For whatsoever truth we come to the clear discovery of, from the knowledge and contemplation of

our own ideas, will always be certainer to us than those which are conveyed to us by traditional revelation. For the knowledge we have, that this revelation came at first from God, can never be so sure, as the knowledge we have from the clear and distinct perception of the agreement or disagreement of our own ideas; *v. g.* if it were revealed some ages since, that the three angles of a triangle were equal to two right ones, I might assent to the truth of that proposition, upon the credit of the tradition, that it was revealed; but that would never amount to so great a certainty as the knowledge of it, upon the comparing and measuring my own ideas of two right angles, and the three angles of a triangle. The like holds in matter of fact, knowable by our senses; *v. g.* the history of the deluge is conveyed to us by writings which had their original from revelation: and yet nobody, I think, will say he has as certain and clear a knowledge of the flood as Noah that saw it; or that he himself would have had, had he then been alive and seen it. For he has no greater assurance than that of his senses that it is writ in the book supposed writ by Moses inspired; but he has not so great an assurance that Moses writ that book as if he had seen Moses write it. So that the assurance of its being a revelation is less still than the assurance of his senses.

5. In propositions then, whose certainty is built upon the clear perception of the agreement or disagreement of our ideas, attained either by immediate intuition, as in self-evident propositions, or by evident deductions of reason in demonstrations, we need not the assistance of revelation, as necessary to gain our assent, and introduce them into our minds. Because the natural ways of knowledge could settle them there, or had done it already; which is the greatest assurance we can possibly have of any thing, unless where God immediately reveals it to us: and there too our assurance can be no greater than our knowledge is, that it is a revelation from God. But yet nothing, I think, can, under that title, shake or over-rule plain knowledge; or rationally prevail with any man to admit it for true, in a direct contradiction to the clear evidence of his own understanding. For since no evidence of our faculties, by which we receive such revelations, can exceed, if equal, the certainty of our intuitive knowledge, we can never receive for a truth any thing that is directly contrary to our clear and distinct knowledge: *v. g.* the ideas of one body, and one place, do so clearly agree, and the mind has so evident a perception of their agreement, that we can never assent to a proposition, that affirms the same body to be in two distant places at once, however it should pretend to the authority of a divine revelation: since the evidence, first, that we deceive not ourselves, in ascribing it to God; secondly, that we understand it right; can never be so great as the evidence of our own intuitive knowledge, whereby we discern it impossible for the same body to be in two places at once. And therefore no proposition can be received for divine revelation, or obtain the assent due to all such, if it be contradictory to our clear intuitive knowledge. Because this would be to subvert the principles and foundations of all knowledge, evidence, and assent whatsoever: and there would be left no difference between truth and falsehood, no

measures of credible and incredible in the world, if doubtful propositions shall take place before self-evident, and what we certainly know give way to what we may possibly be mistaken in. In propositions therefore contrary to the clear perception of the agreement or disagreement of any of our ideas, it will be in vain to urge them as matters of faith. They cannot move our assent, under that or any other title whatsoever. For faith can never convince us of any thing that contradicts our knowledge. Because though faith be founded on the testimony of God (who cannot lie) revealing any proposition to us; yet we cannot have an assurance of the truth of its being a divine revelation greater than our own knowledge: since the whole strength of the certainty depends upon our knowledge that God revealed it; which in this case, where the proposition supposed revealed contradicts our knowledge or reason, will always have this objection hanging to it, viz. that we cannot tell how to conceive that to come from God, the bountiful Author of our being, which, if received for true, must overturn all the principles and foundations of knowledge he has given us; render all our faculties useless; wholly destroy the most excellent part of his workmanship, our understandings; and put a man in a condition, wherein he will have less light, less conduct, than the beast that perisheth. For if the mind of man can never have a clearer (and perhaps not so clear) evidence of any thing to be a divine revelation, as it has of the principles of its own reason, it can never have a ground to quit the clear evidence of its reason, to give a place to a proposition, whose revelation has not a greater evidence than those principles have.

6. Thus far a man has use of reason, and ought to hearken to it, even in immediate and original revelation, where it is supposed to be made to himself: but to all those who pretend not to immediate revelation, but are required to pay obedience, and to receive the truths revealed to others, which by the tradition of writings, or word of mouth, are conveyed down to them; reason has a great deal more to do, and is that only which can induce us to receive them. For matter of faith being only divine revelation, and nothing else; faith, as we use the word, (called commonly divine faith) has to do with no propositions but those which are supposed to be divinely revealed. So that I do not see how those who make revelation alone the sole object of faith, can say, that it is a matter of faith, and not of reason, to believe that such or such a proposition, to be found in such or such a book, is of divine inspiration; unless it be revealed, that that proposition, or all in that book, was communicated by divine inspiration. Without such a revelation, the believing or not believing that proposition or book to be of divine authority can never be matter of faith, but matter of reason; and such as I must come to an assent to only by the use of my reason, which can never require or enable me to believe that which is contrary to itself: it being impossible for reason ever to procure any assent to that, which to itself appears unreasonable.

In all things, therefore, where we have clear evidence from our ideas, and those principles of knowledge I have above-mentioned, reason is the proper judge; and revelation, though it may in consenting with it confirm its dictates, yet cannot in such cases invalidate its decrees: nor can we be obliged, where we have the clear and evident sentence of reason, to quit it for the contrary opinion, under a pretence that it is matter of faith; which can have no authority against the plain and clear dictates of reason.

7. But, thirdly, there being many things, wherein we have very imperfect notions, or none at all; and other things, of whose parts, present, or future existence, by the natural use of our faculties, we can have no knowledge at all; these, as being beyond the discovery of our natural faculties, and above reason, are, when revealed, the proper matter of faith. Thus, that part of the angels rebelled against God, and thereby lost their first happy state; and that the dead shall rise, and live again: these, and the like, being beyond the discovery of reason, are purely matters of faith with which reason has directly nothing to do.

8. But since God in giving us the light of reason has not thereby tied up his own hands from affording us, when he thinks fit, the light of revelation in any of those matters wherein our natural faculties are able to give a probable determination; revelation, where God has been pleased to give it, must carry it against the probable conjectures of reason. Because the mind not being certain of the truth of that it does not evidently know, but only yielding to the probability that appears in it, is bound to give up its assent to such a testimony; which, it is satisfied, comes from one who cannot err; and will not deceive. But yet it still belongs to reason to judge of the truth of its being a revelation, and of the signification of the words wherein it is delivered. Indeed, if any thing shall be thought revelation which is contrary to the plain principles of reason, and the evident knowledge the mind has of its own clear and distinct ideas; there reason must be hearkened to, as to a matter within its province: since a man can never have so certain a knowledge, that a proposition, which contradicts the clear principles and evidence of his own knowledge, was divinely revealed, or that he understands the words rightly wherein it is delivered; as he has, that the contrary is true: and so is bound to consider and judge of it as a matter of reason, and not swallow it, without examination, as a matter of faith.

9. First, whatever proposition is revealed, of whose truth our mind, by its natural faculties and notions, cannot judge; that is purely matter of faith, and above reason.

Secondly, all propositions, whereof the mind, by the use of its natural faculties, can come to determine and judge from naturally acquired ideas, are matter of reason; with this difference still, that in those concerning which it has but an uncertain evidence, and so is persuaded of their truth only upon probable grounds, which still admit a possibility of the contrary to be true, without doing violence to the certain evidence of its own knowledge, and overturning the principles of its own reason; in such probable propositions, I say, an evident revelation ought to determine our assent even against probability. For where the principles of reason have not evidenced a proposition to be certainly true or false, there clear revelation, as another principle of truth, and ground of assent, may determine: and so it may be matter of faith, and be also above reason. Because reason, in that particular matter, being able to reach no higher than probability, faith gave the determination, where reason came short; and revelation discovered on which side the truth lay.

10. Thus far the dominion of faith reaches, and that without any violence or hindrance to reason; which is not injured or disturbed, but assisted and improved, by new discoveries of truth coming from the eternal fountain of all knowledge. Whatever God hath revealed, is certainly true; no doubt can be made of it. This is the proper object of faith; but whether it be a divine revelation or no, reason must judge; which can never permit the mind to reject a greater evidence to embrace what is less evident, nor allow it to entertain probability in opposition to knowledge and certainty. There can be no evidence that any traditional revelation is of divine original, in the words we receive it, and in the sense we understand it, so clear and so certain as that of the principles of reason: and therefore nothing that is contrary to, and inconsistent with, the clear and self-evident dictates of reason, has a right to be urged or assented to as a matter of faith, wherein reason hath nothing to do. Whatsoever is divine revelation ought to over-rule all our opinions, prejudices, and interest, and hath a right to be received with full assent. Such a submission as this, of our reason to faith, takes not away the landmarks of knowledge; this shakes not the foundations of reason, but leaves us that use of our faculties for which they were given us.

11. If the provinces of faith and reason are not kept distinct by these boundaries, there will, in matters of religion, be no room for reason at all; and those extravagant opinions and ceremonies that are to be found in the several religions of the world will not deserve to be blamed. For to this crying up of faith, in opposition to reason, we may, I think, in good measure ascribe those absurdities that fill almost all the religions which possess and divide mankind. For men having been principled with an opinion, that they must not consult reason in the things of religion, however apparently contradictory to common sense, and the very principles of all their knowledge, have let loose their fancies and natural superstition; and have been by them led into so strange opinions, and extravagant practices in religion, that a considerate man cannot but stand amazed at their follies, and judge them so far from being acceptable to the great and wise God, that he cannot avoid thinking them ridiculous, and offensive to a sober good man. So that, in effect, religion, which should most distinguish us from beasts, and ought most peculiarly to elevate us, as rational creatures, above brutes, is that wherein men often appear most irrational and more senseless than beasts themselves. "Credo, quia impossibile est"; I believe, because it is impossible, might in a good man pass for a sally of zeal; but would prove a very ill rule for men to choose their opinions or religion by.

R. G. SWINBURNE[1]

The Christian Wager

On what grounds will the rational man become a Christian? It is often assumed by many, especially non-Christians, that he will become a Christian if and only if he judges that the evidence available to him shows that it is more likely than not that the Christian theological system is true, that, in mathematical terms, on the evidence available to him, the probability of its truth is greater than half. It is the purpose of this paper to investigate whether or not this is a necessary and sufficient condition for the rational man to adopt Christianity.

The Christian is a man who believes a series of propositions (accepts the Christian theological system as basically correct) and tries to act in a certain way (sets himself to live the Christian life). Several recent theologians have claimed that the Christian is a man who enters into a personal relationship with Christ, not a man who accepts a series of propositions. Now indeed there is more to faith than mere belief-that ("Thou believest that God is one; Thou doest well: The devils also believe and shudder." James 2.19). But, as Professor Price painstakingly pointed out[2]—belief "in" always presupposes belief "that." Belief in God presupposes the belief that He exists. A man who believes in the God of the Christians must—of logical necessity—believe that a being with the defining properties of the God of the Christians exists. A man who claims to believe in God may indeed mean much more by his claim than that he believes that God exists; he will often mean that he puts his confidence in God to help in life's difficulties. But to put one's confidence in a person is something one does. Putting one's confidence in God is among the many actions to which the Christian is committed. The man who makes no effort to do any of these actions, to lead the Christian life, cannot be described as a Christian, whatever his beliefs. So the Christian is a man who believes a series of propositions and tries to act in a certain way.

From *Religious Studies* 4 (1969): 217–28. Reprinted with the permission of Cambridge University Press and Richard G. Swinburne.

[1]I am most grateful to G. Wallace and C. J. F. Williams for their helpful criticisms of an earlier version of this paper.

[2]H. H. Price, "Belief 'In' and Belief 'That'." *Religious Studies*, 1965, Vol. I, pp. 5–27.

The rational man is the man who pursues a policy if and only if he judges that the expected gain or mathematical expectation from it exceeds the expected gain (positive or negative) from not pursuing the policy. (If the expected gains from pursuing or not pursuing the policy are equal, the rational man may do either.) The expected gain from a policy is the sum of the values of each possible outcome of the policy, each multiplied by the probability of that outcome. The probability of some outcome O of a policy is the probability of the existence of that state of affairs under which O will be the outcome of the policy. The rational man will thus evaluate the probabilities of the existence of the different states and the value of each outcome, calculate the expected gain from pursuing or not pursuing a policy and act accordingly. Now let us suppose to start with, to simplify the picture, that the only considerations relevant are prudential ones. In that case the rational man is the prudent man, the man who pursues his long-term self-interest. Then the value of an outcome of a policy will be the amount of happiness which it brings to the agent. The rational man will seek to pursue those policies which will maximize his happiness.

Let me give a trivial example to illustrate the above points for those unfamiliar with the terms. A man is deciding between two policies—to bet £1 that Eclipse will win the Derby, or not to bet. There are two possible states of affairs—Eclipse will win, Eclipse will not win. After careful study of the form book, the man estimates the probability that Eclipse will win as 0.2 and so the probability that he will not win as 0.8. The odds offered by bookies are 6–1. Hence if the man bets there are two distinct outcomes—if Eclipse wins, he gains £6; if Eclipse loses, he loses £1. If the man does not bet, the two outcomes are identical—he neither gains nor loses. Now if the value of the outcome for him is measured by their monetary value, then the expected gain of betting is £6 × 0.2 – £1 × 0.8 = £0.4, and the expected gain of not betting is £0 × 0.2 – £0 × 0.8 = £0. Hence the man ought to bet. Of course the value of the outcomes may not be measured by their monetary value—the loss of the £1 may be as undesirable a loss as the win of £6 is a desirable gain. In that case we can represent the gain and loss both by one unit of value. In that case the expected gain of betting will be 1 × 0.2 – 1 × 0.8 = – 0.6, and the expected gain of not betting, as before, 0. Hence in that case the rational man will not bet.

Now it is well known that Pascal's claim that the rational man will become a Christian represented the rational man as choosing between the policies of becoming or not becoming a Christian in this kind of way.

> Let us then examine the point and say "God is," or "He is not." But to which side shall we incline? Reason can decide nothing here…. A game is being played…heads or tails will turn up. What will you wager?[3]

---

[3]B. Pascal, *Pensées*. No. 233.

If you bet on God and win, you win "an infinity of infinitely happy life";[4] whereas if you bet on God and lose, you lose a mere finite amount. If you bet on no God, or, which amounts to the same thing, refuse to bet openly, then, if you win, you gain a mere finite amount, mere temporary happiness, whereas if you lose, you obtain "an eternity of miseries."[5] Hence you ought to bet on God.

> Our proposition is of infinite force: when there is the finite to stake in a game where there are equal risks of gain and loss, and the infinite to gain. This is demonstrable; and if men are capable of any truths this is one.[6]

There is a lot wrong with Pascal's argument, and it is instructive to consider exactly what. I shall ignore, to begin with, the obvious theological objection that God does not consign to eternal Hell those who die non-Christians for no fault of their own. It will later appear that any mistake in describing the fate of non-Christians if the Christian theological system is true, does not necessarily upset the argument.

First, Pascal has stated the alternative states misleadingly. If the alternatives are meant to be "there is a Christian God" and "there is no after-life," then Pascal has ignored other possible states of affairs—e.g. "There is a god who consigns Christians to eternal Hell and non-Christians to eternal Heaven."[7] Alternatively, Pascal may have intended his alternative states to be simply "There is a Christian God" and "There is not a Christian God." But in that case it is unclear what are the outcomes and so the gains and losses on the second alternative of the two policies— Heaven remains a possible outcome for Christian or non-Christian even on this alternative.

Now clearly we can represent the alternative states as two or many or infinite. Yet perhaps the most useful way to represent them is threefold:

(A)   The God of the Christian exists.
(B)   There is no after-life.
(C)   There is an after-life but no Christian God.

The outcomes of the two alternative policies, becoming or not becoming Christian, are then as Pascal stated them for alternatives *A* and *B*; but there are a variety of possible outcomes under the third alternative, and we cannot

---

[4]*Ibid., loc. cit.*

[5]*Ibid.,* No. 195.

[6]B. Pascal, *Pensées*, No. 233.

[7]This point has been well made by (e.g.) Antony Flew. See his *God and Philosophy* (London, 1966), 9.9 *et seq.*

say much definite about them. The outcomes under the alternative policies, however we evaluate them numerically, will be as follows:

		A	B	C
(1)	Becoming Christian	Christian life of worship and service followed by eternal Heaven	Christian life of worship and service	Christian life of worship and service followed by?
(2)	Not becoming Christian	Worldly life followed by eternal Hell	Worldly life	Worldly life followed by?

We will indicate by A_1 the value (positive or negative) of the outcome of policy (1) under state of affairs A, and so on.

A second fault in Pascal's argument is this. Pascal assumed that all men would evaluate in the same way as he the various outcomes. But in fact, rightly or wrongly men will put very different values from each other on the different outcomes. Life in the Christian Heaven appeals to some more than others, and the life of worldly bliss enjoyed by the non-believer also appeals to some more than others. Further of course some men (e.g. the rich) have more opportunity than others to profit from the license of unbelief and so will have a gayer time in consequence. Likewise the Christian religion may demand more sacrifices of some (e.g. the rich) than of others. The different courses of action bring different gains to the twentieth-century business man and the negro in the Ghetto.

Thirdly Pascal supposes (by his remarks "There are equal risks of gain and loss" and "Reason can decide nothing here") that the probabilities of his two alternative states are equal. This claim is, to say the least, arguable. Most of natural theology is devoted to arguing about it. But his argument does not depend on this claim. All we need is some estimate of the probability of alternative states to get the argument off the ground, and, as will be seen, we can reach Pascal's conclusion without having his estimate of probabilities.

Now the rational action for a man will be determined by his estimates of the respective probabilities of the three alternative states and his evaluation of the outcomes under them. The difficulty is that we do not know what our fate will be, after death, if the alternative C be true. Nevertheless men may ascribe probabilities to the other alternative states and evaluate the possible outcomes in such a way that they can judge that one policy would be the best, even if they cannot estimate by how much the best. Thus they may ascribe a probability of zero to alternative C—in which case evaluation of gains and losses under it makes no difference to the calculation. Or, more likely, their scale of values may be such that they can say this much about the gains and losses under alternative C—that C_1 cannot exceed A_1 since Heaven is for them the highest possible bliss, that C_2 can only exceed A_1 by an infinitesimal amount since the maximum gain from life after death, if policy (2) be followed in state of affairs C, can at best only equal that obtained if policy (1) be followed in state of affairs A, and that the very slight difference in happiness on Earth can make very very little difference to the eternal balance sheet.

Once we have in this way assessed the probabilities of alternative states and the values of possible outcomes, we can work out expected gain under the two policies. The expected gain under policy (1)—becoming Christian will be

$$P(A)A_1 + P(B)B_1 + P(C)C_1$$

where $P(A)$ is the probability that A is true, etc. If this exceeds the expected gain under policy (2)

$$P(A)A_2 + P(B)B_2 + P(C)C_2$$

we ought to become Christian; otherwise not. Our estimates will depend on how desirable we consider the different outcomes. If we have Pascal's standards, our evaluation can be represented as follows:

$$A_1 = 1 \qquad\qquad B_1 = 0 \qquad\qquad 1 \le C_1 \le -1$$
$$A_2 = -1 \qquad\qquad B_2 = 0 \qquad\qquad 1 \le C_2 \le -1$$

These standards are Pascal's, since for him the ratio of worldly gains and losses to gains in the life to come, if there is one, is of finite to infinite. It is more convenient for the purposes of my calculation to measure Pascal's comparative evaluations on a scale on which $A_1 = 1$, $B_1 = 0$, etc., rather than one on which $A_1 = \infty$, $B_1 = $ some finite number. However, Pascal's standards are not everyone's, and someone else might evaluate the alternatives as follows:

$$A_1 = 1 \qquad\qquad B_1 = -0.0005 \qquad\qquad 1 \le C_1 \le -1$$
$$A_2 = -1 \qquad\qquad B_2 = +0.0005 \qquad\qquad 1 \le C_2 \le -1$$

Then on this estimate of probabilities

$$P(A) = 0.1;\ P(B) = 0.85;\ P(C) = 0.05,$$

policy (1) ought to be followed. Yet on this estimate $P(A) = 0.0001$, $P(B) = 0.99985$, $P(C) = 0.00005$, policy (2) ought to be followed. On some estimates of probability, it will be unclear which is the rational policy because of the uncertainty of gains and losses, if C be true. In such circumstances, we ought to divide alternative C up into different possible states—e.g. Ca (Afterlife rewards distributed according to Hindu scheme), Cb (Christians go to Hell, non-Christians cease to exist), etc.—in such a way that we can ascribe values and probabilities, so as to get a clear indication of the best policy. I conclude that Pascal's system of evaluating whether the man concerned with his long-term interests ought to become a Christian is perfectly workable, but it does not necessarily yield Pascal's results.

Two points must now be made to tidy up the argument so far. First, Pascal's supposition that every man who dies a non-Christian goes, if the Christian God exists, to eternal Hell, would be denied by most Christians. Many Christians would say that only the culpable non-Christian goes to eternal Hell for his beliefs, whereas the man who was a non-Christian because the Christian alternative was never presented to him or because he mistakenly judged it irrational to become Christian would not go to Hell for his beliefs. However, if this is the fate of the non-Christian under alternative (A), calculations of the best policy based on this supposition will be the same as those based on the original supposition. For the investigator is a man to whom the Christian alternative has been presented and who must assume that he has not made a mistake in his calculations—hence it is irrelevant what happens to the man to whom the Christian alternative has not been presented or to the man who unintentionally miscalculates. But not all Christians believe that anyone will go to Hell. Some Christians would say that the culpable non-Christian merely ceases to exist—this supposition means that $A_2 = B_2$. This supposition may make a different policy the best one—on some estimates of value and probability. Some few Christians would maintain the rather unbiblical view that all men go to Heaven eventually—the man who follows policy (1) simply goes there sooner. On most estimates of probability and evaluations of outcomes on this supposition policy (2) would seem to come out the best. Further of course most Christians today think of Hell, not as the mediaeval place of literal fiery torment, but merely as a state of separation from God. In so far as different suppositions about the fate of the non-Christian on alternative (A) make a difference to what is the best policy, the alternative must be subdivided and probabilities and values ascribed to Aa (Christians go to eternal Heaven; non-Christians to eternal Hell), Ab (Christians go to eternal Heaven; non-Christians cease to exist) etc.

The second relevant point is this. A man who decides to become a Christian does not merely decide to act in a certain way but decides to hold certain beliefs. The convert may not have held, when wondering whether or not to become a Christian, that the Christian theological system was probably true, but in becoming a Christian he must now adopt this view. Is it logically possible for him to do so? Can a man adopt a belief? Certain philosophers from Hume[8] onwards have held that our beliefs are not subject to our control. If they are right, it cannot be rational for us to decide to become Christians, unless we are already convinced of the truth of the Christian theological system, for it cannot be rational for us to do what is not logically possible.

---

[8]David Hume, *A Treatise of Human Nature*, Appendix, p. 624 in the edition edited by L. A. Selby-Bigge (Oxford, 1888).

Now there *may* be something odd about the suggestion that a man could decide to believe something. But there seems nothing odd about the suggestion that a man could decide to take certain action which had the known effect of inducing some belief.[9] A man might, for instance adopt Pascal's own programme—take holy water, have masses said, etc.[10] Or he might say prayers; or he might just think hard about certain kinds of evidence for his proposition. Having considered the difficulty, I shall nevertheless in future, to avoid the cumbersome phrase, often speak of choosing or deciding to believe, rather than of choosing or deciding to take steps with the known effect of inducing a belief. The former expressions are now meant to be mere definitional substitutes for the latter.

So then if the rational man is the prudent man, whether or not he becomes a Christian depends on how he estimates the happiness provided by the different outcomes and how he assigns probabilities to the different alternative states. Now although we shall shortly have to think of the rational man as a less selfish person, the account so far does elucidate two features of Christian apologetic which have been ignored by most philosophers of religion.

The first is that the Christian preacher to the unconverted is often concerned not with proving the Christian religion to be true, but with expounding what it teaches and the new relationship to God and his fellows which the Christian believes that he and only he will enjoy now and hereafter. An extreme form of this kind of preaching, more fashionable in the past than now, was the sermon which contrasted the joys of Heaven with the pains of Hell, and exhorted men to pursue the good life lest they find themselves in Hell forever after death. Another form of such preaching is the sermon which tells of the joy of Christians on Earth and contrasts it with the dreariness of the non-Christian life on Earth. Many sophisticated philosophers of religion would pour scorn on preaching of this kind. What matters, they would urge, is not what the Christian system offers or threatens, but whether or not it is true, and if the preacher is not prepared to produce evidence to show this, his talk is mere rhetoric. If my argument is correct, such philosophers would not be sophisticated enough. What the preacher has been trying to do is to persuade men of the desirability of what the Christian religion offers here and hereafter, and thereby to show it to be rational for men to gamble all to gain it. In so far as the preacher makes men give a higher value to A_1 and a lower value to A_2, then for fixed $P(A)$, he makes it more rational for men to become Christian. The more desirable is Heaven and the less desirable is Hell the more sensible it is to risk much to get to Heaven and avoid Hell, for any given probability that the Christian system is true. Further, in telling of the joy of the Christian life and the dreariness of the non-Christian life on Earth

---

[9]See H. H. Price, "Belief and Will," *Proceedings of the Aristotelian Society Supplementary Volume*, 1954, 28, pp. 1–26, who develops this point at length.

[10]*Ibid.*, No. 233.

the preacher is presenting an immensely powerful argument for becoming Christian. For he is claiming not merely that A_1 vastly exceeds A_2, but that B_1 somewhat exceeds B_2. If he accepts that argument then (if we ignore for a moment the alternative (C), however low he estimates $P(A)$ and however high he estimates $P(B)$,) the rational man will become Christian. The improbability of the truth of the Christian theological system would be quite irrelevant, for the rewards of being Christian exceed the rewards of not being Christian whether or not the Christian theological system is true. This result could be upset by taking alternative C into account, only if—given an after-life but no Christian God—the evidence was that the Christian was less likely to have a happy after-life than was the non-Christian. But, if we ignore this possibility, then, if the preacher can convince men that B_1 exceeds B_2, probabilities are irrelevant and the rational man will straightway become Christian. The humanist is of course perfectly entitled to counter these arguments by pointing out how even Heaven might pall (viz, that A_1 is not very large after all) and by describing the pleasure of his own worldly society.

The second feature of Christian apologetic on which our account sheds light is this. In so far as Christians have attempted to show the truth of their system, they have often been very much concerned to show how much more likely it is to be true than any other religious system, but not so concerned to show that it is more likely to be true than any non-religious system. My analysis brings out why this is so. Non-religious systems limit the duration of human life to life in this world, and hence the gains and losses of following any religious or non-religious policy are, if a non-religious system be true, very small compared with the gains and losses if the Christian system be true. Hence a non-religious system would have to be very much more probable than the Christian system for it to be rational to adopt it. Whereas rival religious systems offer their own eternal rewards and penalties and so, if their probability is anywhere near that of the Christian system, it will be in no way clear which it is rational to adopt. Hence it is important to the Christian preacher to show that their probability is not in that region. If $P(C)$ exceeds $P(A)$ and C_2 considerably exceeds C_1, then the policy of becoming a Christian may be the irrational policy—even if the joys of Christian life in the present exceed the joys of non-Christian life. For $P(A) = 0.05$, $P(B) = 0.85$, $P(C) = 0.1$, $A_1 = +1$, $A_2 = -1$, $B_1 = B_2$, $C_1 = -0.6$, $C_2 = +0.6$, the non-Christian policy will be the rational one. Now, true, in fact $P(C)$ covers many alternatives, on only some of which will the Christian be less well rewarded than the non-Christian, but these alternatives together must be shown to have a low probability, since the rewards and punishments will have a high positive or negative value in the regions respectively of A_1 and A_2. For this reason the Christian must show that Muhammad is no true prophet, and the Book of Mormon no true gospel. From earliest times Christians have been very much concerned to substantiate this kind of claim.

Yet, of course, there is more to religion than prudence. Moral considerations enter into our picture in two crucial ways. First the goals which we ought to seek are not merely those which we judge to be to our long-term advantage, not what we want, but what we ought to want for ourselves as well as for others. The preacher preaching the relative merits of the different systems tells men not merely that they will enjoy, say, Heaven but that life there will alone have meaning and purpose and that it is man's duty to seek such an existence for himself. But introducing morality into the ends does not disturb our calculus. We can use the same calculus to calculate the morally good as to calculate the long-term advantage. Yet although introducing morality into the ends may not upset the form of the calculus, it may make quite a difference to its matter. If we are concerned only with selfish advantage, there may well be some gain in living the non-Christian life. But the preacher may be able to persuade us that there is no moral good in it, and that the only life worth living is the life of Christian service here and hereafter. In that case we would hold that, however small the probability that the Christian theological system is true, we ought to become Christian. On the other hand the humanist preacher may be able to convince us that the Christian ideal of preserving oneself for a life hereafter, albeit a life of service, is not a worthy one. In that case we would hold that, whatever the possible selfish gain from doing so, we ought not to become Christian. Yet, if on the contrary, the evidence shows that the Christian system is probably true, then it shows that all deductive consequences of that system are probably true. One of these is that it is the duty of men to become Christian. However, considerations so far adduced suggest that it could be our duty to become Christian, even when the evidence suggests that the Christian theological system is probably false.

The other moral consideration which enters into our picture is perhaps the most crucial. It is this. We have seen that the Christian is one who believes certain propositions and lives out a certain kind of life. To decide to become a Christian involves—if we do not already believe them—deciding to take steps which would result in believing certain propositions. But even if a man can choose to believe, ought he to do so? Many would consider that it is highly immoral to choose to believe propositions (viz. to regard the evidence as supporting those propositions) when the evidence is now known not to support them. It would seem like lying to oneself. Others may be concerned with the fact that unless one is prepared to sacrifice one's beliefs in the service of the good, one is only half-committed to its pursuit. I do not wish to consider this moral issue in detail, but only to point out the consequences of different views about it. If a man claimed that there was nothing immoral in inducing in oneself any beliefs at all, not supported by present evidence,[11] then the position is as I have so far outlined it in this paper. The joys of Heaven (or the moral desirability of attempting to obtain them) and the horrors of Hell (or the moral wickedness of allowing oneself to risk obtaining them)

---

[11]Price adopts this view in the paper referred to in note 9.

provide reasons for inducing oneself to believe what seems on the evidence improbable. Many however would consider it morally wrong to induce oneself to believe what seems improbable. Yet these might hold a weaker position, that there is nothing immoral in choosing to believe one of two exhaustive alternatives between which we cannot decide by rational assessment of the evidence. By this I do not mean choosing to believe something with—by agreed standards of estimating probability—a probability of half; but choosing to believe something with—by one method of estimating probability—a probability of more than half, and—by another method of estimating—a probability of less than half, when it seems equally legitimate to use either method of estimating probability.

There are certain paradigm cases of events having on certain evidence certain numerical probabilities, and of events and theories being on certain evidence more probable than other events and theories. It is clear what is the probability relative to certain evidence of throwing two heads in a row or three sixes with three dice. But it is not always clear how we are to extrapolate standards of estimating probability from such simple cases to more complicated ones and on one way, one method of estimating probability, some theory T may have a probability of more than half, and on another way less than half. Yet both methods may appear equally natural ways of extrapolating from the paradigm cases. What ought one to do here? On one view one ought to average out the results given by the different methods. But there may be many methods, and the average result for the probability of theories and events from all methods may be all too often near to a half. To average the results yielded by all possible methods might seem no less arbitrary than to decide to adopt one method of estimating probability, and thereby reach definite conclusions on matters previously unsettled. Such a decision would not be a decision to go against the evidence, but, at most, a decision to go beyond it. Yet such a decision would lead one to adopt beliefs previously not held. A man who felt it immoral to induce in himself beliefs not warranted by the evidence might well not feel it immoral to adopt one method of estimating probability rather than another, and this on grounds of which beliefs it would lead him to adopt.

Now the position in metaphysics may well be that there are various methods of estimating the probability of metaphysical theories and they are equally natural extrapolations from paradigm cases of ascribing probability to events and simpler theories. On one natural way of extrapolating from paradigm cases the evidence may indicate that the Christian theological system is probably true and on another way the evidence may indicate that the system is probably false; yet there be no rational grounds for choosing between the ways of assessing probability obtained by extrapolation from paradigm cases. In such circumstances a man might hold that it was not immoral to choose a method of estimating probability. Hence, he would hold, it would not be immoral to choose a method which led to certain assessments of probability rather than others.

Let us see in detail how, given that a man is allowed to choose between two different methods of estimating probability α and β, but not to choose to believe anything shown by both methods to have a probability of less than a half, he will work out the rational religious policy. Let us denote by $P_\alpha(A)$ the probability that state of affairs A holds on the method of α of estimating half, he will work out the rational religious policy. Let us denote by $P_\alpha(A)$ probability, and so on. Let $P_\alpha(A) = 0.55$, $P_\alpha(B) = 0.35$, $P_\alpha(C) = 0.1$, $P_\beta(A) = 0.45$, $P_\beta(B) = 0.45$, $P_\beta(C) = 0.1$. Let the man's estimates of the values of the outcomes be as follows:

$A_1 = 1$	$B_1 = -0.05$	$+1 \leq C_1 \leq -1$
$A_2 = -1$	$B_2 = +0.05$	$+1 \leq C_2 \leq -1$

Then on method α the expressed gain of policy (1) will lie between 0.6325 and 0.4325 and of policy (2) between -0.4325 and -0.6325. On method β the expected gain of policy (1) will lie between 0.5275 and 0.3275, and of policy (2) between -0.3275 and -0.5275. Thus, whichever method of estimating probability be used, the expected gain of policy (1) will far outweigh the expected gain of policy (2). Hence if it is not immoral on other grounds to adopt it policy 1 ought to be adopted on these grounds. It will be immoral on other grounds only if thereby we decide to believe something shown to have a probability of less than a half by all legitimate methods of estimating probability. We do not do so in this case. We are deciding to believe something which, if we adopt a certain legitimate method of estimating probability, will have a probability of more than a half. It will therefore be rational to adopt that method of estimating probability. The numerical example which I chose is in one respect a simple one since the expected gain of one policy is greater than that of the other on both methods of estimating probability. It would be easy enough to devise an example in which the most rational policy will vary with the method of estimating probability which we adopt for calculating expected gain. In that case the pursuit of either policy would seem equally rational.

A man might however consider that the results of different methods of estimating probability ought always to be averaged arithmetically, in which case there will effectively be one resultant method of estimating probability; and that it is only legitimate to believe some system to be true if on that method the evidence now shows it to be probably true. In this case the rational man will become a Christian only if he judges that the evidence indicates that the Christian religion is probably true. He will not however necessarily become Christian even in that case, if we understand by the rational man the prudent man, for he may value so lowly the lives promised by the Christian theological system that the expected gain of becoming a Christian is outweighed by the gain of not becoming a Christian. Even if he judges that $P(A) > \frac{1}{2}$, B_2 may have such a high value in a man's estimation, that policy (2) is for him the most rational policy—so long as by "rational" policy is meant prudential policy. Yet if a man held that $P(A) > \frac{1}{2}$, he would hold that the consequences of the Christian system were probably true and these include the consequence that all men ought to become Christians. In that case if the rational man is the man who pursues the morally right policy, he would become a Christian.

My problem was whether it was a necessary and sufficient condition for the rational man becoming a Christian that he judges that the evidence available to him shows that the probability that the Christian theological system is true is greater than a half. My conclusion is that it depends on how one interprets "rational" and what are one's views about the morality of believing what is probably false. I have illustrated in detail how these considerations affect the issue, and how on some views on the moral issue the cited condition is not a necessary condition, and how on a non-moral understanding of "rational" it is not a sufficient condition, for the rational man to become a Christian.

W. K. CLIFFORD

The Ethics of Belief

A shipowner was about to send to sea an emigrant-ship. He knew that she was old, and not over-well built at the first; that she had seen many seas and climes, and often had needed repairs. Doubts had been suggested to him that possibly she was not seaworthy. These doubts preyed upon his mind, and made him unhappy; he thought that perhaps he ought to have her thoroughly overhauled and refitted, even though this should put him to great expense. Before the ship sailed, however, he succeeded in overcoming these melancholy reflections. He said to himself that she had gone safely through so many voyages and weathered so many storms that it was idle to suppose she would not come safely home from this trip also. He would put his trust in Providence, which could hardly fail to protect all these unhappy families that were leaving their fatherland to seek for better times elsewhere. He would dismiss from his mind all ungenerous suspicions about the honesty of builders and contractors. In such ways he acquired a sincere and comfortable conviction that his vessel was thoroughly safe and seaworthy; he watched her departure with a light heart, and benevolent wishes for the success of the exiles in their strange new home that was to be; and he got his insurance-money when she went down in mid-ocean and told no tales.

What shall we say of him? Surely this, that he was verily guilty of the death of those men. It is admitted that he did sincerely believe in the soundness of his

---

From W. K. Clifford, *Lectures and Essays* (1879).

ship; but the sincerity of his conviction can in no wise help him, because *he had no right to believe on such evidence as was before him.* He had acquired his belief not by honestly earning it in patient investigation, but by stifling his doubts. And although in the end he may have felt so sure about it that he could not think otherwise, yet inasmuch as he had knowingly and willingly worked himself into that frame of mind, he must be held responsible for it.

Let us alter the case a little, and suppose that the ship was not unsound after all; that she made her voyage safely, and many others after it. Will that diminish the guilt of her owner? Not one jot. When an action is once done, it is right or wrong for ever; no accidental failure of its good or evil fruits can possibly alter that. The man would not have been innocent, he would only have been not found out. The question of right or wrong has to do with the origin of his belief, not the matter of it; not what it was, but how he got it; not whether it turned out to be true or false, but whether he had a right to believe on such evidence as was before him.

There was once an island in which some of the inhabitants professed a religion teaching neither the doctrine of original sin nor that of eternal punishment. A suspicion got abroad that the professors of this religion had made use of unfair means to get their doctrines taught to children. They were accused of wresting the laws of their country in such a way as to remove children from the care of their natural and legal guardians; and even of stealing them away and keeping them concealed from their friends and relations. A certain number of men formed themselves into a society for the purpose of agitating the public about this matter. They published grave accusations against individual citizens of the highest position and character, and did all in their power to injure these citizens in the exercise of their professions. So great was the noise they made, that a Commission was appointed to investigate the facts; but after the Commission had carefully inquired into all the evidence that could be got, it appeared that the accused were innocent. Not only had they been accused on insufficient evidence, but the evidence of their innocence was such as the agitators might easily have obtained, if they had attempted a fair inquiry. After these disclosures the inhabitants of that country looked upon the members of the agitating society, not only as persons whose judgment was to be distrusted, but also as no longer to be counted honourable men. For although they had sincerely and conscientiously believed in the charges they had made, yet *they had no right to believe on such evidence as was before them.* Their sincere convictions, instead of being honestly earned by patient inquiring, were stolen by listening to the voice of prejudice and passion.

Let us vary this case also, and suppose, other things remaining as before, that a still more accurate investigation proved the accused to have been really guilty. Would this make any difference in the guilt of the accusers? Clearly not; the question is not whether their belief was true or false, but whether they entertained it on wrong grounds. They would no doubt say, "Now you see that we were right after all; next time perhaps you will believe us." And they might be believed, but they would not thereby become honourable men. They would not be innocent, they would only be not found out. Every one of them, if he chose to examine himself *in foro conscientiae*, would know that he had acquired and nourished a belief, when he had no right to believe on such evidence as was before him; and therein he would know that he had done a wrong thing.

It may be said, however, that in both of these supposed cases it is not the belief which is judged to be wrong, but the action following upon it. The shipowner might say, "I am perfectly certain that my ship is sound, but still I feel it my duty to have her examined, before trusting the lives of so many people to her." And it might be said to the agitator, "However convinced you were of the justice of your cause and the truth of your convictions, you ought not to have made a public attack upon any man's character until you had examined the evidence on both sides with the utmost patience and care."

In the first place, let us admit that, so far as it goes, this view of the case is right and necessary; right, because even when a man's belief is so fixed that he cannot think otherwise, he still has a choice in regard to the action suggested by it, and so cannot escape the duty of investigating on the ground of the strength of his convictions; and necessary, because those who are not yet capable of controlling their feelings and thoughts must have a plain rule dealing with overt acts.

But this being premised as necessary, it becomes clear that it is not sufficient, and that our previous judgment is required to supplement it. For it is not possible so to sever the belief from the action it suggests as to condemn the one without condemning the other. No man holding a strong belief on one side of a question, or even wishing to hold a belief on one side, can investigate it with such fairness and completeness as if he were really in doubt and unbiased; so that the existence of a belief not founded on fair inquiry unfits a man for the performance of this necessary duty.

Nor is that truly a belief at all which has not some influence upon the actions of him who holds it. He who truly believes that which prompts him to an action has looked upon the action to lust after it, he has committed it already in his heart. If a belief is not realized immediately in open deeds, it is stored up for the guidance of the future. It goes to make a part of that aggregate of beliefs which is the link between sensation and action at every moment of all our lives, and which is so organized and compacted together that no part of it can be isolated from the rest, but every new addition modifies the structure of the whole. No real belief, however trifling and fragmentary it may seem, is ever truly insignificant; it prepares us to receive more of its like, confirms those which resembled it before, and weakens others; and so gradually it lays a stealthy train in our inmost thoughts, which may some day explode into overt action, and leave its stamp upon our character for ever.

And no one man's belief is in any case a private matter which concerns himself alone. Our lives are guided by that general conception of the course of things which has been created by society for social purposes. Our words, our phrases, our forms and processes and modes of thought, are common property, fashioned and perfected from age to age; an heirloom which every succeeding generation inherits as a precious deposit and a sacred trust to be handed on to the next one, not unchanged but enlarged and purified, with some clear marks of its proper handiwork. Into this, for good or ill, is woven every belief of every man who has speech of his fellows. An awful privilege, and an awful responsibility, that we should help to create the world in which posterity will live.

In the two supposed cases which have been considered, it has been judged wrong to believe on insufficient evidence, or to nourish belief by suppressing doubts and avoiding investigation. The reason of this judgment is not far to seek: it is that in both these cases the belief held by one man was of great importance to other men. But forasmuch as no belief held by one man, however seemingly trivial the belief, and however obscure the believer, is ever actually insignificant or without its effect on the fate of mankind, we have no choice but to extend our judgment to all cases of belief whatever. Belief, that sacred faculty which prompts the decisions of our will, and knits into harmonious working all the compacted energies of our being, is ours not for ourselves, but for humanity. It is rightly used on truths which have been established by long experience and waiting toil, and which have stood in the fierce light of free and fearless questioning. Then it helps to bind men together, and to strengthen and direct their common action. It is desecrated when given to unproved and unquestioned statements, for the solace and private pleasure of the believer; to add a tinsel splendour to the plain straight road of our life and display a bright mirage beyond it; or even to drown the common sorrows of our kind by a self-deception which allows them not only to cast down, but also to degrade us. Whoso would deserve well of his fellows in this matter will guard the purity of his belief with a very fanaticism of jealous care, lest at any time it should rest on an unworthy object, and catch a stain which can never be wiped away.

It is not only the leader of men, statesman, philosopher, or poet, that owes this bounden duty to mankind. Every rustic who delivers in the village ale-house his slow, infrequent sentences, may help to kill or keep alive the fatal superstitions which clog his race. Every hard-worked wife of an artisan may transmit to her children beliefs which shall knit society together, or rend it in pieces. No simplicity of mind, no obscurity of station, can escape the universal duty of questioning all that we believe.

It is true that this duty is a hard one, and the doubt which comes out of it is often a very bitter thing. It leaves us bare and powerless where we thought that we were safe and strong. To know all about anything is to know how to deal with it under all circumstances. We feel much happier and more secure when we think we know precisely what to do, no matter what happens, than when we have lost our way and do not know where to turn. And if we have supposed ourselves to know all about anything, and to be capable of doing what is fit in regard to it, we naturally do not like to find that we are really ignorant and powerless, that we have to begin again at the beginning, and try to learn what the thing is and how it is to be dealt with—if indeed anything can be learnt about it. It is the sense of power attached to a sense of knowledge that makes men desirous of believing, and afraid of doubting.

This sense of power is the highest and best of pleasures when the belief on which it is founded is a true belief, and has been fairly earned by investigation. For then we may justly feel that it is common property, and hold good for others as well as for ourselves. Then we may be glad, not that *I* have learned secrets by which I am safer and stronger, but that *we men* have got mastery over more of the world; and we shall be strong, not for ourselves, but in the name of Man and in his strength. But if the belief has been accepted on insufficient evidence, the pleasure is a stolen one. Not only does it deceive ourselves by giving us a sense of power which we do not really possess, but it is sinful, because it is stolen in defiance of our duty to mankind. That duty is to guard ourselves from such beliefs as from a pestilence, which may shortly master our own body and then spread to the rest of the town. What would be thought of one who, for the sake of a sweet fruit, should deliberately run the risk of bringing a plague upon his family and his neighbours?

And, as in other such cases, it is not the risk only which has to be considered; for a bad action is always bad at the time when it is done, no matter what happens afterwards. Every time we let ourselves believe for unworthy reasons, we weaken our powers of self-control, of doubting, of judicially and fairly weighing evidence. We all suffer severely enough from the maintenance and support of false beliefs and the fatally wrong actions which they lead to, and the evil born when one such belief is entertained is great and wide. But a greater and wider evil arises when the credulous character is maintained and supported, when a habit of believing for unworthy reasons is fostered and made permanent. If I steal money from any person, there may be no harm done by the mere transfer of possession; he may not feel the loss, or it may prevent him from using the money badly. But I cannot help doing this great wrong towards Man, that I make myself dishonest. What hurts society is not that it should lose its property, but that it should become a den of thieves; for then it must cease to be society. This is why we ought not to do evil that good may come; for at any rate this great evil has come, that we have done evil and are made wicked thereby. In like manner, if I let myself believe anything on insufficient evidence, there may be no great harm done by the mere belief; it may be true after all, or I may never have occasion to exhibit it in outward acts. But I cannot help doing this great wrong towards Man, that I make myself credulous. The danger to society is not merely that it should believe wrong things, though that is great enough; but that it should become credulous, and lose the habit of testing things and inquiring into them; for then it must sink back into savagery.

The harm which is done by credulity in a man is not confined to the fostering of a credulous character in others, and consequent support of false beliefs. Habitual want of care about what I believe leads to habitual want of care in others about the truth of what is told to me. Men speak the truth to one another when each reveres the truth in his own mind and in the other's mind; but how shall my friend revere the truth in my mind when I myself am careless about it, when I believe things because I want to believe them, and because they are comforting and pleasant? Will he not learn to cry, "Peace," to me, when there is no peace? By such a course I shall surround myself with a thick atmosphere of falsehood and fraud, and in that I must live. It may matter little to me, in my cloud-castle of sweet illusions and darling lies; but it matters much to Man that I have made my neighbours ready to deceive. The credulous man is father to the liar and the cheat; he lives in the bosom of this his family, and it is no marvel if he should become even as they are. So closely are our duties knit together, that whoso shall keep the whole law, and yet offend in one point, he is guilty of all.

To sum up: it is wrong always, everywhere, and for anyone, to believe anything upon insufficient evidence.

If a man, holding a belief which he was taught in childhood or persuaded of afterwards, keeps down and pushes away any doubts which arise about it in his mind, purposely avoids the reading of books and the company of men that call in question or discuss it, and regards as impious those questions which cannot easily be asked without disturbing it—the life of that man is one long sin against mankind.

If this judgment seems harsh when applied to those simple souls who have never known better, who have been brought up from the cradle with a horror of doubt, and taught that their eternal welfare depends on *what* they believe, then it leads to the very serious question, *Who hath made Israel to sin?*

It may be permitted me to fortify this judgment with the sentence of Milton—

> A man may be a heretic in the truth; and if he believe things only because his pastor says so, or the assembly so determine, without knowing other reason, though his belief be true, yet the very truth he holds becomes his heresy.

And with this famous aphorism of Coleridge—

> He who begins by loving Christianity better than Truth, will proceed by loving his own sect or Church better than Christianity, and end in loving himself better than all.

Inquiry into the evidence of a doctrine is not to be made once for all, and then taken as finally settled. It is never lawful to stifle a doubt; for either it can be honestly answered by means of the inquiry already made, or else it proves that the inquiry was not complete.

"But," says one, "I am a busy man; I have no time for the long course of study which would be necessary to make me in any degree a competent judge of certain questions, or even able to understand the nature of the arguments." Then he should have no time to believe.

WILLIAM JAMES

The Will to Believe

In the recently published Life by Leslie Stephen of his brother, Fitz-James, there is an account of a school to which the latter went when he was a boy. The teacher, a certain Mr. Guest, used to converse with his pupils in this wise: "Gurney, what is the difference between justification and sanctification?—Stephen, prove the omnipotence of God!" etc. In the midst of our Harvard freethinking and indifference we are prone to imagine that here at your good old orthodox College conversation continues to be somewhat upon this order; and to show you that we at Harvard have not lost all interest in these vital subjects, I have brought with me to-night something like a sermon on justification by faith to read to you,—I mean an essay in justification *of* faith, a defence of our right to adopt a believing attitude in religious matters, in spite of the fact that our merely logical intellect may not have been coerced. "The Will to Believe," accordingly, is the title of my paper.

I have long defended to my own students the lawfulness of voluntarily adopted faith; but as soon as they have got well imbued with the logical spirit, they have as a rule refused to admit my contention to be lawful philosophically, even though in point of fact they were personally all the time chock-full of some faith or other themselves. I am all the while, however, so profoundly convinced that my own position is correct, that your invitation has seemed to me a good occasion to make my statements more clear. Perhaps your minds will be more open than those with which I have hitherto had to deal. I will be as little technical as I can, though I must begin by setting up some technical distinctions that will help us in the end.

I.

Let us give the name of *hypothesis* to anything that may be proposed to our belief; and just as the electricians speak of live and dead wires, let us speak of any hypothesis as either *live* or *dead*. A live hypothesis is one which appeals

---

This essay was originally an address delivered before the Philosophical Clubs of Yale and Brown Universities. It was first published in 1896.

as a real possibility to him to whom it is proposed. If I ask you to believe in the Mahdi, the notion makes no electric connection with your nature,—it refuses to scintillate with any credibility at all. As an hypothesis it is completely dead. To an Arab, however (even if he be not one of the Mahdi's followers), the hypothesis is among the mind's possibilities: it is alive. This shows that deadness and liveness in an hypothesis are not intrinsic properties, but relations to the individual thinker. They are measured by his willingness to act. The maximum of liveness in an hypothesis means willingness to act irrevocably. Practically, that means belief; but there is some believing tendency wherever there is willingness to act at all.

Next, let us call the decision between two hypotheses an *option*. Options may be of several kinds. They may be—1, *living* or *dead;* 2, *forced* or *avoidable;* 3, *momentous* or *trivial;* and for our purposes we may call an option a *genuine* option when it is of the forced, living, and momentous kind.

1. A living option is one in which both hypotheses are live ones. If I say to you: "Be a theosophist or be a Mohammedan," it is probably a dead option, because for you neither hypothesis is likely to be alive. But if I say: "Be an agnostic or be a Christian," it is otherwise: trained as you are, each hypothesis makes some appeal, however small, to your belief.

2. Next, if I say to you: "Choose between going out with your umbrella or without it," I do not offer you a genuine option, for it is not forced. You can easily avoid it by not going out at all. Similarly, if I say, "Either love me or hate me," "Either call my theory true or call it false," your option is avoidable. You may remain indifferent to me, neither loving nor hating, and you may decline to offer any judgment as to my theory. But if I say, "Either accept this truth or go without it," I put on you a forced option, for there is no standing place outside of the alternative. Every dilemma based on a complete logical disjunction, with no possibility of not choosing, is an option of this forced kind.

3. Finally, if I were Dr. Nansen and proposed to you to join my North Pole expedition, your option would be momentous; for this would probably be your only similar opportunity, and your choice now would either exclude you from the North Pole sort of immortality altogether or put at least the chance of it into your hands. He who refuses to embrace a unique opportunity loses the prize as surely as if he tried and failed. *Per contra*, the option is trivial when the opportunity is not unique, when the stake is insignificant, or when the decision is reversible if it later prove unwise. Such trivial options abound in the scientific life. A chemist finds an hypothesis live enough to spend a year in its verification: he believes in it to that extent. But if his experiments prove inconclusive either way, he is quit for his loss of time, no vital harm being done.

It will facilitate our discussion if we keep all these distinctions well in mind.

II.

The next matter to consider is the actual psychology of human opinion. When we look at certain facts, it seems as if our passional and volitional nature lay at the root of all our convictions. When we look at others, it seems as if they could do nothing when the intellect had once said its say. Let us take the latter facts up first.

Does it not seem preposterous on the very face of it to talk of our opinions being modifiable at will? Can our will either help or hinder our intellect in its perceptions of truth? Can we, by just willing it, believe that Abraham Lincoln's existence is a myth, and that the portraits of him in McClure's Magazine are all of some one else? Can we, by any effort of our will, or by any strength of wish that it were true, believe ourselves well and about when we are roaring with rheumatism in bed, or feel certain that the sum of the two one-dollar bills in our pocket must be a hundred dollars? We can *say* any of these things, but we are absolutely impotent to believe them; and of just such things is the whole fabric of the truths that we do believe in made up,—matters of fact, immediate or remote, as Hume said, and relations between ideas, which are either there or not there for us if we see them so, and which if not there cannot be put there by any action of our own.

In Pascal's *Thoughts* there is a celebrated passage known in literature as Pascal's wager. In it he tries to force us into Christianity by reasoning as if our concern with truth resembled our concern with the stakes in a game of chance. Translated freely his words are these: You must either believe or not believe that God is—which will you do? Your human reason cannot say. A game is going on between you and the nature of things which at the day of judgment will bring out either heads or tails. Weigh what your gains and your losses would be if you should stake all you have on heads, or God's existence: if you win in such case, you gain eternal beatitude; if you lose, you lose nothing at all. If there were an infinity of chances, and only one for God in this wager, still you ought to stake your all on God; for though you surely risk a finite loss by this procedure, any finite loss is reasonable, even a certain one is reasonable, if there is but the possibility of infinite gain. Go, then, and take holy water, and have masses said; belief will come and stupefy your scruples,—*Cela vous fera croire et vous abêtira*. Why should you not? At bottom, what have you to lose?

You probably feel that when religious faith expresses itself thus, in the language of the gaming-table, it is put to its last trumps. Surely Pascal's own personal belief in masses and holy water had far other springs; and this celebrated page of his is but an argument for others, a last desperate snatch at a weapon against the hardness of the unbelieving heart. We feel that a faith in masses and holy water adopted wilfully after such a mechanical calculation would lack the inner soul of faith's reality; and if we were ourselves in the place of the Deity, we should probably take particular pleasure in cutting off believers of this pattern from their infinite reward. It is evident that unless there be some pre-existing tendency to believe in masses and holy water, the option offered to the will by Pascal is not a living option. Certainly no Turk ever took to masses and holy water on its account; and even to us Protestants these means of salvation seem such foregone impossibilities that Pascal's logic, invoked for them specifically, leaves us unmoved. As well might the Mahdi write to us, saying, "I am the Expected One whom God has created in his effulgence. You shall be infinitely happy if you confess me; otherwise you shall be cut off from the light of the sun. Weigh, then, your infinite gain if I am genuine against your finite sacrifice if I am not!" His logic would be that of Pascal; but he would vainly use it on us, for the hypothesis he offers us is dead. No tendency to act on it exists in us to any degree.

The talk of believing by our volition seems, then, from one point of view, simply silly. From another point of view it is worse than silly, it is vile. When one turns to the magnificent edifice of the physical sciences, and sees how it was reared; what thousands of disinterested moral lives of men lie buried in its mere foundations; what patience and postponement, what choking down of preference, what submission to the icy laws of outer fact are wrought into its very stones and mortar; how absolutely impersonal it stands in its vast augustness,—then how besotted and contemptible seems every little sentimentalist who comes blowing his voluntary smoke-wreaths, and pretending to decide things from out of his private dream! Can we wonder if those bred in the rugged and manly school of science should feel like spewing such subjectivism out of their mouths? The whole system of loyalties which grow up in the schools of science go dead against its toleration; so that it is only natural that those who have caught the scientific fever should pass over to the opposite extreme, and write sometimes as if the incorruptibly truthful intellect ought positively to prefer bitterness and unacceptableness to the heart in its cup.

> It fortifies my soul to know
> That, though I perish, Truth is so—

sings Clough, while Huxley exclaims: "My only consolation lies in the reflection that, however bad our posterity may become, so far as they hold by the plain rule of not pretending to believe what they have no reason to believe, because it may be to their advantage so to pretend [the word 'pretend' is surely here redundant], they will not have reached the lowest depth of immortality." And that delicious *enfant terrible* Clifford writes: "Belief is desecrated when given to unproved and unquestioned statements for the solace and private pleasure of the believer.... Whoso would deserve well of his fellows in this matter will guard the purity of his belief with a very fanaticism of jealous care, lest at any time it should rest on an unworthy object, and catch a stain which can never be wiped away.... If [a] belief has been accepted on insufficient evidence [even though the belief be true, as Clifford on the same page explains] the pleasure is a stolen one.... It is sinful because it is stolen in defiance of our duty to mankind. That duty is to guard ourselves from such beliefs as from a pestilence which may shortly master our own body and then spread to the rest of the town.... It is wrong always, everywhere, and for every one, to believe anything upon insufficient evidence."

III.

All this strikes one as healthy, even when expressed, as by Clifford, with somewhat too much of robustious pathos in the voice. Free-will and simple wishing do seem, in the matter of our credences, to be only fifth wheels to the coach. Yet if any one should thereupon assume that intellectual insight is what remains after wish and will and sentimental preference have taken wing, or that pure reason is what then settles our opinions, he would fly quite as directly in the teeth of the facts.

It is only our already dead hypotheses that our willing nature is unable to bring to life again. But what has made them dead for us is for the most part a previous action of our willing nature of an antagonistic kind. When I say "willing nature," I do not mean only such deliberate volitions as may have set up habits of belief that we cannot now escape from,—I mean all such factors of belief as fear and hope, prejudice and passion, imitation and partisanship, the circumpressure of our caste and set. As a matter of fact we find ourselves believing, we hardly know how or why. Mr. Balfour gives the name of "authority" to all those influences, born of the intellectual climate, that make hypotheses possible or impossible for us, alive or dead. Here in this room, we all of us believe in molecules and the conservation of energy, in democracy and necessary progress, in Protestant Christianity and the duty of fighting for "the doctrine of the immortal Monroe," all for no reasons worthy of the name. We see into these matters with no more inner clearness, and probably with much less, than any disbeliever in them might possess. His unconventionality would probably have some grounds to show for its conclusions; but for us, not insight, but the *prestige* of the opinions, is what makes the spark shoot from them and light up our sleeping magazines of faith. Our reason is quite satisfied, in nine hundred and ninety-nine cases out of every thousand of us, if it can find a few arguments that will do to recite in case our credulity is criticised by some one else. Our faith is faith in some one else's faith, and in the greatest matters this is most the case. Our belief in truth itself, for instance, that there is a truth, and that our minds and it are made for each other,—what is it but a passionate affirmation of desire, in which our social system backs us up? We want to have a truth; we want to believe that our experiments and studies and discussions must put us in a continually better and better position towards it; and on this line we agree to fight out our thinking lives. But if a pyrrhonistic sceptic asks us *how we know* all this, can our logic find a reply? No! certainly it cannot. It is just one volition against another,—we willing to go in for life upon a trust or assumption which he, for his part, does not care to make.[1]

As a rule we disbelieve all facts and theories for which we have no use. Clifford's cosmic emotions find no use for Christian feelings. Huxley belabors the bishops because there is no use for sacerdotalism in his scheme of life. Newman, on the contrary, goes over to Romanism, and finds all sorts of reasons good for staying there, because a priestly system is for him an organic need and delight. Why do so few "scientists" even look at the evidence for telepathy, so called? Because they think, as a leading biologist, now dead, once said to me, that even if such a thing were true, scientists ought to band together to keep it suppressed and concealed. It would undo the uniformity of Nature and all sorts of other things without which scientists cannot carry on their pursuits. But if this very man had been shown something which as a scientist he might *do* with telepathy, he might not only have examined the evidence, but even have found it good enough. This very law which the logicians would impose upon us—if I may give the name of logicians to those who would rule out our willing nature here—is based on nothing but their own natural wish to exclude all elements for which they, in their professional quality of logicians, can find no use.

Evidently, then, our non-intellectual nature does influence our convictions. There are passional tendencies and volitions which run before and others which come after belief, and it is only the latter that are too late for the fair, and they are not too late when the previous passional work has been already in their own direction. Pascal's argument, instead of being powerless, then seems a regular clincher, and is the last stroke needed to make our faith in masses and holy water complete. The state of things is evidently far from simple; and pure insight and logic, whatever they might do ideally, are not the only things that really do produce our creeds.

IV.

Our next duty, having recognized this mixed-up state of affairs, is to ask whether it be simply reprehensible and pathological, or whether, on the contrary, we must treat it as a normal element in making up our minds. The thesis I defend is, briefly stated, this: *Our passional nature not only lawfully may, but must, decide an option between propositions, whenever it is a genuine option that cannot by its nature be decided on intellectual grounds; for*

---

[1] Compare the admirable p. 310 in S. H. Hodgson's *Time and Space*, London, 1865.

to say, under such circumstances, "Do not decide, but leave the question open," is itself a passional decision,—just like deciding yes or no,—and is attended with the same risk of losing the truth. The thesis thus abstractly expressed will, I trust, soon become quite clear.

• • •

<h2 style="text-align:center">VIII.</h2>

And now, after all this introduction, let us go straight at our question. I have said, and now repeat it, that not only as a matter of fact do we find our passional nature influencing us in our opinions, but that there are some options between opinions in which this influence must be regarded both as an inevitable and as a lawful determinant of our choice.

I fear here that some of you my hearers will begin to scent danger, and lend an inhospitable ear. Two first steps of passion you have indeed had to admit as necessary,—we must think so as to avoid dupery, and we must think so as to gain truth; but the surest path to those ideal consummations, you will probably consider, is from now onwards to take no further passional step.

Well, of course, I agree as far as the facts will allow. Wherever the option between losing truth and gaining it is not momentous, we can throw the chance of *gaining truth* away, and at any rate save ourselves from any chance of *believing falsehood,* by not making up our minds at all till objective evidence has come. In scientific questions, this is almost always the case; and even in human affairs in general, the need of acting is seldom so urgent that a false belief to act on is better than no belief at all. Law courts, indeed, have to decide on the best evidence attainable for the moment, because a judge's duty is to make law as well as to ascertain it, and (as a learned judge once said to me) few cases are worth spending much time over: the great thing is to have them decided on *any* acceptable principle, and got out of the way. But in our dealings with objective nature we obviously are recorders, not makers, of the truth; and decisions for the mere sake of deciding promptly and getting on to the next business would be wholly out of place. Throughout the breadth of physical nature facts are what they are quite independently of us, and seldom is there any such hurry about them that the risks of being duped by believing a premature theory need be faced. The questions here are always trivial options, the hypotheses are hardly living (at any rate not living for us spectators), the choice between believing truth or falsehood is seldom forced. The attitude of sceptical balance is therefore the absolutely wise one if we would escape mistakes. What difference, indeed, does it make to most of us whether we have or have not a theory of the Röntgen rays, whether we believe or not in mind-stuff, or have a conviction about the causality of conscious states? It makes no difference. Such options are not forced on us. On every account it is better not to make them, but still keep weighing reasons *pro et contra* with an indifferent hand.

I speak, of course, here of the purely judging mind. For purposes of discovery such indifference is to be less highly recommended, and science would be far less advanced than she is if the passionate desires of individuals to get their own faiths confirmed had been kept out of the game. See for example the sagacity which Spencer and Weismann now display. On the other hand, if you want an absolute duffer in an investigation, you must, after all, take the man who has no interest whatever in its results: he is the warranted incapable, the positive fool. The most useful investigator, because the most sensitive observer, is always he whose eager interest in one side of the question is balanced by an equally keen nervousness lest he become deceived.[2] Science has organized this nervousness into a regular *technique*, her so-called method of verification; and she has fallen so deeply in love with the method that one may even say she has ceased to care for truth by itself at all. It is only truth as technically verified that interests her. The truth of truths might come in merely affirmative form, and she would decline to touch it. Such truth as that, she might repeat with Clifford, would be stolen in defiance of her duty to mankind. Human passions, however, are stronger than technical rules. "Le coeur a ses raisons," as Pascal says, "que la raison ne connaît pas"; and however indifferent to all but the bare rules of the game the umpire, the abstract intellect, may be, the concrete players who furnish him the materials to judge of are usually each one of them, in love with some pet "live hypothesis" of his own. Let us agree, however, that wherever there is no forced option, the dispassionately judicial intellect with no pet hypothesis, saving us, as it does, from dupery at any rate, ought to be our ideal.

The question next arises: Are there not somewhere forced options in our speculative questions, and can we (as men who may be interested at least as much in positively gaining truth as in merely escaping dupery) always wait with impunity till the coercive evidence shall have arrived? It seems *a priori* improbable that the truth should be so nicely adjusted to our needs and powers as that. In the great boarding-house of nature, the cakes and the butter and the syrup seldom come out so even and leave the plates so clean. Indeed, we should view them with scientific suspicion if they did.

IX.

Moral questions immediately present themselves as questions whose solution cannot wait for sensible proof. A moral question is a question not of what sensibly exists, but of what is good, or would be good if it did exist. Science can tell us what exists; but to compare the *worths*, both of what exists and of what does not exist, we must consult not science, but what Pascal calls our

---

[2]Compare Wilfrid Ward's Essay, "The Wish to Believe," in his *Witnesses to the Unseen*, Macmillan & Co., 1893.

heart. Science herself consults her heart when she lays it down that the infinite ascertainment of fact and correction of false belief are the supreme goods for man. Challenge the statement, and science can only repeat it oracularly, or else prove it by showing that such ascertainment and correction bring man all sorts of other goods which man's heart in turn declares. The question of having moral beliefs at all or not having them is decided by our will. Are our moral preferences true or false, or are they only odd biological phenomena, making things good or bad for *us*, but in themselves indifferent? How can your pure intellect decide? If your heart does not *want* a world of moral reality, your head will assuredly never make you believe in one. Mephistophelian scepticism, indeed, will satisfy the head's play-instincts much better than any rigorous idealism can. Some men (even at the student age) are so naturally cool-hearted that the moralistic hypothesis never has for them any pungent life, and in their supercilious presence the hot young moralist always feels strangely ill at ease. The appearance of knowingness is on their side, of *naïveté* and gullibility on his. Yet, in the inarticulate heart of him, he clings to it that he is not a dupe, and that there is a realm in which (as Emerson says) all their wit and intellectual superiority is no better than the cunning of a fox. Moral scepticism can no more be refuted or proved by logic than intellectual scepticism can. When we stick to it that there *is* truth (be it of either kind), we do so with our whole nature, and resolve to stand or fall by the results. The sceptic with his whole nature adopts the doubting attitude; but which of us is the wiser, Omniscience only knows.

Turn now from these wide questions of good to a certain class of questions of fact, questions concerning personal relations, states of mind between one man and another. *Do you like me or not?*—for example. Whether you do or not depends, in countless instances, on whether I meet you half-way, am willing to assume that you must like me, and show you trust and expectation. The previous faith on my part in your liking's existence is in such cases what makes your liking come. But if I stand aloof, and refuse to budge an inch until I have objective evidence, until you shall have done something apt, as the absolutists say, *ad extorquendum assensum meum*, ten to one your liking never comes. How many women's hearts are vanquished by the mere sanguine insistence of some man that they *must* love him! he will not consent to the hypothesis that they cannot. The desire for a certain kind of truth here brings about that special truth's existence; and so it is in innumerable cases of other sorts. Who gains promotions, boons, appointments, but the man in whose life they are seen to play the part of live hypotheses, who discounts them, sacrifices other things for their sake before they have come, and takes risks for them in advance? His faith acts on the powers above him as a claim, and creates its own verification.

A social organism of any sort whatever, large or small, is what it is because each member proceeds to his own duty with a trust that the other members will simultaneously do theirs. Wherever a desired result is achieved by the co-operation of many independent persons, its existence as a fact is a pure consequence of the precursive faith in one another of those immediately concerned. A government, an army, a commercial system, a ship, a college, an athletic team, all exist on this condition, without which not only is nothing achieved, but nothing is even attempted. A whole train of passengers (individually brave enough) will be looted by a few highwaymen, simply because the latter can count on one another, while each passenger fears that if he makes a movement of resistance, he will be shot before any one else backs him up. If we believed that the whole car-full would rise at once with us, we should each severally rise, and train-robbing would never even be attempted. There are, then, cases where a fact cannot come at all unless a preliminary faith exists in its coming. *And where faith in a fact can help create the fact*, that would be an insane logic which should say that faith running ahead of scientific evidence is the "lowest kind of immorality" into which a thinking being can fall. Yet such is the logic by which our scientific absolutists pretend to regulate our lives!

X.

In truths dependent on our personal action, then, faith based on desire is certainly a lawful and possibly an indispensable thing.

But now, it will be said, these are all childish human cases, and have nothing to do with great cosmical matters, like the question of religious faith. Let us then pass on to that. Religions differ so much in their accidents that in discussing the religious question we must make it very generic and broad. What then do we now mean by the religious hypothesis? Science says things *are*; morality says some things are *better* than other things; and religion says essentially two things.

First, she says that the best things are the more eternal things, the overlapping things, the things in the universe that throw the last stone, so to speak, and say the final word. "Perfection is eternal,"—this phrase of Charles Secrétan seems a good way of putting this first affirmation of religion, an affirmation which obviously cannot yet be verified scientifically at all.

The second affirmation of religion is that we are better off even now if we believe her first affirmation to be true.

Now, let us consider what the logical elements of this situation are *in case the religious hypothesis in both its branches be really true.* (Of course, we must admit that possibility at the outset. If we are to discuss the question at all, it must involve a living option. If for any of you religion be a hypothesis that cannot, by any living possibility be true, then you need go no farther. I speak to the "saving remnant" alone.) So proceeding, we see, first, that religion offers itself as a *momentous* option. We are supposed to gain, even now, by our belief, and to lose by our non-belief, a certain vital good. Secondly, religion is a *forced* option, so far as that good goes. We cannot escape the issue by remaining sceptical and waiting for more light, because, although we do avoid error in that way *if religion be untrue*, we lose the good, *if it be true*, just as certainly as if we positively chose to disbelieve. It is as if a man should hesitate indefinitely to ask a certain woman to marry him because he was not perfectly sure that she would prove an angel after he brought her home. Would he not cut himself off from that particular angel-possibility as decisively as if he went and married some one else? Scepticism, then, is not avoidance of option; it is option of a certain particular kind of risk. *Better risk loss of truth than chance of error,*—that is your faith-vetoer's exact position. He is actively playing his stake as much as the believer is; he is backing the field against the religious hypothesis, just as the believer is backing the religious hypothesis against the field. To preach scepticism to us as a duty until "sufficient evidence" for religion be found, is tantamount therefore to telling us, when in presence of the religious hypothesis, that to yield to our fear of its being error is wiser and better than to yield to our hope that it may be true. It is not intellect against all passions, then; it is only intellect with one passion laying down its law. And by what, forsooth, is the supreme wisdom of this passion warranted? Dupery for dupery, what proof is there that dupery through hope is so much worse than dupery through fear? I, for one, can see no proof; and I simply refuse obedience to the scientist's command to imitate his kind of option, in a case where my own stake is important enough to give me the right to choose my own form of risk. If religion be true and the evidence for it be still insufficient, I do not wish, by putting your extinguisher upon my nature (which feels to me as if it had after all some business in this matter), to forfeit my sole chance in life of getting upon the winning side,—that chance depending, of course, on my willingness to run the risk of acting as if my passional need of taking the world religiously might be prophetic and right.

All this is on the supposition that it really may be prophetic and right, and that, even to us who are discussing the matter, religion is a live hypothesis which may be true. Now, to most of us religion comes in a still further way that makes a veto on our active faith even more illogical. The more perfect and more eternal aspect of the universe is represented in our religions as having personal form. The universe is no longer a mere *It* to us, but a *Thou*, if we are religious; and any relation that may be possible from person to person might be possible here. For instance, although in one sense we are passive portions of the universe, in another we show a curious autonomy, as if we were small active centres on our own account. We feel, too, as if the appeal of religion to us were made to our own active goodwill, as if evidence might be forever withheld from us unless we met the hypothesis half-way. To take a trivial illustration: just as a man who in a company of gentlemen made no advances, asked a warrant for every concession, and believed no one's word without proof, would cut himself off by such churlishness from all the social rewards that a more trusting spirit would earn,—so here, one who should shut himself up in snarling logicality and try to make the gods extort his recognition willy-nilly, or not get it at all, might cut himself off forever from his only opportunity of making the gods' acquaintance. This feeling, forced on us we know not whence, that by obstinately believing that there are gods (although not to do so would be so easy both for our logic and our life) we are doing the universe the deepest service we can, seems parts of the living essence of the religious hypothesis. If the hypothesis *were* true in all its parts, including this one, then pure intellectualism, with its veto on our making willing advances, would be an absurdity; and some participation of our sympathetic nature would be logically required. I, therefore, for one, cannot see my way to accepting the agnostic rules for truth-seeking, or wilfully agree to keep my willing nature out of the game. I cannot do so for this plain reason, that *a rule of thinking which would absolutely prevent me from acknowledging certain kinds of truth if those kinds of truth were really there, would be an irrational rule.* That for me is the long and short of the formal logic of the situation, no matter what the kinds of truth might materially be.

I confess I do not see how this logic can be escaped. But sad experience makes me fear that some of you may still shrink from radically saying with me, *in abstracto*, that we have the right to believe at our own risk any hypothesis that is live enough to tempt our will. I suspect, however, that if this is so, it is because you have got away from the abstract logical point of view altogether, and are thinking (perhaps without realizing it) of some particular religious hypothesis which for you is dead. The freedom to "believe what we will" you apply to the case of some patent superstition; and the faith you think of is the faith defined by the schoolboy when he said, "Faith is when you believe something that you know ain't true." I can only repeat that this is misapprehension. *In concreto*, the freedom to believe can only cover living options which the intellect of the individual cannot by itself resolve; and living options never seem absurdities to him who has them to consider. When I look at the religious question as it really puts itself to concrete men, and when I think of all the possibilities which both practically and theoretically it involves, then this command that we shall put a stopper on our heart, instincts, and courage, and *wait*—acting of course meanwhile more or less as if religion were *not* true[3]—till doomsday, or till such time as our intellect and senses working together may have raked in evidence enough,—this command, I say, seems to me the queerest idol ever manufactured

---

[3]Since belief is measured by action, he who forbids us to believe religion to be true, necessarily also forbids us to act as we should if we did believe it to be true. The whole defence of religious faith hinges upon action. If the action required or inspired by the religious hypothesis is in no way different from that dictated by the naturalistic hypothesis, then religious faith is a pure superfluity, better pruned away, and controversy about its legitimacy is a piece of idle trifling, unworthy of serious minds. I myself believe, of course, that the religious hypothesis gives to the world an expression which specifically determines our reactions, and makes them in a large part unlike what they might be on a purely naturalistic scheme of belief.

in the philosophic cave. Were we scholastic absolutists, there might be more excuse. If we had an infallible intellect with its objective certitudes, we might feel ourselves disloyal to such a perfect organ of knowledge in not trusting to it exclusively, in not waiting for its releasing word. But if we are empiricists, if we believe that no bell in us tolls to let us know for certain when truth is in our grasp, then it seems a piece of idle fantasticality to preach so solemnly our duty of waiting for the bell. Indeed we *may* wait if we will,—I hope you do not think that I am denying that,—but if we do so, we do so at our peril as much as if we believed. In either case we *act*, taking our life in our hands. No one of us ought to issue vetoes to the other, nor should we bandy words of abuse. We ought, on the contrary, delicately and profoundly to respect one another's mental freedom: then only shall we bring about the intellectual republic; then only shall we have that spirit of inner tolerance without which all our outer tolerance is soulless, and which is empiricism's glory; then only shall we live and let live, in speculative as well as in practical things.

I began by a reference to Fitz-James Stephen; let me end by a quotation from him. "What do you think of yourself? What do you think of the world?... These are questions with which all must deal as it seems good to them. They are riddles of the Sphinx, and in some way or other we must deal with them.... In all important transactions of life we have to take a leap in the dark.... If we decide to leave the riddles unanswered, that is a choice; if we waver in our answer, that, too, is a choice: but whatever choice we make, we make it at our peril. If a man chooses to turn his back altogether on God and the future, no one can prevent him; no one can show beyond reasonable doubt that he is mistaken. If a man thinks otherwise and acts as he thinks, I do not see that any one can prove that *he* is mistaken. Each must act as he thinks best; and if he is wrong, so much the worse for him. We stand on a mountain pass in the midst of whirling snow and blinding mist, through which we get glimpses now and then of paths which may be deceptive. If we stand still we shall be frozen to death. If we take the wrong road we shall be dashed to pieces. We do not certainly know whether there is any right one. What must we do? 'Be strong and of good courage.' Act for the best, hope for the best and take what comes.... If death ends all, we cannot meet death better."[4]

---

[4]*Liberty, Equality, Fraternity,* p. 353, 2d ed., London, 1874.

ROBERT MERRIHEW ADAMS

Kierkegaard's Arguments Against Objective Reasoning in Religion

It is sometimes held that there is something in the nature of religious faith itself that renders it useless or undesirable to reason objectively in support of such faith, even if the reasoning should happen to have considerable plausibility. Søren Kierkegaard's *Concluding Unscientific Postscript* is probably the document most commonly cited as representative of this view. In the present essay I shall discuss three arguments for the view. I call them the Approximation Argument, the Postponement Argument, and the Passion Argument; and I suggest they can all be found in the *Postscript*. I shall try to show that the Approximation Argument is a bad argument. The other two will not be so easily disposed of, however. I believe they show that Kierkegaard's conclusion, or something like it, does indeed follow from a certain conception of religiousness—a conception which has some appeal, although for reasons which I shall briefly suggest, I am not prepared to accept it.

Kierkegaard uses the word "objective" and its cognates in several senses, most of which need not concern us here. We are interested in the sense in which he uses it when he says, "it is precisely a misunderstanding to seek an objective assurance," and when he speaks of "an objective uncertainty held fast in the appropriation-process of the most passionate inwardness" (pp. 41, 182).[1] Let us say that a piece of reasoning, R, is *objective reasoning* just in case every (or almost every) intelligent, fair-minded, and sufficiently informed person would regard R as showing or tending to show (in the circumstances in which R is used, and to the extent claimed in R) that R's conclusion is true or probably true. Uses of "objective" and "objectively" in other contexts can be understood from their relation to this one; for example, an objective uncertainty is a proposition which cannot be shown by objective reasoning to be certainly true.

Reprinted from *The Monist*, Vol. 60, No. 2, 1977. Copyright © 1977, *The Monist*, LaSalle, IL 61301. Reprinted by permission of *The Monist*.

[1] Søren Kierkegaard, *Concluding Unscientific Postscript*, translated by David F. Swenson; introduction, notes, and completion of translation by Walter Lowrie (Princeton: Princeton University Press, 1941). Page references in parentheses in the body of the present paper are to this work.

1. THE APPROXIMATION ARGUMENT

"Is it possible to base an eternal happiness upon historical knowledge?" is one of the central questions in the *Postscript*, and in the *Philosophical Fragments* to which it is a "postscript." Part of Kierkegaard's answer to the question is that it is not possible to base an eternal happiness on objective reasoning about historical facts.

> For nothing is more readily evident than that the greatest attainable certainty with respect to anything historical is merely an *approximation*. And an approximation, when viewed as a basis for an eternal happiness, is wholly inadequate, since the incommensurability makes a result impossible. [p. 25]

Kierkegaard maintains that it is possible, however, to base an eternal happiness on a belief in historical facts that is independent of objective evidence for them, and that that is what one must do in order to be a Christian. This is the Approximation Argument for the proposition that Christian faith cannot be based on objective reasoning.[2] (It is assumed that some belief about historical facts is an essential part of Christian faith, so that if religious faith cannot be based on objective historical reasoning, then Christian faith cannot be based on objective reasoning at all.) Let us examine the argument in detail.

Its first premise is Kierkegaard's claim that "the greatest attainable certainty with respect to anything historical is merely an approximation." I take him to mean that historical evidence, objectively considered, never completely excludes the possibility of error. "It goes without saying," he claims, "that it is impossible in the case of historical problems to reach an objective decision so certain that no doubt could disturb it" (p. 41). For Kierkegaard's purposes it does not matter how small the possibility of error is, so long as it is finitely small (that is, so long as it is not literally infinitesimal). He insists (p. 31) that his Approximation Argument makes no appeal to the supposition that the objective evidence for Christian historical beliefs is weaker than the objective evidence for any other historical belief. The argument turns on a claim about *all* historical evidence. The probability of error in our belief that there was an American Civil War in the nineteenth century, for instance, might be as small as $\frac{1}{10^{2,000,000}}$; that would be a large enough chance of error for Kierkegaard's argument.

---

[2]The argument is not original with Kierkegaard. It can be found in works of G. E. Lessing and D. F. Strauss that Kierkegaard had read. See especially Thulstrup's quotation and discussion of a passage from Strauss in the commentary portion of Søren Kierkegaard, *Philosophical Fragments*, translated by David F. Swenson, second edition, translation revised by Howard V. Hong, with introduction and commentary by Niels Thulstrup (Princeton, N.J.: Princeton University Press, 1962), pp. 149–51.

It might be disputed, but let us assume for the sake of argument that there is some such finitely small probability of error in the objective grounds for all historical beliefs, as Kierkegaard held. This need not keep us from saying that we "know," and it is "certain," that there was an American Civil War. For such an absurdly small possibility of error is as good as no possibility of error at all, "for all practical intents and purposes," as we might say. Such a possibility of error is too small to be worth worrying about.

But would it be too small to be worth worrying about if we had an *infinite* passionate interest in the question about the Civil War? If we have an infinite passionate interest in something, there is no limit to how important it is to us. (The nature of such an interest will be discussed more fully in section 3 below.) Kierkegaard maintains that in relation to an infinite passionate interest *no* possibility of error is too small to be worth worrying about. "In relation to an eternal happiness, and an infinite passionate interest in its behalf (in which latter alone the former can exist), an iota is of importance, of infinite importance..." (p. 28). This is the basis for the second premise of the Approximation Argument, which is Kierkegaard's claim that "an approximation, when viewed as a basis for an eternal happiness, is wholly inadequate" (p. 25). "An approximation is essentially incommensurable with an infinite personal interest in an eternal happiness" (p. 26).

At this point in the argument it is important to have some understanding of Kierkegaard's conception of faith, and the way in which he thinks faith excludes doubt. Faith must be decisive; in fact it seems to consist in a sort of decision-making. "The conclusion of belief is not so much a conclusion as a resolution, and it is for this reason that belief excludes doubt."[3] The decision of faith is a decision to disregard the possibility of error—to act on what is believed, without hedging one's bets to take account of any possibility of error.

To disregard the possibility of error is not to be unaware of it, or fail to consider it, or lack anxiety about it. Kierkegaard insists that the believer must be keenly *aware* of the risk of error. "If I wish to preserve myself in faith I must constantly be intent upon holding fast the objective uncertainty, so as to remain out upon the deep, over seventy thousand fathoms of water, still preserving my faith" (p. 182).

For Kierkegaard, then, to ask whether faith in a historical fact can be based on objective reasoning is to ask whether objective reasoning can justify one in disregarding the possibility of error which (he thinks) historical evidence always leaves. Here another aspect of Kierkegaard's conception of faith plays its part in the argument. He thinks that in all genuine religious faith the believer is *infinitely* interested in the object of his faith. And he thinks it follows that objective reasoning cannot justify him in disregarding *any* possibility of error about the object of faith, and therefore cannot lead him all

---

[3]Kierkegaard, *Philosophical Fragments*, p. 104; cf. pp. 102–03.

the way to religious faith where a historical fact is concerned. The farthest it could lead him is to the conclusion that *if* he had only a certain finite (though very great) interest in the matter, the possibility of error would be too small to be worth worrying about and he would be justified in disregarding it. But faith disregards a possibility of error that *is* worth worrying about, since an infinite interest is involved. Thus faith requires a "leap" beyond the evidence, a leap that cannot be justified by objective reasoning (cf. p. 90).

There is something right in what Kierkegaard is saying here, but his Approximation Argument is a bad argument. He is right in holding that grounds of doubt which may be insignificant for most practical purposes can be extremely troubling for the intensity of a religious concern, and that it may require great decisiveness, or something like courage, to overcome them religiously. But he is mistaken in holding that objective reasoning could not justify one in disregarding any possibility of error about something in which one is infinitely interested.

The mistake, I believe, lies in his overlooking the fact that there are at least two different reasons one might have for disregarding a possibility of error. The first is that the possibility is too small to be worth worrying about. The second is that the risk of not disregarding the possibility of error would be greater than the risk of disregarding it. Of these two reasons only the first is ruled out by the infinite passionate interest.

I will illustrate this point with two examples, one secular and one religious. A certain woman has a very great (though not infinite) interest in her husband's love for her. She rightly judges that the objective evidence available to her renders it 99.9 per cent probable that he loves her truly. The intensity of her interest is sufficient to cause her some *anxiety* over the remaining $\frac{1}{1,000}$ chance that he loves her not; for her this chance is not too small to be worth worrying about. (Kierkegaard uses a similar example to support his Approximation Argument; see p. 511.) But she (very reasonably) wants to *disregard* the risk of error, in the sense of not hedging her bets, if he does love her. This desire is at least as strong as her desire not to be deceived if he does not love her. Objective reasoning should therefore suffice to bring her to the conclusion that she ought to disregard the risk of error, since by not disregarding it she would run 999 times as great risk of frustrating one of these desires.

Or suppose you are trying to base your eternal happiness on your relation to Jesus, and therefore have an infinite passionate interest in the question whether he declared Peter and his episcopal successors to be infallible in matters of religious doctrine. You want to be committed to whichever is the true belief on this question, disregarding any possibility of error in it. And suppose, just for the sake of argument, that objective historical evidence renders it 99 per cent probable that Jesus did declare Peter and his successors to be infallible—or 99 per cent probable that he did not—for our present discussion it does not matter which. The one per cent chance of error is enough to make you *anxious*, in view of your infinite interest. But objective reasoning leads to the conclusion that you ought to commit yourself to the more probable opinion, *disregarding* the risk of error, if your strongest desire in the matter is to be so committed to the true opinion. For the only other way to satisfy this desire would be to commit yourself to the less probable opinion, disregarding the risk of error in it. The first way will be successful if and only if the more probable opinion is true, and the second way if and only if the less probable opinion is true. Surely it is prudent to do what gives you a 99 per cent chance of satisfying your strong desire, in preference to what gives you only a one per cent chance of satisfying it.

In this argument your strong desire to be committed to the true opinion is presupposed. The reasonableness of this desire may depend on a belief for which no probability can be established by purely historical reasoning, such as the belief that Jesus is God. But any difficulties arising from this point are distinct from those urged in the Approximation Argument, which itself presupposes the infinite passionate interest in the historical question.

There is some resemblance between my arguments in these examples and Pascal's famous Wager argument. But whereas Pascal's argument turns on weighing an infinite interest against a finite one, mine turn on weighing a large chance of success against a small one. An argument closer to Pascal's will be discussed in section 4 below.

The reader may well have noticed in the foregoing discussion some unclarity about what sort of justification is being demanded and given for religious beliefs about historical facts. There are at least two different types of questions about a proposition which I might try to settle by objective reasoning: (1) Is it probable that the proposition is true? (2) In view of the evidence which I have for and against the proposition, and my interest in the matter, is it prudent for me to have faith in the truth of the proposition, disregarding the possibility of error? Correspondingly, we may distinguish two ways in which a belief can be *based on* objective reasoning. The proposition believed may be the conclusion of a piece of objective reasoning, and accepted because it is that. We may say that such a belief is *objectively probable.* Or one might hold a belief or maintain a religious faith because of a piece of objective reasoning whose conclusion is that it would be prudent, morally right, or otherwise desirable for one to hold that belief or faith. In this latter case let us say that the belief is *objectively advantageous.* It is clear that historical beliefs can be objectively probable; and in the Approximation Argument, Kierkegaard does not deny Christian historical beliefs can be objectively probable. His thesis is, in effect, that in view of an infinite passionate interest in their subject matter, they cannot be objectively advantageous, and therefore cannot be fully justified objectively, even if they are objectively probable. It is this thesis that I have attempted to refute. I have not been discussing the question whether Christian historical beliefs are objectively probable.

2. THE POSTPONEMENT ARGUMENT

The trouble with objective historical reasoning, according to the Approximation Argument, is that it cannot yield complete certainty. But that is not Kierkegaard's only complaint against it as a basis for religious faith. He also objects that objective historical inquiry is never completely finished, so that one who seeks to base his faith on it postpones his religious commitment forever. In the process of historical research "new difficulties arise and are overcome, and new difficulties again arise. Each generation inherits from its predecessor the illusion that the method is quite impeccable, but the learned scholars have not yet succeeded...and so forth.... The infinite personal passionate interest of the subject...vanishes more and more, because the decision is postponed, and postponed as following directly upon the result of the learned inquiry" (p. 28). As soon as we take "an historical document" as "our standard for the determination of Christian truth," we are "involved in a parenthesis whose conclusion is everlastingly prospective" (p. 28)—that is, we are involved in a religious digression which keeps religious commitment forever in the future.[4]

Kierkegaard has such fears about allowing religious faith to rest on *any* empirical reasoning. The danger of postponement of commitment arises not only from the uncertainties of historical scholarship, but also in connection with the design argument for God's existence. In the *Philosophical Fragments* Kierkegaard notes some objections to the attempt to prove God's existence from evidence of "the wisdom in nature, the goodness, the wisdom in the governance of the world," and then says, "even if I began I would never finish, and would in addition have to live constantly in suspense, lest something so terrible should suddenly happen that my bit of proof would be demolished."[5] What we have before us is a quite general sort of objection to the treatment of religious beliefs as empirically testable. On this point many analytical philosophers seem to agree with Kierkegaard. Much discussion in recent analytical philosophy of religion has proceeded from the supposition that religious beliefs are not empirically testable. I think it is far from obvious that that supposition is correct; and it is interesting to consider arguments that may be advanced to support it.

Kierkegaard's statements suggest an argument that I call the Postponement Argument. Its first premise is that one cannot have an authentic religious faith without being totally committed to it. In order to be totally

---

[4]Essentially the same argument can be found in a plea, which has had great influence among more recent theologians, for making Christian faith independent of the results of critical historical study of the Bible: Martin Kähler's famous lecture, first delivered in 1892, *Der sogenannte historische Jesus und der geschichtliche biblische Christus* (München: Christus Kaiser Verlag, 1961), p. 50f.

[5]Kierkegaard, *Philosophical Fragment*, p. 52.

committed to a belief, in the relevant sense, one must be determined not to abandon the belief under any circumstances that one recognizes as epistemically possible.

The second premise is that one cannot yet be totally committed to any belief which one bases on an inquiry in which one recognizes any possibility of a future need to revise the results. Total commitment to any belief so based will necessarily be postponed. I believe that this premise, suitably interpreted, is true. Consider the position of someone who regards himself as committed to a belief on the basis of objective evidence, but who recognizes some possibility that future discoveries will destroy the objective justification of the belief. We must ask how he is disposed to react in the event, however unlikely, that the objective basis of his belief is overthrown. Is he prepared to abandon the belief in that event? If so, he is not totally committed to the belief in the relevant sense. But if he is determined to cling to his belief even if its objective justification is taken away, then he is not basing the belief on the objective justification—or at least he is not basing it solely on the justification.[6]

The conclusion to be drawn from these two premises is that authentic religious faith cannot be based on an inquiry in which one recognizes any possibility of a future need to revise the results. We ought to note that this conclusion embodies two important restrictions on the scope of the argument.

In the first place, we are not given an argument that authentic religious faith cannot *have* an objective justification that is subject to possible future revision. What we are given is an argument that the authentic believer's holding of his religious belief cannot *depend* entirely on such a justification.

In the second place, this conclusion applies only to those who *recognize* some epistemic possibility that the objective results which appear to support their belief may be overturned. I think it would be unreasonable to require, as part of total commitment, a determination with regard to one's response to circumstances that one does not recognize as possible at all. It may be, however, that one does not recognize such a possibility when one ought to.

Kierkegaard needs one further premise in order to arrive at the conclusion that authentic religious faith cannot without error be based on any objective empirical reasoning. This third premise is that in every objective empirical inquiry there is always, objectively considered, some epistemic possibility that the results of the inquiry will need to be revised in view of new evidence or new reasoning. I believe Kierkegaard makes this assumption; he certainly makes it with regard to historical inquiry. From this premise it follows that one is in error if in any objective empirical inquiry one does

---

[6]Kierkegaard notes the possibility that in believing in God's existence "I make so bold as to defy all objections, even those that have not yet been made." But in that case he thinks the belief is not really based on the evidence of God's work in the world; "it is not from the works that I make my proof" (*Philosophical Fragments*, p. 52).

not recognize any possibility of a future need to revise the results. But if one does recognize such a possibility, then according to the conclusion already reached in the Postponement Argument, one cannot base an authentic religious faith on the inquiry.

Some philosophers might attack the third premise of this argument; and certainly it is controversial. But I am more inclined to criticize the first premise. There is undoubtedly something plausible about the claim that authentic religious faith must involve a commitment so complete that the believer is resolved not to abandon his belief under any circumstances that he regards as epistemically possible. If you are willing to abandon your ostensibly religious beliefs for the sake of objective inquiry, mightn't we justly say that objective inquiry is your real religion, the thing to which you are most deeply committed?

There is also something plausible to be said on the other side, however. It has commonly been thought to be an important part of religious ethics that one ought to be humble, teachable, open to correction, new inspiration, and growth of insight, even (and perhaps especially) in important religious beliefs. That view would have to be discarded if we were to concede to Kierkegaard that the heart of commitment in religion is an unconditional determination not to change in one's important religious beliefs. In fact I think there is something radically wrong with this conception of religious commitment. Faith ought not to be thought of as unconditional devotion to a belief. For in the first place the object of religious devotion is not a belief or attitude of one's own, but God. And in the second place it may be doubted that religious devotion to God can or should be completely unconditional. God's love for sinners is sometimes said to be completely unconditional, not being based on any excellence or merit of theirs. But religious devotion to God is generally thought to be based on His goodness and love. It is the part of the strong, not the weak, to love unconditionally. And in relation to God we are weak.

3. THE PASSION ARGUMENT

In Kierkegaard's statements of the Approximation Argument and the Postponement Argument it is assumed that a system of religious beliefs might be objectively probable. It is only for the sake of argument, however, that Kierkegaard allows this assumption. He really holds that religious faith, by its very nature, needs objective *im*probability. "Anything that is almost probable, or probable, or extremely and emphatically probable, is something [one] can almost know, or as good as know, or extremely and emphatically almost *know*—but it is impossible to *believe*" (p. 189). Nor will Kierkegaard countenance the suggestion that religion ought to go beyond belief to some almost-knowledge based on probability. "Faith is the highest passion in a man. There are perhaps many in every generation who do not even reach it, but no one gets further."[7] It would be a betrayal of religion to try to go beyond faith. The suggestion that faith might be replaced by "probabilities and guarantees" is for the believer "a temptation to be resisted with all his strength" (p. 15). The attempt to establish religious beliefs on a foundation of objective probability is therefore no service to religion, but inimical to religion's true interests. The approximation to certainty which might be afforded by objective probability is rejected, not only for the reasons given in the Approximation Argument and Postponement Argument, but also from a deeper motive, "since on the contrary it behooves us to get rid of introductory guarantees of security, proofs from consequences, and the whole mob of public pawnbrokers and guarantors, so as to permit the absurd to stand out in all its clarity—in order that the individual may believe if he wills it; I merely say that it must be strenuous in the highest degree so to believe" (p. 190).

As this last quotation indicates, Kierkegaard thinks that religious belief ought to be based on a strenuous exertion of the will—a passionate striving. His reasons for thinking that objective probability is religiously undesirable have to do with the place of passion in religion, and constitute what I call the Passion Argument. The first premise of the argument is that the most essential and the most valuable feature of religiousness is passion, indeed an infinite passion, a passion of the greatest possible intensity. The second premise is that an infinite passion requires objective improbability. And the conclusion therefore is that that which is most essential and most valuable in religiousness requires objective improbability.

My discussion of this argument will have three parts. (a) First I will try to clarify, very briefly, what it is that is supposed to be objectively improbable. (b) Then we will consider Kierkegaard's reasons for holding that infinite passion requires objective improbability. In so doing we will also gain a clearer understanding of what a Kierkegaardian infinite passion is. (c) Finally I will discuss the first premise of the argument—although issues will arise at that point which I do not pretend to be able to settle by argument.

(a) What are the beliefs whose improbability is needed by religious passion? Kierkegaard will hardly be satisfied with the improbability of just any one belief; it must surely be at least an important belief. On the other hand it would clearly be preposterous to suppose that every belief involved in Christianity must be objectively improbable. (Consider, for example, the belief that the man Jesus did indeed live.) I think that what is demanded in the Passion Argument is the objective improbability of at least one belief which must be true if the goal sought by the religious passion is to be attained.

(b) We can find in the *Postscript* suggestions of several reasons for thinking that an infinite passion needs objective improbability. The two that

---

    [7]Søren Kierkegaard, *Fear and Trembling*, trans. Walter Lowrie, 2d ed. (Princeton: Princeton University Press, 1970; published in one volume with *The Sickness unto Death*), p. 131. Cf. *Postscript*, p. 31f.

seem to me most interesting have to do with (i) the risks accepted and (ii) the costs paid in pursuance of a passionate interest.

(i) One reason that Kierkegaard has for valuing objective improbability is that it increases the *risk* attaching to the religious life, and risk is so essential for the expression of religious passion that "without risk there is no faith" (p. 182). About the nature of an eternal happiness, the goal of religious striving, Kierkegaard says "there is nothing to be said...except that it is the good which is attained by venturing everything absolutely" (p. 382).

> But what then does it mean to venture? A venture is the precise correlative of an uncertainty; when the certainty is there the venture becomes impossible.... If what I hope to gain by venturing is itself certain, I do not risk or venture, but make an exchange.... No, if I am in truth resolved to venture, in truth resolved to strive for the attainment of the highest good, the uncertainty must be there, and I must have room to move, so to speak. But the largest space I can obtain, where there is room for the most vehement gesture of the passion that embraces the infinite, is uncertainty of knowledge with respect to an eternal happiness, or the certain knowledge that the choice is in the finite sense a piece of madness: now there is room, now you can venture! [pp. 380–82]

How is it that objective improbability provides the largest space for the most vehement gesture of infinite passion? Consider two cases. (A) You plunge into a raging torrent to rescue from drowning someone you love, who is crying for help. (B) You plunge into a raging torrent in a desperate attempt to rescue someone you love, who appears to be unconscious and *may* already have drowned. In both cases you manifest a passionate interest in saving the person, risking your own life in order to do so. But I think Kierkegaard would say there is more passion in the second case than in the first. For in the second case you risk your life in what is, objectively considered, a smaller chance that you will be able to save your loved one. A greater passion is required for a more desperate attempt.

A similar assessment may be made of the following pair of cases. (A′) You stake everything on your faith in the truth of Christianity, knowing that it is objectively 99 per cent probable that Christianity is true. (B′) You stake everything on your faith in the truth of Christianity, knowing that the truth of Christianity is, objectively, possible but so improbable that its probability is, say, as small as $\frac{1}{10^{2,000,000}}$. There is passion in both cases, but Kierkegaard will say that there is more passion in the second case than in the first. For to venture the same stake (namely, everything) on a much smaller chance of success shows greater passion.

Acceptance of risk can thus be seen as a *measure* of the intensity of passion. I believe this provides us with one way of understanding what Kierkegaard means when he calls religious passion "infinite." An *infinite* passionate interest in x is an interest so strong that it leads one to make the greatest possible sacrifices in order to obtain x, on the smallest possible chance of success. The infinity of the passion is shown in that there is no sacrifice so great one will not make it, and no chance of success so small one will not act on it. A passion which is infinite in this sense requires, by its very nature, a situation of maximum risk for its expression.

It will doubtless be objected that this argument involves a misunderstanding of what a passionate interest is. Such an interest is a disposition. In order to have a great passionate interest it is not necessary actually to make a great sacrifice with a small chance of success; all that is necessary is to have such an intense interest that one *would* do so if an appropriate occasion should arise. It is therefore a mistake to say that there *is* more passion in case (B) than in case (A), or in (B') than in (A'). More passion is *shown* in (B) than in (A), and in (B') than in (A'); but an equal passion may exist in cases in which there is no occasion to show it.

This objection may well be correct as regards what we normally mean by "passionate interest." But that is not decisive for the argument. The crucial question is what part dispositions, possibly unactualized, ought to play in religious devotion. And here we must have a digression about the position of the *Postscript* on this question—a position that is complex at best and is not obviously consistent.

In the first place I do not think that Kierkegaard would be prepared to think of passion, or a passionate interest, as primarily a disposition that might remain unactualized. He seems to conceive of passion chiefly as an intensity in which one actually does and feels. "Passion is momentary" (p. 178), although capable of continual repetition. And what is momentary in such a way that it must be repeated rather than protracted is presumably an occurrence rather than a disposition. It agrees with this conception of passion that Kierkegaard idealizes a life of "persistent striving," and says that the religious task is to "exercise" the God-relationship and to give "existential expression" to the religious choice (pp. 110, 364, 367).

All of this supports the view that what Kierkegaard means by "an infinite passionate interest" is a pattern of actual decision-making, in which one continually exercises and expresses one's religiousness by making the greatest possible sacrifices on the smallest possible chance of success. In order to actualize such a pattern of life one needs chances of success that are as small as possible. That is the room that is required for "the most vehement gesture" of infinite passion.

But on the other hand Kierkegaard does allow a dispositional element in the religious life, and even precisely in the making of the greatest possible sacrifices. We might suppose that if we are to make the greatest possible sacrifices in our religious devotion, we must do so by abandoning all worldly interests and devoting all our time and attention to religion. That is what monasticism attempts to do, as Kierkegaard sees it; and (in the *Postscript*, at any rate) he rejects the attempt, contrary to what our argument to this point would have led us to expect of him. He holds that "resignation" (pp. 353, 367) or "renunciation" (pp. 362, 386) of *all* finite ends is precisely the first thing that religiousness requires; but he means a renunciation that is compatible with pursuing and enjoying finite ends (pp. 362–71). This renunciation is the practice of a sort of detachment; Kierkegaard uses the image of a dentist loosening the soft tissues around a tooth, while it is still in place, in preparation for pulling it (p. 367). It is partly a matter of not treating finite things with a desperate seriousness, but with a certain coolness or humor, even while one pursues them (pp. 368, 370).

This coolness is not just a disposition. But the renunciation also has a dispositional aspect. "Now if for any individual an eternal happiness is his highest good, this will mean that all finite satisfactions are volitionally relegated to the status of what may have to be renounced in favor of an eternal happiness" (p. 350). The volitional relegation is not a disposition but an act of choice. The object of this choice, however, appears to be a dispositional state—the state of being such that one *would* forgo any finite satisfaction *if* it *were* religiously necessary or advantageous to do so.

It seems clear that Kierkegaard, in the *Postscript*, is willing to admit a dispositional element at one point in the religious venture, but not at another. It is enough in most cases, he thinks, if one is *prepared* to cease for the sake of religion from pursuing some finite end; but it is not enough that one *would* hold to one's belief in the face of objective improbability. The belief must actually be improbable, although the pursuit of the finite need not actually cease. What is not clear is a reason for this disparity. The following hypothesis, admittedly somewhat speculative as interpretation of the text, is the best explanation I can offer.

The admission of a dispositional element in the religious renunciation of the finite is something to which Kierkegaard seems to be driven by the view that there is no alternative to it except idolatry. For suppose one actually ceases from all worldly pursuits and enters a monastery. In the monastery one would pursue a number of particular ends (such as getting up in the middle of the night to say the offices) which, although religious in a way ("churchy," one might say), are still finite. The absolute *telos* or end of religion is no more to be identified with them than with the ends pursued by an alderman (pp. 362–71). To pretend otherwise would be to make an idolatrous identification of the absolute end with some finite end. An existing person cannot have sacrificed everything by actually having ceased from pursuing *all* finite ends. For as long as he lives and acts he is pursuing some finite end. Therefore his renouncing *everything* finite must be at least partly dispositional.

Kierkegaard does not seem happy with this position. He regards it as of the utmost importance that the religious passion should come to expression. The problem of finding an adequate expression for a passion for an infinite end, in the face of the fact that in every concrete action one will be pursuing some finite end, is treated in the *Postscript* as the central problem of religion (see especially pp. 386–468). If the sacrifice of everything finite must remain largely dispositional, then perhaps it is all the more important to Kierkegaard that the smallness of the chance for which it is sacrificed should be fully actual, so that the infinity of the religious passion may be measured by an actuality in at least one aspect of the religious venture.

(ii) According to Kierkegaard, as I have argued, the intensity of a passion is measured in part by the smallness of the chances of success that one acts on. It can also be measured in part by its *costliness*–that is, by how much one gives up or suffers in acting on those chances. This second measure can also be made the basis of an argument for the claim that an infinite passion requires objective improbability. For the objective improbability of a religious belief, if recognized, increases the costliness of holding it. The risk involved in staking everything on an objectively improbable belief gives rise to an anxiety and mental suffering whose acceptance is itself a sacrifice. It seems to follow that if one is not staking everything on a belief one sees to be objectively improbable, one's passion is not infinite in Kierkegaard's sense, since one's sacrifice could be greater if one did adhere to an improbable belief.

Kierkegaard uses an argument similar to this. For God to give us objective knowledge of Himself, eliminating paradox from it, would be "to lower the price of the God-relationship."

> And even if God could be imagined willing, no man with passion in his heart could desire it. To a maiden genuinely in love it could never occur that she had bought her happiness too dear, but rather that she had not bought it dear enough. And just as the passion of the infinite was itself the truth, so in the case of the highest value it holds true that the price is the value, that a low price means a poor value.... [p. 207]

Kierkegaard here appears to hold, first, that an increase in the objective probability of religious belief would reduce its costliness, and second, that the value of a religious life is measured by its cost. I take it his reason for the second of these claims is that passion is the most valuable thing in a religious life and passion is measured by its cost. If we grant Kierkegaard the requisite conception of an infinite passion, we seem once again to have a plausible argument for the view that objective improbability is required for such a passion.

(c) We must therefore consider whether infinite passion, as Kierkegaard conceives of it, ought to be part of the religious ideal of life. Such a passion is a striving, or pattern of decision-making, in which, with the greatest possible intensity of feeling, one continually makes the greatest possible sacrifices on the smallest possible chance of success. This seems to me an impossible ideal. I doubt that any human being could have a passion of this sort, because I doubt that one could make a sacrifice so great that a greater could not be made, or have a (nonzero) chance of success so small that a smaller could not be had.

But even if Kierkegaard's ideal is impossible, one might want to try to approximate it. Intensity of passion might still be measured by the greatness of sacrifices made and the smallness of chances of success acted on, even if we cannot hope for a greatest possible or a smallest possible here. And it could be claimed that the most essential and valuable thing in religiousness is a passion that is very intense (though it cannot be infinite) by this standard—the more intense the better. This claim will not support an argument that objective improbability is absolutely required for religious passion. For a passion could presumably be very intense, involving great sacrifices and risks of some other sort, without an objectively improbable belief. But it could still be argued that objectively improbable religious beliefs enhance the value of the religious life by increasing its sacrifices and diminishing its chances of success, whereas objective probability detracts from the value of religious passion by diminishing its intensity.

The most crucial question about the Passion Argument, then, is whether maximization of sacrifice and risk are so valuable in religion as to make objective improbability a desirable characteristic of religious beliefs. Certainly much religious thought and feeling places a very high value on sacrifice and on passionate intensity. But the doctrine that it is desirable to increase without limit, or to the highest possible degree (if there is one) the cost and risk of a religious life is less plausible (to say the least) than the view that *some* degree of cost and risk may add to the value of a religious life. The former doctrine would set the religious interest at enmity with all other interests, or at least with the best of them. Kierkegaard is surely right in thinking that it would be impossible to live without pursuing some finite ends. But even so it would be possible to exchange the pursuit of better finite ends for the pursuit of worse ones—for example, by exchanging the pursuit of truth, beauty, and satisfying personal relationships for the self-flagellating pursuit of pain. And a way of life would be the costlier for requiring such an exchange. Kierkegaard does not, in the *Postscript*, demand it. But the presuppositions of his Passion Argument seem to imply that such a sacrifice would be religiously desirable. Such a conception of religion is demonic. In a tolerable religious ethics some way must be found to conceive of the religious interest as inclusive rather than exclusive of the best of other interests—including, I think, the interest in having well-grounded beliefs.

4. PASCAL'S WAGER AND KIERKEGAARD'S LEAP

Ironically, Kierkegaard's views about religious passion suggest a way in which his religious beliefs could be based on objective reasoning—not on reasoning which would show them to be objectively probable, but on reasoning which shows them to be objectively advantageous. Consider the situation of a person whom Kierkegaard would regard as a genuine Christian believer.

What would such a person want most of all? He would want above all else to attain the truth through Christianity. That is, he would desire both that Christianity be true and that he himself be related to it as a genuine believer. He would desire that state of affairs (which we may call S) so ardently that he would be willing to sacrifice everything else to obtain it, given only the smallest possible chance of success.

We can therefore construct the following argument, which has an obvious analogy to Pascal's Wager. Let us assume that there is, objectively, some chance, however small, that Christianity is true. This is an assumption which Kierkegaard accepts (p. 31), and I think it is plausible. There are two possibilities, then: either Christianity is true, or it is false. (Others might object to so stark a disjunction, but Kierkegaard will not.) If Christianity is false it is impossible for anyone to obtain S, since S includes the truth of Christianity. It is only if Christianity is true that anything one does will help one or hinder one in obtaining S. And if Christianity is true, one will obtain S just in case one becomes a genuine Christian believer. It seems obvious that one would increase one's chances of becoming a genuine Christian believer by becoming one now (if one can), even if the truth of Christian beliefs is now objectively uncertain or improbable. Hence it would seem to be advantageous for anyone who can to become a genuine Christian believer now, if he wants S so much that he would be willing to sacrifice everything else for the smallest possible chance of obtaining S. Indeed I believe that the argument I have given for this conclusion is a piece of objective reasoning, and that Christian belief is therefore *objectively* advantageous for anyone who wants S as much as a Kierkegaardian genuine Christian must want it.

Of course this argument does not tend at all to show that it is objectively probable that Christianity is true. It only gives a practical, prudential reason for believing, to someone who has a certain desire. Nor does the argument do anything to prove that such an absolutely overriding desire for S is reasonable.[8] It does show, however, that just as Kierkegaard's position has more logical structure than one might at first think, it is more difficult than he probably realized for him to get away entirely from objective justification.[9]

---

[8]It is worth noting, though, that a similar argument might still provide some less overriding justification of belief to someone who had a strong, but less overriding, desire for S.

[9]Versions of this paper have been read to philosophical colloquia at Occidental College and California State University, Fullerton. I am indebted to participants in those discussions, to students in many of my classes, and particularly to Marilyn McCord Adams, Van Harvey, Thomas Kselman, William Laserow, and James Muyskens, for helpful comment on the ideas which are contained in this paper (or which would have been, had it not been for their criticisms).

NORMAN MALCOLM

The Groundlessness of Belief

I.

In his final notebooks Wittgenstein wrote that it is difficult "to realize the groundlessness of our believing."[1] He was thinking of how much mere acceptance, on the basis of no evidence, forms our lives. This is obvious in the case of small children. They are told the names of things. They accept what they are told. They do not ask for grounds. A child does not demand a proof that the person who feeds him is called "Mama." Or are we to suppose that the child reasons to himself as follows: "The others present seem to know this person who is feeding me, and since they call her 'Mama' that probably is her name"? It is obvious on reflection that a child cannot consider evidence or even doubt anything until he has already learned much. As Wittgenstein puts it: "The child learns by believing the adult. Doubt comes *after* belief" (*OC*, 160).

What is more difficult to perceive is that the lives of educated, sophisticated adults are also formed by groundless beliefs. I do not mean eccentric beliefs that are out on the fringes of their lives, but fundamental beliefs. Take the belief that familiar material things (watches, shoes, chairs) do not cease to exist without some physical explanation. They don't "vanish in thin air." It is interesting that we do use that very expression: "I *know* I put the keys right here on this table. They must have vanished in thin air!" But this exclamation is hyperbole; we are not speaking in literal seriousness. I do not know of any adult who would consider, in all gravity, that the keys might have inexplicably ceased to exist.

Reprinted from Norman Malcolm, "The Groundlessness of Belief," in *Reason and Religion*, edited by Stuart C. Brown. Copyright © 1977 by the Royal Institute of Philosophy. Reprinted by permission of the publisher, Cornell University Press.

[1]Ludwig Wittgenstein, *On Certainty*, ed. G. E. M. Anscombe and G. H. von Wright; English translation by D. Paul and G. E. M. Anscombe (Oxford, 1969), paragraph 166. Henceforth I include references to this work in the text, employing the abbreviation "*OC*" followed by paragraph number. References to Wittgenstein's *The Blue and Brown Books* (Oxford, 1958) are indicated in the text by "*BB*" followed by page number. References to his *Philosophical Investigations*, ed. G. E. M. Anscombe and R. Rhees; English translation by Anscombe (Oxford, 1967) are indicated by "*PI*" followed by paragraph number. In *OC* and *PI*, I have mainly used the translations of Paul and Anscombe but with some departures.

Yet it is possible to imagine a society in which it was accepted that sometimes material things do go out of existence without having been crushed, melted, eroded, broken into pieces, burned up, eaten, or destroyed in some other way. The difference between those people and ourselves would not consist in their *saying* something that we don't say ("It vanished in thin air"), since we say it too. I conceive of these people as acting and thinking differently from ourselves in such ways as the following: If one of them could not find his wallet he would give up the search sooner than you or I would; also he would be less inclined to suppose that it was stolen. In general, what we would regard as convincing circumstantial evidence of theft those people would find less convincing. They would take fewer precautions than we would to protect their possessions against loss or theft. They would have less inclination to save money, since it too can just disappear. They would not tend to form strong attachments to material things, animals, or other people. Generally, they would stand in a looser relation to the world than we do. The disappearance of a desired object, which would provoke us to a frantic search, they would be more inclined to accept with a shrug. Of course, their scientific theories would be different; but also their attitude toward experiment, and inference from experimental results, would be more tentative. If the repetition of a familiar chemical experiment did not yield the expected result this *could* be because one of the chemical substances had vanished.

The outlook I have sketched might be thought to be radically incoherent. I do not see that this is so. Although those people consider it to be possible that a wallet might have inexplicably ceased to exist, it is also true that they regard that as unlikely. For things that are lost usually do turn up later; or if not, their fate can often be accounted for. Those people use pretty much the same criteria of identity that we do; their reasoning would resemble ours quite a lot. Their thinking would not be incoherent. But it would be different, since they would leave room for some possibilities that we exclude.

If we compare their view that material things do sometimes go out of existence inexplicably, with our own rejection of that view, it does not appear to me that one position is supported by *better evidence* than is the other. Each position is compatible with ordinary experience. On the one hand it is true that familiar objects (watches, wallets, lawn chairs) occasionally disappear without any adequate explanation. On the other hand it happens, perhaps more frequently, that a satisfying explanation of the disappearance is discovered.

Our attitude in this matter is striking. We would not be willing to consider it as even improbable that a missing lawn chair had "just ceased to exist." We would not entertain such a suggestion. If anyone proposed it we would be sure he was joking. It is no exaggeration to say that this attitude is part of the foundations of our thinking. I do not want to say that this attitude is *un*reasonable; but rather that it is something that we do not *try* to support with grounds. It could be said to belong to "the framework" of our thinking about material things.

Wittgenstein asks: "Does anyone ever test whether this table remains in existence when no one is paying attention to it?" (*OC*, 163). The answer is: Of course not. Is this because we would not call it "a table" if that were to happen? But we do call it "a table" and none of us makes the test. Doesn't this show that we do not regard that occurrence as a possibility? People who did so regard it would seem ludicrous to us. One could imagine that they made ingenious experiments to decide the question; but this research would make us smile. Is this because experiments were conducted by our ancestors that settled the matter once and for all? I don't believe it. The principle that material things do not cease to exist without physical cause is an unreflective part of the framework within which physical investigations are made and physical explanations arrived at.

Wittgenstein suggests that the same is true of what might be called "the principle of the continuity of nature":

> Think of chemical investigations. Lavoisier makes experiments with substances in his laboratory and now concludes that this and that takes place when there is burning. He does not say that it might happen otherwise another time. He has got hold of a world-picture—not of course one that he invented: he learned it as a child. I say world-picture and not hypothesis, because it is the matter-of-course (*selbstverständliche*) foundation for his research and as such also goes unmentioned (*OC*, 167).
>
> But now, what part is played by the presupposition that a substance A always reacts to a substance B in the same way, given the same circumstances? Or is that part of the definition of a substance? (*OC*, 168).

Framework principles such as the continuity of nature or the assumption that material things do not cease to exist without physical cause belong to what Wittgenstein calls a "system." He makes the following observation, which seems to me to be true: "All testing, all confirmation and disconfirmation of a hypothesis takes place already within a system. And this system is not a more or less arbitrary and doubtful point of departure for all our arguments: no, it belongs to the nature of what we call an argument. The system is not so much the point of departure, as the element in which arguments have their life" (*OC*, 105).

A "system" provides the boundaries within which we ask questions, carry out investigations, and make judgments. Hypotheses are put forth, and challenged, *within* a system. Verification, justification, the search for evidence, occur *within* a system. The framework propositions of the system are not put to the test, not backed up by evidence. This is what Wittgenstein means when he says: "Of course there is justification; but justification comes to an end" (*OC*, 192); and when he asks: "Doesn't testing come to an end?" (*OC*, 164); and when he remarks that "whenever we test anything we are already presupposing something that is not tested" (*OC*, 163).

That this is so is not to be attributed to human weakness. It is a conceptual requirement that our inquiries and proofs stay within boundaries. Think, for example, of the activity of calculating a number. Some steps in a calculation we will check for correctness, but others we won't: for example, that $4 + 4 = 8$. More accurately, some beginners might check it, but grown-ups won't. Similarly, some grown-ups would want to determine by calculation whether $25 \times 25 = 625$, whereas others would regard that as laughable. Thus the boundaries of the system within which *you* calculate may not be exactly the same as *mine*. But we do calculate; and, as Wittgenstein remarks, "In certain circumstances...we regard a calculation as sufficiently checked. What gives us a right to do so?... Somewhere we must be finished with justification, and then there remains the proposition that *this* is how we calculate" (*OC*, 212). If someone did not accept any boundaries for calculating this would mean that he had not learned *that* language-game: "If someone supposed that *all* our calculations were uncertain and that we could rely on none of them (justifying himself by saying that mistakes are always possible) perhaps we would say he was crazy. But can we say he is in error? Does he not just react differently? We rely on calculations, he doesn't; we are sure, he isn't" (*OC*, 217). We are taught, or we absorb, the systems within which we raise doubts, make inquiries, draw conclusions. We grow into a framework. We don't question it. We accept it trustingly. But this acceptance is not a consequence of reflection. We do not decide to accept framework propositions. We do not decide that we live on the earth, any more than we decide to learn our native tongue. We do come to adhere to a framework proposition, in the sense that it forms the way we think. The framework propositions that we accept, grow into, are not idiosyncrasies but common ways of speaking and thinking that are pressed on us by our human community. For our acceptances to have been withheld would have meant that we had not learned how to count, to measure, to use names, to play games, or even to *talk*. Wittgenstein remarks that "a language-game is only possible if one trusts something." Not *can*, but *does* trust something (*OC*, 509). I think he means by this trust or acceptance what he calls belief "in the sense of religious belief" (*OC*, 459). What does he mean by belief "in the sense of religious belief"? He explicitly distinguishes it from *conjecture* (*Vermutung*: ibid.) I think this means that there is nothing tentative about it; it is not adopted as a hypothesis that might later be withdrawn in the light of new evidence. This also makes explicit an important feature of Wittgenstein's understanding of belief, in the sense of "religious belief," namely, that it does not rise or fall on the basis of evidence or grounds: it is "groundless."

II.

In our Western academic philosophy, religious belief is commonly regarded as unreasonable and is viewed with condescension or even contempt. It is said that religion is a refuge for those who, because of weakness of intellect or character, are unable to confront the stern realities of the world. The objective, mature, *strong* attitude is to hold beliefs solely on the basis of *evidence*.

It appears to me that philosophical thinking is greatly influenced by this veneration of evidence. We have an aversion to statements, reports, declarations, beliefs, that are not based on grounds. There are many illustrations of this philosophical bent.

For example, in regard to a person's report that he has an image of the Eiffel Tower we have an inclination to think that the image must *resemble* the Eiffel Tower. How else could the person declare so confidently what his image is *of*? *How could he know?*

Another example: A memory-report or memory-belief must be based, we think, on some mental *datum* that is equipped with various features to match the corresponding features of the memory-belief. This datum will include an image that provides the *content* of the belief, and a peculiar feeling that makes one refer the image to a *past* happening, and another feeling that makes one believe that the image is an *accurate* portrayal of the past happening, and still another feeling that informs one that it was *oneself* who witnessed the past happening. The presence of these various features makes memory-beliefs thoroughly reasonable.

Another illustration: If interrupted in speaking one can usually give a confident account, later on, of what one had been *about* to say. How is this possible? Must not one remember a *feeling of tendency to say just those words?* This is one's basis for knowing what one had been about to say. It justifies one's account.

Still another example: After dining at a friend's house you announce your intention to go home. How do you know your intention? One theory proposes that you are presently aware of a particular mental state or bodily feeling which, as you recall from your past experience, has been highly correlated with the behavior of going home; so you infer that *that* is what you are going to do now. A second theory holds that you must be aware of some definite mental state or event which reveals itself, not by experience but *intrinsically*, as the intention to go home. Your awareness of that mental item *informs* you of what action you will take.

Yet another illustration: This is the instructive case of the man who, since birth, has been immune to sensations of bodily pain. On his thirtieth birthday he is kicked in the shins and for the first time he responds by crying out, hopping around on one foot, holding his leg, and exclaiming, "The pain is terrible!" We have an overwhelming inclination to wonder, "How could he tell, *this first time*, that what he felt was *pain?*" Of course, the implication is that *after* the first time there would be no problem. Why not? Because his first experience with pain would provide him with a sample that would be preserved in memory; thereafter he would be equipped to determine whether any sensation he feels is or isn't pain; he would just compare it with the memory-sample to see whether the two match! Thus he will have a justification for believing that what he feels is pain. But the *first time* he will not have this justification. This is why the case is so puzzling. Could it be that this first time he *infers* that he is in pain from his own behavior?

A final illustration: Consider the fact that after a comparatively few examples and bits of instruction a person can go on to carry out a task, apply a word correctly in the future, continue a numerical series from an initial segment, distinguish grammatical from ungrammatical constructions, solve arithmetical problems, and so on. These correct performances will be dealing with new and different examples, situations, combinations. The performance output will be far more varied than the instruction input. How is this possible? What carries the person from the meager instruction to his rich performance? The explanation has to be that an effect of his training was that he abstracted the Idea, perceived the Common Nature, "internalized" the Rule, grasped the Structure. What else could bridge the gap between the poverty of instruction and the wealth of performance? Thus we postulate an intervening mental act or state which removes the inequality and restores the balance.

My illustrations belong to what could be called the *pathology* of philosophy. Wittgenstein speaks of a "general disease of thinking" which attempts to explain occurrences of discernment, recognition, or understanding, by postulating mental states or processes from which those occurrences flow "as from a reservoir" (*BB*, p. 143). These mental intermediaries are assumed to contribute to the causation of the various cognitive performances. More significantly for my present purpose, they are supposed to *justify* them; they provide our *grounds* for saying or doing this rather than that; they *explain how we know*. The Image, or Cognitive State, or Feeling, or Idea, or Sample, or Rule, or Structure, *tells* us. It is like a road map or a signpost. It guides our course.

What is "pathological" about these explanatory constructions and pseudoscientific inferences? Two things at least. First, the movement of thought that demands these intermediaries is circular and empty, unless it provides criteria for determining their presence and nature *other than* the occurrence of the phenomena they are postulated to explain—and, of course, no such criteria are forthcoming. Second, there is the great criticism by Wittgenstein of this movement of philosophical thought: namely, his point that no matter what kind of state, process, paradigm, sample, structure, or rule, is conceived as giving us the necessary guidance, *it* could be taken, or understood, as indicating a *different* direction from the one in which we actually did go. The assumed intermediary Idea, Structure, or Rule, does not and cannot reveal that because of it we went in the only direction it was reasonable to go. Thus the internalized intermediary we are tempted to invoke to bridge the gap between training and performance, as being that which shows us what we must do or say if we are to be rational, cannot do the job it was invented to do. It cannot fill the epistemological gap. It cannot provide the bridge of justification. It cannot put to rest the How-do-we-know? question. Why not? Because it cannot tell us how *it itself* is to be taken, understood, applied. Wittgenstein puts the point briefly and powerfully: "Don't always think that you read off your words from facts; that you portray these in words according to rules. For even so you would have to apply the rule in the particular case without guidance" (*PI*, 292). Without guidance! Like Wittgenstein's signpost arrow that cannot tell us whether to go in the direction of the arrow tip or in the opposite direction, so too the Images, Ideas, Cognitive Structures, or Rules, that we philosophers imagine as devices for guidance, cannot interpret themselves to us. The signpost does not tell the traveler how to read it. A second signpost might tell him how to read the first one; we can imagine such a case. But this can't go on. If the traveler is to continue his journey he will have to do something on his own, without guidance.

The parable of the traveler speaks for *all* of the language-games we learn and practice; even those in which there is the most disciplined instruction and the most rigorous standards of conformity. Suppose that a pupil has been given thorough training in some procedure, whether it is drawing patterns, building fences, or proving theorems. But then he has to carry on by himself in new situations. How does he know what to do? Wittgenstein presents the following dialogue: " 'However you instruct him in the continuation of a pattern—how can he *know* how he is to continue by himself?'—Well, how do *I* know?—If that means 'Have I grounds?', the answer is: the grounds will soon give out. And then I shall act, without grounds" (*PI*, 211). Grounds come to an end. Answers to How-do-we-know? questions come to an end. Evidence comes to an end. We must speak, act, live, without evidence. This is so, not just on the fringes of life and language, but at the center of our most regularized activities. We do learn rules and learn to follow them. But our training was in the past! We had to leave it behind and proceed on our own.

It is an immensely important fact of nature that as people carry on an activity in which they have received a common training, they do largely agree with one another, accepting the same examples and analogies, taking the same steps. We agree in what to say, in how to apply language. We agree in our responses to particular cases.

As Wittgenstein says: "That is not agreement in opinions but in form of life" (*PI*, 241). We cannot explain this agreement by saying that we are just doing what the rules tell us—for our agreement in applying rules, formulae, and signposts is what gives them their *meaning*.

One of the primary pathologies of philosophy is the feeling that we must *justify* our language-games. We want to establish them as well-grounded. But we should consider here Wittgenstein's remark that a language-game "is not based on grounds. It is there—like our life" (*OC*, 559).

Within a language-game there is justification and lack of justification, evidence and proof, mistakes and groundless opinions, good and bad reasoning, correct measurements and incorrect ones. One cannot properly apply these terms to a language-game itself. It may, however, be said to be "groundless," not in the sense of a groundless opinion, but in the sense that we accept it, we live it. We can say, "This is what we do. This is how we are."

In this sense religion is groundless; and so is chemistry. Within each of these two systems of thought and action there is controversy and argument. Within each there are advances and recessions of insight into the secrets of nature or the spiritual condition of humankind and the demands of the Creator, Savior, Judge, Source. Within the framework of each system there is criticism, explanation, justification. But we should not expect that there might be some sort of rational justification of the framework itself.

A chemist will sometimes employ induction. Does he have evidence for a Law of Induction? Wittgenstein observes that it would strike him as nonsense to say, "I know that the Law of Induction is true." ("Imagine such a statement made in a law court.") It would be more correct to say, "I believe in the Law of Induction" (*OC*, 500). This way of putting it is better because it shows that the attitude toward induction is belief in the sense of "religious" belief—that is to say, an acceptance which is not conjecture or surmise and for which there is no reason—it is a groundless acceptance.

It is intellectually troubling for us to conceive that a whole system of thought might be groundless, might have no rational justification. We realize easily enough, however, that grounds soon give out—that we cannot go on giving reasons for our reasons. There arises from this realization the conception of a reason that is *self-justifying*—something whose credentials as a reason cannot be questioned.

This metaphysical conception makes its presence felt at many points—for example, as an explanation of how a person can tell what his mental image is *of*. We feel that the following remarks, imagined by Wittgenstein, are exactly right: " 'The image must be more similar to its object than any picture. For however similar I make the picture to what it is supposed to represent, it can always be the picture of something else. But it is essential to the image that it is the image of *this* and of nothing else' " (*PI*, 389). A pen and ink drawing represents the Eiffel Tower; but it could represent a mine shaft or a new type of automobile jack. Nothing prevents this drawing from being taken as a representation of something other than the Eiffel Tower. But my mental image of the Eiffel Tower is *necessarily* an image of the Eiffel Tower. Therefore it must be a "remarkable" kind of picture. As Wittgenstein observes: "Thus one might come to regard the image as a super-picture" (*ibid.*). Yet we have no intelligible conception of how a super-picture would differ from an ordinary picture. It would seem that it has to be a *super-likeness*—but what does this mean?

There is a familiar linguistic practice in which one person *tells* another what his image is of (or what he intends to do, or what he was about to say) and no question is raised of how the first one *knows* that what he says is true. This question is imposed from outside, artificially, by the philosophical craving for justification. We can see here the significance of these remarks: "It isn't a question of explaining a language-game by means of our experiences, but of noting a language-game" (*PI*, 655). "Look on the language-game as the *primary* thing" (*PI*, 656). Within a system of thinking and acting there occurs, *up to a point*, investigation and criticism of the reasons and justifications that are employed in that system. This inquiry into whether a reason is good or adequate cannot, as said, go on endlessly. We stop it. We bring it to an end. We come upon something that *satisfies* us. It is as if we made a decision or issued an edict: "*This* is an adequate reason!" (or explanation, or justification). Thereby we fix a boundary of our language-game.

There is nothing wrong with this. How else could we have disciplines, systems, games? But our fear of groundlessness makes us conceive that we are under some logical compulsion to terminate at *those particular* stopping points. We imagine that we have confronted the self-evident reason, the self-justifying explanation, the picture or symbol whose meaning cannot be questioned. This obscures from us the *human* aspect of our concepts—the fact that what we call "a reason," "evidence," "explanation," "justification," is what appeals to and satisfies us.

III.

The desire to provide a rational foundation for a form of life is especially prominent in the philosophy of religion, where there is an intense preoccupation with purported proofs of the existence of God. In American universities there must be hundreds of courses in which these proofs are the main topic. We can be sure that nearly always the critical verdict is that the proofs are invalid and consequently that, up to the present time at least, religious belief has received no rational justification.

Well, of course not! The obsessive concern with the proofs reveals the assumption that in order for religious belief to be intellectually respectable it *ought* to have a rational justification. *That* is the misunderstanding. It is like the idea that we are not justified in relying on memory until memory has been proved reliable.

Roger Trigg makes the following remark: "To say that someone acts in a certain way because of his belief in God does seem to be more than a redescription of his action.... It is to give a *reason* for it. The belief is distinct from the commitment which may follow it, and is the justification for it."[2] It is evident from other remarks that by "belief in God" Trigg means "belief in the existence of God" or "belief that God exists." Presumably by the *acts* and *commitments* of a religious person Trigg refers to such things as prayer, worship, confession, thanksgiving, partaking of sacraments, and participation in the life of a religious group.

For myself I have great difficulty with the notion of belief in *the existence* of God, whereas the idea of belief *in* God is to me intelligible. If a man did not ever pray for help or forgiveness, or have any inclination toward it; nor ever felt that it is "a good and joyful thing" to thank God for the blessings of this life; nor was ever concerned about his failure to comply with divine commandments—then, it seems clear to me, he could not be said to believe in God. Belief in God is not an all or none thing; it can be more or less; it can wax and wane. But belief in God in any degree does require, as I understand the words, some religious action, some commitment, or if not, at least a bad conscience.

According to Trigg, if I take him correctly, a man who was entirely devoid of any inclination toward religious action or conscience, might believe in *the existence* of God. What would be the marks of this? Would it be that the man knows some theology, can recite the Creeds, is well-read in Scripture? Or is his belief in the existence of God something different from this? If so, what? What would be the difference between a man who knows some articles of faith, heresies, scriptural writings, and in addition believes in the existence of God, and one who knows these things but does not believe in the existence of God? I assume that both of them are indifferent to the acts and commitments of religious life.

I do not comprehend this notion of belief in *the existence* of God which is thought to be distinct from belief *in* God. It seems to me to be an artificial construction of philosophy, another illustration of the craving for justification.

Religion is a form of life; it is language embedded in action—what Wittgenstein calls a "language-game." Science is another. Neither stands in need of justification, the one no more than the other.

Present-day academic philosophers are far more prone to challenge the credentials of religion than of science, probably for a number of reasons. One

---

[2]*Reason and Commitment* (Cambridge, 1973), p. 75.

may be the illusion that science can justify its own framework. Another is the fact that science is a vastly greater force in our culture. Still another may be the fact that by and large religion is to university people an alien form of life. They do not participate in it and do not understand what it is all about.

Their nonunderstanding is of an interesting nature. It derives, at least in part, from the inclination of academics to suppose that their employment as scholars demands of them the most severe objectivity and dispassionateness. For an academic philosopher to become a religious believer would be a stain on his professional competence! Here I will quote from Nietzsche, who was commenting on the relation of the German scholar of his day to religious belief; yet his remarks continue to have a nice appropriateness for the American and British scholars of our own day:

> Pious or even merely church-going people seldom realize *how much* good will, one might even say wilfulness, it requires nowadays for a German scholar to take the problem of religion seriously; his whole trade...disposes him to a superior, almost good-natured merriment in regard to religion, sometimes mixed with a mild contempt directed at the "uncleanliness" of spirit which he presupposes wherever one still belongs to the church. It is only with the aid of history (thus *not* from his personal experience) that the scholar succeeds in summoning up a reverent seriousness and a certain shy respect towards religion; but if he intensifies his feelings towards it even to the point of feeling grateful to it, he has still in his own person not got so much as a single step closer to that which still exists as church or piety; perhaps the reverse. The practical indifference to religious things in which he was born and raised is as a rule sublimated in him into a caution and cleanliness which avoids contact with religious people and things:...Every age has its own divine kind of naïvety for the invention of which other ages may envy it—and how much naïvety, venerable, childlike and boundlessly stupid naïvety there is in the scholar's belief in his superiority, in the good conscience of his tolerance, in the simple unsuspecting certainty with which his instinct treats the religious man as an inferior and lower type which he himself has grown beyond and above.[3]

---

[3]Friedrich Nietzsche, *Beyond Good and Evil*, trans. R. J. Hollingdale, para. 58.

ALVIN PLANTINGA

The Reformed Objection to Natural Theology

Suppose we think of natural theology as the attempt to prove or demonstrate the existence of God. This enterprise has a long and impressive history—a history stretching back to the dawn of Christendom and boasting among its adherents many of the truly great thinkers of the Western world. One thinks, for example, of Anselm, Aquinas, Scotus, and Ockham, of Descartes, Spinoza, and Leibniz. Recently—since the time of Kant, perhaps—the tradition of natural theology has not been as overwhelming as it once was; yet it continues to have able defenders both within and without officially Catholic philosophy.

Many Christians, however, have been less than totally impressed. In particular Reformed or Calvinist theologians have for the most part taken a dim view of this enterprise. A few Reformed thinkers—B. B. Warfield, for example—endorse the theistic proofs, but for the most part the Reformed attitude has ranged from tepid endorsement, through indifference, to suspicion, hostility, and outright accusations of blasphemy. And this stance is initially puzzling. It looks a little like the attitude some Christians adopt toward faith healing: it can't be done, but even if it could it shouldn't be. What exactly, or even approximately, do these sons and daughters of the Reformation have against proving the existence of God? What *could* they have against it? What could be less objectionable to any but the most obdurate atheist?

A. THE OBJECTION INITIALLY STATED

By way of answering this question, I want to consider three representative Reformed thinkers. Let us begin with the nineteenth-century Dutch theologian Herman Bavinck:

> A distinct natural theology, obtained apart from any revelation, merely through observation and study of the universe in which man lives, does not exist....

Scripture urges us to behold heaven and earth, birds and ants, flowers and lilies, in order that we may see and recognize God in them. "Lift up your eyes on high, and see who hath created these." Is. 40:26. Scripture does not reason in the abstract. It does not make God the conclusion of a syllogism, leaving it to us whether we think the argument holds or not. But it speaks with authority. Both theologically and religiously it proceeds from God as the starting point.

We receive the impression that belief in the existence of God is based entirely upon these proofs. But indeed that would be "a wretched faith, which, before it invokes God, must first prove his existence." The contrary, however, is the truth. There is not a single object the existence of which we hesitate to accept until definite proofs are furnished. Of the existence of self, of the world round about us, of logical and moral laws, etc., we are so deeply convinced because of the indelible impressions which all these things make upon our consciousness that we need no arguments or demonstration. Spontaneously, altogether involuntarily: without any constraint or coercion, we accept that existence. Now the same is true in regard to the existence of God. The so-called proofs are by no means the final grounds of our most certain conviction that God exists. This certainty is established only by faith; that is, by the spontaneous testimony which forces itself upon us from every side.

According to Bavinck, then, belief in the existence of God is not based upon proofs or arguments. By "argument" here I think he means arguments in the style of natural theology—the sort given by Aquinas and Scotus and later by Descartes, Leibniz, Clarke, and others. And what he means to say, I think, is that Christians do not *need* such arguments. Do not need them for what?

Here I think Bavinck means to hold two things. First, arguments or proofs are not, in general, the source of the believer's confidence in God. Typically the believer does not believe in God on the basis of arguments; nor does he believe such truths as that God has created the world on the basis of arguments. Second, argument is not needed for *rational justification;* the believer is entirely within his epistemic right in believing, for example, that God has created the world, even if he has no argument at all for that conclusion. The believer does not need natural theology in order to achieve rationality or epistemic propriety in believing; his belief in God can be perfectly rational even if he knows of no cogent argument, deductive or inductive, for the existence of God—indeed, even if there is no such argument.

Bavinck has three further points. First he means to add, I think, that we cannot come to knowledge of God on the basis of argument; the arguments of natural theology just do not work. (And he follows this passage with a more or less traditional attempt to refute the theistic proofs, including an endorsement of some of Kant's fashionable confusions about the ontological argument.) Second, Scripture "proceeds from God as the starting point," and so should the believer. There is nothing by way of proofs or arguments for God's existence in the Bible; that is simply presupposed. The same should be true of the Christian believer then; he should *start* from belief in God rather than from the premises of some argument whose conclusion is that God exists. What is it that makes those premises a better starting point anyway? And third, Bavinck points out that belief in God relevantly resembles belief in the existence of the self and of the external world—and, we might add, belief in other minds and the past. In none of these areas do we typically *have* proof or arguments, or *need* proofs or arguments.

Suppose we turn next to John Calvin, who is as good a Calvinist as any. According to Calvin God has implanted in us all an innate tendency, or nisus, or disposition to believe in him:

> 'There is within the human mind, and indeed by natural instinct, an awareness of divinity.' This we take to be beyond controversy. To prevent anyone from taking refuge in the pretense of ignorance, God himself has implanted in all men a certain understanding of his divine majesty. Ever renewing its memory, he repeatedly sheds fresh drops. Since, therefore, men one and all perceive that there is a God and that he is their Maker, they are condemned by their own testimony because they have failed to honor him and to consecrate their lives to his will. If ignorance of God is to be looked for anywhere, surely one is most likely to find an example of it among the more backward folk and those more remote from civilization. Yet there is, as the eminent pagan says, no nation so barbarous, no people so savage, that they have not a deep-seated conviction that there is a God. So deeply does the common conception occupy the minds of all, so tenaciously does it inhere in the hearts of all! Therefore, since from the beginning of the world there has been no region, no city, in short, no household, that could do without religion, there lies in this a tacit confession of a sense of deity inscribed in the hearts of all.
>
> Indeed, the perversity of the impious, who though they struggle furiously are unable to extricate themselves from the fear of God, is abundant testimony that this conviction, namely, that *there is some God*, is naturally inborn in all, and is fixed deep within, as it were in the very marrow.... From this we conclude *that it is not a doctrine that must first be learned in school*, but one of which each of us is master from his mother's womb and which nature itself permits no one to forget.

Calvin's claim, then, is that God has created us in such a way that we have a strong tendency or inclination toward belief in him. This tendency has been in part overlaid or suppressed by sin. Were it not for the existence of sin in the world, human beings would believe in God to the same degree and with the same natural spontaneity that we believe in the existence of other persons, an external world, or the past. This is the natural human condition; it is because of our presently unnatural sinful condition that many of us find belief in God difficult or absurd. The fact is, Calvin thinks, one who does not believe in God is in an epistemically substandard position—rather like a man who does not believe that his wife exists, or thinks she is like a cleverly constructed robot and has no thoughts, feelings, or consciousness.

Although this disposition to believe in God is partially suppressed, it is nonetheless universally present. And it is triggered or actuated by a widely realized condition:

> Lest anyone, then, be excluded from access to happiness, he not only sowed in men's minds that seed of religion of which we have spoken, but revealed himself and daily discloses himself in the whole workmanship of the universe. As a consequence, men cannot open their eyes without being compelled to see him.

Like Kant, Calvin is especially impressed in this connection, by the marvelous compages of the starry heavens above:

> Even the common folk and the most untutored, who have been taught only by the aid of the eyes, cannot be unaware of the excellence of divine art, for it reveals itself in this innumerable and yet distinct and well-ordered variety of the heavenly host.

And Calvin's claim is that one who accedes to this tendency and in these circumstances accepts the belief that God has created the world—perhaps upon beholding the starry heavens, or the splendid majesty of the mountains, or the intricate, articulate beauty of a tiny flower—is entirely within his epistemic rights in so doing. It is not that such a person is justified or rational in so believing by virtue of having an implicit argument—some version of the teleological argument, say. No; he does not need any argument for justification or rationality. His belief need not be based on any other propositions at all; under these conditions he is perfectly rational in accepting belief in God in the utter absence of any argument, deductive or inductive. Indeed, a person in these conditions, says Calvin, *knows* that God exists.

Elsewhere Calvin speaks of "arguments from reason" or rational arguments:

> The prophets and apostles do not boast either of their keenness or of anything that obtains credit for them as they speak; nor do they dwell upon rational proofs. Rather, they bring forward God's holy name, that by it the whole world may be brought into obedience to him. Now we ought to see how apparent it is not only by plausible opinion but by clear truth that they do not call upon God's name heedlessly or falsely. If we desire to provide in the best way for our consciences—that they may not be perpetually beset by the instability of doubt or vacillation, and that they may not also boggle at the smallest quibbles—we ought to seek our conviction in a higher place than human reasons, judgments, or conjectures, that is, in the secret testimony of the Spirit.

Here the subject for discussion is not belief in the existence of God, but belief that God is the author of the Scriptures; I think it is clear, however, that Calvin would say the same thing about belief in God's existence. The Christian does not *need* natural theology, either as the source of his confidence or to justify his belief. Furthermore, the Christian *ought* not to believe on the basis of argument; if he does, his faith is likely to be "unstable and wavering," the "subject of perpetual doubt." If my belief in God is based on argument, then if I am to be properly rational, epistemically responsible, I shall have to keep checking the philosophical journals to see whether, say, Anthony Flew has finally come up with a good objection to my favorite argument. This could be bothersome and time-consuming; and what do I do if someone does find a flaw in my argument? Stop going to church? From Calvin's point of view believing in the existence of God on the basis of rational argument is like believing in the existence of your spouse on the basis of the analogical argument for other minds—whimsical at best and unlikely to delight the person concerned.

B. THE BARTHIAN DILEMMA

The twentieth-century theologian Karl Barth is particularly scathing in his disapproval of natural theology. *That* he disapproves is overwhelmingly clear. His *reasons* for thus disapproving, however, are much less clear; his utterances on this topic, as on others, are fascinating but Delphic in everything but length. Sometimes, indeed, he is outrageous, as when he suggests that the mere act of believing or accepting the Christian message is a manifestation of human pride, self-will, contumacy, and sin. Elsewhere, however, he is both more moderate and thoroughly intriguing:

> Now suppose the partner in the conversation [that is, natural theology] discovers that faith is trying to use the well-known artifice of dialectic in relation to him. We are not taking him seriously because we withhold from him what we really want to say and represent. It is only in appearance that we devote ourselves to him, and therefore what we say to him is only an apparent and unreal statement. What will happen then? Well, not without justice—although misconstruing the friendly intention which perhaps motivates us—he will see himself despised and deceived. He will shut himself up and harden himself against the faith which does not speak out frankly, which deserts its own standpoint for the standpoint of unbelief. What use to unbelief is a faith which obviously knows different? And how shocking for unbelief is a faith which only pretends to take up with unbelief a common position.... This dilemma betrays the inner contradiction in every form of a "Christian" natural theology. It must really represent and affirm the standpoint of faith. Its true objective to which it really wants to lead unbelief is the knowability of the real God through Himself in his revelation. But as a "natural" theology, its initial aim is to disguise this and therefore to pretend to share in the life-endeavour of natural man. It therefore thinks that it should appear to engage in the dialectic of unbelief in the expectation that here at least a preliminary decision in regard to faith can and must be reached. Therefore, as a natural theology it speaks and acts improperly.... We cannot experiment with unbelief, even if we think we know

and possess all sorts of interesting and very promising possibilities and recipes for it. We must treat unbelief seriously. Only one thing can be treated more seriously than unbelief; and that is faith itself—or rather, the real God in whom faith believes. But faith itself—or rather, the real God in whom faith believes—must be taken so seriously that there is no place at all for even an apparent transposition to the standpoint of unbelief, for the pedagogic and playful self-lowering into the sphere of its possibilities.

We must try to penetrate a bit deeper into these objections to natural theology, and suppose we start with Barth. Precisely what is the objection to which he is pointing? That somehow it is improper or un-Christian or dishonest or impious to try to prove God's existence; but *how* exactly? Barth speaks here of a *dilemma* that confronts the natural theologian. Dilemmas have horns; what are the horns of this one? The following, I think. In presenting a piece of natural theology, either the believer must adopt what Barth calls "the standpoint of unbelief" or he must pretend to his unbelieving interlocutor to do so. If he does the former, he deserts his Christian standpoint; but if he does the latter, he is dishonest, in bad faith, professing to believe what in fact he does not believe. But what *is* the standpoint of unbelief and what is it to adopt it? And how could one fall into this standpoint just by working at natural theology, just by making a serious attempt to prove the existence of God?

Perhaps Barth is thinking along the following lines. In *arguing* about the existence of God, in attempting to prove it, one implicitly adopts a certain stance. In adopting this stance one presupposes that it is not yet known whether there is a God; that remains to be seen; that is what is up for discussion. In adopting this stance, furthermore, the natural theologian implicitly concedes that what one ought to believe here depends on the result of the inquiry; if there are good arguments *for* the existence of God, then we—that is, we believers and unbelievers who together are engaged in this inquiry—ought to accept God's existence; if there are good arguments *against* the existence of God, we ought to accept its denial; and if the arguments on both sides are equally strong (and equally weak) then perhaps the right thing to do is to remain agnostic.

In adopting this stance one concedes that the rightness or propriety of belief and unbelief depends upon the outcome of a certain inquiry. Belief in God is right and proper only if there is on balance better reason to believe than not to believe—only if, that is, the arguments for the existence of God are stronger than those against it. But of course an inquiry has a starting point, and arguments have premises. In supposing the issue thus dependent upon the outcome of argument, one supposes the appropriate premises are available. What about these premises? In adopting this stance the natural theologian implicitly commits himself to the view that there is a certain set of propositions from which the premises of theistic and antitheistic arguments are to be drawn—a set of propositions such that belief in God is rational or proper only if it stands in the right relation to that set. He concurs with his unbelieving interlocutor that there is a set of propositions both can appeal to, a set of propositions accepted by all or nearly all rational persons; and the propriety or rightness of belief in God depends on its relation to these propositions.

What are these propositions and where do they come from? We shall have to enter that question more deeply later; for the moment let us call them "the deliverances of reason." Then to *prove* or *demonstrate* that God exists is to exhibit a deductive argument whose conclusion is that God exists, whose premises are drawn from the deliverances of reason, and each of whose steps is by way of an argument whose corresponding conditional is among the deliverances of reason. Aquinas' first three ways would be attempts to demonstrate the existence of God in just this sense. A demonstration that God does not exist, of course, would be structurally isomorphic; it would meet the second and third condition just mentioned but have as conclusion the proposition that there is no such person as God. An alleged example would be the deductive argument from evil—the claim that the existence of evil is among the deliverances of reason and is inconsistent with the existence of God.

Of course it might be that the existence of God does not thus follow from the deliverances of reason but is nonetheless *probable* or *likely* with respect to them. One could then give a probabilistic or inductive argument for the existence of God, thus showing that theistic belief is rational, or epistemically proper, in that it is more likely than not with respect to the deliverances of reason. Perhaps Aquinas' Fifth Way and Paley's argument from design can be seen as falling into this category, and perhaps the probabilistic argument from evil—the claim that it is unlikely that God exists, given all the evil there is—can then be seen as a structurally similar argument for the conclusion that unbelief is the proper attitude.

According to Barth, then, the natural theologian implicitly concedes that the propriety of belief in God is to be tested by its relationship to the deliverances of reason. Belief is right, or rational, or rationally acceptable only if it stands in the proper relationship to the deliverances of reason—only if, for example, it is more likely than not or at any rate not unlikely with respect to them.

Now to adopt the standpoint of unbelief is not, as Barth sees it, to reject belief in God. One who enthusiastically accepts and believes in the existence of God can nonetheless be in the standpoint of unbelief. To be in that standpoint it is sufficient to hold that belief in God is rationally permissible for a person *only if he or she has a good argument for it.* To be in the standpoint of unbelief is to hold that belief in God is rationally acceptable *only if it is more likely than not with respect to the deliverances of reason.* One who holds this belief, says Barth, is in the standpoint of unbelief; his ultimate commitment is to the deliverances of reason rather than to God. Such a person "makes reason a judge over Christ," or at any rate over the Christian faith. And to do so, says Barth, is utterly improper for a Christian.

The horns of the Barthian dilemma, then, are bad faith or dishonesty on the one hand and the standpoint of unbelief on the other. Either the natural theologian accepts the standpoint of unbelief or he does not. In the latter case he misleads and deceives his unbelieving interlocutor and thus falls into bad faith. In the former case he makes his ultimate commitment to the deliverances of reason, a posture that is for a Christian totally inappropriate, a manifestation of sinful human pride.

> And this attempt to prove the existence of God certainly cannot end in any other way than with the affirmation that even apart from God's grace, already preceding God's grace, already anticipating it, he is ready for God, so that God is knowable to him otherwise than from and through himself. Not only does it end with this. In principle, it begins with it. For in what does it consist but in the arrogation, preservation and affirmation of the self-sufficiency of man and therefore his likeness with God?

C. REJECTING CLASSICAL FOUNDATIONALISM

Now I think the natural theologian has a sound response to Barth's dilemma: she can execute the maneuver known to dialectician and matador alike as "escaping between the horns." As a natural theologian she offers or endorses theistic arguments, but why suppose that her own belief in God must be based upon such argument? And if it is not, why suppose she must pretend that it is? Perhaps her aim is to point out to the unbeliever that belief in God follows from other things he already believes, so that he can continue in unbelief (and continue to accept these other beliefs) only on pain of inconsistency. We may hope this knowledge will lead him to give up his unbelief, but in any event she can tell him quite frankly that her belief in God is not based on its relation to the deliverances of reason. Indeed, she can follow Calvin in claiming that belief in God *ought* not to be based on arguments from the deliverances of reason or anywhere else. So even if "the standpoint of unbelief" is as reprehensible as Barth says it is, his dilemma seems to evaporate.

What is most interesting here is not Barth's claim that the natural theologian faces this dilemma; here he is probably wrong, or at any rate not clearly right. More interesting is his view that belief in God need not be based on argument. Barth joins Calvin and Bavinck in holding that the believer in God is entirely within his rights in believing as he does even if he does not know of any good theistic argument (deductive or inductive), even if he does not believe there is any such argument, and even if in fact no such argument exists. Like Calvin, Kuyper, and Bavinck, Barth holds that belief in God is *properly basic*—that is, such that it is rational to accept it without accepting it

on the basis of any other propositions or beliefs at all. In fact, they think the
Christian ought not to accept belief in God on the basis of argument; to do
so is to run the risk of a faith that is unstable and wavering, subject to all the
wayward whim and fancy of the latest academic fashion. What the Reformers
held was that a believer is entirely rational, entirely within his epistemic
rights, in *starting with* belief in God, in accepting it as basic, and in taking it
as premise for argument to other conclusions.

In rejecting natural theology, therefore, these Reformed thinkers mean
to say first of all that the propriety or rightness of belief in God in no way
depends upon the success or availability of the sort of theistic arguments that
form the natural theologian's stock in trade. I think this is their central claim
here, and their central insight. As these Reformed thinkers see things, one
who takes belief in God as basic is not thereby violating any epistemic duties
or revealing a defect in his noetic structure; quite the reverse. The correct or
proper way to believe in God, they thought, was not on the basis of arguments from natural theology or anywhere else; the correct way is to take belief
in God as basic.

I spoke earlier of classical foundationalism, a view that incorporates
the following three theses:

> (1) In every rational noetic structure there is a set of beliefs taken as basic—
>   that is, not accepted on the basis of any other beliefs,
>
> (2) In a rational noetic structure nonbasic belief is proportional to support
>   from the foundations,

and

> (3) In a rational noetic structure basic beliefs will be self-evident or incorri-
>   gible or evident to the senses.

Now I think these three Reformed thinkers should be understood as rejecting
classical foundationalism. They may have been inclined to accept (1); they
show no objection to (2); but they were utterly at odds with the idea that the
foundations of a rational noetic structure can at most include propositions
that are self-evident or evident to the senses or incorrigible. In particular, they
were prepared to insist that a rational noetic structure can include belief in
God as basic. As Bavinck put it, "Scripture...does not make God the conclusion of a syllogism, leaving it to us whether we think the argument holds or
not. But it speaks with authority. Both theologically and religiously it proceeds from God as the starting point" (above, p. 75). And of course Bavinck
means to say that we must emulate Scripture here.

In the passages I quoted earlier, Calvin claims the believer does not need
argument—does not need it, among other things, for epistemic respectability.
We may understand him as holding, I think, that a rational noetic structure

may very well contain belief in God among its foundations. Indeed, he means to go further, and in two separate directions. In the first place he thinks a Christian *ought* not believe in God on the basis of other propositions; a proper and well-formed Christian noetic structure will *in fact* have belief in God among its foundations. And in the second place Calvin claims that one who takes belief in God as basic can *know* that God exists. Calvin holds that one can *rationally accept* belief in God as basic; he also claims that one can *know* that God exists even if he has no argument, even if he does not believe on the basis of other propositions. A foundationalist is likely to hold that some properly basic beliefs are such that anyone who accepts them *knows* them. More exactly, he is likely to hold that among the beliefs properly basic for a person *S*, some are such that if *S* accepts them, *S* knows them. He could go on to say that *other* properly basic beliefs cannot be known if taken as basic, but only rationally believed; and he might think of the existence of God as a case in point. Calvin will have none of this; as he sees it, one needs no arguments to know that God exists.

> One who holds this view need not suppose that natural theology is of no use. In the first place, if there *were* good arguments for the existence of God, that would be a fact worth knowing in itself—just as it would be worth knowing (if true) that the analogical argument for other minds is successful, or that there are good arguments from self-evident and incorrigible propositions to the existence of other minds. Second, natural theology could be useful in helping someone move from unbelief to belief. The arguments are not successful from the point of view of classical foundationalism; probably, that is, they do not start from premises that are self-evident, incorrigible, or evident to the sense and then proceed by argument forms that are self-evidently valid to the conclusion that God exists. Nonetheless there may be (in fact there are) people who accept propositions and argument forms out of which a theistic argument can be constructed; for these people theistic arguments can be useful as a means of moving toward what Calvin sees as the best way to believe in God: as basic.

* * *

I take up one final question. In *Reflections on Christian Philosophy* Ralph McInerny suggests that what I have been calling Reformed epistemology is *fideism*. Is he right? Is the Reformed epistemologist perforce a fideist? That depends: it depends, obviously enough, on how we propose to use the term "fideism." According to my dictionary fideism is "exclusive or basic reliance upon faith alone, accompanied by a consequent disparagement of reason and utilized especially in the pursuit of philosophical or religious truth." A fideist therefore urges reliance on faith rather than reason, in matters philosophical and religious; and he may go on to disparage and denigrate reason. We may thus distinguish at least two grades of fideism: moderate fideism, according to which we must rely upon faith rather than reason in religious matters, and extreme fideism, which disparages and denigrates reason.

Now let us ask first whether the Reformed epistemologist is obliged to be an extreme fideist. Of course there is more than one way of disparaging reason. One way to do it is to claim that to take a proposition on faith is higher and better than accepting it on the basis of reason. Another way to disparage reason is to follow Kant in holding that reason left to itself inevitably falls into paradox and antimony on ultimate matters. According to Kant pure reason offers us conclusive argument for supposing that the universe had no beginning, but also, unfortunately, conclusive arguments for the denial of that proposition. I do not think any of the alleged arguments are anywhere nearly conclusive, but if Kant were right, then presumably reason would not deserve to be paid attention to, at least on this topic. According to the most common brand of extreme fideism, however, reason and faith *conflict* or *clash* on matters of religious importance; and when they do, faith is to be preferred and reason suppressed. Thus according to Kierkegaard faith teaches "the absurdity that the eternal is the historical." He means to say, I think, that this proposition is among the deliverances of faith but absurd from the point of view of reason; and it should be accepted despite this absurdity. The turn-of-the-century Russian theologian Shestov carried extreme fideism even further; he held that one can attain religious truth only by rejecting the proposition that $2 + 2 = 4$ and accepting instead $2 + 2 = 5$.

Now it is clear, I suppose, that the Reformed epistemologist need not be an extreme fideist. His views on the proper basicality of belief in God surely do not commit him to thinking that faith and reason conflict. So suppose we ask instead whether the Reformed epistemologist is committed to *moderate* fideism. And again that depends; it depends upon how we propose to use the terms "reason" and "faith." One possibility would be to follow Abraham Kuyper, who proposes to use these terms in such a way that one takes on faith whatever one accepts but does not accept on the basis of argument or inference or demonstration:

> There is thus no objection to the use of the term 'faith' for that function of the soul by which it attains certainty immediately or directly, without the aid of discursive demonstration. This places faith over against demonstration, but *not* over against knowing.

On this use of these terms, anything taken as basic is taken on faith; anything believed on the basis of other beliefs is taken on reason. I take $2 + 1 = 3$ as basic; accordingly, I take it on faith. When I am appropriately appeared to, I take as basic such propositions as *I see a tree before me* or *there is a house over there*; on the present construal I take these things on faith. I remember that I had lunch this noon, but do not accept this belief on the basis of other propositions; this too, then, I take on faith. On the other hand, what I take on the basis of reason is what I believe on the basis of argument or inference from other propositions. Thus I take $2 + 1 = 3$ on faith, but $21 \times 45 = 945$ by reason; for I accept the latter on the basis of calculation, which is a form of argument. Further, suppose I accept supralapsarianism or premillenialism or the doctrine of the virgin birth on the grounds that God proposes these doctrines for our belief and God proposes only truths; then on Kuyper's use of these terms I accept these doctrines not by faith but by reason. Indeed, if with Kierkegaard and Shestov I hold that the eternal is the historical and that $2 + 2 = 5$ because I believe God proposes *these* things for my belief, then on the present construal I take them not on faith but on the basis of reason.

And here we can see, I think, that Kuyper's use of these terms is not the relevant one for the discussion of fideism. For consider Shestov. Shestov is an extreme fideist because he thinks faith and reason conflict; and when they do, he says, it is reason that must be suppressed. To paraphrase the poem, "When faith and reason clash, let reason go to smash!" But he is not holding that faith teaches something—$2 + 2 = 5$, for example—that conflicts with a belief—$2 + 2 = 4$—that one arrives at by reasoning from other propositions. On the contrary, the poignancy of the clash is just that what faith teaches conflicts with an *immediate* teaching of reason—a proposition that is apparently self-evident. On the Kuyperian use of these terms Shestov would be surprised to learn that he is not a fideist after all. For what he takes faith to conflict with here is not something one accepts by reason—that is, on the basis of other propositions. Indeed, on the Kuyperian account Shestov not only does not qualify as a fideist; he probably qualifies as an antifideist. Shestov probably did not recommend taking $2 + 2 = 5$ as basic; he probably held that God proposes this proposition for our belief and that we should therefore accept it. On the other hand, he also believed, no doubt, that $2 + 2 = 4$ is apparently self-evident. So given the Kuyperian use, Shestov would be holding that faith and reason conflict here, but it is $2 + 2 = 4$ that is the deliverance of faith and $2 + 2 = 5$ the deliverance of reason! Since he recommends accepting $2 + 2 = 5$, the deliverance of reason, he thus turns out to be a rationalist or antifideist, at least on this point.

And this shows that Kuyper's use of these terms is not the relevant use. What we take on faith is not simply what we take as basic, and what we accept by reason is not simply what we take on the basis of other propositions. The deliverances of reason include propositions taken as basic, and the deliverances of faith include propositions accepted on the basis of others.

The Reformed epistemologist, therefore, is a fideist only if he holds that some central truths of Christianity are not among the deliverances of reason and must instead be taken on faith. But just what are the deliverances of reason? What do they include? First, clearly enough, self-evident propositions and propositions that follow from them by self-evidently valid arguments are among the deliverances of reason. But we cannot stop there. Consider someone who holds that according to correct scientific reasoning from accurate observation the earth is at least a couple of billion years old; nonetheless, he adds, the fact is it is no more than some 6000 years old, since that is what faith teaches. Such a person is a fideist, even though the proposition *the earth is more than 6000 years old* is neither self-evident nor a consequence of what is self-evident. So the deliverances of reason include more than the self-evident and its consequences. They also include basic perceptual truths (propositions "evident to the senses"), incorrigible propositions, certain memory propositions, certain propositions about other minds, and certain moral or ethical propositions.

But what about the belief that there is such a person as God and that we are responsible to him? Is that among the deliverances of reason or an item of faith? For Calvin it is clearly the former. "There is within the human mind, and indeed by natural instinct, an awareness of divinity.... God himself has implanted in all men a certain understanding of his divine majesty.... men one and all perceive that there is a God and that he is their Maker." (*Institutes* I, 3, 1) According to Calvin everyone, whether in the faith or not, has a tendency or nisus, in certain situations, to apprehend God's existence and to grasp something of his nature and actions. This natural knowledge can be and is suppressed by sin, but the fact remains that a capacity to apprehend God's existence is as much part of our natural noetic equipment as is the capacity to apprehend perceptual truths, truths about the past, and truths about other minds. Belief in the existence of God is in the same boat as belief in other minds, the past, and perceptual objects; in each case God has so constructed us that in the right circumstances we form the belief in question. But then the belief that there is such a person as God is as much among the deliverances of reason as those other beliefs.

From this vantage point we can see, therefore, that the Reformed epistemologist is not a fideist at all with respect to belief in God. He does not hold that there is any conflict between faith and reason here, and he does not even hold that we cannot attain this fundamental truth by reason; he holds, instead, that it is among the deliverances of reason.

Of course the nontheist may disagree; he may deny that the existence of God is part of the deliverances of reason. A former professor of mine for whom I had and have enormous respect once said that theists and nontheists have different conceptions of reason. At the time I did not know what he meant, but now I think I do. On the Reformed view I have been urging, the deliverances of reason include the existence of God just as much as perceptual truths, self-evident truths, memory truths, and the like. It is not that theist and nontheist agree as to what reason delivers, the theist then going on to accept the existence of God by faith; there is, instead, disagreement in the first place as to what are the deliverances of reason. But then the Reformed epistemologist is no more a fideist with respect to belief in God than is, for example, Thomas Aquinas. Like the latter, he will no doubt hold that there are other truths of Christianity that are not to be found among the deliverances of reason—such truths, for example, as that God was in Christ, reconciling the world to himself. But he is not a fideist by virtue of his views on our knowledge of God.

PART TWO

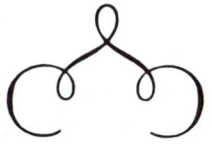

ARGUMENTS FOR AND AGAINST THE EXISTENCE OF GOD

PART INTRODUCTION
AND BIBLIOGRAPHICAL NOTES

In western religions, the most fundamental theological claim is that there is an all-perfect being, God. For that reason, one of the most fundamental questions, if not the most fundamental question, in the philosophy of religion centers on evidence for or against that belief. Is there any reason to suppose that God exists, any proof of his existence? Or is there perhaps some reason to suppose that he does not exist, some proof of his nonexistence? This part of the book is devoted to a consideration of these questions.

There are three classical proofs of the existence of God. One of these, the cosmological argument, argues that there must be a God to create the world or nothing would exist in the world. Another, the teleological argument, argues that there must be a God or the world would not be the orderly, harmonious, purposively adaptive place that it is. Both these arguments are attempts by philosophers to state, in a clear and rigorous fashion, the intuitive arguments that religious believers normally offer for their beliefs. But the ontological argument, the first argument that we will consider carefully, is different in this respect: it bears no relation to the intuitive arguments that ordinary religious believers offer. It is a product of philosophical thought.

The classical statement of the ontological argument occurs in the *Proslogium* of St. Anselm of Canterbury. Anselm begins with the very conception of God as all-perfect—as "that being than which nothing greater can be conceived"—and goes on to argue that God must exist, and that his existence is entailed by his nature. Indeed, says Anselm, the very claim that God does not exist cannot have any more meaning than the equally contradictory claim that fire is water.

Anselm offers several versions of this argument in the first selection in this section. We shall shortly consider whether or not he really has more than one argument. One thing that should be kept in mind, however, is that in all of this discussion, Anselm makes no appeal to any facts about the nature and existence of the world. His proof is a purely a priori proof—a proof based upon pure reason without any appeal to what experience has taught us about the world.

It is often though that the ontological argument was decisively refuted by Immanuel Kant in his *Critique of Pure Reason*. The basic idea behind Kant's objection seems, moreover, to be pretty clear. Anselm, says Kant, is supposing that existence is a perfection—a property that a perfect being must, by its very nature, have. But existence is not a property at all, and therefore certainly not a perfection. So the ontological argument is mistaken.

Kant's claim obviously involves two parts. The first is the idea that the ontological argument really does suppose that existence is a property, a real predicate. The second is the idea that this presupposition is false. But Kant offers no careful analysis of Anselm's argument, so it is difficult to see whether his first claim is true. The recent analytic literature has seen a variety of attempts to formulate the argument carefully; these attempts conclude that Kant was wrong in supposing there to be some objectionable claim about existence being a property that is presupposed by the Anselmian argument.

Norman Malcolm concedes that Anselm's argument presupposes that existence is a perfection and that Anselm is wrong in thinking that this is so. But, claims Malcolm, Anselm offered a different argument in Chapter 3 of the *Proslogium* based upon the idea that necessary existence is a perfection and concluding, therefore, that God must possess necessary existence—that God exists necessarily. Malcolm goes on to argue that, while existence is not a property and therefore not a perfection, necessary existence is both.

Alvin Plantinga, in the next selection, puts forward a version of the ontological argument which doesn't even presuppose that necessary existence is a perfection. Both he and Malcolm are aware however of another objection to the ontological argument. Leibniz had pointed out that the ontological argument presupposes that the conception of God is logically coherent, but had offered no proof of that assumption. Malcolm and Plantinga offer different responses to that objection, and the reader needs to compare these responses carefully.

We turn then to the cosmological argument. The classical statement of the cosmological argument comes in the first two of St. Thomas Aquinas's five ways. Both these arguments begin with noticing some fact about the world. In the case of the first way, what is noted is that some change is occurring. In the case of the second way, what is noted is that something exists. Then, some casual principle (either that changes are caused or that the existence of things is caused) is invoked, and the arguments conclude that there is a series of causes and effects that precede the original thing noted. But, says St. Thomas, there cannot be an infinite regression of causes. So there must be a first cause, and that is God.

There is an obvious objection that can be raised at this point. A crucial assumption of the cosmological argument seems to be the claim that there could not have been an infinite causal regression. But what reason is there to believe that this is so? Why couldn't there be one? Samuel Clarke, in his *A Demonstration of the Being and Attributes of God*, attempted to reformulate the argument so as to meet this objection. Let us concede, says Clarke, that there is no reason why there could not have been an infinite causal regression. And, to be sure, every member of that infinite series has, as its cause, the previous member of the series. This still leaves unanswered, however, one fundamental question. What is the cause of the existence of the whole series? To answer this question, say Clarke, we must bring in God. To put Clarke's point another way, even if we have, in our infinite sequence, a cause of each particular object and of each particular change, we still have to find a cause for everything taken together, for the whole universe. This cause is God.

The standard objection to Clark's reformulation of the argument was first raised by David Hume. It points out that Clarke's argument presupposes that, having explained every member of the causal sequence, we would still have something else left to explain, namely, the sequence as a whole. But, said Hume, that is just a confusion. Once we have explained why each member exists, there is nothing left to explain.

In an extremely important article, William Rowe sets out to defend Clarke's argument against this line of criticism. He begins by clarifying the meaning of the question, "Why does the sequence have any members at all?" Given his interpretation, argues Rowe, the question as to the cause of the existence of the sequence is perfectly meaningful. Now, says Rowe, imagine an infinite causal sequence, each member of which is caused by an earlier member. Given all this causal information, we would still not know why the sequence has any members rather than none at all, for all our causal knowledge would already involve members of the sequence whose existence we are trying to explain. So, contra Hume and his recent followers, even if we have an explanation of the existence of each member of the sequence, we still wouldn't know why the sequence as a whole exists, and to answer that question we must appeal to the existence of God.

St. Thomas was, himself, aware of the objection that there might be an infinite causal regress. Thus, in the course of presenting the first two ways, rather than conceding that possibility and making a Clarkian move, he argued against that possibility. The argument that he presented is very obscure. To begin with, the argument is, on its simplest interpretation, a very bad one. But second, and even more important, there are well-known texts in which St. Thomas allowed not only for the possibility of there being infinite series but even for the possibility of there being certain types of infinite causal regresses.

Patterson Brown's article is concerned with doing two things: (1) explaining the difference between those infinite causal regresses that St. Thomas is prepared to allow as possible and those that he is not and (2) offering an account of why St. Thomas would object to the second type of infinite causal regresses. Brown's crucial idea is that St. Thomas recognized a type of causation in which one did not have the real cause at all until one found the first member of the causal sequence. So, if there were an infinite causal regress, the event in question would have no real cause (in this special Thomistic sense of cause).

Brown recognizes that this interpretation of St. Thomas leads to an obvious problem: Is there any reason to suppose that events do have a cause (in this special Thomistic sense)? If there is not, then the cosmological argument will fail for a new reason; namely, its dependence upon the unsupported claim that every event must have a cause of this special type. Having said that, however, we are immediately reminded that there is still a further general issue about the cosmological argument, one alluded to by Rowe at the beginning of his article. Since every cosmological argument employs some version or another of the principle that every event has a cause, no version of the argument will work unless such a principle can be supported.

We come, finally, to the third famous argument for the existence of God, the teleological argument. Its basic idea is that we must suppose that the universe was created by a wise creator, God, in order to explain the presence in it of order and of purposive adaptiveness—the fact that the parts of natural objects are made and put together in such a way as to enable these objects to perform a variety of tasks. There are many different statements of the argument. We shall study the famous version of it presented by William Paley.

Paley begins by asking us to contrast our reactions when we stumble across a stone and when we stumble across a watch. In the case of the watch, but not of the stone, we would say that it is an artifact—an entity made by some creator and made so as to be able to do certain things. Paley wants to claim that the very reasons that lead us to make such a statement in the case of the watch, the ways in which the parts are designed and put together so as to perform a task, should lead us to make the same statement in the case of the universe as a whole.

Paley goes on to claim that our conclusion would not be weakened in the case of the watch (and should not, therefore, in the case of the universe) just because we have never seen a watch made, or because it didn't always work just right, or because we didn't know the purpose of some parts, and so forth. But there are other, more serious, objections that might be raised. Is it at all legitimate to suppose that the objects are created for the purposes we ascribe to them or would it be better to say—in the case of the natural objects, as opposed to artifacts like watches—that they are used for these purposes just because they happened to be suitable for them? And couldn't we explain the occurrence of this purposive adaptiveness as the result of chance—as one of many possibilities that came about by accident but which continue, unlike the others that died out, just because they work so well? Paley is aware of these objections, and he offers his response to them.

There is still a final question about the argument that Paley considers. Let us grant, for the moment, that the teleological argument succeeds in proving the existence of the creator of the universe. What right has one to suppose that this creator is God, that all-perfect being that is postulated in the Judeo-Christian tradition? Certainly the argument does not prove that. Paley takes a very interesting line in response to this objection. He concedes the point, and suggests that all that the religious person has to suppose about God, such as the immensity of his power and knowledge, is proven by the argument, and that the ideas of infinite power, infinite wisdom, and so forth need not be taken literally. J. S. Mill, in his discussion of this same topic, draws similar conclusions about what conception of God can be validated by appealing to design and order.

Some of the objections that Paley considered are among those raised by David Hume in his classical critique of the teleological argument in his *Dialogues Concerning Natural Religion*. In a large number of ways, Hume was trying to argue that the analogy between artifacts and natural objects that the teleological argument rests upon is not strong enough to support its conclusion. While it has generally been conceded that Hume was right, there has been a recent reevaluation of that claim. R. G. Swinburne's recent article presents an analysis of the logic of analogical arguments and goes on to claim with some force that, in light of this analysis, none of the objections that Hume presents are satisfactory.

There is one further aspect of this issue that we have not yet adequately discussed. Hume raised the possibility of alternative explanations of the order and harmony and purposive adaptiveness in the universe. These alternative explanations involve the idea of the universe existing for a long time and the idea that many possibilities are realized but only the orderly and purposively adaptive ones survive. Indeed, as Hume described it, his conception bears a real resemblance to evolutionary biology and historical cosmology as we know those subjects today. Paley, as we pointed out, attempted to rule out this alternative, but the arguments that he offered are not satisfactory in light of our contemporary scientific knowledge. To meet this objection, Swinburne distinguishes two types of order: regularities of copresence (the type of purposive adaptiveness that Paley was talking about and for which we can offer scientific laws) and regularities of succession (facts about the ways in which, over time, objects behave in accordance with scientific laws). Swinburne wants to claim that, while ordinary regularities of succession can be explained in terms of more basic regularities of succession, the fact that objects obey these most basic regularities of succession can be explained only by the supposition that God created them to behave in such a way.

Swinburne's argument raises certain fundamental issues that need further discussion: (1) are there really such things as the basic regularities of succession or is it the case that, for each such regularity, there is an even more basic one in terms of which the former can be explained? and (2) if there are basic regularities of succession, is there any reason to suppose that they can be explained?

Ian Hacking, in an important but difficult article, suggests that the popular response offered by Hume that improbable purposive order can be explained by a long enough series of chance events is fallacious. He also rejects the anthropic principle that many contemporary cosmologists use to explain purposive order. Instead, he feels that only very strong cosmological principles (such as the principle of plenitude) or cosmological suggestions (such as the view that order is not unusual) can be used to avoid accepting the conclusion of the teleological argument.

In addition to the classical proofs for the existence of God, religious believers have often appealed to two very different sorts of events, miracles and religious experiences, to offer experiential proofs of the existence of God. Let us examine each of these experiential arguments.

A miracle is usually defined as an event which occurs in violation of the laws of nature by virtue of the activity of God. Given this definition, knowledge of the occurrence of a miracle would certainly provide us with knowledge of the existence of God. Can we ever know, however, that a miracle has occurred? That question has two components. Can we know that extraordinary events which violate laws of nature have occurred? And can we know that they are due to the activity of God?

David Hume offered a classical argument to prove that the answer to the first question is no. In any case in which we receive a report of a miracle, says Hume, we have to evaluate the reliability of the testimony as to its occurrence. In evaluating testimony, says Hume, there are many factors to take into account, but one of the most important of them is the intrinsic probability of the event. The more unusual and unlikely the event that is reported, the less credible is the testimony. Now consider a case in which what is reported is the occurrence of a violation of the laws of nature. That is such an extremely improbable event that no testimony is going to establish its occurrence, or, at least, no testimony will do so unless its falsehood would be more miraculous than the event in question.

It should be noted that Hume, in pressing his objection, is really challenging our accepting the occurrence of these extraordinary events. But there is another challenge to be raised. Couldn't one grant that the event in question has occurred, but claim that we have not shown that it is a miracle for we have not proved, and it really is impossible to prove, that the event in question is caused by God?

R. G. Swinburne attempts to meet both of these challenges. Against Hume, he argues that as we collect more and more evidence, particularly of present effects of past purported miracles, we could reach the stage at which it would be reasonable to conclude that the event in question which violates laws of nature did occur. And if the evidence was that the event occurred in certain types of circumstances (say after prayers to some deity for its occurrence) then that would even be evidence that the event was caused by God.

We turn from miracles as evidence for God to mystical experiences as evidence of God's existence. In the case of mystical experiences, there is little doubt that these experiences have occurred. The question raised in the philosophical literature is, instead, whether they provide any evidence for the existence of God. In order to understand why, we need to look more carefully at the nature of these experiences.

As William James pointed out in his classic discussion, mystical experiences are a very special type of experience. According to those who have had them, they do not in any way resemble sensuous experiences, and they are not describable in terms of our concepts and language. It is for this reason that mystics talk of their experiences as being ineffable. It is for this reason, also, that mystics differentiate mystical experiences from visions, and so forth. Those visionary experiences are sensuous experiences, although with most unusual objects, and they can be described using our concepts and language.

While mystics do say that their experiences are in this way ineffable, they want to say that these experiences also involve a deep insight into the nature of things. Naturally, different mystics disagree about what exactly this insight is. But, on the whole, there seems to be at least some agreement that the apprehension is antinaturalistic and otherworldly, and that it says that, behind the pluralistic natural universe, there is another more fundamental unity.

Having described the nature of the mystical experience, James goes on to consider the question of whether it does provide us with some knowledge of how the world really is. James's attitude is rather complicated. On the one hand, he wants to say that the mystic, who has had the experience, has as much right as the ordinary individual to suppose that whatever he has experienced exists. On the other hand, he wants to claim that, despite the impressive agreement among mystics about what they have experienced, the nonmystic is not compelled to admit the reality of what is experienced. The reader will have to (1) see what his reasons are for these claims and (2) decide whether or not the two claims really are compatible.

It is obvious that the crucial and fundamental epistemological question is the one with which James was concerned, namely, whether mystical experiences provide the mystics or anyone else with knowledge of some objective reality (regardless of whether or not it is to be identified with a particular deity). To be sure, the mystic claims that he knows of its existence through his experience, but is that experience of the type that generates knowledge of some reality other than the subjective states of the mystic? It is just this issue that is discussed in C. B. Martin's article.

Martin's main reason for differentiating between the claims of mystic and the claims of the ordinary perceiver is that the latter, but not the former, lend themselves to checking and testing by the perceiver and by others. It might well be suggested that it is just this intersubjective testing that lends credence to the ordinary perceiver's claim that what he has experienced really exists. The fact that such testing is not present in the case of the mystic's experience must certainly cast doubt upon his claim. More fundamentally, however, it means that his claim really resembles, in these important respects, normal claims about one's subjective states. And this naturally raises the question whether it is possible for the mystic to avoid the assimilation of his claim into the latter class of claims, something he surely wants to avoid.

In his article, William Alston argues that Martin's requirement of inter-subjective testability is inappropriate when applied to mystical experiences or other religious experiences. He also argues that other objections often offered either involve double standards or involve applying inappropriate standards to religious experiences. Alston believes that the most difficult problem is that of deciding which religious beliefs are supported by religious experiences given that so many apparently differing beliefs make the claim that they have experiential support. He concludes, in any case, that religious experience can serve as a source of justified belief formation.

We have so far been considering arguments for the existence of God. We turn now to a consideration of the arguments against the existence of God. There is really only one argument that deserves careful consideration, the argument from evil. In a way, this argument is the inverse of the teleological argument. While the teleological argument claims that the nature of the universe indicates that there is a deity, the argument from evil claims that the nature of the universe indicates that there is no deity. In particular, the evil and suffering in the universe indicates that he does not exist.

It is important to understand that the argument from evil is a serious problem just because of the nature of God in the Judeo-Christian tradition. God is all-wise, so he should know how to avoid these evils; he is all-powerful, so he should be able to see that they do not occur; and he is all-good, so he should want to see that they do not occur. Then, if he exists, how is it that they do exist? If, of course, the conception of God were different—if it were supposed that the God that existed did not have these properties—then the argument would collapse. And one of the characters, Philo, in a dialogue by Hume in which this problem is raised, suggests that the way out of it is to suppose that God does not have these attributes in the way that people believe, and that God's true nature is a mystery.

But many theologians have wanted to avoid these conclusions. If God's nature is such a mystery, then what is the content of the belief that God exists? Instead, they have attempted to show that the problem can be avoided in other ways. Many of their attempts are surveyed in the article by H. J. McCloskey. Let us look briefly at some of these defenses. But before doing so, it is important to note the important distinction between two types of evils drawn by McCloskey: moral evils (the evil of bad actions and the bad consequences they produce) and physical evils (evils due to other causes).

The following seem to be the major ways that theologians have adopted for avoiding the problem of evil: (1) evil is an illusion, (2) evil is merely the privation of good, (3) evil has to exist as a counterpart of the good, (4) evil is the by-product of the operations of the laws of nature which are intrinsically good, (5) the presence of evil brings out the good in people, (6) evil is a warning to man or is man's punishment for his sin, and (7) evil is due to man's free will. Of all these, the only one that really has any plausibility is the last. The others are easily shown to be inadequate by McCloskey.

What precisely is the free will solution to the problem of evil? It seems to come to the following: the mere existence of free will, or some of its consequences, are great goods—goods that outweigh any evils that might result from their presence. But the existence of free will entails the possibility of men doing evil actions. It is the actual performance of these actions that produces the evil that exists in the world.

McCloskey raises a variety of objections to this solution. To begin with, it is at best only a solution to the problem of moral evil; it says nothing at all about the problem of physical evil. Second, the claim that free will is a great enough good to outweigh the evil it might produce (and even the evil that it does produce) is questionable. Third, couldn't God have so ordered things (by making the world less conducive to the practice of evil, by making us a bit more predisposed to do the good thing, etc.) that, although we are free, less evil is actually performed? Fourth, and perhaps most important, given that it is possible that all men freely choose to do the right thing, why didn't God see to it that it was this possibility that was actualized? Then, even though there would be free will (with all its attendant goods) and the possibility of evil, there wouldn't be any actual evil.

Alvin Plantinga's article is an important attempt to respond to many of these objections. He begins by considering the crucial fourth objection. His crucial point in response to it is that there are certain logically possible states of affairs that are such that it is logically impossible even for God to bring them about, and that one of these is the state of affairs that all men freely choose to do the right thing. Having done that, he then goes onto demonstrate that the free will defense must be satisfactory. It cannot be incoherent, as McCloskey claims, because it is easy to see that under certain conditions it would be true.

Besides dealing with this crucial fourth objection (and, in a derivative fashion, with the third objection), Plantinga suggests that there is also a way to deal with the first objection. It is, he says, at least logically possible that the physical evil in the world is due to the free actions of the devil or other nonhuman spirits. As Plantinga points out, all that is required to defend the free will solution is that this be a possibility.

Is it really? Is the argument from evil meant to be a proof that God doesn't exist, because there is no possibility of explaining evil in a way that is compatible with the existence of God, or is it meant to be an argument which provides rational support for belief in the nonexistence of God on the grounds that explanations of evil in a world created by God are implausible? William Rowe, in his essay, argues for the latter interpretation, suggesting that evil offers rational support for atheism, even if its existence does not prove that atheism is true. In the latter part of his essay, he develops some unusual implications of thinking about the problem of evil in that way.

In the final essay in this section, Robert Adams argues that the traditional discussion of the problem of evil has mistakenly assumed that a perfect

God would necessarily create the best possible world, and has then gone on to see whether evil as it exists is possibly (or plausibly) viewed as part of the best possible world. Adams argues that there is no reason to believe that assumption providing that one understands the implications for this question of the doctrine of grace, the doctrine that God loves us even if we are not worthy of that love and created us even if he could have created a better world. The reader will have to judge whether Adams is right in supposing that the traditional discussion of evil began with a false assumption.

A tremendous literature exists on the classical arguments for the existence and nonexistence of God. There are two anthologies that collect most of the classical material on the ontological argument: A. Plantinga's *The Ontological Argument* (Anchor, 1965) and J. Hick and A. McGill's *The Many-Faced Argument* (Macmillan, 1965). More recent treatment include J. Barnes's *The Ontological Argument* (Macmillan, 1972) and several important articles including R. Adams's "The Logical Structure of the Ontological Argument," *The Philosophical Review* (1971), and D. Lewis's "Anselm and Actuality," *Noûs* (1970). R. Burrill's *The Cosmological Arguments* collects the classical material on the cosmological argument. Recent treatments of that argument include J. Ross's *Philosophical Theology* (Bobbs Merrill, 1969) and W. Rowe's *The Cosmological Argument* (Princeton University Press, 1975). Recent historical surveys include W. L. Craig's *The Cosmological Argument from Plato to Leibniz* (Macmillan, 1980) and H. Davidson's *Proofs for Eternity, Creation, and the Existence of God in Medieval Islamic and Jewish Philosophy* (Oxford University Press, 1987). The teleological argument has attracted less attention, but two good recent discussions are G. Schlesinger's "Theism and Confirmation," *Pacific Philosophical Quarterly* (1983), and W. Salmon's "Religion and Science: A New Look at Hume's Dialogue," *Philosophical Studies* (1978). Finally, R. Swinburne's *The Existence of God* (Oxford University Press, 1979) and J. L. Mackie's *The Miracle of Theism* (Oxford University Press, 1982) offer two contrasting surveys of all the classical arguments. Overviews of religious experience are contained in such classic works as W. G. Stace's *The Teaching of the Mystics* (New American Library, 1960), E. Underhill's *Mysticism* (Macmillan, 1930), and W. R. Inge's *Mysticism in Religion* (Chicago University Press, 1948). Recent discussions of mysticism include R. Gale's "Mysticism and Philosophy," *Journal of Philosophy* (1960), and William Wainright's "Mysticism and Sense Perception," *Religious Studies* (1973). Finally, J. Hick's *Evil and the God of Love* (Macmillan, 1966), M. B. Ahern's *The Problem of Evil* (Routledge & Kegan Paul, 1971), and E. Madden and P. Hare's *Evil and the Concept of God* (Charles C Thomas, 1968) provide extensive discussions of the problem of evil and citations to the classical literature.

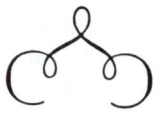

THE ONTOLOGICAL ARGUMENT

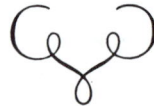

ST. ANSELM

The Ontological Argument

Truly there is a God, although the fool hath said in his heart, There is no God.

And so, Lord, do thou, who dost give understanding to faith, give me, so far as thou knowest it to be profitable, to understand that thou art as we believe; and that thou art that which we believe. And, indeed, we believe that thou art a being than which nothing greater can be conceived. Or is there no such nature, since the fool hath said in his heart, there is no God? (Psalm xiv. 1). But, at any rate, this very fool, when he hears of this being of which I speak—a being than which nothing greater can be conceived—understands what he hears, and what he understands is in his understanding; although he does not understand it to exist.

For, it is one thing for an object to be in the understanding, and another to understand that the object exists. When a painter first conceives of what he will afterwards perform, he has it in his understanding, but he does not yet understand it to be, because he has not yet performed it. But after he has made the painting, he both has it in his understanding, and he understands that it exists, because he has made it.

Hence, even the fool is convinced that something exists in the understanding, at least, than which nothing greater can be conceived. For, when he hears of this, he understands it. And whatever is understood, exists in the understanding. And assuredly that, than which nothing greater can be conceived, cannot exist in the understanding alone. For, suppose it exists in the understanding alone: then it can be conceived to exist in reality; which is greater.

Therefore, if that, than which nothing greater can be conceived, exists in the understanding alone, the very being, than which nothing greater can be

---

From Chapters II–IV of St. Anselm's *Proslogium*.

conceived, is one, than which a greater can be conceived. But obviously this is impossible. Hence, there is no doubt that there exists a being, than which nothing greater can be conceived, and it exists both in the understanding and in reality.

> God cannot be conceived not to exist.—God is that, than which nothing greater can be conceived.—That which can be conceived not to exist is not God.

And it assuredly exists so truly, that it cannot be conceived not to exist. For, it is possible to conceive of a being which cannot be conceived not to exist; and this is greater than one which can be conceived not to exist. Hence, if that, than which nothing greater can be conceived, can be conceived not to exist, it is not that, than which nothing greater can be conceived. But this is an irreconcilable contradiction. There is, then, so truly a being than which nothing greater can be conceived to exist, that it cannot even be conceived not to exist; and this being thou art, O Lord, our God.

So truly, therefore, dost thou exist, O Lord, my God, that thou canst not be conceived not to exist; and rightly. For, if a mind could conceive of a being better than thee, the creature would rise above the Creator; and this is most absurd. And, indeed, whatever else there is, except thee alone, can be conceived not to exist. To thee alone, therefore, it belongs to exist more truly than all other beings, and hence in a higher degree than all others. For, whatever else exists does not exist so truly, and hence in a less degree it belongs to it to exist. Why, then, has the fool said in his heart, there is no God (Psalm xiv. 1), since it is so evident, to a rational mind, that thou dost exist in the highest degree of all? Why, except that he is dull and a fool?

> How the fool has said in his heart what cannot be conceived.—A thing may be conceived in two ways: (1) when the word signifying it is conceived; (2) when the thing itself is understood. As far as the word goes, God can be conceived not to exist; in reality he cannot.

But how has the fool said in his heart what he could not conceive; or how is it that he could not conceive what he said in his heart? since it is the same to say in the heart, and to conceive.

But, if really, nay, since really, he both conceived, because he said in his heart; and did not say in his heart, because he could not conceive; there is more than one way in which a thing is said in the heart or conceived. For, in one sense, an object is conceived, when the word signifying it is conceived; and in another, when the very entity, which the object is, is understood.

In the former sense, then, God can be conceived not to exist; but in the latter, not at all. For no one who understands what fire and water are can conceive fire to be water, in accordance with the nature of the facts themselves, although this is possible according to the words. So, then, no one who understands what God is can conceive that God does not exist, although he says these words in his heart, either without any, or with some foreign, signification. For, God is that than which a greater cannot be conceived. And he who thoroughly understands this, assuredly understands that this being so truly exists, that not even in concept can it be non-existent. Therefore, he who understands that God so exists, cannot conceive that he does not exist.

I thank thee, gracious Lord, I thank thee; because what I formerly believed by thy bounty, I now so understand by thine illumination, that if I were unwilling to believe that thou dost exist, I should not be able not to understand this to be true.

NORMAN MALCOLM

Anselm's Ontological Arguments

I believe that in Anselm's *Proslogion* and *Responsio editoris* there are two different pieces of reasoning which he did not distinguish from one another, and that a good deal of light may be shed on the philosophical problem of "the ontological argument" if we do distinguish them. In Chapter 2 of the *Proslogion*[1] Anselm says that we believe that God is *something a greater than which cannot be conceived*. (The Latin is *aliquid quo nihil maius cogitari posit*. Anselm sometimes uses the alternate expressions *aliquid quo maius nihil cogitari potest, id quo maius cogitari nequit, aliquid quo maius cogitari non valet*.) Even the fool of the Psalm who says in his heart there is no God, when he hears this very thing that Anselm says, namely, "something a greater than which cannot be conceived," understands what he hears, and what he understands is in his understanding though he does not understand that it exists.

Apparently Anselm regards it as tautological to say that whatever is understood is in the understanding (*quidquid intelligitur in intellectu est*): he uses *intelligitur* and *initellectu est* as interchangeable locutions. The same holds for another formula of his: whatever is thought is in thought (*quidquid cogitatur in cogitatione est*).[2]

From *The Philosophical Review*, 69 (1960). Reprinted by permission of the author and *The Philosophical Review*.

[1] I have consulted the Latin text of the *Proslogion*, of *Gaunilonis Pro Insipiente*, and of the *Responsio editoris*, in S. Anselmi, *Opera Omnia*, edited by F. C. Schmitt (Secovii, 1938), vol. I. With numerous modifications, I have used the English translation by S. N. Deane: *St. Anselm* (La Salle, Illinois, 1948).

[2] See *Proslogion* 1 and *Responsio* 2.

Of course many things may exist in the understanding that do not exist in reality; for example, elves. Now, says Anselm, something a greater than which cannot be conceived exists in the understanding. But it cannot exist *only* in the understanding, for to exist in reality is greater. Therefore that thing a greater than which cannot be conceived cannot exist only in the understanding, for then a greater thing could be conceived: namely, one that exists both in the understanding and in reality.[3]

Here I have a question. It is not clear to me whether Anselm means that (a) existence in reality by itself is greater than existence in the understanding, or that (b) existence in reality and existence in the understanding together are greater than existence in the understanding alone. Certainly he accepts (b). But he might also accept (a), as Descartes apparently does in *Meditation III* when he suggests that the mode of being by which a thing is "objectively in the understanding" is *imperfect*.[4] Of course Anselm might accept both (a) and (b). He might hold that in general something is greater if it has both of these "modes of existence" than if it has either one alone, but also that existence in reality is a more perfect mode of existence than existence in the understanding.

In any case, Anselm holds that something is greater if it exists both in the understanding and in reality than if it exists merely in the understanding. An equivalent way of putting this interesting proposition, in a more current terminology, is: something is greater if it is both conceived of and exists than if it is merely conceived of. Anselm's reasoning can be expressed as follows: *id quo maius cogitari nequit* cannot be merely conceived of and not exist, for then it would not be *id quo maius cogitari nequit*. The doctrine that something is greater if it exists in addition to being conceived of, than if it is only conceived of, could be called the doctrine that *existence is a perfection*. Descartes maintained, in so many words, that existence is a perfection,[5] and presumably he was holding Anselm's doctrine, although he does not, in *Meditation V* or elsewhere, argue in the way that Anselm does in *Proslogion 2*.

When Anselm says, "And certainly, that than which nothing greater can be conceived cannot exist merely in the understanding. For suppose it exists merely in the understanding, then it can be conceived to exist in reality, which is greater,"[6] he is claiming that if I conceived of a being of great excellence, that being would be *greater* (more excellent, more perfect) if it existed than if it did not exist. His supposition that "it exists merely

---

[3]Anselm's actual words are: "Et certe id quo maius cogitari nequit, non potest esse in solo intellectu. Si enim vel in solo intellectu est, potest cogitari esse et in re, quod maius est. Si ergo id quo maius cogitari non potest, est in solo intellectu: id ipsum quo maius cogitari non potest, est quo maius cogitari potest. Sed certe hoc esse non potest." *Proslogion* 2.

[4]Haldane and Ross, *The Philosophical Works of Descartes*, 2 vols. (Cambridge, 1931), I, 163.

[5]*Op. cit.*, p. 182.

[6]*Proslogion* 2; Deane, p. 8.

in the understanding" is the supposition that it is conceived of but does not exist. Anselm repeated this claim in his reply to the criticism of the monk Gaunilo. Speaking of the being a greater than which cannot be conceived, he says:

> I have said that if it exists merely in the understanding it can be conceived to exist in reality, which is greater. Therefore, if it exists merely in the understanding obviously the very being a greater than which cannot be conceived, is one a greater than which can be conceived. What, I ask, can follow better than that? For if it exists merely in the understanding, can it not be conceived to exist in reality? And if it can be so conceived does not he who conceives of this conceive of a thing greater than it, if it does exist merely in the understanding? Can anything follow better than this: that if a being a greater than which cannot be conceived exists merely in the understanding, it is something a greater than which can be conceived? What could be plainer?[7]

He is implying, in the first sentence, that if I conceive of something which does not exist then it is possible for it to exist, and *it will be greater if it exists than if it does not exist.*

The doctrine that existence is a perfection is remarkably queer. It makes sense and is true to say that my future house will be a better one if it is insulated than if it is not insulated; but what could it mean to say that it will be a better house if it exists than if it does not? My future child will be a better man if he is honest than if he is not; but who would understand the saying that he will be a better man if he exists than if he does not? Or who understands the saying that if God exists He is more perfect than if He does not exist? One might say, with some intelligibility, that it would be better (for oneself or for mankind) if God exists than if He does not—but that is a different matter.

A king might desire that his next chancellor should have knowledge, wit, and resolution; but it is ludicrous to add that the king's desire is to have a chancellor who exists. Suppose that two royal councilors, A and B, were asked to draw up separately descriptions of the most perfect chancellor they could conceive, and that the descriptions they produced were identical except that A included existence in his list of attributes of a perfect chancellor and B did not. (I do not mean that B put nonexistence in his list.) One and the same person could satisfy both descriptions. More to the point, any person who satisfied A's description would *necessarily* satisfy B's description and *vice versa!* This is to say that A and B did not produce descriptions that differed in any way but rather one and the same description of necessary and desirable qualities in a chancellor. A only made a show of putting down a desirable quality that B had failed to include.

---

[7]*Responsio* 2; Deane, pp. 157–58.

I believe I am merely restating an observation that Kant made in attacking the notion that "existence" or "being" is a "real predicate." He says:

> By whatever and by however many predicates we may think a thing—even if we completely determine it—we do not make the least addition to the thing when we further declare that this thing *is*. Otherwise, it would not be exactly the same thing that exists, but something more than we had thought in the concept; and we could not, therefore, say that the exact object of my concept exists.[8]

Anselm's ontological proof of *Proslogion 2* is fallacious because it rests on the false doctrine that existence is a perfection (and therefore that "existence" is a "real predicate"). It would be desirable to have a rigorous refutation of the doctrine but I have not been able to provide one. I am compelled to leave the matter at the more or less intuitive level of Kant's observation. In any case, I believe that the doctrine does not belong to Anselm's other formulation of the ontological argument. It is worth noting that Gassendi anticipated Kant's criticism when he said, against Descartes:

> Existence is a perfection neither in God nor in anything else; it is rather that in the absence of which there is no perfection.... Hence neither is existence held to exist in a thing in the way that perfections do, nor if the thing lacks existence is it said to be imperfect (or deprived of a perfection), so much as to be nothing.[9]

II.

I take up now the consideration of the second ontological proof, which Anselm presents in the very next chapter of the *Proslogion*. (There is no evidence that he thought of himself as offering two different proofs.) Speaking of the being a greater than which cannot be conceived, he says:

> And it so truly exists that it cannot be conceived not to exist. For it is possible to conceive of a being which cannot be conceived not to exist; and this is greater than one which can be conceived not to exist. Hence, if that, than which nothing greater can be conceived, can be conceived not to exist, it is not that than which nothing greater can be conceived. But this is a contradiction. So truly, therefore, is there something than which nothing greater can be conceived, that it cannot even be conceived not to exist.
>
> And this being thou art, O Lord, our God.[10]

---

[8]*The Critique of Pure Reason*, tr. by Norman Kemp Smith (London, 1929), p. 505.

[9]Haldane and Ross, II, 186.

[10]*Proslogion* 3; Deane, pp. 8–9.

Anselm is saying two things: first, that a being whose nonexistence is logically impossible is "greater" than a being whose nonexistence is logically possible (and therefore that a being a greater than which cannot be conceived must be one whose nonexistence is logically impossible); second, that *God* is a being than which a greater cannot be conceived.

In regard to the second of these assertions, there certainly is *a* use of the word "God," and I think far the more common use, in accordance with which the statements "God is the greatest of all beings," "God is the most perfect being," "God is the supreme being," are *logically* necessary truths, in the same sense that the statement "A square has four sides" is a logically necessary truth. If there is a man named "Jones" who is the tallest man in the world, the statement "Jones is the tallest man in the world" is merely true and is not a logically necessary truth. It is a virtue of Anselm's unusual phrase, "a being a greater than which cannot be conceived,"[11] to make it explicit that the sentence "God is the greatest of all beings" expresses a logically necessary truth and not a mere matter of fact such as the one we imagined about Jones.

With regard to Anselm's first assertion (namely, that a being whose nonexistence is logically impossible is greater than a being whose nonexistence is logically possible) perhaps the most puzzling thing about it is the use of the word "greater." It appears to mean exactly the same as "superior," "more excellent," "more perfect." This equivalence by itself is of no help to us, however, since the latter expressions would be equally puzzling here. What is required is some explanation of their use.

We do think of *knowledge*, say, as an excellence, a good thing. If A has more knowledge of algebra than B we express this in common language by saying that A has a *better* knowledge of algebra than B, or that A's knowledge of algebra is *superior* to B's, whereas we should not say that B has a better or superior *ignorance* of algebra than A. We do say "greater ignorance," but here the word "greater" is used purely quantitatively.

Previously I rejected *existence* as a perfection. Anselm is maintaining in the remarks last quoted, not that existence is a perfection, but that *the logical impossibility of nonexistence is a perfection*. In other words, *necessary existence* is a perfection. His first ontological proof uses the principle that a thing is greater if it exists than if it does not exist. His second proof employs the different principle that a thing is greater if it necessarily exists than if it does not necessarily exist.

Some remarks about the notion of *dependence* may help to make this latter principle intelligible. Many things depend for their existence on other things and events. My house was built by a carpenter: its coming into

---

[11]Professor Robert Calhoun has pointed out to me that a similar locution had been used by Augustine. In *De moribus Manichaeorum* (Bk. II, ch. xi, sec. 24), he says that God is a being *quo esse aut cogitari melius nihil possit* (*Patrologiae Patrum Latinorum*, ed. by J. P. Migne, Paris, 1841–1845, vol. 32: *Augustinus*, vol. 1).

existence was dependent on a certain creative activity. Its continued existence is dependent on many things: that a tree does not crush it, that it is not consumed by fire, and so on. If we reflect on the common meaning of the word "God" (no matter how vague and confused this is), we realize that it is incompatible with this meaning that God's existence should *depend* on anything. Whether we believe in Him or not we must admit that the "almighty and everlasting God" (as several ancient prayers begin), the "Maker of heaven and earth, and of all things visible and invisible" (as is said in the Nicene Creed), cannot be thought of as being brought into existence by anything or as depending for His continued existence on anything. To conceive of anything as dependent upon something else for its existence is to conceive of it as a lesser being than God.

If a housewife has a set of extremely fragile dishes, then as dishes they are *inferior* to those of another set like them in all respects except that they are *not* fragile. Those of the first set are *dependent* for their continued existence on gentle handling; those of the second set are not. There is a definite connection in common language between the notions of dependency and inferiority, and independence and superiority. To say that something which was dependent on nothing whatever was superior to ("greater than") anything that was dependent in any way upon anything is quite in keeping with the everyday use of the terms "superior" and "greater." Correlative with the notions of dependence and independence are the notions of *limited* and *unlimited*. An engine requires fuel and this is a limitation. It is the same thing to say that an engine's operation is *dependent* on as that it is *limited* by its fuel supply. An engine that could accomplish the same work in the same time and was in other respects satisfactory, but did not require fuel, would be a *superior* engine.

God is usually conceived of as an *unlimited* being. He is conceived of as a being who *could not* be limited, that is, as an absolutely unlimited being. This is no less than to conceive of Him as *something a greater than which cannot be conceived*. If God is conceived to be an absolutely unlimited being He must be conceived to be unlimited in regard to His existence as well as His operation. In this conception it will not make sense to say that He depends on anything for coming into or continuing in existence. Nor, as Spinoza observed, will it make sense to say that something could *prevent* Him from existing.[12] Lack of moisture can prevent trees from existing in a certain region of the earth. But it would be contrary to the concept of God as an unlimited being to suppose that anything other than God Himself could prevent Him from existing, and it would be self-contradictory to suppose that He Himself could do it.

Some may be inclined to object that although nothing could prevent God's existence, still it might just *happen* that He did not exist. And if He

---

[12]*Ethics*, pt. I, prop. 11.

did exist that too would be by chance. I think, however, that from the supposition that it could happen that God did not exist it would follow that, if He existed, He would have mere duration and not eternity. It would make sense to ask, "How long has He existed?," "Will He still exist next week?," "He was in existence yesterday but how about today?," and so on. It seems absurd to make God the subject of such questions. According to our ordinary conception of Him, He is an eternal being. And eternity does not mean endless duration, as Spinoza noted. To ascribe eternity to something is to exclude as senseless all sentences that imply that it has duration. If a thing has duration then it would be merely a *contingent* fact, if it was a fact, that its duration was endless. The moon could have endless duration but not eternity. If something has endless duration it will *make sense* (although it will be false) to say that it will cease to exist, and it will make sense (although it will be false) to say that something will *cause* it to cease to exist. A being with endless duration is not, therefore, an absolutely unlimited being. That God is conceived to be eternal follows from the fact that He is conceived to be an absolutely unlimited being.

I have been trying to expand the argument of *Proslogion* 3. In *Responsio* 1 Anselm adds the following acute point: if you can conceive of a certain thing and this thing does not exist then if it *were* to exist its nonexistence would be *possible*. It follows, I believe, that if the thing were to exist it would depend on other things both for coming into and continuing in existence, and also that it would have duration and not eternity. Therefore it would not be, either in reality or in conception, an unlimited being, *aliquid quo nihil maius cogitari possit*.

Anselm states his argument as follows:

> If it [the thing a greater than which cannot be conceived] can be conceived at all it must exist. For no one who denies or doubts the existence of a being a greater than which is inconceivable, denies or doubts that if it did exist its non-existence, either in reality or in the understanding, would be impossible. For otherwise it would not be a being a greater than which cannot be conceived. But as to whatever can be conceived but does not exist: if it were to exist its non-existence either in reality or in the understanding would be possible. Therefore, if a being a greater than which cannot be conceived, can even be conceived, it must exist.[13]

What Anselm has proved is that the notion of contingent existence or of contingent nonexistence cannot have any application to God. His existence must either be logically necessary or logically impossible. The only intelligible way of rejecting Anselm's claim that God's existence is necessary is to maintain that the concept of God, as a being a greater than which cannot be

---

[13]*Responsio* 1; Deane, pp. 154–55.

conceived, is self-contradictory or nonsensical.[14] Supposing that this is false, Anselm is right to deduce God's necessary existence from his characterization of Him as a being a greater than which cannot be conceived.

Let me summarize the proof. If God, a being a greater than which cannot be conceived, does not exist then He cannot *come* into existence. For if He did He would either have been *caused* to come into existence or have *happened* to come into existence, and in either case He would be a limited being, which by our conception of Him He is not. Since He cannot come into existence, if He does not exist His existence is impossible. If He does exist He cannot have come into existence (for the reasons given), nor can He cease to exist, for nothing could cause Him to cease to exist nor could it just happen that He ceased to exist. So if God exists His existence is necessary. Thus God's existence is either impossible or necessary. It can be the former only if the concept of such a being is self-contradictory or in some way logically absurd. Assuming that this is not so, it follows that He necessarily exists.

It may be helpful to express ourselves in the following way: to say, not that *omnipotence* is a property of God, but rather that *necessary omnipotence* is; and to say, not that omniscience is a property of God, but rather that *necessary omniscience* is. We have criteria for determining that a man knows this and that and can do this and that, and for determining that one man has greater knowledge and abilities in a certain subject than another. We could think of various tests to give them. But there is nothing we should wish to describe, seriously and literally, as "testing" God's knowledge and powers. That God is omniscient and omnipotent has not been determined by the application of criteria: rather these are requirements of our conception of Him. They are internal properties of the concept, although they are also rightly said to be properties of God. *Necessary existence* is a property of God in the *same sense* that *necessary omnipotence* and *necessary omniscience* are His properties. And we are not to think that "God necessarily exists" means that it follows necessarily from something that God exists *contingently*. The a priori proposition "God necessarily exists" entails the proposition "God exists," if and only if the latter also is understood as an a priori proposition: in which case the two propositions are equivalent. In this sense Anselm's proof is a proof of God's existence.

---

[14]Gaunilo attacked Anselm's argument on this very point. He would not concede that a being a greater than which cannot be conceived existed in his understanding (*Gaunilonis Pro Insipiente*, secs. 4 and 5; Deane, pp. 148–50). Anselm's reply is: "I call on your faith and conscience to attest that this is most false" (*Responsio* 1; Deane, p. 154). Gaunilo's faith and conscience will attest that it is false that "God is not a being a greater than which is inconceivable," and false that "He is not understood (*intelligitur*) or conceived (*cogitatur*)" (*ibid.*). Descartes also remarks that one would go to "strange extremes" who denied that we understand the words *"that thing which is the most perfect that we can conceive;* for that is what all men call God" (Haldane and Ross, II, 129).

Descartes was somewhat hazy on the question of whether existence is a property of things that exist, but at the same time he saw clearly enough that *necessary existence* is a property of God. Both points are illustrated in his reply to Gassendi's remark, which I quoted above:

> I do not see to what class of reality you wish to assign existence, nor do I see why it may not be said to be a property as well as omnipotence, taking the word property as equivalent to any attribute or anything which can be predicated of a thing, as in the present case it should be by all means regarded. Nay, necessary existence in the case of God is also a true property in the strictest sense of the word, because it belongs to Him and forms part of His essence alone.[15]

Elsewhere he speaks of "the necessity of existence" as being "that crown of perfections without which we cannot comprehend God."[16] He is emphatic on the point that necessary existence applies solely to "an absolutely perfect Being."[17]

III.

I wish to consider now a part of Kant's criticism of the ontological argument which I believe to be wrong. He says:

> If, in an identical proposition, I reject the predicate while retaining the subject, contradiction results; and I therefore say that the former belongs necessarily to the latter. But if we reject subject and predicate alike, there is no contradiction; for nothing is then left that can be contradicted. To post a triangle, and yet to reject its three angles, is self-contradictory; but there is no contradiction in rejecting the triangle together with its three angles. The same holds true of the concept of an absolutely necessary being. If its existence is rejected, we reject the thing itself with all its predicates; and no question of contradiction can then arise. There is nothing outside it that would then be contradicted, since the necessity of the thing is not supposed to be derived from anything external; nor is there anything internal that would be contradicted, since in rejecting the thing itself we have at the same time rejected all its internal properties. "God is omnipotent" is a necessary judgment. The omnipotence cannot be rejected if we posit a Deity, that is, an infinite being; for the two concepts are identical. But if we say, "There is no God," neither the omnipotence nor any other of its predicates is given; they are one and all rejected together with the subject, and there is therefore not the least contradiction in such a judgment.[18]

---

[15]Haldane and Ross, II, 228.

[16]*Ibid.*, I, 445.

[17]E.g., *ibid.*, Principle 15, p. 225.

[18]*Op. cit.*, p. 502.

To these remarks the reply is that when the concept of God is correctly understood one sees that one cannot "reject the subject." "There is no God" is seen to be a necessarily false statement. Anselm's demonstration proves that the proposition "God exists" has the same a priori footing as the proposition "God is omnipotent."

Many present-day philosophers, in agreement with Kant, declare that existence is not a property and think that this overthrows the ontological argument. Although it is an error to regard existence as a property of things that have contingent existence, it does not follow that it is an error to regard necessary existence as a property of God. A recent writer says, against Anselm, that a proof of God's existence "based on the necessities of thought" is "universally regarded as fallacious: it is not thought possible to build bridges between mere abstractions and concrete existence."[19] But this way of putting the matter obscures the distinction we need to make. Does "concrete existence" mean contingent existence? Then to build bridges between concrete existence and mere abstractions would be like inferring the existence of an island from the concept of a perfect island, which both Anselm and Descartes regarded as absurd. What Anselm did was to give a demonstration that the proposition "God necessarily exists" is entailed by the proposition "God is a being a greater than which cannot be conceived" (which is equivalent to "God is an absolutely unlimited being"). Kant declares that when "I think a being as the supreme reality, without any defect, the question still remains whether it exists or not."[20] But once one has grasped Anselm's proof of the necessary existence of a being a greater than which cannot be conceived, no question remains as to whether it exists or not, just as Euclid's demonstration of the existence of an infinity of prime numbers leaves no question on that issue.

Kant says that "every reasonable person" must admit that "all existential propositions are synthetic."[21] Part of the perplexity one has about the ontological argument is in deciding whether or not the proposition "God necessarily exists" is or is not an "existential proposition." But let us look around. Is the Euclidean theorem in number theory, "There exists an infinite number of prime numbers," an "existential proposition"? Do we not want to say that *in some sense* it asserts the existence of something? Cannot we say, with equal justification, that the proposition "God necessarily exists" asserts the existence of something, *in some sense?* What we need to understand, in each case, is the particular sense of the assertion. Neither proposition has the same sort of sense as do the propositions, "A low pressure area exists over the Great Lakes," "There still exists some

---

[19]J. N. Findlay, "Can God's Existence Be Disproved?," *New Essays in Philosophical Theology*, ed. by A. N. Flew and A. MacIntyre (London, 1955), p. 47.

[20]*Op. cit.*, pp. 505–6.

[21]*Ibid.*, pp. 504.

possibility that he will survive," "The pain continues to exist in his abdomen." One good way of seeing the difference in sense of these various propositions is to see the variously different ways in which they are proved or supported. It is wrong to think that all assertions of existence have the same kind of meaning. There are as many kinds of existential propositions as there are kinds of subjects of discourse.

Closely related to Kant's view that all existential propositions are "synthetic" is the contemporary dogma that all existential propositions are contingent. Professor Gilbert Ryle tells us that "Any assertion of the existence of something, like any assertion of the occurrence of something, can be denied without logical absurdity."[22] "All existential statements are contingent," says Mr. I. M. Crombie.[23] Professor J. J. C. Smart remarks that "Existence is not a property" and then goes on to assert that "There can never be any *logical contradiction* in denying that God exists."[24] He declares that "The concept of a logically necessary being is a self-contradictory concept, like the concept of a round square.... No existential proposition can be logically necessary," he maintains, for "the truth of a logically necessary proposition depends only on our symbolism, or to put the same thing in another way, on the relationship of concepts" (p. 38). Professor K. E. M. Baier says, "It is no longer seriously in dispute that the notion of a logically necessary being is self-contradictory. Whatever can be conceived of as existing can equally be conceived of as not existing."[25] This is a repetition of Hume's assertion, "Whatever we conceive as existent, we can also conceive as non-existent. There is no being, therefore, whose non-existence implies a contradiction."[26]

Professor J. N. Findlay ingeniously constructs an ontological *dis*proof of God's existence, based on a "modern view of the nature of "necessity in propositions"": the view, namely, that necessity in propositions "merely reflects our use of words, the arbitrary conventions of our language."[27] Findlay undertakes to characterize what he calls "religious attitude," and here there is a striking agreement between his observations and some of the things I have said in expounding Anselm's proof. Religious attitude, he says, presumes *superiority* in its object and superiority so great that the worshiper is in comparison as nothing. Religious attitude finds it "anomalous to worship anything *limited* in any unthinkable manner.... And hence we are led on irresistibly to demand that our religious object should have an *unsurpassable* supremacy along all avenues, that it should tower *infinitely* above all other objects" (p. 51). We cannot help feeling that "the worthy object of our worship

---

[22]*The Nature of Metaphysics*, ed. by D. F. Pears (New York, 1957), p. 150.

[23]*New Essays in Philosophical Theology*, p. 114.

[24]*Ibid.*, p. 34.

[25]*The Meaning of Life*, Inaugural Lecture, Canberra University College (Canberra, 1957), p. 8.

[26]*Dialogues Concerning Natural Religion*, pt. IX.

[27]Findlay, *op. cit.*, p. 54.

can never be a thing that merely *happens* to exist, nor one on which all other objects merely *happen* to depend. The true object of religious reverence must not be one, merely, to which no *actual* independent realities stand opposed: it must be one to which such opposition is totally *inconceivable....* And not only must the existence of *other* things be unthinkable without Him, but His own non-existence must be wholly unthinkable in any circumstances" (p. 52). And now, says Findlay, when we add up these various requirements, what they entail is "not only that there isn't a God, but that the Divine Existence is either senseless or impossible" (p. 54). For on the one hand, "if God is to satisfy religious claims and needs, He must be a being in every way inescapable, One whose existence and whose possession of certain excellences we cannot possibly conceive away." On the other hand, "modern views make it self-evidently absurd (if they don't make it ungrammatical) to speak of such a Being and attribute existence to Him. It was indeed an ill day for Anselm when he hit upon his famous proof. For on that day he not only laid bare something that is of the essence of an adequate religious object, but also something that entails its necessary non-existence" (p. 55).

Now I am inclined to hold the "modern" view that logically necessary truth "merely reflects our use of words" (although I do not believe that the conventions of language are always *arbitrary*). But I confess that I am unable to see how that view is supposed to lead to the conclusion that "the Divine existence is either senseless or impossible." Findlay does not explain how this result comes about. Surely he cannot mean that this view entails that nothing can have necessary properties: for this would imply that mathematics is "senseless or impossible," which no one wants to hold. Trying to fill in the argument that is missing from his article, the most plausible conjecture I can make is the following: Findlay thinks that the view that logical necessity "reflects the use of words" implies, not that nothing has necessary properties, but that *existence* cannot be a necessary property of anything. That is to say, every proposition of the form "*x* exists," including the proposition "God exists," must be *contingent*.[28] At the same time, our concept of God requires that His existence be *necessary*, that is, that "God exists" be a necessary truth. Therefore, the modern view of necessity proves that what the concept of God requires *cannot* be fulfilled. It proves that God *cannot* exist.

The correct reply is that the view that logical necessity merely reflects the use of words cannot possibly have the implication that every existential proposition must be contingent. That view requires us to *look at* the use of words and not manufacture a priori theses about it. In the Ninetieth Psalm it is said: "Before the mountains were brought forth, or ever thou hadst formed the earth and the world, even from everlasting to everlasting, thou art God."

---

[28]The other philosophers I have just cited may be led to this opinion by the same thinking. Smart, for example, says that "the truth of a logically necessary proposition depends only on our symbolism, or to put the same thing in another way, on the relationship of concepts" (*supra*). This is very similar to saying that it "reflects our use of words."

Here is expressed the idea of the necessary existence and eternity of God, an idea that is essential to the Jewish and Christian religions. In those complex systems of thought, those "language-games," God has the status of a necessary being. Who can doubt that? Here we must say with Wittgenstein, "This language-game is played!"[29] I believe we may rightly take the existence of those religious systems of thought in which God figures as a necessary being to be a disproof of the dogma, affirmed by Hume and others, that no existential proposition can be necessary.

Another way of criticizing the ontological argument is the following. "Granted that the concept of necessary existence follows from the concept of a being a greater than which cannot be conceived, this amounts to no more than granting the *a priori* truth of the *conditional* proposition, 'If such a being exists then it necessarily exists.' This proposition, however, does not entail the *existence of anything*, and one can deny its antecedent without contradiction." Kant, for example, compares the proposition (or "judgment," as he calls it) "A triangle has three angles" with the proposition "God is a necessary being." He allows that the former is "absolutely necessary" and goes on to say:

> The absolute necessity of the judgment is only a conditional necessity of the thing, or of the predicate in the judgment. The above proposition does not declare that three angles are absolutely necessary, but that, under the condition that there is a triangle (that is, that a triangle is given), three angles will necessarily be found in it.[30]

He is saying, quite correctly, that the proposition about triangles is equivalent to the conditional proposition, "If a triangle exists, it has three angles." He then makes the comment that there is no contradiction "in rejecting the triangle together with its three angles." He proceeds to draw the alleged parallel: "The same holds true of the concept of an absolutely necessary being. If its existence is rejected, we reject the thing itself with all its predicates; and no question of contradiction can then arise."[31] The priest, Caterus, made the same objection to Descartes when he said:

> Though it be conceded that an entity of the highest perfection implies its existence by its very name, yet it does not follow that that very existence is anything actual in the real world, but merely that the concept of existence is inseparably united with the concept of highest being. Hence you cannot infer that the existence of God is anything actual, unless you assume that that highest being actually exists; for then it will actually contain all its perfections, together with this perfection of real existence.[32]

I think that Caterus, Kant, and numerous other philosophers have been mistaken in supposing that the proposition "God is a necessary being" (or "God necessarily exists") is equivalent to the conditional proposition "If God

---

[29]*Philosophical Investigations* (New York, 1953), sec. 654.

[30]*Op. cit.*, pp. 501–2.

[31]*Ibid.*, p. 502.

[32]Haldane and Ross, II, 7.

exists then He necessarily exists."[33] For how do they want the antecedent clause, "*If* God exists," to be understood? Clearly they want it to imply that it is *possible* that God does *not* exist.[34] The whole point of Kant's analysis is to try to show that it is possible to "reject the subject." Let us make this implication explicit in the conditional proposition, so that it reads: "If God exists (and it is possible that He does not) then He necessarily exists." But now it is apparent, I think, that these philosophers have arrived at a self-contradictory position. I do not mean that this conditional proposition, taken alone, is self-contradictory. Their position is self-contradictory in the following way. On the one hand, they agree that the proposition "God necessarily exists" is an a priori truth; Kant implies that it is "absolutely necessary," and Caterus says that God's existence is implied by His very name. On the other hand, they think that it is correct to analyze this proposition in such a way that it will entail the proposition "It is possible that God does not exist." But so far from its being the case that the proposition "God necessarily exists" entails the proposition "It is possible that God does not exist," it is rather the case that they are *incompatible* with one another! Can anything be clearer than the conjunction "God necessarily exists but it is possible that He does not exist" is self-contradictory? Is it not just as plainly self-contradictory as the conjunction "A square necessarily has four sides but it is possible for a square not to have four sides"? In short, this familiar criticism of the ontological argument is self-contradictory, because it accepts *both* of two incompatible propositions.[35]

---

[33]I have heard it said by more than one person in discussion that Kant's view was that it is really a misuse of language to speak of a "necessary being," on the grounds that necessity is properly predicated only of propositions (judgments) not of *things*. This is not a correct account of Kant. (See his discussion of "The Postulates of Empirical Thought in General," *op. cit.*, pp. 239–56, esp. p. 239 and pp. 247–48.) But if he had held this, as perhaps the above philosophers think he should have then presumably his view would not have been that the pseudo-proposition "God is a necessary being" is equivalent to the conditional "If God exists then He necessarily exists." Rather his view would have been that the genuine proposition " 'God exists' is necessarily true" is equivalent to the conditional "If God exists then He exists" (*not* "If God exists then He *necessarily* exists," which would be an illegitimate formulation, on the view imaginatively attributed to Kant).

"If God exists then He exists" is a foolish tautology which says nothing different from the tautology "If a new earth satellite exists then it exists." If "If God exists then He exists" were a correct analysis of " 'God exists' is necessarily true," then "If a new earth satellite exists then it exists" would be a correct analysis of " 'A new earth satellite exists' is necessarily true." If the *analysans* is necessarily true then the *analysandum* must be necessarily true, provided the analysis is correct. If this proposed Kantian analysis of " 'God exists' is necessarily true" were correct, we should be presented with the consequence that not only is it necessarily true that God exists, but also it is necessarily true that a new earth satellite exists: which is absurd.

[34]When summarizing Anselm's proof (in part II, *supra*) I said: "If God exists He necessarily exists." But there I was merely stating an entailment. "If God exists" did not have the implication that it is possible He does not exist. And of course I was not regarding the conditional as *equivalent* to "God necessarily exists."

[35]This fallacious criticism of Anselm is implied in the following remarks by Gilson: "To show that the affirmation of necessary existence is analytically implied in the idea of God, would be...to show that God is necessary if He exists, but would not prove that He does exist" (E. Gilson, *The Spirit of Medieval Philosophy*, New York, 1940, p. 62).

One conclusion we may draw from our examination of this criticism is that (contrary to Kant) there is a lack of symmetry, in an important respect, between the propositions "A triangle has three angles" and "God has necessary existence," although both are a priori. The former can be expressed in the conditional assertion, "If a triangle exists (and it is possible that none does) it has three angles." The latter cannot be expressed in the corresponding conditional assertion without contradiction.

IV.

I turn to the question of whether the idea of a being a greater than which cannot be conceived is self-contradictory. Here Leibniz made a contribution to the discussion of the ontological argument. He remarked that the argument of Anselm and Descartes

> is not a paralogism, but it is an imperfect demonstration, which assumes something that must still be proved in order to render it mathematically evident; that is, it is tacitly assumed that this idea of the all-great or all-perfect being is possible, and implies no contradiction. And it is already something that by this remark it is proved that, assuming that God is possible, he exists, which is the privilege of divinity alone.[36]

Leibniz undertook to give a proof that God is possible. He defined a *perfection* as a simple, positive quality in the highest degree.[37] He argued that since perfections are *simple* qualities they must be compatible with one another. Therefore the concept of a being possessing all perfections is consistent.

I will not review his argument because I do not find his definition of a perfection intelligible. For one thing, it assumes that certain qualities or attributes are "positive" in their intrinsic nature, and others "negative" or "privative," and I have not been able clearly to understand that. For another thing, it assumes that some qualities are intrinsically simple. I believe that Wittgenstein has shown in the *Investigations* that nothing is *intrinsically* simple, but that whatever has the status of a simple, an indefinable, in one system of concepts, may have the status of a complex thing, a definable thing, in another system of concepts.

I do not know how to demonstrate that the concept of God—that is, of a being a greater than which cannot be conceived—is not self-contradictory. But I do not think that it is legitimate to demand such a demonstration. I also do not know how to demonstrate that either the concept of a material thing

---

[36]*New Essays Concerning the Human Understanding*, Bk. IV, ch. 10; ed. by A. G. Langley (La Salle, Illinois, 1949), p. 504.

[37]See *Ibid.*, Appendix X, p. 714.

or the concept of *seeing* a material thing is not self-contradictory, and philosophers have argued that both of them are. With respect to any particular reasoning that is offered for holding that the concept of seeing a material thing, for example, is self-contradictory, one may try to show the invalidity of the reasoning and thus free the concept from the charge of being self-contradictory *on that ground*. But I do not understand what it would mean to demonstrate *in general*, and not in respect to any particular reasoning, that the concept is not self-contradictory. So it is with the concept of God. I should think there is no more of a presumption that it is self-contradictory than is the concept of seeing a material thing. Both concepts have a place in the thinking and the lives of human beings.

But even if one allows that Anselm's phrase may be free of self-contradiction, one wants to know how it can have any *meaning* for anyone. Why is it that human beings have even *formed* the concept of an infinite being, a being a greater than which cannot be conceived? This is a legitimate and important question. I am sure there cannot be a deep understanding of that concept without an understanding of the phenomena of human life that give rise to it. To give an account of the latter is beyond my ability. I wish, however, to make one suggestion (which should not be understood as autobiographical).

There is the phenomenon of feeling guilt for something that one has done or thought or felt or for a disposition that one has. One wants to be free of this guilt. But sometimes the guilt is felt to be so great that one is sure that nothing one could do oneself, nor any forgiveness by another human being, would remove it. One feels a guilt that is beyond all measure, a guilt "a greater than which cannot be conceived." Paradoxically, it would seem, one nevertheless has an intense desire to have this incomparable guilt removed. One requires a forgiveness that is beyond all measure, a forgiveness "a greater than which cannot be conceived." Out of such a storm in the soul, I am suggesting, there arises the conception of a forgiving mercy that is limitless, beyond all measure. This is one important feature of the Jewish and Christian conception of God.

I wish to relate this thought to a remark made by Kierkegaard, who was speaking about belief in Christianity but whose remark may have a wider application. He says:

> There is only one proof of the truth of Christianity and that, quite rightly, is from the emotions, when the dread of sin and a heavy conscience torture a man into crossing the narrow line between despair bordering upon madness—and Christendom.[38]

One may think it absurd for a human being to feel a guilt of such magnitude, and even more absurd that, if he feels it, he should *desire* its removal.

---

[38]*The Journals*, tr. by A. Dru (Oxford, 1938), sec. 926.

I have nothing to say about that. It may also be absurd for people to fall in love, but they do it. I wish only to say that there *is* that human phenomenon of an unbearably heavy conscience and that it is importantly connected with the genesis of the concept of God, that is, with the formation of the "grammar" of the word "God." I am sure that this concept is related to human experience in other ways. If one had the acuteness and depth to perceive these connections one could grasp the *sense* of the concept. When we encounter this concept as a problem in philosophy, we do not consider the human phenomena that lie behind it. It is not surprising that many philosophers believe that the idea of a necessary being is an arbitrary and absurd construction.

What is the relation of Anselm's ontological argument to religious belief? This is a difficult question. I can imagine an atheist going through the argument, becoming convinced of its validity, acutely defending it against objections, yet remaining an atheist. The only effect it could have on the fool of the Psalm would be that he stopped saying in his heart "There is no God," because he would now realize that this is something he cannot meaningfully say or think. It is hardly to be expected that a demonstrative argument should, in addition, produce in him a living faith. Surely there is a level at which one can view the argument as a piece of logic, following the deductive moves but not being touched religiously? I think so. But even at this level the argument may not be without religious value, for it may help to remove some philosophical scruples that stand in the way of faith. At a deeper level, I suspect that the argument can be thoroughly understood only by one who has a view of that human "form of life" that gives rise to the idea of an infinitely great being, who views it from the *inside* not just from the outside and who has, therefore, at least some inclination to *partake* in that religious form of life. This inclination, in Kierkegaard's words, is "from the emotions." This inclination can hardly be an *effect* of Anselm's argument, but is rather presupposed in the fullest understanding of it. It would be unreasonable to require that the recognition of Anselm's demonstration as valid must produce a conversion.

ALVIN PLANTINGA

The Argument Restated and Vindicated

Given these ideas, we can restate the present version of the argument in the following more explicit way.

(25) It is possible that there be a being that has maximal greatness.

(26) So there is a possible being that in some world W has maximal greatness.

(27) A Being has maximal greatness in a given world only if it has maximal excellence in every world.

(28) A being has maximal excellence in a given world only if it has omniscience, omnipotence, and moral perfection in that world.

And now we no longer need the supposition that necessary existence is a perfection; for obviously a being can't be omnipotent (or for that matter omniscient or morally perfect) in a given world unless it *exists* in that world. From (25), (27), and (28) it follows that there actually exists a being that is omnipotent, omniscient, and morally perfect; this being, furthermore, exists and has these qualities in every other world as well. For (26), which follows from (25), tells us that there is a possible world W', let's say, in which there exists a being with maximal greatness. That is, had W' been actual, there would have been a being with maximal greatness. But then according to (27) this being has maximal excellence in every world. What this means, according to (28), is that in W' this being has omniscience, omnipotence, and moral perfection *in every world*. That is to say, if W' had been actual, there would have existed a being who was omniscient and omnipotent and morally perfect and who would have had these properties in every possible world. So if W' had been actual, it would have been *impossible* that there be no omnipotent, omniscient, and morally perfect being. But while *contingent* truths vary from world to world, what is logically impossible does not. Therefore, in every possible world W it is impossible that there be no such being; each possible world W is such that if it had been actual, it would have been impossible that there be no such being. And hence it is impossible in the *actual* world (which is one of the possible worlds) that there be no omniscient, omnipotent, and morally

From Alvin Plantinga, "The Argument Restated and Vindicated," in *God, Freedom and Evil* (1974), pp. 108–12. Reprinted with permission of the author.

perfect being. Hence there really does exist a being who is omniscient, omnipotent, and morally perfect and who exists and has these properties in every possible world. Accordingly these premises, (25), (27), and (28), entail that God, so thought of, exists. Indeed, if we regard (27) and (28) as consequences of a *definition*—a definition of maximal greatness—then the only premise of the argument is (25).

But now for a last objection suggested earlier. What about (25)? It says that there is a *possible being* having such and such characteristics. But what *are* possible beings? We know what *actual* beings are—the Taj Mahal, Socrates, you and I, the Grand Teton—these are among the more impressive examples of actually existing beings. But what is a *possible* being? Is there a possible mountain just like Mt. Rainier two miles directly south of the Grand Teton? If so, it is located at the same place as the Middle Teton. Does that matter? Is there another such possible mountain three miles east of the Grand Teton, where Jenny Lake is? Are there possible mountains like this all over the world? Are there also possible oceans at all the places where there are possible mountains? For any place you mention, of course, it is *possible* that there be a mountain there; does it follow that in fact *there is* a possible mountain there?

These are some questions that arise when we ask ourselves whether there are merely possible beings that don't in fact exist. And the version of the ontological argument we've been considering seems to make sense only on the assumption that there are such things. The earlier versions also depended on that assumption; consider for example, this step of the first version we considered:

(18) So there is a possible being x and a world W' such that the greatness of x in W' exceeds the greatness of God in actuality.

This possible being, you recall, was God Himself, supposed not to exist in the actual world. We can make sense of (18), therefore, only if we are prepared to grant that there are possible beings who don't in fact exist. Such beings exist in other worlds, of course; had things been appropriately different, they would have existed. But in fact they don't exist, although nonetheless there *are* such things.

I am inclined to think the supposition that there are such things—things that are possible but don't in fact exist—is either unintelligible or necessarily false. But this doesn't mean that the present version of the ontological argument must be rejected. For we can restate the argument in a way that does not commit us to this questionable idea. Instead of speaking of *possible beings* that do or do not exist in various possible worlds, we may speak of *properties* and the worlds in which they are or are not *instantiated*. Instead of speaking of the possible fat man in the corner, noting that he doesn't exist, we may speak of the property *being a fat man in the corner*, noting that it isn't instantiated (although it could have been). Of course, the *property* in question, like the property *being a unicorn*, exists. It is a perfectly good property which exists with as much equanimity as the property of equanimity, the property of being a horse. But it doesn't happen to apply to anything. That is, in *this* world it doesn't apply to anything; in other possible worlds it does.

10. THE ARGUMENT TRIUMPHANT

Using this idea we can restate this last version of the ontological argument in such a way that it no longer matters whether there are any merely possible beings that do not exist. Instead of speaking of the possible being that has, in some world or other, a maximal degree of greatness, we may speak of *the property of being maximally great* or *maximal greatness*. The premise corresponding to (25) then says simply that maximal greatness is possibly instantiated, i.e., that

(29) There is a possible world in which maximal greatness is instantiated.

And the analogues of (27) and (28) spell out what is involved in maximal greatness:

(30) Necessarily, a being is maximally great only if it has maximal excellence in every world

and

(31) Necessarily, a being has maximal excellence in every world only if it has omniscience, omnipotence, and moral perfection in every world.

Notice that (30) and (31) do not imply that there are possible but nonexistent beings—any more than does, for example,

(32) Necessarily, a thing is a unicorn only if it has one horn.

But if (29) is true, then there is a possible world W such that if it had been actual, then there would have existed a being that was omnipotent, omniscient, and morally perfect; this being, furthermore, would have had these qualities in every possible world. So it follows that if W had been actual, it would have been *impossible* that there be no such being. That is, if W had been actual,

(33) There is no omnipotent, omniscient, and morally perfect being

would have been an impossible proposition. But if a proposition is impossible in at least one possible world, then it is impossible in every possible world;

what is impossible does not vary from world to world. Accordingly (33) is impossible in the *actual* world, i.e., impossible *simpliciter*. But if it is impossible that there be no such being, then there actually exists a being that is omnipotent, omniscient, and morally perfect; this being, furthermore, has these qualities essentially and exists in every possible world.

What shall we say of this argument? It is certainly valid; given its premise, the conclusion follows. The only question of interest, it seems to me, is whether its main premise—that maximal greatness *is* possibly instantiated—is *true*. I think it *is* true; hence I think this version of the ontological argument is sound.

But here we must be careful; we must ask whether this argument is a successful piece of natural theology, whether it *proves* the existence of God. And the answer must be, I think, that it does not. An argument for God's existence may be *sound*, after all, without in any useful sense proving God's existence.[1] Since I believe in God, I think the following argument is sound:

Either God exists or $7 + 5 = 14$
It is false that $7 + 5 = 14$
Therefore God exists.

But obviously this isn't a *proof*; no one who didn't already accept the conclusion, would accept the first premise. The ontological argument we've been examining isn't just like this one, of course, but it must be conceded that not everyone who understands and reflects on its central premise—that the existence of a maximally great being is *possible*—will accept it. Still, it is evident, I think, that there is nothing *contrary to reason* or *irrational* in accepting this premise.[2] What I claim for this argument, therefore, is that it establishes, not the *truth* of theism, but its rational acceptability. And hence it accomplishes at least one of the aims of the tradition of natural theology.

---

[1] See George Mavrodes, *Belief in God* (New York: Macmillan Co., 1970), pp. 22ff.

[2] For more on this see Plantinga, *The Nature of Necessity*, chap. 10, sec. 8.

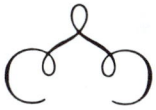

THE COSMOLOGICAL ARGUMENT

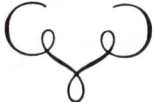

ST. THOMAS AQUINAS

The Five Ways

We proceed thus to the Third Article:—

Objection 1. It seems that God does not exist; because if one of two contraries be infinite, the other would be altogether destroyed. But the name *God* means that He is infinite goodness. If, therefore, God existed, there would be no evil discoverable; but there is evil in the world. Therefore God does not exist.

Obj. 2. Further, it is superfluous to suppose that what can be accounted for by a few principles has been produced by many. But it seems that everything we see in the world can be accounted for by other principles, supposing God did not exist. For all natural things can be reduced to one principle, which is nature; and all voluntary things can be reduced to one principle, which is human reason, or will. Therefore there is no need to suppose God's existence.

On the contrary, It is said in the person of God: *I am Who am* (*Exod.* iii. 14).

I answer that, The existence of God can be proved in five ways.

The first and more manifest way is the argument from motion. It is certain, and evident to our senses, that in the world some things are in motion. Now whatever is moved is moved by another, for nothing can be moved except it is in potentiality to that towards which it is moved; whereas a thing moves inasmuch as it is in act. For motion is nothing else than the reduction of something from potentiality to actuality. But nothing can be reduced from potentiality to actuality, except by something in a state of actuality. Thus that which is actually hot, as fire, makes wood, which is potentially hot, to be actually hot, and thereby moves and changes it. Now it is not possible that the same thing should be at once in actuality and potentiality in the same respect, but only in different respects. For what is actually hot cannot simultaneously be potentially

From *Summa Theologica*, Part I, trans. Dominican Fathers of English Province (New York: Benzinger Bros., Inc., 1947). Reprinted by permission of the publisher.

hot; but it is simultaneously potentially cold. It is therefore impossible that in the same respect and in the same way a thing should be both mover and moved, *i.e.*, that it should move itself. Therefore, whatever is moved must be moved by another. If that by which it is moved be itself moved, then this also must needs be moved by another, and that by another again. But this cannot go on to infinity, because then there would be no first mover, and, consequently, no other mover, seeing that subsequent movers move only inasmuch as they are moved by the first mover; as the staff moves only because it is moved by the hand. Therefore it is necessary to arrive at a first mover, moved by no other; and this everyone understands to be God.

The second way is from the nature of efficient cause. In the world of sensible things we find there is an order of efficient causes. There is no case known (neither is it, indeed, possible) in which a thing is found to be the efficient cause of itself; for so it would be prior to itself, which is impossible. Now in efficient causes it is not possible to go on to infinity, because in all efficient causes following in order, the first is the cause of the intermediate cause, and the intermediate is the cause of the ultimate cause, whether the intermediate cause be several, or one only. Now to take away the cause is to take away the effect. Therefore, if there be no first cause among efficient causes, there will be no ultimate, nor any intermediate, cause. But if in efficient causes it is possible to go on to infinity, there will be no first efficient cause, neither will there be an ultimate effect, nor any intermediate efficient causes; all of which is plainly false. Therefore it is necessary to admit a first efficient cause, to which everyone gives the name of God.

The third way is taken from possibility and necessity, and runs thus. We find in nature things that are possible to be and not to be, since they are found to be generated, and to be corrupted, and consequently, it is possible for them to be and not to be. But it is impossible for these always to exist, for that which can not-be at some time is not. Therefore, if everything can not-be, then at one time there was nothing in existence. Now if this were true, even now there would be nothing in existence, because that which does not exist begins to exist only through something already existing. Therefore, if at one time nothing was in existence, it would have been impossible for anything to have begun to exist; and thus even now nothing would be in existence—which is absurd. Therefore, not all beings are merely possible, but there must exist something the existence of which is necessary. But every necessary thing either has its necessity caused by another, or not. Now it is impossible to go on to infinity in necessary things which have their necessity caused by another, as has been already proved in regard to efficient causes. Therefore we cannot but admit the existence of some being having of itself its own necessity, and not receiving it from another, but rather causing in others their necessity. This all men speak of as God.

The fourth way is taken from the gradation to be found in things. Among beings there are some more and some less good, true, noble, and the like. But *more* and *less* are predicated of different things according as they resemble in their different ways something which is the maximum, as a thing is said to be hotter according as it more nearly resembles that which is hottest; so that there is something which is truest, something best, something noblest, and, consequently, something which is most being, for those things that are greatest in truth are greatest in being, as it is written in *Metaph. ii.* Now the maximum in any genus is the cause of all in that genus, as fire, which is the maximum of heat, is the cause of all hot things, as is said in the same book. Therefore there must also be something which is to all beings the cause of their being, goodness, and every other perfection; and this we call God.

The fifth way is taken from the governance of the world. We see that things which lack knowledge, such as natural bodies, act for an end, and this is evident from their acting always, or nearly always, in the same way, so as to obtain the best result. Hence it is plain that they achieve their end, not fortuitously, but designedly. Now whatever lacks knowledge cannot move towards an end, unless it be directed by some being endowed with knowledge and intelligence; as the arrow is directed by the archer. Therefore some intelligent being exists by whom all natural things are directed to their end; and this being we call God.

Reply Obj. 1. As Augustine says: *Since God is the highest good, He would not allow any evil to exist in His works, unless His omnipotence and goodness were such as to bring good even out of evil.* This is part of the infinite goodness of God, that He should allow evil to exist, and out of it produce good.

Reply Obj. 2. Since nature works for a determinate end under the direction of a higher agent, whatever is done by nature must be traced back to God as to its first cause. So likewise whatever is done voluntarily must be traced back to some higher cause other than human reason and will, since these can change and fail; for all things that are changeable and capable of defect must be traced back to an immovable and self-necessary first principle, as has been shown.

PATTERSON BROWN

Infinite Causal Regression

> The whole modern conception of the world is founded on the illusion that the so-called laws of nature are the explanations of natural phenomena. Thus people today stop at the laws of nature, treating them as something inviolable, just as God and Fate were treated in past ages. And in fact both are right and both wrong: though the view of the ancients is clearer in so far as they have a clear and acknowledged terminus, while the modern system tries to make it look as if *everything* were explained.
>
> WITTGENSTEIN, *Tractatus*, 6.371–6.372

From *The Philosophical Review* 75 (1966): 510–25. Reprinted by permission of *The Philosophical Review.*

Arguments concerning the possibility of an infinite regress of causes have always played a crucial role in metaphysics and in natural theology. And of course this issue was once important in the sciences as well, namely in Aristotelianism. Indeed, the most influential reasons which have been adduced by philosophers and theologians against infinite causal regressions—as, for example, St. Thomas' well-known Five Ways—arose directly and explicitly out of Aristotelian scientific considerations; they are meta-physical proofs, that is, proofs which are supposed to follow on theorizations in physical science. The gist of them is that, if there were an infinite regress of causes, then no adequate scientific explanation would be possible, and observed phenomena would thus be unintelligible—which consequence is absurd. In this paper I shall attempt to delineate the medieval elaboration of this argument, as given by such men as Avicenna, Averroes, Maimonides, Aquinas, and Duns Scotus.

I.

The *locus classicus* of the scholastic discussion was the following passage from Aristotle's *Metaphysics*, wherein he claims that a so-called ascending series of any of his four types of cause must have a first member:

> One thing [cannot] proceed from another, as from matter, *ad infinitum*,...nor can the sources of movement form an endless series.... Similarly the final causes cannot go on *ad infinitum*.... And the case of the essence [that is, of formal causes] is similar. For in the case of intermediates, which have a last term and a term prior to them, the prior must be the cause of the later terms. For if we had to say which of the three is the cause, we should say the first; surely not the last, for the final term is the cause of none; nor even the intermediate, for it is the cause only of one. (It makes no difference whether there is one intermediate or more, nor whether they are finite or infinite in number.) But of series which are infinite in this way,...all the parts down to that now present are alike intermediates; so that if there is no first there is no cause at all.[1]

Early in the eleventh century, Avicenna drew a distinction, as Aristotle had not, between the causality of a *mover* and that of a *maker*.[2] The latter was then called an "efficient" or "agent" cause, and Aristotle's same line of reasoning was directed against there being an infinite regress of such causes of being (see, for example, Aquinas' Second Way). There was, then, one basic argument which the medieval Aristotelians held to demonstrate that neither efficient, moving, formal, final, nor material causal series can regress infinitely.

---

[1] 994a2–19. All quotations from Aristotle will be from R. McKeon (ed.), *The Basic Works of Aristotle* (New York, 1941). "Ascent" in a causal series was defined as proceeding from effect to cause, while "descent" meant proceeding from cause to effect.

[2] Cf. E. Gilson, *History of Christian Philosophy in the Middle Ages* (New York, 1955), pp. 210–12.

It is perhaps commonplace nowadays to assume that the Aristotelian schoolmen were unconditionally opposed to beginningless series, or at least to beginningless causal series. Thus we find W. I. Matson laconically stating that the "contention is defensible only if it is logically impossible for a series to have no first member,...such as the series of all negative integers."[3] This criticism is clearly ineffectual against the Aristotelians, none of whom wished to deny that some series—for example, mathematical ones—may have no termini. After all, consider Aristotle's own definition of an infinite quantity: "A quantity is infinite if it is such that we can always take a part outside what has already been taken."[4] The application of this to the series of negative integers is self-evident. As John Hick has realized, however, the claim was in fact limited to causal series: "Aquinas excludes the possibility of an infinite regress of causes, and so concludes that there must be a first cause, which we call God."[5] Even Hick's remark, however, must be considerably qualified if we are to reach any understanding of the argument, for it was only some among causal series which were held to require a first member. In the course of proving that the world might in principle be everlasting, St. Thomas wrote:

> In efficient causes it is impossible to proceed to infinity *per se*. Thus, there cannot be an infinite number of causes that are *per se* required for a certain effect; for instance, that a stone be moved by a stick, the stick by the hand, and so on to infinity. But it is not impossible to proceed to infinity *accidentally* as regards efficient causes.... [It is, for example,] accidental to this particular man as generator to be generated by another man; for he generates as a man, and not as the son of another man. For all men generating hold one grade in the order of efficient causes—viz., the grade of a particular generator. Hence it is not impossible for a man to be generated by man to infinity.[6]

The claim is, then that causal regresses like a's being begotten by b, b's being begotten by c, and so forth, can go on to infinity, whereas causal regresses like z's being moved by y, y's being moved by x, and so forth, cannot. So not only did the Aristotelians admit the possibility of infinite regresses in general (like—1,—2,—3, and so forth, and even—as we shall see—today, yesterday, day before yesterday, and so forth), but they also admitted the possibility of certain infinite *causal* regresses.

It is important to note that it is the composite causal series, and not the individual constituent causes, which Aquinas is contrasting as either *per se* or *per accidens* in the above quotation. Aristotle had of course differentiated between essential and accidental causes, meaning by the latter an accidental

---

[3]*The Existence of God* (Ithaca, N.Y., 1965), p. 59.

[4]*Physics*, 207a8. See also Aquinas, *Summa Theologica*, ed. by A. C. Pegis (New York, 1945), I, Q. 7, Art. 4, Obj. 1 and Reply (hereafter referred to as ST).

[5]*Philosophy of Religion* (Englewood Cliffs, N.J., 1963), p. 20.

[6]*ST*, I, Q. 46, Art. 2, Reply Obj. 7.

attribute of an essential cause,[7] but that is not the distinction to which St. Thomas is here alluding. This is confirmed by Duns Scotus' comment in his presentation of the argument:

> It is one thing to speak of incidental causes (*causae per accidens*) as contrasted with those which are intended by their nature to produce a certain effect (*causae per se*). It is quite another to speak of causes which are ordered to one another essentially or of themselves (*per se*) and those which are ordered only accidentally (*per accidens*).[8]

There is, then, a difference between essential and accidental *causes* on the one hand, and essential and accidental *ordering* of causes on the other. Moreover, it is the latter distinction which is supposed to be germane to the impossibility of certain infinite causal regressions; infinite causal regression *per accidens* is said to be possible, while infinite causal regression *per se* is said to be impossible. Scotus fortunately tells us in some detail what was understood by the crucial contrast:

> *Per se* or essentially ordered causes differ from accidentally ordered causes.... In essentially ordered causes, the second depends upon the first precisely in its act of causation. In accidentally ordered causes this is not the case, although the second may depend upon the first for its existence, or in some other way. Thus a son depends upon his father for existence but is not dependent upon him in exercising his own causality [that is, in himself begetting a son], since he can act just as well whether his father be living or dead.[9]

I shall now quote what is perhaps the best scholastic statement of the Aristotelian argument against an infinite regress of essentially ordered causes, as found in Aquinas' *Summa contra Gentiles:*

> In an ordered series of movers and things moved (this is a series in which one is moved by another according to an order), it is necessarily the fact that, when the first mover is removed or ceases to move, no other mover will move [another] or be [itself] moved. For the first mover is the cause of motion for all the others. But, if there are movers and things moved following an order to

---

[7]Cf. *Physics*, 195a27 ff., 196b24–29, and 224a21–36, as well as *Metaphysics*, 1013b29. In St. Thomas' words, "If A is the cause of B *per se*, whatever is accidental to A is the accidental cause of B"—*Summa contra Gentiles* (Garden City, N.Y., 1955), III, ch. 14 (hereafter referred to as SCG).

[8]*Opus Oxoniense*, I, Dist. II, Q. 1, as found in A. Wolter (ed.), *Duns Scotus: Philosophical Writings* (Edinburgh, 1962), p. 40.

[9]*Ibid.*, pp. 40–41. From this fundamental criterion Scotus then claims to derive two more: that in essentially ordered causes each step must be to a new order of cause, and that a series of *per se* ordered causes must be instantaneous. See also the selection from Scotus' *Tractatus De Primo Principio*, ch. iii, included in A. Freemantle, *The Age of Belief* (New York, 1955), pp. 189 ff. I gather that this analysis of variously ordered series originated with Avicenna, in Bk. VI of his *Metaphysics*, but no copy of that important work has been available to me.

infinity, there will be no first mover, but all would be as intermediate movers.... [Now] that which moves [another] as an instrumental cause cannot [so] move unless there be a principal moving cause. But, if we proceed to infinity among movers and things moved, all movers will be as instrumental causes, because they will be moved movers and there will be nothing as a principal mover. Therefore, nothing will be moved [which consequence is patently false.][10]

II.

Before going on to consider this argument in any detail, let us first repudiate perhaps the three most common criticisms of it. The first of these[11] takes off from statements like the following, found in St. Thomas' Second Way: "To take away the cause is to take away the effect. Therefore, if there be no first cause among efficient causes, there will be no ultimate, nor any intermediate, cause."[12] This passage may seem to contain an equivocation on "taking away the first cause." It is certainly true that, in any causal sequence, to take away any of the earlier causes—in the sense of removing it from the chain altogether—would break the progression; and this would then preclude any of the subsequent members of the series from coming about at all. But if, with regard to any such catena, we take away any first cause—in the sense of denying that any member is first, that is, uncaused—we do not thereby remove any of the links from the causal chain; the progression is not broken, and so the later members are not precluded. In the hand-stick-stone case, for example, we must differentiate between taking away the stick, and denying that the stick is an uncaused cause of the stone's motion. We might thus think that the Aristotelian rejection of an infinite regress of causes rests on an equivocation between "taking away any first cause" (that is, denying that any cause is first) and "taking away one of the causes" (that is, removing one of the members from the causal series).

Even if we could believe that this glaring fallacy could have gone undetected for two millennia, however, it will hardly do as an objection to the argument. For the above-mentioned polemic cannot account for the distinction between essentially and accidentally ordered causal regresses. If Jacob or Isaac or Abraham *vel cetera* had not copulated, this would in fact have precluded Joseph's existence—just as taking away the motion of the stick or the hand would in fact have resulted in the stone's not moving. In both cases a statement of the effect materially implies a statement of all the string of

---

[10]I, ch. xiii; cf. *ST*, I, Q. 2, Art. 3, First Way. See also Averroes' version in his *Tahafut Al-Tahafut* (London, 1954), I, the Fourth Discussion.

[11]It may be found, e.g., in Paul Edwards' introduction to the section entitled "The Existence of God," in P. Edwards & A. Pap (eds.), *A Modern Introduction to Philosophy* (Glencoe, Ill., 1957), pp. 450–51.

[12]*ST*, I, Q. 2, Art. 3, Second Way.

causes (although in neither instance is there a strict implication; the stone could equally well be caused to move by a hand or a foot, just as Joseph could equally well be descended from Adam or a baboon). It seems highly unlikely that Aristotle and the others would have equivocated in contending that there must be a first mover, and yet have avoided exactly the same type of fallacy in admitting that there need not be a first ancestor.

The second standard criticism of the argument is voiced, for example, by Hick, in his retort that time may never have begun. "The weakness of the argument as Aquinas states it," he writes, "lies in the difficulty (which he himself elsewhere acknowledges) of excluding as impossible an endless regress of events requiring no beginning."[13] A similar point is made by W. T. Blackstone, who objects that "it is perfectly conceivable that time has no beginning, and that every event was preceded by an earlier event."[14] Such comments simply cannot be reconciled with the texts. For of course the Aristotelians notoriously held that causal efficacy must be instantaneous rather than chronological. Aristotle says that "the motion of the moved and the motion of the movent must proceed simultaneously (for the movent is causing motion and the moved is being moved simultaneously)."[15] St. Thomas concurs: "It is clear that when a thing moves because it is moved, the mover and the mobile object are moved simultaneously. For example, if the hand by its own motion moves a staff, the hand and the staff are moved simultaneously."[16] After all, it was only on these grounds that Aristotle could argue both for a First Cause and for the perpetuity of the world.[17] This also explains why Aquinas held it to be of no theological concern that we cannot demonstrate whether or not the world had a beginning in time (leaving it a matter to be settled by revelation alone).[18] The requirement for a Prime Cause is, he thought, the same in either case, since causal chains are necessarily confined to one instant. This same doctrine was later defended by Descartes when he wrote that "all the moments of [the world's] duration are [causally] independent the one from the other";[19] for, he held, "any motion involves a kind of circulation of matter all moving simultaneously."[20]

---

[13]*Op. cit.*, p. 21; the clause in parentheses is footnoted by Hick: *ST*, I, Q. 46, Art. 2, and *SCG*, II, ch. xxxviii.

[14]*The Problem of Religious Knowledge* (Englewood Cliffs, N.J., 1963), p. 164.

[15]*Physics*, 242a23–26.

[16]*Commentary on Aristotle's "Physics"* (New Haven, 1963), Bk. VIII, lec. 2, #892 (hereafter referred to as *On Physics*). Cf. n. 9, *supra*, for Scotus' parallel claim.

[17]Cf. *Physics*, 250b11 ff. and 256a4 ff. Some critics have gone so far as explicitly to claim that Aristotle contradicted himself here; see, e.g., S. van Den Bergh's introduction to Averroes, *op. cit.*, I, xvi.

[18]*ST*, I, Q. 46, *passim*.

[19]Letter to Chanut, quoted by F. Copleston, *History of Philosophy* (London, 1960), IV, 134.

[20]*Principles of Philosophy*, Pt. T. II, xxxix, as found in G. E. M. Anscombe and P. T. Geach (eds.), *Descartes: Philosophical Writings* (Edinburgh, 1954), p. 217; cf. all of pp. 213–19. For a similar doctrine, cp. Aristotle, *Physics*, 214a25–32, 217a10–19, 242a23, and 267a21–b9.

The third commonplace objection is found, for example, in the following remark by C. J. F. Williams:

> The flaw in this argument is its use of the term *moventia secunda* in an attempt to prove the impossibility of an infinite series of causes. For not until we know that such a series is impossible can we know that all movers are properly described as either "a first mover" or as "second movers." This however, is precisely what the argument assumes.[21]

The gravamen of this criticism is, I gather, that to designate anything as a second (intermediate, instrumental, dependent) mover must involve a *petitio principii*, since "second mover" just means "mover dependent for its efficacy on an unmoved mover." This, however, is simply not what the Aristotelians understood by "second mover"; this phrase meant merely "mover dependent for its efficacy on another," with no question-begging stipulation that this other be itself unmoved. In Aquinas' words, "everything which both moves [another] and is moved [by yet another] has the nature of an instrument."[22] Thus, if the hand pushes a stick, the stick in turn pushes a stone, and the stone in turn pushes a clod, then the stone is called an "intermediate" mover just because it depends on the stick for its efficacy; what makes the stick move, and *a fortiori* whether there is an infinite regress of movers, is entirely irrelevant to the classification of the stone as a second mover. There is therefore no begging of the issue in the very introduction of the phrase "second mover."

III.

It is evident that we cannot hope to understand the argument against infinite causal regresses without first getting straight on the supposedly critical contrast between causal series ordered *per se* and those ordered *per accidens*. So let us examine the previously quoted explanation by Scotus that "in essentially ordered series the second [that is, the posterior] depends upon the first [the prior] precisely in its act of causation." I assume that the entire argument would be laid bare if we fully understood this criterion and its application to the two paradigm cases, propulsion and genealogy.

The criterion delineated by Scotus seems straightforward enough; it is simply that each member of an essential series (except of course the first and last *if* there be such) is causally dependent upon its predecessor for its own causal efficacy regarding its successor. The members are each intermediate (secondary, instrumental, dependent) in the sense discussed above. In an accidental series, however, each member is not dependent

---

[21]*"Hic autem...*(St. Thomas Aquinas)," *Mind*, LXIX (1960), 403.

[22]*On Physics*, Bk. VIII, lec. 9, #1044.

upon its predecessor for its own causal efficacy—though it may be dependent in some other regard. Thus a causal series is *per se* ordered if and only if it is throughout of the form: w's being F causes x to be G, x's being G causes y to be H, y's being H causes z to be I,...(here $F\ell$, $G\ell$, $H\ell$, and $I\ell$ may be identical or differing functions). A causal series is ordered *per accidens*, however, if and only if it is throughout of the form: w's being F causes x to be G, x's being H causes y to be I, y's being J causes z to be K,...(here $G\ell \neq H\ell$ and $I\ell \neq J\ell$, but otherwise $F\ell$, $G\ell$, $H\ell$, $I\ell$, $J\ell$, and $K\ell$ may be identical or differing functions). In other words, the two functions of each individual variable must be identical in the essential case, but must differ in the accidental case.

Consider the paradigm case where one's hand pushes a stick which in turn pushes a stone. This causal series is *per se* because it is the same function of the stick (namely, its locomotion) which both is caused by the movement of the hand and causes the movement of the stone. Again, a series where the fire heats the pot and the pot in turn heats the stew, causing it to boil, is also essentially ordered; for the warmth of the pot is both caused by the warmth of the fire and cause of the warmth of the stew, while the warmth of the stew is both caused by the warmth of the pot and cause of the stew's boiling.

On the other hand, consider the paradigm case of Abraham's begetting Isaac, who in turn begets Jacob. Here the series is accidentally ordered because that function of Isaac (namely, his copulating) which causes Jacob's birth is not caused by Abraham's copulation; the latter results in Isaac's *birth*, whereas it is Isaac's *copulation* which causes Jacob to be born. Genealogical series like the following are thus *per accidens*: Abraham's copulation causes Isaac's birth, Isaac's copulation causes Jacob's birth, Jacob's copulation causes Joseph's birth. Each member has one attribute qua effect (being born) and quite another attribute qua cause (copulating).

Now Aristotle and his followers held as a critically important thesis that the constituent relations in an essentially ordered series are *transitive*. This is, I suggest, the point of Aristotle's statement that "everything that is moved is moved by the movent that is further back in the series as well as by that which immediately moves it."[23] If, to use the standard example, the hand propels the stick and the stick in turn propels the stone, then the hand propels the stone by means of the stick. Again, if the fire heats the pot, which heats the stew, which causes the stew to boil, then the fire causes the stew to boil. St. Thomas makes this point in the following passage:

> If that which was given as moved locally is moved by the nearest mover which is increased, and that again is moved by something which is altered, and that again is moved by something which is moved in place, then that which is moved with respect to place will be moved more by the first thing which is moved with respect to place than by the second thing which is altered or by the third thing which is increased.[24]

[23]*Physics*, 257a10–12.

[24]*On Physics*, Bk. VIII, lec. 9, #1047.

Here we have an undisguised claim that "x moves y" is a transitive causal relation.

The Aristotelians claimed such transitivity not only for "x moves y" (moving causation), but also for "x creates y" (Avicennian efficient causation), "y is made out of x" (material causation), "x is the form of y" (formal causation), and "x is the goal of y" (final causation). Maimonides writes:

> A cause must...be sought for each of the four divisions of causes. When we have found for any existing thing those four causes which are in immediate connexion with it, we find for these again causes, and for these again other causes, and so on until we arrive at the first causes. E.g., a certain production has its *agens*, this *agens* has again its *agens*, and so on and on until at last we arrive at a first *agens*, which is the true *agens* throughout all the intervening links. If the letter *aleph* be moved by *bet*, *bet* by *gimel*, *gimel* by *dalet*, and *dalet* by *hé*—and as the series does not extend to infinity, let us stop at *hé*—there is no doubt that the *hé* moves [each of] the letters *aleph*, *bet*, *gimel*, and *dalet*, and we say correctly that the *aleph* is moved by *hé*. In that sense everything occurring in the universe, although indirectly produced by certain nearer causes, is ascribed to the Creator.... [By parity of reasoning] we arrive at length at that form which is necessary for the existence of all intermediate forms, which are the causes of the present [that is, last] form. That form to which the forms of all existing things are traced is God.... The same argument holds good in reference to all final causes.[25]

So, in an essentially ordered series of any type of cause, each member is supposed to be the cause of all those which follow on it, owing to the transitivity of the relations involved. And then, of course, if there is or must be a first member of such series, the transitivity would make it natural to say that the first member was the ultimate cause of every one of the others.

It might be questioned whether these various causal relations are really always transitive. We may suspect that a careful examination of the ordinary uses of, for example, "x moves y" would show it sometimes to be used transitively and sometimes not. But such a discovery would, I think, be irrelevant to the argument, because Aristotle and the others are employing these causal relation statements in refined ways. It can simply be stipulated that "x moves y" and the others be invariably transitive within the Aristotelian scientific model. Nor would this be to use those expressions in ways greatly different from their employment in ordinary language, for they are commonly—even if perhaps not universally—used transitively.

As a counterpart of the foregoing, the Aristotelians held that the constituent relations in an accidentally ordered causal series are *intransitive*. Thus, regarding the paradigm case of "x begets y," if Abraham begets Isaac, who in turn begets Jacob, then Abraham clearly does not beget Jacob.

---

[25]*The Guide for the Perplexed* (New York, 1956), I, ch. lxix.

IV.

Why was an infinite regress thought to be impossible in essentially ordered series, but not in accidentally ordered ones? It has been widely believed that it was the purported simultaneity in the former case which was held to be decisive.[26] Some of Aquinas' statements in particular might seem to support this interpretation; at one place, for instance, he says:

> It is impossible to proceed to infinity in the order of efficient causes which act together at the same time, because in that case the effect would have to depend on an infinite number of actions simultaneously existing. And such cases are essentially infinite, because their infinity is required for the effect caused by them. On the other hand, in the sphere of non-simultaneously acting causes, it is not...impossible to proceed to infinity. And the infinity here is accidental to the causes; thus it is accidental to Socrates' father that he is another man's son or not. But it is not accidental to the stick, in moving the stone, that it be moved by the hand; for the stick moves [the stone] just so far as it is moved [by the hand].[27]

The gist of this argument would seem to be that an instantaneous causal series would have to be essentially ordered, and furthermore that all *per se* ordered series must have a first member. But this is not at all to claim that essentially ordered series must have a beginning just because they are instantaneous; on the contrary, the contention is that instantaneous series must have a beginning just because they are always *per se* ordered. Whatever it is, therefore, that requires essentially ordered causal series to have a first term, we know that it is not their (purported) simultaneity. For example, the argument was not that an infinite series of essentially ordered causes, being instantaneous, would involve an impossible concurrent infinity, whereas an infinite series of accidentally ordered causes, being chronological, would not involve this absurd consequence. For Aristotle and his disciples explicitly state that the argument for a first cause has nothing to do with whether an infinite number of concurrent intermediate causes is possible. Aristotle writes that "it makes no difference whether there is one intermediate or more, nor whether they are infinite or finite in number."[28] St. Thomas concurs, asserting that it does not "make any difference whether there are a finite or an infinite number of intermediates, because so long as they have the nature of intermediate they cannot be the first cause of motion."[29] Finally, we may record Scotus' claim that, "even if the group of beings caused were infinite, they would still depend on something outside the group."[30] I therefore

---

[26]E.g., by Ockham; see his *Quaestiones in lib. I Physicorum*, Qs. 132–36, included in P. Boehner (ed.), *Ockham: Philosophical Writings* (Edinburgh, 1957), pp. 115–25.

[27]*SCG*, II, ch. xxxviii; see *ST*, I, Q. 7, Arts. 3 & 4.

[28]See n. 1, *supra*.

[29]*Commentary on the Metaphysics of Aristotle* (Chicago, 1961), Bk. II, lec. 3, #303.

[30]Wolter, *op. cit.*, p. 42.

conclude that the argument does not rest on the supposed simultaneity of causal series ordered *per se*. Hence it cannot be simply an application of the well-known Aristotelian doctrine that an actualized infinity is impossible.[31]

An interesting recent proposal by G. E. M. Anscombe and P. T. Geach is that the argument involves a composition or grouping together of the members of the causal chain. Anscombe and Geach suggest the following as a paraphrase of the reasoning involved:

> If *B* is the cause of a process going on in *A*, or of *A*'s coming to be, then it may be that this happens because of a process in *B* that is caused by a further thing *C*; and *C* in turn may act because of a process in *C* caused by *D*; and so on. But now let us lump together the chain of things *B*, *C*, *D*,..., and call it *X*. We may predicate of each one of the causes *B*, *C*, *D*,..., *and also* of *X* as a whole, that it causes a process in *A* (or the coming-to-be of *A*) in virtue of being *itself* in process of change. But what is it that maintains this process of change in *X*? Something that cannot itself be in process of change: for if it were, it would just be one of the things in process of change that causes the process in *A* (or the coming-to-be of *A*).[32]

Our first reaction to this presentation of the proof might be to object that it commits the fallacy of composition, in that an inference is made from a common property of the parts *B, C, D*,...to *X*'s having that same attribute. It was this maneuver which Hume had in mind when he wrote: "But the whole [chain of causes and effects], you say, wants a cause. I answer that the uniting of these parts into a whole...is performed merely by an arbitrary act of the mind, and has no influence on the nature of things."[33] Ockham had raised a similar objection: "I reply that the whole multitude of both essentially and accidentally ordered causes is caused, but not by some one thing which is part of this multitude, or which is outside this multitude, but one part is caused by one thing which is part of this multitude, and another by another thing, and so on *ad infinitum*."[34]

It is not at all certain, however, that the Ockhamist-Humean criticism is effective. For although inferences of the form "All the parts of *X* have the property *P*, so therefore *X* has the property *P*" are not formally valid, yet many are valid in virtue of the meanings of the arguments substituted for "*X*" and "*P*."[35] This is the case with, for example, "All the bricks in that wall are red, and so the wall itself is red," and similarly with "Every part of the United States is in the Northern Hemisphere, so therefore the whole U.S. is in the

---

[31]See *Physics*, Bk. III, chs. iv–viii.

[32]*Three Philosophers* (Oxford, 1961), pp. 113–14.

[33]*Dialogues Concerning Natural Religion* (New York, 1948), Pt. IX.

[34]Boehner, *op. cit.*, p. 124.

[35]I am indebted to Geach for bringing this point to my attention. For recent discussion, see W. L. Rowe, "The Fallacy of Composition," *Mind*, LXXI (1962), 87; Y. Bar-Hillel, "More on the Fallacy of Composition," *Mind*, LXXIII (1964), 125; and R. Cole, "A Note on Informal Fallacies," *Mind*, LXXIV (1965), 432.

Northern Hemisphere." On the other hand, many such inferences are quite invalid—as, for example, "Every brick in that wall weighs one pound, and so the entire wall weighs one pound," and "Every part of the U.S. is either east or west of the Mississippi, so therefore the whole U.S. is either east or west of the Mississippi." Thus if the Aristotelian argument really is based on an inference of composition, it cannot be rejected out of hand; each such proof must be considered on its own merits.

It seems to me, however, that Anscombe and Geach have introduced a superfluous issue in making the argument appear to rest primarily on an inference of composition. The *working* parts of their version of the proof are merely the following: the whole world, or at least some substantial part of it, X, is "itself in process of change. But what is it that maintains this process of change in X? Something that cannot itself be in process of change." The grouping together of B, C, D,...to form X is in fact a cog having no important connection with the clockworks; it is merely used to prove the truism that the whole X is undergoing change. Now a mainspring composition argument would be: each part B, C, D,...of X is moved by another, so therefore X itself is moved by another. But neither Aristotle nor his medieval disciples nor Anscombe and Geach even suggest such an inference. The only grouping together employed by the latter pair is the trivial: B, C, D,...are each changing, and so X is changing. This is a sound composition inference, but hardly succeeds in demonstrating the existence of an unchanging cause of X's changing.

V.

I want now to suggest a reading of the argument against infinite causal regresses on the basis of our earlier understanding of the contrast between *per se* and *per accidens* ordering of causal series. I think that the substance of the proof was as follows, again using moving causation as our paradigmatic example. Parallel arguments could obviously be constructed regarding Aristotle's other types of cause, and also regarding Avicennian efficient causes.

The Aristotelian scientific model stipulates that all motions are to be given causal explanations, and that such explanations are to be of the form "x moves y." (Compare the analogous Newtonian stipulation that all accelerations are to be explained in terms of equations of the form "$F = ma$.") Suppose then that we observe something, a, to be moving, and we wish to explain this phenomenon by means of the Aristotelian physics. The explanation must be of the form "x moves a." Suppose further that a is moved by b, b is in turn moved by c, c in turn by d, and so on indefinitely. The issue is whether this series can continue *ad infinitum*. We now ask, what moves a? Well, it has already been stated that b moves a; so it may be suggested that "b moves a" is the desired explanation of a's motion, the desired value of "x moves *a*." But this would be an inadequate account of the matter. For *b* is itself being moved by *c*, which—owing to the transitivity of "*x* moves *y*"—thus yields the implication that *a* is moved by *c*, with *b* serving merely as an instrument or intermediate. But in turn *d* moves *c*; and so *d* moves *a*. But *e* moves *d*; therefore *e* moves *a*. And so on indefinitely. Now, so long as this series continues, we have not found the real mover of *a*; that is to say, we have not found the *explaining* value of the function "*x* moves *a*." The regress is thus a vicious one, in that the required explanation of *a*'s motion is deferred so long as the series continues. With regard to any *x* which moves *a*, if there is a *y* such that *y* moves *x*, then we must infer that *y* moves *a*. And if for any *x* such that *x* moves *a* there were a *y* such that *y* moved *x* (and therefore moved *a* as well), then no explanation of *a*'s motion would be possible with the Aristotelian model. There would of course be any number of *true* statements of the form "*x* moves *a*"—namely, "*b* moves *a*," "*c* moves *a*," "*d* moves *a*," and so forth. But none of these is to count as the Aristotelian *explanation* of *a*'s motion. Nor, it must be noted, is any such explanation given merely by asserting that there is an infinite regress of movers of *a*. "An infinite regress of movers move *a*" is not a possible value of the function "*x* moves *a*," for the variable in the latter ranges over individuals, not classes (and *a fortiori* not over series, finite or infinite). An uncaused motion, however, is no motion at all; in other words, an inexplicable motion would be an unintelligible motion. There must be, therefore, an unmoved mover of *a*.

The foregoing case is to be contrasted with giving an explanation of, for example, Jacob's birth. Such an account is to be of the form "*x* begat Jacob." The complete and unique explanation of that form is that Isaac begat Jacob. We do not get a new value for the function on the grounds that Abraham in turn begat Isaac, since this does not imply that Abraham begat Jacob; on the contrary, it implies that he did not do so. So a full explanation of Jacob's birth can be given regardless of whether his family tree extends back to infinity. An explanation of Isaac's copulation is still required, of course; but that will center on his actions with Rebecca, rather than on his having been sired by Abraham. (The Aristotelians would contend that Isaac's copulation, being a locomotion, must be the termination of an essentially ordered *moving* series. This means that there indeed is a *per se* series which terminates in Jacob's birth, but it does not ascend through Isaac, Abraham, Terah, and so on; rather, it goes back through Isaac's copulation and thence instantaneously back through a series of contiguous movers reaching up to the celestial spheres. Aquinas writes that "whatever generates here below, moves to the production of the species as the instrument of a heavenly body. Thus the Philosopher says that 'man and the sun generate man.' "[36] God is then in turn causally

---

[36] *ST*, I, Q. 115, Art. 3, Reply Obj. 2; the quotation from Aristotle is from *Physics*, 194b13. See also *ST*, I, Q. 118, Art. 1, Reply Obj. 3, where Aquinas asserts that the act of begetting is "concurrent with the power of a heavenly body."

responsible for the locomotion of the heavenly spheres—though not of course by himself changing.[37] In this way each man is supposed to be efficiently caused by God via an essentially ordered series of movers, regardless of whether he has an infinite regress of ancestors in an accidentally ordered genealogy series.)

VI.

What are we to say of the foregoing argument, once so widely accepted? I want to suggest that its salient feature (aside of course, from the transitivity of the relevant causal relations) is the quasi-*legalistic* connotation of "cause" which is employed. It is precisely the sense of a cause as *responsible* for its effect—as against its being merely a concomitant of its effect—which entails that *b*'s being moved by *c* renders the *true* statement "*b* moves *a*" unacceptable as the Aristotelian explanation of *a*'s motion. As it were, the *responsibility* for *a*'s motion is passed on back to *c*, and then on back to *d*, and so on back through the transitive series. Hence Aristotle's assertion: "It is clear that everything that is moved is moved by the movent that is further back in the series as well as by that which immediately moves it; in fact *the earlier movent is that which more strictly moves it*."[38] This seems to be a way of saying that an unmoved mover has some sort of causal *responsibility* in a way that a moved mover has not.

Consider the following case. Mr. Alpha is in his automobile, stopped at an intersection. Immediately behind him sits Mr. Beta in his own car. Behind Mr. Beta is Mr. Gamma, behind whom is Mr. Delta, and so on indefinitely. Suddenly Alpha's car is rammed from the rear, damaging his bumper. So Alpha, desiring to recover the expense of repairing his automobile, accuses Beta of having caused the accident, and brings suit against him. Beta, however, successfully defends himself in court on the grounds that he had himself been rammed into Alpha by Gamma. So Alpha now sues Gamma. But the latter, it turns out, had in turn been rammed by Delta. So Alpha takes legal action against Delta. And so on indefinitely. Now, if this series of rammings extended *ad infinitum*, there would be no one whom Alpha could successfully sue as having caused the dent in his bumper; there would, in short, have been *no* cause for the accident at all. But if there were no cause, no mover, then there would be no effect, no

---

[37] Aristotle held that God is merely the final cause of the celestial rotations; cf. *Metaphysics*, 1072a19 ff. The medievals tended to abuse Avicenna's distinction (n. 2, *supra*) by saying that God is somehow the efficient cause of that locomotion, though perhaps with the intelligences (angels) as intermediates; see E. Gilson, *The Elements of Christian Philosophy* (New York, 1963), pp. 71–74.

[38] *Physics*, 257a10–13; my italics. See also n. 24, *supra*. The etymology of "αἰτί-α" supports my thesis, I think.

moved, either—which is patently false, since Alpha's bumper *is* dented and his car *was* moved. Therefore there cannot be a regress to infinity of ramming automobiles, but rather someone was the first cause of the whole series of accidents; someone can properly be said to have moved Beta into Alpha, Gamma into Beta, Delta into Gamma, and so on. Therefore there is someone from whom Mr. Alpha can collect his expenses.

In this rather queer argument the legalistic sense of "cause" is manifest; the cause of the damage to Alpha's car will lie wherever legal responsibility lies, in this sense of "cause." It seems to me to be an allied (though not identical) notion of causation which is being employed in the Aristotelian argument against infinite regresses in all *per se* ordered causal series.

If my interpretation of the argument is correct, there arise two questions regarding its soundness: (1) whether it is *proper* in scientific explanation to employ a sense of "cause" as being responsible for its effect, or whether only concomitances may be mentioned; and even if the former be proper, (2) whether there could be any *a priori* guarantee that there will always be a *successful* employment of that sense of causation regarding observed phenomena. But answering these questions would obviously require giving a full analysis of the notions of causation and of explanation in natural science—a task far beyond the scope of this paper. I close the present discussion with the following remarks made in another context by J. L. Austin:

> My general opinion about this doctrine is that it is a typically *scholastic* view, attributable, first, to an obsession with a few particular words, the uses of which are over-simplified, not really understood or carefully studied or correctly described; and second, to an obsession with a few (and nearly always the same) half-studied "facts." (I say "scholastic," but I might just as well have said "philosophical"; over-simplification, schematization, and constant obsessive repetition of the same small range of jejune "examples" are...far too common to be dismissed as an occasional weakness of philosophers.)[39]

---

[39]*Sense and Sensibilia* (Oxford, 1962), p. 3. See also the comment in Wittgenstein's *Philosophical Investigations* (Oxford, 1963), #593: "A main cause of philosophical disease—a one-sided diet: one nourishes one's thinking with only one kind of example." One wonders whether the lines of attack mentioned in my last paragraph could be forestalled by elaborating on the next-to-last paragraph of section III above—that is, by means of recently familiar talk about stipulations, conventions, theoretical entities, and the like. So, e.g.: is the Aristotelian God perhaps a theoretical entity in a way not unlike a Newtonian force? Cf. the succinct discussion of "The Nature of Scientific Theory, Illustrated by the Case of Mechanics" in M. Black, *A Companion to Wittgenstein's* Tractatus (Ithaca, 1964), ch. 1xxxi.

SAMUEL CLARKE

An Improved Version of the Argument

There has existed from eternity some one unchangeable and independent being. For since something must needs have been from eternity; as hath been already proved, and is granted on all hands; either there has always existed one unchangeable and *independent* Being, from which all other beings that are or ever were in the universe, have received their original; or else there has been an infinite succession of changeable and *dependent* beings, produced one from another in an endless progression, without any original cause at all: which latter supposition is so very absurd, that tho' all atheism must in its account of most things (as shall be shown hereafter) terminate in it, yet I think very few atheists ever were so weak as openly and directly to defend it. For it is plainly impossible and contradictory to itself. I shall not argue against it from the supposed impossibility of infinite succession, *barely and absolutely considered in itself;* for a reason which shall be mentioned hereafter: but, if we consider such an infinite progression, as *one* entire endless *series* of *dependent* beings; 'tis plain this whole *series* of beings can have no cause *from without,* of its existence; because in it are supposed to be included *all things* that are or ever were in the universe: and 'tis plain it can have no reason *within itself,* of its existence; because no one being in this infinite succession is supposed to be self-existent or *necessary* (which is the only ground or reason of existence of any thing, that can be imagined *within the thing itself,* as will presently more fully appear), but every one *dependent* on the foregoing: and where *no part* is necessary, 'tis manifest *the whole* cannot be necessary; absolute necessity of existence, not being an outward, relative, and accidental determination; but an inward and essential property of the nature of the thing which so exists. An infinite succession therefore of merely *dependent* beings, without any original independent cause; is a *series* of beings, that has neither necessity nor cause, nor any reason *at all* of its existence, neither *within itself* nor *from without:* that is, 'tis an express contradiction and impossibility; 'tis a supposing *something* to be *caused,* (because it's granted in every one of its stages of succession, not to be necessary and from itself); and yet that in the whole it is caused *absolutely by nothing:* Which every man knows is a contradiction to be done *in time;* and because duration in this case makes no difference, 'tis equally a contradiction to suppose it done from eternity: And consequently there must *on the contrary,* of necessity have existed from eternity, *some one* immutable and *independent* Being: Which, what it is, remains in the next place to be inquired.

From Samuel Clarke, *A Demonstration of the Being and Attributes of God* (1705), Part II.

DAVID HUME

Criticism of Clarke's Argument

But if so many difficulties attend the argument *a posteriori*, said Demea, had we not better adhere to that simple and sublime argument *a priori* which, by offering to us infallible demonstration, cuts off at once all doubt and difficulty? By this argument, too, we may prove the *infinity* of the Divine attributes, which, I am afraid, can never be ascertained with certainty from any other topic. For how can an effect which either is finite or, for aught we know, may be so—how can such an effect, I say, prove an infinite cause? The unity, too, of the Divine Nature it is very difficult, if not absolutely impossible, to deduce merely from contemplating the works of nature; nor will the uniformity alone of the plan, even were it allowed, give us any assurance of that attribute. Whereas the argument *a priori*...

You seem to reason, Demea, interposed Cleanthes, as if those advantages and conveniences in the abstract argument were full proofs of its solidity. But it is first proper, in my opinion, to determine what argument of this nature you choose to insist on; and we shall afterwards, from itself, better than from its *useful* consequences, endeavor to determine what value we ought to put upon it.

The argument, replied Demea, which I would insist on is the common one. Whatever exists must have a cause or reason of its existence, it being absolutely impossible for anything to produce itself or be the cause of its own existence. In mounting up, therefore, from effects to causes, we must either go on in tracing an infinite succession, without any ultimate cause at all, or must at last have recourse to some ultimate cause that is *necessarily* existent. Now, that the first supposition is absurd may be thus proved. In the infinite chain or succession of causes and effects, each single effect is determined to exist by the power and efficacy of that cause which immediately preceded; but the whole eternal chain or succession, taken together, is not determined or caused by anything; and yet it is evident that it requires a cause or reason, as much as any particular object which begins to exist in time. The question is still reasonable why this particular succession of causes existed from eternity, and not any other succession or no succession at all. If there be no necessarily existent being, any supposition which can be formed is equally possible; nor is there any more absurdity in nothing's having existed from

From David Hume, *Dialogues Concerning Natural Religion* (1779), Part IX.

eternity than there is in that succession of causes which constitutes the universe. What was it, then, which determined something to exist rather than nothing, and bestowed being on a particular possibility, exclusive of the rest? *External causes*, there are supposed to be none. *Chance* is a word without a meaning. Was it *nothing*? But that can never produce anything. We must, therefore, have recourse to a necessarily existent Being who carries the *reason* of his existence in himself; and who cannot be supposed not to exist, without an express contradiction. There is, consequently, such a Being—that is, there is a Deity.

I shall not leave it to Philo, said Cleanthes (though I know that the starting objections is his chief delight), to point out the weakness of this metaphysical reasoning. It seems to me so obviously ill-grounded, and at the same time of so little consequence to the cause of true piety and religion, that I shall myself venture to show the fallacy of it.

I shall begin with observing that there is an evident absurdity in pretending to demonstrate a matter of fact, or to prove it by any arguments *a priori*. Nothing is demonstrable unless the contrary implies a contradiction. Nothing that is distinctly conceivable implies a contradiction. Whatever we conceive as existent, we can also conceive as non-existent. There is no being, therefore, whose non-existence implies a contradiction. Consequently there is no being whose existence is demonstrable. I propose this argument as entirely decisive, and am willing to rest the whole controversy upon it.

It is pretended that the Deity is a necessarily existent being; and this necessity of his existence is attempted to be explained by asserting that, if we knew his whole essence or nature, we should perceive it to be as impossible for him not to exist, as for twice two not to be four. But it is evident that this can never happen, while our faculties remain the same as at present. It will still be possible for us, at any time, to conceive the non-existence of what we formerly conceived to exist; nor can the mind ever lie under a necessity of supposing any object to remain always in being; in the same manner as we lie under a necessity of always conceiving twice two to be four. The words, therefore, *necessary existence* have no meaning; or, which is the same thing, none that is consistent.

But further, why may not the material universe be the necessarily existent Being, according to this pretended explication of necessity? We dare not affirm that we know all the qualities of matter; and, for aught we can determine, it may contain some qualities which, were they known, would make its nonexistence appear as great a contradiction as that twice two is five. I find only one argument employed to prove that the material world is not the necessarily existent Being; and this argument is derived from the contingency both of the matter and the form of the world. "Any particle of matter," it is said, "may be *conceived* to be annihilated, and any form may be *conceived* to be altered. Such an annihilation or alteration, therefore, is not impossible."[1] But it seems a great partiality not to perceive that the same argument extends equally to the Deity, so far as we have any conception of him; and that the mind can at least imagine him to be non-existent, or his attributes to be altered. It must be some unknown, inconceivable qualities which can make his non-existence appear impossible or his attributes unalterable: And no reason can be assigned why these qualities may not belong to matter. As they are altogether unknown and inconceivable, they can never be proved incompatible with it.

Add to this that in tracing an eternal succession of objects it seems absurd to inquire for a general cause or first author. How can anything that exists from eternity have a cause, since that relation implies a priority in time and a beginning of existence?

In such a chain, too, or succession of objects, each part is caused by that which preceded it, and causes that which succeeds it. Where then is the difficulty? But the *whole*, you say, wants a cause. I answer that the uniting of these parts into a whole, like the uniting of several distinct countries into one kingdom, or several distinct members into one body, is performed merely by an arbitrary act of the mind, and has no influence on the nature of things. Did I show you the particular causes of each individual in a collection of twenty particles of matter, I should think it very unreasonable should you afterwards ask me what was the cause of the whole twenty. This is sufficiently explained in explaining the cause of the parts.

Though the reasonings which you have urged, Cleanthes, may well excuse me, said Philo, from starting any further difficulties; yet I cannot forbear insisting still upon another topic. It is observed by arithmeticians that the products of 9 compose always either 9 or some lesser product of 9 if you add together all the characters of which any of the former products is composed. Thus, of 18, 27, 36, which are products of 9, you make 9 by adding 1 to 8, 2 to 7, 3 to 6. Thus 369 is a product also of 9; and if you add 3, 6, and 9, you make 18, a lesser product of 9.[2] To a superficial observer so wonderful a regularity may be admired as the effect either of chance or design; but a skillful algebraist immediately concludes it to be the work of necessity, and demonstrates that it must forever result from the nature of these numbers. Is it not probable, I ask, that the whole economy of the universe is conducted by a like necessity, though no human algebra can furnish a key which solves the difficulty? And instead of admiring the order of natural beings, may it not happen that, could we penetrate into the intimate nature of bodies, we should clearly see why it was absolutely impossible they could ever admit of any other disposition? So dangerous is it to introduce this idea of necessity into the present question! and so naturally does it afford an inference directly opposite to the religious hypothesis!

---

[1] Dr. Clarke.

[2] *République des Lettres*, Aut 1685.

But dropping all these abstractions, continued Philo, and confining ourselves to more familiar topics, I shall venture to add an observation that the argument *a priori* has seldom been found very convincing, except to people of a metaphysical head who have accustomed themselves to abstract reasoning, and who, finding from mathematics that the understanding frequently leads to truth through obscurity, and contrary to first appearances, have transferred the same habit of thinking to subjects where it ought not to have place. Other people, even of good sense and the best inclined to religion, feel always some deficiency in such arguments, though they are not perhaps able to explain distinctly where it lies—a certain proof that men ever did and ever will derive their religion from other sources than from this species of reasoning.

WILLIAM L. ROWE

Two Criticisms of the Cosmological Argument

In this paper I wish to consider two major criticisms which have been advanced against the Cosmological Argument for the existence of God, criticisms which many philosophers regard as constituting a decisive refutation of that argument. Before stating and examining these objections it will be helpful to have before us a version of the Cosmological Argument. The Cosmological Argument has two distinct parts. The first part is an argument to establish the existence of a necessary being. The second part is an argument to establish that this necessary being is God. The two objections I shall consider are directed against the first part of the Cosmological Argument. using the expression "dependent being" to mean "a being which has the reason for its existence in the causal efficacy or nature of some other being," and that expression "independent being" to mean "a being which has the reason for its existence within its own nature," we may state the argument for the existence of a necessary being as follows:

1. Every being is either a dependent being or an independent being; therefore,
2. Either there exists an independent being or every being is dependent;
3. It is false that every being is dependent; therefore,
4. There exists an independent being; therefore,
5. There exists a necessary being.

From *The Monist*, Vol. 54, No. 3, (1970). Reprinted by permission of the author and The Open Court Publishing Company, LaSalle, IL.

This argument consists of two premises—propositions (1) and (3)—and three inferences. The first inference is from (1) to (2), the second from (2) and (3) to (4), and the third inference is from (4) to (5). Of the premises neither is obviously true, and of the inferences only the first and second are above suspicion. Before discussing the main subject of this paper—the reasoning in support of proposition (3) and the two major objections which have been advanced against that reasoning—I want to say something about the other questionable parts of the argument; namely, proposition (1) and the inference from (4) to (5).

Proposition (1) expresses what we may call the strong form of the Principle of Sufficient Reason. It insists not only that those beings which begin to exist must have a cause or explanation (the weak form of the Principle of Sufficient Reason) but that absolutely every being must have an explanation of its existing rather than not existing—the explanation lying either within the causal efficacy of some other being or within the thing's own nature. In an earlier paper I examined this Principle in some detail.[1] The objections I wish to consider in this paper are, I believe, independent of the Principle of Sufficient Reason. That is, these objections are meant to refute the argument even if the first premise is true. This being so, it will facilitate our examination of these two objections if we take proposition (1) as an unquestioned premise throughout our discussion. Accordingly, in this paper proposition (1) will function as an axiom in our reasoning. This, of course, should not be taken as implying that I think the first premise of the argument is true.

The inference from proposition (4) to proposition (5) is not considered in this paper. Indeed, for purposes of this paper we could have ended the statement of the argument with proposition (4). I have included the inference from (4) to (5) simply because it is an important element in the first part of the Cosmological Argument. Proposition (4) asserts the existence of a being which has the reason or explanation of its existence within its own nature. Proposition (5) asserts the existence of a necessary being. By "a necessary being" is meant a being whose nonexistence is a logical impossibility.[2] Many

---

[1] See "The Cosmological Argument and the Principle of Sufficient Reason," *Man and World*, I, No. 2 (1968).

[2] Not all versions of the Cosmological Argument employ the notion of a logically necessary being. It seems likely, for example, that in Aquinas' Third Way the expression "necessary being" is not used to mean a logically necessary being. (See P. Brown, "St. Thomas' Doctrine of Necessary Being," *The Philosophical Review*, 73 [1964], 76–90.) But in the version we are considering, it is clear that by "necessary being" is meant a being whose existence is logically necessary. Thus Samuel Clarke, from whose work our version has been adapted, remarks: "...the only true idea of a self-existent or necessarily existing being, is the idea of a being the supposition of whose not-existing is an express contradiction" (Samuel Clarke, *A Demonstration of the Being and Attributes of God*, 4th edition, p. 17). David Hume also understands the notion of a necessary being this way. Thus in his statement of the argument, which he adapted from Clarke, he has Demea conclude, "We must, therefore, have recourse to a necessarily existent being, who carries the reason of his existence in himself, and who cannot be supposed not to exist, without an express contradiction" (*Dialogues Concerning Natural Religion*, Part IX).

philosophers have argued that it is logically impossible for there to be a necessary being in this sense of "necessary being." Hence, even if the two objections I shall examine in this paper can be met, the defender of the Cosmological Argument must still face objections not only to the inference from (4) to (5) but to (5) itself. But again, this is a matter which I shall not pursue in this paper. Unlike proposition (1), however, which I treat as an unquestioned assumption, neither proposition (5) nor the inference from (4) to (5) will be appealed to in this paper. In what follows we may simply ignore that part of the argument. Indeed, our attention will be focused entirely on proposition (3), the reasoning which supports it, and the two major criticisms which have been advanced against that reasoning.

Proposition (3) asserts that it is false that every being is dependent. For what reasons? Well, if every being which exists (or ever existed) is dependent, then the whole of existing things, it would seem, consists of a collection of dependent beings, that is, a collection of beings each member of which exists by reason of the causal efficacy of some other being. This collection would have to contain an infinite number of numbers. For suppose it contained a finite number, let us say three *a*, *b*, and *c*. Now if in Scotus' phrase "a circle of causes is inadmissible" then if *c* is caused by *b* and *b* by *a*, *a* would exist without a cause, there being no other member of the collection that could be its cause. But in that case *a* would not be what by supposition it is, namely a *dependent* being. Hence, if we grant that a circle of causes is inadmissible it is impossible that the whole of existing things should consist of a collection of dependent beings *finite* in number.

Suppose, then, that the dependent beings making up the collection are infinite in number. Why is it impossible that the whole of existing things should consist of such a collection? The proponent of the Cosmological Argument answers as follows.[3] The infinite collection *itself*, he argues, requires an explanation of its existence. For since it is true of each member of the collection that it might not have existed, it is true of the whole infinite collection that it might not have existed. But if the entire infinite collection might not have existed there must be some explanation of why it exists rather than not. The explanation cannot lie in the causal efficacy of some being outside of the collection since by supposition the collection includes every being which is or ever was. Nor can the explanation of why there is an infinite collection be found within the collection itself, for since no member of the collection is independent, has the reason of its existence within itself, the collection as a whole cannot have the reason of its existence within itself. Thus the conception of an infinite collection of dependent beings is the conception of something whose existence has no explanation whatever. But since premise (1) tells us that whatever exists has an explanation for its existence, either within itself or in the causal efficacy of some other being, it cannot be that the whole of existing things consists of an infinite collection of dependent beings.

---

[3]See, for example, Samuel Clarke's discussion of Propositions II and III in his *Demonstration*. This discussion is summarized by Hume in Part IX of his *Dialogues*.

The reasoning developed here is exhibited as follows:

1. If every being is dependent then the whole of existing things consists of an infinite collection of dependent beings;
2. If the whole of existing things consists of an infinite collection of dependent beings then the infinite collection itself must have an explanation of its existence;
3. If the existence of the infinite collection of dependent beings has an explanation then the explanation must lie either in the causal efficacy of some being outside the collection or it must lie within the infinite collection itself;
4. The explanation of the existence of the infinite collection of dependent beings cannot lie in the causal efficacy of some being outside the collection;
5. The explanation of the existence of the infinite collection of dependent beings cannot lie within the collection itself; therefore,
6. There is no explanation of the infinite collection of dependent beings (from 3, 4, and 5); therefore,
7. It is false that the whole of existing things consists of an infinite collection of dependent beings (from 2 and 6); therefore,
8. It is false that every being is dependent (from 1 and 7).

Perhaps every premise in this argument is open to criticism. I propose here, however, to consider what I regard as the two major criticisms advanced against this reasoning in support of proposition (3) of the main argument. The first of these criticisms may be construed as directed against premise (2) of the above argument. According to this criticism it *makes no sense* to apply the notion of cause or explanation to the totality of things, and the arguments used to show that the whole of existing things must have a cause or explanation are *fallacious*. Thus in his B.B.C. debate with Father Copleston, Bertrand Russell took the view that the concept of cause is inapplicable to the universe conceived of as the total collection of things. When pressed by Copleston as to how he could rule out "the legitimacy of asking the question how the total, or anything at all comes to be there," Russell responded: "I can illustrate what seems to me your fallacy. Every man who exists has a mother, and it seems to me your argument is that therefore the human race must have a mother, but obviously the human race hasn't a mother—that's a different logical sphere."[4]

The second major criticism is directed at premise (5). According to this criticism it is *intelligible* to ask for an explanation of the existence of the infinite collection of dependent beings. But the answer to this question, so the criticism goes, is provided once we learn that each member of the infinite collection has an explanation of its existence. Thus Hume remarks: "Did I show you the particular causes of each individual in a collection of twenty

---

[4]"The Existence of God, A Debate between Bertrand Russell and Father F. C. Copleston," in John Hick (ed.), *The Existence of God* (New York: Macmillan, 1964), p. 175. The debate was originally broadcast by the British Broadcasting Corporation in 1948. References are to the debate as reprinted in *The Existence of God*.

particles of matter, I should think it very unreasonable, should you afterwards ask me, what was the cause of the whole twenty. This is sufficiently
explained in explaining the cause of the parts."[5]

These two criticisms express the major reasons philosophers have given
for rejecting what undoubtedly is the most important part of the Cosmological
Argument—namely, that portion of the argument which seeks to establish that
not every being can be a dependent being. In this paper my aim is to defend the
Cosmological Argument against both of these criticisms. I shall endeavor to
show that each of these criticisms rests on a philosophical mistake.

The first criticism draws attention to what appears to be a fatal flaw in
the Cosmological Argument. It seems that the proponent of the argument
(i) ascribes to the infinite collection itself a property (having a cause or
explanation) which is applicable only to the members of that collection, and
(ii) does so by means of a fallacious inference from a proposition about the
members of the collection to a proposition about the collection itself. There
are, then, two alleged mistakes committed here. The first error is, perhaps,
a category mistake—the ascription to the collection of a property applicable
only to the members of the collection. As Russell would say, the collection,
in comparison with its members, belongs to a "different logical sphere." The
second error is apparently what leads the proponent of the Cosmological
Argument to make the first error. He ascribes the property of having an
explanation to the infinite collection because he *infers* that the infinite
collection must have a cause or explanation from the premise that each of
its members has a cause. But to infer this, Russell suggests, is as fallacious
as to infer that the human race must have a mother because each member
of the human race has a mother.

That the proponent of the Cosmological Argument ascribes the property of having a cause or explanation to the infinite collection of dependent
beings is certainly true. That to do so is a category mistake is, I think,
questionable. But before pursuing this point I want to deal with the second
charge. The main question we must consider in connection with the second
charge is whether the Cosmological Argument involves the inference: Every
member of the infinite collection has an explanation of its existence; therefore,
the infinite collection itself has an explanation of its existence. As we have
seen, Russell thinks that Copleston has employed this inference in coming to
the conclusion that there must be an explanation for the totality of things,
and not simply for each of the things making up that totality.

Perhaps some proponents of the Cosmological Argument have used
the argument which Russell regards as fallacious. But not all of them
have.[6] Moreover, there is no need to employ such an inference since in its

---

[5]*Dialogues*, Part IX.

[6]Samuel Clarke did not. Nor do we find Hume appealing to this inference in the course
of presenting the Cosmological Argument in Part IX of the *Dialogues*.

first premise the Cosmological Argument has available a principle from which it follows that the infinite collection of dependent beings must have an explanation of its existence. Thus one famous exponent of the argument—Samuel Clarke—reasons that the infinite collection of beings must have an explanation of its existence by appealing to the strong form of the Principle of Sufficient Reason. The principle assures us that whatever exists has an explanation of its existence. But if there exists an infinite succession or collection of dependent beings then that collection or succession, Clarke reasons, must have an explanation of its existence. Hence, we can, I think, safely dismiss the charge that the Cosmological Argument involves an erroneous inference from the premise that the members of a collection have a certain property to the conclusion that the collection itself must have that property.

We must now deal with the question whether it makes *sense* to ascribe the property of having an explanation or cause to the infinite collection of dependent beings. Clearly only if it does make sense is the reasoning in support of proposition (3) of the main argument acceptable. Our question, then, is whether it makes sense to ask for a cause or explanation of the entire universe, conceiving the universe as an infinite collection of dependent beings.

One recent critic of the Cosmological Argument, Ronald Hepburn, has stated our problem as follows:

> When we are seriously speaking of absolutely everything there is, are we speaking of something that requires a cause, in the way that events *in* the universe may require causes? What indeed can be safely said at all about the totality of things? For a great many remarks that one can make with perfect propriety about limited things quite obviously can *not* be made about the cosmos itself. It cannot, for instance, be said meaningfully to be "above" or "below" anything, although things-in-the-universe can be so related to one another. Whatever we might claim to be "*below* the universe" would turn out to be just some more *universe*. We should have been relating part to part, instead of relating the whole to something not-the-universe. The same applies to "outside the universe." We can readily imagine a boundary, a garden wall, shall we say, round something that we want to call the universe. But if we imagine ourselves boring a hole through that wall and pushing a stick out *beyond* it into a nameless zone "outside," we should still not in fact have given meaning to the phrase "outside the universe." For the place into which the stick was intruding would deserve to be called a part of the universe (even if consisting of empty space, no matter) just as much as the area within the walls. We should have demonstrated *not* that the universe has an outside, but that what we took to be the whole universe was not really the whole.
>
> Our problem is this. Supposing we could draw up a list of questions that can be asked about objects in the universe, but cannot be asked about the *whole* universe: would the question, "Has it a cause?" be on that list? One thing is clear. Whether or not this question is on the proscribed list, we are not entitled

to argue as the Cosmological Argument does that *because* things in the world have causes, therefore the sum of things must also have *its* cause. No more (as we have just seen) can we argue from the fact that things in the world have tops and bottoms, insides and outsides, and are related to other things, to the belief that the universe has its top and bottom, inside and outside, and is related to a supra-cosmical something.[7]

In this passage Hepburn (*i*) points out that some properties (e.g., "above," "below," etc.) of things in the universe cannot properly be ascribed to the total universe, (*ii*) raises the question whether "having a cause" is such a property, and (*iii*) concludes that "…we are not entitled to argue as the Cosmological Argument does that *because* things in the world have causes, therefore, the sum of things must also have *its* cause." We noted earlier that the Cosmological Argument (i.e., the version we are examining) does not argue that the sum of things (the infinite collection of dependent beings) must have a cause *because* each being in the collection has a cause. Thus we may safely ignore Hepburn's main objection. However, his other two points are well taken. There certainly are properties which it makes sense to apply to things within a collection but which it makes no sense to apply to the collection itself. What assurance do we have that "having a cause" is not such a property?

Suppose we are holding in our hands a collection of ten marbles. Not only would each marble have a definite weight but the collection itself would have a weight. Indeed, from the premise that each marble weighs more than one ounce we could infer validly that the collection itself weighs more than an ounce. This example shows that it is not always fallacious to infer that a collection has a certain property from the premise that each member of the collection has that property.[8] But the collection in this example is, we might say, *concrete* rather than *abstract*. That is, we are here considering the collection as itself a physical entity, an aggregate of marbles. This, of course, is not a collection in the sense of a class or set of things. Holding several marbles in my hands I can consider the *set* whose members are those marbles. The set itself, being an *abstract* entity, rather than a physical heap, has no weight. Just as the set of human beings has no mother, so the set whose members are marbles in my hand has no weight. Therefore, in considering whether it makes sense to speak of the infinite collection of dependent beings as having a cause or explanation of its existence it is important to decide whether we are speaking of a collection as a *concrete* entity—for example, a physical whole or aggregate—or an *abstract* entity.

---

[7]Ronald W. Hepburn, *Christianity and Paradox* (London: Watts, 1958), pp. 167–68.

[8]For a consideration of inferences of this sort in connection with the fallacy of composition see my paper "The Fallacy of Composition," *Mind*, 71 (January 1962). For some needed corrections of my paper see Yehoshua Bar-Hillel, "More on the Fallacy of Composition," *Mind*, 73 (January 1964).

Suppose we view the infinite collection of dependent beings as itself a concrete entity. As far as the Cosmological Argument is concerned, one advantage of so viewing it is that it is understandable why it might have the property of having a cause or explanation of its existence. For concrete entities—physical objects, events, physical heaps—can be caused. Thus if the infinite collection is a concrete entity it may well make sense to ascribe to it the property of having a cause or explanation.

But such a view of the infinite collection is implausible, if not plainly incorrect. Many collections of physical things cannot possibly be themselves concrete entities. Think, for example, of the collection whose members are the largest prehistoric beast, Socrates, and the Empire State Building. By any stretch of the imagination can we view this collection as itself a concrete thing? Clearly we cannot. Such a collection must be construed as an *abstract* entity, a class or set.[9] But if there are many collections of beings which cannot be concrete entities, what grounds have we for thinking that on the supposition that every being that is or ever was is dependent the collection of those beings would itself be a concrete thing such as a physical heap? At any rate our knowledge of the things (both past and present) comprising the universe and their interrelations would have to be much greater than it currently is before we would be entitled to view the *sum* of concrete things, past and present, as itself something *concrete*.

But if the infinite collection of dependent beings is to be understood as an abstract entity, say the set whose members include all the beings that are or ever were, haven't we conceded the point to Russell? A set or class conceived of as an abstract entity has no weight, is not below or above anything, and cannot be thought of as being caused or brought into being. Thus if the infinite collection is a set, an abstract entity, is not Russell right in charging that it makes no more sense to ascribe the property of having a cause or an explanation to the infinite collection than it does to ascribe the property of having a mother to the human race?

Suppose that every being that is or ever was is dependent. Suppose further that the number of such beings is infinite. Let A be the set consisting of these beings. Thus no being exists or ever existed which is not a member of A. Does it make *sense* to ask for an explanation of A's existence? We do, of course, ask questions about sets which are equivalent to questions about their members. For example, "Is set X included in set Y?" is equivalent to the question "Is every member of X a member of Y?" I suggest that the question "Why does A exist?" be taken to mean "Why does A have the members that it does rather than some other members or none at all?" Consider, for example, the set of men. Let M be this set. The question "Why does M exist?"

---

[9] Of course, the three members of this collection, unlike the members of the collection of dependent beings, presumably are causally unrelated. But it is equally easy to think of collections which cannot possibly be concrete entities whose members are causally related—e.g., the collection whose members are the ancestors of a given man.

is perhaps odd if we understand it as a request for an explanation of the existence of an abstract entity. But the question "Why does M exist?" may be taken to mean "Why does M have the members it has rather than some other members or none at all?" So understood the form of words "Why does M exist?" does, I think, ask an intelligible question. It is a contingent fact that Hitler existed. Indeed, it is a contingent fact that any men exist at all. One of Leibniz' logically possible worlds is a world which includes some members of M, for example Socrates and Plato, but not others, say Hitler and Stalin. Another is a world in which the set of men is entirely empty and therefore identical with the null set. Why is it, then, that M exists? That is, why does M have just the members it has rather than some other members or none at all? Not only is this question intelligible but we seem to have some idea of what its answer is. Presumably, the theory of evolution might be a part of the explanation of why M is not equivalent to the null set and why its members have certain properties rather than others.

But if the question "Why does M exist?" makes sense, why should not the question "Why does A exist?" also make sense? A is the set of dependent beings. In asking why A exists we are not asking for an explanation of the existence of an abstract entity; we are asking why A has the members it has rather than some other members or none at all. I submit that this question does make sense. Moreover, I think that it is precisely this question which the proponents of the Cosmological Argument were asking when they asked for an explanation of the existence of the infinite collection or succession of dependent beings.[10] Of course, it is one thing for a question to make sense and another thing for there to be an answer to it.

The interpretation I have given to the question "Why does A exist?" is somewhat complex. For according to this interpretation what is being asked is not simply why does A have members rather than having none, but also why does A have just the members it has rather than having some other members. Although the proponents of the Cosmological Argument do seem to interpret the question in this way, it will facilitate our discussion if we simplify the interpretation somewhat by focusing our attention solely on the question why A has the members it has rather than having none. Hence, for purposes of simplification, in what follows I shall take the question "Why does A exist?" to mean "Why does A have the members it has rather than not having any?"

For any being to be a member of A it is necessary and sufficient that it have the reason of its existence in the causal efficacy of some other being. Imagine the following state of affairs. A has exactly three members: a_1, a_2, and a_3. a_3 exists by reason of the causal efficacy of a_2, and a_2 exists by reason of

---

[10]Thus in speaking of the infinite succession, Hume has Demea say: "...and yet it is evident that it requires a cause or reason, as much as any particular object which begins to exist in time. The question is still reasonable, *why this particular succession of causes existed from eternity, and not any other succession, or no succession at all*" (*Dialogues*, Part IX; italics mine).

the causal efficacy of a_1. There exists an *eternal* being b which does not exist by reason of the causal efficacy of any other being. Since b is not a dependent being, b is not a member of A. At a certain time a_1 came into existence by reason of the causal efficacy of b. Clearly the question "Why does A exist?" when taken to mean "Why does A have the members it has rather than none at all?" makes sense when asked within the context of this imagined state of affairs. Indeed, part of the answer to the question would involve reference to b and its causal efficacy in bringing about the existence of one of the members of A, namely a_1.

What this case shows is that the question "Why does A exist?" is not always (i.e., in every context) meaningless. If Russell holds that the question is meaningless in the framework of the Cosmological Argument it must be because of some special assumption about A which forms part of the context of the Cosmological Argument. The assumption in question undoubtedly is that absolutely every being is dependent. On this assumption every being which is or ever was has membership in A and A has an infinite number of members.

Perhaps Russell's view is that within the context of the assumption that *every* being is dependent it makes no sense to ask why A has the members it has rather than none at all. It makes no sense, he might argue, for two reasons. First, on the assumption that every being is dependent there could not be such a thing as the *set* A whose members are all dependent beings. For the set A is, although abstract, presumably a being. But if every being is dependent then A would have to be dependent and therefore a member of itself. But apart from whatever difficulties arise when a set is said to be a member of itself, it would seem to make little sense to think of an abstract entity, such as a set, as being caused, as having the reason of its existence within the causal efficacy of some other being.

Second, Russell might argue that the assumption that every being is dependent and therefore a member of A rules out the possibility of any answer to the question why A has the members it has rather than none at all. For on that assumption our question about A is in effect a question about the totality of things. And, as Russell observes, "I see no reason whatsoever to suppose that the total has any cause whatsoever."[11]

Neither of these reasons suffices to show that our question about A is meaningless. The first reason does, however, point up the necessity of introducing some restriction on the assumption "Every being is dependent" in order that abstract entities like numbers and sets not fall within the scope of the expression "Every being." Such a restriction will obviate the difficulty that A is said to be both a member of itself and dependent. I propose the following rough restriction. In speaking of beings we shall restrict ourselves to beings that *could be caused* to exist by some other being or *could be causes* of

---

[11] "Debate," p. 175.

the existence of other beings. God (if he exists), a man, the sun, a stone are beings of this sort. Presumably, numbers, sets, and the like are not. The assumption that every being is dependent is to be understood under this restriction. That is, we are here assuming that every being of the sort described by the restriction is *in fact* a being which exists by reason of the causal efficacy of some other being. The second reason given confuses the issue of whether a question makes sense, is meaningful, with the issue of whether a question has an answer. Of course, given the assumption that every being is a member of A we cannot expect to find the cause or reason of A's existence in some being which is not a member of A. If the explanation for A's existence cannot be found within A itself then we must conclude that there can be no explanation for the infinite collection of dependent beings. But this is to say only that on our assumption that every being is dependent there is no answer to the question "Why does A exist?" It is one thing for a question not to have an answer and quite another thing for the question to be *meaningless*.

We have been examining the first of the two major criticisms philosophers have directed at the reasoning the Cosmological Argument provides in support of the proposition that not every being is dependent. The heart of this criticism is that it *makes no sense* to ascribe the property of having a cause or explanation to the infinite collection of dependent beings. This criticism, I think, has been shown to be correct in one way, but incorrect in another. If we construe the infinite collection of dependent beings as an abstract entity, a set, it perhaps does not make sense to claim that something caused the existence of this abstract entity. But the question "Why does A exist?" may be interpreted to mean "Why does A have the members it has rather than none at all?" I have argued that taken in this way the question "Why does A exist?" is a *meaningful* question.

According to the Principle of Sufficient Reason there must be an answer to the question "Why does A exist?," an explanation of the existence of the infinite collection of dependent beings. Moreover, the explanation either must lie in the causal efficacy of some being outside of the collection or it must lie within the collection itself. But since by supposition every being is dependent—and therefore in the collection—there is no being outside the collection whose causal efficacy might explain the existence of the collection. Therefore, either the collection has the explanation of its existence within itself or there can be no explanation of its existence. If the first alternative is rejected then, since the Principle of Sufficient Reason requires that everything has an explanation of its existence, we must reject the supposition that every being is dependent. For on that supposition there is no explanation for why there is an infinite collection of dependent beings.

The second major criticism argues that the proponent of the Cosmological Argument is mistaken in thinking that the explanation of the existence of the infinite collection cannot be found within the collection itself. The explanation of the existence of the collection is provided, so the criticism goes, once we learn what the explanation is of each of the members of the collection. As we noted earlier, this criticism was succinctly expressed by Hume in his remark: "Did I show you the particular causes of each individual in a collection of twenty particles of matter, I should think it very unreasonable, should you afterwards ask me, what was the cause of the whole twenty. This is sufficiently explained in explaining the cause of the parts." Applying this objection to the infinite collection of dependent beings, we obtain the result that to explain the existence of the infinite collection, A, amounts to no more than explaining the existence of each of its members. Now, of course, A is unlike Hume's collection of twenty particles in that we cannot give *individual* explanations for each of the members of A. For since A has an infinite number of members we would have to give an infinite number of explanations. But our inability to give a particular explanation for each of the members of A does not imply that there is any member of A for whose existence there is no explanation. Indeed, from the fact that each member of A is dependent (i.e., has the reason of its existence in the causal efficacy of some other being), we know that every member of A has an explanation of its existence; from the assumption that every being is a member of A we know that for each member of A the explanation lies in the causal efficacy of some other member of A. But, so the criticism goes, if every member of A has an explanation of its existence then the existence of A has been sufficiently explained. For to explain why a certain collection of things exists it is sufficient to explain the existence of each of its members. Hence, since we know that the existence of every one of A's members is explained we know that the existence of the collection A is explained.

This forceful criticism, originally advanced by Hume, has gained wide acceptance in contemporary philosophy. Indeed, the only remaining problem seems to be to explain why the proponents of the Cosmological Argument failed to see that to explain the existence of all the members of a collection is to explain the existence of the collection. In restating Hume's criticism, Paul Edwards suggests that perhaps they may have been misled by grammar.

> The demand to find the cause of the series as a whole rests on the erroneous assumption that the series is something over and above the members of which it is composed. It is tempting to suppose this, at least by implication, because the word "series" is a noun like "dog" or "man." Like the expression "this dog" or "this man" the phrase "this series" is easily taken to designate an individual object. But reflection shows this to be an error. If we have explained the individual members there is nothing additional left to be explained. Suppose I see a group of five Eskimos standing on the corner of Sixth Avenue and 50th Street and I wish to explain why the group came to New York. Investigation reveals the following stories:
>
> Eskimo No. 1 did not enjoy the extreme cold in the polar region and decided to move to a warmer climate.
>
> No. 2 is the husband of Eskimo No. 1. He loves her dearly and did not wish to live without her.

No. 3 is the son of Eskimos 1 and 2. He is too small and too weak to oppose his parents.

No. 4 saw an advertisement in the *New York Times* for an Eskimo to appear on television.

No. 5 is a private detective engaged by the Pinkerton Agency to keep an eye on Eskimo No. 4.

Let us assume that we have now explained in the case of each of the five Eskimos why he or she is in New York. Somebody then asks: "All right, but what about the group as a whole; why is *it* in New York?" This would plainly be an absurd question. There is no group over and above the five members, and if we have explained why each of the five members is in New York we have *ipso facto* explained why the group is there. It is just as absurd to ask for the cause of the series as a whole as distinct from asking for the causes of the individual members.[12]

The principle underlying the Hume-Edwards criticism may be stated as follows: *If the existence of every member of a set is explained the existence of that set is thereby explained.* This principle seems to be a corollary of our interpretation of the question "Why does this set exist?" For on our interpretation, once it is explained why the set has the members it has rather than none at all it is thereby explained why the set exists. And it would seem that if a set A has, say, three members, a_1, a_2, and a_3, then if we explain the existence of a_1, a_2, and a_3 we have explained why A has the members it has rather than none at all. Thus the principle which underlies the second major criticism seems to be implied by our conception of what is involved in explaining the existence of a set.

The principle underlying the Hume-Edwards criticism seems plausible enough when restricted to finite sets, i.e., sets with a finite number of members. But the principle is false, I believe, when extended to infinite sets in which the explanation of each member's existence is found in the causal efficacy of some other member. Consider M, the set of men. Suppose M consists of an infinite number of members, each member owing its existence to some other member which generated it. Suppose further that to explain the existence of a given man it is sufficient to note that he was begotten by some other man. That is, where x and y are men and x begat y we allow that the existence of y is explained by the causal efficacy of x. On these suppositions it is clear that the antecedent of the principle is satisfied with respect to M. For every member of M has an explanation of its existence. But does it follows that the existence of M has an explanation? I think not. We do not have an explanation of the existence of M until we have an explanation of why M has the members it has rather than none at all. But clearly if *all* we know is that there always have been men and that every man's existence is

---

[12]Paul Edwards, "The Cosmological Argument," in Donald R. Burrill (ed.), *The Cosmological Arguments* (New York: Doubleday, 1967), pp. 113–14. Edwards' paper was originally published in *The Rationalist Annual for the Year 1959*.

explained by the causal efficacy of some other man, we do not know *why* there always have been men rather than none at all. If I ask why M has the members it has rather than none, it is no answer to say that M always had members. We may, I suppose, answer the question "Why does M have the *currently existing* members it has?" by saying that M always had members and there were men who generated the currently existing men. But in asking why M has the members it has rather than none at all we are not asking why M has the currently existing members it has. To make this clear, we may rephrase our question as follows: "Why is it that M has now and always had members rather than never having had any members at all?" Surely we have not learned the answer to this question when we have learned that there always have been members of M and that each member's existence is explained by the causal efficacy of some other member.

What we have just seen is that from the fact that the existence of each member of a collection is explained it does not follow that the existence of the collection is thereby explained. It does not follow because when the collection (set) has an infinite number of members, each member's existence having its explanation in the causal efficacy of *some other member*, it is true that the existence of every member has an explanation, and yet it is still an open question whether the existence of the set has an explanation. To explain the existence of a set we must explain why it has the members it has rather than none. But clearly if every member's existence is explained by some other *member*, then although the existence of every member has an explanation it is still unexplained why the set has the members it has, rather than none at all.

Put somewhat differently, we have seen that the fact (assuming for the moment that it is a fact) that there always have been men, each man's existence brought about by some other man, is insufficient to explain *why* it is a fact that there always have been men rather than a fact that there never have been any men. If someone asks us to explain why there always have been men rather than never having been any it would not suffice for us to observe that there always have been men and each man has been brought into existence by some other man.

I have argued that the second major criticism rests on a false principle, namely, that if the existence of every member of a set is explained then the existence of that set is thereby explained. This principle, so far as I can determine, is true when restricted to sets with a *finite* number of members. For example, if a set A has two members, a_1 and a_2, and if we explain a_2 by a_1 and a_1 by some being b that caused a_1, then, I think, we have explained the existence of A. In any case we have explained why A has members rather than none at all. Thus I am not claiming that the principle underlying Hume's objection is always false. Indeed, as I have just indicated, it is easy to provide an example of a finite set of which the principle is true. And perhaps it is just this feature of the principle—i.e., its plausibility when applied to finite sets such as Hume's collection of twenty particles and Edwards' five Eskimos—which has led Hume and many philosophers since Hume to reject the Cosmological Argument's thesis that even if every member of the infinite succession of dependent beings has an explanation the infinite succession itself is not thereby explained. If so, then the mistake Hume and his successors have made is to assume that a principle which is true of all finite sets also is true of all infinite sets.

We know, for example, that if we have a set B consisting of five members and a set C consisting of three of the members of B, the members of C cannot be put in one-to-one correspondence with those of B. In reflecting on this fact, we are tempted to conclude that for *any* two sets X and Y, if all the members of X are members of Y but some members of Y are not members of X then the members of X cannot be put in one-to-one correspondence with those of Y. Indeed, so long as X and Y are restricted to *finite* sets the principle just stated is true. But if we let X be the set of *even* natural numbers—2, 4, 6,...—and Y be the set of natural numbers—1, 2, 3,...—the principle is shown to be false. For although all the members of X are members of Y and some members of Y—the odd integers—are not members of X, it is not true that the members of X cannot be put in one-to-one correspondence with those of Y. What this example illustrates is that a principle which holds of all finite sets may not hold of all infinite sets. The principle underlying the second major criticism is, I have argued, such a principle.

One final point concerning my reply to the second major criticism needs to be made clear. In rejecting the principle on which the criticism rests I have contended that when a set has an *infinite* number of members, every one of which has an explanation of its existence, it *does not follow* that the existence of the set is thereby explained. In saying this I do not mean to imply that in explaining the existence of every member of an infinite set we never thereby explain the existence of the set, only that we *sometimes* do not. Specifically, we do not, I think, when we explain the existence of each member of the set by some other member of *that set*. Recall our example of M, the set of men. If we think of the members of this set as forming a temporal series stretching infinitely back in time, each member's existence explained by the causal efficacy of the preceding member, we have an example, I think, in which an explanation of the existence of each member of M does not constitute an explanation of the existence of M. Let us suppose that each man is produced not by another man but by some superior being, say a god. What we are supposing is that M is described as before except that instead of every member having the explanation of its existence in some preceding member of M the explanation is found in the causal efficacy of some member of the set of gods. From eternity, then, gods have been producing men. There have always been members of M and every member has an explanation of its existence. Here it does seem true to say that in explaining the existence of every member of M we have thereby explained the existence of M. If someone asks why there now are and always have been men rather than never having been any, we can say in response that there always have been men because there always have been gods producing them. This, if true, would explain why M has always had members.

In this paper I have examined two criticisms which have been advanced against that part of the Cosmological Argument which seeks to establish that not every being can be a dependent being. I have argued that each of these criticisms is mistaken and, therefore, fails as a refutation of the Cosmological Argument. If my arguments are correct, it does not follow, of course, that the Cosmological Argument is a good argument for its conclusion. But it does follow that those philosophers who have rejected the argument for either of the two criticisms discussed in this paper need to re-examine the argument and, if they continue to reject it, provide some *good* reasons for doing so.

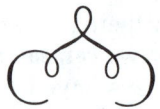

THE
TELEOLOGICAL
ARGUMENT

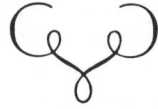

WILLIAM PALEY

The Analogy of the Watch

CHAPTER ONE

In crossing a heath, suppose I pitched my foot against a *stone* and were asked how the stone came to be there, I might possibly answer that for anything I knew to the contrary it had lain there forever; nor would it, perhaps, be very easy to show the absurdity of this answer. But suppose I had found a *watch* upon the ground, and it should be inquired how the watch happened to be in that place, I should hardly think of the answer which I had before given, that for anything I knew the watch might have always been there. Yet why should not this answer serve for the watch as well as for the stone; why is it not as admissible in the second case as in the first? For this reason, and for no other, namely, that when we come to inspect the watch, we perceive—what we could not discover in the stone—that its several parts are framed and put together for a purpose, e.g., that they are so formed and adjusted as to produce motion, and that motion so regulated as to point out the hour of the day; that if the different parts had been differently shaped from what they are, or placed after any other manner or in any other order than that in which they are placed, either no motion at all would have been carried on in the machine, or none which would have answered the use that is now served by it. To reckon up a few of the plainest of these parts and of their offices, all tending to one result: we see a cylindrical box containing a coiled elastic spring, which, by its endeavor to relax itself, turns round the box. We next observe a flexible chain—artificially wrought for the sake of flexure—communicating the action of the spring from the box to the fusee. We then find a series of wheels, the teeth of which catch in and apply to each other,

From William Paley, *Natural Theology* (1802).

conducting the motion from the fusee to the balance and from the balance to the pointer, and at the same time, by the size and shape of those wheels, so regulating that motion as to terminate in causing an index, by an equable and measured progression, to pass over a given space in a given time. We take notice that the wheels are made of brass, in order to keep them from rust; the springs of steel, no other metal being so elastic; that over the face of the watch there is placed a glass, a material employed in no other part of the work, but in the room of which, if there had been any other than a transparent substance, the hour could not be seen without opening the case. This mechanism being observed—it requires indeed an examination of the instrument, and perhaps some previous knowledge of the subject, to perceive and understand it; but being once, as we have said, observed and understood—the inference we think is inevitable, that the watch must have had a maker—that there must have existed, at some time and at some place or other, an artificer or artificers who formed it for the purpose which we find it actually to answer, who completely comprehended its construction and designed its use.

I. Nor would it, I apprehend, weaken the conclusion, that we had never seen a watch made—that we had never known an artist capable of making one—that we were altogether incapable of executing such a piece of workmanship ourselves, or of understanding in what manner it was performed; all this being no more than what is true of some exquisite remains of ancient art, of some lost arts, and, to the generality of mankind, of the more curious productions of modern manufacture. Does one man in a million know how oval frames are turned? Ignorance of this kind exalts our opinion of the unseen and unknown artist's skill, if he be unseen and unknown, but raises no doubt in our minds of the existence and agency of such an artist, at some former time and in some place or other. Nor can I perceive that it varies at all the inference, whether the question arise concerning a human agent or concerning an agent of a different species, or an agent possessing in some respects a different nature.

II. Neither, secondly, would it invalidate our conclusion, that the watch sometimes went wrong or that it seldom went exactly right. The purpose of the machinery, the design, and the designer might be evident, and in the case supposed, would be evident, in whatever way we accounted for the irregularity of the movement, or whether we could account for it or not. It is not necessary that a machine be perfect in order to show with what design it was made: still less necessary, where the only question is whether it were made with any design at all.

III. Nor, thirdly, would it bring any uncertainty into the argument, if there were a few parts of the watch, concerning which we could not discover or had not yet discovered in what manner they conduced to the general effect; or even some parts, concerning which we could not ascertain whether they conduced to that effect in any manner whatever. For, as to the first branch of the case, if by the loss, or disorder, or decay of the parts in question, the movement of the watch were found in fact to be stopped, or disturbed, or retarded, no doubt would remain in our minds as to the utility or intention of these parts, although we should be unable to investigate the manner according to which, or the connection by which, the ultimate effect depended upon their action or assistance; and the more complex the machine, the more likely is this obscurity to arise. Then, as to the second thing supposed, namely, that there were parts which might be spared without prejudice to the movement of the watch, and that we had proved this by experiment, these superfluous parts, even if we were completely assured that they were such, would not vacate the reasoning which we had instituted concerning other parts. The indication of contrivance remained, with respect to them, nearly as it was before.

IV. Nor, fourthly, would any man in his senses think the existence of the watch with its various machinery accounted for, by being told that it was one out of possible combinations of material forms; that whatever he had found in the place where he found the watch, must have contained some internal configuration or other; and that this configuration might be the structure now exhibited, namely, of the works of a watch, as well as a different structure.

V. Nor, fifthly, would it yield his inquiry more satisfaction, to be answered that there existed in things a principle of order, which had disposed the parts of the watch into their present form and situation. He never knew a watch made by the principle of order; nor can he even form to himself an idea of what is meant by a principle of order distinct from the intelligence of the watchmaker.

VI. Sixthly, he would be surprised to hear that the mechanism of the watch was no proof of contrivance, only a motive to induce the mind to think so:

VII. And not less surprised to be informed that the watch in his hand was nothing more than the result of the laws of *metallic* nature. It is a perversion of language to assign any law as the efficient, operative cause of any thing. A law presupposes an agent, for it is only the mode according to which an agent proceeds: it implies a power, for it is the order according to which that power acts. Without this agent, without this power, which are both distinct from itself, the *law* does nothing, is nothing. The expression, "the law of metallic nature," may sound strange and harsh to a philosophic ear; but it seems quite as justifiable as some others which are more familiar to him, such as "the law of vegetable nature," "the law of animal nature," or, indeed, as "the law of nature" in general, when assigned as the cause of phenomena, in exclusion of agency and power, or when it is substituted into the place of these.

VIII. Neither, lastly, would our observer be driven out of his conclusion or from his confidence in its truth by being told that he knew nothing at all about the matter. He knows enough for his argument; he knows the utility of the end; he knows the subserviency and adaptation of the means to the end. These points being known, his ignorance of other points, his doubts concerning other points affect not the certainty of his reasoning. The consciousness of knowing little need not beget a distrust of that which he does know.

CHAPTER TWO

Suppose, in the next place, that the person who found the watch should after some time discover that, in addition to all the properties which he had hitherto observed in it, it possessed the unexpected property of producing in the course of its movement another watch like itself—the thing is conceivable; that it contained within it a mechanism, a system of parts—a mold, for instance, or a complex adjustment of lathes, files, and other tools—evidently and separately calculated for this purpose; let us inquire what effect ought such a discovery to have upon his former conclusion.

I. The first effect would be to increase his admiration of the contrivance, and his conviction of the consummate skill of the contriver. Whether he regarded the object of the contrivance, the distinct apparatus, the intricate, yet in many parts intelligible mechanism by which it was carried on, he would perceive in this new observation nothing but an additional reason for doing what he had already done—for referring the construction of the watch to design and to supreme art. If that construction *without* this property, or, which is the same thing, before this property had been noticed, proved intention and art to have been employed about it, still more strong would the proof appear when he came to the knowledge of this further property, the crown and perfection of all the rest.

II. He would reflect that, though the watch before him were *in some sense* the maker of the watch which was fabricated in the course of its movements, yet it was in a very different sense from that in which a carpenter, for instance, is the maker of a chair—the author of its contrivance, the cause of the relation of its parts to their use. With respect to these, the first watch was no cause at all to the second; in no such sense as this was it the author of the constitution and order, either of the parts which the new watch contained, or of the parts by the aid and instrumentality of which it was produced. We might possibly say, but with great latitude of expression, that a stream of water ground corn; but no latitude of expression would allow us to say, no stretch of conjecture could lead us to think that the stream of water built the mill, though it were too ancient for us to know who the builder was. What the stream of water does in the affair is neither more nor less than this: by the application of an unintelligent impulse to a mechanism previously arranged, arranged independently of it and arranged by intelligence, an effect is produced, namely, the corn is ground. But the effect results from the arrangement. The force of the stream cannot be said to be the cause or the author of the effect, still less of the arrangement. Understanding and plan in the formation of the mill were not the less necessary for any share which the water has in grinding the corn; yet is this share the same as that which the watch would have contributed to the production of the new watch, upon the supposition assumed in the last section. Therefore,

III. Though it be now no longer probable that the individual watch which our observer had found was made immediately by the hand of an artificer, yet this alteration does not in anywise affect the inference that an artificer had been originally employed and concerned in the production. The argument from design remains as it was. Marks of design and contrivance are no more accounted for now than they were before. In the same thing, we may ask for the cause of different properties. We may ask for the cause of the color of a body, of its hardness, of its heat; and these causes may be all different. We are now asking for the cause of that subserviency to a use, that relation to an end, which we have remarked in the watch before us. No answer is given to this question by telling us that a preceding watch produced it. There cannot be design without a designer; contrivance without a contriver; order without choice; arrangement without anything capable of arranging; subserviency and relation to a purpose without that which could intend a purpose; means suitable to an end, and executing their office in accomplishing that end, without the end ever having been contemplated or the means accommodated to it. Arrangement, disposition of parts, subserviency of means to an end, relation of instruments to a use imply the presence of intelligence and mind. No one, therefore, can rationally believe that the insensible, inanimate watch, from which the watch before us issued, was the proper cause of the mechanism we so much admire in it—could be truly said to have constructed the instrument, disposed its parts, assigned their office, determined their order, action, and mutual dependency, combined their several motions into one result, and that also a result connected with the utilities of other beings. All these properties, therefore, are as much unaccounted for as they were before.

IV. Nor is anything gained by running the difficulty farther back, that is, by supposing the watch before us to have been produced from another watch, that from a former, and so on indefinitely. Our going back ever so far brings us no nearer to the least degree of satisfaction upon the subject. Contrivance is still unaccounted for. We still want a contriver. A designing mind is neither supplied by this supposition nor dispensed with. If the difficulty were diminished the farther we went back, by going back indefinitely we might exhaust it. And this is the only case to which this sort of reasoning applies. Where there is a tendency, or, as we increase the number of terms, a continual approach toward a limit, *there*, by supposing the number of terms to be what is called infinite, we may conceive the limit to be attained; but where there is no such tendency or approach, nothing is effected by lengthening the series. There is no difference as to the point in question, whatever there may be as to many points, between one series and another— between a series which is finite and a series which is infinite. A chain composed of an infinite number of links can no more support itself than a chain composed of a finite number of links. And of this we are assured, though we never *can* have tried the experiment; because, by increasing the number of links, from ten, for instance, to a hundred, from a hundred to a thousand, etc., we make not the smallest approach, we observe not the smallest tendency toward self-support. There is no difference in this respect—yet there may be a great difference in several respects—between a chain of a greater or less length, between one chain and another, between one that is finite and one that is infinite. This very much resembles the case before us. The machine which we are inspecting demonstrates, by its construction, contrivance and design. Contrivance must have had a contriver, design a designer, whether the machine immediately proceeded from another machine or not. That circumstance alters not the case. That other machine may, in like manner, have proceeded from a former machine; nor does that alter the case; the contrivance must have had a contriver. That former one from one preceding it: no alteration still; a contriver is still necessary. No tendency is perceived, no approach toward a diminution of this necessity. It is the same with any and every succession of these machines—a succession of ten, of a hundred, of a thousand; with one series, as with another—a series which is finite, as with a series which is infinite. In whatever other respects they may differ, in this they do not. In all equally, contrivance and design are unaccounted for.

The question is not simply, how came the first watch into existence?—which question, it may be pretended, is done away by supposing the series of watches thus produced from one another to have been infinite, and consequently to have had no such *first* for which it was necessary to provide a cause. This, perhaps, would have been nearly the state of the question, if nothing had been before us but an unorganized, unmechanized substance, without mark or indication of contrivance. It might be difficult to show that such substance could not have existed from eternity, either in succession—if it were possible, which I think it is not, for unorganized bodies to spring from one another—or by individual perpetuity. But that is not the question now. To suppose it to be so is to suppose that it made no difference whether he had found a watch or a stone. As it is, the metaphysics of that question have no place; for, in the watch which we are examining are seen contrivance, design, an end, a purpose, means for the end, adaptation to the purpose. And the question which irresistibly presses upon our thoughts is, whence this contrivance and design? The thing required is the intending mind, the adapted hand, the intelligence by which that hand was directed. This question, this demand is not shaken off by increasing a number or succession of substances destitute of these properties; nor the more, by increasing that number to infinity. If it be said that, upon the supposition of one watch being produced from another in the course of that other's movements and by means of the mechanism within it, we have a cause for the watch in my hand, namely, the watch from which it proceeded; I deny that for the design, the contrivance, the suitableness of means to an end, the adaptation of instruments to a use, all of which we discover in the watch, we have any cause whatever. It is in vain, therefore, to assign a series of such causes or to allege that a series may be carried back to infinity; for I do not admit that we have yet any cause at all for the phenomena, still less any series of causes either finite or infinite. Here is contrivance but no contriver; proofs of design, but no designer.

V. Our observer would further also reflect that the maker of the watch before him was in truth and reality the maker of every watch produced from it: there being no difference, except that the latter manifests a more exquisite skill, between the making of another watch with his own hands, by the mediation of files, lathes, chisels, etc., and the disposing, fixing, and inserting of these instruments, or of others equivalent to them, in the body of the watch already made, in such a manner as to form a new watch in the course of the movements which he had given to the old one. It is only working by one set of tools instead of another.

The conclusion which the *first* examination of the watch, of its works, construction, and movement, suggested, was that it must have had, for cause and author of that construction, an artificer who understood its mechanism and designed its use. This conclusion is invincible. A *second* examination presents us with a new discovery. The watch is found, in the course of its movement, to produce another watch similar to itself; and not only so, but we perceive in it a system or organization separately calculated for that purpose. What effect would this discovery have or ought it to have upon our former inference? What, as has already been said, but to increase beyond measure our admiration of the skill which had been employed in the formation of such a machine? Or shall it, instead of this, all at once turn us round to an opposite conclusion, namely, that no art or skill whatever has been concerned in the business, although all other evidences of art and skill remain as they were, and this last and supreme piece of art be now added to the rest? Can this be maintained without absurdity? Yet this is atheism.

CHAPTER FIVE

Every observation which was made in our first chapter concerning the watch may be repeated with strict propriety concerning the eye, concerning animals, concerning plants, concerning, indeed, all the organized parts of the works of nature. As,

I. When we are inquiring simply after the *existence* of an intelligent Creator, imperfection, inaccuracy, liability to disorder, occasional irregularities may subsist in a considerable degree without inducing any doubt into the question; just as a watch may frequently go wrong, seldom perhaps exactly right, may be faulty in some parts, defective in some, without the smallest ground of suspicion from thence arising that it was not a watch, or not made for the purpose ascribed to it. When faults are pointed out, and when a question is started concerning the skill of the artist or the dexterity with which the work is executed, then, indeed, in order to defend these qualities from accusation, we must be able either to expose some intractableness and imperfection in the materials or point out some invincible difficulty in the execution, into which imperfection and difficulty the matter of complaint may be resolved; or, if we cannot do this, we must adduce such specimens of consummate art and contrivance proceeding from the same hand as may convince the inquirer of the existence, in the case before him, of impediments like those which we have mentioned, although, what from the nature of the case is very likely to happen, they be unknown and unperceived by him. This we must do in order to vindicate the artist's skill, or at least the perfection of it; as we must also judge of his intention and of the provisions employed in fulfilling that intention, not from an instance in which they fail but from the great plurality of instances in which they succeed. But, after all, these are different questions from the question of the artist's existence; or, which is the same, whether the thing before us be a work of art or not; and the questions ought always to be kept separate in the mind. So likewise it is in the works of nature. Irregularities and imperfections are of little or no weight in the consideration when that consideration relates simply to the existence of a Creator. When the argument respects his attributes, they are of weight; but are then to be taken in conjunction—the attention is not to rest upon them, but they are to be taken in conjunction with the unexceptional evidences which we possess of skill, power, and benevolence displayed in other instances; which evidences may, in strength, number, and variety, be such and may so overpower apparent blemishes as to induce us, upon the most reasonable ground, to believe that these last ought to be referred to some cause, though we be ignorant of it, other than defect of knowledge or of benevolence in the author.

II. There may be also parts of plants and animals, as there were supposed to be of the watch, of which in some instances the operation, in others the use, is unknown. These form different cases; for the operation may be unknown, yet the use be certain. Thus it is with the lungs of animals. It does not, I think, appear that we are acquainted with the action of the air upon the blood, or in what manner that action is communicated by the lungs; yet we find that a very short suspension of their office destroys the life of the animal. In this case, therefore, we may be said to know the use, nay, we experience the necessity of the organ though we be ignorant of its operation. Nearly the same thing may be observed of what is called the lymphatic system. We suffer grievous inconveniences from its disorder, without being informed of the office which it sustains in the economy of our bodies. There may possibly also be some few examples of the second class in which not only the operation is unknown, but in which experiments may seem to prove that the part is not necessary; or may leave a doubt how far it is even useful to the plant or animal in which it is found. This is said to be the case with the spleen, which has been extracted from dogs without any sensible injury to their vital functions. Instances of the former kind, namely, in which we cannot explain the operation, may be numerous; for they will be so in proportion to our ignorance. They will be more or fewer to different persons, and in different stages of science. Every improvement of knowledge diminishes their number. There is hardly, perhaps, a year passes that does not in the works of nature bring some operation or some mode of operation to light, which was before undiscovered—probably unsuspected. Instances of the second kind, namely, where the part appears to be totally useless, I believe to be extremely rare; compared with the number of those of which the use is evident, they are beneath any assignable proportion and perhaps have been never submitted to trial and examination sufficiently accurate, long enough continued, or often enough repeated. No accounts which I have seen are satisfactory. The mutilated animal may live and grow fat—as was the case of the dog deprived of its spleen—yet may be defective in some other of its functions, which, whether they can all, or in what degree of vigor and perfection, be performed, or how long preserved without the extirpated organ, does not seem to be ascertained by experiment. But to this case, even were it fully made out, may be applied the consideration which we suggested concerning the watch, namely, that these superfluous parts do not negative the reasoning which we instituted concerning those parts which are useful, and of which we know the use; the indication of contrivance with respect to them remains as it was before.

III. One atheistic way of replying to our observations upon the works of nature, and to the proofs of a Deity which we think that we perceive in them, is to tell us that all which we see must necessarily have had some form, and that it might as well be its present form as any other. Let us now apply this answer to the eye, as we did before to the watch. Something or other must have occupied that place in the animal's head, must have filled up, as we say, the socket; we will say also, that it must have been of that sort of substance which we call animal substance, as flesh, bone, membrane, or cartilage, etc. But that it should have been an *eye*, knowing as we do what an eye comprehends, namely, that it should have consisted, first, of a series of transparent lenses—very different, by the by, even in their substance, from the opaque materials of which the rest of the body is, in general at least, composed, and with which the whole of its surface, this single portion of it excepted, is covered; secondly, of a black cloth or canvas—the only membrane in the body which is black—spread out behind these lenses, so as to receive the image formed by pencils of light transmitted through them, and at which alone a distinct image could be formed, namely, at the concourse of the refracted rays; thirdly, of a large nerve communicating between this membrane and the brain, without which the action of light upon the membrane, however modified by the organ, would be lost to the purposes of sensation; that this fortunate conformation of parts should have been the lot not of one individual out of many thousand individuals, like the great prize in a lottery or like some singularity in nature, but the happy chance of a whole species; nor of one species out of many thousand species with which we are acquainted, but of by far the greatest number of all that exist, and that under varieties not causal or capricious, but bearing marks of being suited to their respective exigencies; that all this should have taken place merely because something must have occupied these points on every animal's forehead, or that all this should be thought to be accounted for by the short answer that "whatever was there must have had some form or other" is too absurd to be made more so by any argumentation. We are not contented with this answer; we find no satisfaction in it, by way of accounting for appearances of organization far short of those of the eye, such as we observe in fossil shells, petrified bones, or other substances which bear the vestiges of animal or vegetable recrements, but which, either in respect to utility or of the situation in which they are discovered, may seem accidental enough. It is no way of accounting even for these things, to say that the stone, for instance, which is shown to us—supposing the question to be concerning a petrifaction—must have contained some internal conformation or other. Nor does it mend the answer to add, with respect to the singularity of the conformation, that after the event it is no longer to be computed what the chances were against it. This is always to be computed when the question is whether a useful or imitative conformation be the product of chance or not: I desire no greater certainty in reasoning than that by which chance is excluded from the present disposition of the natural world. Universal experience is against it. What does chance ever do for us? In the human body, for instance, chance, that is, the operation of causes without design, may produce a wen, a wart, a mole, a pimple, but never an eye. Among inanimate substances, a clod, a pebble, a liquid drop might be; but never was a watch, a telescope, an organized body of any kind, answering a valuable purpose by a complicated mechanism, the effect of chance. In no assignable instance has such a thing existed without intention somewhere.

IV. There is another answer which has the same effect as the resolving of things into chance, which answer would persuade us to believe that the eye, the animal to which it belongs, every other animal, every plant, indeed every organized body which we see are only so many out of the possible varieties and combinations of being which the lapse of infinite ages has brought into existence; that the present world is the relic of that variety; millions of other bodily forms and other species having perished, being, by the defect of their constitution, incapable of preservation, or of continuance by generation. Now there is no foundation whatever for this conjecture in any thing which we observe in the works of nature; no such experiments are going on at present—no such energy operates as that which is here supposed, and which should be constantly pushing into existence new varieties of beings. Nor are there any appearances to support an opinion that every possible combination of vegetable or animal structure has formerly been tried. Multitudes of conformation, both of vegetables and animals, may be conceived capable of existence and succession, which yet do not exist. Perhaps almost as many forms of plants might have been found in the fields as figures of plants can be delineated upon paper. A countless variety of animals might have existed which do not exist. Upon the supposition here stated, we should see unicorns and mermaids, sylphs and centaurs, the fancies of painters and the fables of poets, realized by examples. Or, if it be alleged that these may transgress the bounds of possible life and propagation, we might at least have nations of human beings without nails upon their fingers, with more or fewer fingers and toes than ten, some with one eye, others with one ear, with one nostril, or without the sense of smelling at all. All these and a thousand other imaginable varieties might live and propagate. We may modify any one species many different ways, all consistent with life, and with the actions necessary to preservation, although affording different degrees of conveniency and enjoyment to the animal. And if we carry these modifications through the different species which are known to subsist, their number would be incalculable. No reason can be given why, if these deperdits ever existed, they have now disappeared. Yet, if all possible existences have been tried, they must have formed part of the catalogue.

But, moreover, the division of organized substances into animals and vegetables, and the distribution and subdistribution of each into genera and species, which distribution is not an arbitrary act of the mind, but founded in the order which prevails in external nature, appear to me to contradict the supposition of the present world being the remains of an indefinite variety of existences—of a variety which rejects all plan. The hypothesis teaches that every possible variety of being has at one time or other found its way into existence—by what cause or in what manner is not said—and that those which were badly formed perished; but how or why those which survived should be cast, as we see that plants and animals are cast, into regular classes, the hypothesis does not explain; or rather the hypothesis is inconsistent with this phenomenon.

The hypothesis, indeed, is hardly deserving of the consideration which we have given it. What should we think of a man who, because we had never ourselves seen watches, telescopes, stocking mills, steam engines, etc., made, knew not how they were made, nor could prove by testimony when they were made, or by whom, would have us believe that these machines, instead of deriving their curious structures from the thought and design of their inventors and contrivers, in truth derive them from no other origin than this: namely, that a mass of metals and other materials having run, when melted, into all possible figures, and combined themselves in all possible forms and shapes and proportions, these things which we see are what were left from the incident, as best worth preserving, and as such are become the remaining stock of a magazine which at one time or other, has by this means contained every mechanism, useful and useless, convenient and inconvenient, into which such like materials could be thrown? I cannot distinguish the hypothesis, as applied to the works of nature, from this solution, which no one would accept as applied to a collection of machines.

DAVID HUME

Criticisms of the Analogy

Not to lose any time in circumlocutions, said Cleanthes, addressing himself to Demea, much less in replying to the pious declamations of Philo, I shall briefly explain how I conceive this matter. Look round the world: Contemplate the whole and every part of it: You will find it to be nothing but one great machine, subdivided into an infinite number of lesser machines, which again admit of subdivisions to a degree beyond what human senses and faculties can trace and explain. All these various machines, and even their most minute parts, are adjusted to each other with an accuracy which ravishes into admiration all men who have ever contemplated them. The curious adapting of means to ends, throughout all nature, resembles exactly, though it much exceeds, the productions of human contrivance—of human design, thought, wisdom, and intelligence. Since therefore the effects resemble each other, we are led to infer, by all the rules of analogy, that the causes also resemble, and that the Author of Nature is somewhat similar to the mind of man, though possessed of much larger faculties, proportioned to the grandeur of the work which he has executed. By this argument *a posteriori*, and by this argument alone, do we prove at once the existence of a Deity and his similarity to human mind and intelligence.

I shall be so free, Cleanthes, said Demea, as to tell you that from the beginning I could not approve of your conclusion concerning the similarity of the Deity to men, still less can I approve of the mediums by which you endeavor to establish it. What! No demonstration of the Being of God! No abstract arguments! No proofs *a priori!* Are these which have hitherto been so much insisted on by philosophers all fallacy, all sophism? Can we reach no farther in this subject than experience and probability? I will say not that this is betraying the cause of a Deity; but surely, by this affected candor, you give advantages to atheists which they never could obtain by the mere dint of argument and reasoning.

From David Hume, *Dialogues Concerning Natural Religion* (1779), Parts II, V, and VIII.

What I chiefly scruple in this subject, said Philo, is not so much that all religious arguments are by Cleanthes reduced to experience, as that they appear not to be even the most certain and irrefragable of that inferior kind. That a stone will fall, that fire will burn, that the earth has solidity, we have observed a thousand and a thousand times; and when any new instance of this nature is presented, we draw without hesitation the accustomed inference. The exact similarity of the cases gives us a perfect assurance of a similar event, and a stronger evidence is never desired nor sought after. But wherever you depart, in the least, from the similarity of the cases, you diminish proportionably the evidence; and may at last bring it to a very weak *analogy*, which is confessedly liable to error and uncertainty. After having experienced the circulation of the blood in human creatures, we make no doubt that it takes place in Titius and Maevius; but from its circulation in frogs and fishes it is only a presumption, though a strong one, from analogy that it takes place in men and other animals. The analogical reasoning is much weaker when we infer the circulation of the sap in vegetables from our experience that the blood circulates in animals; and those who hastily followed that imperfect analogy are found, by more accurate experiments, to have been mistaken.

If we see a house, Cleanthes, we conclude, with the greatest certainty, that it had an architect or builder because this is precisely that species of effect which we have experienced to proceed from that species of cause. But surely you will not affirm that the universe bears such a resemblance to a house that we can with the same certainty infer a similar cause, or that the analogy is here entire and perfect. The dissimilitude is so striking that the utmost you can here pretend to is a guess, a conjecture, a presumption concerning a similar cause; and how that pretension will be received in the world, I leave you to consider.

It would surely be very ill received, replied Cleanthes; and I should be deservedly blamed and detested did I allow that the proofs of a Deity amounted to no more than a guess or conjecture. But is the whole adjustment of means to ends in a house and in the universe so slight a resemblance? the economy of final causes? the order, proportion, and arrangement of every part? Steps of a stair are plainly contrived that human legs may use them in mounting; and this inference is certain and infallible. Human legs are also contrived for walking and mounting; and this inference, I allow, is not altogether so certain because of the dissimilarity which you remark; but does it, therefore, deserve the name only of presumption or conjecture?

Good God! cried Demea, interrupting him, where are we? Zealous defenders of religion allow that the proofs of a Deity fall short of perfect evidence! And you, Philo, on whose assistance I depended in proving the adorable mysteriousness of the Divine Nature, do you assent to all these extravagant opinions of Cleanthes? For what other name can I give them? or, why spare my censure when such principles are advanced, supported by such an authority, before so young a man as Pamphilus?

You seem not to apprehend, replied Philo, that I argue with Cleanthes in his own way, and, by showing him the dangerous consequences of his tenets, hope at last to reduce him to our opinion. But what sticks most with you, I observe, is the representation which Cleanthes has made of the argument *a posteriori;* and, finding that the argument is likely to escape your hold and vanish into air, you think it so disguised that you can scarcely believe it to be set in its true light. Now, however much I may dissent, in other respects, from the dangerous principle of Cleanthes, I must allow that he has fairly represented that argument, and I shall endeavor so to state the matter to you that you will entertain no further scruples with regard to it.

Were a man to abstract from everything which he knows or has seen, he would be altogether incapable, merely from his own ideas, to determine what kind of scene the universe must be, or to give the preference to one state or situation of things above another. For as nothing which he clearly conceives could be esteemed impossible or implying a contradiction, every chimera of his fancy would be upon an equal footing; nor could he assign any just reason why he adheres to one idea or system, and rejects the others which are equally possible.

Again, after he opens his eyes and contemplates the world as it really is, it would be impossible for him at first to assign the cause of any one event, much less of the whole of things, or of the universe. He might set his fancy a rambling, and she might bring him in an infinite variety of reports and representations. These would all be possible; but, being all equally possible, he would never of himself give a satisfactory account for his preferring one of them to the rest. Experience alone can point out to him the true cause of any phenomenon.

Now, according to this method of reasoning, Demea, it follows (and is, indeed, tacitly allowed by Cleanthes himself) that order, arrangement, or the adjustment of final causes, is not of itself any proof of design, but only so far as it has been experienced to proceed from that principle. For aught we can know *a priori*, matter may contain the source or spring of order originally within itself, as well as mind does; and there is no more difficulty in conceiving that the several elements, from an internal unknown cause, may fall into the most exquisite arrangement, than to conceive that their ideas, in the great universal mind, from a like internal unknown cause, fall into that arrangement. The equal possibility of both these suppositions is allowed. But, by experience, we find (according to Cleanthes) that there is a difference between them. Throw several pieces of steel together, without shape or form, they will never arrange themselves so as to compose a watch. Stone and mortar and wood, without an architect, never erect a house. But the ideas in a human mind, we see, by an unknown, inexplicable economy, arrange themselves so as to form the plan of a watch or house. Experience, therefore, proves that there is an original principle of order in mind, not in matter. From similar effects we infer similar causes. The adjustment of means to ends is alike in the universe, as in a machine of human contrivance. The causes, therefore, must be resembling.

I was from the beginning scandalized, I must own, with this resemblance which is asserted between the Deity and human creatures, and must conceive it to imply such a degradation of the Supreme Being as no sound theist could endure. With your assistance, therefore, Demea, I shall endeavor to defend what you justly call the adorable mysteriousness of the Divine Nature, and shall refute this reasoning of Cleanthes, provided he allows that I have made a fair representation of it.

When Cleanthes had assented, Philo, after a short pause, proceeded in the following manner.

That all inferences, Cleanthes, concerning fact are founded on experience, and that all experimental reasonings are founded on the supposition that similar causes prove similar effects, and similar effects similar causes, I shall not at present much dispute with you. But observe, I entreat you, with what extreme caution all just reasoners proceed in the transferring of experiments to similar cases. Unless the cases be exactly similar, they repose no perfect confidence in applying their past observation to any particular phenomenon. Every alteration of circumstances occasions a doubt concerning the event; and it requires new experiments to prove certainly that the new circumstances are of no moment or importance. A change in bulk, situation, arrangement, age, disposition of the air, or surrounding bodies—any of these particulars may be attended with the most unexpected consequences. And unless the objects be quite familiar to us, it is the highest temerity to expect with assurance, after any of these changes, an event similar to that which before fell under our observation. The slow and deliberate steps of philosophers here, if anywhere, are distinguished from the precipitate march of the vulgar, who, hurried on by the smallest similitude, are incapable of all discernment or consideration.

But can you think, Cleanthes, that your usual phlegm and philosophy have been preserved in so wide a step as you have taken when you compared to the universe houses, ships, furniture, machines; and, from their similarity in some circumstances, inferred a similarity in their causes? Thought, design, intelligence, such as we discover in men and other animals, is no more than one of the springs and principles of the universe, as well as heat or cold, attraction or repulsion, and is a hundred others which fall under daily observation. It is an active cause by which some particular parts of nature, we find, produce alterations on other parts. But can a conclusion, with any propriety, be transferred from parts to the whole? Does not the great disproportion bar all comparison and inference? From observing the growth of a hair, can we learn anything concerning the generation of a man? Would the manner of a leaf's blowing, even though perfectly known, afford us any instruction concerning the vegetation of a tree?

But allowing that we were to take the *operations* of one part of nature upon another for the foundation of our judgment concerning the *origin* of the whole (which never can be admitted), yet why select so minute, so weak, so bounded a principle as the reason and design of animals is found to be upon this planet? What peculiar privilege has this little agitation of the brain which we call *thought*, that we must thus make it the model of the whole universe? Our partiality in our own favor does indeed present it on all occasions, but sound philosophy ought carefully to guard against so natural an illusion.

So far from admitting, continued Philo, that the operations of a part can afford us any just conclusion concerning the origin of the whole, I will not allow any one part to form a rule for another part if the latter be very remote from the former. Is there any reasonable ground to conclude that the inhabitants of other planets possess thought, intelligence, reason, or anything similar to these faculties in men? When nature has so extremely diversified her manner of operation in this small globe, can we imagine that she incessantly copies herself throughout so immense a universe? And if thought, as we may well suppose, be confined merely to this narrow corner and has even there so limited a sphere of action, with what propriety can we assign it for the original cause of all things? The narrow views of a peasant who makes his domestic economy the rule for the government of kingdoms is in comparison a pardonable sophism.

But were we ever so much assured that a thought and reason resembling the human were to be found throughout the whole universe, and were its activity elsewhere vastly greater and more commanding than it appears in this globe; yet I cannot see why the operations of a world constituted, arranged, adjusted, can with any propriety be extended to a world which is in its embryo-state, and is advancing towards that constitution and arrangement. By observation we know somewhat of the economy, action, and nourishment of a finished animal; but we must transfer with great caution that observation to the growth of a foetus in the womb, and still more to the formation of an animalcule in the loins of its male parent. Nature, we find, even from our limited experience, possesses an infinite number of springs and principles which incessantly discover themselves on every change of her position and situation. And what new and unknown principles would actuate her in so new and unknown a situation as that of the formation of a universe, we cannot, without the utmost temerity, pretend to determine.

A very small part of this great system, during a very short time, is very imperfectly discovered to us; and do we thence pronounce decisively concerning the origin of the whole?

Admirable conclusion! Stone, wood, brick, iron, brass, have not, at this time, in this minute globe of earth, an order or arrangement without human art and contrivance; therefore, the universe could not originally attain its order and arrangement without something similar to human art. But is a part of nature a rule for another part very wide of the former? Is it a rule for the whole? Is a very small part a rule for the universe? Is nature in one situation a certain rule for nature in another situation vastly different from the former?

And can you blame me, Cleanthes, if I here imitate the prudent reserve of Simonides, who, according to the noted story, being asked by Hiero, *What God was?* desired a day to think of it, and then two days more; and after that manner continually prolonged the term, without ever bringing in his definition or description? Could you even blame me if I had answered, at first, *that I did not know,* and was sensible that this subject lay vastly beyond the reach of my faculties? You might cry out sceptic and railer, as much as you pleased; but, having found in so many other subjects much more familiar the imperfections and even contradictions of human reason, I never should expect any success from its feeble conjectures in a subject so sublime and so remote from the sphere of our observation. When two *species* of objects have always been observed to be conjoined together, I can *infer,* by custom, the existence of one wherever I *see* the existence of the other; and this I call an argument from experience. But how this argument can have place where the objects, as in the present case, are single, individual, without parallel or specific resemblance, may be difficult to explain. And will any man tell me with a serious countenance that an orderly universe must arise from some thought and art like the human because we have experience of it? To ascertain this reasoning it were requisite that we had experience of the origin of worlds; and it is not sufficient, surely, that we have seen ships and cities arise from human art and contrivance....

Now, Cleanthes, said Philo, with an air of alacrity and triumph, mark the consequences. *First,* by this method of reasoning you renounce all claim to infinity in any of the attributes of the Deity. For, as the cause ought only to be proportioned to the effect, and the effect, so far as it falls under our cognizance, is not infinite, what pretensions have we, upon your suppositions, to ascribe that attribute to the divine Being? You will still insist that, by removing him so much from all similarity to human creatures, we give in to the most arbitrary hypothesis, and at the same time weaken all proofs of his existence.

Secondly, you have no reason, on your theory, for ascribing perfection to the Deity, even in his finite capacity; or for supposing him free from every error, mistake, or incoherence, in his undertakings. There are many inexplicable difficulties in the works of nature which, if we allow a perfect author to be proved *a priori*, are easily solved, and become only seeming difficulties from the narrow capacity of man, who cannot trace infinite relations. But according to your method of reasoning, these difficulties become all real; and, perhaps, will be insisted on as new instances of likeness to human art and contrivance. At least, you must acknowledge that it is impossible for us to tell, from our limited views, whether this system contains any great faults or deserves any considerable praise if compared to other possible and even real systems. Could a peasant, if the *Aeneid* were read to him, pronounce that poem to be absolutely faultless, or even assign to it its proper rank among the productions of human wit, he who had never seen any other production?

But were this world ever so perfect a production, it must still remain uncertain whether all the excellences of the work can justly be ascribed to the workman. If we survey a ship, what an exalted idea must we form of the ingenuity of the carpenter who framed so complicated, useful, and beautiful a machine? And what surprise must we feel when we find him a stupid mechanic who imitated others, and copied an art which, through a long succession of ages, after multiplied trials, mistakes, corrections, deliberations, and controversies, had been gradually improving? Many worlds might have been botched and bungled, throughout an eternity, ere this system was struck out; much labor lost; many fruitless trials made; and a slow but continued improvement carried on during infinite ages in the art of world-making. In such subjects, who can determine where the truth, nay, who can conjecture where the probability lies, amidst a great number of hypotheses which may be proposed, and a still greater which may be imagined?

And what shadow of an argument, continued Philo, can you produce from your hypothesis to prove the unity of the Deity? A great number of men join in building a house or ship, in rearing a city, in framing a commonwealth; why may not several deities combine in contriving and framing a world? This is only so much greater similarity to human affairs. By sharing the work among several, we may so much further limit the attributes of each, and get rid of that extensive power and knowledge which must be supposed in one deity, and which, according to you, can only serve to weaken the proof of his existence. And if such foolish, such vicious creatures as man can yet often unite in framing and executing one plan, how much more those deities or demons, whom we may suppose several degrees more perfect?

To multiply causes without necessity is indeed contrary to true philosophy, but this principle applies not to the present case. Were one deity antecedently proved by your theory who were possessed of every attribute requisite to the production of the universe, it would be needless, I own (though not absurd), to suppose any other deity existent. But while it is still a question whether all these attributes are united in one subject or dispersed among several independent beings; by what phenomena in nature can we pretend to decide the controversy? Where we see a body raised in a scale, we are sure that there is in the opposite scale, however concealed from sight, some counterposing weight equal to it; but it is still allowed to doubt whether that weight be an aggregate of several distinct bodies or one uniform united mass. And if the weight requisite very much exceeds anything which we have ever seen conjoined in any single body, the former supposition becomes still more probable and natural. An intelligent being of such vast power and capacity as is necessary to produce the universe—or, to speak in the language of ancient philosophy, so prodigious an animal—exceeds all analogy and even comprehension.

But further, Cleanthes, men are mortal, and renew their species by generation; and this is common to all living creatures. The two great sexes of male and female, says Milton, animate the world. Why must this circumstance, so universal, so essential, be executed from those numerous and limited deities? Behold, then, the theogeny of ancient times brought back upon us.

And why not become a perfect anthropomorphite? Why not assert the deity or deities to be corporeal, and to have eyes, a nose, mouth, ears, etc.? Epicurus maintained that no man had ever seen reason but in a human figure; therefore, the gods must have a human figure. And this argument, which is deservedly so much ridiculed by Cicero, becomes, according to you, solid and philosophical.

In a word, Cleanthes, a man who follows your hypothesis is able, perhaps, to assert or conjecture that the universe sometime arose from something like design; but beyond that position he cannot ascertain one single circumstance, and is left afterwards to fix every point of his theology by the utmost license of fancy and hypothesis. This world, for aught he knows, is very faulty and imperfect, compared to a superior standard; and was only the first rude essay of some infant deity who afterwards abandoned it, ashamed of his lame performance; it is the work only of some dependent, inferior deity, and is the object of derision to his superiors; it is the production of old age and dotage in some superannuated deity; and ever since his death has run on at adventures, from the first impulse and active force which it received from him. You justly give signs of horror, Demea, at these strange suppositions; but these, and a thousand more of the same kind, are Cleanthes' suppositions, not mine. From the moment the attributes of the Deity are supposed finite, all these have place. And I cannot, for my part, think that so wild and unsettled a system of theology is, in any respect, preferable to none at all....

What you ascribe to the fertility of my invention, replied Philo, is entirely owing to the nature of the subject. In subjects adapted to the narrow compass of human reason there is commonly but one determination which carries probability or conviction with it; and to a man of sound judgment all other suppositions but that one appear entirely absurd and chimerical. But in such questions as the present, a hundred contradictory views may preserve a kind of imperfect analogy, and invention has here full scope to exert itself. Without any great effort of thought, I believe that I could, in an instant, propose other systems of cosmogony which would have some faint appearance of truth; though it is a thousand, a million to one if either yours or any one of mine be the true system.

For instance, what if I should revive the old Epicurean hypothesis? This is commonly, and I believe justly, esteemed the most absurd system that has yet been proposed; yet I know not whether, with a few alterations, it might not be brought to bear a faint appearance of probability. Instead of supposing matter infinite, as Epicurus did, let us suppose it finite. A finite number of particles is only susceptible of finite transpositions; and it must happen, in an eternal duration, that every possible order or position must be tried an infinite number of times. This world, therefore, with all its events, even the most minute, has before been produced and destroyed, and will again be produced and destroyed, without any bounds and limitations. No one who has a conception of the powers of infinite, in comparison of finite, will ever scruple this determination.

But this supposes, said Demea, that matter can acquire motion without any voluntary agent or first mover.

And where is the difficulty, replied Philo, of that supposition? Every event, before experience, is equally difficult and incomprehensible; and every event, after experience, is equally easy and intelligible. Motion, in many instances, from gravity, from elasticity, from electricity, begins in matter, without any known voluntary agent; and to suppose always, in these cases, an unknown voluntary agent is mere hypothesis—and hypothesis attended with no advantages. The beginning of motion in matter itself is as conceivable *a priori* as its communication from mind and intelligence.

Besides, why may not motion have been propagated by impulse through all eternity, and the same stock of it, or nearly the same, be still upheld in the universe? As much as is lost by the composition of motion, as much is gained by its resolution. And whatever the causes are, the fact is certain that matter is and always has been in continual agitation, as far as human experience or tradition reaches. There is not probably, at present, in the whole universe, one particle of matter at absolute rest.

And this very consideration, too, continued Philo, which we have stumbled on in the course of the argument suggests a new hypothesis of cosmogony that is not absolutely absurd and improbable. Is there a system, an order, an economy of things, by which matter can preserve that perpetual agitation which seems essential to it, and yet maintain a constancy in the forms which it produces? There certainly is such an economy, for this is actually the case with the present world. The continual motion of matter, therefore, in less than infinite transpositions, must produce this economy or order; and, by its very nature, that order, when once established, supports itself for many ages if not to eternity. But wherever matter is so poised, arranged, and adjusted, as to continue in perpetual motion, and yet preserve a constancy in the forms, its situation must, of necessity, have all the same appearance of art and contrivance which we observe at present. All the parts of each form must have a relation to each other and to the whole; and the whole itself must have a relation to the other parts of the universe, to the element in which the form subsists, to the materials with which it repairs its waste and decay, and to every other form which is hostile or friendly. A defect in any of these particulars destroys the form; and the matter of which it is composed is again set loose, and is thrown into irregular motions and fermentations till it unite itself to some other regular form. If no such form be prepared to receive it, and if there be a great quantity of this corrupted matter in the universe, the universe itself is entirely disordered, whether it be the feeble embryo of a world in its first beginnings that is thus destroyed or the rotten carcass of one languishing in old age and infirmity. In either case, a chaos ensues till infinite though innumerable revolutions produce, at last, some forms whose parts and organs are so adjusted as to support the forms amidst a continued succession of matter.

Suppose (for we shall endeavor to vary the expression) that matter were thrown into any position by a blind, unguided force; it is evident that this first position must, in all probability, be the most confused and most disorderly imaginable, without any resemblance to those works of human contrivance which, along with a symmetry of parts, discover an adjustment of means to ends and a tendency to self-preservation. If the actuating force cease after this operation, matter must remain forever in disorder, and continue an immense chaos, without any proportion or activity. But suppose that the actuating force, whatever it be, still continues in matter, this first position will immediately give place to a second which will likewise, in all probability, be as disorderly as the first, and so on through many successions of changes and revolutions. No particular order or position ever continues a moment unaltered. The original force, still remaining in activity, gives a perpetual restlessness to matter. Every possible situation is produced, and instantly destroyed. If a glimpse or dawn of order appears for a moment, it is instantly hurried away and confounded by that never-ceasing force which actuates every part of matter.

Thus the universe goes on for many ages in a continued succession of chaos and disorder. But is it not possible that it may settle at last, so as not to lose its motion and active force (for that we have supposed inherent in it), yet so as to preserve a uniformity of appearance, amidst the continual motion and fluctuation of its parts? This we find to be the case with the universe at present. Every individual is perpetually changing, and every part of every individual; and yet the whole remains, in appearance, the same. May we not hope for such a position or rather be assured of it from the eternal revolutions of unguided matter; and may not this account for all the appearing wisdom and contrivance which is in the universe? Let us contemplate the subject a little, and we shall find that this adjustment if attained by matter of a seeming stability in the forms, with a real and perpetual revolution or motion of parts, affords a plausible, if not a true, solution of the difficulty.

It is in vain, therefore, to insist upon the uses of the parts in animals or vegetables, and their curious adjustment to each other. I would fain know how an animal could subsist unless its parts were so adjusted? Do we not find that it immediately perishes whenever this adjustment ceases, and that its matter, corrupting, tries some new form? It happens indeed that the parts of the world are so well adjusted that some regular form immediately lays claim to this corrupted matter; and if it were not so, could the world subsist? Must it not dissolve, as well as the animal, and pass through new positions and situations till in great but finite succession it fall, at last, into the present or some such order?

It is well, replied Cleanthes, you told us that this hypothesis was suggested on a sudden, in the course of the argument. Had you had leisure to examine it, you would soon have perceived the insuperable objections to which it is exposed. No form, you say, can subsist unless it possess those powers and organs requisite for its subsistence; some new order or economy must be tried, and so on, without intermission, till at last some order which can support and maintain itself is fallen upon. But according to this hypothesis, whence arise the many conveniences and advantages which men and all animals possess? Two eyes, two ears are not absolutely necessary for the subsistence of the species. Human race might have been propagated and preserved without horses, dogs, cows, sheep, and those innumerable fruits and products which serve to our satisfaction and enjoyment. If no camels had been created for the use of man in the sandy deserts of Africa and Arabia, would the world have been dissolved? If no loadstone had been framed to give that wonderful and useful direction to the needle, would human society and the human kind have been immediately extinguished? Though the maxims of nature be in general very frugal, yet instances of this kind are far from being rare; and any one of them is a sufficient proof of design—and of a benevolent design—which gave rise to the order and arrangement of the universe.

At least, you may safely infer, said Philo, that the foregoing hypothesis is so far incomplete and imperfect, which I shall not scruple to allow. But can we ever reasonably expect greater success in any attempts of this nature? Or can we ever hope to erect a system of cosmogony that will be liable to no exceptions, and will contain no circumstance repugnant to our limited and imperfect experience of the analogy of nature? Your theory itself cannot surely pretend to any such advantage; even though you have run into *anthropomorphism*, the better to preserve a conformity to common experience. Let us once more put it to trial. In all instances which we have ever seen, ideas are copied from real objects, and are ectypal, not archetypal, to express myself in learned terms. You reverse this order and give thought the precedence. In all instances which we have ever seen, thought has no influence upon matter except where that matter is so conjoined with it as to have an equal reciprocal influence upon it. No animal can move immediately anything but the members of its own body; and, indeed, the equality of action and reaction seems to be an universal law of nature; but your theory implies a contradiction to this experience. These instances, with many more which it were easy to collect (particularly the supposition of a mind or system of thought that is eternal or, in other words, an animal ingenerable and immortal)—these instances, I say, may teach all of us sobriety in condemning each other, and let us see that as no system of this kind ought ever to be received from a slight analogy, so neither ought any to be rejected on account of a small incongruity. For that is an inconvenience from which we can justly pronounce no one to be exempted.

All religious systems, it is confessed, are subject to great and insuperable difficulties. Each disputant triumphs in his turn, while he carries on an offensive war, and exposes the absurdities, barbarities, and pernicious tenets of his antagonist. But all of them, on the whole, prepare a complete triumph for the *sceptic*, who tells them that no system ought ever to be embraced with regard to such subjects; for this plain reason, that no absurdity ought ever to be assented to with regard to any subject. A total suspense of judgment is here our only reasonable resource. And if every attack, as is commonly observed, and no defence among theologians is successful, how complete must be *his* victory who remains always, with all mankind, on the offensive, and has himself no fixed station or abiding city which he is ever, on any occasion, obliged to defend?

J. S. MILL

God's Attributes and the Argument from Design

The question of the existence of a Deity, in its purely scientific aspect, standing as is shown in the First Part, it is next to be considered, given the indications of a Deity, what *sort* of a Deity do they point to? What attributes are we warranted, by the evidence which nature affords of a creative mind, in assigning to that mind?

It needs no showing that the power, if not the intelligence, must be so far superior to that of man as to surpass all human estimate. But from this to omnipotence and omniscience there is a wide interval. And the distinction is of immense practical importance.

It is not too much to say that every indication of design in the cosmos is so much evidence against the omnipotence of the designer. For what is meant by design? Contrivance: the adaptation of means to an end. But the necessity for contrivance—the need of employing means—is a consequence of the limitation of power. Who would have recourse to means if to attain his end his mere word was sufficient? The very idea of means implies that the means have an efficacy which the direct action of the being who employs them has not. Otherwise they are not means but an encumbrance. A man does not use machinery to move his arms. If he did, it could only be when paralysis had deprived him of the power of moving them by volition. But if the employment of contrivance is in itself a sign of limited power, how much more so is the careful and skillful choice of contrivances? Can any wisdom be shown in the selection of means when the means have no efficacy but what is given them by the will of him who employs them, and when his will could have bestowed the same efficacy on any other means? Wisdom and contrivance are shown in overcoming difficulties, and there is no room for them in a being for whom no difficulties exist. The evidences, therefore, of natural theology distinctly imply that the author of the cosmos worked under limitations; that he was obliged to adapt himself to conditions independent of his will and to attain his ends by such arrangements as those conditions admitted of.

And this hypothesis agrees with what we have seen to be the tendency of the evidences in another respect. We found that the appearances in nature point indeed to an origin of the cosmos or order in nature, and indicate that

From J. S. Mill, *Theism*, Part II.

origin to be design, but do not point to any commencement, still less creation, of the two great elements of the universe, the passive element and the active element, matter and force. There is in nature no reason whatever to suppose that either matter or force, or any of their properties, were made by the being who was the author of the collocations by which the world is adapted to what we consider as its purposes; or that he has power to alter any of those properties. It is only when we consent to entertain this negative supposition that there arises a need for wisdom and contrivance in the order of the universe. The Deity had on this hypothesis to work out his ends by combining materials of a given nature and properties. Out of these materials he had to construct a world in which his designs should be carried into effect through given properties of matter and force, working together and fitting into one another. This did require skill and contrivance, and the means by which it is effected are often such as justly excite our wonder and admiration; but exactly because it requires wisdom, it implies limitation of power, or rather the two phrases express different sides of the same fact.

If it be said that an Omnipotent Creator, though under no necessity of employing contrivances such as man must use, thought fit to do so in order to leave traces by which man might recognize his creative hand, the answer is that this equally supposes a limit to his omnipotence. For if it was his will that men should know that they themselves and the world are his work, he, being omnipotent, had only to will that they should be aware of it. Ingenious men have sought for reasons why God might choose to leave his existence so far a matter of doubt that men should not be under an absolute necessity of knowing it, as they are of knowing that three and two make five. These imagined reasons are very unfortunate specimens of casuistry; but even did we admit their validity, they are of no avail on the supposition of omnipotence, since if it did not please God to implant in man a complete conviction of his existence, nothing hindered him from making the conviction fall short of completeness by any margin he chose to leave. It is usual to dispose of arguments of this description by the easy answer that we do not know what wise reasons the Omniscient may have had for leaving undone things which he had the power to do. It is not perceived that this plea itself implies a limit to omnipotence. When a thing is obviously good and obviously in accordance with what all the evidences of creation imply to have been the Creator's design, and we say we do not know what good reason he may have had for not doing it, we mean that we do not know to what other, still better object—to what object still more completely in the line of his purposes, he may have seen fit to postpone it. But the necessity of postponing one thing to another belongs only to limited power. Omnipotence could have made the objects compatible. Omnipotence does not need to weigh one consideration against another. If the Creator, like a human ruler, had to adapt himself to a set of conditions which he did not make, it is as unphilosophical as presumptuous in us to call him to account for any imperfections in his work, to complain that he left anything in it contrary to what, if the indications of design prove anything, he must have intended. He must at least know more than we know, and we cannot judge what greater good would have had to be sacrificed or what greater evil incurred if he had decided to remove this particular blot. Not so if he be omnipotent. If he be that, he must himself have willed that the two desirable objects should be incompatible; he must himself have willed that the obstacle to his supposed design should be insuperable. It cannot therefore *be* his design. It will not do to say that it was, but that he had other designs which interfered with it; for no one purpose imposes necessary limitations on another in the case of a Being not restricted by conditions of possibility.

Omnipotence, therefore, cannot be predicated of the Creator on grounds of natural theology. The fundamental principles of natural religion as deduced from the facts of the universe negate his omnipotence. They do not, in the same manner, exclude omniscience: if we suppose limitation of power, there is nothing to contradict the supposition of perfect knowledge and absolute wisdom. But neither is there anything to prove it. The knowledge of the powers and properties of things necessary for planning and executing the arrangements of the cosmos is no doubt as much in excess of human knowledge as the power implied in creation is in excess of human power. And the skill, the subtlety of contrivance, the ingenuity as it would be called in the case of a human work, is often marvelous. But nothing obliges us to suppose that either the knowledge or the skill is infinite. We are not even compelled to suppose that the contrivances were always the best possible. If we venture to judge them as we judge the works of human artificers, we find abundant defects. The human body, for example, is one of the most striking instances of artful and ingenious contrivance which nature offers, but we may well ask whether so complicated a machine could not have been made to last longer and not to get so easily and frequently out of order. We may ask why the human race should have been so constituted as to grovel in wretchedness and degradation for countless ages before a small portion of it was enabled to lift itself into the very imperfect state of intelligence, goodness, and happiness which we enjoy. The divine power may not have been equal to doing more; the obstacles to a better arrangement of things may have been insuperable. But it is also possible that they were not. The skill of the *demiourgos* was sufficient to produce what we see; but we cannot tell that this skill reached the extreme limit of perfection compatible with the material it employed and the forces it had to work with. I know not how we can even satisfy ourselves on grounds of natural theology that the Creator foresees all the future, that he foreknows all the effects that will issue from his own contrivances. There may be great wisdom without the power of foreseeing and calculating everything; and human workmanship teaches us the possibility that the workman's knowledge of the properties of the things he works on may enable him to make arrangements admirably fitted to produce a given result, while he may have very little power of foreseeing the agencies of another kind which may modify or counteract the operation of the machinery he has made. Perhaps a knowledge of the laws of nature on which organic life depends, not much more perfect than the knowledge which man even now possesses of some other natural laws, would enable man, if he had the same power over the materials and the forces concerned which he has over some of those of inanimate nature, to create organized beings not less wonderful nor less adapted to their conditions of existence than those in nature.

Assuming then that while we confine ourselves to natural religion we must rest content with a Creator less than almighty; the question presents itself, of what nature is the limitation of his power? Does the obstacle at which the power of the Creator stops, which says to it: "Thus far shalt thou go and no further," lie in the power of other intelligent beings, or in the insufficiency and refractoriness of the materials of the universe, or must we resign ourselves to admitting the hypothesis that the author of the cosmos, though wise and knowing, was not all-wise and all-knowing, and may not always have done the best that was possible under the conditions of the problem?

The first of these suppositions has until a very recent period been, and in many quarters still is, the prevalent theory even of Christianity. Though attributing, and in a certain sense sincerely, omnipotence to the Creator, the received religion represents him as for some inscrutable reason tolerating the perpetual counteraction of his purposes by the will of another being of opposite character and of great, though inferior, power, the Devil. The only difference on this matter between popular Christianity and the religion of Ormuzd and Ahriman is that the former pays its good Creator the bad compliment of having been the maker of the Devil and of being at all times able to crush and annihilate him and his evil deeds and counsels, which nevertheless he does not do. But, as I have already remarked, all forms of polytheism, and this among the rest, are with difficulty reconcilable with a universe governed by general laws. Obedience to law is the note of a settled government and not of a conflict always going on. When powers are at war with one another for the rule of the world, the boundary between them is not fixed by constantly fluctuating. This may seem to be the case on our planet as between the powers of good and evil when we look only at the results; but when we consider the inner springs we find that both the good and the evil take place in the common course of nature, by virtue of the same general laws originally impressed—the same machinery turning out now good, now evil things, and oftener still, the two combined. The division of power is only apparently variable, but really so regular that, were we speaking of human potentates, we should declare without hesitation that the share of each must have been fixed by previous consent. Upon that supposition, indeed, the result of the combination of antagonist forces might be much the same as on that of a single creator with divided purposes.

But when we come to consider, not what hypothesis may be conceived and possibly reconciled with known facts, but what supposition is pointed to by the evidences of natural religion, the case is different. The indications of design point strongly in one direction—the preservation of the creatures in whose structure the indications are found. Along with the preserving agencies there are destroying agencies which we might be tempted to ascribe to the will of a different creator; but there are rarely appearances of the recondite contrivance of means of destruction except when the destruction of one creature is the means of preservation to others. Nor can it be supposed that the preserving agencies are wielded by one being, the destroying agencies by another. The destroying agencies are a necessary part of the preserving agencies: the chemical compositions by which life is carried on could not take place without a parallel series of decompositions. The great agent of decay in both organic and inorganic substances is oxidation, and it is only by oxidation that life is continued for even the length of a minute. The imperfections in the attainment of the purposes which the appearances indicate have not the air of having been designed. They are like the unintended results of accidents insufficiently guarded against, or of a little excess or deficiency in the quantity of some of the agencies by which the good purpose is carried on, or else they are consequences of the wearing out of a machinery not made to last forever: they point either to shortcomings in the workmanship as regards its intended purpose, or to external forces not under the control of the workman, but which forces bear no mark of being wielded and aimed by any other and rival intelligence.

We may conclude, then, that there is no ground in natural theology for attributing intelligence or personality to the obstacles which partially thwart what seem the purposes of the Creator. The limitation of his power more probably results either from the qualities of the material—the substances and forces of which the universe is composed not admitting of any arrangements by which his purposes could be more completely fulfilled; or else, the purposes might have been more fully attained, but the Creator did not know how to do it; creative skill, wonderful as it is, was not sufficiently perfect to accomplish his purposes more thoroughly.

We now pass to the moral attributes of the Deity, so far as indicated in the creation; or (stating the problem in the broadest manner) to the question, what indications nature gives of the purposes of its author. This question bears a very different aspect to us from what it bears to those teachers of natural theology who are encumbered with the necessity of admitting the omnipotence of the Creator. We have not to attempt the impossible problem of reconciling infinite benevolence and justice with infinite power in the Creator of such a world as this. The attempt to do so not only involves absolute contradiction in an intellectual point of view but exhibits to excess the revolting spectacle of a jesuitical defense of moral enormities.

On this topic I need not add to the illustrations given of this portion of the subject in my Essay on Nature. At the stage which our argument has reached there is none of this moral perplexity. Grant that creative power was limited by conditions the nature and extent of which are wholly unknown to us, and the goodness and justice of the Creator may be all that the most pious believe; and all in the work that conflicts with those moral attributes may be the fault of the conditions which left to the Creator only a choice of evils.

It is, however, one question whether any given conclusion is consistent with known facts, and another whether there is evidence to prove it; and if we have no means for judging of the design but from the work actually produced, it is a somewhat hazardous speculation to suppose that the work designed was of a different quality from the result realized. Still, though the ground is unsafe we may, with due caution, journey a certain distance on it. Some parts of the order of nature give much more indication of contrivance than others; many, it is not too much to say, give no sign of it at all. The signs of contrivance are most conspicuous in the structure and processes of vegetable and animal life. But for these, it is probable that the appearances in nature would never have seemed to the thinking part of mankind to afford any proofs of a God. But when a God had been inferred from the organization of living beings, other parts of nature, such as the structure of the solar system, seemed to afford evidences, more or less strong, in confirmation of the belief; granting, then, a design in nature, we can best hope to be enlightened as to what that design was by examining it in the parts of nature in which its traces are the most conspicuous.

To what purpose, then, do the expedients in the construction of animals and vegetables, which excite the admiration of naturalists, appear to tend? There is no blinking the fact that they tend principally to no more exalted object than to make the structure remain in life and in working order for a certain time: the individual for a few years, the species or race for a longer but still a limited period. And the similar, though less conspicuous, marks of creation which are recognized in inorganic nature are generally of the same character. The adaptations, for instance, which appear in the solar system consist in placing it under conditions which enable the mutual action of its parts to maintain, instead of destroying, its stability, and even that only for a time, vast indeed if measured against our short span of animated existence, but which can be perceived even by us to be limited; for even the feeble means which we possess of exploring the past are believed by those who have examined the subject by the most recent lights to yield evidence that the solar system was once a vast sphere of nebula or vapor and is going through a process which in the course of ages will reduce it to a single and not very large mass of solid matter frozen up with more than arctic cold. If the machinery of the system is adapted to keep itself at work only for a time, still less perfect is the adaptation of it for the abode of living beings, since it is only adapted to them during the relatively short portion of its total duration which intervenes between the time when each planet was too hot and the time when it became or will become too cold to admit of life under the only conditions in which we have experience of its possibility. Or we should perhaps reverse the statement and say that organization and life are only adapted to the conditions of the solar system during a relatively short portion of the system's existence.

The greater part, therefore, of the design of which there is indication in nature, however wonderful its mechanism, is no evidence of any moral attributes, because the end to which it is directed, and its adaptation to which end is the evidence of its being directed to an end at all, is not a moral end: it is not the good of any sentient creature, it is but the qualified permanence, for a limited period, of the work itself, whether animate or inanimate. The only inference that can be drawn from most of it respecting the character of the Creator is that he does not wish his works to perish as soon as created; he wills them to have a certain duration. From this alone nothing can be justly inferred as to the manner in which he is affected toward his animate or rational creatures.

After deduction of the great number of adaptations which have no apparent object but to keep the machine going, there remain a certain number of provisions for giving pleasure to living beings, and a certain number of provisions for giving them pain. There is no positive certainty that the whole of these ought not to take their place among the contrivances for keeping the creature or its species in existence; for both the pleasures and the pains have a conservative tendency; the pleasures being generally so disposed as to attract to the things which maintain individual or collective existence, the pains so as to deter from such as would destroy it.

When all these things are considered it is evident that a vast deduction must be made from the evidences of a Creator before they can be counted as evidences of a benevolent purpose—so vast indeed that some may doubt whether after such a deduction there remains any balance. Yet endeavoring to look at the question without partiality or prejudice and without allowing wishes to have any influence over judgment, it does appear that granting the existence of design, there is a preponderance of evidence that the Creator desired the pleasure of his creatures. This is indicated by the fact that pleasure of one description or another is afforded by almost everything, the mere play of the faculties, physical and mental, being a never-ending source of pleasure, and even painful things giving pleasure by the satisfaction of curiosity and the agreeable sense of acquiring knowledge; and also that pleasure, when experienced, seems to result from the normal working of the machinery, while pain usually arises from some external interference with it and resembles in each particular case the result of an accident. Even in cases when pain results, like pleasure, from the machinery itself, the appearances do not indicate that contrivance was brought into play purposely to produce pain: what is indicated is rather a clumsiness in the contrivance employed for some other purpose. The author of the machinery is no doubt accountable for having made it susceptible to pain; but this may have been a necessary condition of its susceptibility to pleasure; a supposition which avails nothing on the theory of an omnipotent Creator but is an extremely probable one in the case of a contriver working under the limitation of inexorable laws and indestructible properties of matter. The susceptibility being conceded as a thing which did enter into design, the pain itself usually seems like a thing undesigned; a casual result of the collision of the organism with some outward force to which it was not intended to be exposed, and which, in many cases, provision is even made to hinder it from being exposed to. There is, therefore, much appearance that pleasure is agreeable to the Creator, while there is very little, if any, appearance that pain is so: and there is a certain amount of justification for inferring, on grounds of natural theology alone, that benevolence is one of the attributes of the Creator. But to jump from this to the inference that his sole or chief purposes are those of benevolence, and that the single end and aim of Creation was the happiness of his creatures, is not only not justified by any evidence but is a conclusion in opposition to such evidence as we have. If the motive of the Deity for creating sentient beings was the happiness of the beings he created, his purpose, in our corner of the universe at least, must be pronounced, taking past ages and all countries and races into account, to have been thus far an ignominious failure; and if God had no purpose but our happiness and that of other living creatures it is not credible that he would have called them into existence with the prospect of being so completely baffled. If man had not the power by the exercise of his own energies for the improvement both of himself and of his outward circumstances to do for himself and other creatures vastly more than God had in the first instance done, the Being who called him into existence would deserve something very different from thanks at his hands. Of course it may be said that this very capacity of improving himself and the world was given to him by God, and that the change which he will be thereby enabled ultimately to effect in human existence will be worth purchasing by the sufferings and wasted lives of entire geological periods. This may be so; but to suppose that God could not have given him these blessings at a less frightful cost is to make a very strange supposition concerning the Deity. It is to suppose that God could not, in the first instance, create anything better than a Bosjesman or an Andaman Islander, or something still lower, and yet was able to endow the Bosjesman or the Andaman Islander with the power of raising himself into a Newton or a Fénelon. We certainly do not know the nature of the barriers which limit the divine omnipotence; but it is a very odd notion of them that they enable the Deity to confer on an almost bestial creature the power of producing by a succession of efforts what God himself had no other means of creating.

Such are the indications of natural religion in respect to the divine benevolence. If we look for any other of the moral attributes which a certain class of philosophers are accustomed to distinguish from benevolence, as, for example, justice, we find a total blank. There is no evidence whatever in nature for divine justice, whatever standard of justice our ethical opinions may lead us to recognize. There is no shadow of justice in the general arrangements of nature; and what imperfect realization it obtains in any human society (a most imperfect realization as yet) is the work of man himself, struggling upward against immense natural difficulties into civilization, and making to himself a second nature, far better and more unselfish than he was created with. But on this point enough has been said in another Essay, already referred to: on Nature.

These, then, are the net results of natural theology on the question of the divine attributes. A being of great but limited power, how or by what limited we cannot even conjecture; of great, and perhaps unlimited, intelligence, but perhaps also more narrowly limited than his power; who desires and pays some regard to the happiness of his creatures, but who seems to have other motives of action which he cares more for, and who can hardly be supposed to have created the universe for that purpose alone. Such is the Deity whom natural religion points to; and any idea of God more captivating than this comes only from human wishes or from the teaching of either real or imaginary revelation.

We shall next examine whether the light of nature gives any indications concerning the immortality of the soul and a future life.

R. G. SWINBURNE

The Argument from Design

The object of this paper[1] is to show that there are no valid formal objections to the argument from design, so long as the argument is articulated with sufficient care. In particular I wish to analyse Hume's attack on the argument in *Dialogues Concerning Natural Religion* and to show that none of the formal objections made therein by Philo have any validity against a carefully articulated version of the argument.

From *Philosophy* 43 (1968). Reprinted by permission of the author and the editors.

[1] I am most grateful to Christopher Williams and to colleagues at Hull for their helpful criticisms of an earlier version of this paper.

The argument from design is an argument from the order or regularity of things in the world to a god or, more precisely, a very powerful free non-embodied rational agent, who is responsible for that order. By a body I understand a part of the material universe subject, at any rate partially, to an agent's direct control, to be contrasted with other parts not thus subject. An agent's body marks the limits to what he can directly control; he can only control other parts of the universe by moving his body. An agent who could directly control any part of the universe would not be embodied. Thus ghosts, if they existed, would be non-embodied agents, because there are no particular pieces of matter subject to their direct control, but any piece of matter may be so subject. I use the word "design" in such a way that it is not analytic that if anything evinces design, an agent designed it, and so it becomes a synthetic question whether the design of the world shows the activity of a designer.

The argument, taken by itself, as was admitted in the *Dialogues* by Cleanthes the proponent of the argument, does not show that the designer of the world is omnipotent, omniscient, totally good, etc. Nor does it show that he is the God of Abraham, Isaac, and Jacob. To make these points, further arguments would be needed. The isolation of the argument from design from the web of Christian apologetic is perhaps a somewhat unnatural step, but necessary in order to analyse its structure. My claim is that the argument does not commit any formal fallacy, and by this I mean that it keeps to the canons of argument about matters of fact and does not violate any of them. It is, however, an argument by analogy. It argues from an analogy between the order of the world and the products of human art to a god responsible for the former, in some ways similar to man who is responsible for the latter. And even if there are no formal fallacies in the argument, one unwilling to admit the conclusion might still claim that the analogy was too weak and remote for him to have to admit it, that the argument gave only negligible support to the conclusion which remained improbable. In defending the argument I will leave to the objector this way of escape from its conclusion.

I will begin by setting forward the argument from design in a more careful and precise way than Cleanthes did.

There are in the world two kinds of regularity or order, and all empirical instances of order are such because they evince one or other or both kinds of order. These are the regularities of co-presence or spatial order, and regularities of succession, or temporal order. Regularities of co-presence are patterns of spatial order at some one instant of time. An example of a regularity of co-presence would be a town with all its roads at right angles to each other, or a section of books in a library arranged in alphabetical order of authors. Regularities of succession are simple patterns of behaviour of objects, such as their behaviour in accordance with the laws of nature—for example, Newton's law of gravitation, which holds universally to a very high degree of approximation, that all bodies attract each other with forces proportional to the product of their masses and inversely proportional to the square of their distance apart.

Many of the striking examples of order in the world evince an order which is the result both of a regularity of co-presence and of a regularity of succession. A working car consists of many parts so adjusted to each other that it follows the instructions of the driver delivered by his pulling and pushing a few levers and buttons and turning a wheel to take passengers whither he wishes. Its order arises because its parts are so arranged at some instant (regularity of co-presence) that, the laws of nature being as they are (regularity of succession), it brings about the result neatly and efficiently. The order of living animals and plants likewise results from regularities of both types.

Men who marvel at the order of the world may marvel at either or both of the regularities of co-presence and of succession. The men of the eighteenth century, that great century of "reasonable religion," were struck almost exclusively by the regularities of co-presence. They marvelled at the design and orderly operations of animals and plants; but since they largely took for granted the regularities of succession, what struck them about the animals and plants, as to a lesser extent about machines made by men, was the subtle and coherent arrangement of their millions of parts. Paley's *Natural Theology* dwells mainly on details of comparative anatomy, on eyes and ears and muscles and bones arranged with minute precision so as to operate with high efficiency, and Hume's Cleanthes produces the same kind of examples: "Consider, anatomise the eye, survey its structure and contrivance, and tell me from your own feeling, if the idea of a contriver does not immediately flow in upon you with a force like that of sensation."[2]

Those who argue from the existence of regularities of copresence other than those produced by men to the existence of a god who produced them are, however, in many respects on slippery ground when compared with those who rely for their premises on regularities of succession. We shall see several of these weaknesses later in considering Hume's objections to the argument, but it is worthwhile noting two of them at the outset. First, although the world contains many striking regularities of co-presence (some few of which are caused by human agency), it also contains many examples of spatial disorder. The uniform distribution of the galactic clusters is a marvellous example of spatial order, but the arrangement of trees in an African jungle is a marvellous example of spatial disorder. Although the proponent of the argument may then proceed to argue that in an important sense or from some point of view (e.g., utility to man) the order vastly exceeds the disorder, he has to argue for this in-no-way-obvious proposition.

---

[2]David Hume, *Dialogues Concerning Natural Religion*, ed. H. D. Aiken (New York, 1948), p. 28.

Secondly the proponent of the argument runs the risk that the regularities of co-presence may be explained in terms of something else by a normal scientific explanation[3] in a way that the regularities of succession could not possibly be. A scientist could show that a regularity of co-presence R arose from an apparently disordered state D by means of the normal operation of the laws of nature. This would not entirely "explain away" the regularity of co-presence, because the proponent of this argument from design might then argue that the apparently disordered state D really had a latent order, being the kind of state which, when the laws of nature operate, turns into a manifestly ordered one. As long as only few of the physically possible states of apparent disorder were states of latent order, the existence of many states of latent order would be an important contingent fact which could form a premiss for an argument from design. But there is always the risk that scientists might show that most states of apparent disorder were states of latent order, that is, that if the world lasted long enough considerable order must emerge from whichever of many initial states it began. If a scientist showed that, he would have explained by normal scientific explanation the existence of regularities of co-presence in terms of something completely different. The eighteenth-century proponents of the argument from design did not suspect this danger, and hence the devastating effect of Darwin's Theory of Evolution by Natural Selection on those who accepted their argument. For Darwin showed that the regularities of co-presence of the animal and plant kingdoms had evolved by natural processes from an apparently disordered state and would have evolved equally from many other apparently disordered states. Whether all regularities of co-presence can be fully explained in this kind of way no one yet knows, but the danger remains for the proponent of an argument from design of this kind that they can be.

However, those who argue from the operation of regularities of succession other than those produced by men to the existence of a god who produces them do not run into either of these difficulties. Regularities of succession (other than those produced by men), unlike regularities of co-presence, are all-pervasive. Simple natural laws rule almost all successions of events. Nor can regularities of succession be given a normal scientific explanation in terms of something else. For the normal scientific explanation of the operation of a regularity of succession is in terms of the operation of a yet more general regularity of succession. Note too that a normal scientific explanation of the existence of regularities of co-presence in terms of something different, if it can be provided, is explanation in terms of regularities of succession.

---

[3] I understand by a "normal scientific explanation" one conforming to the pattern of deductive or statistical explanation utilised in paradigm empirical sciences such as physics and chemistry, elucidated in recent years by Hempel, Braithwaite, Popper, and others. Although there are many uncertain points about scientific explanation, those to which I appeal in the text are accepted by all philosophers of science.

For these reasons the proponent of the argument from design does much better to rely for his premiss more on regularities of succession. St. Thomas Aquinas, wiser than the men of the eighteenth century, did just this. He puts forward an argument from design as his fifth and last way to prove the existence of God, and gives his premiss as follows:

"The fifth way is based on the guidedness of nature. An orderedness of actions to an end is observed in all bodies obeying natural laws, even when they lack awareness. For their behaviour hardly ever varies, and will practically always turn out well; which shows that they truly tend to a goal, and do not merely hit it by accident."[4] If we ignore any value judgment in "practically always turn out well," St. Thomas' argument is an argument from regularities of succession.

The most satisfactory premiss for the argument from design is then the operation of regularities of succession other than those produced by men, that is, the operation of natural laws. Almost all things almost always obey simple natural laws and so behave in a strikingly regular way. Given the premiss, what is our justification for proceeding to the conclusion that a very powerful free non-embodied rational agent is responsible for their behaving in that way? The justification which Aquinas gives is that "Nothing...that lacks awareness tends to a goal, except under the direction of someone with awareness and with understanding; the arrow, for example, requires an archer. Everything in nature, therefore, is directed to its goal by someone with understanding, and this we call 'God'."[5] A similar argument has been given by many religious apologists since Aquinas, but clearly as it stands it is guilty of the grossest *petitio principii*. Certainly *some* things which tend to a goal, tend to a goal because of a direction imposed upon them by someone "with awareness and with understanding." Did not the archer place the arrow and pull the string in a certain way the arrow would not tend to its goal. But whether *all* things which tend to a goal tend to a goal for this reason is the very question at issue, and that they do cannot be used as a premiss to prove the conclusion. We must therefore reconstruct the argument in a more satisfactory way.

The structure of any plausible argument from design can only be that the existence of a god responsible for the order in the world is a hypothesis well-confirmed on the basis of the evidence—viz., that contained in the premiss which we have now stated, and better confirmed than any other hypothesis. I shall begin by showing that there can be no other possible explanation for the operation of natural laws than the activity of a god, and then see to what extent the hypothesis is well confirmed on the basis of the evidence.

---

[4]St. Thomas Aquinas, *Summa Theologiae*, Ia.2.3. Trans. Timothy McDermott, O.P. (London, 1964).

[5]*Ibid.*

Almost all phenomena can, as we have seen, be explained by a normal scientific explanation in terms of the operation of natural laws on preceding states. There is, however, one other way of explaining natural phenomena, and that is explaining in terms of the rational choice of a free agent. When a man marries Jane rather than Anne, becomes a solicitor rather than a barrister, kills rather than shows mercy after considering arguments in favour of each course, he brings about a state of the world by his free and rational choice. To all appearances this is an entirely different way whereby states of the world may come about than through the operation of laws of nature on preceding states. Someone may object that it is necessary that physiological or other scientific laws operate in order for the agent to bring about effects. My answer is that certainly it is necessary that such laws operate in order for effects brought about directly by the agent to have ulterior consequences. But unless there are some effects which the agent brings about directly without the operation of scientific laws' acting on preceding physical states bringing them about, then these laws and states could fully explain the effects and there would be no need to refer in explaining them to the rational choice of an agent. True, the apparent freedom and rationality of the human will *may* prove an illusion. Many may have no more option what to do than a machine and be guided by an argument no more than is a piece of iron. But this has never yet been shown, and, in the absence of good philosophical and scientific argument to show it, I assume, what is apparent, that when a man acts by free and rational choice, his agency is the operation of a different kind of causality from that of scientific laws. The free choice of a rational agent is the only way of accounting for natural phenomena other than the way of normal scientific explanation, which is recognised as such by all men and has not been reduced to normal scientific explanation.

Almost all regularities of succession are the result of the normal operation of scientific laws. But to say this is simply to say that these regularities are instances of more general regularities. The operation of the most fundamental regularities clearly cannot be given a normal scientific explanation. If their operation is to receive an explanation and not merely to be left as a brute fact, that explanation must therefore be in terms of the rational choice of a free agent. What, then, are grounds for adopting this hypothesis, given that it is the only possible one?

The grounds are that we can explain some few regularities of succession as produced by rational agents and that the other regularities cannot be explained except in this way. Among the typical products of a rational agent acting freely are regularities both of co-presence and of succession. The alphabetical order of books on a library shelf is the result of the activity of the librarian who chose to arrange them thus. The order of the cards of a pack by suits and seniority in each suit is the result of the activity of the card-player who arranged them thus. Among examples of regularities of succession produced by men are the notes of a song sung by a singer or the movements of a dancer's body when he performs a dance in time with the accompanying instrument. Hence, knowing that some regularities of succession have such a cause, we postulate that they all have. An agent produces the celestial harmony like a man who sings a song. But at this point an obvious difficulty arises. The regularities of succession, such as songs which are produced by men, are produced by agents of comparatively small power, whose bodies we can locate. If an agent is responsible for the operation of the laws of nature, he must act directly on the whole universe, as we act directly on our bodies. Also he must be of immense power and intelligence compared with men. Hence he can only be somewhat similar to men, having, like them, intelligence and freedom of choice, yet unlike them in the degree of these and in not possessing a body. For a body, as I have distinguished it earlier, is a part of the universe subject to an agent's direct control, to be contrasted with other parts not thus subject. The fact that we are obliged to postulate on the basis of differences in the effects, differences in the causes, men and the god, weakens the argument. How much it weakens it depends on how great these differences are.

Our argument thus proves to be an argument by analogy and to exemplify a pattern common in scientific inference. As are caused by Bs, A*s are similar to As. Therefore—given that there is no more satisfactory explanation of the existence of A*s—they are produced by B*s similar to Bs. B*s are postulated to be similar in all respects to Bs except in so far as shown otherwise, viz., except in so far as the dissimilarities between As and A*s force us to postulate a difference. A well-known scientific example of this type of inference is as follows. Certain pressures (As) on the walls of containers are produced by billiard balls (Bs) with certain motions. Similar pressures (A*s) are produced on the walls of containers which contain not billiard balls but gases. Therefore, since we have no better explanation of the existence of the pressures, gases consist of particles (B*s) similar to billiard balls except in certain respects—e.g., size. By similar arguments, scientists have argued for the existence of many unobservables. Such an argument becomes weaker in so far as the properties which we are forced to attribute to the B*s because of the differences between the As and the A*s become different from those of the Bs. Nineteenth-century physicists postulated the existence of an elastic solid, the aether, to account for the propagation of light. But the way in which light was propagated turned out to have such differences (despite the similarities) from the way in which waves in solids are normally propagated that the physicists had to say that if there was an aether it had very many peculiar properties not possessed by normal liquids or solids. Hence they concluded that the argument for its existence was very weak. The proponent of the argument from design stresses the similarities between the regularities of succession produced by man and those which are laws of nature and so between men and the agent which he postulates as responsible for the laws of nature. The opponent of the argument stresses the dissimilarities. The degree of support which the conclusion obtains from the evidence depends on how great the similarities are.

The degree of support for the conclusion of an argument from analogy does not, however, depend merely on the similarities between the types of evidence but on the degree to which the resulting theory makes explanation of empirical matters more simple and coherent. In the case of the argument from design, the conclusion has an enormous simplifying effect on explanations of empirical matters. For if the conclusion is true, if a very powerful non-embodied rational agent is responsible for the operation of the laws of nature, then normal scientific explanation would prove to be personal explanation. That is, explanation of some phenomenon in terms of the operation of a natural law would ultimately be an explanation in terms of the operation of an agent. Hence (given an initial arrangement of matter) the principles of explanation of phenomena would have been reduced from two to one. It is a basic principle of explanation that we should postulate as few as possible kinds of explanation. To take a more mundane example—if we have as possible alternatives to explain physical phenomena by the operation of two kinds of force, the electromagnetic and the gravitational, and to explain physical phenomena in terms of the operation of only one kind of force, the gravitational, we ought always—*ceteris paribus*—to prefer the latter alternative. Since, as we have seen, we are obliged, at any rate at present, to use explanation in terms of the free choice of a rational agent in explaining many empirical phenomena, then if the amount of similarity between the order in the universe not produced by human agents and that produced by human agents makes it at all plausible to do so, we ought to postulate that an agent is responsible for the former as well as for the latter. So then in so far as regularities of succession produced by the operation of natural laws are similar to those produced by human agents, to postulate that a rational agent is responsible for them would indeed provide a simple unifying and coherent explanation of natural phenomena. What is there against taking this step? Simply that celebrated principle of explanation—*entia non sunt multiplicanda praeter necessitatem*—do not add a god to your ontology unless you have to. The issue turns on whether the evidence constitutes enough of a *necessitas* to compel us to multiply entities. Whether it does depends on how strong the analogy is between the regularities of succession produced by human agents and those produced by the operation of natural laws. I do not propose to assess the strength of the analogy but only to claim that everything turns on it. I claim that the inference from natural laws to a god responsible for them is of a perfectly proper type for inference about matters of fact, and that the only issue is whether the evidence is strong enough to allow us to affirm that it is probable that the conclusion is true.

Now that I have reconstructed the argument from design in what is, I hope, a logically impeccable form, I turn to consider Hume's criticisms of it, and I shall argue that all his criticisms alleging formal fallacies in the argument do not apply to it in the form in which I have stated it. This, we shall see, is largely because the criticisms are bad criticisms of the argument in any form but also in small part because Hume directed his fire against that form of the argument which used as its premiss the existence of regularities of co-presence other than those produced by men, and did not appeal to the operation of regularities of succession. I shall begin by considering one general point which he makes only in the *Enquiry* and then consider in turn all the objections which appear on the pages of the *Dialogues*.

1. The point which appears at the beginning of Hume's discussion of the argument in section XI of the *Enquiry* is a point which reveals the fundamental weakness of Hume's sceptical position. In discussing the argument, Hume puts forward as a general principle that "when we infer any particular cause from an effect, we must proportion the one to the other, and can never be allowed to ascribe to the cause any qualities but what are exactly sufficient to produce the effect."[6] Now, it is true that Hume uses this principle mainly to show that we are not justified in inferring that the god responsible for the design of the universe is totally good, omnipotent, and omniscient. I accept, as Cleanthes did, that the argument does not by itself lead to that conclusion. But Hume's use of the principle tends to cast doubt on the validity of the argument in the weaker form in which I am discussing it, for it seems to suggest that although we may conclude that whatever produced the regularity of the world was a regularity-producing object, we cannot go further and conclude that it is an agent who acts by choice, etc., for this would be to suppose more than we need in order to account for the effect. It is, therefore, important to realise that the principle is clearly false on our normal understanding of what are the criteria of inference about empirical matters. For the universal adoption of this celebrated principle would lead to the abandonment of science. Any scientist who told us only that the cause of E and E-producing characteristics would not add an iota to our knowledge. Explanation of matters of fact consists in postulating on reasonable grounds that the cause of an effect has certain characteristics other than those sufficient to produce the effect.

2. Two objections seem to be telescoped in the following passage of the *Dialogues*. "When two *species* of objects have always been observed to be conjoined together, I can *infer* by custom the existence of one wherever I *see* the existence of the other; and this I call an argument from experience. But how this argument can have place where the objects, as in the present case, are single, individual, without parallel or specific resemblance, may be difficult to explain."[7] One argument here seems to be that we can only infer

---

[6]David Hume, *An Enquiry Concerning Human Understanding*, ed. L. A. Selby-Bigge (2nd ed., 1902), p. 136.

[7]*Dialogues*, p. 23.

from an observed A to an unobserved B when we have frequently observed As and Bs together, and that we cannot infer to a B unless we have actually observed other Bs. Hence we cannot infer from regularities of succession to an unobserved god on the analogy of the connection between observed regularities and human agents, unless we have observed at other times other gods. This argument, like the first, reveals Hume's inadequate appreciation of scientific method. As we saw in the scientific examples which I cited, a more developed science than Hume knew has taught us that when observed As have a relation R to observed Bs, it is often perfectly reasonable to postulate that observed A*s, similar to As, have the same relation to unobserved and unobservable B*s similar to Bs.

3. The other objection which seems to be involved in the above passage is that we cannot reach conclusions about an object which is the only one of its kind, and, as the universe is such an object, we cannot reach conclusions about the regularities characteristic of it as a whole.[8] But cosmologists are reaching very well-tested scientific conclusions about the universe as a whole, as are physical anthropologists about the origins of our human race, even though it is the only human race of which we have knowledge and perhaps the only human race there is. The principle quoted in the objections is obviously wrong. There is no space here to analyze its errors in detail, but suffice it to point out that it becomes hopelessly confused by ignoring the fact that uniqueness is relative to description. Nothing describable is unique under all descriptions (the universe is, like the solar system, a number of material bodies distributed in empty space), and everything describable is unique under some description.

4. The next argument which we meet in the *Dialogues* is that the postulated existence of a rational agent who produces the order of the world would itself need explaining. Picturing such an agent as a mind, and a mind as an arrangement of ideas, Hume phrases the objection as follows: "a mental world or Universe of ideas requires a cause as much as does a material world or Universe of objects."[9] Hume himself provides the obvious answer to this—that it is no objection to explaining X by Y that we cannot explain Y. But then he suggests that the Y in this case, the mind, is just as mysterious as the ordered universe. Men never "thought it satisfactory to explain a particular effect by a particular cause which was no more to be accounted for than the effect itself."[10] On the contrary, scientists have always thought it reasonable to postulate entities merely to explain effects, so long as the postulated entities accounted simply and coherently for the characteristics of the effects. The existence of molecules with their characteristic behaviour

---

[8]For this argument see also *Enquiry*, pp. 147f.

[9]*Dialogues*, p. 33.

[10]*Ibid.*, p. 36.

was "no more to be accounted for" than observable phenomena, but the postulation of their existence gave a neat and simple explanation of a whole host of chemical and physical phenomena, and that was the justification for postulating their existence.

5. Next, Hume argues that if we are going to use the analogy of a human agent we ought to go the whole way and postulate that the god who gives order to the universe is like men in many other respects. "Why not become a perfect anthropomorphite? Why not assert the deity or deities to be corporeal, and to have eyes, a nose, mouths, ears, etc."[11] The argument from design is, as we have seen, an argument by analogy. All analogies break down somewhere; otherwise they would not be analogies. In saying that the relation of A to B is analogous to a relation of A* to a postulated B*, we do not claim that B* is in all respects like B, but only in such respects as to account for the existence of the relation and also in other respects except in so far as we have contrary evidence. For the activity of a god to account for the regularities, he must be free, rational, and very powerful. But it is not necessary that he, like men, should only be able to act on a limited part of the universe, a body, and by acting on that control the rest of the universe. And there is good reason to suppose that the god does not operate in this way. For, if his direct control was confined to a part of the universe, scientific laws outside his control must operate to ensure that his actions have effects in the rest of the universe. Hence the postulation of the existence of the god would not explain the operations of those laws: yet to explain the operation of all scientific laws was the point of postulating the existence of the god. The hypothesis that the god is not embodied thus explains more and explains more coherently than the hypothesis that he is embodied. Hume's objection would, however, have weight against an argument from regularities of co-presence which did not appeal to the operation of regularities of succession. For one could suppose an embodied god just as well as a disembodied god to have made the animal kingdom and then left it alone, as a man makes a machine, or, like a landscape gardener, to have laid out the galactic clusters. The explanatory force of such an hypothesis is as great as that of the hypothesis that a disembodied god did these things, and argument from analogy would suggest the hypothesis of an embodied god to be more probable. Incidentally, a god whose prior existence was shown by the existence of regularities of co-presence might now be dead, but a god whose existence was shown by the present operation of regularities of succession could not be, since the existence of an agent is contemporaneous with the temporal regularities which he produces.

6. Hume urges: why should we not postulate many gods to give order to the universe, not merely one? "A great number of men join in building a house or a ship, in rearing a city, in framing a commonwealth, why may not several

---

[11]*Ibid.*, p. 40.

deities combine in framing a world?"[12] Hume again is aware of the obvious counter-objection to his suggestion—"To multiply causes without necessity is...contrary to true philosophy."[13] He claims, however, that the counter-objection does not apply here, because it is an open question whether there is a god with sufficient power to put the whole universe in order. The principle, however, still applies whether or not we have prior information that a being of sufficient power exists. When postulating entities, postulate as few as possible. Always suppose only one murderer, unless the evidence forces you to suppose a second. If there were more than one deity responsible for the order of the universe, we should expect to see characteristic marks of the handiwork of different deities in different parts of the universe, just as we see different kinds of workmanship in the different houses of a city. We should expect to find an inverse square law of gravitation obeyed in one part of the universe, and in another part a law which was just short of being an inverse square law—without the difference's being explicable in terms of a more general law. But it is enough to draw this absurd conclusion to see how ridiculous the Humean objection is.

7. Hume argues that there are in the universe other things than rational agents which bestow order. "A tree bestows order and organisation on that tree which springs from it, without knowing the order; an animal in the same manner on its offspring."[14] It would, therefore, Hume argues, be equally reasonable if we are arguing from analogy, to suppose the cause of the regularities in the world "to be something similar or analogous to generation or vegetation."[15] This suggestion makes perfectly good sense if it is the regularities of co-presence which we are attempting to explain. But as analogous processes to explain regularities of succession, generation or vegetation will not do, because they only produce regularities of co-presence—and those through the operation of regularities of succession outside their control. The seed only produces the plant because of the continued operation of the laws of biochemistry.

8. The last distinct objection which I can discover in the *Dialogues* is the following. Why should we not suppose, Hume urges, that this ordered universe is a mere accident among the chance arrangements of eternal matter? In the course of eternity, matter arranges itself in all kinds of ways. We just happen to live in a period when it is characterised by order, and mistakenly conclude that matter is always ordered. Now, as Hume phrases this objection, it is directed against an argument from design which uses as its premiss the existence of the regularities of co-presence. "The continual motion of matter...in less than infinite transpositions must produce this

---

[12]*Ibid.*, p. 39.

[13]*Ibid.*, p. 40.

[14]*Ibid.*, p. 50.

[15]*Ibid.*, p. 47.

economy or order, and by its very nature, that order, when once established supports itself for many ages if not to eternity."[16] Hume thus relies here partly on chance and partly on the operation of regularities of succession (the preservation of order) to account for the existence of regularities of co-presence. In so far as it relies on regularities of succession to explain regularities of co-presence, such an argument has, as we saw earlier, some plausibility. But in so far as it relies on chance, it does not—if the amount of order to be accounted for is very striking. An attempt to attribute the operation of regularities of succession to chance would not thus be very plausible. The claim would be that there are no laws of nature which always apply to matter; matter evinces in the course of eternity all kinds of patterns of behaviour; it is just chance that at the moment the states of the universe are succeeding each other in a regular way. But if we say that it is chance that in 1960 matter is behaving in a regular way, our claim becomes less and less plausible as we find that in 1961 and 1962 and so on it continues to behave in a regular way. An appeal to chance to account for order becomes less and less plausible, the greater the order. We would be justified in attributing a typewritten version of collected works of Shakespeare to the activity of monkeys typing eternally on eternal typewriters if we had some evidence of the existence of an infinite quantity of paper randomly covered with type, as well as the collected works. In the absence of any evidence that matter behaved irregularly at other temporal periods, we are not justified in attributing its present regular behaviour to chance.

In addition to the objections which I have stated, the *Dialogues* contain a lengthy presentation of the argument that the existence of evil in the world shows that the god who made it and gave it order is not both totally good and omnipotent. But this does not affect the argument from design which, as Cleanthes admits, does not purport to show that the designer of the universe does have these characteristics. The eight objections which I have stated are all the distinct objections to the argument from design which I can find in the *Enquiry* and in the *Dialogues*, which claim that in some formal respect the argument does not work. As well as claiming that the argument from design is deficient in some formal respect, Hume makes the point that the analogy of the order produced by men to the other order of the universe is too remote for us to postulate similar causes.[17] I have argued earlier that if there is a weakness in the argument it is here that it is to be found. The only way to deal with this point would be to start drawing the parallels or stressing the dissimilarities, and these are perhaps tasks more appropriate for the preacher and the poet than for the philosopher. The philosopher will be content to have shown that though perhaps weak, the argument has some force. How much force depends on the strength of the analogy.

---

[16]*Ibid.*, p. 53.

[17]See, for example, *Dialogues*, pp. 18 and 37.

IAN HACKING

The Inverse Gambler's Fallacy: The Argument from Design. The Anthropic Principle Applied to Wheeler Universes

The point of this paper is far less formidable than its title. I present an elementary fallacy in probability reasoning. It seems not to have been noticed previously. An analogy with the so-called gambler's fallacy leads me to call it the inverse gambler's fallacy. Its interest is twofold. Firstly, the most popular objection to the traditional argument from design for the existence of God commits this fallacy. In exposing the error I do not advocate the design argument. I note only that the most common ground for dismissing it is facile. Secondly, I observe that one use of the recently propounded anthropic principle commits the same fallacy. This use is connected with an idea of John Wheeler's about sequential universes. The anthropic principle as used by Brandon Carter for coexistent universes does not commit the fallacy.

The argument from design for the existence of God begins with a *premiss* of the following sort: Our world is orderly, complex, law-governed, and with a fine adjustment of means to ends. Such order and adjustment, the argument continues, form far too delicate a balance to have arisen by mere chance. The explanation must lie elsewhere. We should infer the existence of an intelligent designer and creator of the universe.

The argument was at its apogee in the Established Church of England between 1680 and 1810. Royal Society divines (as they have been called)[1] found this the most comfortable proof of God. But the argument—or ways to circumvent it—has recently provoked some interest among cosmologists and students of the life sciences alike. Their most assiduous and faithful interpreter for philosophers has been John Leslie.[2]

From *Mind*, Vol. 96 (1987), pp. 331–40. Reprinted by permission of Oxford University Press.

[1] Anders Jeffner, *Butler and Hume on Religion, a Comparative Analysis*, Stockholm, 1966.

[2] 'Anthropic Principle, World Ensemble and Design', *American Philosophical Quarterly*, 1982, pp. 141–51. 'Cosmology, Probability and the Need to Explain Life', in N. Rescher, ed., *Scientific Explanation and Understanding*, University Press of America, Lanham, Md., 1983. 'Observership in Cosmology: The Anthropic Principle', *Mind*, 1983, pp. 573–9. Leslie has already replied to the present paper in 'Anthropological Explanations in Cosmology', *PSA 1986*.

There are surprisingly many interesting questions to ask about the premiss for the argument from design.[3] To what extent is the universe 'fine-tuned'? That is a matter for cosmology, geophysics, and biology. There are also questions of a logical sort. How are we to measure the surprise, degree of coincidence, or improbability of our universe? But here I wish to address a trivial matter. Suppose we do accept some version of the premiss for the argument from design, and pass by the important questions of physics, biology, and logic. I assert that there is a trifling fallacy that occurs in almost all popular rejections of the argument from design. I speak not of those who reject the premiss, on the ground, perhaps, that the universe is not fine-tuned, or on the ground that its degree of tuning should occasion no surprise. I speak of a *popular objection* to what is supposed to follow from the premiss.

Why dwell upon a trivial matter when matters of moment lurk in the wings? Because the fallacy in what I call the popular objection is so widely circulated, and so little noticed, that it is a logician's task to display it. Demonstration of the fallacy does have one unexpected corollary. It shows that there is a fundamental logical difference between two present-day competing cosmologies that are usually taken to be very similar.

The 'popular objection' says: It is indeed extremely improbable that a random concatenation of the forces, energies, particles, and fields of the universe (or whatever we think are its building blocks) should, in a single trial, form into anything orderly, let alone something that supports our form of intelligent life. But why suppose the universe to be made by one single roll of myriad dice? Think instead of a sequence of indefinitely or infinitely many chance events. Sooner or later, mere chance would give an organization like ours. We need invoke nothing but chance to explain the order in the universe and the fine adjustment of means to ends.

I believe that almost all who accept the premiss of the argument from design (the world is orderly) but reject the conclusion, believe the above objection to be sound. I urge that this objection commits an elementary fallacy.

The objection, in its popular form, clearly models itself on common ideas about chance devices and random events. Let us recall the model, in the form of a fair device for rolling a pair of fair dice. Trials are independent, and the chance of getting double six on a pair of dice is, for example, 1/36. Let it be assumed (or empirically determined) that our device has the property that we call fairness, namely, equal chances for each face, no interaction between dice, and no memory, so that rolls are independent.

---

[3]See, for example, the numerous works cited by Leslie, and the results of a three-day multidisciplinary conference under the auspices of the Royal Society of Canada, 1985, forthcoming as: J. Robson, ed., *Origin and Evolution of the Universe: Evidence for Design?*, Queens/McGill University Press, Montreal.

We should distinguish three propositions. The first is correct: The more often the pair of dice is rolled, the greater the chance that, in the sequence of rolls, we will obtain at least one double six. In thirty-six rolls, the chance of getting at least one double six is about $2/3$. In a thousand rolls we are almost certain to get at least one double six. Or let us consider repeated shufflings and dealings of a normal pack of cards. In an ideal pack (which never wears out) and which is shuffled by a fair device (very hard to manufacture) the chance of dealing the pack in order, from the ace of spades down, is only $1/52$, that is, only slightly better than one chance in 10^{68}. Nevertheless, in 10^{100} ideal shuffles, one would have a good chance of getting at least one 'perfectly orderly' deal. Let us call this line of reasoning R, intended to recall the idea that repetition improves the chances of getting at least one rare event in a sequence of trials.

Now we pass to a familiar fallacy, commonly explained—not always with success—to schoolchildren taking elementary lessons in probability. A gambler, fully accepting the premiss of a fair-rolling device, observed a sequence of, say, 35 rolls without a single double six. He reasons that the chance of double six in 36 rolls is about $2/3$, so it is smart to bet that double six will occur on the next toss. This error is called the gambler's fallacy. This is the fallacy of someone who reasons that, relative to the evidence of a string of 35 non-double sixes, it is rather likely that a double six will occur at the next roll. But on the assumption of fairness, which I take to include independence of trials, it is not likely. The probability of double six, relative to the evidence, is still $1/36$.

I now turn to a second and less familiar fallacy. Its diagnosis seems not to occur in any literature. I call it the inverse gambler's fallacy.

I imagine it in two forms, A and B. In the former, think of a gambler coming into a room, walking to the fair device, and seeing it roll double six. A kibitzer asks, 'Do you think this is the first roll of the evening? Or have there been many rolls?' The gambler reasons that since double six occurs seldom, there have probably been many rolls.

In case B, we have what looks like a more sophisticated gambler. He enters the room as a roll is about to be made. The kibitzer asks, 'Is this the first roll of the dice, do you think, or have we made many a one earlier tonight?' The gambler takes a quick look around the room, and determines his own personal or subjective probability distribution as to his judgement among the possibilities that this is the first roll, the thirty-sixth roll, or the hundredth roll, and so forth. But slyly, he says, 'Can I wait until I see how this roll comes out, before I lay my bet with you on the number of past plays made tonight?' The kibitzer, no fool, agrees, although charging a slight fee for allowing this extra 'information'. The roll is double six. The gambler foolishly says, 'Ha, that makes a difference—I think there have been quite a few rolls.'

Gambler A and gambler B reason fallaciously. In case B, a trifling computation by Bayes's rule shows that the gambler's posterior subjective probabilities (after seeing the outcome of the most recent roll) should be identical to his prior subjective probabilities (based simply on his hunches about the time of night, the demeanour of the players, and so forth).[4]

The inverse gambler's fallacy is closely related to the gambler's fallacy. The point is that the information available to the gambler is that double six occurred at this throw. It is no more probable that double six should occur at this throw, on the supposition of many previous throws, than it is that it should occur at this throw, on the supposition that this is the first throw tonight, or with this device and newly made pair of dice, or whatever.

There is, however, an important difference between the gambler's fallacy and the inverse gambler's fallacy. The former works upon assumptions of fairness that exclude any information as being relevant, except these assumptions themselves. The only pertinent information to the gambler is the sequence of past throws, plus the built-in assumptions about the dice-rolling device. But in the inverse case, the gambler may have other reasons to suspect that the game has been in play for some time—it is now three in the morning, the other gamblers are frenzied, a kibitzer is trying to bet with him, and the like. Inevitably this creates a personal probability distribution for the 'Bayesian' gambler. However, this distribution is not affected one jot by adding the extra information that on the only actually observed throw of the dice—the only one known to have been made, tonight—double six was observed.

Thus, a difference between the gambler's fallacy and the inverse gambler's fallacy is that all relevant prior probabilities are built into the story of the gambler's fallacy. In the inverse fallacy, there is always room for subjective, personal, or rational prior probabilities. Then the point is that observing double six has no effect whatsoever on those priors. The inverse gambler's fallacy is that of thinking that 'double-six' is relevant information that should affect his priors. To pun a little, the inverse gambler's fallacy is a mistake in what used to be called inverse probability reasoning, and which is now more commonly called Bayesian.

A second difference between the fallacies is that the relation to R is different. R, it will be recalled, is the true proposition to the effect that rare events are more likely to occur somewhere or other in a long run of trials than in a short one.

---

[4]Let S = This roll has outcome double six.
F = This is the first roll of the night.
G = This is not the first roll of the night.

Then the prior subjective probability of F is $\Pr(F)$, and the posterior, in the light of the evidence, is $\Pr(F/S)$. Knowing S makes no difference, because $\Pr(F/S) = \Pr(F)$. For we have $\Pr(F) + \Pr(G) = 1$, and $\Pr(S/F) = \Pr(S/G) = 1/36$. Hence, using Bayes's rule,

$$\Pr(F/S) = \frac{\Pr(F)\Pr(S/F)}{\Pr(F)\Pr(S/F) + \Pr(G)\Pr(S/G)} = \Pr(F).$$

The gambler's fallacy makes a *prediction* on the basis of R: double six will likely turn up soon. The relationship between R and the inverse gambler's fallacy is what is sometimes called the inverse of prediction, namely *explanation*.

There is a controversial mode of reasoning to which Gilbert Harman was the first to give the handy name, 'inference to the best explanation'.[5] We think that we have good ground to believe, or accept, or bet on, proposition p if it is the best explanation of an otherwise puzzling fact reported in the proposition q. An inverse gambler may think as follows. There is something puzzling: double six just occurred. The best available explanation may be that many trials have been made, for double six occurs often enough in many trials. Therefore, I infer to the best explanation, namely, many trials have been made. I'll bet on that.

But the known fact is that double six occurred in the last trial. This event is exactly as probable $(1/36)$ on the hundredth trial or the first trial. It is in no way explained by a long sequence of preceding trials.

There was once a longish debate, among philosophers of science, about what constitutes a statistical explanation. On one view, propounded by C. G. Hempel and others, a probabilistic explanation E of an observed fact F would have to be such that F was more probable given E than otherwise. Such matters have been much discussed since, but here let us record Richard Jeffrey's correct view that the only explanation of why an unusual event (of probability $1/36$, say) occurred may be that an unusual event occurred. That is the explanation of why double six occurred last time, before the inverse gambler's eyes.[6]

It may be objected that there is *another* fact which one seeks to explain. This is the fact that double six occurred somewhere or other in a sequence of trials. I reply in two parts. Firstly, if this means that we know that double six occurs at least once in many trials, then the fact is not known at all. Indeed, it begs the question, for what is at issue is whether there is reason to think that there have been many trials.

Secondly, however, it may correctly be urged that since we know that double six has just occurred, we know the disjunctive fact that double six occurred at least once in a sequence of one trial, or of two trials, or of three trials...or of many trials. Since we know double six occurred in the most recent trial, we know that this disjunctive fact is a fact. Is *it* not explained by R plus the inference that there have been many trials?

Here we must make a remark about inference to the best explanation. If F is known, and E is the best explanation of F, then we are supposed to infer E. However, we cannot give this rule *carte blanche*. If F is known, then FvG is

---

[5]'Inference to the Best Explanation', *The Philosophical Review*, 1966, pp. 241–7.

[6]'Statistical Explanation vs. Statistical Inference', in A. R. Anderson *et al.*, eds., *Essays in Honor of C. G. Hempel*, Reidel, Dordrecht, 1969, pp. 104–13.

known, but E^* might be the best explanation of FvG, and yet knowledge of F gives not the slightest reason to believe E^*. (John, an excellent swimmer, drowns in Lake Ontario. Therefore he drowns in either Lake Ontario or the Gulf of Mexico. At the time of his death, a hurricane is ravaging the Gulf. So the best explanation of why he drowned is that he was overtaken by a hurricane, which is absurd.) We must insist that F, the fact to be explained, is the most specific version of what is known and not a disjunctive consequence of what is known. In the case of double six the most specific version is that double six has just occurred. That is the fact to be explained, and a long run of previous trials is of no value in explaining that fact.

Evidently these reflections have something to do with the 'popular objection' to the argument from design. I shall draw connections with four different positions: the popular argument, Hume's (or Philo's) modified Epicureanism, the Brandon Carter principle of plenitude cosmology, and the Boltzmann–Wheeler notion of an unending succession of universes. In every case, the position accepts the premiss of the argument from design—our universe is very unusual, improbable, or whatever.

The popular argument says, the universe has been around for ever so long, so it is not in the least surprising that it should have got into its present orderly state. Given an old enough universe, we would expect our order to arrive by mere chance.

This is the inverse gambler's fallacy. Think of it first in the eighteenth century, when considered opinion would appraise the infinitely old universe as very improbable indeed. There would be no ground for believing we have an old universe, except that it explains the present order. But it does not explain the present order. So there is no ground for believing in an old universe. Even if there were, it would in no way explain the present order in the universe. The only anti-design explanation is that something very unusual has occurred, namely us.

But the objector may protest: Whatever was thought in the eighteenth century, modern science teaches that we have an ancient universe. Won't that do? No. On the contrary, modern science teaches of the big bang and of the universe that we know being curiously finely tuned from the start. Chance hardly had the opportunity to get its sticky little fingers in after the first three minutes. To restart the objection to design, we would have to invent a sequence of universes, of which ours is the most recent. That takes us to Wheeler, with whom I shall conclude.

Next we pass to Hume's Philo, in Part VIII of *Dialogues Concerning Natural Religion*. Philo has caustic words for the Epicurean hypothesis of endless atoms wandering through endless space and time. But let's revive it by revising it, he suggests. Postulate that the universe is infinitely old, but has only finitely many particles. Postulate that configurations of particles occur by chance, but that there are only finitely many. Postulate that transition times between configurations are finite (Hume omitted that, and also neglected to exclude a closed-loop universe in which some logically possible configurations never get to occur). Well then, every possible configuration of the universe will occur, indeed recur indefinitely often.

Do these postulates, suitably toughened up, explain the existence of our orderly universe? Yes. Our universe is a possible one (it exists, therefore is possible). All possible universes come to pass, hence ours does. Why are we observing an orderly universe: why is it that the most recent universe is orderly? Question wrongly posed: we can exist only in an orderly universe. So of course the one we are observing is orderly. No surprise. No need for a creator. There are a few lapses in my version, far less elegant than Hume's, who has his own lapses. I make only one point. Although revised Epicureanism may speak of chance transitions between configurations of particles, *chance and probability have nothing to do with the explanatory power of this retort to theism*. The argument is entirely deductive. All possible universes exist, so we do. The question we must turn to is: But why is an orderly universe possible at all? That is what Philo takes up next. One must not confuse Hume with what I call the popular response to the argument from design. Hume here presents a strategic case of the principle of plenitude, that everything exists sooner or later.

Philo was able to make some progress away from chance, by proposing infinite time, finite configurations, and finite transition times. That is no longer an option for a physicist. But the principle of plenitude has been revived by Brandon Carter, Stephen Hawking, and other cosmologists at Cambridge University.[7] They start with the assumption that a classical big-bang theory is true, in which the laws of the universe are constant, and not altering as in some 'exotic' speculations. They are then able to consider all possible outcomes of a big bang, and conclude, by imposing plausible topological measures over the space of possibilities, that a universe with anything like our features is logically possible but highly improbable, even of probability-measure zero. This is a rather rigorous quantification of the assertion, that our orderly world is extremely rare, or unusual, or improbable.

Do we need the intelligent designer, then? No; Carter brings back the principle of plenitude, *with the supposition that all logically possible universes consistent with classical big-bang cosmology actually coexist.*

Why do we exist? Because we are a possible universe, and all possible ones exist. Why are we in an orderly universe? Because the only universes that we could observe are orderly ones that support our form of life. In an even stronger way than with Hume, nothing is left to chance. Everything in this reasoning is deductive. It has nothing to do with the inverse gambler's fallacy.

---

[7]Brandon Carter, 'Large Number Coincidences and the Anthropic Principle in Cosmology', in M. S. Longair, ed., *Confrontation of Cosmological Theories with Observational Data*, Reidel, Dordrecht, pp. 291–8. C. B. Collins and S. W. Hawking, 'The Anisotropy of the Universe', *Astrophysical Journal*, 1973, pp. 317–26. Without venturing any judgement of merit in cosmology, a logician will find these sounder than much subsequent work.

A quite different idea has everything to do with the fallacy. It has been attributed to Boltzmann,[8] and numbers John Wheeler among its champions.[9] Here we have the idea of a sequence of universes. Every universe goes through its life history, and finally expires, collapsing, or whatever. Then a new universe comes into being, and goes through its history. Most universes will have precious little history, for they collapse into themselves almost at once, or go off as light and nothing else. It is important to this view that universes have no memories. There is effectively no trace in a universe of its predecessors. Recall that the postulate of independence of a chance device is sometimes put: The device has no memory. A fair die does not remember how it fell last time. Likewise, Wheeler universes have no memories.

It is often thought that the Wheeler and Carter models are in close analogy. One is a model of succession, one of coexistence. But even their cardinalities are not coincident. Coexistence, if understood in physical terms, more readily allows of larger sets than ordinal succession. But there is a more interesting logical difference between them.

It is a matter of the inverse gambler's fallacy. I wish to contrast Wheeler's hypothesis *W*, that there have been many successive universes before ours, and Carter's hypothesis *C*, that all possible big-bang universes coexist. According to *W* itself, there can be no empirical evidence for *W*, because according to *W* our universe has no traces of preceding universes. Much the same is true of *C*. There remain two kinds of ground for conjecturing that *W* or *C* is true.

(1) An inference to the best explanation.

(2) 'A priori physics': simplicity, symmetry, etc.

Now, an inference to the best explanation may fail for two distinct reasons.

(a) The explanans may be deemed unacceptable because it is known to be false, or because it is too bizarre, or because it is less likely than a rival explanans.

(b) The explanans does not explain the explanandum: the explanandum is not deducible from the explanans, nor made more probable by it, nor does it satisfy, e.g., W. C. Salmon's more modest requirements of an explanation.

Wheeler's hypothesis *W* cannot be supported by (1), an inference to the best explanation. It fails on ground (b). The explanans *W* does not explain the explanandum; that is, a long string of previous universes does not explain the present existence of our orderly universe. Our present orderly universe is not made more probable on the assumption of many previous universes spontaneously forming by chance. To suppose otherwise is to commit the inverse gambler's fallacy.

---

[8]What Boltzmann believed is open to some interpretation. Some of my colleagues in the history of nineteenth-century physics resist drawing him towards the Wheeler model. P. C. W. Davies kindly drew my attention to the following paper which, in his opinion, expresses the Wheeler idea: L. Boltzmann, 'Hrn. Zermelos Abhandlung, "Uber die mechanische Erklärung irreversibiler Vorgänge" ', *Annalen der Physik*, 1897, pp. 392–8, esp. p. 396.

[9] C. W. Misner, K. S. Thorne, and J. A. Wheeler, *Gravitation*, Foresman, San Francisco, 1973, ch. 44.

Naturally there may be reasons other than (1) for believing W. These would be 'a priori' considerations of type (2). Perhaps W is true, and perhaps arguments of type (2) may convince someone of that. Even so, belief in W would go no way at all towards explaining or helping to understand the existence of our present orderly universe. To suppose otherwise is to commit the inverse gambler's fallacy.

To emphasize the point we may distinguish three propositions. W_1: The world (or metauniverse) is such that there will be a sequence of universes each of which goes out of existence but is followed by a new universe whose structure is determined by chance. W_2: Our universe has been preceded by a very large number of universes. W_3: Ours is the very first Wheeler universe; just by chance, a very orderly universe came up first. (W_2 and W_3 are contraries, exactly analogous to G and F of n. 4 above.) Now, we might have 'a priori' arguments of type (2) for W_1. These arguments could not possibly lead us to prefer W_2 to W_3 or vice versa. The Wheeler picture that has regularly been urged by its proponents is W_1 & W_2 combined with the thought that somehow our present orderly universe is explained by its being late in a sequence, i.e. by the assumption of W_2. That is a mistake. If you like the Wheeler account, stick to W_1 and do not speculate on whether we are the first Wheeler universe in the world, or merely the latest in a long sequence.

The situation is different with Carter's hypothesis C of coexistence universes. As with W, C may be supported by arguments of types (1) and (2). In the case of W, we found that an inference to the best explanation, type (1), is defective on ground (b). W does not make our present orderly universe more probable. But C cannot be faulted in this way. C, if true, really would explain our present orderly universe. For our universe follows deductively from C. Of course, we could still fault an argument of type (1) for C. For we could reject it on ground (a), holding for example that C is simply too bizarre or too unintelligible to deserve credence. (The same can be done for W.) But, to continue the contrast between W and C, if we did have arguments of type (2) for C, then we really would have explained the existence of our present orderly universe.

To complete the contrast, note that C does not factor in the way in which W factors into W_1 & W_2. Of course, we can say that C = (Every possible big-bang universe exists) & (Our possible big-bang universe exists). But the latter conjunct follows from the former, whereas W_2 does not follow from, nor is it made probable by, W_1.

Carter coined the phrase 'anthropic principle' to name the self-evident and trivial fact that humans can observe only a universe orderly enough to maintain human life. (He also has a far from trivial 'strong anthropic principle' that I ignore here.) His explanation of the existence of an orderly universe that we know about is twofold. (i) The existence of our universe follows deductively from the co-existence of all possible universes. (ii) As the anthropic principle states, if we are observing anything at all, it is orderly. Note that (ii) by itself does not explain why there is an orderly universe. How could something akin to a tautology do that? The explanation is furnished by (i) alone.

The anthropic principle of course applies to the Wheeler story too, and indeed to anything at all, as is the habit of tautologies. The 'explanation', of why we are observing an orderly universe is, if you like, that we exist; that is an obfuscating banality that applies equally to Carter, to Wheeler, to Epicurus, and to creationism. If the Wheeler story is true, then our universe is indeed the latest in a sequence of universes, and it is sufficiently orderly to maintain human life. But the 'latest' could (as W_3 asserts) well be the very first Wheeler universe. All we can say, on the Wheeler story, is that our universe arose by chance. We cannot say that it arose inevitably because the world of universes has been running for so long that we were bound to turn up. To suppose otherwise is to commit the inverse gambler's fallacy.

Philosophical discussions of the anthropic principle—whether written by a philosopher, such as John Leslie, or an articulate physicist, such as P. C. W. Davies—commonly regard Carter and Wheeler cosmologies as interchangeable.[10] Both are held to explain the existence of our orderly universe. This is incorrect. The two cosmologies may seem analogous until one considers the inverse gambler's fallacy. It is an historical fact that Carter was led to his world view in part by thinking about Wheeler universes. But physicist Carter, not only the inventor of the anthropic principle but also quite the most careful philosopher of anthropism, deliberately replaced Wheeler universes by his own. We should follow his example. The anthropic principle—effectively a tautology—is of the slightest help only when added to that very substantive (and almost incredible) proposition, the principle of plenitude.

None of my observations provides a ground for theism. They show only that the confrontation between those who advocate the design argument and those who reject it is of an unusually banal nature. The popular objection tries not to be banal and to say that in an ancient enough universe or sequence of universes, our universe would be bound to turn up, and so is not surprising enough to postulate a designer and creator.

Instead the opponent should be saying only this: 'The world is very unusual, but unusual things do occur by chance.' To which the design argument retorts, 'The world is very unusual, so it must be made by an intelligent creator.' That is the *whole* of the controversy unless a principle of plenitude is introduced. To suppose otherwise is to bungle your probabilities.

---

[10]Leslie repeatedly says so, and responds to my present argument in the final paper cited in n. 2. One physicist who has written extensively on these matters, and who denies any significant difference between Carter and Wheeler universes in this logical respect, is P. C. W. Davies, *The Accidental Universe*, CUP Cambridge, 1982 and *God and the New Physics*, Simon and Shuster, New York, 1983.

As I said at the start, there is a quite different group of questions, none of which is banal. Is the *premiss* true? *Is* our universe unusual? That takes us to deep questions of cosmology. It also leads to questions of the logic of coincidence that are by no means easy of resolution.[11]

---

[11]My own attempt to analyse the logic of coincidence in the cosmological context is, 'Coincidences: Mundane and Cosmological', in the conference proceedings cited in n. 3.

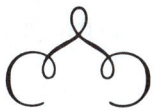

MIRACLES
AND MYSTICAL
EXPERIENCES

DAVID HUME

Skeptical Challenge to the Belief in Miracles

There is, in Dr. Tillotson's writings, an argument against the *real presence* which is as concise and elegant and strong as any argument can possibly be supposed against a doctrine so little worthy of a serious refutation. It is acknowledged on all hands, says that learned prelate, that the authority either of the Scripture or of tradition is founded merely on the testimony of the Apostles, who were eyewitnesses to those miracles of our Saviour by which he proved his divine mission. Our evidence, then, for the truth of the *Christian* religion is less than the evidence for the truth of our senses, because, even in the first authors of our religion, it was no greater; and it is evident it must diminish in passing from them to their disciples, nor can anyone rest such confidence in their testimony as in the immediate object of his senses. But a weaker evidence can never destroy a stronger; and therefore, were the doctrine of the real presence ever so clearly revealed in Scripture, it were directly contrary to the rules of just reasoning to give our assent to it. It contradicts sense, though both the Scripture and tradition, on which it is supposed to be built, carry not such evidence with them as sense when they are considered merely as external evidences, and are not brought home to everyone's breast by the immediate operation of the Holy Spirit.

Nothing is so convenient as a decisive argument of this kind, which must at least *silence* the most arrogant bigotry and superstition and free us from their impertinent solicitations. I flatter myself that I have discovered an argument of a like nature which, if just, will, with the wise and learned, be an everlasting check to all kinds of superstitious delusion, and consequently will be useful as long as the world endures; for so long, I presume, will the accounts of miracles and prodigies be found in all history, sacred and profane.

From David Hume, *An Inquiry Concerning Human Understanding* (1748), section X.

Though experience be our only guide in reasoning concerning matters of fact, it must be acknowledged that this guide is not altogether infallible, but in some cases is apt to lead us into errors. One who in our climate should expect better weather in any week of June than in one of December would reason justly and conformably to experience, but it is certain that he may happen, in the event, to find himself mistaken. However, we may observe that in such a case he would have no cause to complain of experience, because it commonly informs us beforehand of the uncertainty by that contrariety of events which we may learn from a diligent observation. All effects follow not with like certainty from their supposed causes. Some events are found, in all countries and all ages, to have been constantly conjoined together; others are found to have been more variable, and sometimes to disappoint our expectations, so that in our reasonings concerning matter of fact there are all imaginable degrees of assurance, from the highest certainty to the lowest species of moral evidence.

A wise man, therefore, proportions his belief to the evidence. In such conclusions as are founded on an infallible experience, he expects the event with the last degree of assurance and regards his past experience as a full *proof* of the future existence of that event. In other cases he proceeds with more caution: he weighs the opposite experiments; he considers which side is supported by the greater number of experiments—to that side he inclines with doubt and hesitation; and when at last he fixes his judgment, the evidence exceeds not what we properly call "probability." All probability, then, supposes an opposition of experiments and observations where the one side is found to overbalance the other and to produce a degree of evidence proportioned to the superiority. A hundred instances or experiments on one side, and fifty on another, afford a doubtful expectation of any event, though a hundred uniform experiments, with only one that is contradictory, reasonably beget a pretty strong degree of assurance. In all cases we must balance the opposite experiments where they are opposite, and deduct the smaller number from the greater in order to know the exact force of the superior evidence.

To apply these principles to a particular instance, we may observe that there is no species of reasoning more common, more useful, and even necessary to human life than that which is derived from the testimony of men and the reports of eyewitnesses and spectators. This species of reasoning, perhaps, one may deny to be founded on the relation of cause and effect. I shall not dispute about a word. It will be sufficient to observe that our assurance in any argument of this kind is derived from no other principle than our observation of the veracity of human testimony and of the usual conformity of facts to the report of witnesses. It being a general maxim that no objects have any discoverable connection together, and that all the inferences which we can draw from one to another are founded merely on our experience of their constant and regular conjunction, it is evident that we ought not to make an exception to this maxim in favor of human testimony whose connection with any event seems in itself as little necessary as any other. Were not the memory tenacious to a certain degree, had not men commonly an inclination to truth and a principle of probity, were they not sensible to shame when detected in a falsehood—were not these, I say, discovered by *experience* to be qualities inherent in human nature, we should never repose the least confidence in human testimony. A man delirious or noted for falsehood and villainy has no manner of authority with us.

And as the evidence derived from witnesses and human testimony is founded on past experience, so it varies with the experience and is regarded either as a *proof* or a *probability*, according as the conjunction between any particular kind of report and any kind of object has been found to be constant or variable. There are a number of circumstances to be taken into consideration in all judgments of this kind; and the ultimate standard by which we determine all disputes that may arise concerning them is always derived from experience and observation. Where this experience is not entirely uniform on any side, it is attended with an unavoidable contrariety in our judgments and with the same opposition and mutual destruction of argument as in every other kind of evidence. We frequently hesitate concerning the reports of others. We balance the opposite circumstances which cause any doubt or uncertainty; and when we discover a superiority on any side, we incline to it, but still with a diminution of assurance, in proportion to the force of its antagonist.

This contrariety of evidence, in the present case, may be derived from several different causes: from the opposition of contrary testimony, from the character or number of the witnesses, from the manner of their delivering their testimony, or from the union of all these circumstances. We entertain a suspicion concerning any matter of fact when the witnesses contradict each other, when they are but few or of a doubtful character, when they have an interest in what they affirm, when they deliver their testimony with hesitation or, on the contrary, with too violent asseverations. There are many other particulars of the same kind which may diminish or destroy the force of any argument derived from human testimony.

Suppose, for instance, that the fact which the testimony endeavors to establish partakes of the extraordinary and the marvelous—in that case the evidence resulting from the testimony admits of a diminution, greater or less in proportion as the fact is more or less unusual. The reason why we place any credit in witnesses and historians is not derived from any *connection* which we perceive *a priori* between testimony and reality, but because we are accustomed to find a conformity between them. But when the fact attested is such a one as has seldom fallen under our observation, here is a contest of two opposite experiences, of which the one destroys the other as far as its force goes, and the superior can only operate on the mind by the force which remains. The very same principle of experience which gives us a certain degree of assurance in the testimony of witnesses gives us also, in this case, another degree of assurance against the fact which they endeavor to establish; from which contradiction there necessarily arises a counterpoise and mutual destruction of belief and authority.

"I should not believe such a story were it told me by Cato" was a proverbial saying in Rome, even during the lifetime of that philosophical patriot. The incredibility of a fact, it was allowed, might invalidate so great an authority.

The Indian prince who refused to believe the first relations concerning the effects of frost reasoned justly, and it naturally required very strong testimony to engage his assent to facts that arose from a state of nature with which he was unacquainted, and which bore so little analogy to those events of which he had had constant and uniform experience. Though they were not contrary to his experience, they were not conformable to it.

But in order to increase the probability against the testimony of witnesses, let us suppose that the fact which they affirm, instead of being only marvelous, is really miraculous; and suppose also that the testimony, considered apart and in itself, amounts to an entire proof—in that case there is proof against proof, of which the strongest must prevail, but still with a diminution of its force, in proportion to that of its antagonist.

A miracle is a violation of the laws of nature; and as a firm and unalterable experience has established these laws, the proof against a miracle, from the very nature of the fact, is as entire as any argument from experience can possibly be imagined. Why is it more than probable that all men must die, that lead cannot of itself remain suspended in the air, that fire consumes wood and is extinguished by water, unless it be that these events are found agreeable to the laws of nature, and there is required a violation of these laws, or, in other words, a miracle to prevent them? Nothing is esteemed a miracle if it ever happen in the common course of nature. It is no miracle that a man, seemingly in good health, should die on a sudden, because such a kind of death, though more unusual than any other, has yet been frequently observed to happen. But it is a miracle that a dead man should come to life, because that has never been observed in any age or country. There must, therefore, be a uniform experience against every miraculous event, otherwise the event would not merit that appellation. And as a uniform experience amounts to a proof, there is here a direct and full *proof*, from the nature of the fact, against the existence of any miracle, nor can such a proof be destroyed or the miracle rendered credible but by an opposite proof which is superior.

The plain consequence is (and it is a general maxim worthy of our attention) that no testimony is sufficient to establish a miracle unless the testimony be of such a kind that its falsehood would be more miraculous than the fact which it endeavors to establish. And even in that case there is a mutual destruction of arguments, and the superior only gives us an assurance suitable to that degree of force which remains after deducting the inferior.

When anyone tells me that he saw a dead man restored to life, I immediately consider with myself whether it be more probable that this person should either deceive or be deceived, or that the fact which he relates should really have happened. I weigh the one miracle against the other, and according to the superiority which I discover I pronounce my decision, and always reject the greater miracle. If the falsehood of his testimony would be more miraculous than the event which he relates, then, and not till then, can he pretend to command my belief or opinion.

R. G. SWINBURNE

Miracles[1]

In this article I wish to investigate whether there could be strong historical evidence for the occurrence of miracles, and contrary to much writing which has derived from Hume's celebrated chapter "Of Miracles", I shall argue that there could be. I understand by a miracle a violation of a law of Nature by a god, that is, a very powerful rational being who is not a material object (viz., is invisible and intangible). My definition of a miracle is thus approximately the same as Hume's: "a transgression of a law of nature by a particular volition of the Deity or by the interposition of some invisible agent".[2] It has been questioned by many biblical scholars whether this is what the biblical writers understood by the terms translated into English 'miracle.' I do not propose to enter into this controversy. Suffice it to say that many subsequent Christian theologians have understood by 'miracle' roughly what I understand by the term and that much medieval and modern apologetic which appeals to purported miracles as evidence of the truth of the Christian revelation has had a similar understanding of miracle to mine.

I shall take the question in two parts. I shall enquire first whether there could be evidence that a law of nature has been violated, and secondly, if there can be such evidence, whether there could be evidence that the violation was due to a god.

From *The Philosophical Quarterly*, Vol. 18, No. 73, October 1968. Reprinted by permission of the publisher, Basil Blackwell, London.

[1]I am most grateful to Edgar Page and Christopher Williams for their helpful criticisms of an earlier version of this paper.

[2]David Hume, *An Enquiry Concerning Human Understanding*, ed. L. A. Selby-Bigge (Oxford, 2nd ed., 1902), p. 115, footnote.

First, then, can there be evidence that a law of nature has been violated? It seems natural to understand, as Ninian Smart[3] does, by a violation of a law of nature, an occurrence of a non-repeatable counter-instance to a law of nature. Clearly, as Hume admitted, events contrary to predictions of formulae which we had good reason to believe to be laws of nature often occur. But if we have good reason to believe that they have occurred and good reason to believe that similar events would occur in similar circumstances, then we have good reason to believe that the formulae which we previously believed to be the laws of nature were not in fact such laws. Repeatable counter-instances do not violate laws of nature, they just show propositions purporting to state laws of nature to be false. But if we have good reason to believe that an event E has occurred contrary to predictions of a formula L which we have good reason to believe to be a law of nature, and we have good reason to believe that events similar to E would not occur in circumstances as similar as we like in any respect to those of the original occurence, then we do not have reason to believe that L is not a law of nature. For any modified formula which allowed us to predict E would allow us to predict similar events in similar circumstances and hence, we have good reason to believe, would give false predictions. Whereas if we leave the formula L unmodified, it will, we have good reason to believe, give correct predictions in all other conceivable circumstances. Hence if we are to say that any law of nature is operative in the field in question we must say that it is L. This seems a natural thing to say rather than to say that no law of nature operates in the field. Yet E is contrary to the predictions of L. Hence, for want of a better expression, we say that E has violated the law of nature L. If the use of the word 'violated' suggests too close an analogy between laws of nature and civil or moral laws, that is unfortunate. Once we have explained, as above, what is meant by a violation of a law of nature, no subsequent confusion need arise.

The crucial question, not adequately discussed by Smart, however, is what would be good reason for believing that an event E, if it occurred, was a nonrepeatable as opposed to a repeatable counter-instance to a formula L which we have on all other evidence good reason to believe to be a law of nature. The evidence that E is a repeatable counter-instance would be that a new formula L^1 fairly well confirmed by the data as a law of nature can be set up. A formula is confirmed by data, if the data obtained so far are predicted by the formula, if new predictions are successful and if the formula is a simple and coherent one relative to the collection of the data.

Compatible with any finite set of data, there will always be an infinite number of possible formulae from which the data can be predicted. We can rule out many by further tests, but however many tests we make we shall still have only a finite number of data and hence an infinite number of formulae compatible with them.

---

[3]Ninian Smart, *Philosophers and Religious Truth* (London, 1964), Ch. II.

But some of these formulae will be highly complex relative to the data, so that no scientist would consider that the data were evidence that those formulae were true laws of nature. Others are very simple formulae such that the data can be said to provide evidence that they are true laws of nature. Thus suppose the scientist's task is to find a formula accounting for marks on a graph, observed at $(1, 1)$, $(2, 2)$, $(3, 3)$, and $(4, 4)$, the first number of each pair being the x co-ordinate and the second the y co-ordinate. One formula which would predict these marks is $x = y$. Another one is $(x - 1) (x - 2) (x - 3) (x - 4) + x = y$. But clearly we would not regard the data as supporting the second formula. It is too clumsy a formula to explain four observations. Among simple formulae supported by the data, the simplest is the best supported and regarded, provisionally, as correct. If the formula survives further tests, that increases the evidence in its favour as a true law.

Now if for E and for all other relevant data we can construct a formula L^1 from which the data can be derived and which either makes successful predictions in other circumstances where L makes bad predictions, or is a fairly simple formula, so that from the fact that it can predict E, and L cannot, we have reason to believe that its predictions, if tested, would be better than those of L in other circumstances, then we have good reason to believe that L^1 is the true law in the field. The formula will indicate under what circumstances divergencies from L similar to E will occur. The evidence thus indicates that they will occur under these circumstances and hence that E is a repeatable counter-instance to the original formula L.

Suppose, however, that for E and all the other data of the field we can construct no new formula L^1 which yields more successful predictions than L in other examined circumstances, nor one which is fairly simple relative to the data; but for all the other data except E the simple formula L does yield good predictions. And suppose that as the data continue to accumulate, L remains a completely successful predictor and there remains no reason to suppose that a simple formula L^1 from which all the other data and E can be derived can be constructed. The evidence then indicates that the divergence from L will not be repeated and hence that E is a non-repeatable counter-instance to a law of nature L.

Here is an example. Suppose E to be the levitation (viz., rising into the air and remaining floating on it) of a certain holy person. E is a counterinstance to otherwise well substantiated laws of mechanics L. We could show E to be a repeatable counter-instance if we could construct a formula L^1 which predicted E and also successfully predicted other divergences from L, as well as all other tested predictions of L; or if we could construct L^1 which was comparatively simple relative to the data and predicted E and all the other tested predictions of L, but predicted divergences from L which had not yet been tested. L^1 might differ from L in that, according to it, under certain circumstances bodies exercise a gravitational repulsion on each other, and the circumstance in which E occurred was one of those circumstances. If L^1

satisfied either of the above two conditions, we would adopt it, and we would then say that under certain circumstances people do levitate and so E was not a counter-instance to a law of nature. However, it might be that any modification which we made to the laws of mechanics to allow them to predict E might not yield any more successful predictions than L and they [might] be so clumsy that there [would be] no reason to believe that their predictions not yet tested would be successful. Under these circumstances we would have good reasons to believe that the levitation of the holy person violated the laws of nature.

If the laws of nature are statistical and not deterministic, it is not in all cases so clear what counts as a counter-instance to them. How improbable does an event have to be to constitute a counter-instance to a statistical law? But this problem is a general one in the philosophy of science and does not raise any issues peculiar to the topic of miracles.

It is clear that all claims about what does or does not violate the laws of nature are corrigible. New scientific knowledge may force us to revise any such claims. But all claims to knowledge about matters of fact are corrigible, and we must reach provisional conclusions about them on the evidence available to us. We have to some extent good evidence about what are the laws of nature, and some of them are so well established and account for so many data that any modifications to them which we could suggest to account for the odd counter-instance would be so clumsy and *ad hoc* as to upset the whole structure of science. In such cases the evidence is strong that if the purported counter-instance occurred it was a violation of the laws of nature. There is good reason to believe that the following events, if they occurred, would be violations of the laws of nature: levitation; resurrection from the dead in full health of a man whose heart has not been beating for twenty-four hours and who was, by other criteria also, dead; water turning into wine without the assistance of chemical apparatus or catalysts; a man getting better from polio in a minute.

So then we could have the evidence that an event E if it occurred was a non-repeatable counter-instance to a true law of nature L. But Hume's argument here runs as follows. The evidence, which *ex hypothesi* is good evidence, that L is a true law of nature is evidence that E did not occur. We have certain other evidence that E did occur. In such circumstances, writes Hume, the wise man "weighs the opposite experiments. He considers which side is supported by the greater number of experiments."[4] Since he supposes that the evidence that E occurred would be that of testimony, Hume concludes "that no testimony is sufficient to establish a miracle, unless the testimony be of such a kind, that its falsehood would be more miraculous, than the fact which it endeavours to establish."[5] He considers that this condition is not in fact satisfied by any purported miracle, though he seems at times to allow that it is logically possible that it might be.

---

[4]*Op. cit.*, p. 111.
[5]*Op. cit.*, p. 116.

One wonders here at Hume's scale of evidence. Suppose two hundred witnesses claiming to have observed some event E, an event which, if it occurred, would be a non-repeatable counter-instance to a law of nature. Suppose these to be witnesses able and anxious to show that E did not occur if there were grounds for doing so. Would not their combined evidence give us good reason to believe that E occurred? Hume's answer which we can see from his discussion of two apparently equally well authenticated miracles is—No. But then, one is inclined to say, is not Hume just being bigoted, refusing to face facts? It would be virtually impossible to draw up a table showing how many witnesses and of what kind we need to establish the occurrence of an event which, if it occurred, would be a non-repeatable counter-instance to a law of nature. Each purported instance has to be considered on its merits. But certainly one feels that Hume's standards of evidence are too high. What, one wonders, would Hume himself say if he saw such an event?

But behind Hume's excessively stringent demands on evidence there may be a philosophical point which he has not fully brought out. This is a point made by Flew in justification of Hume's standards of evidence: "The justification for giving the 'scientific' this ultimate precedence here over the 'historical' lies in the nature of the propositions concerned and in the evidence which can be displayed to sustain them...the candidate historical proposition will be particular, often singular, and in the past tense.... But just by reason of this very pastness and particularity it is no longer possible for anyone to examine the subject directly for himself...the law of nature will, unlike the candidate historical proposition, be a general nomological. It can thus in theory, though obviously not always in practice, be tested at any time by any person".[6]

Flew's contrast is, however, mistaken. Particular experiments on particular occasions only give a certain and far from conclusive support to claims that a purported scientific law is true. Any person can test for the truth of a purported scientific law, but a positive result to one test will only give limited support to the claim. Exactly the same holds for purported historical truths. Anyone can examine the evidence, but a particular piece of evidence only gives limited support to the claim that the historical proposition is true. But in the historical as in the scientific case, there is no limit to the amount of evidence. We can go on and on testing for the truth of historical as well as scientific propositions. We can look for more and more data which can only be explained as effects of some specified past event, and data incompatible with its occurrence, just as we can look for more and more data for or against the truth of some physical law. Hence the truth of the historical proposition can also "be tested at any time by any person."

What Hume seems to suppose is that the only evidence about whether an event E happened is the written or verbal testimony of those who would

---

[6]Antony Flew, *Hume's Philosophy of Belief* (London, 1961), pp. 207 ff.

have been in a position to witness it, had it occurred. And as there will be only a finite number of such pieces of testimony, the evidence about whether or not E happened would be finite. But this is not the only testimony which is relevant—we need testimony about the character and competence of the original witnesses. Nor is testimony the only type of evidence. All effects of what happened at the time of the alleged occurrence of E are also relevant. Far more than in Hume's day we are today often in a position to assess what occurred by studying the physical traces of the event. Hume had never met Sherlock Holmes with his ability to assess what happened in the room from the way in which the furniture lay, or where the witness was yesterday from the mud on his boot. As the effects of what happened at the time of the occurrence of E are always with us in some form, we can always go on examining them yet more carefully. Further, we need to investigate whether E, if it did occur, would in fact have brought about the present effects, and whether any other cause could have brought about just these effects. To investigate these issues involves investigating which scientific laws operate (other than the law L of which it is claimed that E was a violation), and this involves doing experiments *ad lib*. Hence there is no end to the amount of new evidence which can be had. The evidence that the event E occurred can go on mounting up in the way that evidence that L is a law of nature can do. The wise man in these circumstances will surely say that he has good reason to believe that E occurred, but also that L is a true law of nature and so that E was a violation of it.

So we could have good reason to believe that a law of nature has been violated. But for a violation of a law of nature to be a miracle, it has to be caused by a god, that is, a very powerful rational being who is not a material object. What could be evidence that it was?

To explain an event as brought about by a rational agent with intentions and purposes is to give an entirely different kind of explanation of its occurrence from an explanation by scientific laws acting on precedent causes. Our normal grounds for attributing an event to the agency of an embodied rational agent A is that we or others perceived A bringing it about *or* that it is the sort of event that A typically brings about and that A, and no one else of whom we have knowledge, was in a position to bring it about. The second kind of ground is only applicable when we have prior knowledge of the existence of A. In considering evidence for a violation E of a law of nature being due to the agency of a god, I will distinguish two cases, one where we have good reason on grounds other than the occurrence of violations of laws of nature to believe that there exists at least one god, and one where we do not.

Let us take the second case first. Suppose we have no other good reason for believing that a god exists, but an event E then occurs which, our evidence indicates, is a non-repeatable counter-instance to a true law of nature. Now we cannot attribute E to the agency of a god by seeing the god's body bring

E about, for gods do not have bodies. But suppose that E occurs in ways and circumstances C strongly analogous to those in which occur events brought about by human agents, and that other violations occur in such circumstances. We would then be justified in claiming that E and other such violations are, like effects of human actions, brought about by agents, but ones unlike men in not being material objects. This inference would be justified because, if an analogy between effects is strong enough, we are always justified in postulating slight difference in causes to account for slight difference in effects. Thus if because of its other observable behaviour we say that light is a disturbance in a medium, then the fact that the medium, if it exists, does not, like other media, slow down material bodies passing through it, is not by itself (viz., if there are no other disanalogies) a reason for saying that the light is not a disturbance in a medium, but only for saying that the medium in which light is a disturbance has the peculiar property of not resisting the passage of material bodies. So if, because of very strong similarity between the ways and circumstances of the occurrence of E and other violations of laws of nature to the ways and circumstances in which effects are produced by human agents, we postulate a similar cause—a rational agent, the fact there are certain disanalogies (viz., we cannot point to the agent, say where his body is) does not mean that our explanation is wrong. It only means that the agent is unlike humans in not having a body. But this move is only justified if the similarities are otherwise strong. Nineteenth-century scientists eventually concluded that for light the similarities were not strong enough to outweigh the dissimilarities and justify postulating the medium with the peculiar property.

Now what similiarities in the ways and circumstances C of their occurrence could there be between E (and other violations of laws of nature) and the effects of human actions to justify the postulation of similar causes? Suppose that E occurred in answer to a request. Thus E might be an explosion in my room, totally inexplicable by the laws of nature, when at the time of its occurrence there were in a room on the other side of the corridor men in turbans chanting "O God of the Sikhs, may there be an explosion in Swinburne's room." Suppose, too, that when E occurs a voice, but not the voice of an embodied agent, is heard giving reasonable reasons for granting the request. When the explosion occurs in my room, a voice emanating from no man or animal or man-made machine is heard saying "Your request is granted. He deserves a lesson." Would not all this be good reason for postulating a rational agent other than a material object who brought about E and the other violations, an agent powerful enough to change instantaneously by intervention the properties of things, viz., a god? Clearly if the analogy were strong enough between the ways and circumstances in which violations of laws of nature and effects of human action occur, it would be. If furthermore the prayers which were answered by miracles were prayers for certain kinds of events (e.g., relief of suffering, punishment of ill-doers) and those which were not answered by miracles were for events of different kinds, then this would show something about the character of the god. Normally, of course, the evidence adduced by theists for the occurrence of miracles is not as strong as I have indicated that very strong evidence would be. Violations are often reported as occurring subsequent to prayer for them to occur, and seldom otherwise; but voices giving reasons for answering such a request are rare indeed. Whether in cases where voices are not heard but the occurrence of a violation E and of prayer for its occurrence were both well confirmed, we would be justified in concluding that the existence of a god who brought E about is a matter of whether the analogy is strong enough as it stands. The question of exactly when an analogy is strong enough to justify an inference based on it is a difficult one. But my only point here is that if the analogy were strong enough, the inference would be justified.

Suppose now that we have other evidence for the existence of a god. Then if E occurs in the circumstances C, previously described, that E is due to the activity of a god is more adequately substantiated, and the occurrence of E gives further support to the evidence for the existence of a god. But if we already have reason to believe in the existence of a god, the occurrence of E not under circumstances as similar as C to those under which human agents often bring about results, could nevertheless sometimes be justifiably attributed to his activity. Thus, if the occurrence of E is the sort of thing that the only god of whose existence we have evidence would wish to bring about if he has the character suggested by the other evidence for his existence, we can reasonably hold him responsible for the occurrence of E which would otherwise be unexplained. The healing of a faithful blind Christian contrary to the laws of nature could reasonably be attributed to the God of the Christians, if there were other evidence for his existence, whether or not the blind man or other Christians had ever prayed for that result.

For these reasons I conclude that we can have good reason to believe that a violation of a law of nature was caused by a god, and so was a miracle.

I would like to make two final points, one to tidy up the argument and the other to meet a further argument put forward by Hume which I have not previously discussed.

Entia non sunt multiplicanda praeter necessitatem.— Unless we have good reason to do so we ought not to postulate the existence of more than one god, but to suppose that the same being answers all prayers. But there could be good reason to postulate the existence of more than one god, and evidence to this effect could be provided by miracles. One way in which this could happen is that prayers for a certain kind of result, for example, shipwreck, which began "O, Neptune" were often answered, and also prayers for a different kind of result, for example, success in love, which began "O, Venus" were also often answered, but prayers for a result of the first kind beginning

"O, Venus", and for a result of the second kind beginning "O, Neptune" were never answered. Evidence for the existence of one god would in general support, not oppose, evidence for the existence of a second one since, by suggesting that there is one rational being other than those whom we can see, it makes more reasonable the postulation of another one.

The second point is that there is no reason at all to suppose that Hume is in general right to claim that "every miracle...pretended to have been wrought in any...(religion)...as its direct scope is to establish the particular system to which it is attributed; so has it the same force, though more indirectly, to overthrow every other system. In destroying a rival system it likewise destroys the credit of those miracles on which that system was established".[7] If Hume were right to claim that evidence for the miracles of one religion was evidence against the miracles of any other, then indeed evidence for miracles in each would be poor. But in fact evidence for a miracle "wrought in one religion" is only evidence against the occurrence of a miracle "wrought in another religion" if the two miracles, if they occurred, would be evidence for propositions of the two religious systems incompatible with each other. It is hard to think of pairs of alleged miracles of this type. If there were evidence for a Roman Catholic miracle which was evidence for the doctrine of transubstantiation and evidence for a Protestant miracle which was evidence against it, here we would have a case of the conflict of evidence which, Hume claims, occurs generally with alleged miracles. But it is enough to give this example to see that most alleged miracles do not give rise to conflicts of this kind. Most alleged miracles, if they occurred, would only show the power of god or gods and their concern for the needs of men, and little else.

My main conclusion, to repeat it, is that there are no logical difficulties in supposing that there could be strong historical evidence for the occurence of miracles. Whether there is such evidence is, of course, another matter.

---

[7] *Op. cit.*, pp. 121 ff.

WILLIAM JAMES

Mysticism

Over and over again in these lectures I have raised points and left them open and unfinished until we should have come to the subject of Mysticism. Some of you, I fear, may have smiled as you noted my reiterated postponements. But now the hour has come when mysticism must be faced in good earnest, and those broken threads wound up together. One may say truly, I think, that personal religious experience has its root and centre in mystical states of consciousness; so for us, who in these lectures are treating personal experience as the exclusive subject of our study, such states of consciousness ought to form the vital chapter from which the other chapters get their light. Whether my treatment of mystical states will shed more light or darkness, I do not know, for my own constitution shuts me out from their enjoyment almost entirely, and I can speak of them only at second hand. But though forced to look upon the subject so externally, I will be as objective and receptive as I can; and I think I shall at least succeed in convincing you of the reality of the states in question, and of the paramount importance of their function.

First of all, then, I ask, What does the expression "mystical states of consciousness" mean? How do we part off mystical states from other states?

The words "mysticism" and "mystical" are often used as terms of mere reproach, to throw at any opinion which we regard as vague and vast and sentimental, and without a base in either facts or logic. For some writers a "mystic" is any person who believes in thought-transference, or spirit-return. Employed in this way the word has little value: there are too many less ambiguous synonyms. So, to keep it useful by restricting it, I will do what I did in the case of the word "religion," and simply propose to you four marks which, when an experience has them, may justify us in calling it mystical for the purpose of the present lectures. In this way we shall save verbal disputation, and the recriminations that generally go therewith.

1. *Ineffability.*—The handiest of the marks by which I classify a state of mind as mystical is negative. The subject of it immediately says that it defies expression, that no adequate report of its contents can be given in words. It follows from this that its quality must be directly experienced; it cannot be imparted or transferred to others. In this peculiarity mystical states are more

---

From William James, *The Varieties of Religious Experience* (1902).

like states of feeling than like states of intellect. No one can make clear to another who has never had a certain feeling, in what the quality or worth of it consists. One must have musical ears to know the value of a symphony; one must have been in love one's self to understand a lover's state of mind. Lacking the heart or ear, we cannot interpret the musician or the lover justly, and are even likely to consider him weak-minded or absurd. The mystic finds that most of us accord to his experiences an equally incompetent treatment.

2. *Noetic quality.*—Although so similar to states of feeling, mystical states seem to those who experience them to be also states of knowledge. They are states of insight into depths of truth unplumbed by the discursive intellect. They are illuminations, revelations, full of significance and importance, all inarticulate though they remain; and as a rule they carry with them a curious sense of authority for aftertime.

These two characters will entitle any state to be called mystical, in the sense in which I use the word. Two other qualities are less sharply marked, but are usually found. These are:—

3. *Transiency.*—Mystical states cannot be sustained for long. Except in rare instances, half an hour, or at most an hour or two, seems to be the limit beyond which they fade into the light of common day. Often, when faded, their quality can but imperfectly be reproduced in memory; but when they recur it is recognized; and from one recurrence to another it is susceptible of continuous development in what is felt as inner richness and importance.

4. *Passivity.*—Although the oncoming of mystical states may be facilitated by preliminary voluntary operations, as by fixing the attention, or going through certain bodily performances, or in other ways which manuals of mysticism prescribe; yet when the characteristic sort of consciousness once has set in, the mystic feels as if his own will were in abeyance, and indeed sometimes as if he were grasped and held by a superior power. This latter peculiarity connects mystical states with certain definite phenomena of secondary or alternative personality, such as prophetic speech, automatic writing, or the mediumistic trance. When these latter conditions are well pronounced, however, there may be no recollection whatever of the phenomenon, and it may have no significance for the subject's usual inner life, to which, as it were, it makes a mere interruption. Mystical states, strictly so-called, are never merely interruptive. Some memory of their content always remains, and a profound sense of their importance. They modify the inner life of the subject between the times of their recurrence. Sharp divisions in this region are, however, difficult to make, and we find all sorts of gradations and mixtures.

These four characteristics are sufficient to mark out a group of states of consciousness peculiar enough to deserve a special name and to call for careful study. Let it then be called the mystical group....

In India, training in mystical insight has been known from time immemorial under the name of yoga. Yoga means the experimental union of the individual with the divine. It is based on persevering exercise; and the diet, posture, breathing, intellectual concentration, and moral discipline vary slightly in the different systems which teach it. The yogi, or disciple, who has by these means overcome the obscurations of his lower nature sufficiently, enters into the condition termed *samâdhi*, "and comes face to face with facts which no instinct or reason can ever know." He learns—

> That the mind itself has a higher state of existence, beyond reason, a super-conscious state, and that when the mind gets to that higher state, then this knowledge beyond reasoning comes.... All the different steps in yoga are intended to bring us scientifically to the superconscious state or Samâdhi.... Just as unconscious work is beneath consciousness, so there is another work which is above consciousness, and which, also, is not accompanied with the feeling of egoism.... There is no feeling of *I*, and yet the mind works, desireless, free from restlessness, objectless, bodiless. Then the Truth shines in its full effulgence, and we know ourselves—for Samâdhi lies potential in us all—for what we truly are, free, immortal, omnipotent, loosed from the finite, and its contrasts of good and evil altogether, and identical with the Atman or Universal Soul.

The Vedantists say that one may stumble into superconsciousness sporadically, without the previous discipline, but it is then impure. Their tests of its purity, like our test of religion's value, is empirical: its fruits must be good for life. When a man comes out of Samâdhi, they assure us that he remains "enlightened, a sage, a prophet, a saint, his whole character changed, his life changed, illumined."

The Buddhists used the word "samâdhi" as well as the Hindus; but "dyhâna" is their special word for higher states of contemplation. There seem to be four stages recognized in dyhâna. The first stage comes through concentration of the mind upon one point. It excludes desire, but not discernment or judgment: it is still intellectual. In the second stage the intellectual functions drop off, and the satisfied sense of unity remains. In the third stage the satisfaction departs, and indifference begins, along with memory and self-consciousness. In the fourth stage the indifference, memory, and self-consciousness are perfected. [Just what "memory" and "self-consciousness" mean in this connection is doubtful. They cannot be the faculties familiar to us in the lower life.] Higher stages still of contemplation are mentioned—a region where there exists nothing, and where the mediator says: "There exists absolutely nothing," and stops. Then he reaches another region where he says: "There are neither ideas nor absence of ideas," and stops again. Then another region where, "having reached the end of both idea and perception, he stops finally." This would seem to be, not yet Nirvâna, but as close an approach to it as this life affords.

In the Mohammedan world the Sufi sect and various dervish bodies are the possessors of the mystical tradition. The Sufis have existed in Persia from the earliest times, and as their pantheism is so at variance with the hot and rigid monotheism of the Arab mind, it has been suggested that Sufism must have been inoculated into Islam by Hindu influences. We Christians know little of Sufism, for its secrets are disclosed only to those initiated. To give its existence a certain liveliness in your minds, I will quote a Moslem document, and pass away from the subject.

Al-Ghazzali, a Persian philosopher and theologian, who flourished in the eleventh century, and ranks as one of the greatest doctors of the Moslem church, has left us one of the few autobiographies to be found outside of Christian literature. Strange that a species of book so abundant among ourselves should be so little represented elsewhere—the absence of strictly personal confessions is the chief difficulty to the purely literary student who would like to become acquainted with the inwardness of religions other than the Christian.

M. Schmölders has translated a part of Al-Ghazzali's autobiography into French:—

> The Science of the Sufis (says the Moslem author) aims at detaching the heart from all that is not God, and at giving to it for sole occupation the meditation of the divine being. Theory being more easy for me than practice, I read [certain books] until I understood all that can be learned by study and hearsay. Then I recognized that what pertains most exclusively to their method is just what no study can grasp, but only transport, ecstasy, and the transformation of the soul. How great, for example, is the difference between knowing the definitions of health, of satiety, with their causes and conditions, and being really healthy or filled. How different to know in what drunkenness consists—as being a state occasioned by a vapor that rises from the stomach—and *being* drunk effectively. Without doubt, the drunken man knows neither the definition of drunkenness nor what makes it interesting for science. Being drunk, he knows nothing; whilst the physician, although not drunk, knows well in what drunkenness consists, and what are its pre-disposing conditions. Similarly there is a difference between knowing the nature of abstinence, and *being* abstinent or having one's soul detached from the world.—Thus I had learned what words could teach of Sufism, but what was left could be learned neither by study nor through the ears, but solely by giving one's self up to ecstasy and leading a pious life.
>
> Reflecting on my situation, I found myself tied down by a multitude of bonds—temptations on every side. Considering my teaching, I found it was impure before God. I saw myself struggling with all my might to achieve glory and to spread my name. [Here follows an account of his six months' hesitation to break away from the conditions of his life at Bagdad, at the end of which he fell ill with a paralysis of the tongue.] Then, feeling my own weakness, and having entirely given up my own will, I repaired to God like a man in distress who has no more resources. He answered, as he answers the wretch who invokes him. My heart no longer felt any difficulty in renouncing glory, wealth, and my children. So I quitted Bagdad, and reserving from my fortune only what was indispensable for my subsistence, I distributed the rest. I went to Syria, where I remained about two years, with no other occupation than living in retreat and solitude, conquering my desires, combating my passions,

training myself to purify my soul, to make my character perfect, to prepare my heart for meditating on God—all according to the methods of the Sufis, as I had read of them.

This retreat only increased my desire to live in solitude, and to complete the purification of my heart and fit it for meditation. But the vicissitudes of the times, the affairs of the family, the need of subsistence, changed in some respects my primitive resolve, and interfered with my plans for a purely solitary life. I had never yet found myself completely in ecstasy, save in a few single hours; nevertheless, I kept the hope of attaining this state. Every time that the accidents led me astray, I sought to return; and in this situation I spent ten years. During this solitary state things were revealed to me which it is impossible either to describe or to point out. I recognized for certain that the Sufis are assuredly walking in the path of God. Both in their acts and their inaction, whether internal or external, they are illumined by the light which proceeds from the prophetic source. The first condition for a Sufi is to purge his heart entirely of all that is not God. The next key of the contemplative life consists in the humble prayers which escape from the fervent soul, and in the meditations on God in which the heart is swallowed up entirely. But in reality this is only the beginning of the Sufi life, the end of Sufism being total absorption in God. The intuitions and all that precede are, so to speak, only the threshold for those who enter. From the beginning, revelations take place in so flagrant a shape that the Sufis see before them, whilst wide awake, the angels and the souls of the prophets. They hear their voices and obtain their favors. Then the transport rises from the perception of forms and figures to a degree which escapes all expression, and which no man may seek to give an account of without his words involving sin.

Whosoever has had no experience of the transport knows of the true nature of prophetism nothing but the name. He may meanwhile be sure of its existence, both by experience and by what he hears the Sufis say. As there are men endowed only with the sensitive faculty who reject what is offered them in the way of objects of the pure understanding, so there are intellectual men who reject and avoid the things perceived by the prophetic faculty. A blind man can understand nothing of colors save what he has learned by narration and hearsay. Yet God has brought prophetism near to men in giving them all a state analogous to it in its principal characters. This state is sleep. If you were to tell a man who was himself without experience of such a phenomenon that there are people who at times swoon away so as to resemble dead men, and who [in dreams] yet perceive things that are hidden, he would deny it [and give his reasons]. Nevertheless, his arguments would be refuted by actual experience. Wherefore, just as the understanding is a stage of human life in which an eye opens to discern various intellectual objects uncomprehended by sensation; just so in the prophetic the sight is illumined by a light which uncovers hidden things and objects which the intellect fails to reach. The chief properties of prophetism are perceptible only during the transport, by those who embrace the Sufi life. The prophet is endowed with qualities to which you possess nothing analogous, and which consequently you cannot possibly understand. How should you know their true nature, since one knows only what one can comprehend? But the transport which one attains by the method of the Sufis is like an immediate perception, as if one touched the objects with one's hand.

This incommunicableness of the transport is the keynote of all mysticism. Mystical truth exists for the individual who has the transport, but for no one else. In this, as I have said, it resembles the knowledge given to us in sensations more than that given by conceptual thought. Thought, with its remoteness and abstractness, has often enough in the history of philosophy been contrasted unfavorably with sensation. It is a commonplace of metaphysics that God's knowledge cannot be discursive but must be intuitive, that is, must be constructed more after the pattern of what in ourselves is called immediate feeling, that after that of proposition and judgment. But *our* immediate feelings have no content but what the five senses supply; and we have seen and shall see again that mystics may emphatically deny that the senses play any part in the very highest type of knowledge which their transports yield.

In the Christian church there have always been mystics. Although many of them have been viewed with suspicion, some have gained favor in the eyes of the authorities. The experiences of these have been treated as precedents, and a codified system of mystical theology has been based upon them, in which everything legitimate finds its place. The basis of the system is "orison" or meditation, the methodical elevation of the soul towards God. Through the practice of orison the higher levels of mystical experience may be attained. It is odd that Protestantism, especially evangelical Protestantism, should seemingly have abandoned everything methodical in this line. Apart from what prayer may lead to, Protestant mystical experience appears to have been almost exclusively sporadic. It has been left to our mindcurers to reintroduce methodical meditation into our religious life.

The first thing to be aimed at in orison is the mind's detachment from outer sensations for these interfere with its concentration upon ideal things. Such manuals as Saint Ignatius's Spiritual Exercises recommend the disciple to expel sensation by a graduated series of efforts to imagine holy scenes. The acme of this kind of discipline would be a semi-hallucinatory mono-ideism— an imaginary figure of Christ, for example, coming fully to occupy the mind. Sensorial images of this sort, whether literal or symbolic, play an enormous part in mysticism. But in certain cases imagery may fall away entirely, and in the very highest raptures it ends to do so. The state of consciousness becomes then insusceptible of any verbal description. Mystical teachers are unanimous as to this. Saint John of the Cross, for instance, one of the best of them, thus describes the condition called the "union of love," which, he says, is reached by "dark contemplation." In this the Deity compenetrates the soul, but in such a hidden way that the soul—

> finds no terms, no means, no comparison whereby to render the sublimity of the wisdom and the delicacy of the spiritual feeling with which she is filled.... We receive this mystical knowledge of God clothed in none of the kinds of images, in none of the sensible representations, which our mind makes use of in other circumstances. Accordingly in this knowledge, since the senses and the

imagination are not employed, we get neither form nor impression, nor can we give any account or furnish any likeness, although the mysterious and sweet-tasting wisdom comes home so clearly to the inmost parts of our soul. Fancy a man seeing a certain kind of thing for the first time in his life. He can understand it, use and enjoy it, but he cannot apply a name to it, nor communicate any idea of it, even though all the while it be a mere thing of sense. How much greater will be his powerlessness when it goes beyond the senses! This is the peculiarity of the divine language. The more infused, intimate, spiritual, and supersensible it is, the more does it exceed the senses, both inner and outer, and impose silence upon them.... The soul then feels as if placed in a vast and profound solitude, to which no created thing has access, in an immense and boundless desert, desert the more delicious the more solitary it is. There, in this abyss of wisdom, the soul grows by what it drinks in from the well-springs of the comprehension of love,...and recognizes, however sublime and learned may be the terms we employ, how utterly vile, insignificant, and improper they are, when we seek to discourse of divine things by their means.

I cannot pretend to detail to you the sundry stages of the Christian mystical life. Our time would not suffice, for one thing; and moreover, I confess that the subdivisions and names which we find in the Catholic books seem to me to represent nothing objectively distinct. So many men, so many minds; I imagine that these experiences can be as infinitely varied as are the idiosyncrasies of individuals.

The cognitive aspects of them, their value in the way of revelation, is what we are directly concerned with, and it is easy to show by citation how strong an impression they leave of being revelations of new depths of truth. Saint Teresa is the expert of experts in describing such conditions, so I will turn immediately to what she says of one of the highest of them, the "orison of union."

In the orison of union (says Saint Teresa) the soul is fully awake as regards God, but wholly asleep as regards things of this world and in respect of herself. During the short time the union lasts, she is as it were deprived of every feeling, and even if she would, she could not think of any single thing. Thus she needs to employ no artifice in order to arrest the use of her understanding: it remains so stricken with inactivity that she neither knows what she loves, nor in what manner she loves, nor what she wills. In short, she is utterly dead to the things of the world and lives solely in God.... I do not even know whether in this state she has enough life left to breathe. It seems to me she has not; or at least that if she does breathe, she is unaware of it. Her intellect would fain understand something of what is going on within her, but it has so little force now that it can act in no way whatsoever. So a person who falls into a deep faint appears as if dead....

Thus does God, when he raises a soul to union with himself, suspend the natural action of all her faculties. She neither sees, hears, nor understands, so long as she is united with God. But this time is always short, and it seems even shorter than it is. God establishes himself in the interior of this soul in such a way, that when she returns to herself, it is wholly impossible for her to doubt that she has been in God, and God in her. This truth remains so strongly impressed on her that, even though many years should pass without the condition returning, she can neither forget the favor she received, nor doubt of its reality. If you, nevertheless, ask how it is possible that the soul can see and understand that she has been in God, since during the union she has neither sight nor understanding, I reply that she does not see it then, but that she sees it clearly later, after she has returned to herself, not by any vision, but by a certitude which abides with her and which God alone can give her. I knew a person who was ignorant of the truth that God's mode of being in everything must be either by presence, by power, or by essence, but who, after having received the grace of which I am speaking, believed this truth in the most unshakable manner. So much so that, having consulted a half-learned man who was as ignorant on this point as she had been before she was enlightened, when he replied that God is in us only by "grace," she disbelieved his reply, so sure she was of the true answer; and when she came to ask wiser doctors, they confirmed her in her belief, which much consoled her....

But how, you will repeat, *can* one have such certainty in respect to what one does not see? This question, I am powerless to answer. These are secrets of God's omnipotence which it does not appertain to me to penetrate. All that I know is that I tell the truth; and I shall never believe that any soul who does not possess this certainty has ever been really united to God.

The kinds of truth communicable in mystical ways, whether these be sensible or supersensible, are various. Some of them relate to this world—visions of the future, the reading of hearts, the sudden understanding of tests, the knowledge of distant events, for example; but the most important revelations are theological or metaphysical.

Saint Ignatius confessed one day to Father Laynez that a single hour of meditation at Manresa had taught him more truths about heavenly things than all the teachings of all the doctors put together could have taught him.... One day in orison, on the steps of the choir of the Dominican church, he saw in a distinct manner the plan of divine wisdom in the creation of the world. On another occasion, during a procession, his spirit was ravished in God, and it was given him to contemplate, in a form and images fitted to the weak understanding of a dweller on the earth, the deep mystery of the holy Trinity. This last vision flooded his heart with such sweetness, that the mere memory of it in after times made him shed abundant tears.

Similarly with Saint Teresa.

One day, being in orison (she writes), it was granted me to perceive in one instant how all things are seen and contained in God. I did not perceive them in their proper form, and nevertheless the view I had of them was of a sovereign clearness, and has remained vividly impressed upon my soul. It is one of the most signal of all the graces which the Lord has granted me.... The view was so subtle and delicate that the understanding cannot grasp it.

She goes on to tell how it was as if the Deity were an enormous and sovereignly limpid diamond, in which all our actions were contained in such a way that their full sinfulness appeared evident as never before. On another day, she relates, while she was reciting the Athanasian Creed—

> Our Lord made me comprehend in what way it is that one God can be in three persons. He made me see it so clearly that I remained as extremely surprised as I was comforted,...and now, when I think of the holy Trinity, or hear It spoken of, I understand how the three adorable Persons form only one God and I experience an unspeakable happiness.

On still another occasion, it was given to Saint Teresa to see and understand in what wise the Mother of God had been assumed into her place in Heaven.

The deliciousness of some of these states seems to be beyond anything known in ordinary consciousness. It evidently involves organic sensibilities, for it is spoken of as something too extreme to be borne, and as verging on bodily pain. But it is too subtle and piercing a delight for ordinary words to denote. God's touches, the wounds of his spear, references to ebriety and to nuptial union have to figure in the phraseology by which it is shadowed forth. Intellect and senses both swoon away in these highest states of ecstasy. "If our understanding comprehends," says Saint Teresa, "it is in a mode which remains unknown to it, and it can understand nothing of what it comprehends. For my own part, I do not believe that it does comprehend, because, as I said, it does not understand itself to do so. I confess that it is all a mystery in which I am lost." In the condition called *raptus* or ravishment by theologians, breathing and circulation are so depressed that it is a question among the doctors whether the soul be or be not temporarily disseuered from the body. One must read Saint Teresa's descriptions and the very exact distinctions which she makes, to persuade one's self that one is dealing, not with imaginary experiences, but with phenomena which, however rare, follow perfectly definite psychological types.

To the medical mind these ecstasies signify nothing but suggested and imitated hypnoid states, on an intellectual basis of superstition, and a corporeal one of degeneration and hysteria. Undoubtedly these pathological conditions have existed in many and possibly in all the cases, but that fact tells us nothing about the value for knowledge of the consciousness which they induce. To pass a spiritual judgment upon these states, we must not content ourselves with superficial medical talk, but inquire into their fruits for life.

Their fruits appear to have been various. Stupefaction, for one thing, seems not to have been altogether absent as a result. You may remember the helplessness in the kitchen and schoolroom of poor Margaret Mary Alacoque. Many other ecstatics would have perished but for the care taken of them by admiring followers. The "other-worldliness" encouraged by the mystical consciousness makes this over-abstraction from practical life peculiarly liable to befall mystics in whom the character is naturally passive and the intellect feeble; but in natively strong minds and characters we find quite opposite results. The great Spanish mystics, who carried the habit of ecstasy as far as it has often been carried, appear for the most part to have shown indomitable spirit and energy, and all the more so for the trances in which they indulged.

Saint Ignatius was a mystic, but his mysticism made him assuredly one of the most powerfully practical human engines that ever lived. Saint John of the Cross, writing of the intuitions and "touches" by which God reaches the substance of the soul, tells us that—

> They enrich it marvelously. A single one of them may be sufficient to abolish at a stroke certain imperfections of which the soul during its whole life had vainly tried to rid itself, and to leave it adorned with virtues and loaded with supernatural gifts. A single one of these intoxicating consolations may reward it for all the labors undergone in its life—even were they numberless. Invested with an invincible courage, filled with an impassioned desire to suffer for its God, the soul then is seized with a strange torment—that of not being allowed to suffer enough.

Saint Teresa is as emphatic, and much more detailed. You may perhaps remember a passage I quoted from her in my first lecture. There are many similar pages in her autobiography. Where in literature is a more evidently veracious account of the formation of a new center of spiritual energy, than is given in her description of the effects of certain ecstasies which in departing leave the soul upon a higher level of emotional excitement?

> Often, infirm and wrought upon with dreadful pains before the ecstasy, the soul emerges from it full of health and admirably disposed for action...as if God had willed that the body itself, already obedient to the soul's desires, should share in the soul's happiness.... The soul after such a favor is animated with a degree of courage so great that if at that moment its body should be torn to pieces for the cause of God, it would feel nothing but the liveliest comfort. Then it is that promises and heroic resolutions spring up in profusion in us, soaring desires, horror of the world, and the clear perception of our proper nothingness.... What empire is comparable to that of a soul who, from this sublime summit to which God has raised her, sees all the things of earth beneath her feet, and is captivated by no one of them? How ashamed she is of her former attachments! How amazed at her blindness! What lively pity she feels for those whom she recognizes still shrouded in the darkness!... She groans at having ever been sensitive to points of honor, at the illusion that made her ever see as honor what the world calls by that name. Now she sees in this name nothing more than an immense lie of which the world remains a victim. She discovers, in the new light from above, that in genuine honor there is nothing spurious, that to be faithful to this honor is to give our respect to what deserves to be respected really, and to consider as nothing, or as less than nothing, whatsoever perishes and is not agreeable to God.... She laughs when she sees grave persons, persons of orison,

caring for points of honor for which she now feels profoundest contempt. It is suitable to the dignity of their rank to act thus, they pretend, and it makes them more useful to others. But she knows that in despising the dignity of their rank for the pure love of God they would do more good in a single day than they would effect in ten years by preserving it.... She laughs at herself that there should ever have been a time in her life when she made any case of money, when she ever desired it.... Oh! if human beings might only agree together to regard it as so much useless mud, what harmony would then reign in the world! With what friendship we would all treat each other if our interest in honor and in money could but disappear from earth! For my own part, I feel as if it would be a remedy for all our ills.

Mystical conditions may, therefore, render the soul more energetic in the lines which their inspiration favors. But this could be reckoned an advantage only in case the inspiration were a true one. If the inspiration were erroneous, the energy would be all the more mistaken and misbegotten. So we stand once more before the problem of truth which confronted us at the end of the lectures on saintliness. You will remember that we turned to mysticism precisely to get some light on truth. Do mystical states establish the truth of those theological affections in which the saintly life has its root?

In spite of their repudiation of articulate self-description, mystical states in general assert a pretty distinct theoretic drift. It is possible to give the outcome of the majority of them in terms that point in definite philosophical directions. One of these directions is optimism, and the other is monism. We pass into mystical states from out of ordinary consciousness as from a less into a more, as from a smallness into a vastness, and at the same time as from an unrest to a rest. We feel them as reconciling, unifying states. They appeal to the yes-function more than to the no-function in us. In them the unlimited absorbs the limits and peacefully closes the account. Their very denial of every adjective you may propose as applicable to the ultimate truth—He, the Self, the Atman, is to be described by "No! no!" only, say the Upanishads— though it seems on the surface to be a no-function, is a denial made on behalf of a deeper yes. Whoso calls the Absolute anything in particular, or says that it is *this*, seems implicitly to shut it off from being *that*—it is as if he lessened it. So we deny the "this," negating the negation which it seems to us to imply, in the interests of the higher affirmative attitude by which we are possessed. The fountainhead of Christian mysticism is Dionysius the Areopagite. He describes the absolute truth by negatives exclusively.

> The cause of all things is neither soul nor intellect; nor has it imagination, opinion, or reason, or intelligence; nor is it reason or intelligence; nor is it spoken or thought. It is neither number, nor order, nor magnitude, nor littleness, nor equality, nor inequality, nor similarity, nor dissimilarity. It neither stands, nor moves, nor rests.... It is neither essence, nor eternity, nor time. Even intellectual contact does not belong to it. It is neither science nor truth. It is not even royalty or wisdom; not one; not unity; not divinity or goodness; nor even spirit as we know it (etc., *ad libitum*).

But these qualifications are denied by Dionysius, not because the truth falls short of them, but because it so infinitely excels them. It is above them. It is *super*-lucent, *super*-splendent, *super*-essential, *super*-sublime, *super every-thing* that can be named. Like Hegel in his logic, mystics journey towards the positive pole of truth only by the "Methode der Absoluten Negativität."

Thus comes the paradoxical expressions that so abound in mystical writings. As when Eckhart tells of the still desert of the Godhead, "where never was seen difference, neither Father, Son, nor Holy Ghost, where there is no one at home, yet where the spark of the soul is more at peace than in itself." As when Boehme writes of the Primal Love, that "it may fitly be compared to Nothing, for it is deeper than any Thing, and is as nothing with respect to all things, forasmuch as it is not comprehensible by any of them. And because it is nothing respectively, it is therefore free from all things, and is that only good, which a man cannot express or utter what it is, there being nothing to which it may be compared, to express it by." Or as when Angelus Silesius sings:—

> Gott ist ein lauter Nichts, ihn rührt kein Nun noch Hier;
> Je mehr du nach ihm greiffst, je mehr entwind er dir.

To this dialectical use, by the intellect, of negation as a mode of passage towards a higher kind of affirmation, there is correlated the subtlest of moral counterparts in the sphere of the personal will. Since denial of the finite self and its wants, since asceticism of some sort, is found in religious experience to be the only doorway to the larger and more blessed life, this moral mystery intertwines and combines with the intellectual mystery in all mystical writings.

> Love (continues Behmen) [is Nothing, for] when thou art gone forth wholly from the Creature and from that which is visible, and art become Nothing to all that is Nature and Creature, then thou art in that eternal One, which is God himself, and then thou shalt feel within thee the highest virtue of Love.... The treasure of treasures for the soul is where she goeth out of the Somewhat into that Nothing out of which all things may be made. The soul here saith, *I have nothing*, for I am utterly stripped and naked; *I can do nothing*, for I have no manner of power, but am as water poured out; *I am nothing*, for all that I am is no more than an image of Being, and only God is to me I AM; and so, sitting down in my own Nothingness, I give glory to the eternal Being, and *will nothing* of myself, that so God may will all in me, being unto me my God and all things.

In Paul's language, I live, yet not I, but Christ liveth in me. Only when I become as nothing can God enter in and no difference between his life and mine remain outstanding.

This overcoming of all the usual barriers between the individual and the Absolute is the great mystic achievement. In mystic states we both become one with the Absolute and we become aware of our oneness. This is the everlasting and triumphant mystical tradition, hardly altered by differences of clime or creed. In Hinduism, in Neoplatonism, in Sufism, in Christian mysticism, in Whitmanism, we find the same recurring note, so that there is about mystical utterances an eternal unanimity which ought to make a critic stop and think, and which brings it about that the mystical classics have, as has been said, neither birthday nor native land. Perpetually telling of the unity of man with God, their speech antedates languages, and they do not grow old.

"That are Thou!" says the Upanishads, and the Vedantists add: "Not a part, not a mode of That, but identically That, that absolute Spirit of the World." "As pure water poured into pure water remains the same, thus, O Gautama, is the Self of a thinker who knows. Water in water, fire in fire, ether in ether, no one can distinguish them: likewise a man whose mind has entered into the self." 'Everyman,' says the Sufi Gulshan-Râz, whose heart is no longer shaken by any doubts, knows with certainty that there is no being save only One.... In his divine majesty the *me*, and *we*, the *thou*, are not found, for in the One there can be no distinction. Every being who is annulled and entirely separated from himself, hears resound outside of him this voice and this echo: *I am God:* he has an eternal way of existing, and is no longer subject to death.' " In the vision of God, says Plotinus, "what sees is not our reason, but something prior and superior to our reason.... He who thus sees does not properly see, does not distinguish or imagine two things. He changes, he ceases to be himself, preserves nothing of himself. Absorbed in God, he makes but one with him, like a centre of a circle coinciding with another centre." "Here," writes Suso, "the spirit dies, and yet is all alive in the marvels of the Godhead...and is lost in the stillness of the glorious dazzling obscurity and of the naked simple unity. It is in this modeless *where* that the highest bliss is to be found." "Ich bin so gross als Gott," sings Angelus Silesius again, "Er ist als ich so klein; Er kann nich über mich, ich unter ihm nicht sein."

In mystical literature such self-contradictory phrases as "dazzling obscurity," "whispering silence," "teeming desert," are continually met with. They prove that not conceptual speech, but music rather, is the element through which we are best spoken to by mystical truth. Many mystical scriptures are indeed little more than musical compositions.

> He who would hear the voice of Nada, "the Soundless Sound," and comprehend it, he has to learn the nature of Dhârana.... When to himself his form appears unreal, as do on waking all the forms he sees in dreams; when he has ceased to hear the many, he may discern the ONE—the inner sound which kills the outer.... For then the soul will hear, and will remember. And then to the inner ear will speak THE VOICE OF THE SILENCE.... And now thy *Self* is lost in SELF, *thyself* unto THYSELF, merged in that SELF from which thou first didst radiate.... Behold! thou hast become the Light, thou hast become the Sound, thou art thy

Master and thy God. Thou art THYSELF the object of thy search: the VOICE unbroken, that resounds throughout eternities, exempt from change, from sin exempt, the seven sounds in one, the VOICE OF THE SILENCE. *Om tat Sat.*

These words, if they do not awaken laughter as you receive them, probably stir chords within you which music and language touch in common. Music gives us ontological messages which non-musical criticism is unable to contradict, though it may laugh at our foolishness in minding them. There is a verge of the mind which these things haunt; and whispers therefrom mingle with the operations of our understanding, even as the waters of the infinite ocean send their waves to break among the pebbles that lie upon our shores.

Here begins the sea that ends not till the world's end. Where we stand,
Could we know the next high sea-mark set beyond these waves that gleam,
We should know what never man hath known, nor eye of man hath scanned....
Ah, but here man's heart leaps, yearning towards the gloom with venturous glee,
From the shore that hath no shore beyond it, set in all the sea.

That doctrine, for example, that eternity is timeless, that our "immortality," if we live in the eternal, is not so much future as already now and here, which we find so often expressed to-day in certain philosophical circles, finds its support in a "hear, hear!" or an "amen," which floats up from that mysteriously deeper level. We recognize the passwords to the mystical region as we hear them, but we cannot use them ourselves; it alone has the keeping of "the password primeval."

I have now sketched with extreme brevity and insufficiency, but as fairly as I am able in the time allowed, the general traits of the mystic range of consciousness. *It is on the whole pantheistic and optimistic, or at least the opposite of pessimistic. It is anti-naturalistic, and harmonizes best with twice-bornness and so-called other-worldly states of mind.*

My next task is to inquire whether we can invoke it as authoritative. Does it furnish any *warrant for the truth* of the twice-bornness and supernaturality and pantheism which it favors? I must give my answer to this question as concisely as I can.

In brief my answer is this—and I will divide it into three parts:—

(1) Mystical states, when well developed, usually are, and have the right to be, absolutely authoritative over the individuals to whom they come.

(2) No authority emanates from them which should make it a duty for those who stand outside of them to accept their revelations uncritically.

(3) They break down the authority of the non-mystical or rationalistic consciousness, based upon the understanding and the senses alone. They show it to be only one kind of consciousness. They open out the possibility of other orders of truth, in which, so far as anything in us vitally responds to them, we may freely continue to have faith.

I will take up these points one by one.

1. As a matter of psychological fact, mystical states of a well-pronounced and emphatic sort *are* usually authoritative over those who have them. They have been "there," and know. It is vain for rationalism to grumble about this. If the mystical truth that comes to a man proves to be a force that he can live by, what mandate have we of the majority to order him to live in another way? We can throw him into a prison or a madhouse, but we cannot change his mind—we commonly attach it only the more stubbornly to its beliefs. It mocks our utmost efforts, as a matter of fact, and in point of logic it absolutely escapes our jurisdiction. Our own more "rational" beliefs are based on evidence exactly similar in nature to that which mystics quote for theirs. Our senses, namely, have assured us of certain states of fact; but mystical experiences are as direct perceptions of fact for those who have them as any sensations ever were for us. The records show that even though the five senses be in abeyance in them, they are absolutely sensational in their epistemological quality, if I may be pardoned the barbarous expression—that is, they are face to face presentations of what seems immediately to exist.

The mystic is, in short, *invulnerable*, and must be left, whether we relish it or not, in undisturbed enjoyment of his creed. Faith, says Tolstoy, is that by which men live. And faith-state and mystic state are practically convertible terms.

2. But I now proceed to add that mystics have no right to claim that we ought to accept the deliverance of their peculiar experiences, if we are ourselves outsiders and feel no private call thereto. The utmost they can ever ask of us in this life is to admit that they establish a presumption. They form a consensus and have an unequivocal outcome; and it would be odd, mystics might say, if such a unanimous type of experience should prove to be altogether wrong. At bottom, however, this would only be an appeal to numbers, like the appeal of rationalism the other way; and the appeal to numbers has no logical force. If we acknowledge it, it is for "suggestive," not for logical reasons: we follow the majority because to do so suits our life.

But even this presumption from the unanimity of mystics is far from being strong. In characterizing mystic states as pantheistic, optimistic, etc., I am afraid I over-simplified the truth. I did so for expository reasons, and to keep the closer to the classic mystical tradition. The classic religious mysticism, it now must be confessed, is only a "privileged case." It is an *extract*, kept true to type by the selection of the fittest specimens and their preservation in "schools." It is carved out from a much larger mass; and if we take the larger mass as seriously as religious mysticism has historically taken itself, we find that the supposed unanimity largely disappears. To begin with, even religious mysticism itself, the kind that accumulates traditions and makes schools, is much less unanimous than I have allowed. It has been both ascetic and antinomianly self-indulgent within the Christian church. It is dualistic in Sankhya, and monistic in Vedanta philosophy. I called it pantheistic; but the great Spanish mystics are anything but pantheists. They are with few exceptions non-metaphysical minds, for whom "the category of personality" is absolute. The "union" of man with God is for them much more like an occasional miracle than like an original identity. How different again, apart from the happiness common to all, is the mysticism of Walt Whitman, Edward Carpenter, Richard Jefferies, and other naturalistic pantheists, from the more distinctively Christian sort. The fact is that the mystical feeling of enlargement, union, and emancipation has no specific intellectual content whatever of its own. It is capable of forming matrimonial alliances with material furnished by the most diverse philosophies and theologies, provided only they can find a place in their framework for its peculiar emotional mood. We have no right, therefore, to invoke its prestige as distinctively in favor of any special belief, such as that in absolute idealism, or in the absolute monistic identity, or in the absolute goodness, of the world. It is only relatively in favor of all these things—it passes out of common human consciousness in the direction in which they lie.

So much for religious mysticism proper. But more remains to be told, for religious mysticism is only one half of mysticism. The other half has no accumulated traditions except those which the text-books on insanity supply. Open any one of these, and you will find abundant cases in which "mystical ideas" are cited as characteristic symptoms of enfeebled or deluded states of mind. In delusional insanity, paranoia, as they sometimes call it, we may have a *diabolical* mysticism, a sort of religious mysticism turned upside down. The same sense of ineffable importance in the smallest events, the same texts and words coming with new meanings, the same voices and visions and leadings and missions, the same controlling by extraneous powers; only this time the emotion is pessimistic: instead of consolations we have desolations; the meanings are dreadful; and the powers are enemies to life. It is evident from the point of view of their psychological mechanism, the classic mysticism and these lower mysticisms spring from the same mental level, from that great subliminal or transmarginal region of which science is beginning to admit the existence, but of which so little is really known. That region contains every kind of matter: "seraph and snake" abide there side by side. To come from thence is no infallible credential. What comes must be sifted and tested, and run the gauntlet of confrontation with the total context of experience, just like what comes from the outer world of sense. Its value must be ascertained by empirical methods, so long as we are not mystics ourselves.

Once more, then, I repeat that non-mystics are under no obligation to acknowledge in mystical states a superior authority conferred on them by their intrinsic nature.

3. Yet, I repeat once more, the existence of mystical states absolutely overthrows the pretension of non-mystical states to be the sole and ultimate dictators of what we may believe. As a rule, mystical states merely add a super-sensuous meaning to the ordinary outward data of consciousness.

They are excitements like the emotions of love or ambition, gifts to our spirit by means of which facts already objectively before us fall into a new expressiveness and make a new connection with our active life. They do not contradict these facts as such, or deny anything that our senses have immediately seized. It is the rationalistic critic rather who plays the part of denier in the controversy, and his denials have no strength, for there never can be a state of facts to which new meaning may not truthfully be added, provided the mind ascend to a more enveloping point of view. It must always remain an open question whether mystical states may not possibly be such superior points of view, windows through which the mind looks out upon a more extensive and inclusive world. The difference of the views seen from the different mystical windows need not prevent us from entertaining this supposition. The wider world would in that case prove to have a mixed constitution like that of this world, that is all. It would have its celestial and its infernal regions, its tempting and its saving moments, its valid experiences and its counterfeit ones, just as our world has them; but it would be a wider world all the same. We should have to use its experiences by selecting and subordinating and substituting just as is our custom in this ordinary naturalistic world; we should be liable to error just as we are now; yet the counting in of that wider world of meanings, and the serious dealing with it, might, in spite of all the perplexity, be indispensable stages in our approach to the final fullness of the truth.

In this shape, I think, we have to leave the subject. Mystical states indeed wield no authority due simply to their being mystical states. But the higher ones among them point in directions to which the religious sentiments even of non-mystical men incline. They tell of the supremacy of the ideal, of vastness, of union, of safety, and of rest. They offer us *hypotheses*, hypotheses which we may voluntarily ignore, but which as thinkers we cannot possibly upset. The supernaturalism and optimism to which they would persuade us may, interpreted in one way or another, be after all the truest of insights into the meaning of this life.

"Oh, the little more, and how much it is; and the little less, and what worlds away!" It may be that possibility and permission of this sort are all that our religious consciousness requires to live on. In my last lecture I shall have to try to persuade you that this is the case. Meanwhile, however, I am sure that for many of my readers this diet is too slender. If supernaturalism and inner union with the divine are true, you think, then not so much permission, as compulsion to believe, ought to be found. Philosophy has always professed to prove religious truth by coercive argument; and the construction of philosophies of this kind has always been one favorite function of the religious life, if we use this term in the large historic sense. But religious philosophy is an enormous subject, and in my next lecture I can only give that brief glance at it which my limits will allow.

C. B. MARTIN

A Religious Way of Knowing

I.

Some theologians support their claim to knowledge of the existence of God on the basis of direct experience of God. I shall attempt to point out some of the eccentricities of this alleged way of knowing. The two main sources which I shall use are Professor J. Baillie's *Our Knowledge of God* and Professor H. H. Farmer's *Towards Belief in God*.

> We are rejecting logical argument of any kind as the first chapter of our theology or as representing the process by which God comes to be known. We are holding that our knowledge of God rests rather on the revelation of His personal Presence as Father, Son, and Holy Spirit.... Of such a Presence it must be true that to those who have never been confronted with it argument is useless, while to those who have it is superfluous. [BAILLIE, p. 132.]
>
> It is not as the result of an inference of any kind, whether explicit or implicit, whether laboriously excogitated or swiftly intuited, that the knowledge of God's reality comes to us. It comes rather through our direct, personal encounter with Him in the Person of Jesus Christ His Son our Lord. [*Ibid.*, p. 143.]
>
> If now we ask how we would expect such a reality (God) to disclose itself to us, the answer can only be that we can have no expectancy about the matter at all; for in the nature of the case there are no parallels, no analogies on which expectancy may be based. The divine reality is, by definition, unique. Or, in other words, we would expect that if we know the reality of God in respect of this fundamental aspect of His being at all, we shall just know that we are dealing with God, the ultimate source and disposer of all things, including ourselves, and there will be nothing more to be said. It will not be possible to describe the compelling touch of God otherwise than as the compelling touch of God. To anyone who has no such awareness of God, leading as it does to the typically religious attitudes of obeisance and worship, it will be quite impossible to indicate what is meant; one can only hope to evoke it, on the assumption that the capacity to become aware of God is part of normal human nature like the capacity to see light or to hear sound. [FARMER, p. 40.]

From *Mind* 61:244 (October 1952). Reprinted by permission of the author and the publisher Basil Blackwell, London.

The arguments of the theologians quoted have been taken out of context. I do not want to suggest that the quotations give a faithful or complete impression of their total argument. The following quotations from Professor Farmer indicate two further lines of argument which cannot be discussed here.

Reflection

For what we have now in mind is no demonstrative proofs *from* the world, but rather confirmatory considerations which present themselves to us when we bring belief in God with us *to* the world. It is a matter of the coherence of the belief with other facts. If we find that the religious intuition which has arisen from other sources provides the mind with a thought in terms of which much else can without forcing be construed, then that is an intellectual satisfaction, and a legitimate confirmation of belief, which it would be absurd to despise. [FARMER, p. 113.]

Pragmatic Element

We shall first speak in general terms of what may be called the human situation and need, and thereafter we shall try to show how belief in God, as particularized in its Christian form (though still broadly set forth), fits onto this situation and need. [*Ibid.*, p. 62.]

II.

The alleged theological way of knowing may be described as follows:

"I have direct experience (knowledge, acquaintance, apprehension) of God, therefore I have valid reason to believe that God exists."

A. By this it may be meant that the statement "I have had direct experience of God, but God does not exist" is contradictory. Thus, the assertion that "I have had direct experience of God" commits one to the assertion that God exists. From this it follows that "I have had direct experience of God" is more than a psychological statement, because it claims more than the fact that I have certain sensations—it claims that God exists. Thus as it stands this is a correct form of deductive argument. The assertion "I have direct experience of God" includes the assertion "God exists" thus, the conclusion "therefore, God exists" follows tautologically.

B. Unfortunately, this deduction is useless. The addition of the existential claim "God exists" to the psychological claim of having religious experiences must be shown to be warrantable. It cannot be shown to be warrantable by any deductive argument, because psychological statements of the form:

(1) I feel as if an unseen person were interested in (willed) my welfare.

(2) I feel an elation quite unlike any I have ever felt before.

(3) I have feelings of guilt and shame at my sinfulness.

(4) I feel as if I were committed to bending all of my efforts to living in a certain way, etc., etc.

can make the claim only that I have these complex feelings and sensations. Nothing else follows deductively. No matter what the existential statement might be that is added to the psychological statement, it is always logically possible for future psychological statements to call this existential claim in doubt. The only thing that I can establish beyond correction on the basis of having certain feelings and sensations is that I have these feelings and sensations. No matter how unique an experience may be claimed to be, it cannot do the impossible.

There is an influential and subtle group of religious thinkers who would not insist upon any existential claim. My remarks are largely irrelevant to this group. It would be hasty to describe their religious belief as "psychological" or employ any other such general descriptive term. For example, the "call," in even the most liberal and "subjective" Quaker sects, could not be reduced to feeling statements, etc. The "call," among other things, implies a mission or intricate programme of behaviour. The non-subjective element of the "call" is evident because in so far as one failed to live in accordance with a mission just so far would the genuineness of the "call" be questioned. It will be seen that this verification procedure is necessarily not available in the religious way of knowing to be examined.

C. Neither is the addition of the existential claim "God exists" to the psychological claim made good by any inductive argument. There are no tests agreed upon to establish genuine experience of God and distinguish it decisively from the ungenuine. Indeed, many theologians deny the possibility of any such test or set of tests. Nor is there any increased capacity for prediction produced in the Christian believer which we cannot explain on a secular basis. However, just such a capacity is implied by those who talk of religious experience as if it were due to some kind of sixth sense.

(1) The believer may persuade us that something extraordinary has happened by saying, "I am a changed man since 6:37 p.m., 6th May, 1939." This is a straightforward empirical statement. We can test this by noticing whether or not he has given up bad habits, etc. We may allow the truth of the statement, even if he has not given up bad habits, etc. because we may find evidence of bad conscience, self-searchings and remorse that had not been present before that date.

(2) However, if the believer says, "I had a direct experience of God at 6:37 p.m., 6th May, 1939," this is not an empirical statement in the way that the other statement is. The checking procedure is very far from clear. No matter how much or how little his subsequent behaviour such as giving up bad habits, etc., is affected, it could never prove or disprove his statement.

An important point to note is that the theologian discourages any detailed description of the required experience ("apprehension of God"). The more naturalistic and detailed the description of the required experience became, the easier would it become to deny the existential claim. One could say, "Yes, I had those very experiences, but they certainly did not convince me of God's existence." The only sure defence here would be for the theologian to make the claim analytic—"You *couldn't* have those experiences and at the same time sincerely deny God's existence."

D. The way in which many theologians talk would seem to show that they think of knowing God as something requiring a kind of sixth sense.

(1) The Divine Light is not merely of a colour usually visible only to eagles and the Voice of God is not merely of a pitch usually audible only to dogs. No matter how much more keen our senses became, we should be no better off than before. This sixth sense, therefore, must be very different from the other five.

(a) This supposed religious sense has no vocabulary of its own, but depends upon metaphors drawn from the other senses. There are no terms which apply to it and it alone. There is a vocabulary for what is sensed but not for the sense. We "see" the Holy, the Numinous, the Divine, etc. This linguistic predicament may be compared with the similar one of the intuitionists when they talk of "seeing" a logical connection. It also may be compared with "hearing" the Voice of Conscience.

(b) The intuitionists seldom differ from the rest of us in the number of facts referred to in describing how we come to understand logical statements and their relations. The intuitionist, however, emphasizes the fact that often we come to understand the point of an argument or problem in logic very suddenly. We mark this occurrence by such phrases as "the light dawned," "understood it in a flash." Such events are usually described in terms of a complete assurance that one's interpretation is correct and a confidence that one will tend to be able to reproduce or recognize the argument or problem in various contexts in the future. A vitally important distinction between this "seeing" and the religious "seeing" is that there is checking procedure for the former, but not for the latter. If the intuitionist finds that his boasted insight was wrong, then he says, "I couldn't really have 'seen' it." No matter how passionate his claims he cannot have "seen" that $2 + 2 = 5$.

III.

The religious way of knowing is described as being unique.

A. No one can deny the existence of feelings and experiences which the believer calls "religious" and no one can deny their power. Because of this and because the way of knowing by direct experience is neither inductive nor deductive, theologians have tried to give this way of knowing a special status. One way in which this has been done has been to claim that religious experience is unique and incommunicable. There is a sense in which this is true. This sense may be brought out by a list such as the following:

(1) You don't know what the experience of God is until you have had it.
(2) You don't know what a blue sky is until you have been to Naples.
(3) You don't know what poverty is until you have been poor.
(4) "We can only know a person by the direct communion of sympathetic intercourse." (William Temple).

Professor Baillie, in likening our knowledge of God to our knowledge of other minds, says that it is

> like our knowledge of tridimensional space and all other primary modes of knowledge, something that cannot be imagined by one who does not already possess it, since it cannot be described to him in terms of anything else than itself. [BAILLIE, p. 217.]

What Professor Baillie does not see is that according to his criteria anything can qualify as a primary mode of knowledge. Each one of the statements in the above list is unique and incommunicable in just this way. You must go to Naples and not just to Venice. A postcard is no substitute.

B. That this sort of uniqueness is not to the point in supporting the existential claim "God exists" can be seen by examining the following two samples:

(1) You don't know what the experience of God is until you have had it.
(2) You don't know what the colour blue is until you have seen it.

Professor Farmer says,

> All the basic elements in our experience are incommunicable. Who could describe light and colour to one who has known nothing but darkness? [FARMER, p. 41.]

Just in so far as the experience of God is unique and incommunicable in this way, then just so far is it not to the point in supporting the existential claim "God exists."

All that this proves is that a description of one group of sensations A in terms of another set of sensations B is never sufficient for knowing group A. According to this definition of "know," in order to know one must have those sensations. Thus, all that is proved is that in order to know what religious experience is one must have a religious experience. This helps in no way at all to prove that such experience is direct apprehension of God and helps in no way to support the existential claim "God exists."

C. Professor Farmer makes the point that describing the experience of God to an unbeliever is like describing colour to a blind man. So it is, in the sense that the believer has usually had experiences which the unbeliever has not. However, it is also very much unlike. The analogy breaks down at some vital points.

(1) The blind man may have genuine though incomplete knowledge of colour. He may have an instrument for detecting wave lengths, etc. Indeed, he may even increase our knowledge of colour. More important still, the blind man may realize the differences in powers of prediction between himself and the man of normal eyesight. He is well aware of the fact, unlike himself, the man of normal eyesight does not have to wait to hear the rush of the bull in order to be warned.

(2) This point is connected with the problem of how we are to know when someone has the direct experience of God or even when we ourselves have the direct experience of God. It was shown above how the situation is easier in the case of the blind man. It is easy also, in the case of knowing a blue sky in Naples. One can look at street signs and maps in order to be sure that this is the really blue sky in question. It is only when one comes to such a case as knowing God that the society of tests and check-up procedures that surround other instances of knowing, completely vanishes. What is put in the place of these tests and checking procedures is an immediacy of knowledge that is supposed to carry its own guarantee. This feature will be examined later.

D. It is true that the man of normal vision has a way of knowing colour which the blind man does not have. Namely, he can see coloured objects. However, as we have seen, it would be wrong to insist that this is the only way of knowing colour and that the blind man has *no* way of knowing colour. There is a tendency to deny this and to maintain that having colour sensations is *the* way of knowing colour. Perhaps Professor Farmer has this in mind when he tries to make an analogy between the incommunicability of the believer's direct knowledge of God to the unbeliever and the incommunicability of the normal man's knowledge of colour to the blind man. The analogy is justified if "knowing colour" is made synonymous with "having colour sensations."

(1) On this account, no matter how good his hearing and reliable his colour-detecting instruments, etc., the blind man could not know colour and the man of normal vision could not communicate to him just what this knowledge would be like.

(2) The believer has had certain unusual experiences which, presumably, the unbeliever has not had. If "having direct experience of God" is made synonymous with "having certain religious experiences," and the believer has had these and the unbeliever has not, then we may say that the believer's knowledge is incommunicable to the unbeliever in that it has already been legislated that in order to know what the direct experience of God is one must have had certain religious experiences.

> To anyone who has no such awareness of God, leading as it does to the typically religious attitudes of obeisance and worship, it will be quite impossible to indicate what is meant; one can only hope to evoke it.... [FARMER, p. 40.]

Reading theological textbooks and watching the behaviour of believers is not sufficient.

E. The theologian has made the above analogy hold at the cost of endangering the existential claim about God which he hoped to establish.

(1) If "knowing colour" is made synonymous with "having colour sensations" and "having direct experience of God" is made synonymous with "having certain religious experiences," then it is certainly true that a blind man cannot "know colour" and that a non-religious man cannot "have direct experience of God." By definition, also, it is true that the blind man and the non-religious man cannot know the meaning of the phrases "knowing colour" and "having direct experience of God," because it has been previously legislated that one cannot know their meaning without having the relevant experiences.

(2) If this analogy is kept then the phrases "knowing colour" and "having direct experience of God" seem to make no claim beyond the psychological claims about one's colour sensations and religious feelings.

(3) If this analogy is not kept then there is no sense in the comparison between the incommunicability between the man of normal vision and the blind man and the incommunicability between the believer and the unbeliever.

(4) If "knowing colour" is to be shaken loose from its purely psychological implications and made to have an existential reference concerning certain features of the world then a whole society of tests and check-up procedures which would be wholly irrelevant to the support of the psychological claim about one's own colour sensations become relevant. E.g., what other people see and the existence of light waves and the description of their characteristics needing the testimony of research workers and scientific instruments.

F. Because "having direct experience of God" does not admit the relevance of a society of tests and checking procedures it places itself in the company of the other ways of knowing which preserve their self-sufficiency, "uniqueness" and "incommunicability" by making a psychological and not an existential claim. E.g. "I seem to see a blue piece of paper." This statement requires no further test or checking procedure in order to be considered true. Indeed, if A makes the statement "I seem to see a blue piece of paper," then not only does A need no further corroboration, but there could be no disproof of his statement for him, for, if B says to A, "It does not seem to me as if I were now seeing a blue piece of paper," then B's statement does *not* call A's statement in doubt for A though it does for B. However, if A makes the statement, "I see a piece of blue paper," and B says in the same place and at the same time, "I do not see a piece of blue paper," then B's statement *does* call A's statement in doubt for A. Further investigation will then be proper and if no piece of paper can be felt and other investigators cannot see or feel the paper and photographs reveal nothing, then A's statement will be shown to have been false. A's only refuge will be to say, "Well, I certainly seem to see a piece of blue paper." This is a perfect refuge because no one can prove him wrong, but its unassailability has been bought at the price of making no claim about the world beyond the claim about his own state of mind.

G. Another way of bringing out the closeness of the religious statement to the psychological statement is the following.

(1) When A wishes to support the assertion that a certain physical object exists, the tests and checking procedures made by A himself are not the only things relevant to the truth of his assertion. Testimony of what B, C, D, etc. see, hear, etc. is also relevant. That is, if A wanted to know whether it was really a star that he saw, he could not only take photographs, look through a telescope, etc., but also ask others if they saw the star. If a large proportion of a large number of people denied seeing the star, A's claim about the star's existence would be weakened. Of course, he might still trust his telescope. However, let us now imagine that A does not make use of the tests and checking procedures (photographs and telescopes) but is left with the testimony of what he sees and the testimony of others concerning what they see. In this case, it is so much to the point if a large number of people deny seeing the star, that A will be considered irrational or mad if he goes on asserting its existence. His only irrefutable position is to reduce his physical object claim to an announcement concerning his own sensations. Then the testimony of men and angels cannot disturb his certitude. These sensations of the moment he knows directly and immediately and the indirect and non-immediate testimony of men and angels is irrelevant. Absolute confidence, and absolute indifference to the majority judgment, is bought at the price of reducing the existential to the psychological.

(2) The religious claim is similar to, though not identical with, the above case in certain important features. We have seen that there are no tests or checking procedures open to the believer to support his existential claim about God. Thus, he is left with the testimony of his own experience and the similar testimony of the experience of others. And, of course, he is not left wanting for such testimony, for religious communities seem to fulfill just this sort of need.

(3) Let us imagine a case comparable to the one concerning the existence of a physical object. In this case A is a professor of Divinity and he believes that he has come to know of the existence of God through direct experience of God. In order to understand the intricate character of what Professor A is asserting we must imagine a highly unusual situation. The other members of the faculty and the members of Professor A's religious community suddenly begin sincerely to deny his and what has been their assertion. Perhaps they still attend church services and pray as often as they used to, and

perhaps they claim to have the same sort of experiences as they had when they were believers, but they refuse to accept the conclusion that God exists. Whether they give a Freudian explanation or some other explanation or no explanation of their experiences, they are agreed in refusing to accept the existential claim (about God) made by Professor A. How does this affect Professor A and his claim? It may affect Professor A very deeply—indeed, he may die of broken-hearted disappointment at the loss of his fellow-believers. However, the loss of fellow-believers may not weaken his confidence in the truth of his assertion or in the testimony of his experience. In this matter his experience may be all that ultimately counts for him in establishing his confidence in the truth of his claim about the existence of God. It has been said that religious experience carries its own guarantee and perhaps the above account describes what is meant by this.

H. It is quite obvious from the examples given above that the religious statement ("I have direct experience of God") is of a different status from the physical object statement ("I can see a star") and shows a distressing similarity to the psychological statement ("I seem to see a star"). The bulk of this paper has been devoted to showing some of the many forms this similarity takes. Does this mean then that the religious statement and its existential claim concerning God amount to no more than a reference to the complex feelings and sensations of the believer?

I. Perhaps the best way to answer this last question is to take a typical psychological statement and see if there is anything which must be said of it and all other psychological statements which cannot be said of the religious statement.

(1) One way of differentiating a physical object statement from a psychological statement is by means of prefixing the phrase "I seem...." For instance, the statement "I can see a star" may be transformed from a statement concerning the existence of a certain physical object to a statement concerning my sensations by translating it into the form "I seem to see a star." The first statement involves a claim about the existence of an object as well as an announcement concerning my sensations and therefore subjects itself to the risk of being wrong concerning that further claim. Being wrong in this case is determined by a society of tests and checking procedures such as taking photographs and looking through telescopes, and by the testimony of others that they see or do not see a star. The second statement involves no claim about the existence of an object and so requires no such tests and no testimony of others; indeed, the sole judge of the truth of the statement is the person making it. If no existential claim is lost by the addition of this phrase to a statement then the statement is psychological. For instance, the statement "I feel pain" loses nothing by the addition of "I seem to feel pain."

(2) In the case of the religious statement "I have direct experience of God" the addition of the phrase is fatal to all that the believer wants to

assert. "I seem to be having direct experience of God" is a statement concerning my feelings and sensations of the moment and as such it makes no claim about the existence of God. Thus, the original statement "I have direct experience of God" is not a psychological statement. This should not surprise us. We should have known it all along, for isn't it an assertion that one comes to know something, namely God, by means of one's feelings and sensations and this something is not reducible to them? The statement is not a psychological one just because it is used to assert the existence of something. Whether this assertion is warranted and what exactly it amounts to is quite another question.

We are tempted to think that the religious statement *must* be of one sort or another. The truth is that *per impossibile* it is both at once. The theologian must use it in both ways and which way he is to emphasize at a particular time depends upon the circumstances of its use; and most particularly upon the direction of our probings.

(3) The statement "I seem to be having direct experience of God" is an eccentric one. It is eccentric not only because introspective announcements are unusual and because statements about God have a peculiar obscurity, but for a further and more important reason. This peculiarity may be brought out by comparing this statement with others having the same form. A first formulation of this may be put in the following way. In reference to things other than our sensations of the moment knowledge is prior to seeming as if.

The statement "I seem to be looking directly at a chair" has a meaning only in so far as I already *know* what it is like to look directly at a chair. The statement "I seem to be listening to a choir" has a meaning only in so far as I already *know* what it is like to be listening to a choir. The assumption of knowledge in both of these cases is one which all normal people are expected to make or do in fact make.

The statement "I seem to be having direct experience of God" does not lend itself so easily to the criterion for meaning exemplified in the above, because if this statement has meaning only in so far as one already *knows* what it is like to have direct experience of God, then the assumption of such knowledge is certainly not one which all normal people may be expected to be able or do in fact make.

However, it may be said that the assumption of such knowledge as knowledge of what it is like to see a gorgon may not be assumed of all normal people and, therefore, the case of religious knowledge is in no peculiar position.

The answer to this objection and the discovery of the peculiarity of the religious statement may come about by asking the question "How do we come to learn what it would be like to look directly at a chair, hear a choir, see a gorgon, have direct experience of God?"

It is not that there are no answers to the question concerning how we come to learn what it would be like to have direct experience of God. We are not left completely in the dark. Instead, the point is that the answers to this question are quite different from those referring to the questions concerning how we come to learn what it would be like to look directly at a chair, hear a choir, and see a gorgon.

No one has ever seen a gorgon, yet there certainly are people who, by means of their specialized knowledge of mythical literature, may claim in a perfectly meaningful manner that it now seems to them as if they were seeing a gorgon.

Let us imagine a society in which there are no chairs and no one knows anything at all about chairs. If we were to try to teach one of the members of this society what it would be like to see a chair and if we were not allowed to construct a chair, what sort of thing might we do? We might look around at the furniture and say, "A chair is a kind of narrow settee. It is used to sit on." This would be a beginning. Then we might compare different settees as to which are more chair-like. We might draw pictures of chairs, make gestures with our hands showing the general shape and size of different sorts of chairs. If, on the following day, he said, "I had a most unusual dream last night. I seemed to be looking directly at a chair," we should admit that his statement was closer in meaning to a similar one which we who have seen chairs might make than it would be to a similar one which another member might make who had no information or instruction or experience of chairs. We would insist that we had better knowledge of what it is to see a chair than does the instructed member of society who has still actually to see a chair. However, to know pictures of chairs is to know chairs in a legitimate sense.

But let us now imagine a utopian society in which none of the members has ever been in the least sad or unhappy. If we were to try to teach one of the members of this society what it would be like to feel sad, how would we go about it? It can be said that giving definitions, no matter how ingenious, would be no help, drawing pictures of unhappy faces, no matter how well drawn, would be no help, so long as these measures failed to evoke a feeling of sadness in this person. Comparing the emotion of sadness with other emotions would be no help, because no matter how like other emotions (weariness, etc.) are to sadness they fail just because they are not sadness. No, sadness is unique and incomparable.

To anyone who has no such awareness of sadness, leading as it does to the typically unhappy behaviour of tears and drawn faces, it will be quite impossible to indicate what is meant, one can only hope to evoke it, on the assumption that the capacity to become aware of sadness is part of normal human nature like the capacity to see light or to hear sound.

This last paragraph is a play upon a quotation given at the very beginning of the paper. The following is the original version.

> To anyone who has no such awareness of God, leading as it does to the typically religious attitudes of obeisance and worship, it will be quite impossible to

indicate what is meant; one can only hope to evoke it, on the assumption that the capacity to become aware of God is part of normal human nature like the capacity to see light or to hear sound. [FARMER, p. 40.]

(4)

> We are rejecting logical argument of any kind as the first chapter of our epistemology of aesthetics, or as representing the process by which beauty comes to be known....
>
> It is not as the result of an inference of any kind, whether explicit or implicit, whether laboriously excogitated or swiftly intuited, that the knowledge of beauty comes to us.
>
> ...to those who have never been confronted with the experience of seeing the beauty of something, argument is useless.

As these statements stand they are plainly false. Professors of aesthetics and professional art critics often do help us to come to "knowledge of beauty" by all kinds of inference and arguments. They may, and often do, help us to come to a finer appreciation of beautiful things. Knowledge of the rules of perspective and understanding of an artist's departure from them is relevant to an aesthetic appreciation of his work.

However, it is possible to interpret these statements as true and this is more important for our purpose.

There is sense in saying that an art critic, who has vastly increased our aesthetic sensitivity and whose books of art criticism are the very best, may never have known beauty. If there are no signs of this critic ever having been stirred by any work of art, then no matter how subtle his analyses, there is sense in claiming that he has never been confronted with the experience of seeing the beauty of something. This sense just is that we are determined not to say that a person has seen the beauty of something or has knowledge of beauty if he does not at some time have certain complex emotions and feelings which are typically associated with looking at paintings, hearing music and reading poetry. To "know beauty" or to "see beauty of something" means, among other things, to have certain sorts of emotions and feelings.

The quotation given above was a play on a quotation given at the beginning of the paper. The following is the original version with the appropriate cuts.

> We are rejecting logical argument of any kind as the first chapter of our theology or as representing the process by which God comes to be known....
>
> It is not as the result of an inference of any kind, whether explicit or implicit, whether laboriously excogitated or swiftly intuited, that the knowledge of God comes to us.
>
> ...to those who have never been confronted with it [direct, personal encounter with God] argument is useless.

As these statements stand they are plainly false. Professors of divinity and clergymen are expected to do what Professor Baillie claims cannot be done.

However, it is possible to interpret these statements as true and this is more important for our purpose.

There is sense in saying that a theologian (who has vastly increased our religious sensitivity and whose books of theology are the very best) may never have known God. If there are no signs of this theologian ever having been stirred by any religious ritual or act of worship, then no matter how subtle his analyses, there is sense in claiming that he has never been confronted with God's personal Presence. This sense just *is* that we are determined not to say that a person has knowledge of God if he does not at some time have certain complex emotions and feelings which are associated with attending religious services, praying and reading the Bible. To "know God" or to be confronted with God's "personal Presence" means, of necessity, having certain sorts of emotions and feelings.

(5) The analogy suggested above between aesthetic experience and religious experience and between aesthetic knowledge and religious knowledge cannot be examined further in this paper. However, certain preliminary suggestions may be made. The following quotations set the problem.

> In it [art] also there is an awareness, however unformulated and inarticulate, of a world of beauty which can be grasped and actualized in creative activity, yet it will never be possible fully to grasp it and actualize it in all its infinite reach and depth. In the appreciation of beauty in artistic products something of the same sense of an "infinite beyond" disclosing itself through, yet transcending, what is contemplated and enjoyed, is present. It is precisely this that marks the difference between, say, a Beethoven symphony and a shallow and "tinny" jazz-dance. [FARMER, *Towards Belief in God*, p. 56.]

After quoting Santayana's remark, "Religions are better or worse, never true or false," Professor Farmer says:

> It is sufficient answer to this suggestion to say that it is utterly false both to art and to religion. It is a central element in the artistic consciousness that it is, in its work, seeking to grasp and express an ideal world which in spite of its ideality is real and in some sense stands objectively over against the artist; it is never apprehended as merely a source of internal satisfaction and delights. Without this neither the work of artistic production nor its product would internally satisfy or delight. This is even more obviously true of religion. In religion the reality-interest is paramount. Once persuade the religious man that the reality with which he supposes himself to be dealing is not "there" in the sense in which he supposes it to be "there" and his religion vanishes away. [FARMER, *Towards Belief in God*, p. 176.]

One may select a group of statements to compare and analyse. The following would be samples of such statements.

"The Believer experiences God."

"The Sensitive Listener experiences Beauty in the music."

"The Believer experiences something of the infinite goodness of God."

"The Sensitive Listener experiences the subtlety, sadness, colour, etc., of the music as part of what is the Beauty in the music."

"One may hear God through prayer."

"One may hear the Beautiful above or in the voices of the actors and the instruments of the orchestra."

"What the artist experiences and knows, namely Beauty, is ultimately incommunicable."

"What the Believer experiences and knows, namely God, is ultimately incommunicable."

"One may learn to come to know God."

"One may learn to come to know Beauty."

"One may learn to come to know one's wife."

Going over the complex uses of such statements may help one to discover something of the intricate logic of certain kinds of religious statements.

In this paper the analogy between seeing blue and experiencing God has been examined and found to be misleading. The suggested analogy between experiencing the Beautiful and experiencing God has further complexities and requires another examination which, among other things, would show how religious experience is and is not another experience in the way in which seeing red may be said to be another experience to seeing blue or hearing a nightingale.

Another important subject with which this paper has not dealt is the connection between what the believer expects from immortality and his religious belief. This peculiar kind of test or verification has special difficulties which cannot be treated here.

IV.

Conclusion

It must be made clear in conclusion that the lack of tests and checking procedures which has been noted is not merely an unfortunate result of human frailty. It is necessarily the nature of the case. If tests and checking procedures were devised they would not, could not, support the claim of the believer. They may do for the detection of saints and perhaps even angels, but never of God. Of course, in a way theologians know this.

This paper has been an attempt to indicate how statements concerning a certain alleged religious way of knowing betray a logic extraordinarily like that of statements concerning introspective and subjective ways of knowing. It is not my wish to go from a correct suggestion that the logic is *very, very* like to an incorrect suggestion that the logic is *just* like.

WILLIAM P. ALSTON

Perceiving God*

I want to explore and defend the idea that the experience, or, as I shall say, the *perception*, of God plays an epistemic role with respect to beliefs about God importantly analogous to that played by sense perception with respect to beliefs about the physical world. The nature of that latter role is, of course, a matter of controversy, and I have no time here to go into those controversies. It is admitted, however, on (almost) all hands that sense perception provides us with knowledge (justified belief) about current states of affairs in the immediate environment of the perceiver and that knowledge of this sort is somehow required for any further knowledge of the physical world. The possibility I wish to explore is that what a person takes to be an experience of God can provide him/her with knowledge (justified beliefs) about what God is doing, or how God is "situated," vis-à-vis that subject at that moment. Thus, by experiencing the presence and activity of God, *S* can come to know (justifiably believe) that God is sustaining her in being, filling her with His love, strengthening her, or communicating a certain message to her. Let's call beliefs as to how God is currently related to the subject *M-beliefs* ('M' for manifestation); these are the "perceptual beliefs" of the theological sphere. I shall suppose that here too the "perceptual" knowledge one acquires from experience is crucial for whatever else we can learn about God, though I won't have time to explore and defend that part of the position; I will have my hands full defending the claim that M-beliefs are justified. I will just make two quick points about the role of M-beliefs in the larger scheme. First, just as with our knowledge of the physical world, the recognition of a crucial role for perceptual knowledge is compatible with a wide variety of views as to just how it figures in the total system and as to what else is involved. Second, an important difference between the two spheres is that in the theological sphere perceptual beliefs as to what God has "said" (communicated, revealed) to one or another person play a major role.

*Presented at an APA symposium on "Religious Experience and Religious Knowledge," December 29, 1986. Terence Penelhum commented; see *The Journal of Philosophy*, 1986, 665/6.

From *The Journal of Philosophy*, Vol. LXXXIII, 11 (November 1986), pp. 655–65. Reprinted by permission of *The Journal of Philosophy* and the author.

I have been speaking alternatively of perceptual *knowledge* and of the *justification* of perceptual beliefs. In this paper I shall concentrate on justification, leaving to one side whatever else is involved in knowledge. It will be my contention that (putative) experience of God is a source of justification for M-beliefs, somewhat in the way that sense experience is a source of justification for perceptual beliefs. Again, it is quite controversial what this latter way is. I shall be thinking of it in terms of a direct-realist construal of sense perception, according to which I can be justified in supposing that my dog is wagging his tail just because something is visually presenting itself to me as (looks like) my dog wagging his tail; that is, it looks to me in such a way that I am thereby justified in thereby supposing it to be my dog wagging his tail. Analogously I think of the "experience of God" as a matter of something's presenting itself to one's experience as God (doing so and so); so that here too the subject is justified in believing that God is present to her, or is doing so and so vis-à-vis her, just because that is the way in which the object is presented to her experience. (For the purposes of this paper let's focus on those cases in which this presentation is not via any *sensory* qualities or sensorily perceivable objects. The experience involved will be non-sensory in character.) It is because I think of the experience of God as having basically the same structure as the sense perception of physical objects that I feel entitled to speak of "perceiving God." But though I construe the matter in direct-realist terms, most of what I have to say here will be relevant to a defense of the more general claim that the experiential justification of M-beliefs is importantly parallel to the experiential justification of perceptual beliefs about the physical environment, on any halfway plausible construal of the latter, at least on any halfway plausible realist construal.

I shall develop the position by way of responding to a number of objections. This procedure reflects my conviction that the very considerable incidence of putative perceptions of God creates a certain initial presumption that these experiences are what they seem to be and that something can thereby be learned about God.

Objection I. What reason do we have for supposing that anyone ever does really perceive God? In order for S to perceive God it would have to be the case that (1) God exists, and (2) God is related to S or to his experience in such a way as to be perceivable by him. Only after we have seen reason to accept all that will we take seriously any claim to perceive God.

Answer. It all depends on what you will take as a reason. What you have in mind, presumably, are reasons drawn from some source other than perceptions of God, e.g., metaphysical arguments for the existence and nature of God. But why do you think you are justified in that restriction? We don't proceed in this way with respect to sense perception. Although in determining whether a particular alleged perception was genuine we don't make use of the results of *that* perception, we do utilize what has been observed in many other cases. And what alternative is there? The conditions of veridical sense perception have to do with states of affairs and causal interactions in the physical world, matters to which we have no cognitive access that is not based on sense perception. In like fashion, if there is a divine reality why suppose that the conditions of veridically perceiving it could be ascertained without relying on perceptions of *it?* In requiring external validation in this case but not the other you are arbitrarily imposing a double standard.

Objection II. There are many contradictions in the body of M-beliefs. In particular, persons report communications from God that contradict other reported communications. How, then, can one claim that all M-beliefs are justified?

Answer. What is (should be) claimed is only *prima facie* justification. When a person believes that God is experientially present to him, that belief is justified *unless* the subject has sufficient reasons to suppose it to be false or to suppose that the experience is not, in these circumstances, sufficiently indicative of the truth of the belief. This is, of course, precisely the status of individual perceptual beliefs about the physical environment. When, seeming to see a lake, I believe there to be a lake in front of me, my belief is thereby justified unless I have sufficient reason to suppose it false or to suppose that, in these circumstances, the experience is not sufficiently indicative of the truth of the belief.

Objection III. It is rational to form beliefs about the physical environment on the basis of the way that environment appears to us in sense experience (call this practice of belief formation *SP*) because that is a generally reliable mode of belief formation. And it is reliable just because, in normal conditions, sense experience varies concomitantly with variations in what we take ourselves to be perceiving. But we have no reason to suppose any such regular covariation for putative perception of God. And hence we lack reason for regarding as rational the parallel practice of forming M-beliefs on the basis of what is taken to be a perception of God (call that practice *RE*).

Answer. This is another use of a double standard. How do we know that normal sense experience varies concomitantly with perceived objects? We don't know this a priori. Rather, we have strong empirical evidence for it. That is, by relying on sense perception for our data we have piled up evidence for the reliability of SP. Let's call the kind of circularity exhibited here *epistemic circularity*. It is involved whenever the premises in an argument for the reliability or rationality of a belief-forming practice have themselves been acquired by that practice.[1] If we allow epistemically circular arguments, the reliability of RE can be supported in the same way. Among the things people have claimed to learn from RE is that God will enable people to

---

[1]See my "Epistemic Circularity," *Philosophy and Phenomenological Research*, XLVII, 1(September 1986): 1–30.

experience His presence and activity from time to time in a veridical way. By relying on what one learns from the practice of RE, one can show that RE is a reliable belief-forming practice. On the other hand, if epistemically circular arguments are not countenanced, there can be no significant basis for a reliability claim in either case.

Objection IV. A claim to perceive X, and so to form reliable perceptual beliefs about X on the basis of this, presupposes that the experience involved is best explained by the activity of X, *inter alia*. But it seems that we can give adequate explanations of putative experiences of God in purely naturalistic terms, without bringing God into the explanation at all. Whereas we can't give adequate explanations of normal sense experience without bringing the experienced external objects into the explanation. Hence RE, but not SP, is discredited by these considerations.

Answer. I do not believe that much of a case can be made for the adequacy of any naturalistic explanation of experiences of God. But for present purposes I want to concentrate on the way in which this objection once more depends on a double standard. You will have no case at all for your claim unless you, question-beggingly, restrict yourself to sources of evidence that exclude RE. For from RE and systems built up on its output we learn that God is involved in the explanation of every fact whatever. But you would not proceed in that way with SP. If it is a question of determining the best explanation of sense experience you will, of course, make use of what you think you have learned from SP. Again, you have arbitrarily applied different standards to the two practices.

Here is another point. Suppose that one could give a purely psychological or physiological explanation of the experiences in question. That is quite compatible with God's figuring among their causes and, hence, coming into an ideally complete explanation. After all, it is presumably possible to give an adequate causal explanation of sense experience in terms of what goes on within the skull, but that is quite compatible with the external perceived objects' figuring further back along the causal chain.

Objection V. You have been accusing me of *arbitrarily* employing a double standard. But I maintain that RE differs from SP in ways that make different standards appropriate. SP is a pervasive and inescapable feature of our lives. Sense experience is insistent, omnipresent, vivid, and richly detailed. We use it as a source of information during all our waking hours. RE, by contrast, is not universally shared; and even for its devotees its practice is relatively infrequent. Moreover, its deliverances are, by comparison, meager, obscure, and uncertain. Thus when an output of RE does pop up, it is naturally greeted with more skepticism, and one properly demands more for its validation than in the case of so regular and central part of our lives as SP.

Answer. I don't want to deny either the existence or the importance of these differences. I want to deny only that they have the alleged bearing on the epistemic situation. Why should we suppose that a cognitive access enjoyed only by a part of the population is less likely to be reliable than one that is universally distributed? Why should we suppose that a source that yields less detailed and less fully understood beliefs is more suspect than a richer source? A priori it would seem just as likely that some aspects of reality are accessible only to persons that satisfy certain conditions not satisfied by all human beings as that some aspects are equally accessible to all. A priori it would seem just as likely that some aspects of reality are humanly graspable only in a fragmentary and opaque manner as that some aspects are graspable in a more nearly complete and pellucid fashion. Why view the one sort of cognitive claim with more suspicion than the other? I will agree that the spotty distribution of RE calls for explanation, as does the various cognitively unsatisfactory features of its output. But, for that matter, so does the universal distribution and cognitive richness of SP. And in both cases explanations are forthcoming, though in both cases the outputs of the practices are utilized in order to achieve those explanations. As for RE, the limited distribution may be explained by the fact that many persons are not prepared to meet the moral and other "way of life" conditions that God has set for awareness of Himself. And the cognitively unsatisfactory features of the doxastic output are explained by the fact that God infinitely exceeds our cognitive powers.

Objection VI. When someone claims to see a spruce tree in a certain spot, the claim is checkable. Other people can take a look, photographs can be taken, the subject's condition can be diagnosed, and so on. But there are no comparable checks and tests available in RE. And how can we take seriously a claim to have perceived an objective state of affairs if there is, in principle, no intersubjective way of determining whether that claim is correct?

Answer. The answer to this objection is implicit in a point made earlier, viz., that putative experience of God yields only prima facie justification, justification (unqualifiedly) provided there are no sufficient overriding considerations. This notion has a significant application only where there is what we may call an *overrider system*, i.e., ways of determining whether the facts are such as to indicate a belief from the range in question to be false and ways of determining whether conditions are such that the basis of the belief is sufficiently indicative of its truth. SP does contain such a system. What about RE? Here we must confront a salient difference between the two spheres. If we consider the way in which a body of beliefs has been developed on the basis of SP we find pretty much the same system across all cultures. But our encounters with God have spawned a number of different religious communities with beliefs and practices of worship which are quite different, though with some considerable overlap. These differences carry with them differences in overrider systems. But it remains true that if we consider any particular religious community which exhibits a significant commonality in doctrine and worship it will feature a more or less definite overrider system. For concreteness let's think of what I will call the *mainline Christian community*. (From this point onward I will use the term 'RE' for the practice of forming M-beliefs as it goes on in this community.) In that community a body of doctrine has developed concerning the nature of God, His purposes, and His interactions with mankind, including His appearances to us. If an M-belief contradicts this system that is a reason for deeming it false. Moreover there is a long and varied history of experiential encounters with God, embodied in written accounts as well as oral transmission. This provides bases for regarding particular experiences as more or less likely to be veridical, given the conditions, psychological or otherwise, in which they occurred, the character of the subject, and the effects in the life of the subject. Thus a socially established religious doxastic practice like RE will contain a rich system of overriders that provides resources for checking the acceptability of any particular M-belief.

But perhaps your point is rather that there are no *external* checks on a particular report, none that do not rely on other claims of the same sort. Let's agree that this is the case. But why suppose that to be any black mark against RE? Here is the double standard again. After all, particular claims within SP cannot be checked without relying on what we have learned from SP. Suppose I claim to see a fir tree in a certain spot. To check on this one would have to rely on other persons' perceptual reports as to what is at that spot, our general empirical knowledge of the likelihood of a fir tree in that locality, and so on. Apart from what we take ourselves to have learned from SP, we would have nothing to go on. One can hardly determine whether my report was accurate by intuiting self-evident truths or by consulting divine revelation. But if SP counts as having a system of checks even though this system involves relying on some outputs of the practice in order to put others to the test, why should RE be deemed to have no such system when its procedures exhibit the same structure? Once more you are, arbitrarily, setting quite different requirements for different practices.

Perhaps your point was that RE's system of checks is unlike SP's. In particular, the following difference can be discerned. Suppose I report seeing a morel at a certain spot in the forest. Now suppose that a number of qualified observers take a good look at that spot at that time and report that no morel is to be seen. In that case my report would have been decisively disconfirmed. But nothing like that is possible in RE. We can't lay down any conditions (of a sort the satisfaction of which we can determine) under which a properly qualified person will experience the presence of God if God is "there" to be experienced. Hence a particular report cannot be decisively disconfirmed by the experience of others.

But what epistemic relevance does this difference have? Why should we suppose that RE is rendered dubious for lacking checkability of this sort?

Let's consider what makes this kind of intersubjective test possible for SP. Clearly it is that we have discovered fairly firm regularities in the behavior of physical things, including human sense perception. Since there are stable regularities in the ways in which physical objects disclose themselves to our perception, we can be assured that if X exists at a certain time and place and if S satisfies appropriate conditions then S is sure to perceive X. But no such tight regularities are discoverable in God's appearances to our experience. We can say something about the way in which such matters as the distribution of attention and the moral and spiritual state of the subject are conducive to such appearances; but these most emphatically do not add up to the sort of lawlike connections we get with SP. Now what about this difference? Is it to the epistemic discredit of RE that it does not enable us to discover such regularities? Well, that all depends on what it would be reasonable to expect if RE does put us into effective cognitive contact with God. Given what we have learned about God and our relations to Him (from RE, supplemented by whatever other sources there be), should we expect to be able to discover such realities if God really exists? Clearly not. There are several important points here, but the most important is that it is contrary to God's plans for us to give us that much control, cognitive and practical. Hence it is quite understandable, if God exists and is as RE leads us to suppose, that we should not be able to ascertain the kinds of regularities that would make possible the kinds of intersubjective tests exhibited by SP. Hence, the epistemic status of RE is in no way diminished by its lack of such tests. Once more RE is subjected to an inappropriate standard. This time, however, it is not a double standard, but rather an inappropriate single standard. RE is being graded down for lacking positive features of other practices, where these features cannot reasonably be supposed to be generally necessary conditions of epistemic excellence, even for experiential practices. Thus my critic is exhibiting what we might term *epistemic chauvinism*, judging alien forms of life according to whether they conform to the home situation, a procedure as much to be deplored in the epistemic as in the political sphere.

Objection VII. How can it be rational to take RE as a source of justification when there are incompatible rivals that can lay claim to that status on exactly the same grounds? M-beliefs of different religious communities conflict to a considerable extent, particularly those concerning alleged divine messages, and the bodies of doctrine they support conflict even more. We get incompatible accounts of God's plans for us and requirements on us, of the conditions of salvation, and so on. This being the case, how can we pick out just one of these communal practices as yielding justified belief?

Answer. I take this to be by far the most serious difficulty with my position. I have chosen to concentrate on what I take to be less serious problems, partly because their consideration brings out better the main lineaments of the position, and partly because any serious treatment of this last problem would spill beyond the confines of this paper.[2] Here I shall have to content myself with making one basic point. We are not faced with the necessity of choosing only one such practice as yielding prima facie justified M-beliefs. The fact that there are incompatibilities between systems of religious beliefs in M-beliefs and elsewhere, shows that not all M-beliefs can be true, but not that they cannot all be prima facie justified. After all, incompatible beliefs *within* a system can all be prima facie justified; that's the point of the prima facie qualification. When we are faced with a situation like that, the hope is that the overrider system and other winnowing devices will weed out the inconsistencies. To be sure, intersystem winnowing devices are hazier and more meager than those which are available within a system; but consistency, consonance with other well-entrenched beliefs and doxastic practices, and general reasonability and plausibility give us something to go on. Moreover, it may be that some religious ways of life fulfill their own promises more fully than others. Of course, there is never any guarantee that a unique way of resolving incompatibilities will present itself, even with a system. But where there are established practices of forming beliefs on the basis of experience, I believe the rational course is to regard each such belief as thereby prima facie justified, hoping that future developments, perhaps unforeseeable at present, will resolve fundamental incompatibilities.

In conclusion I will make explicit the general epistemological orientation I have been presupposing in my defense of RE. I take our human situation to be such that we engage in a plurality of basic doxastic practices, each of which involves a distinctive sort of input to belief-forming "mechanisms," a distinctive range of belief contents (a "subject matter" and ways of conceiving it), and a set of functions that determine belief contents as a function of input features. Each practice is socially established: socially shared, inculcated, reinforced, and propagated. In addition to experiential practices, with which we have been concerned in this paper, there are, e.g., inferential practices, the input of which consists of beliefs, and the practice of forming memory beliefs. A doxastic practice is not restricted to the formation of first-level beliefs; it will also typically involve criteria and procedures of criticism of the beliefs thus formed; here we will find the "overrider systems" of which we were speaking earlier. In general, we learn these practices and engage in them long before we arrive at the stage of explicitly formulating their principles and subjecting them to critical reflection. Theory is deeply rooted in practice.

Nor, having arrived at the age of reason, can we turn our back on all that and take a fresh start, in the Cartesian spirit, choosing our epistemic procedures and criteria anew, on a purely "rational" basis. Apart from reliance on doxastic tendencies with which we find ourselves, we literally

---

[2]For an extended treatment of this issue see my "Religious Experience and Religious Diversity," forthcoming in *Christian Scholars' Review*.

have nothing to go on. Indeed, what Descartes did, as Thomas Reid trenchantly pointed out, was arbitrarily to pick one doxastic practice he found himself engaged in—accepting propositions that seem self-evident—and set that as a judge over all the others, with what results we are all too familiar. This is not to say that we must acquiesce in our prereflective doxastic tendencies in every respect. We can tidy things up, modify our established practices so as to make each more internally consistent and more consistent with the others. But, on the whole and for the most part, we have no choice but to continue to form beliefs in accordance with these practices and to take these ways of forming beliefs as paradigmatically conferring epistemic justification. And this is the way that epistemology has in fact gone, except for some arbitrary partiality. Of course it would be satisfying to economize our basic commitments by taking one or a few of these practices as basic and using them to validate the others; but we have made little progress in this enterprise over the centuries. It is not self-evident that sense perception is reliable, nor can we establish its reliability if we restrict ourselves to premises drawn from introspection; we cannot show that deductive reasoning is valid without using deductive reasoning to do so; and so on. We are endowed with strong tendencies to engage in a number of distinct doxastic practices, none of which can be warranted on the basis of others. It is clearly the better part of wisdom to recognize beliefs that emerge from these practices to be rational and justified, at least once they are properly sifted and refined.

In this paper I have undertaken to extend this account to doxastic practices that are not universally practiced. Except for that matter of distribution and the other peripheral matters mentioned in Objection V and except for being faced with actually existing rivals, a religious experiential doxastic practice like RE seems to me to be on all fours with SP and other universal practices. It too involves a distinctive range of inputs, a range of belief contents, and functions that map features of the former onto contents of the latter. It is socially established within a certain community. It involves higher-level procedures of correction and modification of its first-level beliefs. Though it *may* be acquired in a deliberate and self-conscious fashion, it is more typically acquired in a practical, prereflective form. Though it is obviously evitable in a way SP, e.g., is not, for many of its practitioners it is just about as firmly entrenched.

These similarities lead me to the conclusion that if, as it seems we must concede, a belief is prima facie justified by virtue of emerging from one of the universal basic practices, we should also concede the same status to the products of RE. I have sought to show that various plausible-sounding objections to this position depend on the use of a double standard or reflect arbitrary epistemic chauvinism. They involve subjecting RE to inappropriate standards. Once we appreciate these points, we can see the strength of the case for RE as one more epistemically autonomous practice of belief formation and source of justification.

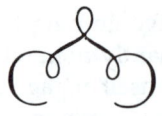

THE
PROBLEM
OF EVIL

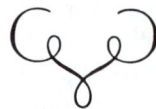

DAVID HUME

The Argument from Evil

It is my opinion, I own, replied Demea, that each man feels, in a manner, the truth of religion within his own breast; and, from a consciousness of his imbecility and misery rather than from any reasoning, is led to seek protection from that Being on whom he and all nature are dependent. So anxious or so tedious are even the best scenes of life that futurity is still the object of all our hopes and fears. We incessantly look forward and endeavor, by prayers, adoration, and sacrifice, to appease those unknown powers whom we find, by experience, so able to afflict and oppress us. Wretched creatures that we are! What resource for us amidst the innumerable ills of life did not religion suggest some methods of atonement, and appease those terrors with which we are incessantly agitated and tormented?

I am indeed persuaded, said Philo, that the best and indeed the only method of bringing everyone to a due sense of religion is by just representations of the misery and wickedness of men. And for that purpose a talent of eloquence and strong imagery is more requisite than that of reasoning and argument. For is it necessary to prove what everyone feels within himself? It is only necessary to make us feel it, if possible, more intimately and sensibly.

The people, indeed, replied Demea, are sufficiently convinced of this great and melancholy truth. The miseries of life, the unhappiness of man, the general corruptions of our nature, the unsatisfactory enjoyment of pleasures, riches, honors—these phrases have become almost proverbial in all languages. And who can doubt of what all men declare from their own immediate feeling and experience?

From David Hume, *Dialogues Concerning Natural Religion* (1779), Part X.

In this point, said Philo, the learned are perfectly agreed with the vulgar; and in all letters, *sacred* and *profane,* the topic of human misery has been insisted on with the most pathetic eloquence that sorrow and melancholy could inspire. The poets, who speak from sentiment, without a system, and whose testimony has therefore the more authority, abound in images of this nature. From Homer down to Dr. Young, the whole inspired tribe have ever been sensible that no other representation of things would suit the feeling and observation of each individual.

As to authorities, replied Demea, you need not seek them. Look round this library of Cleanthes. I shall venture to affirm that, except authors of particular sciences, such as chemistry or botany, who have no occasion to treat of human life, there is scarce one of those innumerable writers from whom the sense of human misery has not, in some passage or other, extorted a complaint and confession of it. At least, the chance is entirely on that side; and no one author has ever, so far as I can recollect, been so extravagant as to deny it.

There you must excuse me, said Philo: Leibniz has denied it, and is perhaps the first[1] who ventured upon so bold and paradoxical an opinion; at least, the first who made it essential to his philosophical system.

And by being the first, replied Demea, might he not have been sensible of his error? For is this a subject in which philosophers can propose to make discoveries especially in so late an age? And can any man hope by a simple denial (for the subject scarcely admits of reasoning) to bear down the united testimony of mankind, founded on sense and consciousness?

And why should man, added he, pretend to an exemption from the lot of all other animals? The whole earth, believe me, Philo, is cursed and polluted. A perpetual war is kindled amongst all living creatures. Necessity, hunger, want stimulate the strong and courageous; fear, anxiety, terror agitate the weak and infirm. The first entrance into life gives anguish to the new-born infant and to its wretched parent; weakness, impotence, distress attend each stage of that life, and it is, at last, finished in agony and horror.

Observe, too, says Philo, the curious artifices of nature in order to embitter the life of every living being. The stronger prey upon the weaker and keep them in perpetual terror and anxiety. The weaker, too, in their turn, often prey upon the stronger, and vex and molest them without relaxation. Consider that innumerable race of insects, which either are bred on the body of each animal or, flying about, infix their stings in him. These insects have others still less than themselves which torment them. And thus on each hand, before and behind, above and below, every animal is surrounded with enemies which incessantly seek his misery and destruction.

---

[1]That sentiment had been maintained by Dr. King and some few others before Leibniz, though by none of so great fame as that German philosopher.

Man alone, said Demea, seems to be, in part, an exception to this rule. For by combination in society he can easily master lions, tigers, and bears, whose greater strength and agility naturally enable them to prey upon him.

On the contrary, it is here chiefly, cried Philo, that the uniform and equal maxims of nature are most apparent. Man, it is true, can, by combination, surmount all his *real* enemies and become master of the whole animal creation; but does he not immediately raise up to himself *imaginary* enemies, the demons of his fancy, who haunt him with superstitious terrors and blast every enjoyment of life? His pleasure, as he imagines, becomes in their eyes a crime; his food and repose give them umbrage and offence; his very sleep and dreams furnish new materials to anxious fear; and even death, his refuge from every other ill, presents only the dread of endless and innumerable woes. Nor does the wolf molest more the timid flock than superstition does the anxious beast of wretched mortals.

Besides, consider, Demea: This very society by which we surmount those wild beasts, our natural enemies, what new enemies does it not raise to us? What woe and misery does it not occasion? Man is the greatest enemy of man. Oppression, injustice, contempt, contumely, violence, sedition, war, calumny, treachery, fraud—by these they mutually torment each other, and they would soon dissolve that society which they had formed were it not for the dread of still greater ills which must attend their separation.

But though these external insults, said Demea, from animals, from men, from all the elements, which assault us form a frightful catalogue of woes, they are nothing in comparison of those which arise within ourselves, from the distempered condition of our mind and body. How many lie under the lingering torment of disease? Hear the pathetic enumeration of the great poet.

> Intestine stone and ulcer, colic-pangs,
> Demoniac frenzy, moping melancholy,
> And moon-struck madness, pining atrophy,
> Marasmus, and wide-wasting pestilence.
> Dire was the tossing, deep the groans: *Despair*
> Tended the sick, busiest from couch to couch.
> And over them triumphant *Death* his dart
> Shook: but delay'd to strike, though oft invok'd
> With vows, as their chief good and final hope.

The disorders of the mind, continued Demea, though more secret, are not perhaps less dismal and vexatious. Remorse, shame, anguish, rage, disappointment, anxiety, fear, dejection, despair—who has ever passed through life without cruel inroads from these tormentors? How many have scarcely ever felt any better sensations? Labor and poverty, so abhorred by everyone, are the certain lot of the far greater number; and those few privileged persons who enjoy ease and opulence never reach contentment or true felicity. All the goods of life united would not make a very happy man, but all the ills united would make a wretch indeed; and any one of them almost (and who can be free from every one), nay, often the absence of one good (and who can possess all) is sufficient to render life ineligible.

Were a stranger to drop on a sudden into this world, I would show him, as a specimen of its ills, a hospital full of diseases, a prison crowded with malefactors and debtors, a field of battle strewed with carcases, a fleet foundering in the ocean, a nation languishing under tyranny, famine, or pestilence. To turn the gay side of life to him and give him a notion of its pleasures—whither should I conduct him? To a ball, to an opera, to court? He might justly think that I was only showing him a diversity of distress and sorrow.

There is no evading such striking instances, said Philo, but by apologies which still further aggravate the charge. Why have all men, I ask, in all ages, complained incessantly of the miseries of life?... They have no just reason, says one: These complaints proceed only from their discontented, repining, anxious disposition.... And can there possibly, I reply, be a more certain foundation of misery than such a wretched temper?

But if they were really as unhappy as they pretend, says my antagonist, why do they remain in life?...

> Not satisfied with life, afraid of death.

This is the secret chain, say I, that holds us. We are terrified, not bribed to the continuance of our existence.

It is only a false delicacy, he may insist, which a few refined spirits indulge, and which has spread these complaints among the whole race of mankind.... And what is this delicacy, I ask, which you blame? Is it anything but a greater sensibility to all the pleasures and pains of life? And if the man of a delicate, refined temper, by being so much more alive than the rest of the world, is only so much more unhappy, what judgment must we form in general of human life?

Let men remain at rest, says our adversary, and they will be easy. They are willing artificers of their own misery.... No! reply I: An anxious languor follows their repose; disappointment, vexation, trouble, their activity and ambition.

I can observe something like what you mention in some others, replied Cleanthes; but I confess I feel little or nothing of it in myself, and hope that it is not so common as you represent it.

If you feel not human misery yourself, cried Demea, I congratulate you on so happy a singularity. Others, seemingly the most prosperous, have not been ashamed to vent their complaints in the most melancholy strains. Let us attend to the great, the fortunate emperor, Charles V, when, tired with human grandeur, he resigned all his extensive dominions into the hands of his son. In the last harangue which he made on that memorable occasion, he publicly avowed *that the greatest prosperities which he had ever enjoyed had been mixed with so many adversities that he might truly say he had never enjoyed any satisfaction or contentment*. But did the retired life in which he sought for shelter afford him any greater happiness? If we may credit his son's account, his repentance commenced the very day of his resignation.

Cicero's fortune, from small beginnings, rose to the greatest luster and renown; yet what pathetic complaints of the ills of life do his familiar letters, as well as philosophical discourses, contain? And suitably to his own experience, he introduces Cato, the great, the fortunate Cato protesting in his old age that had he a new life in his offer he would reject the present.

Ask yourself, ask any of your acquaintance, whether they would live over again the last ten or twenty years of their life. No! but the next twenty, they say, will be better:

> And from the dregs of life, hope to receive
> What the first sprightly running could not give.

Thus, at last, they find (such is the greatness of human misery, it reconciles even contradictions) that they complain at once of the shortness of life and of its vanity and sorrow.

And is it possible, Cleanthes, said Philo, that after all these reflections, and infinitely more which might be suggested, you can still persevere in your anthropomorphism, and assert the moral attributes of the Deity, his justice, benevolence, mercy, and rectitude, to be of the same nature with these virtues in human creatures? His power, we allow, is infinite; whatever he wills is executed; but neither man nor any other animal is happy; therefore, he does not will their happiness. His wisdom is infinite; he is never mistaken in choosing the means to any end; but the course of nature tends not to human or animal felicity; therefore, it is not established for that purpose. Through the whole compass of human knowledge there are no inferences more certain and infallible than these. In what respect, then, do his benevolence and mercy resemble the benevolence and mercy of men?

Epicurus' old questions are yet unanswered.

Is he willing to prevent evil, but not able? then is he impotent. Is he able, but not willing? then is he malevolent. Is he both able and willing? whence then is evil?

You ascribe, Cleanthes (and I believe justly), a purpose and intention to nature. But what, I beseech you, is the object of that curious artifice and machinery which she has displayed in all animals—the preservation alone of individuals, and propagation of the species? It seems enough for her purpose, if such a rank be barely upheld in the universe, without any care or concern for the happiness of the members that compose it. No resource for this purpose: no machinery in order merely to give pleasure or ease: no fund of pure joy and contentment: no indulgence without some want or necessity accompanying it. At least, the few phenomena of this nature are overbalanced by opposite phenomena of still greater importance.

Our sense of music, harmony, and indeed beauty of all kinds, gives satisfaction, without being absolutely necessary to the preservation and propagation of the species. But what racking pains, on the other hand, arise from gouts, gravels, megrims, toothaches, rheumatisms, where the injury to the animal machinery is either small or incurable? Mirth, laughter, play, frolic seem gratuitous satisfactions which have no further tendency; spleen, melancholy, discontent, superstition are pains of the same nature. How then does the divine benevolence display itself, in the sense of you anthropomorphites? None but we mystics, as you were pleased to call us, can account for this strange mixture of phenomena, by deriving it from attributes infinitely perfect but incomprehensible.

And have you, at last, said Cleanthes smiling, betrayed your intentions, Philo? Your long agreement with Demea did indeed a little surprise me, but I find you were all the while erecting a concealed battery against me. And I must confess that you have now fallen upon a subject worthy of your noble spirit of opposition and controversy. If you can make out the present point, and prove mankind to be unhappy or corrupted, there is an end at once of all religion. For to what purpose establish the natural attributes of the Deity, while the moral are still doubtful and uncertain?

You take umbrage very easily, replied Demea, at opinions the most innocent and the most generally received, even amongst the religious and devout themselves; and nothing can be more surprising than to find a topic like this—concerning the wickedness and misery of man—charged with no less than atheism and profaneness. Have not all pious divines and preachers who have indulged their rhetoric on so fertile a subject; have they not easily, I say, given a solution of any difficulties which may attend it? This world is but a point in comparison of the universe; this life but a moment in comparison of eternity. The present evil phenomena, therefore, are rectified in other regions, and in some future period of existence. And the eyes of men, being then opened to larger views of things, see the whole connection of general laws, and trace, with adoration, the benevolence and rectitude of the Deity through all the mazes and intricacies of his providence.

No! replied Cleanthes, no! These arbitrary suppositions can never be admitted, contrary to matter of fact, visible and uncontroverted. Whence can any cause be known but from its known effects? Whence can any hypothesis be proved but from the apparent phenomena? To establish one hypothesis upon another is building entirely in the air; and the utmost we ever attain by these conjectures and fictions is to ascertain the bare possibility of our opinion, but never can we, upon such terms, establish its reality.

The only method of supporting divine benevolence—and it is what I willingly embrace—is to deny absolutely the misery and wickedness of man. Your representations are exaggerated; your melancholy views mostly fictitious; your inferences contrary to fact and experience. Health is more common than sickness; pleasure than pain; happiness than misery.

And for one vexation which we meet with, we attain, upon computation, a hundred enjoyments.

Admitting your position, replied Philo, which yet is extremely doubtful, you must at the same time allow that, if pain be less frequent than pleasure, it is infinitely more violent and durable. One hour of it is often able to outweigh a day, a week, a month of our common insipid enjoyments; and how many days, weeks, and months are passed by several in the most acute torments? Pleasure, scarcely in one instance, is ever able to reach ecstasy and rapture; and in no one instance can it continue for any time at its highest pitch and altitude. The spirits evaporate, the nerves relax, the fabric is disordered, and the enjoyment quickly degenerates into fatigue and uneasiness. But pain often, good God, how often! rises to torture and agony; and the longer it continues, it becomes still more genuine agony and torture. Patience is exhausted, courage languishes, melancholy seizes us, and nothing terminates our misery but the removal of its cause or another event which is the sole cure of all evil, but which, from our natural folly, we regard with still greater horror and consternation.

But not to insist upon these topics, continued Philo, though most obvious, certain, and important, I must use the freedom to admonish you, Cleanthes, that you have put the controversy upon a most dangerous issue, and are unawares introducing a total scepticism into the most essential articles of natural and revealed theology. What! no method of fixing a just foundation for religion unless we allow the happiness of human life, and maintain a continued existence even in this world, with all our present pains, infirmities, vexations, and follies, to be eligible and desirable! But this is contrary to everyone's feeling and experience; it is contrary to an authority so established as nothing can subvert. No decisive proofs can ever be produced against this authority; nor is it possible for you to compute, estimate, and compare all the pains and all the pleasures in the lives of all men and of all animals; and thus, by your resting the whole system of religion on a point which, from its very nature, must forever be uncertain, you tacitly confess that that system is equally uncertain.

But allowing you what never will be believed, at least, what you never possibly can prove, that animal or, at least, human happiness in this life exceeds its misery, you have yet done nothing; for this is not, by any means, what we expect from infinite power, infinite wisdom, and infinite goodness. Why is there any misery at all in the world? Not by chance, surely. From some cause then. Is it from the intention of the Deity? But he is perfectly benevolent. Is it contrary to his intention? But he is almighty. Nothing can shake the solidity of this reasoning, so short, so clear, so decisive, except we assert that these subjects exceed all human capacity, and that our common measures of truth and falsehood are not applicable to them—a topic which I have all along insisted on, but which you have, from the beginning, rejected with scorn and indignation.

But I will be contented to retire still from this intrenchment, for I deny that you can ever force me in it. I will allow that pain or misery in man is *compatible* with infinite power and goodness in the Deity, even in your sense of these attributes: what are you advanced by all these concessions? A mere possible compatibility is not sufficient. You must *prove* these pure, unmixed and uncontrollable attributes from the present mixed and confused phenomena, and from these alone. A hopeful undertaking! Were the phenomena ever so pure and unmixed, yet, being finite, they would be insufficient for that purpose. How much more, where they are also so jarring and discordant!

Here, Cleanthes, I find myself at ease in my argument. Here I triumph. Formerly, when we argued concerning the natural attributes of intelligence and design, I needed all my sceptical and metaphysical subtilty to elude your grasp. In many views of the universe and of its parts, particularly the latter, the beauty and fitness of final causes strike us with such irresistible force that all objections appear (what I believe they really are) mere cavils and sophisms; nor can we then imagine how it was ever possible for us to repose any weight on them. But there is no view of human life or of the condition of mankind from which, without the greatest violence, we can infer the moral attributes or learn that infinite benevolence, conjoined with infinite power and infinite wisdom, which we must discover by the eyes of faith alone. It is your turn now to tug the laboring oar, and to support your philosophical subtitles against the dictates of plain reason and experience.

H. J. MCCLOSKEY

God and Evil

A. THE PROBLEM STATED

Evil is a problem for the theist in that a contradiction is involved in the fact of evil on the one hand, and the belief in the omnipotence and perfection of God on the other. God cannot be both all-powerful and perfectly good if evil is real. This contradiction is well set out in its detail by Mackie in his discussion of the problem.[1] In his discussion Mackie seeks to show that this contradiction cannot be resolved in terms of man's free will. In arguing in this way Mackie neglects a large number of important points, and concedes far too much to the theist. He implicitly allows that whilst physical evil creates a problem, this problem is reducible to the problem of moral evil and

---

From *The Philosophical Quarterly* 10 (1960). Reprinted by permission of the author and *The Philosophical Quarterly*.

[1]Evil and Omnipotence," *Mind*, 1955.

that therefore the satisfactoriness of solutions of the problem of evil turns on the compatibility of free will and absolute goodness. In fact physical evils create a number of distinct problems which are not reducible to the problem of moral evil. Further, the proposed solution of the problem of moral evil in terms of free will renders the attempt to account for physical evil in terms of moral good, and the attempt thereby to reduce the problem of evil to the problem of moral evil, completely untenable. Moreover, the account of moral evil in terms of free will breaks down on more obvious and less disputable grounds than those indicated by Mackie. Moral evil can be shown to remain a problem whether or not free will is compatible with absolute goodness. I therefore propose in this paper to reopen the discussion of "the problem of evil," by approaching it from a more general standpoint, examining a wider variety of solutions than those considered by Mackie and his critics.

The fact of evil creates a problem for the theist; but there are a number of simple solutions available to a theist who is content seriously to modify his theism. He can either admit a limit to God's power, or he can deny God's moral perfection. He can assert either (1) that God is not powerful enough to make a world that does not contain evil, or (2) that God created only the good in the universe and that some other power created the evil, or (3) that God is all-powerful but morally imperfect, and chose to create an imperfect universe. Few Christians accept these solutions, and this is no doubt partly because such "solutions" ignore the real inspiration of religious beliefs, and partly because they introduce embarrassing complications for the theist in his attempts to deal with other serious problems. However, if any one of these "solutions" is accepted, then the problem of evil is avoided, and a weakened version of theism is made secure from attacks based upon the fact of the occurrence of evil.

For more orthodox theism, according to which God is both omnipotent and perfectly good, evil creates a real problem; and this problem is well-stated by the Jesuit, Father G. H. Joyce. Joyce writes:

> The existence of evil in the world must at all times be the greatest of all problems which the mind encounters when it reflects on God and His relation to the world. If He is, indeed, all-good and all-powerful, how has evil any place in the world which He has made? Whence came it? Why is it here? If He is all-good why did He allow it to arise? If all-powerful why does He not deliver us from the burden? Alike in the physical and moral order creation seems so grievously marred that we find it hard to understand how it can derive in its entirety from God.[2]

The facts which give rise to the problem are of two general kinds, and give rise to two distinct types of problems. These two general kinds of evil

---

[2]Joyce: *Principles of Natural Theology*, ch. XVII. All subsequent quotations from Joyce in this paper are from this chapter of this work.

are usually referred to as "physical" and as "moral" evil. These terms are by no means apt—suffering for instance is not strictly physical evil—and they conceal significant differences. However, this terminology is too widely accepted, and too convenient to be dispensed with here, the more especially as the various kinds of evil, whilst important as distinct kinds, need not for our purposes be designated by separate names.

Physical evil and moral evil then are the two general forms of evil which independently and jointly constitute conclusive grounds for denying the existence of God in the sense defined, namely as an all-powerful, perfect Being. The acuteness of these two general problems is evident when we consider the nature and extent of the evils of which account must be given. To take physical evils, looking first at the less important of these.

(a) Physical evils. Physical evils are involved in the very constitution of the earth and animal kingdom. There are deserts and icebound areas; there are dangerous animals of prey, as well as creatures such as scorpions and snakes. There are also pests such as flies and fleas and the hosts of other insect pests, as well as the multitude of lower parasites such as tapeworms, hookworms and the like. Secondly, there are the various natural calamities and the immense human suffering that follows in their wake—fires, floods, tempests, tidal-waves, volcanoes, earthquakes, droughts and famines. Thirdly, there are the vast numbers of diseases that torment and ravage man. Diseases such as leprosy, cancer, poliomyelitis, appear *prima facie* not to be creations which are to be expected of a benevolent Creator. Fourthly, there are the evils with which so many are born—the various physical deformities and defects such as misshapen limbs, blindness, deafness, dumbness, mental deficiency and insanity. Most of these evils contribute towards increasing human pain and suffering: but not all physical evils are reducible simply to pain. Many of these evils are evils whether or not they result in pain. This is important, for it means that, unless there is one solution to such diverse evils, it is both inaccurate and positively misleading to speak of *the* problem of physical evil. Shortly I shall be arguing that no one "solution" covers all these evils, so we shall have to conclude that physical evils create not one problem but a number of distinct problems for the theist.

The nature of the various difficulties referred to by the theist as the problem of physical evil is indicated by Joyce in a way not untypical among the more honest, philosophical theists, as follows:

> The actual amount of suffering which the human race endures is immense. Disease has store and to spare of torments for the body: and disease and death are the lot to which we must all look forward. At all times, too, great numbers of the race are pinched by want. Nor is the world ever free for very long from the terrible sufferings which follow in the track of war. If we concentrate our attention on human woes, to the exclusion of the joys of life, we gain an appalling picture of the ills to which the flesh is heir. So too if we fasten our attention on the sterner side of nature, on the pains which men endure from

natural forces—on the storms which wreck their ships, the cold which freezes them to death, the fire which consumes them—if we contemplate this aspect of nature alone we may be led to wonder how God came to deal so harshly with His Creatures as to provide them with such a home.

Many such statements of the problem proceed by suggesting, if not by stating, that the problem arises at least in part by concentrating one's attention too exclusively on one aspect of the world. This is quite contrary to the facts. The problem is not one that results from looking at only one aspect of the universe. It may be the case that over-all pleasure predominates over pain, and that physical goods in general predominate over physical evils, but the opposite may equally well be the case. It is both practically impossible and logically impossible for this question to be resolved. However, it is not an unreasonable presumption, with the large bulk of mankind inadequately fed and housed and without adequate medical and health services, to suppose that physical evils at present predominate over physical goods. In the light of the facts at our disposal, this would seem to be a much more reasonable conclusion than the conclusion hinted at by Joyce and openly advanced by less cautious theists, namely, that physical goods in fact outweigh physical evils in the world.

However, the question is not, which predominates, physical good or physical evil? The problem of physical evil remains a problem whether the balance in the universe is on the side of physical good or not, because the problem is that of accounting for the fact that physical evil occurs at all.

(b) Moral evil. Physical evils create one of the groups of problems referred to by the theist as "the problem of evil." Moral evil creates quite a distinct problem. Moral evil is simply immorality—evils such as selfishness, envy, greed, deceit, cruelty, callousness, cowardice and the larger scale evils such as wars and the atrocities they involve.

Moral evil is commonly regarded as constituting an even more serious problem than physical evil. Joyce so regards it, observing:

> The man who sins thereby offends God.... We are called on to explain how God came to create an order of things in which rebellion and even final rejection have such a place. Since a choice from among an infinite number of possible worlds lay open to God, how came He to choose one in which these occur? Is not such a choice in flagrant opposition to the Divine Goodness?

Some theists seek a solution by denying the reality of evil or by describing it as a "privation" or absence of good. They hope thereby to explain it away as not needing a solution. This, in the case of most of the evils which require explanation, seems to amount to little more than an attempt to sidestep the problem simply by changing the name of that which has to be explained. It can be exposed for what it is simply by describing some of the evils which have to be explained. That is why a survey of the data to be accounted for is a most important part of the discussion of the problem of evil.

In *The Brothers Karamazov*, Dostoievsky introduces a discussion of the problem of evil by reference to some then recently committed atrocities. Ivan states the problem:

> "By the way, a Bulgarian I met lately in Moscow," Ivan went on... "told me about the crimes committed by Turks in all parts of Bulgaria through fear of a general rising of the Slavs. They burn villages, murder, outrage women and children, and nail their prisoners by the ears to the fences, leave them till morning, and in the morning hang them—all sorts of things you can't imagine. People talk sometimes of bestial cruelty, but that's a great injustice and insult to the beasts; a beast can never be so cruel as a man, so artistically cruel. The tiger only tears and gnaws and that's all he can do. He would never think of nailing people by the ears, even if he were able to do it. These Turks took a pleasure in torturing children too; cutting the unborn child from the mother's womb, and tossing babies up in the air and catching them on the points of their bayonets before their mothers' eyes. Doing it before the mother's eyes was what gave zest to the amusement. Here is another scene that I thought very interesting. Imagine a trembling mother with her baby in her arms, a circle of invading Turks around her. They've planned a diversion: they pet the baby to make it laugh. They succeed; the baby laughs. At that moment, a Turk points a pistol four inches from the baby's face. The baby laughs with glee, holds out its little hands to the pistol, and he pulls the trigger in the baby's face and blows out its brains. Artistic, wasn't it?"[3]

Ivan's statement of the problem was based on historical events. Such happenings did not cease in the nineteenth century. *The Scourge of the Swastika* by Lord Russell of Liverpool contains little else than descriptions of such atrocities; and it is simply one of a host of writings giving documented lists of instances of evils, both physical and moral.

Thus the problem of evil is both real and acute. There is a clear *prima facie* case that evil and God are incompatible—both cannot exist. Most theists admit this, and that the onus is on them to show that the conflict is not fatal to theism; but a consequence is that a host of proposed solutions are advanced.

The mere fact of such a multiplicity of proposed solutions, and the widespread repudiation of each other's solutions by theists, in itself suggests that the fact of evil is an insuperable obstacle to theism as defined here. It also makes it impossible to treat of all proposed solutions, and all that can be attempted here is an examination of those proposed solutions which are most commonly invoked and most generally thought to be important by theists.

Some theists admit the reality of the problem of evil, and then seek to sidestep it, declaring it to be a great mystery which we poor humans cannot hope to comprehend. Other theists adopt a rational approach and advance rational arguments to show that evil, properly understood, is compatible

---

[3]P. 244, Garnett translation, Heinemann.

with, and even a consequence of God's goodness. The arguments to be advanced in this paper are directed against the arguments of the latter theists; but in so far as these arguments are successful against the rational theists, to that extent they are also effective in showing that the non-rational approach in terms of great mysteries is positively irrational.

B. PROPOSED SOLUTIONS
TO THE PROBLEM OF PHYSICAL EVIL

Of the large variety of arguments advanced by theists as solutions to the problem of physical evil, five popularly used and philosophically significant solution will be examined. They are, in brief: (i) Physical good (pleasure) requires physical evil (pain) to exist at all; (ii) Physical evil is God's punishment of sinners; (iii) Physical evil is God's warning and reminder to man; (iv) Physical evil is the result of the natural laws, the operations of which are on the whole good; (v) Physical evil increases the total good.

(i) *Physical Good is Impossible without Physical Evil.* Pleasure is possible only by way of contrast with pain. Here the analogy of colour is used. If everything were blue we should, it is argued, understand neither what colour is nor what blue is. So with pleasure and pain.

The most obvious defect of such an argument is that it does not cover all physical goods and evils. It is an argument commonly invoked by those who think of physical evil as creating only one problem, namely the problem of human pain. However, the problems of physical evils are not reducible to the one problem, the problem of pain; hence the argument is simply irrelevant to much physical evil. Disease and insanity are evils, but health and sanity are possible in the total absence of disease and insanity. Further, if the argument were in any way valid even in respect of pain, it would imply the existence of only a speck of pain, and not the immense amount of pain in the universe. A speck of yellow is all that is needed for an appreciation of blueness and of colour generally. The argument is therefore seen to be seriously defective on two counts even if its underlying principle is left unquestioned. If its underlying principle is questioned, the argument is seen to be essentially invalid. Can it seriously be maintained that if an individual were born crippled and deformed and never in his life experienced pleasure, that he could not experience pain, not even if he were severely injured? It is clear that pain is possible in the absence of pleasure. It is true that it might not be distinguished by a special name and called "pain," but the state we now describe as a painful state would nonetheless be possible in the total absence of pleasure. So too the converse would seem to apply. Plato brings this out very clearly in Book 9 of the *Republic* in respect of the pleasures of taste and smell. These pleasures seem not to depend for their existence on any prior experience of pain. Thus the argument is unsound in respect of its main contention; and in being unsound in this respect, it is at the same time ascribing a serious limitation to God's power. It maintains that God cannot create pleasure without creating pain, although as we have seen, pleasure and pain are not correlatives.

(ii) *Physical Evil is God's Punishment for Sin.* This kind of explanation was advanced to explain the terrible Lisbon earthquake in the 18th century, in which 40,000 people were killed. There are many replies to this argument, for instance Voltaire's. Voltaire asked: "Did God in this earthquake select the 40,000 least virtuous of the Portuguese citizens?" The distribution of disease and pain is in no obvious way related to the virtue of the persons afflicted, and popular saying has it that the distribution is slanted in the opposite direction. The only way of meeting the fact that evils are not distributed proportunately to the evil of the sufferer is by suggesting that all human beings, including children, are such miserable sinners, that our offenses are of such enormity, that God would be justified in punishing all of us as severely as it is possible for humans to be punished; but even then, God's apparent caprice in the selection of His victims requires explanation. In any case it is by no means clear that young children who very often suffer severely are guilty of sin of such an enormity as would be necessary to justify their sufferings as punishment.

Further, many physical evils are simultaneous with birth—insanity, mental defectiveness, blindness, deformities, as well as much disease. No crime or sin of *the child* can explain and justify these physical evils as punishment; and, for a parent's sin to be punished in the child is injustice or evil of another kind.

Similarly, the sufferings of animals cannot be accounted for as punishment. For these various reasons, therefore, this argument must be rejected. In fact it has dropped out of favour in philosophical and theological circles, but it continues to be invoked at the popular level.

(iii) *Physical Evil is God's Warning to Men.* It is argued, for instance of physical calamities, that "they serve a moral end which compensates the physical evil which they cause. The awful nature of these phenomena, the overwhelming power of the forces at work, and man's utter helplessness before them, rouse him from the religious indifference to which he is so prone. They inspire a reverential awe of the Creator who made them, and controls them, and a salutary fear of violating the laws which He has imposed" (Joyce). This is where immortality is often alluded to as justifying evil.

This argument proceeds from a proposition that is plainly false; and that the proposition from which it proceeds is false is conceded implicitly by most theologians. Natural calamities do not necessarily turn people to God, but rather present the problem of evil in an acute form; and the problem of evil is said to account for more defections from religion than any other cause. Thus if God's object in bringing about natural calamities is to inspire reverence and awe, He is a bungler. There are many more reliable methods of achieving this end. Equally important, the use of physical evil to achieve this object is hardly the course one would expect a benevolent God to adopt when other, more effective, less evil methods are available to Him, for example, miracles, special revelation, etc.

(iv) *Evils are the Results of the Operation of Laws of Nature.* This fourth argument relates to most physical evil, but it is more usually used to account for animal suffering and physical calamities. These evils are said to result from the operation of the natural laws which govern these objects, the relevant natural laws being the various causal laws, the law of pleasure-pain as a law governing sentient beings, etc. The theist argues that the non-occurrence of these evils would involve either the constant intervention by God in a miraculous way, and contrary to his own natural laws, or else the construction of a universe with different components subject to different laws of nature; for God, in creating a certain kind of being, must create it subject to its appropriate laws; He cannot create it and subject it to any law of His own choosing. Hence He creates a world which has components and laws good in their total effect, although calamitous in some particular effects.

Against this argument three objections are to be urged. First, it does not cover all physical evil. Clearly not all disease can be accounted for along these lines. Secondly, it is not to give a reason against God's miraculous intervention simply to assert that it would be unreasonable for Him constantly to intervene in the operation of His own laws. Yet this is the only reason that theists seem to offer here. If, by intervening in respect to the operation of His laws, God could thereby eliminate an evil, it would seem to be unreasonable and evil of Him not to do so. Some theists seek a way out of this difficulty by denying that God has the power miraculously to intervene; but this is to ascribe a severe limitation to His power. It amounts to asserting that when His Creation has been effected, God can do nothing else except contemplate it. The third objection is related to this, and is to the effect that it is already to ascribe a serious limitation to God's omnipotence to suggest that He could not make sentient beings which did not experience pain, nor sentient beings without deformities and deficiencies, nor natural phenomena with different laws of nature governing them. There is no reason why better laws of nature governing the existing objects are not possible on the divine hypothesis. Surely, if God is all-powerful, He could have made a better universe in the first place, or one with better laws of nature governing it, so that the operation of its laws did not produce calamities and pain. To maintain this is not to suggest that an omnipotent God should be capable of achieving what is logically impossible. All that has been indicated here is logically possible, and therefore not beyond the powers of a being Who is really omnipotent.

This fourth argument seeks to exonerate God by explaining that He created a universe sound on the whole, but such that He had no direct control over the laws governing His creations, and had control only in His selection of His creations. The previous two arguments attribute the detailed results of the operations of these laws directly to God's will. Theists commonly use all three arguments. It is not without significance that they betray such uncertainty as to whether God is to be *commended* or *exonerated*.

(v) *The Universe is Better with Evil in it.* This is the important argument. One version of it runs:

> Just as the human artist has in view the beauty of his composition as a whole, not making it his aim to give to each several part the highest degree of brilliancy, but that measure of adornment which most contributes to the combined effect, so it is with God. [Joyce]

Another version of this general type of argument explains evil not so much as *a component* of a good whole, seen out of its context as a mere component, but rather as *a means* to a greater good. Different as these versions are, they may be treated here as one general type of argument, for the same criticisms are fatal to both versions.

This kind of argument if valid simply shows that some evil may enrich the Universe; it tells us nothing about *how much* evil will enrich this particular universe, and how much will be too much. So, even if valid in principle—and shortly I shall argue that it is not valid—such an argument does not in itself provide a justification for the evil in the universe. It shows simply that the evil which occurs might have a justification. In view of the immense amount of evil the probabilities are against it.

This is the main point made by Wisdom in his discussion of this argument. Wisdom sums up his criticism as follows:

> It remains to add that, unless there are independent arguments in favour of this world's being the best logically possible world, it is probable that some of the evils in it are not logically necessary to a compensating good; it is probable because there are so many evils.[4]

Wisdom's reply brings out that the person who relies upon this argument as a conclusive and complete argument is seriously mistaken. The argument, if valid, justifies only some evil. A belief that it justifies all the evil that occurs in the world is mistaken, for a second argument, by way of a supplement to it, is needed. This supplementary argument would take the form of a proof that all the evil that occurs is *in fact* valuable and necessary as a means to greater good. Such a supplementary proof is in principle impossible; so, at best, this fifth argument can be taken to show only that some evil *may be* necessary for the production of good, and that the evil in the world may perhaps have a justification on this account. This is not to justify a physical evil, but simply to suggest that physical evil might nonetheless have a justification, although we may never come to know this justification.

---

[4]*Mind*, 1931.

Thus the argument even if it is valid as a general form of reasoning is unsatisfactory because inconclusive. It is, however, also unsatisfactory in that it follows on the principle of the argument that, just as it is possible that evil in the total context contributes to increasing the total ultimate good, so equally, it will hold that good in the total context may increase the ultimate evil. Thus if the principle of the argument were sound, we could never know whether evil is really evil, or good really good. (Aesthetic analogies may be used to illustrate this point.) By implication it follows that it would be dangerous to eliminate evil because we may thereby introduce a discordant element into the divine symphony of the universe; and, conversely, it may be wrong to condemn the elimination of what is good, because the latter may result in the production of more, higher goods.

So it follows that, even if the general principle of the argument is not questioned, it is still seen to be a defective argument. On the one hand, it proves too little—it justifies only some evil and not necessarily all the evil in the universe; on the other hand it proves too much because it creates doubts about the goodness of apparent goods. These criticisms in themselves are fatal to the argument as a solution to the problem of physical evil. However, because this is one of the most popular and plausible accounts of physical evil, it is worthwhile considering whether it can properly be claimed to establish even the very weak conclusion indicated above.

Why, and in what way, is it supposed that physical evils such as pain and misery, disease and deformity, will heighten the total effect and add to the value of the moral? The answer given is that physical evil enriches the whole by giving rise to moral goodness. Disease, insanity, physical suffering and the like are said to bring into being the noble moral virtues—courage, endurance, benevolence, sympathy and the like. This is what the talk about the enriched whole comes to. W. D. Niven makes this explicit in his version of the argument:

> Physical evil has been the goad which has impelled men to most of those achievements which made the history of man so wonderful. Hardship is a stern but fecund parent of invention. Where life is easy because physical ills are at a minimum we find man degenerating in body, mind, and character.

And Niven concludes by asking:

> Which is preferable—a grim fight with the possibility of splendid triumph; or no battle at all?[5]

Joyce's corresponding argument runs:

> Pain is the great stimulant to action. Man no less than animals is impelled to work by the sense of hunger. Experience shows that, were it not for this motive the majority of men would be content to live in indolent ease. Man must earn his bread.

---

[5]W. D. Niven, *Encyclopedia of Religion and Ethics.*

> One reason plainly why God permits suffering is that man may rise to a height of heroism which would otherwise have been beyond his scope. Nor are these the only benefits which it confers. That sympathy for others which is one of the most precious parts of our experience, and one of the most fruitful sources of well-doing, has its origin in the fellow-feeling engendered by endurance of similar trials. Furthermore, were it not for these trials, man would think little enough of a future existence, and of the need of striving after his last end. He would be perfectly content with his existence, and would wreck little of any higher good. These considerations here briefly advanced suffice at least to show how important is the office filled by pain in human life, and with what little reason it is asserted that the existence of so much suffering is irreconcilable with the wisdom of the Creator.

And:

> It may be asked whether the Creator could not have brought man to perfection without the use of suffering. Most certainly He could have conferred upon him a similar degree of virtue without requiring any effort on his part. Yet it is easy to see that there is a special value attaching to a conquest of difficulties such as man's actual demands, and that in God's eyes this may well be an adequate reason for assigning this life to us in preference to another.... Pain has value in respect to the next life, but also in respect to this. The advance of scientific discovery, the gradual improvement of the organization of the community, the growth of material civilization are due in no small degree to the stimulus afforded by pain.

The argument is: Physical evil brings moral good into being, and in fact is an essential precondition for the existence of some moral goods. Further, it is sometimes argued in this context that those moral goods which are possible in the total absence of physical evils are more valuable in themselves if they are achieved as a result of a struggle. Hence physical evil is said to be justified on the grounds that moral good plus physical evil is better than the absence of physical evil.

A common reply, and an obvious one, is that urged by Mackie.[6] Mackie argues that whilst it is true that moral good plus physical evil together are better than physical good alone, the issue is not as simple as that, for physical evil also gives rise to and makes possible many moral evils that would not or could not occur in the absence of physical evil. It is then urged that it is not clear that physical evils (for example, disease and pain) plus some moral goods (for example courage) plus some moral evil (for example, brutality) are better than physical good and those moral goods which are possible and which would occur in the absence of physical evil.

This sort of reply, however, is not completely satisfactory. The objection it raises is a sound one, but it proceeds by conceding too much to the theist, and by overlooking two more basic defects of the argument. It allows

---

[6]Mackie, "Evil and Omnipotence," *Mind*, 1955.

implicitly that the problem of physical evil may be reduced to the problem of moral evil; and it neglects the two objections which show that the problem of physical evil cannot be so reduced.

The theist therefore happily accepts this kind of reply, and argues that, if he can give a satisfactory account of moral evil he will then have accounted for both physical and moral evil. He then goes on to account for moral evil in terms of the value of free will and/or its goods. This general argument is deceptively plausible. It breaks down for the two reasons indicated here, but it breaks down at another point as well. If free will alone is used to justify moral evil, then even if no moral good occurred, moral evil would still be said to be justified; but physical evil would have no justification. Physical evil is not essential to free will; it is only justified if moral good actually occurs, and if the moral good which results from physical evils outweighs the moral evils. This means that the argument from free will cannot alone justify physical evil along these lines; and it means that the argument from free will and its goods does not justify physical evil, because such an argument is incomplete, and necessarily incomplete. It needs to be supplemented by factual evidence that it is logically and practically impossible to obtain.

The correct reply, therefore, is first that the argument is irrelevant to many instances of physical evil, and secondly that it is not true that physical evil plus the moral good it produces is better than physical good and its moral goods. Much pain and suffering, in fact much physical evil generally, for example in children who die in infancy, animals and the insane passes unnoticed; it therefore has no morally uplifting effects upon others, and cannot by virtue of the examples chosen have such effects on the sufferers. Further, there are physical evils such as insanity and much disease to which the argument is inapplicable. So there is a large group of significant cases not covered by the argument. And where the argument is relevant, its premiss is plainly false. It can be shown to be false by exposing its implications in the following way.

We either have obligations to lessen physical evil or we have not. If we have obligations to lessen physical evil then we are thereby reducing the total good in the universe. If, on the other hand, our obligation is to increase the total good in the universe it is our duty to prevent the reduction of physical evil and possibly even to increase the total amount of physical evil. Theists usually hold that we are obliged to reduce the physical evil in the universe; but in maintaining this, the theist is, in terms of this account of physical evil, maintaining that it is his duty to reduce the total amount of real good in the universe, and thereby to make the universe worse. Conversely, if by eliminating the physical evil he is not making the universe worse, then that amount of evil which he eliminates was unnecessary and in need of justification. It is relevant to notice here that evil is not always eliminated for morally praiseworthy reasons. Some discoveries have been due to positively unworthy motives, and many other discoveries which have resulted in a lessening of the sufferings of mankind have been due to no higher a motive than a scientist's desire to earn a reasonable living wage.

This reply to the theist's argument brings out its untenability. The theist's argument is seen to imply that war plus courage plus the many other moral virtues war brings into play are better than peace and its virtues; that famine and its moral virtues are better than plenty; that disease and its moral virtues are better than health. Some Christians in the past, in consistency with this mode of reasoning, opposed the use of anaesthetics to leave scope for the virtues of endurance and courage, and they opposed state aid to the sick and needy to leave scope for the virtues of charity and sympathy. Some have even contended that war is a good in disguise, again in consistency with this argument. Similarly the theist should, in terms of this fifth argument, in his heart if not aloud regret the discovery of the Salk polio vaccine because Dr. Salk has in one blow destroyed infinite possibilities of moral good.

There are three important points that need to be made concerning this kind of account of physical evil. (a) We are told, as by Niven, Joyce and others, that pain is a goad to action and that part of its justification lies in this fact. This claim is empirically false as a generalization about all people and all pain. Much pain frustrates action and wrecks people and personalities. On the other hand many men work and work well without being goaded by pain or discomfort. Further, to assert that men need goading is to ascribe another evil to God, for it is to claim that God made men naturally lazy. There is no reason why God should not have made men naturally industrious; the one is no more incompatible with free will than the other. Thus the argument from physical evil being a goad to man breaks down on three distinct counts. Pain often frustrates human endeavour, pain is not essential as a goad with many men, and where pain is a goad to higher endeavours, it is clear that less evil means to this same end are available to an omnipotent God. (b) The real fallacy in the argument is in the assumption that all or the highest moral excellence results from physical evil. As we have already seen, this assumption is completely false. Neither all moral goodness nor the highest moral goodness is triumph in the face of adversity or benevolence towards others in suffering. Christ Himself stressed this when He observed that the two great commandments were commandments to love. Love does not depend for its possibility on the existence and conquest of evil. (c) The "negative" moral virtues which are brought into play by the various evils—courage, endurance, charity, sympathy and the like—besides not representing the highest forms of moral virtue, are in fact commonly supposed by the theist and atheist alike not to have the value this fifth argument ascribes to them. We—theists and atheists alike—reveal our comparative valuations of these virtues and of physical evil when we insist on state aid for the needy; when we strive for peace, for plenty, and for harmony within the state.

In brief, the good man, the morally admirable man, is he who loves what is good knowing that it is good and preferring it because it is good. He does not need to be torn by suffering or by the spectacle of another's sufferings to be morally admirable. Fortitude in his own sufferings, and sympathetic kindness in others' may reveal to us his goodness; but his goodness is not necessarily increased by such things.

Five arguments concerning physical evil have now been examined. We have seen that the problem of physical evil is a problem in its own right, and one that cannot be reduced to the problem of moral evil; and further, we have seen that physical evil creates not one but a number of problems to which no one nor any combination of the arguments examined offers a solution.

C. PROPOSED SOLUTIONS
TO THE PROBLEM OF MORAL EVIL

The problem of moral evil is commonly regarded as being the greater of the problems concerning evil. As we shall see, it does create what appears to be insuperable difficulties for the theist; but so too, apparently, do physical evils.

For the theist moral evil must be interpreted as a breach of God's law and as a rejection of God himself. It may involve the eternal damnation of the sinner, and in many of its forms it involves the infliction of suffering on other persons. Thus it aggravates the problem of physical evil, but its own peculiar character consists in the fact of sin. How could a morally perfect, all-powerful God create a universe in which occur such moral evils as cruelty, cowardice and hatred, the more especially as these evils constitute a rejection of God Himself by His creations, and as such involve them in eternal damnation?

The two main solutions advanced relate to free will and to the fact that moral evil is a consequence of free will. There is a third kind of solution more often invoked implicitly than as an explicit and serious argument, which need not be examined here as its weaknesses are plainly evident. This third solution is to the effect that moral evils and even the most brutal atrocities have their justification in the moral goodness they make possible or bring into being.

(i) *Free will alone provides a justification for moral evil.* This is perhaps the more popular of the serious attempts to explain moral evil. The argument in brief runs: men have free will; moral evil is a consequence of free will; a universe in which men exercise free will even with lapses into moral evil is better than a universe in which men become *automata* doing good always because predestined to do so. Thus on this argument it is the mere fact of the supreme value of free will itself that is taken to provide a justification for its corollary moral evil.

(ii) *The goods made possible by free will provide a basis for accounting for moral evil.* According to this second argument, it is not the mere fact of free will that is claimed to be of such value as to provide a justification of moral evil, but the fact that free will makes certain goods possible. Some indicate the various moral virtues as the goods that free will makes possible, whilst others point to beatitude, and others again to beatitude achieved by man's own efforts or the virtues achieved as a result of one's own efforts. What all these have in common is the claim that the good consequences of free will provide a justification of the bad consequences of free will, namely moral evil.

Each of these two proposed solutions encounters two specific criticisms, which are fatal to their claims to be real solutions.

(i) To consider first the difficulties to which the former proposed solution is exposed. (*a*) A difficulty for the first argument—that it is free will alone that provides a justification for moral evil—lies in the fact that the theist who argues in this way has to allow that it is logically possible on the free will hypothesis that all men should always will what is evil, and that even so, a universe of completely evil men possessing free will is better than one in which men are predestined to virtuous living. It has to be contended that the value of free will itself is so immense that it more than outweighs the total moral evil, the eternal punishment of the wicked, and the sufferings inflicted on others by the sinners in their evilness. It is this paradox that leads to the formulation of the second argument; and it is to be noted that the explanation of moral evil switches to the second argument or to a combination of the first and second argument, immediately the theist refuses to face the logical possibility of complete wickedness, and insists instead that in fact men do not always choose what is evil.

(*b*) The second difficulty encountered by the first argument relates to the possibility that free will is compatible with less evil, and even with no evil, that is, with absolute goodness. If it could be shown that free will is compatible with absolute goodness, or even with less moral evil than actually occurs, then all or at least some evil will be left unexplained by free will alone.

Mackie, in his recent paper, and Joyce, in his discussion of this argument, both contend that free will is compatible with absolute goodness. Mackie argues that if it is not possible for God to confer free-will on men and at the same time ensure that no moral evil is committed, He cannot really be omnipotent. Joyce directs his argument rather to fellow-theists, and it is more of an *ad hominem* argument addressed to them. He writes:

> Free will need not (as is often assumed) involve the power to choose wrong. Our ability to misuse the gift is due to the conditions under which it is exercised here. In our present state we are able to reject what is truly good, and exercise our power of preference in favour of some baser attraction. Yet it is not necessary that it should be so. And all who accept Christian revelation admit that those who attain their final beatitude exercise freedom of will, and yet cannot choose aught but what is truly good. They possess the knowledge of Essential Goodness; and to it, not simply to good in general, they refer every choice. Moreover, even in our present condition it is open to omnipotence so to order our

circumstances and to confer on the will such instinctive impulses that we should in every election adopt the right course and not the wrong one.

To this objection, that free will is compatible with absolute goodness and that therefore a benevolent, omnipotent God would have given man free will and ensured his absolute virtue, it is replied that God is being required to perform what is logically impossible. It is logically impossible, so it is argued, for free will and absolute goodness to be combined, and hence, if God lacks omnipotence only in this respect. He cannot be claimed to lack omnipotence in any sense in which serious theists have ascribed it to Him.

Quite clearly, if free will and absolute goodness are logically incompatible, then God, in not being able to confer both on man does not lack omnipotence in any important sense of the term. However, it is not clear that free will and absolute goodness are logically opposed; and Joyce does point to considerations which suggest that they are not logical incompatibles. For my own part I am uncertain on this point; but my uncertainty is not a factual one but one concerning a point of usage. It is clear that an omnipotent God could create rational agents predestined always to make virtuous "decisions"; what is not clear is whether we should describe such agents as having free will. The considerations to which Joyce points have something of the status of test cases, and they would suggest that we should describe such agents as having free will. However, no matter how we resolve the linguistic point, the question remains—Which is more desirable, free will and moral evil and the physical evil to which free will gives rise, or this special free will or pseudo-free will which goes with absolute goodness? I suggest that the latter is clearly preferable. Later I shall endeavour to defend this conclusion; for the moment I am content to indicate the nature of the value judgement on which the question turns at this point.

The second objection to the proposed solution of the problem of moral evil in terms of free will alone, related to the contention that free will is compatible with less moral evil than occurs, and possibly with no moral evil. We have seen what is involved in the latter contention. We may now consider what is involved in the former. It may be argued that free will is compatible with less moral evil than in fact occurs on various grounds. (1) God, if He were all-powerful, could miraculously intervene to prevent some or perhaps all moral evil; and He is said to do so on occasion in answer to prayers, (for example, to prevent wars) or of His own initiative (for instance, by producing calamities which serve as warnings, or by working miracles, etc.). (2) God has made man with a certain nature. This nature is often interpreted by theologians as having a bias to evil. Clearly God could have created man with a strong bias to good, whilst still leaving scope for a decision to act evilly. Such a bias to good would be compatible with freedom of the will. (3) An omnipotent God could so have ordered the world that it was less conducive to the practice of evil.

These are all considerations advanced by Joyce, and separately and jointly, they establish that God could have conferred free will upon us, and at least very considerably *reduced* the amount of moral evil that would have resulted from the exercise of free will. This is sufficient to show that *not all* the moral evil that exists can be justified by reference to free will alone. This conclusion is fatal to the account of moral evil in terms of free will alone. The more extreme conclusion that Mackie seeks to establish—that absolute goodness is compatible with free will—is not essential as a basis for refuting the free will argument. The difficulty is as fatal to the claims of theism whether all moral evil or only some moral evil is unaccountable. However, whether Mackie's contentions are sound is still a matter of logical interest, although not of any real moment in the context of the case against theism, once the fact that less moral evil is compatible with free will has been established.

(ii) The second free will argument arises out of an attempt to circumvent these objections. It is not free will, but the value of the goods achieved through free will that is said to be so great as to provide a justification for moral evil.

(*a*) This second argument meets a difficulty in that it is now necessary for it to be supplemented by a proof that the number of people who practice moral virtue or who attain beatitude and/or virtue after a struggle is sufficient to outweigh the evilness of moral evil, the evilness of their eternal damnation and the physical evil they cause to others. This is a serious defect in the argument, because it means that the argument can at best show that moral evil *may have* a justification, and not that it has a justification. It is both logically and practically impossible to supplement and complete the argument. It is necessarily incomplete and inconclusive even if its general principle is sound.

(*b*) This second argument is designed also to avoid the other difficulty of the first argument—that free will may be compatible with no evil and certainly with less evil. It is argued that even if free will is compatible with absolute goodness it is still better that virtue and beatitude be attained after a genuine personal struggle; and this, it is said, would not occur if God is conferring free will nonetheless prevented moral evil or reduced the risk of it. Joyce argues in this way:

> To receive our final beatitude as the fruit of our labours, and as the recompense of a hard-won victory, is an incomparably higher destiny than to receive it without any effort on our part. And since God in His wisdom has seen fit to give us such a lot as this, it was inevitable that man should have the power to choose wrong. We could not be called to merit the reward due to victory without being exposed to the possibility of defeat.

There are various objections which may be urged here. First, this argument implies that the more intense the struggle, the greater is the triumph and resultant good, and the better the world; hence we should apparently, on this argument, court temptation and moral struggles to attain greater virtue and to be more worthy of our reward. Secondly, it may be urged that

God is being said to be demanding too high a price for the goods produced. He is omniscient. He knows that many will sin and not attain the goods or the Good free will is said to make possible. He creates men with free will, with the natures men have, in the world as it is constituted, knowing that in His doing so He is committing many to moral evil and eternal damnation. He could avoid all this evil by creating men with rational wills predestined to virtue, or He could eliminate much of it by making men's natures and the conditions in the world more conducive to the practice of virtue. He is said not to choose to do this. Instead, at the cost of the sacrifice of the many, He is said to have ordered things so as to allow fewer men to attain this higher virtue and higher beatitude that result from the more intense struggle.

In attributing such behaviour to God, and in attempting to account for moral evil along these lines, theist are, I suggest, attributing to God immoral behaviour of a serious kind—of a kind we should all unhesitatingly condemn in a fellow human being.

We do not commend people for putting temptation in the way of others. On the contrary, anyone who today advocated, or even allowed where he could prevent it, the occurrence of evil and the sacrifice of the many—even as a result of their own freely chosen actions—for the sake of the higher virtue of the few, would be condemned as an immoralist. To put severe temptation in the way of the many, knowing that many and perhaps even most will succumb to the temptation, for the sake of the higher virtue of the few, would be blatant immorality; and it would be immoral whether or not those who yielded to the temptation possessed free will. This point can be brought out by considering how a conscientious moral agent would answer the question: Which should I choose for other people, a world in which there are intense moral struggles and the possibility of magnificent triumphs and the certainty of many defeats, or a world in which there are less intense struggles, less magnificent triumphs and fewer defeats, or a world in which there are no struggles, no triumphs and no defeats? We are constantly answering less easy questions than this in a way that conflicts with the theist's contentions. If by modifying our own behaviour we can save someone else from an intense moral struggle and almost certain moral evil for example if by refraining from gambling or excessive drinking ourselves we can help a weaker person not to become a confirmed gambler or an alcoholic, or if by locking our car and not leaving it unlocked and with the key in it we can prevent people yielding to the temptation to become car thieves, we feel obliged to act accordingly, even though the persons concerned would freely choose the evil course of conduct. How much clearer is the decision with which God is said to be faced—the choice between the higher virtue of some and the evil of others, or the higher but less high virtue of many more, and the evil of many fewer. Neither alternative denies free will to men.

These various difficulties dispose of each of the main arguments relating to moral evil. There are in addition to these difficulties two other objections that might be urged.

If it could be shown that man has not free will both arguments collapse; and even if it could be shown that God's omniscience is incompatible with free will they would still break down. The issues raised here are too great to be pursued in this paper; and they can simply be noted as possible additional grounds for which criticisms of the main proposed solutions of the problem of moral evil may be advanced.

The other general objection is by way of a follow-up to points made in objections (*b*) to both arguments (i) and (ii). It concerns the relative value of free will and its goods and evils and the value of the best of the alternatives to free will and its goods. Are free will and its goods so much more valuable than the next best alternatives that their superior value can really justify the immense amount of evil that is introduced into the world by free will?

Theologians who discuss this issue ask, Which is better—men with free will striving to work out their own destinies, or automata-machine-like creatures, who never make mistakes because they never make decisions? When put in this form we naturally doubt whether free will plus moral evil plus the possibility of the eternal damnation of the many and the physical evil of untold billions are quite so unjustified after all; but the fact of the matter is that the question has not been fairly put. The real alternative is, on the one hand, rational agents with free wills making many bad and some good decisions on rational and non-rational grounds, and "rational" agents predestined always "to choose" the right things for the right reasons—that is, if the language of automata must be used, rational automata. Predestination does not imply the absence of rationality in all senses of that term. God, were He omnipotent, could preordain the decisions and the reasons upon which they were based; and such a mode of existence would seem to be in itself a worthy mode of existence, and one preferable to an existence with free will, irrationality and evil.

D. CONCLUSION

In this paper it has been maintained that God, were He all-powerful and perfectly good, would have created a world in which there was no unnecessary evil. It has not been argued that God ought to have created a perfect world, nor that He should have made one that is in any way logically impossible. It has simply been argued that a benevolent God could, and would, have created a world devoid of superfluous evil. It has been contended that there is evil in this world—unnecessary evil—and that the more popular and philosophically more significant of the many attempts to explain this evil are completely unsatisfactory. Hence we must conclude from the existence of evil that there cannot be an omnipotent, benevolent God.

ALVIN PLANTINGA

The Free Will Defence

Since the days of Epicurus many philosophers have suggested that the existence of evil constitutes a problem for those who accept theistic belief.[1] Those contemporaries who follow Epicurus here claim, for the most part, to detect logical inconsistency in such belief. So McCloskey:

> Evil is a problem for the theist in that a *contradiction* is involved in the fact of evil, on the one hand, and the belief in the omnipotence and perfection of God on the other.[2]

and Mackie:

> I think, however, that a more telling criticism can be made by way of the traditional problem of evil. Here it can be shown, not that religious beliefs lack rational support, but that they are positively irrational, that the several parts of the essential theological doctrine are *inconsistent* with one another....[3]

and essentially the same charge is made by Professor Aiken in an article entitled "God and Evil."[4]

These philosophers, then, and many others besides, hold that traditional theistic belief is self-contradictory and that the problem of evil, for the theist, is that of deciding which of the relevant propositions he is to abandon. But just which propositions are involved? What is the set of theistic beliefs whose conjunction yields a contradiction? The authors referred to above take the following five propositions to be essential to traditional theism: (*a*) that God exists, (*b*) that God is omnipotent, (*c*) that God is omniscient, (*d*) that God is wholly good, and (*e*) that evil exists. Here they are certainly right: each of these propositions is indeed an essential feature of orthodox theism. And it is just these five propositions whose conjunction is said, by our atheologians,[5] to be self-contradictory.

From *Philosophy in America*, edited by Max Black. Reprinted by permission of Unwin Hyman Ltd., London.

[1]David Hume and some of the French encyclopedists, for example, as well as F. H. Bradley, J. McTaggart, and J. S. Mill.

[2]H. J. McCloskey, "God and Evil." *The Philosophical Quarterly*, Vol. 10 (April 1960), p. 97.

[3]"Evil and Omnipotence." J. L. Mackie, *Mind*, Vol. 64, No. 254 (April 1955), p. 200.

[4]*Ethics*, Vol. 48 (1957–58), p. 79.

[5]*Natural* theology is the attempt to infer central religious beliefs from premises that are either obvious to common sense (e.g., *that some things are in motion*) or logically necessary. *Natural atheology* is the attempt to infer the falsity of such religious beliefs from premises of the same sort.

Apologists for theism, of course, have been quick to repel the charge. A line of resistance they have often employed is called *The Free Will Defence*; in this paper I shall discuss and develop that idea.

First of all, a distinction must be made between *moral evil* and *physical evil*. The former, roughly, is the evil which results from human choice or volition; the latter is that which does not. Suffering due to an earthquake, for example, would be a case of physical evil; suffering resulting from human cruelty would be a case of moral evil. This distinction, of course, is not very clear and many questions could be raised about it; but perhaps it is not necessary to deal with these questions here. Given this distinction, the Free Will Defence is usually stated in something like the following way. A world containing creatures who freely perform both good and evil actions—and do more good than evil—is more valuable than a world containing quasiautomata who always do what is right because they are unable to do otherwise. Now God can create free creatures, but He cannot causally or otherwise determine them to do only what is right; for if he does so then they do not do what is right *freely*. To create creatures capable of moral good, therefore, he must create creatures capable of moral evil; but he cannot create the possibility of moral evil and at the same time prohibit its actuality. And as it turned out, some of the free creatures God created exercised their freedom to do what is wrong: hence moral evil. The fact that free creatures sometimes err, however, in no way tells against God's omnipotence or against his goodness; for he could forestall the occurrence of moral evil only by removing the possibility of moral good.

In this way some traditional theists have tried to explain or justify part of the evil that occurs by ascribing it to the will of man rather than to the will of God. At least three kinds of objections to this idea are to be found both in the tradition and in the current literature. I shall try to develop and clarify the Free Will Defence by restating it in the face of these objections.

I.

The first objection challenges the assumption, implicit in the above statement of the Free Will Defence, that free will and causal determinism are logically incompatible. So Flew:

> ...to say that a person could have helped doing something is not to say that what he did was in principle unpredictable nor that there were no causes anywhere which determined that he would as a matter of fact act in this way. It is to say that if he had chosen to do otherwise he would have been able to do so; that there were alternatives, within the capacities of one of his physical strength, of his I.Q., of his knowledge, open to a person in his situation.
>
> ...There is no contradiction involved in saying that a particular action or choice was: *both* free, and could have been helped, and so on; *and* predictable, or even foreknown, and explicable in terms of caused causes.

...if it is really logically possible for an action to be both freely chosen and yet fully determined by caused causes, then the keystone argument of the Free Will Defense, that there is contradiction in speaking of God so arranging the laws of nature that all men always as a matter of fact freely choose to do the right, cannot hold.[6]

Flew's objection, I think, can be dealt with in a fairly summary fashion. He does not, in the paper in question, explain what he means by 'causal determination' (and of course in that paper this omission is quite proper and justifiable). But presumably he means to use the locution in question in such a way that to say of Jones' action *A* that it is *causally determined* is to say that the action in question has causes and that given these causes, Jones could not have refrained from doing *A*. That is to say, Flew's use of 'causally determined', presumably, is such that one or both of the following sentences, or some sentences very much like them, express necessarily true propositions:

(a) If Jones' action *A* is causally determined, then a set *S* of events has occurred prior to Jones' doing *A* such that, given *S*, it is causally impossible for Jones to refrain from doing *A*.

(b) If Jones' action *A* is causally determined, then there is a set *S* of propositions describing events occurring before *A* and a set *L* of propositions expressing natural laws such that

(1) the conjunction of *S*'s members does not entail that Jones does *A*, and

(2) the conjunction of the members of *S* with the members of *L* does entail that Jones does *A*.

And Flew's thesis, then, is that there is no contradiction in saying of a man, both that all of his actions are causally determined (in the sense just explained) and that some of them are free.

Now it seems to me altogether paradoxical to say of anyone all of whose actions are causally determined, that on some occasions he acts freely. When we say that Jones acts freely on a given occasion, what we say entails, I should think, that either his action on that occasion is not causally determined, or else he has previously performed an undetermined action which is a causal ancestor of the one in question. But this is a difficult and debatable issue; fortunately we need not settle it in order to assess the force of Flew's objection to the Free Will Defence. The Free Will Defender claims that the sentence 'Not all free actions are causally determined' expresses a necessary truth; Flew denies this claim. This strongly suggests that Flew and the Free Will Defender are not using the words 'free' and 'freedom' in the same way. The Free Will Defender, apparently, uses the words in question in such a way that sentences 'Some of Jones' actions are free' and 'Jones did action *A* freely' express

---

[6]"Divine Omnipotence and Human Freedom," in *New Essays in Philosophical Theology*, ed. A. Flew and A. MacIntyre, London 1955, pp. 150, 151, 153.

propositions which are inconsistent with the proposition that all of Jones' actions are causally determined. Flew, on the other hand, claims that with respect to the ordinary use of these words, there is no such inconsistency. It is my opinion that Flew is mistaken here; I think it is he who is using these words in a non-standard, unordinary way. But we need not try to resolve that issue; for the Free Will Defender can simply make Flew a present of the word 'freedom' and state his case using other locutions. He might now hold, for example, not that God made men free and that a world in which men freely do both good and evil is more valuable than a world in which they unfreely do only what is good; but rather that God made men such that some of their actions are *unfettered* (both free in Flew's sense and also causally undetermined) and that a world in which men perform both good and evil unfettered actions is superior to one in which they perform only good, but fettered, actions. By substituting 'unfettered' for 'free' throughout this account, the Free Will Defender can elude Flew's objection altogether.[7] So whether Flew is right or wrong about the ordinary sense of 'freedom' is of no consequence; his objection is in an important sense merely verbal and thus altogether fails to damage the Free Will Defence.

II.

Flew's objection, in essence, is the claim that an omnipotent being could have created men in such a way that although free they would be *causally determined* to perform only right actions. According to a closely allied objection, an omnipotent being could have made men in such a way that although free, and free from any such causal determination, they would nonetheless *freely refrain* from performing any evil actions. Here the contemporary spokesman is Mackie:

> ...if God has made men such that in their free choices they sometimes prefer what is good and sometimes what is evil, why could he not have made men such that they always freely choose the good? If there is no logical impossibility in a man's freely choosing the good on one, or on several occasions, there cannot be a logical impossibility in his freely choosing the good on every occasion. God was not, then, faced with a choice between making innocent automata and making beings who, in acting freely, would sometimes go wrong; there was open to him the obviously better possibility of making beings who would act freely but always go right. Clearly, his failure to avail himself of this possibility is inconsistent with his being both omnipotent and wholly good.[8]

---

[7]And since this is so in what follows I shall continue to use the words "free" and "freedom" in the way the Free Will Defender uses them.

[8]*Op. cit.*, p. 17.

The objection is more serious than Flew's and must be dealt with more fully. Now the Free Will Defence is an argument for the conclusion that (*a*) is not contradictory or necessarily false.[9]

(*a*) God is omnipotent, omniscient, and all-good and God creates free men who sometimes perform morally evil actions.

What Mackie says, I think, may best be construed as an argument for the conclusion that (*a*) *is* necessarily false; in other words, that *God is omnipotent, omniscient and all good* entails *no free men He creates ever perform morally evil actions*. Mackie's argument seems to have the following structure:

     (1) God is omnipotent and omniscient and all-good.
     (2) If God is omnipotent, He can create any logically possible state of affairs.
∴ (3) God can create any logically possible state of affairs.   (1, 2)
     (4) That all free men do what is right on every occasion is a logically possible state of affairs.
∴ (5) God can create free men such that they always do what is right.   (4, 3)
     (6) If God can create free men such that they always do what is right and God is all-good, then any free men created by God always do what is right.
∴ (7) Any free men created by God always do what is right.   (1, 5, 6)
∴ (8) No free men created by God ever perform morally evil actions.   (7)

Doubtless the Free Will Defender will concede the truth of (4); there is a difficulty with (2), however; for

(*a*) That there are men who are not created by God is a logically possible state of affairs

is clearly true. But (2) and (*a*) entail

(*b*) If God is omnipotent, God can create men who are not created by God.

And (*b*), of course, is false; (2) must be revised. The obvious way to repair it seems to be something like the following:

(2′) If God is omnipotent, then God can create any state of affairs S such that *God creates S* is consistent.

Similarly, (3) must be revised:

---

[9]And of course if (*a*) is consistent, so is the set (*a*)–(*e*) mentioned on page 187, for (*a*) entails each member of that set.

(3′) God can create any state of affairs *S* such that *God creates S* is consistent.

(1′) and (3′) do not seem to suffer from the faults besetting (1) and (3); but now it is not at all evident that (3′) and (4) entail

(5) God can create free men such that they always do what is right

as the original argument claims. To see this, we must note that (5) is true only if

(5*a*) God creates free men such that they always do what is right

is consistent. But (5*a*), one might think, is equivalent to:

(5*b*) God creates free men and brings it about that they always freely do what is right.

And (5*b*), of course, is *not* consistent; for if God *brings it about* that the men He creates always do what is right, then they do not do what is right *freely*. So if (5*a*) is taken to express (5*b*), then (5) is clearly false and clearly not entailed by (3′) and (4).

On the other hand, (5*a*) could conceivably be used to express:

(5*c*) God creates free men and these free men always do what is right.

(5*c*) is surely consistent; it is indeed logically possible that God creates free men and that the free men created by Him always do what is right. And conceivably the objector is using (5) to express this possibility—i.e., it may be that (5) is meant to express:

(5*d*) the proposition *God creates free men and the free men created by God always do what is right* is consistent.

If (5) is equivalent to (5*d*), then (5) is true—in fact necessarily true (and hence trivially entailed by (3′) and (4)). But now the difficulty crops up with respect to (6) which, given the equivalence of (5) and (5*d*) is equivalent to

(6′) If God is all-good and the proposition *God creates free men and the free men He creates always do what is right* is consistent, then any free men created by God always do what is right.

Now Mackie's aim is to show that the proposition *God is omnipotent, omniscient and all-good* entails the proposition *no free men created by God ever perform morally evil actions*. His attempt, as I outlined it, is to show this by constructing a valid argument whose premise is the former and whose conclusion is the latter. But then any additional premise appealed to in the deduction must be necessarily true if Mackie's argument is to succeed. (6') is one such additional premise; but there seems to be no reason for supposing that (6') is true at all, let alone necessarily true. Whether the free men created by God would always do what is right would presumably be up to them; for all we know they might sometimes exercise their freedom to do what is wrong. Put in a nutshell the difficulty with the argument is the following. (5a) (God creates free men such that they always do what is right) is susceptible of two interpretations ((5b) and (5c)). Under one of these interpretations (5) turns out to be false and the argument therefore fails. Under the other interpretation (6) turns out to be utterly groundless and question begging, and again the argument fails.

So far, then, the Free Will Defence has emerged unscathed from Mackie's objection. One has the feeling, however, that more can be said here; that there is something to Mackie's argument. What more? Well, perhaps something along the following lines. It is agreed that it is logically possible that all men always do only what is right. Now God is said to be omniscient and hence knows, with respect to any person he proposes to create, whether that person would or would not commit morally evil acts. For every person P who in fact performs morally evil actions, there is, evidently, a possible person P' who is exactly like P in every respect except that P' never performs any evil actions. If God is omnipotent, He could have created these possible persons instead of the persons He in fact did create. And if He is also all-good, He *would*, presumably, have created them, since they differ from the persons He did create only in being morally better than they are.

Can we make coherent sense out of this revised version of Mackie's objection? What, in particular, could the objector mean by 'possible person'? and what are we to make of the suggestion that God could have created possible persons? I think these questions can be answered. Let us consider first the set of all those properties it is logically possible for human beings to have. Examples of properties *not* in this set are the properties of *being over a mile long; being a hippopotamus; being a prime number; being divisible by four;* and the like. Included in the set are such properties as *having red hair; being present at the Battle of Waterloo; being the President of the United States; being born in 1889;* and *being a pipe-smoker.* Also included are such moral properties as *being kind to one's maiden aunt, being a scoundrel, performing at least one morally wrong action,* and so on. Let us call the properties in this set H properties. The complement $\overline{P}$ of an H property P is the property a thing has just in case it does not have P. And a *consistent set of H* properties is a set of H properties such that it is logically possible that there be a human being having every property in the set. Now we can define "possible person" in the following way:

> x is a possible person = x is a consistent set of H properties such that for every H property P, either P or $\overline{P}$ is a member of x.

To *instantiate* a possible person *P* is to create a human being having every property in *P*. And a set *S* of possible persons is a *co-possible set of possible persons* just in case it is logically possible that every member of *S* is instantiated.[10]

Given this technical terminology, Mackie's objection can be summarily restated. It is granted by everyone that there is no absurdity in the claim that some man who is free to do what is wrong never, in fact, performs any wrong action. It follows that there are many possible persons containing the property *is free to do wrong but always does right*. And since it is logically possible that all men always freely do what is right, there are presumably several co-possible sets of possible persons such that each member of each set contains the property in question. Now God, if he is omnipotent, can instantiate any possible person and any co-possible set of possible persons he chooses. Hence, if He were all-good, He would have instantiated one of the sets of co-possible persons all of whose members freely do only what is right.

In spite of its imposing paraphernalia the argument, thus restated, suffers from substantially the same defect that afflicts Mackie's original version. There are *some* possible persons God obviously cannot instantiate—those, for example, containing the property *is not created by God*. Accordingly it is *false* that God can instantiate just any possible person, He chooses. But of course the interesting question is whether

(1) God can instantiate possible persons containing the property of always freely doing what is right

is true; for perhaps Mackie could substitute (1) for the premise just shown to be false.

Is (1) true? Perhaps we can approach this question in the following way. Let *P* be any possible person containing the property *always freely does what is right*. Then there must be some action *A* such that *P* contains the property of being free with respect to *A* (i.e., the property of being free to perform *A* and free to refrain from performing *A*). The *instantiation* of a possible person, *S*, I shall say, is a person having every property in *S*; and let us suppose that if *P* were instantiated, its instantiation would be doing something morally wrong in performing *A*. And finally, let us suppose that God wishes to instantiate *P*. Now *P* contains many properties in addition to the ones already mentioned. Among them, for example, we might find the following: *is born in 1910, has red hair, is born in Stuttgart, has feeble-minded ancestors, is six feet tall at the age of fourteen*, and the like. And there is no difficulty in God's creating a person with these properties. Further, there is no difficulty in God's bringing it about that this person (let's call him Smith) is free with respect to *A*. But if God *also* brings it about that Smith refrains from performing *A* (as he must

---

[10]The definiens must not be confused with: For every member *M* of *S*, it is logically possible that *M* is instantiated.

to be the instantiation of *P*) then Smith is no longer free with respect to *A* and is hence not the instantiation of *P* after all. God cannot cause Smith to refrain from performing *A*, while allowing him to be free with respect to *A*; and therefore whether or not Smith does *A* will be entirely up to Smith; it will be a matter of free choice for him. Accordingly, whether God can instantiate *P* depends upon what Smith would freely decide to do.

This point may be put more accurately as follows: First, we shall say that an *H* property *Q* is *indeterminate* if *God creates a person and causes him to have Q* is necessarily false; an *H* property is *determinate* if it is not indeterminate. Of the properties we ascribed to *P*, all are determinate except *freely refrains from doing A* and *always freely does what is right*. Now consider P_1 the subset of *P* containing just the determinate members of *P*. In order to instantiate *P* God must instantiate P_1. It is evident that there is at most one instantiation of P_1, for among the members of P_1 will be some such individuating properties as for example, *is the third son of Richard and Lena Dykstra*. P_1 also contains the property of being free with respect to *A*; and if P_1 is instantiated, its instantiation will either perform *A* or refrain from performing *A*. It is, of course, possible that P_1 is such that if it is instantiated its instantiation *I* will perform *A*. If so, then if God allows *I* to remain free with respect to *A*, *I* will do *A*; and if God prevents *I* from doing *A*, then *I* is not free with respect to *A* and hence not the instantiation of *P* after all. Hence in neither case does God succeed in instantiating *P*. And accordingly God can instantiate *P* only if P_1 is *not* such that if it is instantiated, its instantiation will perform *A*. Hence it is possible that God cannot instantiate *P*. And evidently it is also possible, further, that *every* possible person containing the property *always freely does what is right* is such that neither God nor anyone else can instantiate it.

Now we merely supposed that P_1 is such that if it is instantiated, its instantiation will perform *A*. And this supposition, if true at all, is merely contingently true. It might be suggested, therefore, that God could instantiate *P* by instantiating P_1 and bringing it about that P_1 is *not* such that if it is instantiated, its instantiation will perform *A*. But to do this God must instantiate P_1 and bring it about that P_1 is such that if it is instantiated, its instantiation *I* will *refrain* from performing *A*. And if God does this then God brings it about that *I* will not perform *A*. But then *I* is not free to perform *A* and hence once more is not the instantiation of *P*.

It is possible, then, that God cannot instantiate any possible person containing the property *always freely does what is right*. It is also possible, of course, that He *can* instantiate some such possible persons. But *that* He can, if indeed He can, is a contingent truth. And since Mackie's project is to prove an entailment, he cannot employ any contingent propositions as added premises. Hence the reconstructed argument fails.

Now the difficulty with the reconstructed argument is the fact that God cannot instantiate just any possible person he chooses, and the possibility that God cannot instantiate any possible persons containing the property of always freely doing what is right. But perhaps the objector can circumvent this difficulty.

The H properties that make trouble for the objector are the indeterminate properties—those which God cannot cause anyone to have. It is because possible persons contain indeterminate properties that God cannot instantiate just any possible person He wishes. And so perhaps the objector can reformulate his definition of 'possible person' in such a way that a possible person is a consistent set S of *determinate* properties such that for any determinate H property P or $\bar{P}$ is a member of S. Unfortunately the following difficulty arises. Where I is any indeterminate H property and D a determinate H property, D or I (the property a person has if he has either D or I) is determinate. And so, of course, is D. The same difficulty, accordingly, arises all over again— there will be some possible persons God can't instantiate (those containing the properties *is not created by God or has red hair* and *does not have red hair*, for example). We must add, therefore, that no possible person *entails* an indeterminate property.[11]

Even so our difficulties are not at an end. For the definition as so stated entails that there are no *possible free persons,* i.e., possible persons containing the property *on some occasions free to do what is right and free to do what is wrong.*[12] We may see this as follows: Let P be any possible free person. P then contains the property of being free with respect to some action A. Furthermore, P would contain either the property of performing A (since that is a determinate property) or the property of refraining from performing A. But if P contains the property of performing A and the property of being free with respect to A, then P entails the property of freely performing A—which is an indeterminate property. And the same holds in case P contains the property of refraining from performing A. Hence in either case P entails an indeterminate property and accordingly is not a possible person.

Clearly the objector must revise the definition of 'possible person' in such a way that for any action with respect to which a given possible person P is free, P contains neither the property of performing that action nor the property of refraining from performing it. This may be accomplished in the following way. Let us say that a person S is *free with respect to a property P* just in case there is some action A with respect to which S is free and which is such that S has P if and only if he performs A. So, for example, if a person is free to leave town and free to stay, then he is free with respect to the property *leaves town.* And let us say that a set of

---

[11]Where a set of S of properties entails a property P if and only it is necessarily true that anything having every property in S also has P.

[12]This was pointed out to me by Mr. Lewis Creary.

properties is free with respect to a given property P just in case it contains the property is *free with respect to P*. Now we can restate the definition of 'possible person' as follows:

> x is a possible person = x is a consistent set of determinate H properties such that (1) for every determinate H property P with respect to which x is not free, either P or $\overline{P}$ is a member of x, and (2) x does not entail any indeterminate property.

Now let us add the following new definition:

> Possibly person P has indeterminate property I = if P were instantiated, P's instantiation would have I.

Under the revised definition of 'possible person' it seems apparent that God, if he is omnipotent, can instantiate any possible person, and any co-possible set of possible persons, he chooses. But, the objector continues, if God is also all-good, He will, presumably, instantiate only those possible persons who have some such indeterminate H property as that of *always freely doing what is right*. And here the Free Will Defender can no longer make the objection which held against the previous versions of Mackie's argument. For if God can instantiate any possible person he chooses, he can instantiate any possible free person he chooses.

The Free Will Defender can, however raise what is essentially the same difficulty in a new guise: what reason is there for supposing that there are *any* possible persons, in the present sense of 'possible person', having the indeterminate property in question? For it is clear that, given any indeterminate H property I, the proposition *no possible person has I* is a contingent proposition. Further, the proposition *every possible free person freely performs at least one morally wrong action* is possibly true. But if every *possible* free person performs at least one wrong action, then every *actual* free person also freely performs at least one wrong action; hence if every possible free person performs at least one wrong action, God could create a universe without moral evil only by refusing to create any free persons at all. And, the Free Will Defender adds, a world containing free persons and moral evil (provided that it contained more moral good than moral evil) would be superior to one lacking both free persons and moral good and evil. Once again, then, the objection seems to fail.

The definitions offered during the discussion of Mackie's objection afford the opportunity of stating the Free Will Defence more formally. I said above that the Free Will Defence is in essence an argument for the conclusion that (*a*) is consistent:

> (*a*) God is omnipotent, omniscient, and all-good and God creates persons who sometimes perform morally evil actions.

One way of showing (*a*) to be consistent is to show that its first conjunct does not entail the negation of its second conjunct, i.e., that (*b*) God is omnipotent, omniscient and all-good

does not entail

(*c*) God does not create persons who perform morally evil actions.

Now one can show that a given proposition *p* does not entail another proposition *q* by producing a third proposition *r* which is such that (1) the conjunction of *p* and *r* is consistent and (2) the conjunction of *p* and *r* entails the negation of *q*. What we need here, then, is a proposition whose conjunction with (*b*) is both logically consistent and a logically sufficient condition of the denial of (*c*).

Consider the following argument:

(*b*) God is omnipotent, omniscient and all-good.
(*r*1) God creates some free persons.
(*r*2) Every possible free person performs at least one wrong action.
∴ (*d*) Every actual free person performs at least one wrong action. (*r*2)
∴ (*e*) God creates persons who perform morally evil actions. ((*r*1), (*d*))

This argument is valid (and can easily be expanded so that it is *formally* valid). Furthermore, the conjunction of (*b*), (*r*1) and (*r*2) is evidently consistent. And as the argument shows, (*b*), (*r*1) and (*r*2) *jointly entail* (*e*). But (*e*) is the denial of (*c*); hence (*b*) and (*r*) jointly entail the denial of (*c*). Accordingly (*b*) does not entail (*c*), and (*a*) (God is omnipotent, omniscient and all-good and God creates persons who perform morally evil acts) is shown to be consistent. So stated, therefore, the Free Will Defence appears to be successful.

At this juncture it might be objected that even if the Free Will Defence, as explained above, shows that there is no contradiction in the supposition that God, who is all-good, omnipotent and omniscient, creates persons who engage in moral evil, it does nothing to show that an all-good, omnipotent and omniscient Being could create a universe containing as *much* moral evil as this one seems to contain. The objection has a point, although the fact that there seems to be no way of measuring or specifying amounts of moral evil makes it exceedingly hard to state the objection in any way which does not leave it vague and merely suggestive. But let us suppose, for purposes of argument, that there is a way of measuring moral evil (and moral good) and that the moral evil present in the universe amounts to ø. The problem then is to show that

(*b*) God is omnipresent, omniscient and all-good

is consistent with

(*f*) God creates a set of free persons who produce ø moral evil. Here the Free Will Defender can produce an argument to show that (*b*) is consistent with (*f*) which exactly parallels the argument for the consistency of (*b*) with (*c*):

(*b*) God is omnipotent, omniscient and all-good.

(*r*3) God creates a set *S* of free persons such that there is a balance of moral good over moral evil with respect to the members of *S*.

(*r*4) There is exactly one co-possible set *S'* of free possible persons such that there is a balance of moral good over moral evil with respect to its members; and the members of *S'* produce ø *moral evil*.

Set *S* is evidently the instantiation of *S'* (i.e. every member of *S* is an instantiation of some members of *S'* and every member of *S'* is instantiated by some member of *S*); hence the members of *S* produce ø moral evil. Accordingly, (*b*), (*r*3) and (*r*4) jointly entail (*f*); but the conjunction of (*b*), (*r*3) and (*r*4) is consistent; hence (*b*) is consistent with (*f*).

III.

The preceding discussion enables us to conclude, I believe, that the Free Will Defence succeeds in showing that there is no inconsistency in the assertion that God creates a universe containing as much moral evil as the universe in fact contains. There remains but one objection to be considered. McCloskey, Flew and others charge that the Free Will Defence, even if it is successful, accounts for only *part* of the evil we find; it accounts only for moral evil, leaving physical evil as intractable as before. The atheologian can therefore restate his position, maintaining that the existence of *physical evil*, which cannot be ascribed to the free actions of human beings, is inconsistent with the existence of an omniscient, omnipotent and all-good Deity.

To make this claim, however, is to overlook an important part of traditional theistic belief; it is part of much traditional belief to attribute a good deal of the evil we find to Satan, or to Satan and his cohorts. Satan, so the traditional doctrine goes, is a mighty non-human spirit, who, along with many other angels, was created long before God created men. Unlike most of his colleagues, Satan rebelled against God and has since been creating whatever havoc he could; the result, of course, is physical evil. But now we see that the moves available to the Free Will Defender in the case of moral evil are equally available to him in the case of physical evil. First he provides definitions of "possible non-human spirit," "free non-human spirit," etc., which exactly parallel their counterparts where it was moral evil that was at stake. Then he points out that it is logically possible that

(*r*5) God creates a set *S* of free non-human spirits such that the members of *S* do more good than evil, and

(r6) there is exactly one co-possible set S' of possible free non-human spirits such that the members of S' do more good than evil and

(r7) all of the physical evil in the world is due to the actions of the members of S.

He points out further that (r5), (r6), and (r7) are jointly consistent and that their conjunction is consistent with the proposition that God is omnipotent, omniscient and all-good. But (r5) through (r7) jointly entail that God creates a universe containing as much physical evil as the universe in fact contains; it follows then, that the existence of physical evil is not inconsistent with the existence of an omniscient, omnipotent, all-good Deity.

Now it must be conceded that views involving devils and other non-human spirits do not at present enjoy either the extensive popularity or the high esteem of (say) the Theory of Relativity. Flew, for example, has this to say about the view in question:

> To make this more than just another desperate *ad hoc* expedient of apologetic it is necessary to produce independent evidence for launching such an hypothesis (if "hypothesis" is not too flattering a term for it).[13]

But in the present context this claim is surely incorrect; to rebut the charge of contradiction the theist need not hold that the hypothesis in question is probable or even true. He need hold only that it is not inconsistent with the proposition that God exists. Flew suspects that "hypothesis" may be too flattering a term for the sort of view in question. Perhaps this suspicion reflects his doubts as to the meaningfulness of the proposed view. But it is hard to see how one could plausibly argue that the views in question are nonsensical (in the requisite sense) without invoking some version of the Verifiability Criterion, a doctrine whose harrowing vicissitudes are well known. Furthermore, it is likely that any premises worth considering which yield the conclusion that hypotheses about devils are nonsensical will yield the same conclusion about the hypothesis that God exists. And if *God exists* is nonsensical, then presumably theism is not self-contradictory after all.

We may therefore conclude that the Free Will Defence successfully rebuts the charge of contradiction brought against the theist. The Problem of Evil (if indeed evil constitutes a problem for the theist) does not lie in any inconsistency in the belief that God, who is omniscient, omnipotent and all-good, has created a world containing moral and physical evil.

---

[13]*Op. cit.*, p. 17.

WILLIAM L. ROWE

The Problem of Evil and Some Varieties of Atheism

This paper is concerned with three interrelated questions. The first is: Is there an argument for atheism based on the existence of evil that may rationally justify someone in being an atheist? To this first question I give an affirmative answer and try to support that answer by setting forth a strong argument for atheism based on the existence of evil.[1] The second question is: How can the theist best defend his position against the argument for atheism based on the existence of evil? In response to this question I try to describe what may be an adequate rational defense for theism against any argument for atheism based on the existence of evil. The final question is: What position should the informed atheist take concerning the rationality of theistic belief? Three different answers an atheist may give to this question serve to distinguish three varieties of atheism: unfriendly atheism, indifferent atheism, and friendly atheism. In the final part of the paper I discuss and defend the position of friendly atheism.

Before we consider the argument from evil, we need to distinguish a narrow and a broad sense of the terms "theist," "atheist," and "agnostic." By a "theist" in the narrow sense I mean someone who believes in the existence of an omnipotent, omniscient, eternal, supremely good being who created the world. By a "theist" in the broad sense I mean someone who believes in the existence of some sort of divine being or divine reality. To be a theist in the narrow sense is also to be a theist in the broad sense, but one may be a theist in the broad sense—as was Paul Tillich—without believing that there is a supremely good, omnipotent, omniscient, eternal being who created the world. Similar distinctions must be made between a narrow and a broad sense of the terms "atheist" and "agnostic." To be an atheist in the broad sense

---

From *American Philosophical Quarterly* (1979), pp. 335–41. Reprinted by permission of the editor.

[1]Some philosophers have contended that the existence of evil is *logically inconsistent* with the existence of the theistic God. No one, I think, has succeeded in establishing such an extravagant claim. Indeed, granted incompatibilism, there is a fairly compelling argument for the view that the existence of evil is logically consistent with the existence of the theistic God. (For a lucid statement of this argument see Alvin Plantinga, *God, Freedom, and Evil* (New York, 1974), pp. 29–59.) There remains, however, what we may call the *evidential* form—as opposed to the *logical* form—of the problem of evil: the view that the variety and profusion of evil in our world, although perhaps not logically inconsistent with the existence of the theistic God, provides, nevertheless, *rational support* for atheism. In this paper I shall be concerned solely with the evidential form of the problem, the form of the problem which, I think, presents a rather severe difficulty for theism.

is to deny the existence of any sort of divine being or divine reality. Tillich was not an atheist in the broad sense. But he was an atheist in the narrow sense, for he denied that there exists a divine being that is all-knowing, all-powerful and perfectly good. In this paper I will be using the terms "theism," "theist," "atheism," "atheist," "agnosticism," and "agnostic" in the narrow sense, not in the broad sense.

I.

In developing the argument for atheism based on the existence of evil, it will be useful to focus on some particular evil that our world contains in considerable abundance. Intense human and animal suffering, for example, occurs daily and in great plenitude in our world. Such intense suffering is a clear case of evil. Of course, if the intense suffering leads to some greater good, a good we could not have obtained without undergoing the suffering in question, we might conclude that the suffering is justified, but it remains an evil nevertheless. For we must not confuse the intense suffering in and of itself with the good things to which it sometimes leads or of which it may be a necessary part. Intense human or animal suffering is in itself bad, an evil, even though it may sometimes be justified by virtue of being a part of, or leading to, some good which is unobtainable without it. What is evil in itself may sometimes be good as a means because it leads to something that is good in itself. In such a case, while remaining an evil in itself, the intense human or animal suffering is, nevertheless, an evil which someone might be morally justified in permitting.

Taking human and animal suffering as a clear instance of evil which occurs with great frequency in our world, the argument for atheism based on evil can be stated as follows:

1. There exist instances of intense suffering which an omnipotent, omniscient being could have prevented without thereby losing some greater good or permitting some evil equally bad or worse.[2]
2. An omniscient, wholly good being would prevent the occurrence of any intense suffering it could, unless it could not do so without thereby losing some greater good or permitting some evil equally bad or worse.

---

3. There does not exist an omnipotent, omniscient, wholly good being.

---

[2]If there is some good, G, greater than any evil. (1) will be false for the trivial reason that no matter what evil, E, we pick the conjunctive good state of affairs consisting of G and E will outweigh E and be such that an omnipotent being could not obtain it without permitting E. (See Alvin Plantinga, *God and Other Minds* [Ithaca, 1967], p. 167.) To avoid this objection we may insert "unreplaceable" into our premises (1) and (2) between "some" and "greater." If E isn't required for G, and G is better than G plus E, then the good conjunctive state of affairs composed of G and E would be *replaceable* by the greater good of G alone. For the sake of simplicity, however, I will ignore this complication both in the formulation and discussion of premises (1) and (2).

What are we to say about this argument for atheism, an argument based on the profusion of one sort of evil in our world? The argument is valid; therefore, if we have rational grounds for accepting its premises, to that extent we have rational grounds for accepting atheism. Do we, however, have rational grounds for accepting the premises of this argument?

Let's begin with the second premise. Let s_1 be an instance of intense human or animal suffering which an omniscient, wholly good being could prevent. We will also suppose that things are such that s_1 will occur unless prevented by the omniscient, wholly good (OG) being. We might be interested in determining what would be a *sufficient* condition of OG failing to prevent s_1. But, for our purpose here, we need only try to state a *necessary* condition for OG failing to prevent s_1. That condition, so it seems to me, is this:

> *Either* (i) there is some greater good, G, such that G is obtainable by OG only if OG permits s_1,[3]
>
> *or* (ii) there is some greater good, G, such that G is obtainable by OG only if OG permits either s_1 or some evil equally bad or worse,
>
> *or* (iii) s_1 is such that it is preventable by OG only if OG permits some evil equally bad or worse.

It is important to recognize that (iii) is not included in (i). For losing a good greater than s_1 is not the same as permitting an evil greater than s_1. And this because the *absence* of a good state of affairs need not itself be an evil state of affairs. It is also important to recognize that s_1 might be such that it is preventable by OG *without* losing G (so condition (i) is not satisfied) but also such that if OG did prevent it, G would be loss *unless* OG permitted some evil equal to or worse than s_1. If this were so, it does not seem correct to require that OG prevent s_1. Thus, condition (ii) takes into account an important possibility not encompassed in condition (i).

Is it true that if an omniscient, wholly good being permits the occurrence of some intense suffering it could have prevented, then either (i) or (ii) or (iii) obtains? It seems to me that it is true. But if it is true then so is premise (2) of the argument for atheism. For that premise merely states in more compact form what we have suggested must be true if an omniscient, wholly

---

[3]Three clarifying points need to be made in connection with (i). First, by "good" I don't mean to exclude the fulfillment of certain moral principles. Perhaps preventing s_1 would preclude certain actions prescribed by the principles of justice. I shall allow that the satisfaction of certain principles of justice may be a good that outweighs the evil of s_1. Second, even though (i) may suggest it, I don't mean to limit the good in question to something that would *follow in time* the occurrence of s_1. And, finally, we should perhaps not fault OG if the good G, that would be loss were s_1 prevented, is not actually greater than s_1, but merely such that allowing s_1 and G, as opposed to preventing s_1 and thereby losing G, would not alter the balance between good and evil. For reasons of simplicity, I have left this point out in stating (i), with the result that (i) is perhaps a bit stronger than it should be.

good being fails to prevent some intense suffering it could prevent. Premise (2) says that an omniscient, wholly good being would prevent the occurrence of any intense suffering it could, unless it could not do so without thereby losing some greater good or permitting some evil equally bad or worse. This premise (or something not too distant from it) is, I think, held in common by many atheists and nontheists. Of course, there may be disagreement about whether something is good, and whether, if it is good, one would be morally justified in permitting some intense suffering to occur in order to obtain it. Someone might hold, for example, that no good is great enough to justify permitting an innocent child to suffer terribly.[4] Again, someone might hold that the mere fact that a given good outweighs some suffering and would be loss if the suffering were prevented, is not a morally sufficient reason for permitting the suffering. But to hold either of these views is not to deny (2). For (2) claims only that *if* an omniscient, wholly good being permits intense suffering *then* either there is some greater good that would have been loss, or some equally bad or worse evil that would have occurred, had the intense suffering been prevented. (2) does not purport to describe what might be a *sufficient* condition for an omniscient, wholly good being to permit intense suffering, only what is a *necessary* condition. So stated, (2) seems to express a belief that accords with our basic moral principles, principles shared by both theists and nontheists. If we are to fault the argument for atheism, therefore, it seems we must find some fault with its first premise.

Suppose in some distant forest lightning strikes a dead tree, resulting in a forest fire. In the fire a fawn is trapped, horribly burned, and lies in terrible agony for several days before death relieves its suffering. So far as we can see, the fawn's intense suffering is pointless. For there does not appear to be any greater good such that the prevention of the fawn's suffering would require either the loss of that good or the occurrence of an evil equally bad or worse. Nor does there seem to be any equally bad or worse evil so connected to the fawn's suffering that it would have had to occur had the fawn's suffering been prevented. Could an omnipotent, omniscient being have prevented the fawn's apparently pointless suffering? The answer is obvious, as even the theist will insist. An omnipotent, omniscient being could have easily prevented the fawn from being horribly burned, or, given the burning, could have spared the fawn the intense suffering by quickly ending its life, rather than allowing the fawn to lie in terrible agony for several days. Since the fawn's intense suffering was preventable and, so far as we can see, pointless, doesn't it appear that premise (1) of the argument is true, that there do exist instances of intense suffering which an omnipotent, omniscient being could have prevented without thereby losing some greater good or permitting some evil equally bad or worse.

---

[4]See Ivan's speech in Book V, Chapter IV of *The Brothers Karamazov*.

It must be acknowledged that the case of the fawn's apparently pointless suffering does not *prove* that (1) is true. For even though we cannot see how the fawn's suffering is required to obtain some greater good (or to prevent some equally bad or worse evil), it hardly follows that it is not so required. After all, we are often surprised by how things we thought to be unconnected turn out to be intimately connected. Perhaps, for all we know, there is some familiar good outweighing the fawn's suffering to which that suffering is connected in a way we do not see. Furthermore, there may well be unfamiliar goods, goods we haven't dreamed of, to which the fawn's suffering is inextricably connected. Indeed, it would seem to require something like omniscience on our part before we could lay claim to *knowing* that there is no greater good connected to the fawn's suffering in such a manner than an omnipotent, omniscient being could not have achieved that good without permitting that suffering or some evil equally bad or worse. So the case of the fawn's suffering surely does not enable us to *establish* the truth of (1).

The truth is that we are not in a position to prove that (1) is true. We cannot know with certainty that instances of suffering of the sort described in (1) do occur in our world. But it is one thing to *know* or *prove* that (1) is true and quite another thing to have *rational grounds* for believing (1) to be true. We are often in the position where in the light of our experience and knowledge it is rational to believe that a certain statement is true, even though we are not in a position to prove or to know with certainty that the statement is true. In the light of our past experience and knowledge it is, for example, very reasonable to believe that neither Goldwater nor McGovern will ever be elected President, but we are scarcely in the position of knowing with certainty that neither will ever be elected President. So, too, with (1), although we cannot know with certainty that it is true, it perhaps can be rationally supported, shown to be a rational belief.

Consider again the case of the fawn's suffering. Is it reasonable to believe that there is some greater good so intimately connected to that suffering that even an omnipotent, omniscient being could not have obtained that good without permitting that suffering or some evil at least as bad? It certainly does not appear reasonable to believe this. Nor does it seem reasonable to believe that there is some evil at least as bad as the fawn's suffering such that an omnipotent being simply could not have prevented it without permitting the fawn's suffering. But even if it should somehow be reasonable to believe either of these things of the fawn's suffering, we must then ask whether it is reasonable to believe either of these things of *all* the instances of seemingly pointless human and animal suffering that occur daily in our world. And surely the answer to this more general question must be no. It seems quite unlikely that *all* the instances of intense suffering occurring daily in our world are intimately related to the occurrence of greater goods or the prevention of evils at least as bad; and even more unlikely, should they somehow all be so related, than an omnipotent, omniscient being could not have achieved at least some of those goods (or prevented some of those evils) without permitting the instances of intense suffering that are supposedly related to them. In the light of our experience and knowledge of the variety and scale of human and animal suffering in our world, the idea that none of this suffering could have been prevented by an omnipotent being without thereby losing a greater good or permitting an evil at least as bad seems an extraordinary absurd idea, quite beyond our belief. It seems then that although we cannot *prove* that (1) is true, it is, nevertheless, altogether *reasonable* to believe that (1) is true, that (1) is a *rational* belief.[5]

Returning now to our argument for atheism, we've seen that the second premise expresses a basic belief common to many theists and nontheists. We've also seen that our experience and knowledge of the variety and profusion of suffering in our world provides *rational support* for the first premise. Seeing that the conclusion, "There does not exist an omnipotent, omniscient, wholly good being" follows from these two premises, it does seem that we have *rational support* for atheism, that it is reasonable for us to believe that the theistic God does not exist.

II.

Can theism be rationally defended against the argument for atheism we have just examined? If it can, how might the theist best respond to that argument? Since the argument from (1) and (2) to (3) is valid, and since the theist, no less than the nontheist, is more than likely committed to (2), it's clear that the

---

[5]One might object that the conclusion of this paragraph is stronger than the reasons given warrant. For it is one thing to argue that it is unreasonable to think that (1) is false and another thing to conclude that we are therefore justified in accepting (1) as true. There are propositions such that believing them is much more reasonable than disbelieving them, and yet are such that *withholding judgment* about them is more reasonable than believing them. To take an example of Chisholm's: it is more reasonable to believe that the Pope will be in Rome (on some arbitrarily picked future date) than to believe that he won't; but it is perhaps more reasonable to suspend judgment on the question of the Pope's whereabouts on that particular date, than to believe that he will be in Rome. Thus, it might be objected, that while we've shown that believing (1) is more reasonable than disbelieving (1), we haven't shown that believing (1) is more reasonable than withholding belief. My answer to this objection is that there are things we know which render (1) probable to the degree that it is more reasonable to believe (1) than to suspend judgment on (1). What are these things we know? First, I think, is the fact that there is an enormous variety and profusion of intense human and animal suffering in our world. Second, is the fact that much of this suffering seems quite unrelated to any greater goods (or the absence of equal or greater evils) that might justify it. And, finally, there is the fact that such suffering as is related to greater goods (or the absence of equal or greater evils) does not, in many cases, seem so intimately related as to require its permission by an omnipotent being bent on securing those goods (the absence of those evils). These facts, I am claiming, make it more reasonable to accept (1) than to withhold judgment on (1).

theist can reject this atheistic argument only by rejecting its first premise, the premise that states that there are instances of intense suffering which an omnipotent, omniscient being could have prevented without thereby losing some greater good or permitting some evil equally bad or worse. How, then, can the theist best respond to this premise and the considerations advanced in its support?

There are basically three responses a theist can make. First, he might argue not that (1) is false or probably false, but only that the reasoning given in support of it is in some way *defective*. He may do this either by arguing that the reasons given in support of (1) are *in themselves* insufficient to justify accepting (1), or by arguing that there are other things we know which, when taken in conjunction with these reasons, do not justify us in accepting (1). I suppose some theists would be content with this rather modest response to the basic argument for atheism. But given the validity of the basic argument and the theist's likely acceptance of (2), he is thereby committed to the view that (1) is false, not just that we have no good reasons for accepting (1) as true. The second two responses are aimed at showing that it is reasonable to believe that (1) is false. Since the theist is committed to this view I shall focus the discussion on these two attempts, attempts which we can distinguish as "the direct attack" and "the indirect attack."

By a direct attack, I mean an attempt to reject (1) by pointing out goods, for example, to which suffering may well be connected, goods which an omnipotent, omniscient being could not achieve without permitting suffering. It is doubtful, however, that the direct attack can succeed. The theist may point out that some suffering leads to moral and spiritual development impossible without suffering. But it's reasonably clear that suffering often occurs in a degree far beyond what is required for character development. The theist may say that some suffering results from free choices of human beings and might be preventable only by preventing some measure of human freedom. But, again, it's clear that much intense suffering occurs not as a result of human free choices. The general difficulty with this direct attack on premise (1) is twofold. First, it cannot succeed, for the theist does not know what greater goods might be served, or evils prevented, by each instance of intense human or animal suffering. Second, the theist's own religious tradition usually maintains that in this life it is not given to us to know God's purpose in allowing particular instances of suffering. Hence, the direct attack against premise (1) cannot succeed and violates basic beliefs associated with theism.

The best procedure for the theist to follow in rejecting premise (1) is the indirect procedure. This procedure I shall call "the G. E. Moore shift," so-called in honor of the twentieth century philosopher, G. E. Moore, who used it to great effect in dealing with the arguments of the skeptics. Skeptical philosophers such as David Hume have advanced ingenious arguments to prove that no one can know of the existence of any material object. The premises of their arguments employ plausible principles, principles which many philosophers have tried to reject directly, but only with questionable success. Moore's procedure was altogether different. Instead of arguing directly against the premises of the skeptic's arguments, he simply noted that the premises implied, for example, that he (Moore) did not know of the existence of a pencil. Moore then proceeded indirectly against the skeptic's premises by arguing:

> I do know that this pencil exists.
> If the skeptic's principles are correct I cannot know of the existence of this pencil.
>
> ∴ The skeptic's principles (at least one) must be incorrect.

Moore then noted that his argument is just as valid as the skeptic's, that both of their arguments contain the premise "If the skeptic's principles are correct Moore cannot know of the existence of this pencil," and concluded that the only way to choose between the two arguments (Moore's and the skeptic's) is by deciding which of the first premises it is more rational to believe—Moore's premise "I do know that this pencil exists" or the skeptic's premise asserting that his skeptical principles are correct. Moore concluded that his own first premise was the more rational of the two.[6]

Before we see how the theist may apply the G. E. Moore shift to the basic argument for atheism, we should note the general strategy of the shift. We're given an argument: p, q, therefore, r. Instead of arguing directly against p, another argument is constructed—not-r, q, therefore, not-p—which begins with the denial of the conclusion of the first argument, keeps its second premise, and ends with the denial of the first premise as its conclusion. Compare, for example, these two:

I.	p	II.	not-r
	q		q
	———		———
	r		not-p

It is a truth of logic that If I is valid II must be valid as well. Since the arguments are the same so far as the second premise is concerned, any choice between them must concern their respective first premises. To argue against the first premise (p) by constructing the counter argument II is to employ the G. E. Moore shift.

---

[6]See, for example, the two chapters on Hume in G. E. Moore, *Some Main Problems of Philosophy* (London, 1953).

Applying the G. E. Moore shift against the first premise of the basic argument for atheism, the theist can argue as follows:

not-3. There exists an omnipotent, omniscient, wholly good being.

2. An omniscient, wholly good being would prevent the occurrence of any intense suffering it could, unless it could not do so without thereby losing some greater good or permitting some evil equally bad or worse.

therefore,

not-1. It is not the case that there exist instances of intense suffering which an omnipotent, omniscient being could have prevented without thereby losing some greater good or permitting some evil equally bad or worse.

We now have two arguments: the basic argument for atheism from (1) and (2) to (3), and the theist's best response, the argument from (not-3) and (2) to (not-1). What the theist then says about (1) is that he has rational grounds for believing in the existence of the theistic God (not-3), accepts (2) as true, and sees that (not-1) follows from (not-3) and (2). He concludes, therefore, that he has rational grounds for rejecting (1). Having rational grounds for rejecting (1), the theist concludes that the basic argument for atheism is mistaken.

III.

We've had a look at a forceful argument for atheism and what seems to be the theist's best response to that argument. If one is persuaded by the argument for atheism, as I find myself to be, how might one best view the position of the theist. Of course, he will view the theist as having a false belief, just as the theist will view the atheist as having a false belief. But what position should the atheist take concerning the *rationality* of the theist's belief? There are three major positions an atheist might take, positions which we may think of as some varieties of atheism. First, the atheist may believe that no one is rationally justified in believing that the theist God exists. Let us call this position "unfriendly atheism." Second, the atheist may hold no belief concerning whether any theist is or isn't rationally justified in believing that the theistic God exists. Let us call this view "indifferent atheism." Finally, the atheist may believe that some theists are rationally justified in believing that the theistic God exists. This view we shall call "friendly atheism." In this final part of the paper I propose to discuss and defend the position of friendly atheism.

If no one can be rationally justified in believing a false proposition then friendly atheism is a paradoxical, if not incoherent position. But surely the truth of a belief is not a necessary condition of someone's being rationally justified in having that belief. So in holding that someone is rationally justified in believing that the theistic God exists, the friendly atheist is not committed to thinking that the theist has a true belief. What he is committed to is that the theist has rational grounds for his belief, a belief the atheist rejects and is convinced he is rationally justified in rejecting. But is this possible? Can someone, like our friendly atheist, hold a belief, be convinced that he is rationally justified in holding that belief, and yet believe that someone else is equally justified in believing the opposite? Surely this is possible. Suppose your friends see you off on a flight to Hawaii. Hours after take-off they learn that your plane has gone down at sea. After a twenty-four hour search, no survivors have been found. Under these circumstances they are rationally justified in believing that you have perished. But it is hardly rational for you to believe this, as you bob up and down in your life vest, wondering why the search planes have failed to spot you. Indeed, to amuse yourself while awaiting your fate, you might very well reflect on the fact that your friends are rationally justified in believing that you are now dead, a proposition you disbelieve and are rationally justified in disbelieving. So, too, perhaps an atheist may be rationally justified in his atheistic belief and yet hold that some theists are rationally justified in believing just the opposite of what he believes.

What sort of grounds might a theist have for believing that God exists? Well, he might endeavor to justify his belief by appealing to one or more of the traditional arguments: Ontological, Cosmological, Teleological, Moral, etc. Second, he might appeal to certain aspects of religious experience, perhaps even his own religious experience. Third, he might try to justify theism as a plausible theory in terms of which we can account for a variety of phenomena. Although an atheist must hold that the theistic God does not exist, can he not also believe, and be justified in so believing, that some of these "justifications of theism" do actually rationally justify some theists in their belief that there exists a supremely good, omnipotent, omniscient being? It seems to me that he can.

If we think of the long history of theistic belief and the special situations in which people are sometimes placed, it is perhaps as absurd to think that no one was ever rationally justified in believing that the theistic God exists as it is to think that no one was ever justified in believing that human being would never walk on the moon. But in suggesting that friendly atheism is preferable to unfriendly atheism, I don't mean to rest the case on what some human beings might reasonably have believed in the eleventh or thirteenth century. The more interesting question is whether some people in modern society, people who are aware of the usual grounds for belief and disbelief and are acquainted to some degree with modern science, are yet rationally justified in accepting theism. Friendly atheism is a significant position only if it answers this question in the affirmative.

It is not difficult for an atheist to be friendly when he has reason to believe that the theist could not reasonably be expected to be acquainted with the grounds for disbelief that he (the atheist) possesses. For then the atheist may take the view that some theists are rationally justified in holding to theism, but would not be so were they to be acquainted with the grounds for disbelief—those grounds being sufficient to tip the scale in favor of atheism when balanced against the reasons the theist has in support of his belief.

Friendly atheism become paradoxical, however, when the atheist contemplates believing that the theist has all the grounds for atheism that he, the atheist, has, and yet is rationally justified in maintaining his theistic belief. But even so excessively friendly a view as this perhaps can be held by the atheist if he also has some reason to think that the grounds for theism are not as telling as the theist is justified in taking them to be.[7]

In this paper I've presented what I take to be a strong argument for atheism, pointed out what I think is the theist's best response to that argument, distinguished three positions an atheist might take concerning the rationality of theistic belief, and made some remarks in defense of the position called "friendly atheism." I'm aware that the central points of the paper are not likely to be warmly received by many philosophers. Philosophers who are atheists tend to be tough minded—holding that there are no good reasons for supposing that theism is true. And theists tend either to reject the view that the existence of evil provides rational grounds for atheism or to hold that religious belief has nothing to do with reason and evidence at all. But such is the way of philosophy.[8]

---

[7]Suppose that I add a long sum of numbers three times and get result x. I inform you of this so that you have pretty much the same evidence I have for the claim that the sum of the numbers is x. You then use your calculator twice over and arrive at result y. You, then, are justified in believing that the sum of the numbers is *not* x. However, knowing that your calculator has been damaged and is therefore unreliable, and that you have no reason to think that it is damaged, I may reasonably believe not only that the sum of the numbers is x, but also that you are justified in believing that the sum is not x. Here is a case, then, where you have all of my evidence for p, and yet I can reasonably believe that you are justified in believing not-p—for I have reason to believe that your grounds for not-p are not as telling as you are justified in taking them to be.

[8]I am indebted to my colleagues at Purdue University, particularly to Ted Ulrich and Lilly Russow, and to philosophers at The University of Nebraska, Indiana State University, and The University of Wisconsin at Milwaukee for helpful criticisms of earlier versions of this paper.

ROBERT MERRIHEW ADAMS

Must God Create the Best?

I.

Many philosophers and theologians have accepted the following propositions:

> (P) If a perfectly good moral agent created any world at all, it would have to be the very best world that he could create.

The best world that an omnipotent God could create is the best of all logically possible worlds. Accordingly, it has been supposed that if the actual world was created by an omnipotent, perfectly good God, it must be the best of all logically possible worlds.

In this paper I shall argue that ethical views typical of the Judaeo-Christian religious tradition do not require the Judaeo-Christian theist to accept (P). He must hold that the actual world is a good world. But he need not maintain that it is the best of all possible worlds, or the best world that God could have made.[1]

The position which I am claiming that he can consistently hold is that *even if* there is a best among possible worlds, God could create another instead of it, and still be perfectly good. I do not in fact see any good reason to believe that there is a best among possible worlds. Why can't it be that for every possible world there is another that is better? And if there is no maximum degree of perfection among possible worlds, it would be unreasonable to blame God, or to think less highly of his goodness, because he created a world less excellent than he could have created.[2] But I do not claim to be able to prove that there is no best among possible worlds, and in this essay I shall assume for the sake of argument that there is one.

From *The Philosophical Review*, Vol. 81 (1972), pp. 317–32. Reprinted by permission of the publisher and the author.

[1]What I am saying in this paper is obviously relevant to the problem of evil. But I make no claim to be offering a complete theodicy here.

[2]Leibniz held (in his *Theodicy*, pt. i, s. 8) that if there were no best among possible worlds, a perfectly good God would have created nothing at all. But Leibniz is mistaken if he supposes that in this way God could avoid choosing an alternative less excellent than others He could have chosen. For the existence of no created world at all would surely be a less excellent state of affairs than the existence of some of the worlds that God could have created.

Whether we accept proposition (*P*) will depend on what we believe are the requirements for perfect goodness. If we apply an act-utilitarian standard of moral goodness, we will have to accept (*P*). For by act-utilitarian standards it is a moral obligation to bring about the best state of affairs that one can. It is interesting to note that the ethics of Leibniz, the best-known advocate of (*P*), is basically utilitarian.[3] In his *Theodicy* (part I, s. 25) he maintains, in effect, that men, because of their ignorance of many of the consequences of their actions, ought to follow a rule-utilitarian code, but that God, being omniscient, must be a perfect act utilitarian in order to be perfectly good.

I believe that utilitarian views are not typical of the Judaeo-Christian ethical tradition, although Leibniz is by no means the only Christian utilitarian. In this essay I shall assume that we are working with standards of moral goodness which are not utilitarian. But I shall not try either to show that utilitarianism is wrong or to justify the standards that I take to be more typical of Judaeo-Christian religious ethics. To attempt either of these tasks would unmanageably enlarge the scope of the paper. What I can hope to establish here is therefore limited to the claim that the rejection of (*P*) is consistent with Judaeo-Christian religious ethics.

Assuming that we are not using utilitarian standards of moral goodness, I see only two types of reason that could be given for (*P*). (1) It might be claimed that a creator would necessarily wrong someone (violate someone's rights), or be less kind to someone than a perfectly good moral agent must be, if he knowingly created a less excellent world instead of the best that he could. Or (2) it might be claimed that, even if no one would be wronged or treated unkindly by the creation of an inferior world, the creator's choice of an inferior world must manifest a defect of character. I will argue against the first of these claims in section II. Then I will suggest, in section III, that God's choice of a less excellent world could be accounted for in terms of his grace, which is considered a virtue rather than a defect of character in Judaeo-Christian ethics. A counter-example, which is the basis for the most persuasive objections to my position that I have encountered, will be considered in sections IV and V.

II.

Is there someone *to* whom a creator would have an obligation to create the best world he could? Is there someone whose rights would be violated, or who would be treated unkindly, if the creator created a less excellent world? Let us suppose that our creator is God, and that there does not exist any being, other than himself, which he has not created. It follows that if God has wronged anyone, or been unkind to anyone, in creating whatever world he

---

[3]See Gaston Grua, *Jurisprudence universelle et théodicée selon Leibniz* (Paris, 1953), pp. 210–18.

has created, this must be one of his own creatures. To which of his creatures, then, might God have an obligation to create the best of all possible worlds? (For that is the best world he could create.)

Might he have an obligation to the creatures in the best possible world, to create them? Have they been wronged, or even treated unkindly, if God has created a less excellent world, in which they do not exist, instead of creating them? I think not. The difference between actual beings and merely possible beings is of fundamental moral importance here. The moral community consists of actual beings. It is they who have actual rights, and it is to them that there are actual obligations. A merely possible being cannot be (actually) wronged or treated unkindly. A being who never exists is not wronged by not being created, and there is no obligation to any possible being to bring it into existence.

Perhaps it will be objected that we believe we have obligations to future generations, who are not yet actual and may never be actual. We do say such things, but I think what we mean is something like the following. There is not merely a logical possibility, but a probability greater than zero, that future generations will really exist; and *if* they will in fact exist, we will have wronged them if we act or fail to act in certain ways. On this analysis we cannot have an obligation to future generations to bring them into existence.

I argue, then, that God does not have an obligation to the creatures in the best of all possible worlds to create them. If God has chosen to create a world less excellent than the best possible, he has not thereby wronged any creatures whom he has chosen not to create. He has not even been unkind to them. If any creatures are wronged, or treated unkindly, by such a choice of the creator, they can only be creatures that exist in the world he has created.

I think it is fairly plausible to suppose that God could create a world which would have the following characteristics:

(1) None of the individual creatures in it would exist in the best of all possible worlds.
(2) None of the creatures in it has a life which is so miserable on the whole that it would be better for that creature if it had never existed.
(3) Every individual creature in the world is at least as happy on the whole as it would have been in any other possible world in which it could have existed.

It seems obvious that, if God creates such a world, he does not thereby wrong any of the creatures in it, and does not thereby treat any of them with less than perfect kindness. For none of them would have been benefited by his creating any other world instead.[4]

---

[4]Perhaps I can have a right to something which would not benefit me (e.g., if it has been promised to me). But if there are such non-beneficial rights, I do not see any plausible reason for supposing that a right not to be created could be among them.

If there are doubts about the possibility of God's creating such a world, they will probably have to do with the third characteristic. It may be worth while to consider two questions, on the supposition (which I am not endorsing) that no possible world less excellent than the best would have characteristic (3), and that God has created a world which has characteristics (1) and (2) but not (3). In such a case, must God have wronged one of his creatures? Must He have been less than perfectly kind to one of His creatures?

I do not think it can reasonably be argued that in such a case God must have wronged one of his creatures. Suppose a creature in such a case were to complain that God had violated its rights by creating it in a world in which it was less happy on the whole than it would have been in some other world in which God could have created it. The complaint might express a claim to special treatment: 'God ought to have created *me* in more favourable circumstances (even though that would involve his creating some *other* creature in less favourable circumstances than he could have created it in).' Such a complaint would not be reasonable, and would not establish that there had been any violation of the complaining creature's rights.

Alternatively, the creature might make the more principled complaint, 'God has wronged me by not following the principle of refraining from creating any world in which there is a creature that would have been happier in another world he could have made.' This also is an unreasonable complaint. For if God followed the stated principle, he would not create any world that lacked characteristic (3). And we are assuming that no world less excellent than the best possible would have characteristic (3). It follows that, if God acted on the stated principle, he would not create any world less excellent than the best possible. But the complaining creature would not exist in the best of all possible worlds; for we are assuming that this creature exists in a world which has characteristic (1). The complaining creature, therefore, would never have existed if God had followed the principle that is urged in the complaint. There could not possibly be any advantage to this creature from God's having followed that principle; and the creature has not been wronged by God's not following the principle. (It would not be better for the creature if it had never existed; for we are assuming that the world God created has characteristic (2).)

The question of whether in the assumed case God must have been unkind to one of his creatures is more complicated than the question of whether he must have wronged one of them. In fact it is too complicated to be discussed adequately here. I will just make three observations about it. The first is that it is no clearer that the best of all possible worlds would possess characteristic (3) than that some less excellent world would possess it. In fact, it has often been supposed that the best possible world might not possess it. The problem we are now discussing can therefore arise also for those who believe that God has created the best of all possible worlds.

My second observation is that, if kindness to a person is the same as a tendency to promote his happiness, God has been less than perfectly (completely, unqualifiedly) kind to any creature whom he could have made somewhat happier than he has made it. (I shall not discuss here whether kindness to a person is indeed the same as a tendency to promote his happiness; they are at least closely related.)

But in the third place I would observe that such qualified kindness (if that is what it is) toward some creatures is consistent with God's being perfectly good, and with his being very kind to all his creatures. It is consistent with his being very kind to all his creatures because he may have prepared for all of them a very satisfying existence even though some of them might have been slightly happier in some other possible world. It is consistent with his being perfectly good because even a perfectly good moral agent may be led, by other considerations of sufficient weight, to qualify his kindness or beneficence toward some person. It has sometimes been held that a perfectly good God might cause or permit a person to have less happiness than he might otherwise have had, in order to punish him, or to avoid interfering with the freedom of another person, or in order to create the best of all possible worlds. I would suggest that the desire to create and love all of a certain group of possible creatures (assuming that all of them would have satisfying lives on the whole) might be an adequate ground for a perfectly good God to create them, even if his creating *all* of them must have the result that some of them are less happy than they might otherwise have been. And they need not be the best of all possible creatures, or included in the best of all possible worlds, in order for this qualification of his kindness to be consistent with his perfect goodness. The desire to create *those* creatures is as legitimate a ground for him to qualify his kindness toward some, as is the desire to create the best of all possible worlds. This suggestion seems to me to be in keeping with the aspect of the Judaeo-Christian moral ideal which will be discussed in section III.

These matters would doubtless have to be discussed more fully if we were considering whether the *actual* world can have been created by a perfectly good God. For our present purposes, however, enough may have been said—especially since, as I have noted, it seems a plausible assumption that God could make a world having characteristics (1), (2) and (3). In that case he could certainly make a less excellent world than the best of all possible worlds without wronging any of his creatures or failing in kindness to any of them. (I have, of course, *not* been arguing that there is *no* way in which God could wrong anyone or be less kind to anyone than a perfectly good moral agent must be.)

III.

Plato is one of those who held that a perfectly good creator would make the very best world he could. He thought that if the creator chose to make a world less good than he could have made, that could be understood only in terms of some defect in the creator's character. Envy is the defect that Plato suggests.[5] It may be thought that the creation of a world inferior to the best that he could make would manifest a defect in the creator's character even if no one were thereby wronged or treated unkindly. For the perfectly good moral agent must not only be kind and refrain from violating the rights of others, but must also have other virtues. For instance, he must be noble, generous, high-minded, and free from envy. He must satisfy the moral ideal.

There are differences of opinion, however, about what is to be included in the moral ideal. One important element in the Judaeo-Christian moral ideal is *grace*. For present purposes, grace may be defined as a disposition to love which is not dependent on the merit of the person loved. The gracious person loves without worrying about whether the person he loves is worthy of his love. Or perhaps it would be better to say that the gracious person sees what is valuable in the person he loves, and does not worry about whether it is more or less valuable than what could be found in someone else he might have loved. In the Judaeo-Christian tradition, it is typically believed that grace is a virtue which God does have and men ought to have.

A God who is gracious with respect to creating might well choose to create and love less excellent creatures than he could have chosen. This is not to suggest that grace in creation consists in a preference for imperfection as such. God could have chosen to create the best of all possible creatures, and still have been gracious in choosing them. God's graciousness in creation does not imply that the creatures he has chosen to create must be less excellent than the best possible. It implies, rather, that even if they are the best possible creatures, that is not the ground for his choosing them. And it implies that there is nothing in God's nature or character which would require him to act on the principle of choosing the best possible creatures to be the object of his creative powers.

Grace, as I have described it, is not part of everyone's moral ideal. For instance, it was not part of Plato's moral ideal. The thought that it may be the expression of a virtue, rather than a defect of character, in a creator, *not* to act on the principle of creating the best creatures he possibly could, is quite foreign to Plato's ethical viewpoint. But I believe that thought is not at all foreign to a Judaeo-Christian ethical viewpoint.

This interpretation of the Judaeo-Christian tradition is confirmed by the religious and devotional attitudes toward God's creation which prevail in the tradition. The man who worships God does not normally praise him for his moral rectitude and good judgement in creating *us*. He thanks God for his existence as for an undeserved personal favour. Religious writings frequently deprecate the intrinsic worth of human beings, considered apart from God's love for them, and express surprise that God should concern himself with them at all.

---

[5]*Timaeus*, 29E–30A.

> When I look at thy heavens, the work of thy fingers, the moon and the stars which thou hast established;
> What is man that thou art mindful of him, and the son of man that thou dost care for him?
> Yet thou hast made him little less than God, and dost crown him with glory and honour.
> Thou hast given him dominion over the works of thy hands; thou hast put all things under his feet [Psalm 8: 3–6].

Such utterances seem quite incongruous with the idea that God created us because if he had not he would have failed to bring about the best possible state of affairs. They suggest that God has created human beings and made them dominant on this planet although he could have created intrinsically better states of affairs instead.

I believe that in the Judaeo-Christian tradition the typical religious attitude (or at any rate the attitude typically encouraged) toward the fact of our existence is something like the following. 'I am glad that I exist, and I thank God for the life he has given me. I am also glad that other people exist, and I thank God for them. Doubtless there could be more excellent creatures than we. But I believe that God, in his grace, created us and loves us; and I accept that gladly and gratefully.' (Such an attitude need not be complacent; for the task of struggling against certain evils may be seen as precisely a part of the life that the religious person is to accept and be glad in.) When people who have or endorse such an attitude say that God is perfectly good, we will not take them as committing themselves to the view that God is the kind of being who would not create any other world than the best possible. For they regard grace as an important part of perfect goodness.

IV.

On more than one occasion, when I have argued for the positions I have taken in sections II and III above, a counter-example of the following sort has been proposed. It is the case of a person who, knowing that she intends to conceive a child and that a certain drug invariably causes severe mental retardation in children conceived by those who have taken it, takes the drug and conceives a severely retarded child. We all, I imagine, have a strong inclination to say that such a person has done something wrong. It is objected to me that our moral intuitions in this case (presumably including the moral intuitions of religious Jews and Christians) are inconsistent with the views I have advanced above. It is claimed that consistency requires me to abandon those views unless I am prepared to make moral judgements that none of us are in fact willing to make.

I will try to meet these objections. I will begin by stating the case in some detail, in the most relevant form I can think of. Then I will discuss objections based on it. In this section I will discuss an objection against what I have said in section II, and a more general objection against the rejection of proposition (*P*) will be discussed in section V.

Let us call this case (*A*). A certain couple become so interested in retarded children that they develop a strong desire to have a retarded child of their own—to love it, to help it realize its potentialities (such as they are) to the full, to see that it is as happy as it can be. (For some reason it is impossible for them to *adopt* such a child.) They act on their desire. They take a drug which is known to cause damaged genes and abnormal chromosome structure in reproductive cells, resulting in severe mental retardation of children conceived by those who have taken it. A severely retarded child is conceived and born. They lavish affection on the child. They have ample means, so that they are able to provide for special needs, and to ensure that others will never be called on to pay for the child's support. They give themselves unstintedly, and do develop the child's capacities as much as possible. The child is, on the whole, happy, though incapable of many of the higher intellectual, aesthetic, and social joys. It suffers some pains and frustrations, of course, but does not feel miserable on the whole.

The first objection founded on this case is based, not just on the claim that the parents have done something wrong (which I certainly grant), but on the more specific claim that they have *wronged the child*. I maintained, in effect, in section II that a creature has not been wronged by its creator's creating it if both of the following conditions are satisfied.[6] (4) The creature is not, on the whole, so miserable that it would be better for him if he had never existed. (5) No being who came into existence in better or happier circumstances would have been the same individual as the creature in question. If we apply an analogous principle to the parent—child relationship in case (*A*), it would seem to follow that the retarded child has not been wronged by its parents. Condition (4) is satisfied: the child is happy rather than miserable on the whole. And condition (5) also seems to be satisfied. For the retardation in case (*A*), as described, is not due to pre-natal injury but to the genetic constitution of the child. Any normal child the parents might have conceived (indeed any normal child at all) would have had a different genetic constitution, and would therefore have been a different person, from the retarded child they actually did conceive. But—it is objected to me—we do regard the parents in case (*A*) as having wronged the child, and therefore we cannot consistently accept the principle that I maintained in section II.

---

[6] I am not holding that these are necessary conditions, but only that they are jointly sufficient conditions, for a creature's not being wronged by its creator's creating it. I have numbered these conditions in such a way as to avoid confusion with the numbered characteristics of worlds in section II.

My reply is that if conditions (4) and (5) are really satisfied the child cannot have been wronged by its parents' taking the drug and conceiving it. If we think otherwise we are being led, perhaps by our emotions, into a confusion. If the child is not worse off than if it had never existed, and if *its* never existing would have been a sure consequence of its not having been brought into existence as retarded, I do not see how *its* interests can have been injured, or *its* rights violated, by the parents' bringing it into existence as retarded.

It is easy to understand how the parents might come to feel that they had wronged the child. They might come to feel guilty (and rightly so), and the child would provide a focus for the guilt. Moreover, it would be easy, psychologically, to assimilate case (*A*) to cases of culpability for pre-natal injury, in which it is more reasonable to think of the child as having been wronged.[7] And we often think very carelessly about counter-factual personal identity, asking ourselves questions of doubtful intelligibility, such as, 'What if I had been born in the Middle Ages?' It is very easy to fail to consider the objection, 'But that would not have been the same person.'

It is also possible that an inclination to say that the child has been wronged may be based, at least in part, on a doubt that conditions (4) and (5) are really satisfied in case (*A*). Perhaps one is not convinced that in real life the parents could ever have a reasonable confidence that the child would be happy rather than miserable. Maybe it will be doubted that a few changes in chromosome structure, and the difference between damaged and undamaged genes, are enough to establish that the retarded child is a different person from any normal child that the couple could have had. Of course, if conditions (4) and (5) are not satisfied, the case does not constitute a counterexample to my claims in section II. But I would not rest any of the weight of my argument on doubts about the satisfaction of the conditions in case (*A*), because I think it is plausible to suppose that they would be satisfied in case (*A*) or in some very similar case.

V.

Even if the parents in case (*A*) have not wronged the child, I assume that they have done something wrong. It may be asked *what* they have done wrong, or *why* their action is regarded as wrong. And these questions may give rise to an objection, not specifically to what I said in section II, but more generally to my rejection of proposition (*P*). For it may be suggested that what is wrong

---

[7]It may be questioned whether even the pre-natally injured child is the same person as any unimpaired child that might have been born. I am inclined to think it is the same person. At any rate there is *more* basis for regarding it as the same person as a possible normal child than there is for so regarding a child with abnormal genetic constitution.

about the action of the parents in case (A) is that they have violated the following principle:

> (Q) It is wrong to bring into existence, knowingly, a being less excellent than one could have brought into existence.[8]

If we accept this principle we must surely agree that it would be wrong for a creator to make a world that was less excellent than the best he could make, and therefore that a perfectly good creator would not do such a thing. In other words, (Q) implies (P).

I do not think (Q) is a very plausible principle. It is not difficult to think of counter-examples to it.

Case (B): A man breeds goldfish, thereby bringing about their existence. We do not normally think it is wrong, or even *prima facie* wrong, for a man to do this, even though he could equally well have brought about the existence of more excellent beings, more intelligent and capable of higher satisfactions. (He could have bred dogs or pigs, for example.) The deliberate breeding of human beings of subnormal intelligence is morally offensive; the deliberate breeding of species far less intelligent than retarded human children is not morally offensive.

Case (C): Suppose it has been discovered that if intending parents take a certain drug before conceiving a child, they will have a child whose abnormal genetic constitution will give it vastly superhuman intelligence and superior prospects of happiness. Other things being equal, would it be wrong for intending parents to have normal children instead of taking the drug? There may be considerable disagreement of moral judgement about this. I do not think that the parents who chose to have normal children rather than take the drug would be doing anything wrong, nor that they would necessarily be manifesting any weakness or defect of moral character. Parents' choosing to have a normal rather than a super-human child would not, at any rate, elicit the strong and universal or almost universal disapproval that would be elicited by the action of the parents in case (A). Even with respect to the offspring of human beings, the principle we all confidently endorse is not that it is wrong to bring about, knowingly and voluntarily, the procreation of offspring less excellent than could have been procreated, but that it is wrong to bring about, knowingly and voluntarily, the procreation of a human offspring which is deficient by comparison with normal human beings.

Such counter-examples as these suggest that our disapproval of the action of the parents in case (A) is not based on principle (Q), but on a less general and more plausible principle such as the following:

---

[8]Anyone who was applying this principle to human actions would doubtless insert an 'other things being equal' clause. But let us ignore that, since such a clause would presumably provide no excuse for an agent who was deciding an issue so important as what world to create.

(R) It is wrong for human beings to cause, knowingly and voluntarily, the procreation of an offspring of human parents which is notably deficient, by comparison with normal human beings, in mental or physical capacity.

One who rejects (Q) while maintaining (R) might be held to face a problem of explanation. It may seem arbitrary to maintain such a specific moral principle as (R), unless one can explain it as based on a more general principle, such as (Q). I believe, however, that principle (R) might well be explained in something like the following way in a theological ethics in the Judaeo-Christian tradition, consistently with the rejection of (Q) and (P).[9]

God, in his grace, has chosen to have human beings among his creatures. In creating us he has certain intentions about the qualities and goals of human life. He has these intentions for us, not just as individuals, but as members of a community which in principle includes the whole human race. And his intentions for human beings as such extend to the offspring (if any) of human beings. Some of these intentions are to be realized by human voluntary action, and it is our duty to act in accordance with them.

It seems increasingly possible for human voluntary action to influence the genetic constitution of human offspring. The religious believer in the Judaeo-Christian tradition will want to be extremely cautious about this. For he is to be thankful that we exist as the beings we are, and will be concerned lest he bring about the procreation of human offspring who would be deficient in their capacity to enter fully into the purposes that God has for human beings as such. We are not God. We are his creatures, and we belong to him. Any offspring we have will belong to him in a much more fundamental way than they can belong to their human parents. We have not the right to try to have as our offspring just any kind of being whose existence might on the whole be pleasant and of some value (for instance, a being of very low intelligence but highly specialized for the enjoyment of aesthetic pleasures of smell and taste). If we do intervene to affect the genetic constitution of human offspring, it must be in ways which seem likely to make them *more* able to enter fully into what we believe to be the purposes of God for human beings as such. The deliberate procreation of children deficient in mental or physical capacity would be an intervention which could hardly be expected to result in offspring more able to enter fully into God's purposes for human life. It would therefore be sinful, and inconsistent with a proper respect for the human life which God has given us.

On this view of the matter, our obligation to refrain from bringing about the procreation of deficient human offspring is rooted in our obligation to God, as his creatures, to respect his purposes for human life. In

---

[9]I am able to give here, of course, only a very incomplete sketch of a theological position on the issue of 'biological engineering'.

adopting this theological rationale for the acceptance of principle (R), one in no way commits oneself to proposition (P). For one does not base (R) on any principle to the effect that one must always try to bring into existence the most excellent things that one can. And the claim that, because of his intentions for human life, we have an obligation to God not to try to have as our offspring beings of certain sorts does not imply that it would be wrong for God to create such beings in other ways. Much less does it imply that it would be wrong for God to create a world less excellent than the best possible.

In this essay I have argued that a creator would not necessarily wrong anyone, or be less kind to anyone than a perfectly good moral agent must be, if he created a world of creatures who would not exist in the best world he could make. I have also argued that from the standpoint of Judaeo-Christian religious ethics, a creator's choice of a less excellent world need not be regarded as manifesting a defect of character. It could be understood in terms of his *grace*, which (in that ethics) is considered an important part of perfect goodness. In this way I think the rejection of proposition (P) can be seen to be congruous with the attitude of gratitude and respect for human life as God's gracious gift which is encouraged in the Judaeo-Christian religious tradition. And that attitude (rather than any belief that one ought to bring into existence only the best beings one can) can be seen as a basis for the disapproval of the deliberate procreation of deficient human offspring.[10]

---

[10]Among the many to whom I am indebted for help in working out the thoughts contained in this paper, and for criticisms of earlier drafts of it, I must mention Marilyn McCord Adams, Richard Brandt, Eric Lerner, the members of my graduate class on theism and ethics in the Fall term of 1970 at the University of Michigan, and the editors of the *Philosophical Review*.

PART THREE

GOD'S ATTRIBUTES

PART INTRODUCTION
AND BIBLIOGRAPHICAL NOTES

Religious people talk of God as existing, as the creator of the world, as all-powerful and all-knowing, and so forth. Much of the philosophy of religion discusses the evidence we have for the truth and/or falsity of these claims. But equally important is the philosophical problem of the meaningfulness and consistency of these claims. This part of the book is devoted to these issues of meaningfulness and consistency.

In the opening section, we begin with the classical discussion of how we can meaningfully attribute any characteristics to God. This discussion was emphasized in the medieval period. Why did the medievals suppose that problems would arise if we attributed properties to God? There seem to have been several different problems that they envisaged. Maimonides felt the crucial problem was that attributing properties to God would in some way involve God's being a composite being, thus giving up the idea that God is an absolute unity. St. Thomas envisaged several other problems: (1) all predicates are such that their being predicated of an object presupposes that the object in question has some of the conditions of corporeality (like temporality, composition, etc.)—but since God is incorporeal, he has none of these conditions and the predicates cannot be truly attributed to him—and (2) there is an important sense in which it is true that God is incomprehensible, but if we could attribute properties to him, he would not be incomprehensible.

There are several classical responses that the medievals adopted to these problems. The first is the view that all attributions of properties to God must really be understood as denying other positive attributions. Thus, to say that God is alive is really to say only that his being is not like the being of dead bodies. This view is expressed by Maimonides in the selection reprinted here. St. Thomas, however, rejects that view for several reasons. To begin with, one could equally well say, on the Maimonidean account, that God is dead since his being is not like the being of living things (people, plants, etc). Obviously—and this leads us to St. Thomas's second point—we want to say that God is more unlike dead things than living things, that is, that God is more like a live thing than a dead thing. But then we really are, in some way, saying something positive about what God is like, and Maimonides's theory collapses.

St. Thomas also rejects two other views that had been adopted by other medieval philosophers. The first is that the predicates we positively attribute to God mean the same thing when attributed to him as when attributed to ordinary creatures. This view he rejects, partially because it involves no solution to the problems mentioned and partially because such a view obscures the way in which God has these properties perfectly and other creatures do not. The second is that the predicates we positively attribute to God mean something entirely different in such attributions from what they mean when they are attributed to other creatures. St. Thomas rejects this view, as well, on the grounds (really not argued for) that it would rule out the possibility that we could come to know something about the nature of God from an examination of ordinary creatures. Instead, Aquinas's own solution to this problem is to claim that predicates, when applied to God, have a meaning analogous to the meaning that they have when applied to ordinary things.

This medieval debate has been continued by several contemporary authors. One of the most interesting contributions is found in the selection by William Alston. In that article, Professor Alston argues that the tremendous difference between the divine and the human does not prevent there from being common abstract features that make the attribution to God and to humans of certain characteristics a univocal attribution. Drawing upon certain popular ideas in the philosophy of mind, Alston develops this approach as a way of understanding how we can attribute to God the same psychological attributes (e.g., knowledge) that we attribute to humans.

We turn from this general discussion of God's attributes to a discussion of specific attributes, beginning with the question of what it means to attribute to God the role of creator, and with the related question of how that impacts on God's temporality. Many religious people want to claim that there is a special relationship between God and the world, the relationship of creator to created. Although they may disagree as to whether God created the world from nothing (creation *ex nihilo*) or whether he molded, shaped, and gave order to preexisting matter, they all agree that the universe, as we know it now, is a product of the creative activity of God. This doctrine of creation raises a variety of philosophical problems, some of which are examined in this section.

We begin with a variety of problems raised by the idea that, at some given point in time, God created the universe. Stated simply, these problems arise out of the question, "Why did God create the universe when he did rather than at some other time?" St. Augustine raises one version of the problem as follows: if God is eternal and immutable, then his creative activity must be so as well (or else, it would involve a change in him). But if it is, then why hasn't the universe existed eternally? How could it be that it only came into existence at a given moment in time? Leibniz raises another version of the problem as follows: there must be a reason why a given event occurs rather than some other event. Now suppose that God created the universe at some given time. Why did that event occur rather than the other event of his having created it a year earlier? Given empty time without anything in it, there could, says Leibniz, be no reason why the one event should occur rather than the other.

In attempting to deal with these problems, both Augustine and Leibniz are forced into adopting certain theories about the nature of time and of God's relation to time. For St. Augustine, time is a created entity that was created, like all other such entities, by God. There was then no time before God's creative activity, and so it is true that the universe has existed for all time. But that does not mean, of course, that the universe is eternal like God. God's eternity involves his not being in time at all, and not his existing successively at all times.

Leibniz adopts, instead, a very different theory about the nature of time. According to his theory, time is not an entity at all. Instead, it is a series of relations (the relations we call the temporal relations) between entities. And if these relations remain the same, there is not a change in the time in question. Consequently, if the temporal relations among the events in the history of universe remain the same, it is meaningless to talk of the possibility of God's having created the universe a year earlier.

Leibniz offers this solution to his problem as an alternative to the solution proposed by Samuel Clarke. Clarke could not see why there is a problem; after all, he argued, God might have his reasons as to why he created the universe at some given time rather than at some earlier time. Clarke, it should be noted, was forced into adopting this position since, as a good Newtonian, he wanted to insist that space and time were things (contra Leibniz) that were infinite in extension no matter what is the extension of the universe (contra Augustine). But, of course, Clarke's position will not do. As Leibniz points out, given the homogeneity of empty time, what reason could God have?

It should be noted that, even on Leibniz's position, the universe could have existed longer than it has. But this would require there existing things and events that preceded all that has actually existed. And, of course, there would then be no problem about God's having his reasons why he created the actual universe rather than any of these possible universes; his reasons could be based upon the merits of having these additional things and events.

The question of God's temporality is explicitly debated in the selections by Nicholas Wolterstorff and in the selection by Eleonore Stump and Norman Kretzmann. Wolterstorff argues that God is ever-lasting (existing within time at all times) rather than eternal (existing outside of time), as Augustine and others had thought, because God as portrayed in the Bible is an agent acting within history. In particular, a God who remembers what has occurred and who plans to bring about various occurrences, argues Wolterstorff, is a God who is in time rather than eternal. Stump and Kretzmann disagree. After offering an analysis of eternity, they present an analysis of how an eternal entity can act in time, with their crucial point being that an eternal act, even if not itself in time, can bring about effects located in time, and that is all that is required for an eternal God to act in history. Near the end of their essay, they specifically consider Wolterstorff's concern about God knowing what people have done (e.g., that they have prayed) and responding to the human action. The reader will have to judge whether their account of God's acting in history while being eternal is satisfactory.

God is often viewed as all-powerful. This concept (omnipotency) has proven to be as troubling as the concept of God as creator, and the next four selections are devoted to a discussion of God's omnipotence. One way to understand these problems is to look at certain paradoxes that the idea of omnipotency gives rise to. One is the paradox of the stone—can God create a stone so heavy that he cannot lift it? If he can, then he is not omnipotent (since there is something—lift that stone—that he cannot do); and if he cannot, then he is also not omnipotent (since there is something—create that stone—that he cannot do). In either case, God cannot be omnipotent. The second is the paradox of God's sinning—can God sin? If he can, then he is not all-perfect. If he cannot, then he is still not all-perfect because he cannot do something (sin) and is not therefore omnipotent.

It is obvious that both these paradoxes raise, each in their own way, the same issue. Do we want to say that God can do anything? And if we do, won't this idea get us into trouble? On the other hand, if we want in some way to limit God's power (so as to avoid these paradoxes), what is left of the idea that God is omnipotent?

St. Thomas Aquinas, like many other theologians, adopted the idea that God can do anything that is logically possible, but that he cannot do anything that is not logically possible. St. Thomas felt that this was really no limitation on God's power, since the logically impossible is not some task that God cannot perform. In light of this Thomistic principle, George I. Mavrodes argues that the paradox of the stone can be resolved, since even if God cannot create a stone so heavy that he cannot lift it, that is no challenge to his omnipotence, since creating a stone so heavy that God cannot lift it is a logically impossible task. Similarly, others have used this Thomistic thought to deal with the paradox of God's sinning. God, they say, cannot sin, but that is no challenge to his omnipotence, since God's committing a sin is not a logically possible task.

Not all philosophers have, however, been satisfied with this approach. As Harry G. Frankfurt points out, there are many theologians who are unhappy with the idea that God cannot do logically impossible tasks, that he is in this way bound by the laws of logic. Intuitively speaking, their motivation is the following: just as God is not bound in his actions by the laws of nature, since it is only by his will that ordinary objects act in accordance with these laws, so God is not bound by the laws of logic, since it is only by his will that the world is in accordance with these laws. Descartes, for example, held this view. Now it is obvious that this dispute between Aquinas and Descartes hinges upon fundamental issues having to do with the nature of the laws of logic, so it would seem desirable to see if the paradoxes could be avoided without having to resolve those very difficult issues.

Frankfurt's own solution is rather straightforward. Suppose, he says, that God can do the impossible, so he can create the stone so heavy he can't lift it. There would still be no limitation upon his power, for if he can do the impossible, then he can also lift the stone he can't lift. In short, suggests Frankfurt, if we do want to stick with the idea of God being able to do anything at all, we need not be troubled by the paradox of the stone.

In the last selection, Anthony Kenny reviews these and other suggestions and argues that none of them will do. He is sympathetic to a suggestion of Geach that the whole concept of omnipotence might be dropped, and that religious people would do better to talk of God as almighty (as having power over all things). But at the end, he offers an account of omnipotence as having every power which it is logically possible for God to possess, and argues that it is better to define omnipotence in terms of powers than in terms of the ability to bring about all logically possible states of affairs.

We turn finally to the attribute of omniscience (knowing everything). The main philosophical problem here has not been with understanding what it means to claim that God is omniscient. Instead, the problem has been in understanding how God's omniscience is compatible with human freedom. Religious believers have wanted to say that God has foreknowledge of what each of us will do (as part of his omniscience) but that we are free to choose what we shall do. The question is whether these two claims are compatible.

Aquinas's discussion of the topic involves two major observations. The first is based upon his view that God is eternal and out of his time so that his knowledge of all things is not strictly speaking foreknowledge. The second is that while it is necessarily true that everything which God knows will occur, it is not true that what God knows will occur will necessarily occur, and it is only that latter false claim that would be incompatible with human freedom and contingency.

Jonathan Edwards, an American Calvinist theologian, disagreed and felt that there is a major problem with believing in human freedom and God's foreknowledge. He developed the following argument:

1. Everything that has already occurred is now necessary (cannot be changed).
2. Suppose that a man will do A at some future.
3. Then God already knows that he will do A.
4. It follows from (1) and (3) that it is necessary that God knows that he will do A.
5. It is necessary, as Aquinas agrees, that if God knows that the man will do A, then he will do A.
6. It follows from (4) and (5) that it is necessary that he will do A.

This argument has been restated in recent times by Nelson Pike in a classic article reprinted as our third selection. Pike correctly points out that the argument rests upon believing that God exists at all times and has beliefs at all times about what people will later do. In Edwards's argument, that is what lies behind (3). The argument might not be a problem for those who believe in God's eternity as opposed to God's everlasting existence.

One of the major attempts to resolve this problem is the Ockhamist solution found in the selection from Marilyn Adams. William of Ockham, a great medieval philosopher, had claimed that not every proposition about the past is necessary in the sense that it cannot be changed. In particular, those propositions about the past which are true because of certain future events, including some about God's knowledge of what we will do, are not necessarily true. Such propositions are said to express "soft" facts about the past. In effect, Ockham's position would deny step (1) and therefore also step (4) in the above argument.

In the beginning of her paper, Marilyn Adams attempts to clarify the distinction between "soft facts" and "hard facts." In the rest of her paper, she argues that Pike's argument fails precisely because the relevant facts about the past (the existence of an essentially omniscient and everlasting God) are not hard facts. In his critique of her ideas, John Fischer argues both that Adams's account of the hard fact/soft fact distinction is inadequate and that there are theological reasons for doubting that any satisfactory account can be given.

A very different approach to the problem is adopted by William Alston in the final selection in this section. Professor Alston points out that very little attribution has been devoted in the literature about this problem to the meaning of freedom. He distinguishes two very different notions of freedom, a libertarian account of freedom and a compatibilist account. He goes on to argue that while Pike (and, presumably, Edwards before him) was arguing that divine foreknowledge is incompatible with freedom in a libertarian sense of that term, defenders of human freedom often seem to be adopting a compatibilist account. Alston does not himself conclude which conception of freedom is more appropriate in this setting, and that is a question which the reader will have to consider very carefully.

The different sections of this part have quite distinct literatures associated with them, but good overviews of the discussions of the attributes of God include Stephen Davis's *Logic and the Nature of God* (Eerdmans, 1982), Anthony Kenny's *The God of the Philosophers* (Oxford University Press, 1979), and Richard Swinburne's *The Coherency of Theism* (Oxford University Press, 1978). J. Ross's *Philosophical Theology* (Bobbs Merrill, 1969) has an extensive discussion of omnipotence, while L. Urban and D. Walton's *The Power of God* (Oxford University Press, 1976) collects many fine articles on omnipotence. N. Pike's *God and Timelessness* (Shocken, 1970) is a classic work on God's relation to temporality, while John Martin Fischer's *God, Foreknowledge, and Freedom* (Stanford University Press, 1989) collects most of the important recent articles on divine foreknowledge and human freedom.

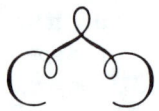

BASIC NATURE
OF ATTRIBUTIONS
TO GOD

MAIMONIDES

Negative Predication

More obscure than what preceded. Know that the description of God, may He be cherished and exalted, by means of negations is the correct description—a description that is not affected by an indulgence in facile language and does not imply any deficiency with respect to God in general or in any particular mode. On the other hand, if one describes Him by means of affirmations, one implies, as we have made clear, that He is associated with that which is not He and implies a deficiency in Him. I must make it clear to you in the first place how negations are in a certain respect attributes and how they differ from the affirmative attributes. After that I shall make it clear to you that we have no way of describing Him unless it be through negations and not otherwise.

I shall say accordingly that an attribute does not particularize any object of which it is predicated in such a way that it is not associated by virtue of that particular attribute with other things. On the contrary, the attribute is sometimes attributed to the object of which it is predicated in spite of the fact that the latter has it in common with other things and is not particularized through it. For instance, if you would see a man at some distance and if you would ask: What is this thing that is seen? and were told: This is a living being—this affirmation would indubitably be an attribute predicated of the thing seen though it does not particularize the latter, distinguishing it from everything else. However, a certain particularization is achieved through it; namely, it may be learnt from it that the thing seen is not a body belonging to the species of plants or to that of the minerals. Similarly if there were a man

From Maimonides, *Guide of the Perplexed*, Chap. 58, trans. S. Pines (Chicago: University of Chicago Press, 1963). Reprinted by permission of the publisher.

in this house and you knew that some body is in it without knowing what it is and would ask, saying: What is in this house? and the one who answered you would say: There is no mineral in it and no body of a plant—a certain particularization would be achieved and you would know that a living being is in the house though you would not know which animal. Thus the attributes of negation have in this respect something in common with the attributes of affirmation, for the former undoubtedly bring about some particularization even if the particularization due to them only exists in the exclusion of what has been negated from the sum total of things that we had thought of as not being negated. Now as to the respect in which the attributes of negation differ from the attributes of affirmation: The attributes of affirmation, even if they do not particularize, indicate a part of the thing the knowledge of which is sought, that part being either a part of its substance or one of its accidents; whereas the attributes of negation do not give us knowledge in any respect whatever of the essence the knowledge of which is sought, unless this happens by accident as in the example we have given.

After this preface, I shall say that it has already been demonstrated that God, may He be honored and magnified, is existent of necessity and that there is no composition in Him, as we shall demonstrate, and that we are only able to apprehend the fact that He is and cannot apprehend His quiddity. It is consequently impossible that He should have affirmative attributes. For he has no "That" outside of His "What," and hence an attribute cannot be indicative of one of the two; all the more His "What" is not compound so that an attribute cannot be indicative of its two parts; and all the more, He cannot have accidents so that an attribute cannot be indicative of them. Accordingly He cannot have an affirmative attribute in any respect.

As for the negative attributes, they are those that must be used in order to conduct the mind toward that which must be believed with regard to Him, may He be exalted, for no notion of multiplicity can attach to Him in any respect on account of them; and, moreover, they conduct the mind toward the utmost reach that man may attain in the apprehension of Him, may He be exalted. For instance, it has been demonstrated to us that it is necessary that something exists other than those essences apprehended by means of the senses and whose knowledge is encompassed by means of the intellect. Of this thing we say that it exists, the meaning being that its nonexistence is impossible. We apprehend further that this being is not like the being of the elements, for example, which are dead bodies. We say accordingly that this being is living, the meaning being that He, may He be exalted, is not dead. We apprehend further that this being is not like the being of the heaven, which is a living body. We say accordingly that He is not a body. We apprehend further that this being is not like the being of the intellect, which is neither a body nor dead, but is caused. We say accordingly that He, may He be exalted, is eternal, the meaning being that He has no cause that has brought Him into existence. We apprehend further that the existence of this being, which is its essence, suffices not only for His being existent, but also for many other existents flowing from it, and that this overflow—unlike that of heat from fire and unlike the proceeding of light from the sun—is an overflow that, as we shall make clear, constantly procures for those existents duration and order by means of wisely contrived governance. Accordingly we say of Him, because of these notions, that He is powerful and knowing and willing. The intention in ascribing these attributes to Him is to signify that He is neither powerless nor ignorant nor inattentive nor negligent. Now the meaning of our saying that He is not powerless is to signify that His existence suffices for the bringing into existence of things other than He. The meaning of our saying that He is not ignorant is to signify that He apprehends—that is, is living, for every apprehending thing is living. And the meaning of our saying that He is not inattentive or negligent is to signify that all the existent things in question proceed from their cause according to a certain order and governance—not in a neglected way so as to be generated as chance would have it, but rather as all the things are generated that a willing being governs by means of purpose and will. We apprehend further that no other thing is like that being. Accordingly our saying that He is one signifies the denial of multiplicity.

ST. THOMAS AQUINAS

Analogical Predication

After the consideration of those things which belong to the divine knowledge, we now proceed to the consideration of the divine names. For everything is named by us according to our knowledge of it.

Under this head, there are twelve points for inquiry.[1] (1) Whether God can be named by us? (2) Whether any names applied to God are predicated of Him substantially? (3) Whether any names applied to God are said of Him properly, or are all to be taken metaphorically? (4) Whether any names applied to God are synonymous? (5) Whether some names are applied to God and to creatures univocally or equivocally? (6) Whether, supposing they are applied analogically, they are applied first to God or to creatures? (7) Whether

---

From *Summa Theologica*, Part I, trans. Dominican Fathers of English Province (New York: Benziger Bros., Inc., 1947). Reprinted by permission of the publisher.

[1]Only the first five are included below—ED.

any names are applicable to God from time? (8) Whether this name *God* is a name of nature, or of operation? (9) Whether this name *God* is a communicable name? (10) Whether it is taken univocally or equivocally as signifying God, by nature, by participation, and by opinion? (11) Whether this name, *Who is*, is the supremely appropriate name of God? (12) Whether affirmative propositions can be formed about God?

1. WHETHER A NAME CAN BE GIVEN TO GOD

We proceed thus to the First Article:—

Objection 1. It seems that no name can be given to God. For Dionysius says that, *Of Him there is neither name, nor can one be found of Him;* and it is written: *What is His name, and what is the name of His Son, if thou knowest?* (*Prov.* xxx. 4).

Obj. 2. Further, every name is either abstract or concrete. But concrete names do not belong to God, since He is simple, nor do abstract names belong to Him, since they do not signify any perfect subsisting thing. Therefore no name can be said of God.

Obj. 3. Further, nouns signify substance with quality; verbs and participles signify substance with time; pronouns the same with demonstration or relation. But none of these can be applied to God, for He has not quality, or accident, or time; moreover, He cannot be felt, so as to be pointed out; nor can He be described by relation, inasmuch as relations serve to recall a thing mentioned before by nouns, participles, or demonstrative pronouns. Therefore God cannot in any way be named by us.

On the contrary, It is written (*Exod.* xv. 3): *The Lord is a man of war, Almighty is His name.*

I *answer that,* Since, according to the Philosopher, words are signs of ideas, and ideas the similitudes of things, it is evident that words function in the signification of things through the conception of the intellect. It follows therefore that we can give a name to anything in so far as we can understand it. Now it was shown above that in this life we cannot see the essence of God; but we know God from creatures as their cause, and also by way of excellence and remotion. In this way therefore He can be named by us from creatures, yet not so that the name which signifies Him expresses the divine essence in itself in the way that the name *man* expresses the essence of man in himself, since it signifies the definition which manifests his essence. For the idea expressed by the name is the definition.

Reply Obj. 1. The reason why God has no name, or is said to be above being named, is because His essence is above all that we understand about God and signify in words.

Reply Obj. 2. Because we come to know and name God from creatures, the names we attribute to God signify what belongs to material creatures, of which the knowledge is natural to us, as was shown above. And because in creatures of this kind what is perfect and subsistent is composite, whereas their form is not a complete subsisting thing, but rather is that whereby a thing is, hence it follows that all names used by us to signify a complete subsisting thing must have a concrete meaning, as befits composite things. On the other hand, names given to signify simple forms signify a thing not as subsisting, but as that whereby a thing is; as, for instance, whiteness signifies that whereby a thing is white. And since God is simple and subsisting, we attribute to Him simple and abstract names to signify His simplicity, and concrete names to signify His subsistence and perfection; although both these kinds of names fail to express His mode of being, because our intellect does not know Him in this life as He is.

Reply Obj. 3. To signify substance with quality is to signify the *suppositum* with a nature or determined form in which it subsists. Hence, as some things are said of God in a concrete sense, to signify His subsistence and perfection, so likewise nouns are applied to God signifying substance with quality. Further, verbs and participles, which signify time, are applied to Him because His eternity includes all time. For as we can apprehend and signify simple subsistents only by way of composite things, so we can understand and express simple eternity only by way of temporal things, because our intellect has a natural proportion to composite and temporal things. But demonstrative pronouns are applied to God as pointing to what is understood, not to what is sensed. For we can point to Him only as far as we understand Him. Thus, according as nouns, participles and demonstrative pronouns are applicable to God, so far can He be signified by relative pronouns.

2. WHETHER ANY NAME CAN BE APPLIED TO GOD SUBSTANTIALLY

We proceed thus to the Second Article:—

Objection 1. It seems that no name can be applied to God substantially. For Damascene says: *Everything said of God must not signify His substance, but rather show forth what He is not; or express some relation, or something following from His nature or operation.*

Obj. 2. Further, Dionysius says: *You will find a chorus of holy doctors addressed to the end of distinguishing clearly and praiseworthy the divine processions in the denominations of God.* This means that the names applied by the holy doctors in praising God are distinguished according to the divine processions themselves. But what expresses the procession of anything does not signify anything pertaining to its essence. Therefore the names said of God are not said of Him substantially.

Obj. 3. Further, a thing is named by us according as we understand it. But in this life God is not understood by us in His substance. Therefore neither is any name we can use applied substantially to God.

On the contrary, Augustine says: *For God to be is to be strong or wise, or whatever else we may say of that simplicity whereby His substance is signified.* Therefore all names of this kind signify the divine substance.

I answer that, Names which are said of God negatively or which signify His relation to creatures manifestly do not at all signify His substance, but rather express the distance of the creature from Him, or His relation to something else, or rather, the relation of creatures to Himself.

But as regards names of God said absolutely and affirmatively, as *good, wise*, and the like, various and many opinions have been held. For some have said that all such names, although they are applied to God affirmatively, nevertheless have been brought into use more to remove something from God than to posit something in Him. Hence they assert that when we say that God lives, we mean that God is not like an inanimate thing; and the same in like manner applies to other names. This was taught by Rabbi Moses. Others say that these names applied to God signify His relationship towards creatures: thus in the words, *God is good*, we mean God is the cause of goodness in things; and the same interpretation applies to other names.

Both of these opinions, however, seem to be untrue for three reasons. First, because in neither of them could a reason be assigned why some names more than others should be applied to God. For He is assuredly the cause of bodies in the same way as He is the cause of good things; therefore if the words *God is good* signified no more than, *God is the cause of good things*, it might in like manner be said that God is a body, inasmuch as He is the cause of bodies. So also to say that He is a body implies that He is not a mere potentiality, as is primary matter. Secondly, because it would follow that all names applied to God would be said of Him by way of being taken in a secondary sense, as healthy is secondarily said of medicine, because it signifies only the cause of health in the animal which primarily is called healthy. Thirdly, because this is against the intention of those who speak of God. For in saying that God lives, they assuredly mean more than to say that He is the cause of our life, or that He differs from inanimate bodies.

Therefore we must hold a different doctrine—viz., that these names signify the divine substance, and are predicated substantially of God, although they fall short of representing Him. Which is proved thus. For these names express God, so far as our intellects know Him. Now since our intellect knows God from creatures, it knows Him as far as creatures represent Him. But it was shown above that God prepossesses in Himself all the perfections of creatures, being Himself absolutely and universally perfect. Hence every creature represents Him, and is like Him, so far as it possesses some perfection: yet not so far as to represent Him as something of the same species or genus, but as the excelling source of whose form the effects fall short, although they derive some kind of likeness thereto, even as the forms of inferior bodies represent the power of the sun. This was explained above in treating of the divine perfection. Therefore, the aforesaid names signify the divine substance, but in an imperfect manner, even as creatures represent it imperfectly. So when we say, *God is good*, the meaning is not, *God is the cause of goodness*, or, *God is not evil*; but the meaning is, *Whatever good we attribute to creatures pre-exists in God*, and in a higher way. Hence it does not follow that God is good because He causes goodness; but rather, on the contrary, He causes goodness in things because He is good. As Augustine says, *Because He is good, we are*.

Reply Obj. 1. Damascene says that these names do not signify what God is because by none of these names is what He is perfectly expressed; but each one signifies Him in an imperfect manner, even as creatures represent Him imperfectly.

Reply Obj. 2. In the signification of names, that from which the name is derived is different sometimes from what it is intended to signify, as for instance this name *stone* [*lapis*] is imposed from the fact that it hurts the *foot* [*lædit pedem*]; yet it is not imposed to signify that which hurts the foot, but rather to signify a certain kind of body; otherwise everything that hurts the foot would be a stone. So we must say that such divine names are imposed from the divine processions; for as according to the diverse processions of their perfections, creatures are the representations of God, although in an imperfect manner, so likewise our intellect knows and names God according to each kind of procession. But nevertheless these names are not imposed to signify the processions themselves, as if when we say *God lives*, the sense were, *life proceeds from Him*, but to signify the principle itself of things, in so far as life pre-exists in Him, although it pre-exists in Him a more eminent way than is understood or signified.

Reply Obj. 3. In this life, we cannot know the essence of God as it is in itself, but we know it according as it is represented in the perfections of creatures; and it is thus that the names imposed by us signify it.

3. WHETHER ANY NAME CAN BE APPLIED TO GOD PROPERLY

We proceed thus to the Third Article:—

Objection 1. It seems that no name is applied properly to God. For all names which we apply to God are taken from creatures, as was explained above. But the names of creatures are applied to God metaphorically, as when we say, God is a stone, or a lion, or the like. Therefore names are applied to God in a metaphorical sense.

Obj. 2. Further, no name can be applied properly to anything if it should be more truly denied of it than given to it. But all such names as *good, wise*, and the like, are more truly denied of God than given to Him; as appears from what Dionysius says. Therefore none of these names is said of God properly.

Obj. 3. Further, corporeal names are applied to God in a metaphorical sense only, since He is incorporeal. But all such names imply some kind of corporeal condition; for their meaning is bound up with time and composition and like corporeal conditions. Therefore all these names are applied to God in a metaphorical sense.

On the contrary, Ambrose says, *Some names there are which express evidently the property of the divinity, and some which express the clear truth of the divine majesty; but others there are which are said of God metaphorically by way of similitude.* Therefore not all names are applied to God in a metaphorical sense, but there are some which are said of Him properly.

I answer that, According to the preceding article, our knowledge of God is derived from the perfections which flow from Him to creatures; which perfections are in God in a more eminent way than in creatures. Now our intellect apprehends them as they are in creatures, and as it apprehends them thus does it signify them by names. Therefore, as to the names applied to God, there are two things to be considered—viz., the perfections themselves which they signify, such as goodness, life, and the like, and their mode of signification. As regards what is signified by these names, they belong properly to God, and more properly than they belong to creatures, and are applied primarily to Him. But as regards their mode of signification, they do not properly and strictly apply to God; for their mode of signification befits creatures.

Reply Obj. 1. There are some names which signify these perfections flowing from God to creatures in such a way that the imperfect way in which creatures receive the divine perfection is part of the very signification of the name itself, as stone signifies a material being; and names of this kind can be applied to God only in a metaphorical sense. Other names, however, express the perfections themselves absolutely, without any such mode of participation being part of their signification, as the words *being, good, living,* and the like; and such names can be applied to God properly.

Reply Obj. 2. Such names as these, as Dionysius shows, are denied of God for the reason that what the name signifies does not belong to Him in the ordinary sense of its signification, but in a more eminent way. Hence Dionysius says also that God is above all substance and all life.

Reply Obj. 3. These names which are applied to God properly imply corporeal conditions, not in the thing signified, but as regards their mode of signification; whereas those which are applied to God metaphorically imply and mean a corporeal condition in the thing signified.

4. WHETHER NAMES APPLIED
TO GOD ARE SYNONYMOUS

We proceed thus to the Fourth Article:—

Objection 1. It seems that these names applied to God are synonymous names. For synonymous names are those which mean exactly the same. But these names applied to God mean entirely the same thing in God; for the goodness of God is His essence, and likewise it is His wisdom. Therefore these names are entirely synonymous.

Obj. 2. Further, if it be said that these names signify one and the same thing in reality, but differ in idea, it can be objected that an idea to which no reality corresponds is an empty notion. Therefore if these ideas are many, and the thing is one, it seems also that all these ideas are empty notions.

Obj. 3. Further, a thing which is one in reality and in idea is more one than what is one in reality and many in idea. But God is supremely one. Therefore it seems that He is not one in reality and many in idea; and thus the names applied to God do not have different meanings. Hence they are synonymous.

On the contrary, All synonyms united with each other are redundant, as when we say, *vesture clothing.* Therefore if all names applied to God are synonymous, we cannot properly say *good God,* or the like; and yet it is written, *O most mighty, great and powerful, the Lord of hosts is Thy name* (Jer. XXXII. 18).

I answer that, These names spoken of God are not synonymous. This would be easy to understand, if we said that these names are used to remove or to express the relation of cause to creatures; for thus it would follow that there are different ideas as regards the diverse things denied of God, or as regards diverse effects connoted. But according to what was said above, namely, that these names signify the divine substance, although in an imperfect manner, it is also clear from what has been said that they have diverse meanings. For the idea signified by the name is the conception in the intellect of the thing signified by the name. But since our intellect knows God from creatures, in order to understand God it forms conceptions proportioned to the perfections flowing from God to creatures. These perfections pre-exist in God unitedly and simply, whereas in creatures they are received divided and multiplied. Just as, therefore, to the diverse perfections of creatures there corresponds one simple principle represented by the diverse perfections of creatures in a various and manifold manner, so also to the various and multiplied conceptions of our intellect there corresponds one altogether simple principle, imperfectly understood through these conceptions. Therefore, although the names applied to God signify one reality, still, because they signify that reality under many and diverse aspects, they are not synonymous.

Thus appears the solution of the First Objection, since synonymous names signify one thing under one aspect; for names which signify different aspects of one thing do not signify primarily and absolutely one thing, because a name signifies a thing only through the medium of the intellectual conception, as was said above.

Reply Obj. 2. The many aspects of these names are not useless and empty, for there corresponds to all of them one simple reality represented by them in a manifold and imperfect manner.

Reply Obj. 3. The perfect unity of God requires that what are manifold and divided in others should exist in Him simply and unitedly. Thus it comes about that He is one in reality, and yet multiple in idea, because our intellect apprehends Him in a manifold manner, as things represent Him.

5. WHETHER WHAT IS SAID OF GOD AND OF CREATURES IS UNIVOCALLY PREDICATED OF THEM

We proceed thus to the Fifth Article:—

Objection 1. It seems that the things attributed to God and creatures are univocal. For every equivocal term is reduced to the univocal, as many are reduced to one: for if the name *dog* be said equivocally of the barking dog and of the dogfish, it must be said of some univocally—viz., of all barking dogs; otherwise we proceed to infinitude. Now there are some univocal agents which agree with their effects in name and definition, as man generates man; and there are some agents which are equivocal, as the sun which causes heat, although the sun is hot only in an equivocal sense. Therefore it seems that the first agent, to which all other agents are reduced, is a univocal agent: and thus what is said of God and creatures is predicated univocally.

Obj. 2. Further, no likeness is understood through equivocal names. Therefore, as creatures have a certain likeness to God, according to the text of *Genesis* (i. 26), *Let us make man to our image and likeness*, it seems that something can be said of God and creatures univocally.

Obj. 3. Further, measure is homogeneous with the thing measured, as is said in *Metaph.* X. But God is the first measure of all beings. Therefore God is homogeneous with creatures; and thus a name may be applied univocally to God and to creatures.

On the contrary, Whatever is predicated of various things under the same name but not in the same sense is predicated equivocally. But no name belongs to God in the same sense that it belongs to creatures; for instance, wisdom in creatures is a quality, but not in God. Now a change in genus changes an essence, since the genus is part of the definition; and the same applies to other things. Therefore whatever is said of God and of creatures is predicated equivocally.

Further, God is more distant from creatures than any creatures are from each other. But the distance of some creatures makes any univocal predication of them impossible, as in the case of those things which are not in the same genus. Therefore much less can anything be predicated univocally of God and creatures; and so only equivocal predication can be applied to them.

I answer that, Univocal predication is impossible between God and creatures. The reason of this is that every effect which is not a proportioned result of the power of the efficient cause receives the similitude of the agent not in its full degree, but in a measure that falls short; so that what is divided and multiplied in the effects resides in the agent simply, and in an unvaried manner. For example, the sun by the exercise of its one power produces manifold and various forms in these sublunary things. In the same way, as was said above, all perfections existing in creatures divided and multiplied pre-exist in God unitedly. Hence, when any name expressing perfection is applied to a creature, it signifies that perfection as distinct from the others according to the nature of its definition; as, for instance, by this term *wise* applied to a man, we signify some perfection distinct from a man's essence, and distinct from his power and his being, and from all similar things. But when we apply *wise* to God, we do not mean to signify anything distinct from His essence or power or being. And thus when this term *wise* is applied to man, in some degree it circumscribes and comprehends the thing signified; whereas this is not the case when it is applied to God, but it leaves the thing signified as uncomprehended and as exceeding the signification of the name. Hence it is evident that this term *wise* is not applied in the same way to God and to man. The same applies to other terms. Hence, no name is predicated univocally of God and of creatures.

Neither, on the other hand, are names applied to God and creatures in a purely equivocal sense, as some have said. Because if that were so, it follows that from creatures nothing at all could be known or demonstrated about God; for the reasoning would always be exposed to the fallacy of equivocation. Such a view is against the Philosopher, who proves many things about God, and also against what the Apostle says: *The invisible things of God are clearly seen being understood by the things that are made* (*Rom.* i. 20). Therefore it must be said that these names are said of God and creatures in an *analogous* sense, that is, according to proportion.

This can happen in two ways: either according as many things are proportioned to one (thus, for example *healthy* is predicated of medicine and urine in relation and in proportion to health of body, of which the latter is the sign and the former the cause), or according as one thing is proportioned to another (thus, *healthy* is said of medicine and an animal, since medicine is the cause of health in the animal body). And in this way some things are said of God and creatures analogically, and not in a purely equivocal nor in a purely univocal sense. For we can name God only from creatures. Hence, whatever is said of God and creatures is said according as there is some relation of the creature to God as to its principle and cause, wherein all the perfections of things pre-exist excellently. Now this mode of community is a mean between pure equivocation and simple univocation. For in analogies the idea is not, as it is in univocals, one and the same; yet it is not totally diverse as in equivocals; but the name which is thus used in a multiple sense signifies various proportions to some one thing: *e.g.*, *healthy*, applied to urine, signifies the sign of animal health; but applied to medicine, it signifies the cause of the same health.

Reply Obj. 1. Although in predications all equivocals must be reduced to univocals, still in actions the non-univocal agent must precede the univocal agent. For the non-univocal agent is the universal cause of the whole species, as the sun is the cause of the generation of all men. But the univocal agent is not the universal efficient cause of the whole species (otherwise it would be the cause of itself, since it is contained in the species), but is a particular cause of this individual which it places under the species by way of participation. Therefore the universal cause of the whole species is not a univocal agent: and the universal cause comes before the particular cause. But this universal agent, while not univocal, nevertheless is not altogether equivocal (otherwise it could not produce its own likeness); but it can be called an analogical agent, just as in predications all univocal names are reduced to one first non-univocal analogical name which is *being*.

Reply Obj. 2. The likeness of the creature to God is imperfect, for it does not represent the same thing even generically.

Reply Obj. 3. God is not a measure proportioned to the things measured; hence it is not necessary that God and creatures should be in the same genus.

The arguments adduced in the contrary sense prove indeed that these names are not predicated univocally of God and creatures; yet they do not prove that they are predicated equivocally.

WILLIAM P. ALSTON

Functionalism and Theological Language

I.

Thoughtful theists have long felt a tension between the radical 'otherness' of God and the fact that we speak of God in terms drawn from our talk of creatures. If God is radically other than creatures, how can we properly think and speak of Him as acting, loving, knowing, and purposing? Wouldn't that imply that God shares features with creatures and hence is not 'wholly other'?

To be sure, whether there is a problem here, and if so just what problem, depends both on the precise way(s) in which God is 'other', and on the way in which the creaturely terms are used. Let's take a brief look at both issues.

The respects in which God has been thought to differ from creatures can be roughly arranged in a scale of increasingly radical 'otherness'. Without aspiring to range over all possible creatures, including angels, let's just think of the ways in which one or another thinker has deemed God to be different from human beings:

From *American Philosophical Quarterly*, Vol. 22, (1985), pp. 221–30. Reprinted by permission of the editor.

(A) Incorporeality

(B) Infinity. This can be divided into:

   B_1. The unlimited realization of each 'perfection'.

   B_2. The exemplification of all perfections, every thing else equal it is better to be than not to be.

(C) Timelessness

(D) Absolute simplicity. No composition of any sort.

(E) Not *a* being. (God is rather 'Being-itself'.)

Even if (D) and (E) rule out any commonality of properties between God and man, it may still be, as I shall be arguing in this paper, that (A)–(C) do not.

As for the other side of the problem, let's first note the impossibility of avoiding *all* creaturely terms in thinking and speaking of God. We can avoid the crudest anthropomorphisms, speaking of God's hands, arms, and other bodily parts. But we cannot so easily avoid psychological and agential terms ('know', 'love', 'forgive', 'make') that are taken from our talk about ourselves. Suppose that we do carry out so heroic a renunciation and restrict ourselves to speaking of God in such terms as 'being itself', 'ground of being', 'supreme unity', and the like. Even so, we would not be avoiding all terms that apply to creatures, for example, 'being' and 'unity'. The notion of a 'ground' is presumably derived from the notion of *causality*, or perhaps the notion of a *necessary condition*, and both these terms apply to creatures. So long as we say anything at all, we will be using terms that apply to creatures, or terms derivative therefrom. Hence, so far as the aim at avoiding creaturely language is concerned, we may as well retain the more concrete mentalistic and agential concepts that are so central to the religious life.

But of course there are various ways in which creaturely terms can be used in speaking of God; and some of these may be ruled out by a certain form of otherness, and not others. These ways include:

(1) Straight univocity. Ordinary terms are used in the same ordinary senses of God and human beings.

(2) Modified univocity. Meanings can be defined or otherwise established such that terms can be used with those meanings of both God and human beings.

(3) Special literal meanings. Terms can be given, or otherwise take on, special technical senses in which they apply only to God.

(4) Analogy. Terms for creatures can be given analogical extensions so as to be applicable to God.

(5) Metaphor. Terms that apply literally to creatures can be metaphorically applied to God.

(6) Symbol. Ditto for 'symbol', in one or another meaning of that term.

The most radical partisans of otherness, from Dionysius through Aquinas to Tillich, plump for something in the (4)–(6) range and explicitly reject (1). The possibility of (3) has been almost wholly ignored, and (2) has not fared much better.

I can use this background to explain what I will do in this paper. First I shall be concentrating on the psychological terms we apply to God—'know', 'will', 'intend', 'love', and so on. I do not suppose it needs stressing that these are quite central to the way God is thought of in theistic religion. As creator, governor, and redeemer of the world God acts in the light of his perfect knowledge to carry out his purposes and intentions, and as an expression of his love for his creation. As is implicit in this last sentence, the divine psychology comes into our religious dealings with God as an essential background to divine action. God impinges on our lives primarily as agent, as one who does things—creates, guides, enjoins, punishes, redeems, and speaks. But action is an outgrowth of knowledge, purpose, and intention; unless we could credit these to God we would not be able to think of him as acting in these ways or in any other ways.

Second, I am going to work with a conception of God that involves modes of otherness (A)–(C), but stops short of a doctrine of absolute simplicity and does not deny that God is in any sense a being. There is no opportunity here to defend that choice; I will only say that I find the arguments for (D) and (E) quite unconvincing, and that this particular packaging has been a common one. Third, I shall seek to show that these modes of otherness are compatible with a degree of univocity in divine–human predication. I shall not go so far as to defend (1), though my position will be compatible with that strong a claim. I shall be arguing that, even if God differs from creatures as radically as this, we can still identify a common core of meaning in terms for human and divine psychological states, and that we can, at least, introduce terms to carry that meaning. If ordinary terms already carry just that meaning, so much the better. But whether or not that is the case, it will at least be possible to speak univocally, in an abstract fashion, of divine and human knowledge and purpose.

As my title indicates, I am going to exhibit this divine–human commonality by exploiting a functionalist account of human psychological concepts. But before getting into the details of that, I want to give a more general characterization of the sort of view of which my functionalist account is one version.

The most general idea behind the argument of this paper is that the common possession of abstract features is compatible with as great a difference as you like in the way in which these features are realized. A meeting and a train of thought can both be 'orderly', even though what it is for the one to be orderly is enormously different from what it is for the other to be orderly. A new computer and a new acquaintance can both be 'intriguing' in a single sense of the term, even though what makes the one intriguing is very different from what makes the other intriguing. This general point suggests the possibility that the radical otherness of God might manifest itself in the *way* in which common abstract features are realized in the divine being, rather than in the absence of common features. What it is for God to *make something* is radically different from what it is for a human being to make something; but that does not rule out an abstract feature in common, for example, that *by the exercise of agency something comes into existence.* It is something like the way in which a man and a wasp may both be *trying to reach a goal*, even though what it is for the one to try is enormously different from what it is for the other to try. Many theistic thinkers have moved too quickly from radical otherness to the impossibility of any univocity, neglecting this possibility that the otherness may come from the way in which common features are realized.[1]

More specifically, I shall be suggesting that there are abstract common properties that underlie the enormous differences between divine and human psychological states. By extricating and specifying these properties, we can form terms that apply univocally to God and man.

II.

The tools I shall use to exhibit this commonality are drawn from the movement in contemporary philosophy of mind called 'functionalism'. Functionalism has been propounded as a theory of the meaning of psychological terms in ordinary language and as a theory of the nature of psychological states and processes, whatever we mean by our ordinary terms for them.[2] Since we are concerned here with meanings of terms, I shall restrict attention to the former version. The basic idea, the source of the name, is that the concept[3] of a belief, desire, or intention is the concept of a particular *function* in the psychological economy, a particular 'job' done by the psyche. A belief is a structure that performs that job, and what psychological state it is—that it is a belief and a belief with that particular content—is determined by what that job is. In saying of a subject, S, that S believes that it will rain tomorrow, what we are attributing to S is a structure that performs this function. Our ordinary psychological terms carry no implications as to the intrinsic nature of the structure, its neurophysiological or soul-stuff character. No such information is embedded in our common-sense psychological conceptual scheme. Thus, on this view, psychological concepts are functional in the same way as many concepts of artefacts, for example, the concept of a loudspeaker. A loudspeaker is something the function of which is to convert electronic signals to sound. Its composition, its internal mechanism, and its external appearance

---

[1]The general thrust of the preceding paragraph is reminiscent of St Thomas's distinction between the property signified by a term and the mode of signifying (or the mode signified). Thomas says that for certain predicates that are applied both to God and to man, e.g. 'good', the property signified is common but the mode of signifying is not (*Summa Theologiae* Iae, xiii, 3; *Summa Contra Gentiles*, i, 30). That naturally suggests an elaboration in terms of underlying common abstract features that are realized in quite different ways. But neither Thomas nor the Thomistic tradition has seized the opportunity to locate an area of univocal predication.

[2]The latter version may be accompanied by proposals as to how psychological terms should be given meaning for theoretical purpose.

[3]I shall use 'The concept of *x* is...' interchangeably with 'The term '*x*' means...'.

can vary widely so long as it has that function. In thinking of something as a loudspeaker, we are thinking of it *in terms of* its function.

If this basic insight is to be exploited, we will have to specify the defining functions of various kinds of psychological states. One of the guiding principles of functionalism is that the basic function of the psyche is the regulation of behaviour. The point of having desires, aversions, likes and dislikes, interests and attitudes, is that they set goals for behaviour; and the point of having knowledge, beliefs, memories, perceptions, is that they provide us with the information we need to get around in our environment in the pursuit of those goals. In seeking to exploit these commonplaces in the analysis of psychological concepts, functionalism is following the lead of analytical behaviourism, one of its ancestors. Analytical behaviourism sought to construe a belief or a desire as a disposition to behave in a certain way, given certain conditions. Thus a belief that it is raining might be thought of as a set of dispositions that includes, for example, the disposition to carry an umbrella if one goes out. Behaviourism failed because it was committed to the thesis that each *individual* psychological state determines a set of dispositions to behaviour. Human beings just are not wired that simply. Whether I will carry an umbrella if I go out is determined not just by whether I believe that it is raining, but rather by that factor in conjunction with my desire to keep dry, my preferences with respect to alternative ways of keeping dry, my beliefs about the other consequences of carrying an umbrella, and so on. Even if I believe that it is raining I might not carry an umbrella, if I am wearing a raincoat and hat and I believe that is sufficient, or if I do not object to getting wet, or if I believe that I will project an unwanted image by carrying an umbrella. What I do is a function not just of a single psychological state but rather of the total psychological 'field' at the moment.

Functionalism, as an improved version of behaviourism, seeks to preserve the basic insight that the function of the psyche is the guidance of behaviour, while avoiding the simple-minded idea that each psychological state determines behavioural dispositions all by itself. It tries to bring this off by thinking of a belief, for example, as, indeed, related to potential behaviour, but only through the mediation of other psychological states. A belief that it is raining is, *inter alia*, a disposition to carry an umbrella if one is going outside, provided one has such-and-such other beliefs, desires, aversions, attitudes, etc. The concept of a belief is (in part) the concept of a certain way in which a state combines with other states and processes to determine behaviour.[4] And since other

---

[4]When the matter is put in this way, in terms of the *determination* of behaviour, it looks as if functionalism is committed to psychological determinism, and to the denial of free will in any sense in which it is incompatible with determinism. But the theory need not be stated in those terms. We could hold that one's current psychological state, at most, renders certain lines of behaviour more probable than others, and still state functionalism in terms of these probabilistic relationships.

psychological states have to be mentioned anyway, there is no bar to bringing purely intra-psychic transactions into the picture. Functionalism recognizes that a belief has the function of combining with other beliefs to produce inferentially still other beliefs, the function of combining with desires and aversions and other beliefs to produce other desires and aversions (as when my belief that I can't get a wanted object without earning money gives rise to a derivative desire to earn money), and the function of combining with desires to produce affective reactions (as when my belief that I have not been accepted to medical school combines with my desire to go to medical school to produce disappointment), as well as the function of combining with other psychological states to influence behaviour. Clearly a complete analysis of a psychological concept along functionalist lines would be an enormously complicated affair and perhaps beyond human power to achieve.[5]

Most contemporary formulations of functionalism are even wider than we have yet suggested. A typical recent statement is the following. 'Functionalism is the doctrine that pain (for example) is identical to a certain functional state, a state definable in terms of its causal relations to inputs, outputs, and other mental states.'[6] This brings into the picture the way in which sensory inputs create or affect psychological states, as well as the way the latter interact in the guidance of behaviour. Because of the focus of this paper, we will not be concerned about 'inputs' or any other influences on the genesis of psychological states. Since we are looking for concepts that could be applied to a timeless deity (as will appear in due course), such concepts will have nothing to say about how a state originates. And even apart from timelessness, a being of perfect, unlimited knowledge, power, and goodness will not acquire his knowledge via any sort of process. He will have it just by virtue of being what he is. Hence in this essay I shall restrict even human functionalist concepts to those that specify the ways in which a given kind of psychological state combines with another to affect behavioural output and other psychological states.

Behaviourism was a reductive theory, one that aspired to show that each psychological concept could be explained in purely non-psychological terms—physical antecedent conditions, physical behavioural response, plus

---

[5]For important formulations of functionalism, see N. Block, 'Troubles with Functionalism', in C. W. Savage (ed.), *Perception and Cognition: Issues in the Foundations of Psychology* (Minneapolis, 1978), and 'Are Absent Qualia Impossible?', *Philosophical Review* 89 (1980), pp. 257–74; D. Lewis, 'Psychophysical and Theoretical Identifications', *Australasian Journal of Philosophy* 50 (1972), pp. 249–58; and 'Mad Pain and Martian Pain', in N. Block (ed.), *Readings in the Philosophy of Psychology* (Cambridge, Mass., 1980); H. Putnam, *Philosophical Papers*, vol. 2, *Mind, Language and Reality* (Cambridge, 1981), chs. 18–21; S. Shoemaker, 'Some Varieties of Functionalism', *Philosophical Topics* 12 (1981); and R. van Gulick, 'Functionalism, Information, and Content', *Nature and System* 2 (1980), pp. 139–62.

[6]Block, 'Are Absent Qualia Impossible?', p. 257. The reference to 'inputs' and 'outputs' reflects the computer orientation of functionalism, of which more below. The 'output' on which we have been concentrating is behaviour.

the overall dispositional structure. But since functionalism does not take psychological states individually to determine behavioural dispositions, it cannot aspire to reduce or eliminate psychological concepts one by one. A functional definition of any given psychological term will include many other psychological terms. If any such reduction is to be effected, it will have to be a wholesale affair.[7] For our purposes we are not interested in functionalism as a reductive theory. For that matter, the use to which I am going to put functionalism does not even require that any (much less every) psychological concept has to do solely with functional role. Critics of functionalism have contended that a belief cannot be completely characterized in functional terms, since that leaves out the distinctive 'intentionality', the 'about-ness', characteristic of the mind. And it has also been contended that feelings and sensations cannot be adequately characterized in terms of functional role, since that leaves out their distinctive 'qualitative' or 'phenomenal' character. For our purposes it doesn't matter whether those criticisms are justified; it doesn't matter whether a concept of a functional role does the whole job. As will appear in the sequel, it will be enough if our concept of a given type of psychological state is, *in part*, the concept of a functional role.

III.

With this background we are in a position to bring out how functionalism can help us to reconcile a degree of univocity with the radical otherness of the divine. The crucial point is one that was just now made in passing, viz., that a functional concept of X is non-committal as to the intrinsic nature, character, composition or structure of X. In conceiving of a 0 in functional terms we are simply thinking of a 0 in terms of its function (or some of its functions), in terms of the job(s) it is fitted to do. So long as something has that function it will count as a 0, whatever sort of thing it is otherwise, whatever it is like in itself. One of the main sources of functionalism in the philosophy of mind is the attempt to use our knowledge of computers to throw light on the mind and mental functioning, and, conversely, to understand the sense in which mental terms can be used to characterize the activities of computers. Functionalism is well fitted to bring out a sense in which it might well be true that mental terms (or some of them) apply univocally to human beings and to computers. For if the concept of recalling that p or the concept of perceiving that p is a concept of a certain *function*, then this same concept might well apply to beings as different in their composition, nature, and structure

---

[7] For a suggestion as to how this can be done, see Lewis, 'Psychophysical and Theoretical Identifications'.

as a human organism and a computer.[8] Since in saying that S recalled that *p* we are, on the functionalist interpretation, not committing ourselves as to whether a neurophysiological, an electronic, or a purely spiritual process was involved, the concept might apply in the same sense to systems of all those sorts. This point is often put by saying that a given functional property or state can have different, even radically different, 'realizations'.

The application to theological predication should be obvious, in its main lines. The same functional concept of knowledge that *p*, or of purpose to bring about R, could be applicable to God and to man, even though the realization of that function is radically different, even though what it is to know that *p* is radically different in the two cases. We can preserve the point that the divine life is wholly mysterious to us, that we can form no notion of what it is like to be God, to know or to purpose as God does, while still thinking of God in terms that we understand because they apply to us.

But of course the obviousness of the application is no guarantee that it will work. Even if functional psychological terms apply univocally to man and computer, to man and beast, and even to man and angel, there could still be Creator–creature differences that make common functions impossible. So we will have to get down to the details.

Whether any functional properties can be common to God and man, and if so which, depends on what divine–human differences there are. It will be recalled that we are working with a conception of God as differing from human beings in three main respects: incorporeality, timelessness, and infinity. We shall consider them in turn.

Can an immaterial spiritual being perform (some of) the same psychological functions as an embodied human being? Are functional psychological concepts neutral as between physical and non-physical realizations, as well as between different sorts of physical realizations? It would seem so.[9] If a functional concept really is non-committal as to what kind of mechanism, structure, or agency carries out the function, then it should be non-committal as to whether this is any kind of physical agency, as well as to what kind of physical agency it is if physical. To be sure, if human psychological functioning is, in large part, the guidance of behaviour, then behaviour guidance will figure heavily in human psychological concepts. The concept of the belief that it is raining will be, in considerable part, the concept of some state that joins with psychological states of various other kinds in certain ways to produce tendencies to behaviour. If such concepts are to apply to God, then God will have to be capable of behaviour, and it

---

[8]I am by no means endorsing the view that psychological terms apply univocally to human beings and computers. I am merely indicating one application that has been made of the feature of functional concepts under discussion.

[9]A prominent functionalist without dualist or theological sympathies, Hilary Putnam, has stressed this conceptual possibility (*Mind, Language and Reality*, p. 436).

might be thought that this is impossible without a body. If God has no body to move, how can he *do* anything, in the same sense in which an embodied human being does things? But this is not an insuperable difficulty. The core concept of human action is not *movement of one's own body*, but rather *bringing about a change in the world—directly or indirectly—by an act of will, decision, or intention.* That concept can be intelligibly applied to a purely spiritual deity. It is just that we will have to think of God as bringing about changes in the 'external' world directly by an act of will—not indirectly through moving his body, as in our case.[10]

Timelessness, like immateriality, may seem to inhibit the application of functional concepts. How can an atemporal being *carry out* or *perform* a function, something that, like all activities, requires a temporal duration? This consideration does show that we shall have to abandon the term 'function' in its strictest sense; but that does not mean that we shall have to give up the project of applying to God what functionalism calls 'functional concepts'. We have already noted that functionalists broaden out the strict notion of a function into the view that a functional concept of a state, S, is the concept of the causal relations in which S stands to inputs, outputs, and other states. Now if causality is thought to require temporal succession, such concepts too will be inapplicable to a timeless being. Rather than get into an argument over that, I will loosen the requirements one more notch and say that a functional concept of S is a concept of *law-like connections* in which S stands with other states and with outputs.[11] Some such connections involve temporal sequence (as with causal laws of the 'Lighting the fuse produces an explosion' type) and some do not. For an example of the latter type, consider: 'If S wants X more than anything else and realizes that doing A is necessary for getting X, and believes that doing A is possible, then S will intend to do A.' This is a 'law of co-existence'. It tells us what intention S has now if S's current beliefs, desires, etc., are related *now* as specified. Of course a human being would normally have arrived at these desires, beliefs, etc., by some kind of process, which would often have included some process of deliberation, but this particular law-like statement doesn't get into any of that. It simply specifies what intention a subject will have at a given time, provided it has the other psychological states specified at that time. There is no reason why such regularities should not enter into a functional psychological concept, and a concept wholly made up of such regularities could apply to a timeless being.

To be sure, common-sense concepts of human psychological states are not made up wholly of such 'laws of co-existence', but also include

---

[10]For a detailed exposition of the point, see my 'Can We Speak Literally of God?', in A. D. Steuer and J. W. McClendon, Jr. (eds.), *Is God GOD?* (Nashville, 1981).

[11]See above for the explanation of why 'input' has been omitted.

'laws of temporal succession', such as: 'If S considers whether it is the case that *p*, and in the course of this consideration brings to consciousness his beliefs that *If q then p* and *q*, then S will come to believe that *p*.' And this suffices to show that our ordinary concepts of human psychological states cannot be applied in their entirety to a timeless being. But I have already disavowed any intention to show that any of the psychological terms we commonly apply to creatures can, in precisely the same sense, be applied to God. I am only seeking to show that terms for psychological functions can be devised that apply in just the same sense to God and to creature. What the above considerations show is that we could form functional psychological concepts that are made up wholly of laws of co-existence, and that could apply univocally to creatures and to a timeless Creator. Or at least these considerations indicate that the timelessness of the Creator is no bar to this.

IV.

In considering the infinity of God we will have to further restrict the range of functional psychological concepts that are applicable to God. We are understanding 'infinity' here as the absence of any imperfections and the possession of all perfections. Thus among the modes of divine infinity will be omnipotence, omniscience, and perfect goodness.

Let's begin by considering the sort of behaviour guidance principle that functionalists take to be partly constitutive of the concepts of beliefs and wants. Here is the most simple-minded version.

(1) If S wants that *p* and believes that doing A will bring it about that *p*, then S will do A.

This will not do. The antecedent might be true and yet S not do A, and this for a number of reasons.

(A) S may want something else more than she wants *p*.
(B) S may have a stronger aversion to doing A or to something she believes to be a consequence or accompaniment of *p*.
(C) S may believe that doing B would also lead to *p* and may prefer doing B to doing A.
(D) S may have scruples against doing A.
(E) S may not have the capacity or opportunity to do A.
(F) S may be prevented from carrying out an intention to do A by some emotional upset.

A natural way of taking account of these complexities is to change (1) to:

(2) If S wants that p and believes that doing A will bring about p, then S has a *tendency* to do A.

Having a tendency to do A is a state that will lead to doing A, given ability and opportunity, provided it is not opposed by stronger tendencies. At a given moment the 'motivational field' will contain a number of competing tendencies, and what is actually done will depend on which of these tendencies is the strongest.[12]

Now let's consider whether this kind of law-like connection could be partly constitutive of any divine psychological state, and if not what modifications would be required. The first point that may strike the reader is the inappropriateness of attributing wants to the deity. And so it is, if 'want' is taken to imply lack or deficiency. However, even if this is true of the most common psychological sense of the term (and I doubt that it is), it is easy to modify that sense so as to avoid that implication. What we need for our purposes, and for purposes of human psychology, is a sense in which a want is any 'goal-setting' state. This sense is sufficiently characterized by (2). Anyone in whom a belief that A *will lead to p* increases the tendency to do A, thereby has a want for p in this sense.

In this broad sense 'want' ranges over a vast diversity of goal-setting human psychological states—aversions, likes, interests, attitudes, internalized moral standards, and so on. It is an important question for human motivation whether all 'wants', in the broad sense, operate according to the same dynamic laws. But be this as it may, it is noteworthy for our present concerns that there is no such diversity in the divine psyche. God is subject to no biological cravings, rooted in the needs for survival. Since God is perfectly good, he wants nothing that runs contrary to what he sees to be best, and so there is no discrepancy between what he wants and what he recognizes to be right and good. He does not pursue goals in sudden gusts of passion or uncontrollable longing. And so on. This means that a lot of the complexity of human motivation drops out. 'Recognizing that it is good that p' would be a better term for the 'goal-setting' state in the divine psyche.

Here is another simplification. In human motivation we can think of the various current action tendencies as interacting to produce a winner, an intention to do something right away. Whether this intention to do A actually issues in doing A will depend on the current state of S's abilities, and on co-operation from the environment. But God's abilities are always in perfect condition, and he needs no such co-operation. Therefore there can never be a gap between divine intention and action. But then is there any point in inserting intention as an intermediary between the field of tendencies and

---

[12]Again, this may seem to rule out free will. However, if we wish we can include the will as one source of tendencies, and hold that whenever a subject makes a strong enough effort of will, the tendency so engendered will be stronger than any other tendency.

action? Can't we just say that what God sees to be best (or what he chooses between incompatible equal goods) he *does?* So it would seem.

I have been talking as if God apprehends or recognizes the comparative goodness of various possible states of affairs and acts accordingly, actualizing those that are good enough to warrant it. This presupposes that the values are independent of God's will, that he *recognizes* them to be as they are. But many theologians have protested against this, on the ground that it limits God's sovereignty by assuming a realm of values that exists and is what it is independently of his creative activity. The 'voluntarists' who put forward this argument think of values as themselves being created by an act of the divine will. Hence God's will is not guided by his apprehension of values, at least not primordially. I will not try to decide between these two powerful theological traditions in this paper. Instead I will point out that a functionalist account of the divine psychology can accommodate either, though the precise form taken by the account will be correspondingly different. On a voluntarist view there will either be a single primordial act of will that sets up values and standards, after which action is guided by apprehensions of the values so constituted; or else many divine decisions are constitutive of value. However, on either version there will still be many divine acts that are guided by the values so constituted. Whereas, on the opposite view, 'intellectualism' as we might call it, all divine volition and action is guided by divine apprehension of the inherent value qualities of alternative possibilities. Thus the main bearing of these differences on functionalism stems from the fact that for voluntarism, but not for intellectualism, there is at least one action that is not guided by apprehensions of value. Nevertheless, the general account of the function of cognition and wants in the guidance of behaviour will be the same on both views.

Turning now to the cognitive side of behaviour guidance, there are problems about the application of 'belief' to God, somewhat analogous to the problems about 'want'. 'Belief' in the sense in which it is contrasted with knowledge, 'mere belief', does not apply to God. Since God is a perfect cognizer, he has no beliefs that do not count as knowledge. But even if we are thinking of a wider sense of 'belief', in which when S believes that p, S may or may not know that p, the whole point of having that sense is that a subject *may* believe that p without knowing that p. Since that possibility is lacking for God, the term 'belief' loses its point in application to him. Therefore we will speak most felicitously about the divine motivation if we simply substitute 'know' for 'believe' wherever cognition enters in.

Where does this leave us with respect to the cognitive guidance of behaviour in the divine psychology? To turn the question around, what behaviour guidance principles figure in concepts of divine cognitive states? First of all, as we have seen, evaluative apprehensions play a crucial role on an intellectualist construal and a lesser role on a voluntarist construal. Second, does God's knowledge of the existing situation exercise any guiding role? Here we must take account of another theological controversy, this time over whether God determines every detail of creation. Those who hold that he does will not recognize any action of God, with respect to the created world, other than His creation of that world in all its details. There is nothing else for him to do. *We* may think of God as reacting to successive stages of the world as they unfold, but that is because we are, illegitimately, thinking of God as moving through time, responding to successive phases of the world process as it unfolds. If God is timeless, he decides on and constitutes the entire affair in one act of will—the beginning of the universe and all of its successive stages, including anything that looks to us like *ad hoc* responses of God at a particular time. From this perspective, God's knowledge of how things are in the world plays no guiding role in his behaviour, which wholly consists of the one complex act of determining every detail of the world. That act is not guided by an awareness of how things are in the world, since apart from the completed act there is no way in which things are. Cognitive guidance of behaviour is limited to evaluative apprehension.

Suppose, on the other hand, that God does not determine every detail of creation. He voluntarily abstains from determining the choices of free agents like human beings. This means that there will be certain aspects of creation that he does not know about just by knowing his own creative acts. With respect to the choices of free agents and states of affairs affected by them, he will have to 'look and see' how things came out in order to know what they are. If he is timeless he does not have to '*wait* and see'; all of his knowledge and activity is comprised in one 'eternal now'. Nevertheless, his activity *vis-à-vis* the world is divided into (*a*) original creation *ex nihilo*, and (*b*) activity directed to states of affairs that, in part, are what they are independently of divine fiat. Creative activity of this latter sort *will* be guided by his knowledge of these states of affairs.

Next, let's turn to another sort of regularity that enters into concepts of human cognitive states, viz., that based on inferential relations. One of the functions that makes a belief that *p* the state it is, is its tendency to enter with other beliefs into inferences that generate further beliefs. Thus the belief that Jim is Sam's only blood-related uncle tends to give rise to the belief that Sam's parents have only one brother between them; it also tends to combine with the beliefs that Jim is childless and that Sam has no aunt to produce the belief that Sam has no first cousins.

Now a timeless deity will not carry out inferences, since this requires a temporal duration. Indeed, an omniscient deity will not *derive* any of its knowledge from inference, or even from an atemporal analogue of inference; for any true proposition, *p*, such a deity will automatically know that *p* without needing to base it on something else he knows. So inferential regularities cannot be even partly constitutive of concepts that apply to God. But suitable analogues of such regularities may be available. It will still be true that, whatever God knows, he knows all the logical consequences thereof, knows that all probabilistic consequences thereof are probable, knows that all contradictories thereof are false, and so on. That is, there is a certain structure to divine knowledge that corresponds to logical relationships, and corresponds much more closely than any body of human knowledge.

The discussion of this section indicates that the divine psyche is much simpler than the human psyche in the variety of its constituents. Assuming God to be atemporal, it involves no processes or activities, no sequences of events. There are no beliefs as distinct from knowledge, and hence no distinction of degrees of firmness of belief. Propositional knowledge is all intuitive, the simple recognition that p. There is no distinction between wants, cravings, longings, and the sense that something ought to be done. There is only one kind of goal-setting state, which could perhaps best be characterized as the recognition that something is good or right. There are no bursts of passion or emotional upsets to interfere with rational motivational processes. There is no point in distinguishing between a present intention to do A and doing A intentionally. Though God may not be as simple as St Thomas supposed, it is true that much of the complexity of human psychological functioning drops out. The complexity of human psychology is largely due to our limitations: to the fallibility of our cognition, the internal opposition to rational decision making, the limitations of our capacities, and the relative irrationality of our intellectual processes.

V.

Where do all these differences leave our project of identifying psychological commonalities in God and human beings? We have discovered a vast reduction in the number of distinct types of divine psychological states, in comparison with the human estate. But that is quite compatible with important commonalities in states of those types. How does the matter stand in that regard? Let's see just how divine psychological states could be functionally construed, adopting a non-voluntarist position for the sake of illustration. As for the cognitive side, a divine recognition that it would be good that p can be construed, in part, as a state that will give rise to the action of bringing about p unless God recognizes something logically incompatible with p as a greater or equal good.[13] On the cognitive side, God's knowledge that p can be construed as a state that (a) will carry with it the knowledge of everything logically entailed by p and exclude the knowledge of anything contradictory to p, and (b) gives rise to action that is appropriate to p, given what God sees to be good.[14] Do functional concepts like this apply to human beings?

---

[13]If God apprehended something incompatible to be equally good, he still might bring about p, but he would not necessarily do so.

[14]As we saw earlier, (b) is applicable only if God does not determine every detail of the created world.

They do not apply just as they stand, because of the human limitations we have just noted. A human being does not know, or believe, everything entailed by what she knows or believes, nor does she fail to believe everything logically incompatible with what she believes. A human being does not always (or even usually) do what she recognizes to be the best thing to do in the circumstances, even assuming that she correctly assesses the circumstances. But these differences do not prevent a significant commonality in functional psychological states. This commonality can best be brought out by constructing tendency versions of the law-like generalizations imbedded in the functional concepts just articulated, and attributing them to human beings. Thus we can ascribe to a human being a *tendency* to believe whatever is entailed by what she knows or believes, and a tendency to reject what is incompatible with what she knows or believes. And we can regard these tendencies as partly constitutive of the concepts of belief and knowledge. Likewise, we can say of a human being that she will tend to do what she can to bring about what she recognizes to be best in a given situation, and we can take this tendency to be partly constitutive of the concept of recognizing something to be best. We can then formulate the divine regularities in tendency terms also. Thus it will be true of God also that if he recognizes that it is good that p he will tend to bring about p in so far as he can, unless he recognizes something incompatible with p to be a greater good.[15] These tendency statements about God constitute a limiting case in which the qualifications are vacuous, since God can do anything he chooses to do, and since God is not subject to non-rational interferences in carrying out what he recognizes to be good. Nevertheless, they are true of God.

I take it that this brings out a significant commonality of meaning between psychological terms applicable to God and to man. Even though there is no carry-over of the complete package from one side of the divide to the other, there is a core of meaning in common. And the distinctive features on the divine side simply consist in the dropping out of creaturely limitations. Thus a functional approach to psychological concepts makes it possible to start with human psychological concepts and create psychological concepts that literally apply to God, thus generating theological statements that un-problematically possess truth values.[16] This saves us from the morass of an unqualified pan-symbolism, and makes possible a modicum of unquestionably cognitive discourse about God.[17]

---

[15]The 'or equal' (see note 13 and text above) drops out when the generalization is in terms of a tendency. God will still have a tendency to bring about p even if something incompatible is equally good, and even if that other alternative is chosen.

[16]Or at least the predicates present no bar to the attribution of truth values.

[17]This paper has profited from comments by Jonathan Bennett.

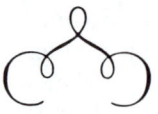

SPACE, TIME, AND CREATION

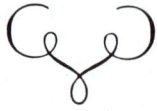

ST. AUGUSTINE

God's Will and the Beginning of the Universe

In this Beginning, O God, hast Thou made heaven and earth, in Thy Word, in Thy Son, in Thy Power, in Thy Wisdom, in Thy Truth; wondrously speaking, and wondrously making. Who shall comprehend? Who declare it? What is that which gleams through me, and strikes my heart without hurting it; and I shudder and kindle? I shudder, inasmuch as I am unlike it; I kindle, inasmuch as I am like it. It is Wisdom, Wisdom's self which gleameth through me; severing my cloudiness which yet again mantles over me, fainting from it, through the darkness which for my punishment gathers upon me. For my strength is brought down in need, so that I cannot support my blessings, till Thou, Lord, Who hast been gracious to all mine iniquities, shalt heal all my infirmities. For Thou shalt also redeem my life from corruption, and crown me with loving kindness and tender mercies, and shalt satisfy my desire with good things, because my youth shall be renewed like an eagle's. For in hope we are saved, wherefore we through patience wait for Thy promises. Let him that is able hear Thee inwardly discoursing out of Thy oracle: I will boldly cry out. How wonderful are Thy works, O Lord, in Wisdom hast Thou made them all; and this Wisdom is the Beginning, and in that Beginning didst Thou make heaven and earth.

Lo, are they not full of their old leaven who say to us, "What was God doing before He made heaven and earth? For if (say they) He were unemployed and wrought not, why does He not also henceforth, and for ever, as He did heretofore? For did any new motion arise in God, and a new will to make a creature which He had never before made, how then would that be a true eternity, where there ariseth a will which was not? For the will of God

From St. Augustine's *Confessions* (397–401), Book XI.

is not a creature, but before the creature; seeing nothing could be created, unless the will of the Creator had preceded. The will of God then belongeth to His very Substance. And if aught have arisen in God's Substance which before was not, that Substance cannot be truly called eternal. But if the will of God has been from eternity that the creature should be, why was not the creature also from eternity?"

Who speak thus, do not yet understand Thee, O Wisdom of God, Light of souls, understand not yet how the things be made, which by Thee and in Thee are made; yet they strive to comprehend things eternal, whilst their heart fluttereth between the motions of things past and to come, and is still unstable. Who shall hold it, and fix it, that it be settled awhile, and awhile catch the glory of that ever-fixed Eternity, and compare it with the times which are never fixed, and see that it cannot be compared; and that a long time cannot become long, but out of many motions passing by, which cannot be prolonged altogether; but that in the Eternal nothing passeth, but the whole is present; whereas no time is all at once present; and that all time past is driven on by time to come, and all to come followeth upon the past; and all past and to come is created, and flows out of that which is ever present? Who shall hold the heart of man, that it may stand still, and see how eternity, ever still-standing, neither past nor to come, uttereth the times past and to come? Can my hand do this, or the hand of my mouth by speech bring about a thing so great?

See, I answer him that asketh, "What did God before He made heaven and earth?" I answer not as one is said to have done merrily (eluding the pressure of the question): "He was preparing hell (saith he) for pryers into mysteries." It is one thing to answer enquiries, another to make sport of enquirers. So I answer not; for rather had I answer, "I know not" what I know not, than so as to raise a laugh at him who asketh deep things and gain praise for one who answereth false things. But I say that Thou, our God, art the Creator of every creature; and, if by the name "heaven and earth" every creature be understood, I boldly say, "that before God made heaven and earth, He did not make anything. For if He made, what did He make but a creature?" And would I knew whatsoever I desire to know to my profit, as I know that no creature was made before there was made any creature.

But if any excursive brain rove over the images of forepassed times, and wonder that Thou the God Almighty and All-creating and All-supporting, Maker of heaven and earth, didst for innumerable ages forbear from so great a work, before Thou wouldest make it; let him awake and consider that he wonders at false conceits. For whence could innumerable ages pass by, which Thou madest not, Thou the Author and Creator of all ages? or what times should there be, which were not made by Thee? or how should they pass by, if they never were? Seeing then Thou art the Creator of all times, if any time was before Thou madest heaven and earth, why say they that Thou didst forego working? For that very time didst Thou make, nor could times pass by before thou madest those times. But if before heaven and earth there was no time, why is it demanded what Thou then didst? For there was no "then," when there was no time.

Nor dost Thou by time precede time; else shouldest Thou not precede all times. But Thou precedest all things past, by the sublimity of an ever-present eternity; and surpassest all future because they are future, and when they come, they shall be past; but "Thou art the Same, and Thy years fail not." Thy years neither come nor go; whereas ours both come and go, that they all may come. Thy years stand together, because they do stand; nor are departing thrust out by coming years, for they pass not away; but ours shall all be, when they shall no more be. Thy years are one day; and Thy day is not daily, but Today, seeing Thy Today gives not place unto tomorrow, for neither doth it replace yesterday. Thy Today is Eternity; therefore didst Thou beget the Coeternal, to whom Thou saidst, "This day have I begotten Thee." Thou hast made all things; and before all times Thou art; neither in any time was time not.

G. W. LEIBNIZ AND SAMUEL CLARKE

Controversy on Time and Creation

G. W. LEIBNIZ:

3. These gentlemen maintain therefore, that space is a real absolute being. But this involves them in great difficulties; for such a being must needs be eternal and infinite. Hence some have believed it to be God himself, or, one of his attributes, his immensity. But since space consists of parts, it is not a thing which can belong to God.

4. As for my own opinion, I have said more than once, that I hold space to be something merely relative, as time is; that I hold it to be an order of co-existences, as time is an order of successions. For space denotes, in terms of possibility, an order of things which exist at the same time, considered as existing together; without enquiring into their manner of existing. And when many things are seen together, one perceives that order of things among themselves.

From the Leibniz–Clarke Correspondence, published 1717.

5. I have many demonstrations, to confute the fancy of those who take space to be a substance, or at least an absolute being. But I shall only use, at the present, one demonstration, which the author here gives me occasion to insist upon. I say then, that if space was an absolute being, there would something happen for which it would be impossible there should be a sufficient reason. Which is against my axiom. And I prove it thus. Space is something absolutely uniform; and, without the things placed in it, one point of space does not absolutely differ in any respect whatsoever from another point of space. Now from hence it follows, (supposing space to be something in itself, besides the order of bodies among themselves,) that 'tis impossible there should be a reason, why God, preserving the same situations of bodies among themselves, should have placed them in space after one certain particular manner, and not otherwise; why every thing was not placed the quite contrary way, for instance, by changing East into West. But if space is nothing else, but that order or relation; and is nothing at all without bodies, but the possibility of placing them; then those two states, the one such as it now is, the other supposed to be the quite contrary way, would not at all differ from one another. Their difference therefore is only to be found in our chimerical supposition of the reality of space in itself. But in truth the one would exactly be the same thing as the other, they being absolutely indiscernible; and consequently there is no room to enquire after a reason of the preference of the one to the other.

6. The case is the same with respect to time. Supposing any one should ask, why God did not create every thing a year sooner; and the same person should infer from thence, that God has done something, concerning which 'tis not possible there should be a reason, why he did it so, and not otherwise: the answer is, that his inference would be right, if time was any thing distinct from things existing in time. For it would be impossible there should be any reason, why things should be applied to such particular instants, rather than to others, their succession continuing the same. But then the same argument proves, that instants, consider'd without the things, are nothing at all; and that they consist only in the successive order of things: which order remaining the same, one of the two states, viz. that of a supposed anticipation, would not at all differ, nor could be discerned from, the other which now is.

7. It appears from what I have said, that my axiom has not been well understood; and that the author denies it, tho' he seems to grant it. 'Tis true, says he, that there is nothing without a sufficient reason why it is, and why it is thus, rather than otherwise: but he adds, that this sufficient reason, is often the simple or mere will of God: as, when it is asked why matter was not placed otherwhere in space; the same situations of bodies among themselves being preserved. But this is plainly maintaining, that God wills something, without any sufficient reason for his will: against the axiom, or the general

rule of whatever happens. This is falling back into the loose indifference, which I have confuted at large, and showed to be absolutely chimerical even in creatures, and contrary to the wisdom of God, as if he could operate without acting by reason.

8. The author objects against me, that if we don't admit this simple and mere will, we take away from God the power of choosing, and bring in a fatality. But the quite contrary is true. I maintain that God has the power of choosing, since I ground that power upon the reason of a choice agreeable to his wisdom. And 'tis not this fatality, (which is only the wisest order of providence) but a blind fatality or necessity, void of all wisdom and choice, which we ought to avoid.

SAMUEL CLARKE:

4. If space was nothing but the order of things coexisting; it would follow, that if God should remove in a straight line the whole material world entire, with any swiftness whatsoever; yet it would still always continue in the same place: and that nothing would receive any shock upon the most sudden stopping of that motion. And if time was nothing but the order of succession of created things; it would follow, that if God had created the world millions of ages sooner than he did, yet it would not have been created at all the sooner. Further: space and time are quantities; which situation and order are not.

5. The argument in this paragraph, is; that because space is uniform or alike, and one part does not differ from another; therefore the bodies created in one place, if they had been created in another place, (supposing them to keep the same situation with regard to each other,) would still have been created in the same place as before: which is a manifest contradiction. The uniformity of space, does indeed prove, that there could be no (external) reason why God should create things in one place rather than in another: but does that hinder his own will, from being to itself a sufficient reason of acting in any place, when all places are indifferent or alike, and there be good reason to act in some place?

6. The same reasoning takes place here, as in the foregoing.

7 and 8. Where there is any difference in the nature of things, there the consideration of that difference always determines an intelligent and perfectly wise agent. But when two ways of acting are equally and alike good, (as in the instances before mentioned;) to affirm in such case, that God cannot act at all, or that 'tis no perfection in him to be able to act, because he can have no external reason to move him to act one way rather than the other, seems to be a denying God to have in himself any original principle or power of beginning to act, but that he must needs (as it were mechanically) be always determined by things extrinsic.

NICHOLAS WOLTERSTORFF

God Everlasting

All Christian theologians agree that God is without beginning and without end. The vast majority have held, in addition, that God is *eternal*, existing outside of time. Only a small minority have contended that God is *everlasting*, existing within time.[1] In what follows I shall take up the cudgels for that minority, arguing that God as conceived and presented by the biblical writers is a being whose own life and existence is temporal.

The biblical writers do not present God as some passive factor within reality but as an agent in it. Further, they present him as acting within *human* history. The god they present is neither the impassive god of the Oriental nor the nonhistorical god of the Deist. Indeed, so basic to the biblical writings is their speaking of God as agent within history that if one viewed God as only an impassive factor in reality, or as one whose agency does not occur within human history, one would have to regard the biblical speech about God as at best one long sequence of metaphors pointing to a reality for which they are singularly inept, and as at worst one long sequence of falsehoods.

More specifically, the biblical writers present God as a redeeming God. From times most ancient, man has departed from the pattern of responsibilities awarded him at his creation by God. A multitude of evils has followed. But God was not content to leave man in the mire of his misery. Aware of what is going on, he has resolved, in response to man's sin and its resultant evils, to bring about renewal. He has, indeed, already been acting in accord with that resolve, centrally and decisively in the life, death, and resurrection of Jesus Christ.

What I shall argue is that if we are to accept this picture of God as acting for the renewal of human life, we must conceive of him as everlasting rather than eternal. God the Redeemer cannot be a God eternal. This is so because God the Redeemer is a God who *changes*. And any being which changes is a being among whose states there is temporal succession. Of course, there is an important sense in which God as presented in the Scriptures is changeless: he is steadfast in his redeeming intent and ever faithful to his children. Yet, *ontologically*, God cannot be a redeeming God without there being changeful variation among his states.

[1]The most noteworthy contemporary example is Oscar Cullmann, *Christ and Time* (Eng. tr., Philadelphia, 1950).

If this argument proves correct the importance of the issue here confronting us for Christian theology can scarcely be exaggerated. A theology which opts for God as eternal cannot avoid being in conflict with the confession of God as redeemer. And given the obvious fact that God is presented in the Bible as a God who redeems, a theology which opts for God as eternal cannot be a theology faithful to the biblical witness.

Our line of argument will prove to be neither subtle nor complicated. So the question will insistently arise, why have Christian theologians so massively contended that God is eternal? Why has not the dominant tradition of Christian theology been that of God everlasting?

Our argument will depend heavily on taking with seriousness a certain feature of temporality which has been neglected in Western philosophy. But the massiveness of the God eternal tradition cannot, I am persuaded, be attributed merely to philosophical oversight. There are, I think, two factors more fundamental. One is the feeling, deep-seated in much of human culture, that the flowing of events into an irrecoverable and unchangeable past is a matter for deep regret. Our bright actions and shining moments do not long endure. The gnawing tooth of time bites all. And our evil deeds can never be undone. They are forever to be regretted. Of course, the philosopher is inclined to distinguish the mere fact of temporality from the actual pattern of the events in history and to argue that regrets about the latter should not slosh over into regrets about the former. The philosopher is right. The regrettableness of what transpires in time is not good ground for regretting that there is time. Yet where the philosopher sees the possibility and the need for a distinction, most people have seen none. Regrets over the pervasive pattern of what transpires within time have led whole societies to place the divine outside of time— freed from the "bondage" of temporality.

But I am persuaded that William Kneale is correct when he contends that the most important factor accounting for the tradition of God eternal within Christian theology was the influence of the classical Greek philosophers on the early theologians.[2] The distinction between eternal being and everlasting being was drawn for the first time in the history of thought by Plato (*Timaeus* 37–38), though the language he uses is reminiscent of words used still earlier by Parmenides. Plato does not connect eternity and divinity, but he does make clear his conviction that eternal being is the highest form of reality. This was enough to influence the early Christian theologians, who did their thinking within the milieu of Hellenic and Hellenistic thought, to assign eternity to God. Thus was the fateful choice made.

---

[2]William Kneale, "Time and Eternity in Theology," *Proceedings of the Aristotelian Society* (1961).

A good many twentieth-century theologians have been engaged in what one might call the dehellenization of Christian theology. If Kneale's contention is correct, then in this essay I am participating in that activity. Of course, not every bit of dehellenization is laudatory from the Christian standpoint, for not everything that the Greeks said is false. What is the case, though, is that the patterns of classical Greek thought are incompatible with the pattern of biblical thought. And in facing the issue of God everlasting versus God eternal we are dealing with the fundamental pattern of biblical thought. Indeed, I am persuaded that unless the tradition of God eternal is renounced, fundamental dehellenizing will perpetually occupy itself in the suburbs, never advancing to the city center. Every attempt to purge Christian theology of the traces of incompatible Hellenic patterns of thought must fail unless it removes the roadblock of the God eternal tradition. Around this barricade there are no detours.

I.

Before we can discuss whether God is outside of time we must ask what it would be for something to be outside of time. That is, before we can ask whether God is eternal we must ask what it would be for something to be eternal. But this in turn demands that we are clear on what it would be for something to be a temporal entity. We need not be clear on all the features which something has by virtue of being temporal—on all facets of temporality—but we must at least be able to say what is necessary and sufficient for something's being in time.

For our purposes we can take as the decisive feature of temporality the exemplification of the temporal ordering-relations of precedence, succession, and simultaneity. Unless some entities did stand to each other in one or the other of these relations, there would be no temporal reality. Conversely, if there is temporal reality then there are pairs of entities whose members stand to each other in the relation of one occurring before (precedence) or one occurring after (succession) or one occurring simultaneously with (simultaneity) the other.

We must ask in turn what sort of entity is such that its examples can stand to each other in the relations of precedence, succession, and simultaneity. For not every sort of entity is such. The members of a pair of trees cannot stand in these relations. The golden chain tree outside my back door neither occurs before nor after nor simultaneously with the shingle oak outside my front door. Of course, *the sprouting of the former* stands in one of these relations to *the sprouting of the latter;* and so too does *the demise of the latter* to *the demise of the former.* But the trees themselves do not. They do not occur at all.

We have in this example a good clue, though, as to the sort of entity whose examples can stand in the relations of precedence, succession, and simultaneity. It is just such entities as *the demise of my golden chain tree* and *the sprouting of my shingle oak*. It is, in short, what I shall call events that stand in these relations.

As I conceive of an event, it consists in something's actually having some property, or something's actually performing some action, or something's actually standing in some relation to something. Events as I conceive them are all actual occurrences. They are not what *can have* occurrences. They are, rather, themselves occurrences. Furthermore, as I conceive of events, there may be two or more events consisting in a given entity's having a given property (or performing a given action). For example, my golden chain tree flowered last spring and is flowering again this spring. So there are two events each consisting in the flowering of my golden chain tree. One began and ended last year. The other began and will end this year.

Such events as I have thus far offered by way of example are all temporally limited, in the sense that there are times at which the event is not occurring. There are times at which it has not yet begun or has already ended. Last year's flowering of my golden chain tree is such. It began at some time last spring and has now for about a year or so ceased. But there are other events which are not in this way temporally limited; 3's *being prime*, for example. If time itself begins and ends, then this event, too, occurs wholly within a finite interval. Yet even then there is no time at which it does not occur.

I said that every event consists in something's actually having some property, actually performing some action, or actually standing in some relation to something. So consider some event e which consists in some entity a having some property or performing some action or standing in some relation. Let us call a, a *subject* of e. And let us call e an *aspect* of a. A given event may well have more than one subject. For example, an event consisting of my sitting under my shingle oak has both me and the shingle oak as subjects. Indeed, I think it can also be viewed as having the relation of *sitting under* as subject. I see nothing against regarding an event consisting of my sitting under my shingle oak as identical with an event consisting of the relation of *sitting under* being exemplified by me with respect to my shingle oak.

Now consider that set of a given entity's aspects such that each member bears a temporal order-relation to every member of the set and none bears a temporal order-relation to any aspect not a member of the set. Let us call that set, provided that it is not empty, the *time-strand* of that entity. I assume it to be true that every entity has at most one time-strand. That is, I assume that no entity has two or more sets of temporally interrelated aspects such that no member of the one set bears any temporal order-relation to any member of the other. I do not, however, assume that each of the aspects of every entity which has a time-strand belongs to the strand. And as to whether every entity has at least one time-strand—that of course is involved in the question as to whether anything is eternal.

Consider, next, a set of events such that each member stands to every member in one of the temporal order-relations, and such that no member stands to any event which is not a member in any of these relations. I shall call such a set a *temporal array*. A temporal array is of course just the union of a set of time-strands such that every member of each member strand bears some temporal order-relation to every member of every other member strand, and such that no member of any member strand bears any temporal order-relation to any member of any strand which is not a member of the set. In what follows I assume that there is but one temporal array. I assume, that is, that every member of every time-strand bears a temporal order-relation to every member of every time-strand.

Now suppose that there is some entity all of whose aspects are such that they are to be found in no temporal array whatsoever. Such an entity would be, in the most radical way possible, outside of time. Accordingly, I shall define "eternal" thus:

> Def. 1: x is eternal if and only if x has no aspect which is a member of the temporal array.

An alternative definition would have been this: "x is eternal if and only if x has no time-strand." The difference between the two definitions is that, on the latter, an entity is eternal if none of its aspects bears any temporal order-relation to any of those events which are *its* aspects; whereas on the former, what is required of an entity for it to be eternal is that none of its aspects be related by any temporal order-relation to *any event whatsoever*. Of course, if every event which bears any temporal order-relation to any event whatsoever is also simultaneous with itself, then everything which fails to satisfy the "temporal array" definition of "eternal" will also fail to satisfy the "time-strand" definition.

At this point, certain ambiguities in the concepts of precedence, succession, and simultaneity should be resolved. By saying that event e_1 occurs *simultaneously with* event e_2, I mean that there is some time at which both e_1 and e_2 are occurring. I do *not* mean—though indeed this might reasonably also have been meant by the words—that there is *no* time at which one of e_1 and e_2 is occurring and the other is not. When two events stand in that latter relation I shall say that they are *wholly simultaneous*. By saying that e_1 preceeds e_2, I mean that there is some time at which e_1 but not e_2 is occurring, which precedes all times at which e_2 is occurring. I do not mean that every time at which e_1 occurs precedes every time at which e_2 occurs. When e_1 stands to e_2 in this latter relationship, I shall say that *it wholly precedes* e_2. Lastly, by saying that e_1 *succeeds* e_2, I mean that there is some time at which e_1 but not e_2 is occurring which succeeds all times at which e_2 is occurring. This, as in the case of precedence, allows for overlap. And, as in the case of precedence, an overlapping case of succession may be distinguished from a case in which one event *wholly succeeds* another.

When "simultaneity," "precedence," and "succession" are understood thus, they do not stand for exclusive relations. An event e_1 may precede, occur simultaneously with, and succeed, another event e_2. But of course e_1 cannot *wholly* precede e_2 while also being *wholly* simultaneous with it, and so forth for the other combinations.

Reflecting on the consequences of the above definitions and explanations, someone might protest that the definition of eternal is altogether too stringent. For consider, say, the number 3. This, no doubt, was referred to by Euclid and also by Cantor. So, by our explanation of "aspect," *3's being referred to by Euclid* was an aspect of the number 3, and *3's being referred to by Cantor* was another aspect thereof. And of course the former preceded the latter. So, by our definition, 3 is not eternal. But—it may be protested—the fact that something is successively referred to should not be regarded as ground for concluding that it is not eternal. For after all, successive references to something do not produce any change in it. Although they produce variation among its aspects, they do not produce a changeful variation among them.

In response to this protest it must be emphasized that the concept of an eternal being is not identical with the concept of an unchanging being. The root idea behind the concept of an eternal being is not that of one which does not change but rather that of one which is outside of time. And a question of substance is whether an unchanging being may fail to be eternal. The most thoroughgoing and radical way possible for an entity to be outside of time is that which something enjoys if it satisfies our definition of "eternal." And it must simply be acknowledged that if an entity is successively referred to, then it is not in the most thoroughgoing way outside of time. There is temporal succession among its aspects.

However, the idea of change could be used by the protester in another way. It is indeed true that not every variation among the aspects of an entity constitutes change therein. Only variation among some of them—call them its *change-relevant* aspects—does so. So on the ground that the change-relevant aspects of an entity are more basic to it, we might distinguish between something being *fundamentally* noneternal and something being *trivially* noneternal. Something is *fundamentally* noneternal if it fails to satisfy the concept of being eternal by virtue of some of its change-relevant aspects. Something is *trivially* noneternal if its failure to satisfy the concept of being eternal is not by virtue of any of its change-relevant aspects.

Now in fact it will be change-relevant aspects of God to which I will appeal in arguing that he is not eternal. Thus my argument will be that God is *fundamentally* noneternal.

II.

In order to present our argument that God is fundamentally noneternal we must now take note of a second basic feature of temporality; namely, that all temporal reality comes in the three modes of past, present, and future.[3]

An important fact about the temporal array is that some events within it are *present:* they *are occurring;* some are *past:* they *were occurring;* some are *future:* they *will be occurring.* Indeed, every event is either past or present or future. And not only *is* this the case now. It always was the case in the past that every event was either past or present or future. And it always will be the case in the future that every event is either past or present or future. Further, every event in the array is such that it either was present or is present or will be present. No event can be past unless it was present. No event can be future unless it will be present. Thus the present is the most basic of the three modes of temporality. To be past is just to have been present. To be future is just to be going to be present. Further, if an event is past, it *presently* is past. If an event is future, it *presently* is future. In this way, too, the present is fundamental.

The reason every event in the temporal array is either past, present, or future is as follows: in order to be in the array at all, an event must occur either before or after or at the same time as some other event. But then, of course, it must occur sometime. And when an event is occurring it is present. So consider any event *e* which is to be found in the temporal array. If *e* is occurring, *e* is present. If, on the other hand, *e* is not occurring, then *e* either precedes or succeeds what is occurring. For *some* event is presently occurring. And every event in the array either precedes or succeeds or is wholly simultaneous with every other. But if *e* were wholly simultaneous with what is occurring, *e* itself would be occurring. So *e* either succeeds or precedes what is occurring if it is not itself occurring. Now for any event *x* to precede any event *y* is just for *x* sometime to be past when *y* is not past. So if *e* precedes what is occurring and is not itself occurring, then *e* is past. On the other hand, for any event *x* to succeed any event *y* is just for *x* sometime to be future when *y* is not future. So if *e* succeeds what is occurring and is not itself occurring, then *e* is future. Hence everything to be found in the temporal array is either past, present, or future.

In contemporary Western philosophy the phenomenon of temporal modality has been pervasively neglected or ignored in favor of the phenomena of temporal order-relationships, temporal location, and temporal duration. Thus time has been "spatialized." For though space provides us with

---

[3]There are two other basic features of temporality: one is the phenomenon of temporal location—the fact that events occur at or within intervals. The other is the phenomenon of temporal duration—the fact that intervals have lengths. In our preceding discussion we repeatedly made appeal to the phenomenon of temporal location without calling attention to our doing so.

close analogues to all three of these latter phenomena, it provides us with no analogue whatever to the past/present/future distinction.[4]

Perhaps the most fundamental and consequential manifestation of this neglect is to be found in the pervasive assumption that all propositions expressed with tensed sentences are mode-indifferent and dated. Consider for example the tensed sentence "My golden chain tree is flowering." The assumption is that what I would assert if I now (June 5, 1974) assertively uttered this sentence with normal sense is *that my golden chain tree is or was or will be flowering on June 5, 1974*. And that the proposition I would be asserting if I assertively uttered the same sentence on June 4, 1975, is *that my golden chain tree is or was or will be flowering on June 4, 1975*. And so forth.

In order to see clearly what the assumption in question comes to, it will be helpful to introduce a way of expressing tenses alternative to that found in our natural language.[5] We begin by introducing the three tense operators, *P, T,* and *F*. These are to be read, respectively, as "it was the case that," "it is the case that," and "it will be the case that." They are to be attached as prefixes either to sentences in the present tense which lack any such prefix,[6] or to compound sentences which consist of sentences in the present tense with one or more such prefixes attached. And the result of attaching one such operator to a sentence is to yield a new sentence. For example: P (my golden chain tree is flowering), to be read as, *"it was the case that my golden chain tree is flowering."* And: F[P (my golden chain tree is flowering)], to be read as: *"it will be the case that it was the case that my golden chain tree is flowering."*

So consider any sentence *s* which is either a present tense sentence with no operators prefixed or a compound sentence consisting of a present tense sentence with one or more operators prefixed. The proposition expressed by *P(s)* is true if and only if the proposition expressed by *s* was true (in the past). The proposition expressed by *T(s)* is true if and only if the proposition expressed by *s* is true (now, in the present).[7] And the proposition expressed by *F(s)* is true if and only if the proposition expressed by *s* will be true (in the future).

---

[4]A recent example of the neglect of temporal modality in favor of temporal location is to be found in David Lewis, "Anselm and Actuality," *NOÛS,* 4 (May 1970). Concluding several paragraphs of discussion he says, "If we take a timeless view and ignore our own location in time, the big difference between the present time and other times vanishes."

[5]See the writings of Arthur Prior, especially *Time and Modality* (Oxford, 1957); *Past, Present and Future* (Oxford, 1967); and *Time and Tense* (Oxford, 1968).

[6]This reflects the fact that the past is what was *present;* the future what will be *present.*

[7]Thus, strictly speaking, the *T* operator is unnecessary. Attaching *T* to any sentence *s* always yields a sentence which expresses the same proposition as does *s* by itself. This reflects the fact that what is past is *presently* past, what is future is *presently* future, and, of course what is present is *presently* present.

Any proposition expressed by a tensed sentence from ordinary speech can be expressed by a sentence in this alternative language. Thus "My golden chain tree was flowering" has as its translational equivalent "P (my golden chain tree is flowering)." And "My golden chain tree will have been flowering" has as its translational equivalent "F[P (my golden chain tree is flowering)]."

Let us now introduce a fourth tense operator, *D*, defining this one in terms of the preceding three thus:

Def. 2: D(...), if and only if P(...) or T(...) or F(...).

And let us read it as: "It was or is or will be the case that...." Let us call this the *tense-indifference* tense operator. And, correspondingly, let us call a sentence which has at least one tense operator and all of whose tense operators are tense-indifferent, a *wholly tense-indifferent* sentence. Furthermore, as the ordinary language counterpart to the tense-indifferent operator let us use the verb in its present tense with a bar over it, thus: "My golden chain tree is flowering." Or "My golden chain tree flowers."

Finally, let us add to our linguistic stock a certain set of modifiers of these tense operators—modifiers of the form "at *t*," "before *t*," and "after *t*," where *t* stands in for some expression designating a time which is such that that expression can be used to designate that time no matter whether that time is in the past, present, or future. These modifiers are to be attached to our tense operators, thus: *P at 1974* (...). The result of attaching one to an operator is to yield an operator of a new form—what one might call a *dated* tense operator. The proposition expressed by a sentence of the form *P at t(s)* is true if and only if the proposition expressed by *s* was true at or within time *t*. The proposition expressed by *T at t(s)* is true if and only if the proposition expressed by *s* is true at or within time *t*. And the proposition expressed by *F at t(s)* is true if and only if the proposition expressed by *s* will be true at or within time *t*. Thus the proposition expressed by "P at 1973 (my golden chain tree is flowering)" is true if and only if my golden chain tree was flowering at or within 1973. Similarly, the proposition expressed by a sentence of the form *P before t(s)* is true if and only if the proposition expressed by *s* was true before *t*; likewise for *T before t(s)* and *F before t(s)*. And the proposition expressed by a sentence of the form *P after t(s)* is true if and only if the proposition expressed by *s* was true after *t*; likewise for *T after t(s)* and *F after t(s)*. Let us call a sentence which has tense operators and all of whose tense operators are dated ones, a *fully dated* sentence.

The assumption underlying a great deal of contemporary philosophy can now be stated thus: every proposition expressed by a sentence which is not wholly tense-indifferent and not fully dated is a proposition which can be expressed by some sentence which is wholly tense-indifferent and fully dated. Consider, for example, the sentence "T (my golden chain tree is flowering)"—the translational equivalent of the ordinary sentence, "My golden chain tree is flowering." Suppose that I assertively utter this sentence on June 5, 1974. The assumption is that the proposition I assert by uttering this sentence is that which is expressed by "D at June 5, 1974 (my golden chain tree is flowering)." And in general, where s is some present tense sentence, the assumption is that the proposition asserted by assertively uttering s at time t is just that which would be asserted by assertively uttering D *at* $t(s)$. Similarly, it is assumed that the proposition asserted by assertively uttering $P(s)$ at time t is that which would be asserted by assertively uttering D *before* $t(s)$. And it is assumed that the proposition asserted by assertively uttering $F(s)$ at time t is that which would be asserted by assertively uttering D *after* $t(s)$.

On this view, tense-committed sentences are characteristically used to assert different propositions on different occasions of use. For example, if the sentence "My golden chain tree is flowering" is assertively uttered on June 5, it is being used to assert that it is or was or will be the case on June 5 that my golden chain tree is flowering; whereas, if uttered on June 4, it is being used to assert that it is or was or will be the case on June 4 that my golden chain tree is flowering. Whether this view is correct will be considered shortly. If it is, then tense-committed sentences are in that way different from wholly tense-indifferent sentences. For these latter are used to assert the same proposition on all occasions of utterance.

I think we now have the assumption in question clearly enough before us to weigh its acceptability. It is in fact clearly false. To see this, suppose that I now (June 5, 1974) assertively utter the sentence "My golden chain tree is flowering" and "D at June 5, 1974 (my golden chain tree is flowering)." The proposition asserted with the former entails that the flowering of my golden chain tree is something that *is* occurring, *now, presently*. But the latter does not entail this at all. In general, if someone assertively utters a present tense sentence s at t, what he asserts is true if and only if the proposition "D at $t(s)$" is true. Yet "s" and "D at $t(s)$" are distinct propositions. So also, if I now assertively utter "My golden chain tree was flowering," what I assert entails that the flowering of my golden chain tree is something that *did* take place, in the past. Whereas the proposition asserted with "D before June 5, 1974 (my golden chain tree is flowering)" does not entail this. And this nonidentity of the propositions holds even though it is the case that if someone assertively utters $P(s)$ at t, what he asserts is true if and only if the proposition D *before* $t(s)$ is true.

Just as a wholly tense-indifferent sentence is used to assert the same proposition no matter what the time of utterance, so, too, the proposition asserted with such a sentence does not vary in truth value. If it is ever true, it is always true, that *D at June 5, 1974 (my golden chain tree is flowering)*. And if it is ever false, it is always false. Such a proposition is constant in its truth value. But an implication of the failure of the contemporary assumption is that the same cannot be said for the propositions expressed by tense-committed sentences. At least some of these are such that they are sometimes true, sometimes false. They are variable in their truth value. For example, "My golden chain tree is flowering" is now true; but two weeks ago it was false.

So the situation is not that in successively uttering a tense-committed sentence we are asserting distinct propositions, each of which is constant in truth value and each of which could also be expressed with wholly tense indifferent, fully dated, sentences. The situation is rather that we are repeatedly asserting a proposition which is variable in its truth value. Contemporary philosophers, along with assuming the dispensability of the temporal modes, have assumed that all propositions are constant in truth value. Plato's lust for eternity lingers on.

Though philosophers have ignored the modes of time in their theories, we as human beings are all aware of the past/present/future distinction. For without such knowledge we would be lost in the temporal array. Suppose one knew, for each event x, which events $\overline{\text{occur}}$ simultaneously with x, which $\overline{\text{occur}}$ before x, and which $\overline{\text{occur}}$ after x. (Recall the significance of the bar over a present-tense verb.) Then with respect to, say, Luther's posting of his theses, one would know which events $\overline{\text{occur}}$ simultaneously therewith, which $\overline{\text{occur}}$ before it, and which $\overline{\text{occur}}$ after it. And so forth, for all other temporal interrelations of events. There would then still be something of enormous importance which one would not on that account know. One would not know where we are in the array of temporally ordered events. For one would not know which events are occurring, which were occurring, and which will be occurring. To know this it is not sufficient to know, with respect to every event, which events $\overline{\text{occur}}$ simultaneously therewith, which $\overline{\text{occur}}$ before, and which $\overline{\text{occur}}$ after.

Nor, as we have seen above, is such knowledge gained by knowing what $\overline{\text{occurs}}$ at what time. If all I know with respect to events $e_1 ... e_n$ is that they all $\overline{\text{occur}}$ at the time, say, of the inauguration of the first post-Nixon President, then I do not yet know whether those events are in the past, in the present, or in the future. And if all my knowledge with respect to every event and every interval is of that deficient sort, I do not know where we are in the temporal array. For I do not know which events are present, which are past, and which are future.

III.

It might seem obvious that God, as described by the biblical writers, is a being who changes, and who accordingly is fundamentally noneternal. For God is described as a being who *acts*—in creation, in providence, and for the renewal of mankind. He is an agent, not an impassive factor in reality. And from the manner in which his acts are described, it seems obvious that many of them have beginnings and endings, that accordingly they stand in succession relations to each other, and that these successive acts are of such a sort that their presence and absence on God's time-strand constitutes changes thereon. Thus it seems obvious that God is fundamentally noneternal.

God is spoken of as calling Abraham to leave Chaldea and later instructing Moses to return to Egypt. So does not the event of *God's instructing Moses* succeed that of *God's calling Abraham?* And does not this sort of succession constitute a change on God's time-strand—not a change in his "essence," but nonetheless a change on his time-strand? Again, God is spoken of as leading Israel through the Red Sea and later sending his Son into the world. So does not his doing the latter succeed his doing the former? And does not the fact of this sort of succession constitute a change along God's time-strand?

In short, it seems evident that the biblical writers regard God as having a time-strand of his own on which actions on his part are to be found, and that some at least of these actions vary in such a way that there are changes along the strand. It seems evident that they do not regard changes on time-strands as confined to entities in God's creation. The God who acts, in the way in which the biblical writers speak of God as acting, seems clearly to change.

Furthermore, is it not clear from how they speak that the biblical writers regarded many of God's acts as bearing temporal order-relations to events which are not aspects of him but rather aspects of the earth, of ancient human beings, and so forth? The four cited above, for example, seem all to be described thus. It seems obvious that God's actions as described by the biblical writers stand in temporal order-relations to all the other events in our own time-array.

However, I think it is not at all so obvious as on first glance it might appear that the biblical writers do in fact describe God as changing. Granted that the language they use suggests this. It is not at once clear that this is what they wished to say with this language. It is not clear that this is how they were describing God. Let us begin to see why this is so by reflecting on the following passage from St. Thomas Aquinas:

> Nor, if the action of the first agent is eternal, does it follow that His effect is eternal,...God acts voluntarily in the production of things,...God's act of understanding and willing is, necessarily, His act of making. Now, an effect follows from the intellect and the will according to the determination of the intellect and the command of the will. Moreover, just as the intellect determines every other condition of the thing made, so does it prescribe the time of its making; for art determines not only that this thing is to be such and such, but that it is to be at this particular time, even as a physician determines that a dose of medicine is to be drunk at such and such a particular time, so that, if his act of will were of itself sufficient to produce the effect, the effect would follow anew from his previous decision, without any new action on his part. Nothing, therefore, prevents our saying that God's action existed from all eternity, whereas its effect was not present from eternity, but existed at that time when, from all eternity, He ordained it (*Summa Contra Gentiles* II.35; cf. II.36, 4).

Let us henceforth call an event which neither begins nor ends an *everlasting event*. And let us call an event which either begins or ends, a *temporal* event. In the passage above, St. Thomas is considering God's acts of bringing about temporal events. So consider some such act; say, that of God's bringing about Israel's deliverance from Egypt. The temporal event in question, Israel's deliverance from Egypt, occurred (let us say) in 1225 B.C. But from the fact that what God brought about occurred in 1225 it does not follow, says Aquinas, that God's act of bringing it about occurred in 1225. In fact, it does not follow that this act had any beginning or ending whatsoever. And in general, suppose that God brings about some temporal event *e*. From the fact that *e* is temporal it does not follow, says Aquinas, that God's act of bringing about *e*'s occurrence is temporal. The temporality of the event which God brings about does not infect God's act of bringing it about. God's act of bringing it about may well be everlasting. This can perhaps more easily be seen, he says, if we remember that God, unlike us, does not have to "take steps" so as to bring about the occurrence of some event. He need only will that it occur. If God just wants it to be the case that *e* occur at *t*, *e* occurs at *t*.

Thus God can bring about changes in our history without himself changing. The occurrence of the event of Israel's deliverance from Egypt constitutes a change in our history. But there is no counterpart change among God's aspects by virtue of his bringing this event about.

Now let us suppose that the four acts of God cited above—instructing Moses, calling Abraham, leading Israel through the Red Sea, and sending his Son into the world—regardless of the impression we might gain from the biblical language used to describe them, also have the structure of God's bringing about the occurrence of some temporal event. Suppose, for example, that God's leading Israel through the Red Sea has the structure of God's bringing it about that Israel's passage through the Red Sea occurs. And suppose Aquinas is right that the temporality of Israel's passage does not infect with temporality God's act of bringing about this passage. Then what is strictly speaking the case is not that God's leading Israel through the Red Sea occurs during 1225. What is rather the case is that Israel's passage through the Red Sea occurs during 1225, and that God brings this passage about. And the temporality of the passage does not entail the temporality of God's bringing it about. This latter may be everlasting. So, likewise, the fact that the occurrence of this passage marks a change in our history does not entail that God's bringing it about marks a change among God's aspects. God may unchangingly bring about historical changes.

It is natural, at this point, to wonder whether we do not have in hand here a general strategy for interpreting the biblical language about God acting. Is it not perhaps the case that all those acts of God which the biblical writers speak of as beginning or as ending really consist in God performing the everlasting event of bringing about the occurrence of some temporal event?

Well, God does other things with respect to temporal events than bringing about their occurrence. For example, he also *knows* them. Why then should it be thought that the best way to interpret all the temporal-event language used to describe God's actions is by reference to God's action of bringing about the occurrence of some event? May it not be that the best way to interpret what is said with some of such language is by reference to one of those other acts which God performs with respect to temporal events? But then if God is not to change, it is not only necessary that the temporality of *e* not infect God's act of *bringing about* the occurrence of *e*, but also that *every* act of God such that he performs it with respect to *e* not be infected by the temporality of *e*. For example, if God *knows* some temporal event *e*, his knowledge of *e* must not be infected by the temporality of *e*.

So the best way of extrapolating from Aquinas' hint would probably be along the lines of the following theory concerning God's actions and the biblical speech about them. All God's actions are everlasting. None has either beginning or ending. Of these everlasting acts, the structure of some consists in God's performing some action with respect to some event. And at least some of the events that God acts with respect to are temporal events. However, in no case does the temporality of the event that God acts with respect to infect the event of his acting. On the contrary, his acting with respect to some temporal event is itself invariably an everlasting event. So whenever the biblical writers use temporal-event language to describe God's actions, they are to be interpreted as thereby claiming that God acts with respect to some temporal event. They are not to be interpreted as claiming that God's acting is itself a temporal event. God as described by the biblical writers is to be interpreted as acting, and as acting with respect to temporal events. But he is not to be interpreted as changing. All his acts are everlasting.

This, I think, is a fascinating theory. If true, it provides a way of harmonizing the fundamental biblical teaching that God is a being who acts in our history, with the conviction that God does not change. How far the proposed line of biblical interpretation can be carried out, I do not know. I am not aware of any theologian who has ever tried to carry it out, though there are a great many theologians who might have relieved the tension in their thought by developing and espousing it. But what concerns us here is not so much what the theory can adequately deal with as what it cannot adequately deal with. Does the theory in fact provide us with a wholly satisfactory way of harmonizing the biblical presentation of God as acting in history with the conviction that God is fundamentally eternal?

Before we set about looking for a refutation of the theory it should be observed, though, that even if the theory were true God would still not be eternal. For consider God's acts of bringing about Abraham's leaving of Chaldea and of bringing about Israel's passage through the Red Sea. These would both be, on the theory, *everlasting* acts. Both are always occurring. Hence they occur simultaneously. They stand to each other in the temporal order-relation of simultaneity. And since both are aspects of God, God accordingly has a time-strand on which these acts are to be found. Hence God is not eternal. Further, these are surely change-relevant aspects of God. Hence God is fundamentally noneternal.[8]

Though I myself think that this argument is sound, it would not be decisive if presented to Aquinas. For Aquinas held that God is simple. And an implication of this contention on his part is that all aspects of God are identical. Hence in God's case there are no two aspects which are simultaneous with each other; for there are no two aspects at all.

A reply is possible. For consider that which is, on Aquinas' theory, God's single aspect; and refer to it as you will—say, as *God's being omnipotent*. This aspect presumably occurs at the same time as itself. Whenever it occurs, it is itself occurring. It is simultaneous with itself. Furthermore, it occurs simultaneously with every temporal event whatsoever. Since God's being omnipotent is always occurring, it "overlaps" all temporal events whatsoever. So once again we have the conclusion: God is noneternal, indeed, he is fundamentally noneternal.

It is true, though, that even if Aquinas were to accept this last argument he would not *say*, in conclusion, that God was noneternal. For Aquinas defined an eternal being as one which is without beginning and without end, and which has no *succession* among its aspects (*Summa Theologica*, I.I q 10 a 1). Thus as Aquinas defined eternal, an eternal being may very well have aspects which stand to each other in the temporal order-relation of simultaneity. What Aquinas ruled out was just aspects standing in the temporal order-relation of succession. Our own definition of "eternal," which disallows simultaneity as well as succession, is in this way more thoroughgoing than is Aquinas'. For a being at least one of whose aspects occurs simultaneously with some event is not yet, in the most radical way possible, outside of time. However, in refutation of the extrapolated Thomistic theory sketched out above I shall now offer an argument against God's being eternal which establishes that there is not only simultaneity but succession among God's aspects, and not just succession but *changeful* succession. This argument will be as relevant to the issue of God's being eternal on Aquinas' definition of eternal as it is on my own definition.

To refute the extrapolated Thomistic theory we would have to do one or the other of two things. We would have to show that some of the temporal-event language the biblical writers use in speaking of God's actions cannot properly be construed in the suggested way—that is, cannot be

---

[8]By a similar argument the number 3 can be seen to be fundamentally noneternal. Surely 3's *being odd* and 3's *being prime* are both change-relevant aspects of 3. If either of these were for a while an aspect of 3 and then for a while not, we would conclude that 3 had changed. But these two aspects occur simultaneously with each other. They stand to each other in the temporal order-relation of simultaneity. Hence 3 is fundamentally noneternal.

construed as used to put forth the claim that God acts in some way with respect to some temporal events. Or, alternatively, we would have to show that some of the actions that God performs with respect to temporal events are themselves temporal, either because they are infected by the temporality of the events or for some other reason.

One way of developing this latter alternative would be to show that some of God's actions must be understood as a response to the free actions of human beings—that what God does he sometimes does in response to what some human being does. I think this is in fact the case. And I think it follows, given that all human actions are temporal, that those actions of God which are "response" actions are temporal as well. But to develop this line of thought would be to plunge us deep into questions of divine omniscience and human freedom. So I shall make a simpler, though I think equally effective objection to the theory, arguing that in the case of certain of God's actions the temporality of the event that God acts on infects his own action with temporality.

Three such acts are the diverse though similar acts of knowing about some temporal event that it is occurring (that it is *present*), of knowing about some temporal event that it was occurring (that it is *past*), and of knowing about some temporal event that it will be occurring (that it is *future*). Consider the first of these. No one can know about some temporal event e that it is occurring except when it is occurring. Before e has begun to occur one cannot know that it is occurring, for it is not. Nor after e has ceased to occur can one know that it is occurring, for it is not. So suppose that e has a beginning. Then P's knowing about e that it is occurring cannot occur until e begins. And suppose that e has an ending. Then P's knowing about e that it is occurring cannot occur beyond e's cessation. But every temporal event has (by definition) either a beginning or an ending. So every case of knowing about some temporal event that it is occurring itself either begins or ends (or both). Hence the act of knowing about e that it is occurring is infected by the temporality of e. So also, the act of knowing about e that it *was* occurring, and the act of knowing about e that it *will be* occurring, are infected by the temporality of e.

But God, as the biblical writers describe him, performs all three of these acts, and performs them on temporal events. He knows what is happening in our history, what has happened, and what will happen. Hence, some of God's actions are themselves temporal events. But surely the nonoccurrence followed by the occurrence followed by the nonoccurrence of such knowings constitutes a change on God's time-strand. Accordingly, God is fundamentally noneternal.[9]

---

[9]This line of argument is adumbrated by Arthur Prior here and there in his essay "Formalities of Omniscience," in *Time and Tense*. It is also adumbrated by Norman Kretzmann, "Omniscience and Immutability," *Journal of Philosophy*, 63 (1966). The essence of the argument is missed in discussions of Kretzmann's paper by Hector Castaneda, "Omniscience and Indexical Reference," *Journal of Philosophy*, 64 (1967); and Nelson Pike, *God and Timelessness* (New York, 1970), ch. 5. Castaneda and Pike fail to take the *modes* of time with full seriousness; as a partial defense of them it should perhaps be admitted as not wholly clear that Kretzmann himself does so.

It is important, if the force of this argument is to be discerned, that one distinguish between, on the one hand, the act of knowing about some event *e* that it occurs at some time *t* (recall the significance of the bar) and, on the other hand, the act of knowing about *e* that it is occurring or of knowing that it was occurring or of knowing that it will be occurring. Knowing about *e* that it occurs at *t* is an act not infected by the temporality of the event known. *That Calvin's flight from Geneva occurs in 1537* is something that can be known at any and every time whatsoever. For it is both true, and constant in its truth value. But *that Calvin's flight from Geneva is occurring* is variable in its truth value. It once was true, it now is false. And since one can know only what is true, this proposition cannot be known at every time. It cannot be known now. God can know, concerning every temporal event whatsoever, what time that event occurs at, without such knowledge of his being temporal. But he cannot know concerning any temporal event whatsoever that it is occurring, or know that it was occurring, or know that it will be occurring, without that knowledge being itself temporal.

Similarly, we must distinguish between, on the one hand, the act of knowing about some temporal event *e* that it occurs simultaneously with events $e_1...e_n$, after events $f_1...f_n$, and before events $g_1...g_n$; and, on the other hand, the act of knowing about *e* that it is occurring or of knowing that it was occurring or of knowing that it will be occurring. Knowledge of the former sort is not infected by the temporality of the event whose temporal order-relationships are known. Knowledge of the latter sort is. I know now that Calvin's flight from Geneva occurs after Luther's posting of his theses occurs. But once again, I do not and cannot now know that Calvin's flight *is* occurring. Because it is not. So too, God once knew that Calvin's flight from Geneva was occurring. But he no longer knows this. For he, too, does not know that which is not so. Thus, in this respect his knowledge has changed. But God always knows that Calvin's flight from Geneva occurs after Luther's posting of his theses occurs. Only if time lacked modes and only if propositions were all constant in truth value could God's knowledge be unchanging—assuming that God's knowledge comprises temporal as well as everlasting events.

The act of *remembering* that *e* has occurred is also an act infected by the temporality of *e* (remembering is, of course, a species of knowing). For one can only remember that *e* has occurred after *e* has occurred. "*P* remembers that *e* occurs" entails that *e* has occurred. So if *e* is an event that has a beginning, then the act of remembering that *e* has occurred has a beginning. But some events with beginnings are such that God remembers their occurrence. Consequently this act on God's part is also a temporal event. It too cannot be everlasting.

God is also described by the biblical writers as planning that he would bring about certain events which he does. This, too, is impossible if God does not change. For consider some event which someone brings about, and suppose that he planned to bring it about. His planning to bring it about must occur before the planned event occurs. For otherwise it is not a case of planning.

So in conclusion, if God were eternal he could not be aware, concerning any temporal event, that it is occurring nor aware that it was occurring nor aware that it will be occurring; nor could he remember that it has occurred; nor could he plan to bring it about and do so. But all of such actions are presupposed by, and essential to, the biblical presentation of God as a redeeming God. Hence God as presented by the biblical writers is fundamentally noneternal. He is fundamentally in time.

IV.

As with any argument, one can here choose to deny the premisses rather than to accept the conclusion. Instead of agreeing that God is fundamentally noneternal because he changes with respect to his knowledge, his memory, and his planning, one could try to save one's conviction that God is eternal by denying that he knows what is or was or will be occurring, that he remembers what has occurred, and that he brings about what he has planned. It seems to me, however, that this is clearly to give up the notion of God as a redeeming God; and in turn it seems to me that to give this up is to give up what is central to the biblical vision of God. To sustain this latter claim would of course require an extensive hermeneutical inquiry. But lest someone be tempted to go this route of trying to save God's eternity by treating all the biblical language about God the redeemer as either false or misleadingly metaphorical, let me observe that if God were eternal he could not be the object of any human action whatsoever.

Consider, for example, my act of referring to something, X. The event consisting of *my referring to X* is a temporal event. It both begins and ends, as do all my acts. Now the event of *my referring to X* is identical with the event of *X's being referred to by me*. And this event is an aspect both of X and of me. So if X is a being which lasts longer than my act of referring to X does, then for a while X has this aspect and for a while not. And thus X would have *succession* on its time-strand. And so X would not be eternal. Thus if God were eternal, no human being could ever refer to him—or perform any other temporal act with respect to him. If he were eternal, one could not know him. In particular, one could not know that he was eternal, or even believe that he was. Indeed, if God were eternal one could not predicate of him that he is eternal. For predicating is also a temporal act. So this is the calamitous consequence of claiming of God that he is eternal: if one predicates of him that he is eternal, then he is not.

ELEONORE STUMP AND NORMAN KRETZMANN

Eternity

The concept of eternity makes a significant difference in the consideration of a variety of issues in the philosophy of religion, including, for instance, the apparent incompatibility of divine omniscience with human freedom, of divine immutability with the efficacy of petitionary prayer, and of divine omniscience with divine immutability; but, because it has been misunderstood or cursorily dismissed as incoherent, it has not received the attention it deserves from contemporary philosophers of religion.[1] In this paper we expound the concept as it is presented by Boethius (whose definition of eternity was the *locus classicus* for medieval discussions of the concept), analyse implications of the concept, examine reasons for considering it incoherent, and sample the results of bringing it to bear on issues in the philosophy of religion.

Eternality—the condition of having eternity as one's mode of existence—is misunderstood most often in either of two ways. Sometimes it is confused with limitless duration in time—sempiternality—and sometimes it is construed simply as atemporality, eternity being understood in that case as roughly analogous to an isolated, static instance. The second misunderstanding of eternality is not so far off the mark as the first; but a consideration of the views of the philosophers who contributed most to the development of the concept shows that atemporality alone does not exhaust eternality as they conceived of it, and that the picture of eternity as a frozen instant is a radical distortion of the classic concept.

From *The Journal of Philosophy*, Vol. LXXVIII, 8 (August 1981), pp. 429–53. Reprinted by permission of the authors and *The Journal of Philosophy*.

[1]At least one contemporary philosopher of religion has recently turned his attention to the concept of divine eternality in order to reject it as incompatible with biblical theology and, in particular, with the doctrine of divine redemption. 'God the Redeemer cannot be a God eternal. This is so because God the Redeemer is a God who changes' (Nicholas Wolterstorff, 'God Everlasting', in Clifton J. Orlebeke and Lewis B. Smedes (eds.), *God and the Good* (Grand Rapids, Mich., 1975), pp. 181–203, p. 182). (We are grateful to Kenneth Konyndyk for having supplied us with copies of this article, which is obviously highly relevant to our purposes in this paper. The work we are presenting here was substantially complete by the time we had access to Professor Wolterstorff's work.) Although it is no part of our purposes here to discuss Wolterstorff's arguments, it will become clear that we think he is mistaken in his assessment of the logical relationship between the doctrine of divine eternality and other doctrines of orthodox Christianity, including the doctrine of redemption, even in their Biblical formulations. Passages that have been or might be offered in evidence of a Biblical conception of divine eternality include Malachi 3: 6; John 8: 58; James I: 17.

I. BOETHIUS'S DEFINITION

Boethius discusses eternity in two places: *The Consolation of Philosophy*, book 5, prose 6, and *De Trinitate*, chapter 4.[2] The immediately relevant passages are these:

CP:

That God is eternal, then, is the common judgment of all who live by reason. Let us therefore consider what eternity is, for this makes plain to us both the divine nature and knowledge. Eternity, then, is the complete possession all at once of illimitable life. This becomes clearer by comparison with temporal things. For whatever lives in time proceeds as something present from the past into the future, and there is nothing placed in time that can embrace the whole extent of its life equally. Indeed, on the contrary, it does not yet grasp tomorrow but yesterday it has already lost; and even in the life of today you live no more fully than in a mobile, transitory moment.... Therefore, whatever includes and possesses the whole fullness of illimitable life at once and is such that nothing future is absent from it and nothing past has flowed away, this is rightly judged to be eternal, and of this it is necessary both that being in full possession of itself it be always present to itself and that it have the infinity of mobile time present [to it]. (*CP*, 422.5–424.31)

DT:

What is said of God, [namely, that] he is always, indeed signifies a unity, as if he had been in all the past, is in all the present—however that might be—[and] will be in all the future. That can be said, according to the philosophers, of the heaven and of the imperishable bodies; but it cannot be said of God in the same way. For he is always in that for him *always* has to do with present time. And there is this great difference between the present of our affairs, which is *now*, and that of the divine: our now makes time and sempiternity, as if it were running along; but the divine now, remaining, and not moving, and standing still, makes eternity. If you add *'semper'* to 'eternity', you get sempiternity, the perpetual running resulting from the flowing, tireless now. (*DT*, 20.64–22.77)[3]

The definition Boethius presents and explains in *CP* and elucidates in the earlier *DT* is not original with him,[4] nor does he argue for it in those passages.[5]

---

[2]Ed. E. K. Rand, in H. F. Stewart, E. K. Rand, and S. J. Tester, *Boethius: The Theological Tractates and The Consolation of Philosophy* (London and Cambridge, Mass., 1973).

[3]There are at least two misleading features of this passage. In the first place, Boethius says that God's eternality *always* has to do with present *time*. In the second place, Boethius's etymology of 'sempiternity' is mistaken. *'Sempiternitas'* is an abstract noun constructed directly on *'semper,'* somewhat as we might construct 'alwaysness'. His etymology is not only false but misleading, associating 'sempiternity' with 'eternity' in a context in which he has been distinguishing between sempiternity and eternity.

[4]Its elements stem from Parmenides via Plato, and Plotinus had already framed a definition of eternity on which Boethius's seems to have been based. See note 6 below. Cf. Romano Amerio, 'Probabile fonte della nozione boeziana di eternità', *Filosofia* 1 (1950), pp. 365–73.

[5]The argument that is concluded in the last sentence of passage *CP* is based on premises about God's eternality and omniscience, and is not an argument in support of the definition.

Similarly, we mean to do no more in this section of our paper than to present and explain a concept that has been important in Christian and pre-Christian theology and metaphysics. We will not argue here, for instance, that there is an eternal entity, or even that God must be eternal if he exists. It is a matter of fact that many ancient and medieval philosophers and theologians were committed to the doctrine of God's eternality in the form in which Boethius presents it, and our purpose in this section of the paper is simply to elucidate the doctrine they held.

Boethius's definition is this: *Eternity is the complete possession all at once of illimitable life.*[6]

We want to call attention to four ingredients in this definition. It is clear, first of all, that anything that is eternal has life. In this sense of 'eternal', then, it will not do to say that a number, a truth, or the world is eternal, although one might want to say of the first two that they are atemporal and of the third that it is sempiternal—that it has beginningless, endless temporal existence.[7]

The second and equally explicit element in the definition is illimitability: the life of an eternal being cannot be limited; it is impossible that there be a beginning or an end to it. The natural understanding of such a claim is that the existence in question is infinite duration, unlimited in either 'direction'. But there is another interpretation that must be considered in this context despite its apparent unnaturalness. Conceivably, the existence of an eternal entity is said to be illimitable in the way in which a point or an instant may be said to be illimitable: what cannot be extended cannot be limited in its extent. There are passages that can be read as suggesting that this second interpretation is what Boethius intends. In *CP* eternal existence is expressly contrasted with temporal existence described as extending from the past

---

[6]'*Aeternitas igitur est interminabilis vitae tota simul et perfecta possessio*', *De Trinitate*, p. 422.9–11. This definition closely parallels the definition developed by Plotinus in *Enneads* iii 7: 'The life, then, which belongs to that which exists and is in being, all together and full, completely without-extension-or-interval, is what we are looking for, eternity' (A. H. Armstrong (ed.), *Plotinus* (London and Cambridge, Mass., 1967), vol. 3, p. 304.37–39). The way in which Boethius introduces eternity suggests that he considers himself to be presenting a familiar philosophical concept associated with a recognized definition. The parallel between the Plotinian and Boethian definitions is closest in their middle elements: '*zōē homou pasa kai plērēs*'/'*vitae tota simul et perfecta*'. Plotinus describes the possessor of this life, and Boethius does not; but, in view of the fact that Boethius is talking about God, he, too, would surely describe the possessor of eternality as 'that which exists and is in being'. The most interesting difference between the two definitions is that the Plotinian has 'completely without-extension-or-interval' and the Boethian has 'illimitable', which suggests that Boethius takes eternity to include duration but Plotinus does not. In the rest of *Enneads* iii 7, however, Plotinus goes on to derive duration from his definition and to stress its importance in the concept. For an excellent presentation and discussion of Plotinus on eternity and time, see Werner Beierwaltes, *Plotin über Ewigkeit und Zeit* (*Enneade* iii 7) (Frankfurt am Main, 1967).

[7]The many medieval discussions of the possibility that the world is 'eternal' really concern the possibility that it is sempiternal, and most often their concern is only with the possibility that the world had no beginning in time. Thomas Aquinas provides an important summary and critique of such discussions in *Summa Contra Gentiles*, bk. ii, chs. 32–8.

through the present into the future, and what is eternal is described con-
trastingly as possessing its entire life *at once*. Boethius's insistence in *DT* that
the eternal now is unlike the temporal now in being fixed and unchanging
strengthens that hint with the suggestion that the eternal present is to be
understood in terms of the present instant 'standing still'. Nevertheless, there
are good reasons, in these passages themselves and in the history of the
concept of eternity before and after Boethius, for rejecting this less natural
interpretation. In the first place, some of the terminology Boethius uses
would be inappropriate to eternity if eternity were to be conceived as illimitable in virtue of being unextended. He speaks in *CP* more than once of the
fullness of eternal life. In *DT*, and in *The Consolation of Philosophy* immediately
following our passage *CP*, he speaks of the eternal present or an eternal entity
as *remaining* and *enduring*.[8] And he claims in *DT* that it is correct to say of God
that he is *always*, explaining the use of 'always' in reference to God in such a
way that he can scarcely have had in mind a life illimitable in virtue of being
essentially durationless. The more natural reading of 'illimitable', then, also
provides the more natural reading of these texts. In the second place, the
weight of tradition both before and after Boethius strongly favours interpreting illimitable life as involving infinite duration, beginningless as well as
endless. Boethius throughout the *Consolation*, and especially in passage *CP*,
is plainly working in the Platonic tradition, and both Plato and Plotinus
understand eternal existence in that sense.[9] Medieval philosophers after
Boethius, who depend on him for their conception of eternity, also clearly
understand 'illimitable' in this way.[10] So, for both these sets of reasons, we
understand this part of Boethius's definition to mean that the life of an eternal
entity is characterized by beginningless, endless, infinite duration.

The concept of duration that emerges in the interpretation of 'illimitable
life' is the third ingredient we mean to call attention to. Illimitable life entails
duration of a special sort, as we have just seen, but it would be reasonable to
think that any mode of existence that could be called a life must involve
duration, and so there may seem to be no point in explicitly listing duration
as an ingredient in Boethius's concept of eternality. We call attention to it here,
however, because of its importance as part of the background against which
the fourth ingredient must be viewed. The fourth ingredient is presented in
the only phrase of the definition still to be considered: 'The complete possession all at once'. As Boethius's explanation of the definition in *CP* makes clear,

---

[8]See, e.g., p. 424.51–56.

[9]See Plato, *Timaeus* 37D–38C; Plotinus, *Enneads* iii 7 (and cf. note 6 above).

[10]See, e.g., Thomas Aquinas, *Summa Theologiae*, pt. i, q. 10. Augustine, who is an earlier
and in general an even more important source for medieval philosophy and theology than
Boethius and who is even more clearly in the Platonist tradition, understands and uses this classic
concept of eternity (see, e.g., *Confessions*, bk. xi, ch. 11; *The City of God*, bk. xi, ch. 21); but his
influence on the medieval discussion of eternity seems not to have been so direct or important
as Boethius's.

he conceives of an eternal entity as atemporal, and he thinks of its atemporality as conveyed by just that phrase in the definition. What he says shows that something like the following line of thought leads to his use of those words. A living temporal entity may be said to possess a life, but, since the events constituting the life of any temporal entity occur sequentially, some later than others, it cannot be said to possess all its life *at once.* And since everything in the life of a temporal entity that is not present is either past and so no longer in its possession or future and so not yet in its possession, it cannot be said to have the *complete* possession of its life.[11] So whatever has the complete possession of all its life at once cannot be temporal. The life that is the mode of an eternal entity's existence is thus characterized not only by duration but also by atemporality.

With the possible exception of Parmenides, none of the ancients or medievals who accepted eternity as a real, atemporal mode of existence meant thereby to deny the reality of time or to suggest that all temporal experiences are illusory. In introducing the concept of eternity, such philosophers, and Boethius in particular, were proposing two separate modes of real existence. Eternity is a mode of existence that is, on Boethius's view, neither reducible to time nor incompatible with the reality of time.

In the next two sections of this paper, we will investigate the apparent incoherence of this concept of eternity. We will begin with a consideration of the meaning of atemporality in this connection, including an examination of the relationship between eternity and time; and we will go on to consider the apparent incoherence generated by combining atemporality with duration and with life.

II. THE ATEMPORALITY OF AN ETERNAL ENTITY: PRESENTNESS AND SIMULTANEITY

Because an eternal entity is atemporal, there is no past or future, no earlier or later, *within* its life; that is, the events constituting its life cannot be ordered sequentially from the standpoint of eternity. But, in addition, no temporal entity or event can be earlier or later than or past or future with respect to the whole life of an eternal entity, because otherwise such an eternal life or entity would itself be part of a temporal series. Here it should be evident that, although the stipulation that an eternal entity completely possesses its life all at once entails that it is not part of any sequence, it does not rule out the attribution of presentness or simultaneity to the life and relationships of such an entity, nor should it. In so far as an entity *is,* or *has,* life, completely or otherwise, it is appropriate to say

---

[11]Notice that these characteristics of a temporal entity's possession of its life apply not just to finite temporal lives but even to a temporal life of beginningless, endless duration—a sempiternal life.

that it has present existence in some sense of 'present'; and unless its life consists in only one event or it is impossible to relate an event in its life to any temporal entity or event, we need to be able to consider an eternal entity or event as one of the *relata* in a simultaneity relationship. We will consider briefly the applicability of presentness to something eternal and then consider in some detail the applicability of simultaneity.

If anything exists eternally, it exists. But the existing of an eternal entity is a duration without succession, and, because eternity excludes succession, no eternal entity has existed or will exist; it *only* exists. It is in this sense that an eternal entity is said to have present existence. But since that present is not flanked by past and future, it is obviously not the temporal present. And, furthermore, the eternal, pastless, futureless present is not instantaneous but extended, because eternity entails duration. The temporal present is a durationless instant, a present that cannot be extended conceptually without falling apart entirely into past and future intervals. The eternal present, on the other hand, is by definition an infinitely extended, pastless, futureless duration.

Simultaneity is of course generally and unreflectively taken to mean existence or occurrence at one and the same time. But to attribute to an eternal entity or event simultaneity with anything we need a coherent characterization of simultaneity that does not make it altogether temporal. It is easy to provide a coherent characterization of a simultaneity relationship that is not temporal in case both the *relata* are eternal entities or events. Suppose we designate the ordinary understanding of temporal simultaneity *T-simultaneity*:

(T) T-simultaneity = existence or occurrence at one and the same time.

Then we can easily enough construct a second species of simultaneity, a relationship obtaining between two eternal entities or events:

(E) E-simultaneity = existence or occurrence at one and the same eternal present.

What really interests us among species of simultaneity, however, and what we need for our present purposes, is not E-simultaneity so much as a simultaneity relationship between two *relata* of which one is eternal and the other temporal. We have to be able to characterize such a relationship coherently if we are to be able to claim that there is any connection between an eternal and a temporal entity or event. An eternal entity or event cannot be earlier or later than, or past or future with respect to, any temporal entity or event. If there is to be any relationship between what is eternal and what is temporal, then, it must be some species of simultaneity.

Now in forming the species T-simultaneity and E-simultaneity, we have in effect been taking the genus of those species to be something like this:

(G) Simultaneity = existence or occurrence at once (i.e., together).

And we have formed those two species by giving specific content to the broad expression 'at once'. In each case, we have spelled out 'at once' as meaning at one and the same *something*—time, in the case of T-simultaneity; eternal present, in the case of E-simultaneity. In other words, the *relata* for T-simultaneity occur together at the same time, and the *relata* for E-simultaneity occur together at the same eternal present. What we want now is a species of simultaneity—call it *ET-simultaneity* (for eternal–temporal simultaneity)—that can obtain between what is eternal and what is temporal. It is only natural to try to construct a definition for ET-simultaneity as we did for the two preceding species of simultaneity, by making the broad 'at once' in (G) more precise. Doing so requires starting with the phrase 'at one and the same _____' and filling in the blank appropriately. To fill in that blank appropriately, however, would be to specify a single mode of existence in which the two *relata* exist or occur together, as the *relata* for T-simultaneity coexist (or co-occur) in time and the *relata* for E-simultaneity coexist (or co-occur) in eternity.[12] But, on the view we are explaining and defending, it is theoretically impossible to specify a single mode of existence for two *relata* of which one is eternal and the other temporal. To do so would be to reduce what is temporal to what is eternal (thus making time illusory), or what is eternal to what is temporal (thus making eternity illusory), or both what is temporal and what is eternal to some *third* mode of existence; and all three of these alternatives are ruled out. The medieval adherents of the concept of eternity held that both time and eternity are real and that there is no mode of existence besides those two.[13]

Against this background, then, it is not conceptually possible to construct a definition for ET-simultaneity analogous to the definitions for the other two species of simultaneity, by spelling out 'at once' as 'at one and the same _____' and filling in the blank appropriately. What is temporal and what is eternal can coexist, on the view we are adopting and defending, but not within the same mode of existence; and there is no single mode of existence that can be referred to in filling in the blank in such a definition of ET-simultaneity.

The significance of this difficulty and its implications for a working definition of ET-simultaneity can be better appreciated by returning to the definition of T-simultaneity for a closer look. Philosophers of physics, explaining the special theory of relativity, have taught us to be cautious even

---

[12]In the interest of simplicity and brevity, we will for the most part speak only of coexistence in what follows, taking it as covering co-occurrence too.

[13]The medieval concept of the *aevum* or of *aeviternitas* seems to us to be not the concept of a third mode of existence, on a par with time and eternity. See, e.g., Thomas Aquinas, *Summa Theologiae*, pt. i, q. 10, arts. 5 and 6.

about the notion of temporal simultaneity; in fact, the claim that temporal simultaneity is relative rather than absolute is fundamental to the special theory of relativity.

For all ordinary practical purposes, and also for our theoretical purposes in this paper, time can be thought of as absolute, along Newtonian lines. But, simply in order to set the stage for our characterization of ET-simultaneity, it will be helpful to look at a standard philosophical presentation of temporal simultaneity along Einsteinian lines.[14] Imagine a train travelling *very* fast, at six-tenths the speed of light. One observer (the 'ground observer') is stationed on the embankment beside the track; another observer (the 'train observer') is stationed on the train. Suppose that two lightning bolts strike the train, one at each end, and suppose that the ground observer sees those two lightning bolts simultaneously. The train observer also sees the two lightning bolts, but, since he is travelling toward the light ray emanating from the bolt that strikes the front of the train and away from the bolt that strikes the rear of the train, he will see the lightning bolt strike the front of the train before he sees the other strike the rear of the train. This, then, is the fundamental result: events occurring at different places which are simultaneous in one frame of reference will not be simultaneous in another frame of reference which is moving with respect to the first. This is known as *the relativity of simultaneity'*.[15]

We want to leave to one side the philosophical issues raised by this example and simply accept it for our present purposes as a standard example illustrating Einstein's notion of the relativity of temporal simultaneity. According to this example, the very same two lightning flashes are simultaneous (with respect to the reference frame of the ground observer) and not simultaneous (with respect to the reference frame of the train observer). If we interpret 'simultaneous' here in accordance with our definition of T-simultaneity, we will have to say that the same two lightning flashes occur at the same time and do not occur at the same time; that is, it will be both true and false that these two lightning flashes occur at the same time. The incoherence of this result is generated by filling in the blank for the definition of T-simultaneity with a reference to one and the same time, where time is understood as one single uniform mode of existence. The special theory of relativity takes time itself to be relative and so calls for a more complicated definition of temporal simultaneity than the common, unreflective definition given in (T), such as this relativized version of temporal simultaneity:

(RT) RT-simultaneity = existence or occurrence at the same time within the reference frame of a given observer.

---

[14]Our adaptation of this example is a simplified version of Wesley C. Salmon's presentation of it in his *Space, Time, and Motion* (Encino, Cal., 1975), pp. 73–81. We mean to do little more here than cite the example. An understanding of its significance for relativity theory requires a consideration of a presentation as full (and clear) as Salmon's.

[15]Salmon, *Space, Time, and Motion*, p. 76.

This relativizing of time to the reference frame of a given observer resolves the apparent incoherence in saying that the same two lightning flashes occur and do not occur at one and the same time. They occur at the same time in the reference frame of one observer and do not occur at the same time in the reference frame of a different observer.[16]

Once this is understood, we can see that, if we persist in asking whether or not the two lightning bolts are *really* simultaneous, we are asking an incoherent question, one that cannot be answered. The question is asked about what is assumed to be a feature of reality, although in fact there is no such feature of reality; such a question is on a par with 'Is Uris Library *really* to the left of Morrill Hall?' There is no absolute state of being temporally simultaneous with, any more than there is an absolute state of being to the left of. We determine the obtaining of the one relationship as we determine the obtaining of the other, by reference to an observer and the observer's point of view. The two lightning flashes, then, are RT-simultaneous in virtue of occurring at the same time within the reference frame of the ground observer and not RT-simultaneous in virtue of occurring at different times within the reference frame of the train observer. And, Einstein's theory argues, there is no privileged observer (or reference frame) such that with respect to it we can determine whether the two events are *really* simultaneous; simultaneity is irreducibly relative to observers and their reference frames, and so is time itself. Consequently, it would be a mistake to think that there is one single uniform mode of existence that can be referred to in specifying 'at once' in (G) in order to derive a definition of temporal simultaneity.

These difficulties in spelling out even a very crude acceptable definition for temporal simultaneity in the light of relativity theory foreshadow and are analogous to the difficulties in spelling out an acceptable definition of ET-simultaneity. More significantly, they demonstrate that the difficulties defenders of the concept of eternity encounter in formulating such a definition are by no means unique to their undertaking, and cannot be assumed to be difficulties in the concepts of ET-simultaneity or of eternity themselves. Finally, and most importantly, the way in which we cope with such difficulties in working out a definition for RT-simultaneity suggests the sort of definition needed for ET-simultaneity. Because one of the *relata* for ET-simultaneity is eternal, the definition for this relationship, like that for E-simultaneity, must refer to one and the same present rather than to one and the same time. And because in ET-simultaneity we are dealing with two equally real modes of existence, neither of which is reducible to any other mode of existence, the definition must be constructed in terms of *two*

---

[16]It is important to understand that by 'observer' we mean only that thing, animate or inanimate, with respect to which the reference frame is picked out and with respect to which the simultaneity of events within the reference frame is determined. In the train example we have two human observers, but the example could have been set up just as well if the observers had been nothing more than devices, primitive or sophisticated, for recording flashes of light.

reference frames and *two* observers. So we can characterize ET-simultaneity in this way. Let 'x' and 'y' range over entities and events. Then:

(ET) for every x and for every y, x and y are ET-simultaneous iff

    (i) either x is eternal and y is temporal, or vice versa; and

    (ii) for some observer, A, in the unique eternal reference frame, x and y are both present—i.e., either x is eternally present and y is observed as temporally present, or vice versa; and

    (iii) for some observer, B, in one of the infinitely many temporal reference frames, x and y are both present—i.e., either x is observed as eternally present and y is temporally present, or vice versa.

Given the concept of eternity, condition (ii) provides that a temporal entity or event observed as temporally present by some eternal observer A is ET-simultaneous with every eternal entity or event; and condition (iii) provides that an eternal entity or event observed as eternally present (or simply as eternal) by some temporal observer B is ET-simultaneous with every temporal entity or event.

On our definition, if x and y are ET-simultaneous, then x is neither earlier nor later than, neither past nor future with respect to, y—a feature essential to any relationship that can be considered a species of simultaneity. Further, if x and y are ET-simultaneous, x and y are not temporally simultaneous; since either x or y must be eternal, it cannot be the case that x and y both exist *at one and the same time* within a given observer's reference frame. ET-simultaneity is symmetric, of course; but, since no temporal or eternal entity or event is ET-simultaneous with itself, the relationship is not reflexive; and the fact that there are different domains for its *relata* means that it is not transitive. The propositions

    (1) x is ET-simultaneous with y.

and

    (2) y is ET-simultaneous with z.

do not entail

    (3) x is ET-simultaneous with z.

And even if we conjoin with (1) and (2)

    (4) x and z are temporal.

(1), (2), and (4) together do not entail

    (5) x and z are temporally simultaneous.

(RT) and the Einsteinian conception of time as relative have served the only purpose we have for them in this paper, now that they have provided an introductory analogue for our characterization of ET-simultaneity, and we can now revert to a Newtonian conception of time, which will simplify the discussion without involving any relevant loss of precision. In the first place, at least one of the theological issues we are going to be discussing—the problem of omniscience and immutability—depends on the concept of an absolute present, a concept that is often thought to be dependent on a Newtonian conception of absolute time. But the concept of an absolute present which is essential to our discussion is not discredited by relativity theory.[17] Every conscious temporal observer has an undeniable, indispensable sense of the absolute present, *now*, and that thoroughly pervasive feature of temporal consciousness is all we need. We do not need and we will not try to provide a philosophical justification for the concept of an absolute present; we will simply assume it for our present purposes. And if it must be said that the absolute present is absolute only within a given observer's reference frame, that will not affect our use of the concept here. In the second place, in ordinary human circumstances, all human observers may be said—*should* be said—to share one and the same reference frame, and distinguishing individual reference frames for our discussion of time in the rest of this paper would be as inappropriate as taking an Einsteinian view of time in a discussion of historical chronology.

III. IMPLICATIONS OF ET-SIMULTANEITY

If x and z are temporal entities, they coexist if and only if there is some time during which both x and z exist. But if anything exists eternally, its existence, although infinitely extended, is fully realized, all present at once. Thus the entire life of any eternal entity is coexistent with any temporal entity at any time at which that temporal entity exists.[18] From a temporal standpoint, the present is ET-simultaneous with the whole infinite extent of an eternal

---

[17]On this issue see William Godfrey Smith, 'Special Relativity and the Present', *Philosophical Studies*, 36(3) (Oct. 1979), pp. 233–44.

[18]Since no eternal entity or event can itself be an element in a temporal series, no temporal entity or event can be earlier or later than the whole life or than any part of the life of an eternal entity. It is not clear that it makes sense to think in terms of parts of atemporal duration (cf. Aquinas, *Summa Theologiae*, pt. i, q. 10, art. 1, ad. 3); but even if it does, it cannot make sense to think of any such part as earlier or later than anything temporal. If the Battle of Waterloo were earlier than some part of atemporal duration, it would be uniquely simultaneous with one other part of atemporal duration, in which case one part of atemporal duration would be earlier than another, which is impossible.

entity's life. From the standpoint of eternity, every time is present, co-occur-
rent with the whole of infinite atemporal duration.[19]

We can show the implications of this account of ET-simultaneity by
considering the relationship between an eternal entity and a future contingent event. Suppose that Richard Nixon will die at noon on 9 August 1990,
precisely sixteen years after he resigned the Presidency. Nixon's death some
years from now *will be* present to those who will be at his death-bed, but it *is*
present to an eternal entity. It cannot be that an eternal entity has a vision of
Nixon's death before it occurs; in that case an eternal event would be earlier
than a temporal event. Instead, the actual occasion of Nixon's dying is present
to an eternal entity. It is not that the future pre-exists somehow, so that it can
be inspected by an entity that is outside time, but rather that an eternal entity
that is wholly ET-simultaneous with 9 August 1974, and with today, is wholly
ET-simultaneous with 9 August 1990, as well. It is *now* true to say 'The whole
of eternity is ET-simultaneous with the present'; and of course it was true to
say just the same at noon of 9 August 1974, and it will be true to say it at noon
of 9 August 1990. But since it is one and the same eternal present that is
ET-simultaneous with each of those times, there is a sense in which it is now
true to say that Nixon at the hour of his death is present to an eternal entity;
and in that same sense it is now true to say that Nixon's resigning of the

---

[19]In the development of the classic concept of eternity, geometric models were sometimes
introduced in an attempt to clarify the relationship we are calling ET-simultaneity. There is a
passage in Boethius, for instance (*Consolation*, bk. iv, prose 6; *De trinitate*, pp. 364.78–366.82),
which suggests that he took the relationship between time and eternity to be analogous to that
between the circumference and the centre of a circle. Aquinas developed this sort of analogy in
connection with an account of an eternal entity's apprehension of temporal events: 'Furthermore,
God's understanding, just like his being, does not have succession; it is, therefore, always
enduring all at once, which belongs to the nature of eternity. The duration of time, on the other
hand, is extended in the succession of before and after. Thus the relationship of eternity to the
whole duration of time is like the relationship of an indivisible to a continuum—not indeed of
an indivisible that is a limit of the continuum, which is not present to each part of the continuum
(an instant of time bears a likeness to that), but of the indivisible that is outside the continuum
and nevertheless coexists with each part of the continuum or with a designated point in the
continuum. For, since time does not extend beyond change, eternity, which is entirely beyond
change, is nothing belonging to time; on the other hand, since the being of what is eternal is never
lacking, eternity in its presentness is present to each time or instant of time. A sort of example of
this can be seen in a circle. For a designated point on the circumference, although it is an
indivisible, does not coexist together with another point as regards position since it is the order
of position that produces the continuity of the circumference. But the centre, which is outside
the circumference, is directly opposite any designated point on the circumference. In this way,
whatever is in any part of time coexists with what is eternal as being present to it even though
past or future with respect to another part of time. But nothing can coexist with what is eternal
in its presentness except as a whole, for it does not have the duration of succession. And so in its
eternity the divine understanding perceives as present whatever takes place during the whole
course of time. It is not the case, however, that what takes place in a certain part of time has been
existent always. It remains, therefore, that God has knowledge of those things that, as regards
the course of time, are not yet' (*Summa Contra Gentiles*, bk. i, ch. 66).

Presidency is present to an eternal entity. If we are considering an eternal entity that is omniscient, it is true to say that that entity is *at once* aware of Nixon resigning the Presidency and of Nixon on his death-bed (although of course an omniscient entity understands that those events occur sequentially and knows the sequence and the dating of them); and it is true to say also that for such an entity both those events are present at once.[20]

Such an account of ET-simultaneity suggests at least a radical epistemological or even metaphysical relativism, and perhaps plain incoherence. We *know* that Nixon is now alive. An omniscient eternal entity *knows* that Nixon is now dead. Still worse, an omniscient eternal entity also *knows* that Nixon is now alive, and so Nixon is apparently both alive and dead at once in the eternal present.

These absurdities appear to be entailed partly because the full implications of the concept of eternity have not been taken into account. We have said enough to induce caution regarding 'present' and 'simultaneous', but it is not difficult to overlook the concomitant ambiguity in such expressions as 'now' and 'at once'. To say that we know that Nixon is now alive although an eternal entity knows that Nixon is now dead does not mean that an eternal entity knows the opposite of what we know. What we know is that:

(6) Nixon is alive in the temporal present.

What an eternal entity knows is that

(7) Nixon is dead in the eternal present.

and (6) is not incompatible with (7). Still, this simple observation does nothing to dispel the appearance of incompatibility between (7) and

(8) Nixon is alive in the eternal present.

and, on the basis of what has been said so far, both (7) and (8) are true. But Nixon is temporal, not eternal, and so are his life and death. The conjunction of (7) and (8), then, cannot be taken to mean that the temporal entity Nixon exists in eternity, where he is simultaneously alive and dead, but rather something more nearly like this. One and the same eternal present is ET-simultaneous with Nixon's being alive and is also ET-simultaneous with Nixon's dying; so Nixon's life is ET-simultaneous with and hence present to an eternal entity, and Nixon's death is ET-simultaneous with and hence

---

[20]In *The Consolation of Philosophy* Boethius introduces and develops the concept of eternity primarily in order to argue that divine omniscience is compatible with human freedom, and he does so by demonstrating that omniscience on the part of an eternal entity need not, cannot, involve *fore*knowledge. See also section VI below.

present to an eternal entity, although Nixon's life and Nixon's death are themselves neither eternal nor simultaneous.

These considerations also explain the appearance of metaphysical relativism inherent in the claim that Nixon's death is really future for us and really present for an eternal entity. It is not that there are two objective realities, in one of which Nixon's death is really future and in the other of which Nixon's death and life are really present; that *would* be incoherent. What the concept of eternity implies instead is that there is one objective reality that contains two modes of real existence in which für two different sorts of duration are measured by two irreducibly different sorts of measure: time and eternity. Given the relations between time and eternity spelled out in section II of this paper, Nixon's death is really future or not depending on which sort of entity, temporal or eternal, it is being related to. An eternal entity's mode of existence is such that its whole life is ET-simultaneous with each and every temporal entity or event, and so Nixon's death, like every other event involving Nixon, is really ET-simultaneous with the life of an eternal entity. But when Nixon's death is being related to *us*, today, then, given our location in the temporal continuum, Nixon's death is not simultaneous (temporally or in any other way) with respect to us, but really future.[21]

IV. ATEMPORAL DURATION AND ATEMPORAL LIFE

With this understanding of the atemporality of an eternal entity's existence, we want to consider now the apparent incoherence generated by combining atemporality with duration and with life in the definition of eternity.

The notion of atemporal duration is the heart of the concept of eternity and, in our view, the original motivation for its development. The most efficient way in which to dispel the apparent incoherence of the notion of atemporal duration is to consider, even if only very briefly, the development of the concept of eternity. The concept can be found in Parmenides, we think,[22] but it finds its first detailed formulation in Plato, who makes use of

---

[21]The claim that Nixon's death is really future rests on the assumption around which we all organize our lives, the view that the temporal present is absolute, that the expressions 'the present', 'the past', and 'the future' are uniquely (and differently) referring expressions on each occasion of their use, that 'now' is an essential indexical. On the notion of an essential indexical see John Perry, 'The Problem of the Essential Indexical', *Noûs* 13(1) (March 1979), pp. 3–21. We are grateful to Marilyn Adams for letting us see some of her unpublished work which brings out the importance of the notion of the absolute present in discussions of this sort, particularly in the discussion we will take up in section VI below, and for calling our attention to Perry's article.

[22]Most clearly in fr. 8, as we read it. For excellent examples of both sides of the controversy over the presence of the concept of eternity in Parmenides, see G. E. L. Owen, 'Plato and Parmenides on the Timeless Present', *Monist* L (3) (July 1966), pp. 317–340; and Malcolm Schofield, 'Did Parmenides Discover Eternity?', *Archiv für Geschichte der Philosophie* 52 (1970), pp. 113–35.

it in working out the distinction between the realms of being and becoming; and it receives its fullest exposition in pagan antiquity in the work of Plotinus.[23] The thought that originally stimulated this Greek development of the concept of eternity was apparently something like this. Our *experience* of temporal duration gives us an impression of permanence and persistence which an analysis of time convinces us is an illusion or at least a distortion. Reflection shows us that, contrary to our familiar but superficial impression, temporal duration is only apparent duration, just what one would expect to find in the realm of becoming. The existence of a typical existent temporal entity, such as a human being, is spread over years of the past, through the present, and into years of the future; but the past is not, the future is not, and the present must be understood as no time at all, a durationless instant, a mere point at which the past is continuous with the future.[24] Such radically evanescent existence cannot be the foundation of existence. Being, the persistent, permanent, utterly immutable actuality that seems required as the bedrock underlying the evanescence of becoming, must be characterized by genuine duration, of which temporal duration is only the flickering image. Genuine duration is fully realized duration—not only extended existence (even *that* is theoretically impossible in time) but also existence *none* of which is already gone and *none* of which is yet to come—and such fully realized duration must be atemporal duration. Whatever has atemporal duration as its mode of existence is 'such that nothing future is absent from it and nothing past has flowed away', whereas of everything that has temporal duration it may be said that from it *everything* future is absent and *everything* past has flowed away. What has temporal duration 'does not yet grasp tomorrow but yesterday it has already lost'; even today it exists only 'in a mobile, transitory moment', the present instant. To say of something that it is future is to say that it is not (yet), and to say of something that it is past is to say that it is not (any longer). Atemporal duration is duration none of which is not—none of which is absent (and hence future) or flowed away (and hence past). Eternity, not time, is the mode of existence that admits of fully realized duration.

The ancient Greek philosophers who developed the concept of eternity were using the word '*aiōn*', which corresponds in its original sense to our word 'duration', in a way that departed from ordinary usage in order to introduce a notion which, however counter-intuitive it may be, can reasonably be said to preserve and even to enhance the original sense of the word. It would not be out of keeping with the tradition that runs through Parmenides, Plato, and Plotinus into Augustine, Boethius, and Aquinas to claim that it is only the discovery of eternity that enables us to make genuinely literal use of words

---

[23]See notes 6 and 9 above.

[24]For some discussion of this analysis of time in Aristotle and Augustine, see Fred Miller, 'Aristotle on the Reality of Time', *Archiv für Geschichte der Philosophie* 61 (1974), pp. 132–55; and Norman Kretzmann, 'Time Exists—But Hardly, or Obscurely (*Physics* iv, 10; 217b29–218a33)', *Aristotelian Society Supplementary Volume* I (1976), pp. 91–114.

for duration, words such as 'permanence' and 'persistence', which in their ordinary, temporal application turn out to have been unintended metaphors. 'Atemporal duration', like the ancient technical use of '*aiōn*' itself, violates established usage; but an attempt to convey a new philosophical or scientific concept by adapting familiar expressions is not to be rejected on the basis of its violation of ordinary usage. The apparent incoherence in the concept is primarily a consequence of continuing to think of duration only as 'persistence *through time*'.

Since a life is a kind of duration, some of the apparent incoherence in the notion of an atemporal life may be dispelled in rendering the notion of atemporal duration less readily dismissible. But life is in addition ordinarily associated with processes of various sorts, and processes are essentially temporal, and so the notion of an atemporal entity that has life seems incoherent.[25] Now what Aquinas, for example, is thinking of when he attributes life to eternal God is the doctrine that God is a mind. (Obviously what is atemporal cannot consist of physical matter; we assume for the sake of the argument that there is nothing incoherent in the notion of a wholly immaterial, independently existent mind.) Since God is atemporal, the mind that is God must be different in important ways from a temporal, human mind. Considered as an atemporal mind, God cannot deliberate, anticipate, remember, or plan ahead, for instance; all these mental activities essentially involve time, either in taking time to be performed (like deliberation) or in requiring a temporal viewpoint as a prerequisite to performance (like remembering). But it is clear that there are other mental activities that do not require a temporal interval or viewpoint. Knowing seems to be the paradigm case; learning, reasoning, inferring take time, as knowing does not. In reply to the question 'What have you been doing for the past two hours?' it makes sense to say 'Studying logic' or 'Proving theorems', but not 'Knowing logic'. Similarly, it makes sense to say 'I'm learning logic', but not 'I'm knowing logic'. And knowing is not the only mental activity requiring neither a temporal interval nor a temporal viewpoint. Willing, for example, unlike wishing or desiring, seems to be another. Perceiving is impossible in any literal sense for a mind that is disembodied, but nothing in the nature of incorporeality or atemporality seems to rule out the possibility of awareness. And though *feeling* angry is impossible for an atemporal entity—if feelings of anger are essentially associated, as they seem to be, with bodily states—we do not see that anything prevents such an entity from *being* angry, a state the components of which might be, for instance, being aware of an injustice, disapproving of it, and willing its punishment. It seems, then, that the notion

---

[25]William Kneale has taken this notion to be genuinely incoherent and among the most important reasons for rejecting the classic concept of eternity. See his 'Time and Eternity in Theology', *Proceedings of the Aristotelian Society* 61 (1960), pp. 87–108; also his article 'Eternity' in Paul Edwards (ed.), *The Encyclopedia of Philosophy* (New York, 1967), vol. 3, pp. 63–6. Cf. Martha Kneale, 'Eternity and Sempiternity', *Proceedings of the Aristotelian Society*, 69 (1968–9), pp. 223–38.

of an atemporal mind is not incoherent, but that, on the contrary, it is possible that such a mind might have a variety of faculties or activities. Our informal, incomplete consideration of that possibility is not even the beginning of an argument for such a conclusion, but it is enough for our purposes here to suggest the line along which such an argument might develop. The notion of an atemporal mind is not *prima facie* absurd, and so neither is the notion of an atemporal life absurd; for any entity that has or is a mind must be considered to be *ipso facto* alive, whatever characteristics of other living beings it may lack.

V. THE NOTION OF AN ETERNAL ENTITY'S ACTING IN TIME

The difficulties we have considered so far are difficulties in the concept of eternity itself. We have by no means dealt explicitly with all the objections to the concept which have been raised in contemporary discussions; but many of those objections involve difficulties over simultaneity, and such objections can, we think, be dealt with adequately in the light of our previous discussion of ET-simultaneity. We hope, for instance, to have revealed the misunderstanding underlying such attempted reductions of the concept to absurdity as this one:

> But, on St Thomas' view, my typing of this paper is simultaneous with the whole of eternity. Again, on his view, the great fire of Rome is simultaneous with the whole of eternity. Therefore, while I type these very words, Nero fiddles heartlessly on.[26]

We want now to turn to fundamental difficulties in theological applications of the concept, particularly those which arise in considering the possibility of interaction between eternal and temporal entities.

There are several reasons for thinking that an eternal entity, as we have characterized it, could not affect or respond to temporal entities, events, or state of affairs. Just as an eternal entity cannot exist in time, so, we might suppose, (I) an eternal entity cannot act in time. It might seem, furthermore, that (II) the nature of a temporal action is such that the agent itself must be temporal. Nelson Pike provides the following case in point:

> Let us suppose that yesterday a mountain, 17,000 feet high, came into existence on the flatlands of Illinois. One of the local theists explains this occurrence by reference to divine creative action. He claims that God produced (created, brought about) the mountain. Of course, if God is timeless,

---

[26]Anthony Kenny, 'Divine Foreknowledge and Human Freedom', in Kenny (ed.), *Aquinas: A Collection of Critical Essays* (Garden City, NY, 1969), pp. 255–70, 264.

He could not have produced the mountain *yesterday*. This would require that God's creative-activity and thus the individual whose activity it is have position in time. The theist's claim is that God *timelessly* brought it about that yesterday, a 17,000 feet high mountain came into existence on the flatlands of Illinois.... [But] The claim that God *timelessly* produced a temporal object (such as the mountain) is absurd.[27]

On this basis Pike denies that God, considered as atemporal, could produce or create anything; whatever is produced or created begins to exist and so has a position in time. And it might be argued along similar lines that (III) an atemporal entity could not preserve anything temporal in existence because to do so would require temporal duration on the part of the preserver.

If God is taken to be eternal, considerations I, II, and III are incompatible with some doctrines central to most versions of theism, such as the divine creation and preservation of the world, and divine response to petitionary prayer. More specifically, they militate against the central doctrine of Christianity, since the Incarnation of Christ entails that the second person of the Trinity has a temporal nature and performs temporal actions during a certain period of time.

We think all three of these considerations are confused. In connection with consideration I, a distinction must be drawn between (*a*) acting in such a way that the action itself can be located in time and (*b*) acting in such a way that the effect of the action can be located in time. For temporal agents the distinction between (*a*) and (*b*) is generally nugatory; for an atemporal entity, however, (*a*) is impossible. An agent's action is an event in the agent's life, and there can be no temporal event in the atemporal life of God. But such an observation does not tell against (*b*). If an eternal God is also omnipotent, he can do anything it is not logically impossible for him to do. Even though his actions cannot be located in time, he can bring about effects in time unless doing so is logically impossible for him.

Considerations II and III may be construed as providing reasons for thinking that it is indeed logically impossible for an atemporal entity to produce temporal effects. Pike's version of consideration II, however, involves a confusion like the confusion just sorted out for consideration I. He says:

(9) '[I]f God is timeless, He could not have produced the mountain *yesterday*.'
(10) 'The claim that God *timelessly* produced a temporal object (such as the mountain) is absurd.'

Both these propositions are ambiguous because of the possibility of assigning different scopes to 'yesterday' and to 'timelessly' (or 'atemporally'), and the ambiguities can be sorted out in this way:

---

[27]Nelson Pike, *God and Timelessness* (London, 1970), pp. 104–5.

(9)(*a*) If God is atemporal, he cannot yesterday have brought it about that a temporal object came into existence.

(9)(*b*) If God is atemporal, he cannot (atemporally) bring it about that a temporal object came into existence yesterday.

(10)(*a*) It is absurd to claim that God atemporally brings it about that a temporal object came into existence.

(10)(*b*) It is absurd to claim that God brings it about that a temporal object came into existence atemporally.[28]

Apparently without taking account of the ambiguity of propositions (9) and (10), Pike understands them as (9)(*a*) and (10)(*b*) respectively. Propositions (9)(*a*) and (10)(*b*) are indeed true, but they do not support Pike's inference that an atemporal God cannot produce a temporal object. In drawing that inference, Pike seems to be relying on an assumption about a temporal relationship that must hold between an action and its effect. The assumption is not entirely clear; in some passages of his *God and Timelessness* it looks as if Pike thinks that an action and its effect must be simultaneous, an assumption that is plainly false in general regarding actions and their effects as ordinarily conceived of. But if we do adopt co-occurrence as a theoretically justifiable condition on causal connection between an action and its effect, we can point out that any and every action of an eternal entity is ET-simultaneous with any temporal effect ascribed to it. And, since it would simply beg the question to insist that only *temporal* simultaneity between an action and its effect can satisfy this necessary condition of causal connection, we see no reason for denying of an eternal, omnipotent entity that its atemporal act of willing could bring it about that a mountain came into existence on [yesterday's date]. Consequently, we can see no reason for thinking it absurd to claim that a divine action resulting in the existence of a temporal entity is an atemporal action. In other words, we think that propositions (9)(*b*) and (10)(*a*) are false, although they are legitimate senses of the ambiguous propositions (9) and (10). And so we reject consideration II as well as I.

Our reasons for rejecting these first two considerations apply as well, *mutatis mutandis*, to consideration III. If it is not impossible for an omnipotent, eternal entity to act in eternity (by atemporally willing) in such a way as to bring it about that a temporal entity begins to exist at a particular time, it is not impossible for an omnipotent, eternal entity to act in eternity (by atemporally willing) in such a way that that temporal entity continues to exist during a particular temporal interval.

---

[28]These ambiguities, like the two interpretations provided for consideration I above, are of the sort extensively investigated by medieval logicians under their distinction between the compounded and divided senses of propositions. Thus (9)(*a*) and (10)(*a*) present the compounded senses of propositions (9) and (10), whereas (9)(*b*) and (10)(*b*) present their divided senses.

A different sort of difficulty arises in connection with answering prayers or punishing injustice, for instance, since in such cases it seems necessary that the eternal action occur later than the temporal action; and so our reasons for rejecting considerations I, II, and III, based on the ET-simultaneity of eternal actions with temporal events, seem inapplicable. The problem of answering prayers is typical of difficulties of this sort. An answer to a prayer must be later than the prayer, it seems, just because

(11) Something constitutes an answer to a prayer only if it is done because of the prayer.

and

(12) Something is done because of a prayer only if it is done later than the praying of the prayer.

We think that (11) is true; (12), on the other hand, seems doubtful even as applied to temporal entities. If at 3 o'clock a mother prepares a snack for her little boy because she believes that when he gets home at 3.30 he will ask for one, it does not seem unreasonable to describe her as preparing the food because of the child's request, even though in this case the response is earlier than the request. Whatever may be true regarding temporal entities, however, if (12) is true, it obviously rules out the possibility of an eternal entity's responding to prayers. But consider the case of Hannah's praying on a certain day to have a child and her conceiving several days afterward.[29] Both the day of her prayer and the day of her conceiving are ET-simultaneous with the life of an eternal entity. If such an entity atemporally wills that Hannah conceive on a certain day after the day of her prayer, then such an entity's bringing it about that Hannah conceives on that day is clearly a response to her prayer, even though the willing is ET-simultaneous with the prayer rather than later than it. If ET-simultaneity is a sufficient condition for the possibility of a causal connection in the case of God's bringing about the existence of temporal entity, it is likewise sufficient for the possibility of his acting because of a prayer prayed at a particular time.[30]

The principal difficulty in the doctrine of the Incarnation seems intractable to considerations of the sort with which we have been trying to alleviate difficulties associated with an eternal entity's willing to bring about a temporal event, because according to the doctrine of the Incarnation an eternal entity itself entered time. If we take the essence of the doctrine to be expressed in

---

[29]I Samuel 1: 9–20.

[30]For a discussion of other philosophical problems associated with petitionary prayer see Eleonore Stump, 'Petitionary Prayer', *American Philosophical Quarterly*, 16(1) (Jan. 1979), pp. 81–91.

(13) 'When the fulness of the time was come, God sent forth his Son, born of a woman' (Galatians 4: 4).

it is not difficult to see, in the light of our discussion so far, how to provide an interpretation that shows that, as regards God's sending his Son, the doctrine is compatible with God's eternality:

(13') God atemporally wills that his Son be born of a woman at the appointed time.

But the possibility of making sense of an eternal action with a temporal effect does not settle this issue, because the principal difficulty here does not lie in the nature of the relationship between an eternal agent and a temporal effect. The difficulty here is rather that an eternal entity is also a *component* of the temporal effect—an effect which is, to put it simplistically, an eternal entity's having become temporal without having ceased (*per impossibile*) to exist eternally. Formulating the difficulty in the doctrine of the Incarnation simplistically, however, simply exacerbates it. And whereas this formulation of it may present an insuperable difficulty for one or more of the heresies of the Patristic period that took the person of Christ to be only divine or only human, it is ineffective against the orthodox doctrines of the Trinity and the dual nature of Christ. A full treatment of those philosophically intricate doctrines lies outside the scope of this paper, but we will consider them very briefly on the basis of our limited understanding of them in order to suggest some reasons for supposing that the doctrine of the Incarnation is not incompatible with the doctrine of God's eternality.

The doctrine of the Trinity maintains that God, although one substance, consists in three persons, the second of which is God the Son. The doctrine of the dual nature maintains that the second person of the Trinity has not merely one essence or nature, like every other person divine or human, but two: one the divine nature common to all the persons of the Trinity, the other the human nature of the Incarnation. One of the explicitly intended consequences of the doctrine of the dual nature is that any statement predicating something of Christ is ambiguous unless it contains a phrase specifying one or the other or both of his two natures. That is, the proposition

(14) Christ died.

is ambiguous among these three readings:

(14)(*a*) Christ with respect to his divine nature (or *qua* God) died.
(14)(*b*) Christ with respect to his human nature (or *qua* man) died.
(14)(*c*) Christ with respect to his divine and human natures (or *qua* both God and man) died.

From the standpoint of orthodox Christianity (14)(*a*) and (14)(*c*) are false, and (14)(*b*) is true. (14)(*b*) is not to be interpreted as denying that God died, however—such a denial forms the basis of at least one Christian heresy—but to deny that God, the second person of the Trinity, died with respect to his divine nature. Such an account is loaded with at least apparent paradox, and it is not part of our purpose here even to sketch an analysis of it; but, whatever its internal difficulties may be, the doctrine of the dual nature provides *prima facie* grounds for denying the incompatibility of God's eternality and God's becoming man.

A Boethian account of the compatibility of divine eternality and the Incarnation might be developed along these lines, we think.[31] The divine nature of the second person of the Trinity, like the divine nature of either of the other persons of the Trinity, cannot become temporal; nor could the second person at some time acquire a human nature he does not eternally have. Instead, the second person eternally has two natures; and at some temporal instants, all of which are ET-simultaneous with both these natures in their entirety, the human nature of the second person has been temporally actual. At those times and only in that nature the second person directly participates in temporal events. We need no theologian to tell us how rudimentary this outline is, and no other philosopher to tell us how paradoxical it looks; but we are not now willing or able or required by our main purpose in this paper to undertake an analysis or defence of the role of the doctrine of the dual nature in establishing the compatibility of divine eternality and the Incarnation. We hope simply to have pointed out that the doctrine of the Incarnation cannot be reduced to the belief that God became temporal and that, if it is understood as including the doctrine of the dual nature, it can be seen to have been constructed in just such a way as to avoid being reduced to that simple belief. And those observations are all we need for now in order to allay the suspicion that eternality must be incompatible with the central doctrine of orthodox Christianity.

It seems to us, then, that the concept of eternity is coherent and that there is no logical impossibility in the notion of an eternal being's acting in time, provided that acting in time is understood as we have explained it here.

---

[31]Although Boethius treats of the Incarnation and the dual nature of Christ in his theological tractates, especially in his *Contra Eutychen et Nestorium* (in Stewart, Rand, and Tester, *Boethius*), he does not apply his concept of eternity in those discussions as we think it ought to be applied.

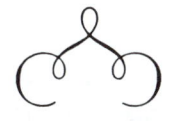

OMNIPOTENCE

ST. THOMAS AQUINAS

The Limits on God's Abilities

We proceed thus to the Third Article:—

Objection 1. It seems that God is not omnipotent. For movement and passiveness belong to everything. But this is impossible for God, since He is immovable, as was said above. Therefore He is not omnipotent.

Obj. 2. Further, sin is an act of some kind. But God cannot sin, nor *deny Himself,* as it is said 2 *Tim.* ii. 13. Therefore He is not omnipotent.

Obj. 3. Further, it is said of God that He manifests His omnipotence *especially by sparing and having mercy.* Therefore the greatest act possible to the divine power is to spare and have mercy. There are things much greater, however, than sparing and having mercy; for example, to create another world, and the like. Therefore God is not omnipotent.

Obj. 4. Further, upon the text, *God hath made foolish the wisdom of this world* (*I Cor.* i. 20), the *Gloss* says: *God hath made the wisdom of this world foolish* by showing those things to be possible which it judges to be impossible. Whence it seems that nothing is to be judged possible or impossible in reference to inferior causes, as the wisdom of this world judges them; but in reference to the divine power. If God, then were omnipotent, all things would be possible; nothing, therefore, impossible. But if we take away the impossible, then we destroy also the necessary; for what necessarily exists cannot possibly not exist. Therefore, there would be nothing at all that is necessary in things if God were omnipotent. But this is an impossibility. Therefore God is not omnipotent.

On the contrary, It is said: *No word shall be impossible with God* (*Luke* i. 37).

I answer that, All confess that God is omnipotent; but it seems difficult to explain in what His omnipotence precisely consists. For there may be a doubt as to the precise meaning of the word "all" when we say that God can do all things. If, however, we consider the matter aright, since power is said in reference to possible things, this phrase, *God can do all things*, is rightly understood to mean that God can do all things that are possible; and for this reason He is said to be omnipotent. Now according to the Philosopher a thing is said to be possible in two ways. First, in relation to some power; thus whatever is subject to human power is said to be possible to man. Now God cannot be said to be omnipotent through being able to do all things that are possible to created nature; for the divine power extends farther than that. If, however, we were to say that God is omnipotent because He can do all things that are possible to His power, there would be a vicious circle in explaining the nature of His power. For this would be saying nothing else but that God is omnipotent because He can do all that He is able to do.

It remains, therefore, that God is called omnipotent because He can do all things that are possible absolutely; which is the second way of saying a thing is possible. For a thing is said to be possible or impossible absolutely, according to the relation in which the very terms stand to one another: possible, if the predicate is not incompatible with the subject, as that Socrates sits; and absolutely impossible when the predicate is altogether incompatible with the subject, as, for instance, that a man is an ass.

It must, however, be remembered that since every agent produces an effect like itself, to each active power there corresponds a thing possible as its proper object according to the nature of that act on which its active power is founded; for instance, the power of giving warmth is related, as to its proper object, to the being capable of being warmed. The divine being, however, upon which the nature of power in God is founded, is infinite; it is not limited to any class of being, but possesses within itself the perfection of all being. Whence, whatsoever has or can have the nature of being is numbered among the absolute possible, in respect of which God is called omnipotent.

Now nothing is opposed to the notion of being except non-being. Therefore, that which at the same time implies being and non-being is repugnant to the notion of an absolute possible, which is subject to the divine omnipotence. For such cannot come under the divine omnipotence; not indeed because of any defect in the power of God, but because it has not the nature of a feasible or possible thing. Therefore, everything that does not imply a contradiction in terms is numbered among those possibles in respect of which God is called omnipotent; whereas whatever implies contradiction does not come within the scope of divine omnipotence, because it cannot have the aspect of possibility. Hence it is more appropriate to say that such things cannot be done, than that God cannot do them. Nor is this contrary to the word of the angel, saying: *No word shall be impossible with God* (*Luke* i. 37). For whatever implies a contradiction cannot be a word, because no intellect can possibly conceive such a thing.

Reply Obj. 1. God is said to be omnipotent in respect to active power, not to passive power, as was shown above. Whence the fact that He is immovable or impassible is not repugnant to His omnipotence.

Reply Obj. 2. To sin is to fall short of a perfect action; hence to be able to sin is to be able to fall short in action, which is repugnant to omnipotence. Therefore it is that God cannot sin, because of His omnipotence. Now it is true that the Philosopher says that *God can deliberately do what is evil.* But this must be understood either on a condition, the antecedent of which is impossible—as, for instance, if we were to say that God can do evil things if He will. For there is no reason why a conditional proposition should not be true, though both the antecedent and consequent are impossible: as if one were to say: *If man is an ass, he has four feet.* Or he may be understood to mean that God can do some things which now seem to be evil: which, however, if He did them, would then be good. Or he is, perhaps, speaking after the common manner of the pagans, who thought that men became gods, like Jupiter or Mercury.

Reply Obj. 3. God's omnipotence is particularly shown in sharing and having mercy, because in this it is made manifest that God has supreme power, namely, that He freely forgives sins. For it is not for one who is bound by laws of a superior to forgive sins of his own free choice. Or, it is thus shown because by sparing and having mercy upon men, He leads them to the participation of an infinite good; which is the ultimate effect of the divine power. Or it is thus shown because, as was said above, the effect of the divine mercy is the foundation of all the divine works. For nothing is due anyone, except because of something already given him gratuitously by God. In this way the divine omnipotence is particularly made manifest, because to it pertains the first foundation of all good things.

Reply Obj. 4. The absolute possible is not so called in reference either to higher causes, or to inferior causes, but in reference to itself. But that which is called possible in reference to some power is named possible in reference to its proximate cause. Hence those things which it belongs to God alone to do immediately—as, for example, to create, to justify, and the like—are said to be possible in reference to a higher cause. Those things, however, which are such as to be done by inferior causes, are said to be possible in reference to those inferior causes. For it is according to the condition of the proximate cause that the effect has contingency or necessity, as was shown above. Thus it is that the wisdom of the world is deemed foolish, because what is impossible to nature it judges to be impossible to God. So it is clear that the omnipotence of God does not take away from things their impossibility and necessity.

GEORGE I. MAVRODES

Some Puzzles Concerning Omnipotence

The doctrine of God's omnipotence appears to claim that God can do anything. Consequently, there have been attempts to refute the doctrine by giving examples of things which God cannot do; for example, He cannot draw a square circle.

Responding to objections of this type, St. Thomas pointed out that "anything" should be here construed to refer only to objects, actions, or states of affairs whose descriptions are not self-contradictory.[1] For it is only such things whose nonexistence might plausibly be attributed to a lack of power in some agent. My failure to draw a circle on the exam may indicate my lack of geometrical skill, but my failure to draw a square circle does not indicate any such lack. Therefore, the fact that it is false (or perhaps meaningless) to say that God could draw one does no damage to the doctrine of His omnipotence.

A more involved problem, however, is posed by this type of question: can God create a stone too heavy for Him to lift? This appears to be stronger than the first problem, for it poses a dilemma. If we say that God can create a stone, then it seems that there might be such a stone. And if there might be a stone too heavy for Him to lift, then He is evidently not omnipotent. But if we deny that God can create such a stone, we seem to have given up His omnipotence already. Both answers lead us to the same conclusion.

Further, this problem does not seem obviously open to St. Thomas' solution. The form "x is able to draw a square circle" seems plainly to involve a contradiction, while "x is able to make a thing too heavy for x to lift" does not. For it may easily be true that I am able to make a boat too heavy for me to lift. So why should it not be possible for God to make a stone too heavy for Him to lift?

Despite this apparent difference, this second puzzle *is* open to essentially the same answer as the first. The dilemma fails because it consists of asking whether God can do a self-contradictory thing. And the reply that He cannot does no damage to the doctrine of omnipotence.

The specious nature of the problem may be seen in this way. God is either omnipotent or not.[2] Let us assume first that He is not. In that case the phrase "a stone too heavy for God to lift" may not be self-contradictory. And

From *The Philosophical Review* 72 (1963): 221–23. Reprinted by permission of the author and *The Philosophical Review*

[1] St. Thomas Aquinas, *Summa Theologiae*, Ia, q. 25, a. 3.

[2] I assume, of course, the existence of God, since that is not being brought in question here.

then, of course, if we assert either that God is able or that He is not able to create such a stone, we may conclude that He is not omnipotent. But this is no more than the assumption with which we began, meeting us again after our roundabout journey. If this were all that the dilemma could establish it would be trivial. To be significant it must derive this same conclusion *from the assumption that God is omnipotent;* that is, it must show that the assumption of the omnipotence of God leads to a *reductio*. But does it?

On the assumption that God is omnipotent, the phrase "a stone too heavy for God to lift" becomes self-contradictory. For it becomes "a stone which cannot be lifted by Him whose power is sufficient for lifting anything." But the "thing" described by a self-contradictory phrase is absolutely impossible and hence has nothing to do with the doctrine of omnipotence. Not being an object of power at all, its failure to exist cannot be the result of some lack in the power of God. And, interestingly, it is the very omnipotence of God which makes the existence of such a stone absolutely impossible, while it is the fact that I am finite in power which makes it possible for me to make a boat too heavy for me to lift.

But suppose that some die-hard objector takes the bit in his teeth and denies that the phrase "a stone too heavy for God to lift" is self-contradictory, even on the assumption that God is omnipotent. In other words, he contends that the description "a stone too heavy for an omnipotent God to lift" is self-coherent and therefore describes an absolutely possible object. Must I then attempt to prove the contradiction which I assume above as intuitively obvious? Not necessarily. Let me reply simply that if the objector is right in this contention, then the answer to the original question is "Yes, God can create such a stone." It may seem that this reply will force us into the original dilemma. But it does not. For now the objector can draw no damaging conclusion from this answer. And the reason is that he has just now contended that such a stone is compatible with the omnipotence of God. Therefore, from the possibility of God's creating such a stone it cannot be concluded that God is not omnipotent. The objector cannot have it both ways. The conclusion which he himself wishes to draw from an affirmative answer to the original question is itself the required proof that the descriptive phrase which appears there is self-contradictory. And "it is more appropriate to say that such things cannot be done, than that God cannot do them."[3]

The specious nature of this problem may also be seen in a somewhat different way.[4] Suppose that some theologian is convinced by this dilemma that he must give up the doctrine of omnipotence. But he resolves to give up as little as possible, just enough to meet the argument. One way he can do so is by retaining the infinite power of God with regard to lifting, while placing a restriction on the sort of stone He is able to create. The only restriction required here, however, is that God must not be able to create a stone too heavy for Him

---

[3]St. Thomas, *loc. cit.*

[4]But this method rests finally on the same logical relations as the preceding one.

to lift. Beyond that the dilemma has not even suggested any necessary restriction. Our theologian has, in effect, answered the original question in the negative, and he now regretfully supposes that this has required him to give up the full doctrine of omnipotence. He is now retaining what he supposes to be the more modest remnants which he has salvaged from that doctrine.

We must ask, however, what it is which he has in fact given up. Is it the unlimited power of God to create stones? No doubt. But what stone is it which God is now precluded from creating? The stone too heavy for Him to lift, of course. But we must remember that nothing in the argument required the theologian to admit any limit on God's power with regard to the lifting of stones. He still holds that to be unlimited. And if God's power to lift is infinite, then His power to create may run to infinity also without outstripping that first power. The supposed limitation turns out to be no limitation at all, since it is specified only by reference to another power which is itself infinite. Our theologian need have no regrets, for he has given up nothing. The doctrine of the power of God remains just what it was before.

Nothing I have said above, of course, goes to prove that God is, in fact, omnipotent. All I have intended to show is that certain arguments intended to prove that He is not omnipotent fail. They fail because they propose, as tests of God's power, putative tasks whose descriptions are self-contradictory. Such pseudo-tasks, not falling within the realm of possibility, are not objects of power at all. Hence the fact that they cannot be performed implies no limit on the power of God, and hence no defect in the doctrine of omnipotence.

HARRY G. FRANKFURT

The Logic of Omnipotence

George Mavrodes has recently presented an analysis designed to show that, despite some appearances to the contrary, a certain well-known puzzle actually raises no serious difficulties in the notion of divine omnipotence.[1] The puzzle suggests a test of God's power—can He create a stone too heavy for Him to lift?—which, it seems, cannot fail to reveal that His power is limited. For He must, it would appear, either show His limitations by being unable to create such a stone or by being unable to lift it once He had created it.

From *The Philosophical Review* 73 (1964). Reprinted by permission of the author and *The Philosophical Review*.

[1]George Mavrodes, "Some Puzzles Concerning Omnipotence," *The Philosophical Review* 72 (1963), 221–23.

In dealing with this puzzle, Mavrodes points out that it involves the setting of a task whose description is self-contradictory—the task of creating a stone too heavy for an omnipotent being to lift. He calls such tasks "pseudo-tasks" and he says of them: "Such pseudo-tasks, not falling within the realm of possibility, are not objects of power at all. Hence the fact that they cannot be performed implies no limit on the power of God, and hence no defect in the doctrine of omnipotence."[2] Thus his way of dealing with the puzzle relies upon the principle that an omnipotent being need not be supposed capable of performing tasks whose descriptions are self-contradictory.

Now this principle is one which Mavrodes apparently regards as self-evident, since he offers no support for it whatever except some references which indicate that it was also accepted by Saint Thomas Aquinas. I do not wish to suggest that the principle is false. Indeed, for all I know it may even be self-evident. But it happens to be a principle which has been rejected by some important philosophers.[3] Accordingly, it might be preferable to have an analysis of the puzzle in question which does not require the use of this principle. And in fact, such an analysis is easy to provide.

Suppose, then, that God's omnipotence enables Him to do even what is logically impossible and that He actually creates a stone too heavy for Him to lift. The critic of the notion of divine omnipotence is quite mistaken if he thinks that this supposition plays into his hands. What the critic wishes to claim, of course, is that when God has created a stone which He cannot lift He is then faced with a task beyond His ability and is therefore seen to be limited in power. But this claim is not justified.

---

[2]*Ibid.*, p. 223.

[3]Descartes, for instance, who in fact thought it blasphemous to maintain that God can do only what can be described in a logically coherent way: "The truths of mathematics...were established by God and entirely depend on Him, as much as do all the rest of His creatures. Actually, it would be to speak of God as a Jupiter or Saturn and to subject Him to the Styx and to the Fates, to say that these truths are independent of Him.... You will be told that if God established these truths He would be able to change them, as a king does his laws; to which it is necessary to reply that this is correct.... In general we can be quite certain that God can do whatever we are able to understand, but not that He cannot do what we are unable to understand. For it would be presumptuous to think that our imagination extends as far as His power" (letter to Mersenne, 15 April 1630). "God was as free to make it false that all the radii of a circle are equal as to refrain from creating the world" (letter to Mersenne, 27 May 1630). "I would not even dare to say that God cannot arrange that a mountain should exist without a valley, or that one and two should not make three; but I only say that He has given me a mind of such a nature that I cannot conceive a mountain without a valley or a sum of one and two which would not be three, and so on, and that such things imply contradictions in my conception" (letter to Arnauld, 29 July 1648). "As for the difficulty in conceiving how it was a matter of freedom and indifference to God to make it true that the three angles of a triangle should equal two right angles, or generally that contradictions should not be able to be together, one can easily remove it by considering that the power of God can have no limit.... God cannot have been determined to make it true that contradictions cannot be together, and consequently He could have done the contrary" (letter to Mesland, 2 May 1644).

For why should God not be able to perform the task in question? To be sure, it is a task—the task of lifting a stone which He cannot lift—whose description is self-contradictory. But if God is supposed capable of performing one task whose description is self-contradictory—that of creating the problematic stone in the first place—why should He not be supposed capable of performing another—that of lifting the stone? After all, is there any greater trick in performing two logically impossible tasks than there is in performing one?

If an omnipotent being can do what is logically impossible, then he can not only create situations which he cannot handle but also, since he is not bound by the limits of consistency, he can handle situations which he cannot handle.

ANTHONY KENNY

The Definition of Omnipotence

It is by no means easy to state concisely and coherently what is meant by 'omnipotence'. Omniscience appears to be analogous to omnipotence: just as omniscience is knowing everything, so omnipotence is being able to do everything. But whereas it is easy to define what it is to be omniscient, it is not so easy to define omnipotence. A being X is omniscient if, for all p, if p, then X knows that p. We cannot offer a simply parallel definition of omnipotence: X is omnipotent if, for all p, if p, then X can bring it about that p. For this, though it would attribute considerable power to X, would not attribute to him power to do anything which has not already been done, or will not sometime be done. On the other hand, if we drop the if-clause, and say that X is omnipotent iff for all p, X can bring it about that p, then we attribute to X a power far beyond what has traditionally been ascribed to God. For, with the possible exception of Descartes, no theologian or philosopher has seriously maintained that God can bring it about that contradictories are true together. But if, for all p, God can bring it about that p, then, by substitution we can conclude that he can bring it about that both p and not p; that mice are both larger and smaller than elephants, or what you will. Nor can one say that, for all ϕ, God can ϕ; for it seems clear that there will be some substitutions for 'ϕ' which will not give truths when applied to God, such as 'cough', 'sin', or 'die'.

Aquinas rehearses some of the difficulties about omnipotence in the seventh article of the first question of the *De Potentia*. He concludes that God cannot be said to be omnipotent in the sense of being simply able to do everything (*quia omnia possit absolute*). He considers a number of other suggestions. One, attributed to St. Augustine, is that God is omnipotent in the sense that he can do whatever he wants to do. But to this there are serious objections. The blessed in heaven, St. Thomas says, and perhaps even the happy on earth, can do whatever they want; otherwise there would be something lacking in their happiness. But they are not called omnipotent. So it is not enough for the omnipotence which is a divine attribute that God should be able to do whatever he wants. Indeed, a wise man restricts his wants to what is within his power. If he succeeds in this degree of self-control, it will be true of him that he can do whatever he wants. But it is not true that every wise man is an omnipotent man.

Aquinas turns to the formulation: God can do whatever is possible. He raises the question: what does 'possible' mean here? Does it mean: whatever is naturally possible, or whatever is supernaturally possible, i.e. possible to God? If the former, then divine omnipotence does not exceed the power of nature and is no great thing. If the latter, then to say that God is omnipotent is a tautology and the analysis a circumlocution: to say that God is omnipotent is merely to say that God can do all that God can do. And once again, in this sense one can claim that everyone is as omnipotent as God: for everyone can do what he can do.

Aquinas's own account is tantamount to the proposal that the omnipotence of God is the ability to do whatever is logically possible. 'We are left with the alternative', he wrote in the *Summa Theologiae*, 'that he is omnipotent because he can do everything that is absolutely possible.' This possibility is absolute possibility in contrast to the relative just discussed which was possibility relative to a particular agent's powers. 'Something is judged to be possible or impossible from the relationship between its terms: possible when the predicate is compatible with the subject, as, for Socrates to sit; impossible when it is not compatible, as for a man to be a donkey.'

St. Thomas offers a rather dubious reason for this, saying that as God is pure being, not being of any particular kind, anything which qualifies as being (*habet rationem entis*) is a fit object of God's action. He goes on:

> Whatever implies being and not being simultaneously is incompatible with the absolute possibility which falls under the divine omnipotence. Such a contradiction is not subject to it, not from any impotence in God, but because it simply does not have the nature of being feasible or possible. Whatever, then, does not involve a contradiction is in that realm of the possible with respect to which God is called omnipotent. Whatever involves a contradiction is not within the scope of omnipotence because it cannot qualify for possibility. Better, however, to say that it cannot be done, rather than that God cannot do it. (*S.Th.* Ia. 25, 3)

Aquinas's solution, however, does not solve the difficulties. We cannot define omnipotence by saying 'For all p, if it is logically possible that p, then God can bring it about that p.' For there are many counter-examples to this which St. Thomas would himself have admitted as counter-examples. For instance, it is no doubt logically possible that Troy did not fall, but according to the common view God cannot (now at any rate) bring it about that Troy did not fall. Moreover, by itself Aquinas's formula does not show us how to deal with a number of familiar puzzles about the idea of omnipotence. It does not show us, for instance, how to answer such questions as 'Can God make an object too heavy for him to lift?' 'Has God the power to make an immovable lamp-post and the power to make an irresistible cannonball?'

St. Thomas does indeed mention some difficulties of this kind; but before considering them it is worth noting that he seems to prefer the formulation 'God's power is infinite' to the formulation 'God is omnipotent.' I shall later argue that this is a sound instinct. However, St. Thomas's argument to this effect is unconvincing. God's active power, he says, is in proportion to his actual being; his actual being is infinite; therefore his active power is infinite. Or, in slightly different terms: The more perfect an agent's form, the more powerful it is (e.g. the hotter something is, the better it can heat); therefore, since God's form or essence is infinite so is his power.

The sense in which God's being is infinite is, however, obscure. From time to time St. Thomas explains it along the following lines: while I am a man and this is a table, there are all kinds of things which I am not and which this table is not; e.g. I am not a horse and this table is not a chair. In the case of God, however, he just *is* and his being is not limited by having any cramping predicates stuck on after the copula. Or, as he puts it in the present article, 'God's being is infinite in so far as it is not limited by any container (*recipiens*).' *Esse* appears to be pictured as a sort of fluid which is boundless in itself and is given form and boundaries by being poured into a particular object as into a bucket. In reading Aquinas on Being, one is constantly torn between considering *esse* in terms of vivid but inapplicable metaphors, and abstract but ill-formed formulas. (See Kenny, 1969, 70 ff.)

Among the difficulties which Aquinas raises for his account of omnipotence, however, there is one which deserves to be pondered: 'Every power is manifested by its effects; otherwise it would be a vain power. So if God's power were infinite he could produce an infinite effect.' In the *Summa* the answer is given that God is not a univocal agent (i.e. not an agent whose effect is something of the same kind as itself). A human begetter, being an univocal agent, cannot do anything more than breed men, so that the whole of its power is manifested in its effect. The case is different with analogous agents like God and (in Aristotelian cosmology) the sun. The *De Potentia* gives an alternative answer; the very notion of *being made* or *being an effect* is incompatible with infinity because whatever is made from nothing has some defect. Hence the notion of an infinite effect is incoherent. But might one not go on to conclude that the notion of an infinite power is no less incoherent than the notion of an infinite effect?

Aquinas's objection is an ancestor of a number of modern difficulties. We may consider an instructive question posed by John Mackie in his article 'Evil and Omnipotence':

> Can an omnipotent being make things which he cannot control? It is clear that this is a paradox; the question cannot be answered satisfactorily either in the affirmative or in the negative. If we answer 'Yes' it follows that if God actually makes things which he cannot control, he is not omnipotent once he has made them: there are then things which he cannot do. But if we answer 'No' we are immediately asserting that there are things which he cannot do, that is to say that he is already not omnipotent. (Mackie, 1955, 210)

It is, I think, clear that the answer to Mackie's question is 'No, he cannot': the problem is to show how this answer is not incompatible with omnipotence.

This cannot be done simply by appeal to the notion of logical impossibility: for whether 'There exists a being whom an omnipotent God cannot control' is a logically possible state of affairs or not depends on what definition we give of omnipotence, and whether the concept is a coherent one.

On the other hand, it seems that we can reverse Mackie's dilemma and ask: Does it make sense to say 'X is a being which even an omnipotent being cannot control'? If it does, then God can make such a being without any loss to his omnipotence, since the ascribing of sense to the formula, however it is done, will have shown that failure to control X is not incompatible with omnipotence. If it does not, then it is no limitation on God's omnipotence to say that God cannot bring it about that such a being exists.

Of course 'X makes a being which X cannot control' is not an impossible sentence-frame; but that does not mean that it will give a possibility with every substitution for 'X', especially if we allow as substitutions phrases like 'a being which can control everything'. Similarly, the fact that both 'X shaves Y' and 'X shaves X' are possible sentence-frames does not mean that there can be a barber who shaves all and only those who do not shave themselves.

In discussing Mackie's paradox Plantinga (1967, 168) considers a suggested definition of omnipotence different from those we have been criticizing:

> X is omnipotent iff X is capable of performing any logically possible action.

This will not do, Plantinga says, because making a table that God did not make is a logically possible action, but God cannot make a table which God did not make. Nor can we say:

> X is omnipotent iff X is capable of performing any action A such that the proposition 'X performs A' is logically possible.

For the unfortunate man who is capable only of scratching his ear is capable of performing any action A such that the proposition 'the man who is capable only of scratching his ear performs A' is logically possible, for the only such action A is the action of scratching his ear:

> We might consider the suggestion that God is omnipotent iff God can do any A such that 'God does A' is logically possible.

This, of course, would not be a definition of omnipotence but only an explication of divine omnipotence. But even so, Plantinga remarks, it would be an unsuccessful explication. For let A be the action of 'doing what I am thinking of'. Then 'God does A' will be logically possible: it is logically possible for God to do what I am thinking of; but if what I am thinking of is creating a square circle, then God cannot do what I am thinking of.

Plantinga in the end abandons the search for a totally satisfactory account of omnipotence, believing rightly that such an account is not necessary in order to counter Mackie's argument. More recently Geach (1973, 7 ff.) has concluded, from difficulties such as the ones we have considered, that the notion of omnipotence is incapable of coherent formulation, and suggests that it be abandoned in favour of the notion of being *almighty*, i.e. as having power over all things. And Swinburne (1977, 156) thinks that in answer to puzzles like Mackie's we must say that an omnipotent being can indeed create a being which he cannot control, but that he can exercise this power only at the cost of thereby ceasing to be omnipotent.

I agree with Plantinga that it is difficult to formulate a coherent and elegant definition of omnipotence; and I agree with Geach that the notion of God as almighty is a more essential element in Western theism than the comparatively philosophical notion of omnipotence. But I think that an account of divine omnipotence simpler than Swinburne's can be devised to avoid the difficulties we have been discussing.

Let us consider the following definition of omnipotence: A being is omnipotent if it has every power which it is logically possible to possess.[1]

The definition must first of all be supplemented with an account of when it is logically possible to possess a power. It is logically possible to possess a power, I suggest, if the exercise of the power does not as such involve any logical impossibility. When I say that the exercise of the power does not *as such* involve any logical possibility I mean that there is no logical incoherence in the description of what it is to exercise the power. For a power to be a logically possible power it is not necessary that every exercise of it should be coherently conceivable, but only that some exercise of it should be.

---

[1]The reader may be disappointed that this definition is not given quasi-logical form like the definitions rejected above. This is no accident. I have argued, in my paper 'Human Abilities and Logical Modalities' (Tuomela, 1974), that the current resources of logic are inadequate to analyse the relevant notion of power.

I shall try to explain the definition, and bring out its merits, by applying to some of the difficult cases current in the literature.

An omnipotent being can make an irresistible cannonball, and he can make an immovable lamp-post; there is nothing incoherent in the supposition that these powers are exercised. Of course there would be an incoherence in the idea of them both being exercised simultaneously; but our definition of the logical possibility of possessing a power did not imply that every formulatable exercise of that power should be logically possible, but only that some should.

The man who is capable only of scratching his ear is not omnipotent by our definition; for there are many logically possible powers which he does not possess (e.g. the ability to create a world).

An omnipotent being has the power to do what I am thinking of. It is true that if I am thinking of something which it is impossible to do, then an omnipotent God cannot, on that occasion, exercise the power he has of doing what I am thinking about. But powers are not tied to particular occasions, and it is not necessary, for a power to be genuinely possessed, that it can be coherently exercised on all occasions and in all circumstances. Though God has the power to do what I am thinking of, he cannot exercise this power if I am thinking a nonsensical thought; just as, though he possesses the power to make an immovable lamp-post, he cannot exercise that power if he has just then exercised his power to make an irresistible cannonball.

It will be seen that the definition of omnipotence by generalizing over powers is an attempt to preserve the merits, without the disadvantages, of St. Thomas's formulation of omnipotence as infinite power. St. Thomas was, I think, right in saying that powers are manifested by their effects or, as he elsewhere puts it, specified by their exercises. That is to say, the power to ϕ can only be defined and understood by someone who knows what ϕ-ing is. But it is not true that powers are specified by their effects in such a way that an infinite power must have an infinite effect. No power, whether finite or infinite, is logically exhausted by its effect: even the human power to beget, with which Aquinas contrasts divine power, is not a limited power in the sense that the power to beget children is a power to beget some specified number of children.

There are advantages, then, in defining omnipotence as the totality of logically possible powers rather than as the power to perform all logically possible actions or to bring about all logically possible states of affairs. But even so defined as the totality of logically possible powers omnipotence cannot be ascribed to God. For there are many powers which it is logically possible to have which God cannot have, such as the power to make a table which God has not made. The power to change, to sin, and to die are instances of powers which it is logically possible to have—since we human beings have them—and yet which traditional theism denies to God.

Divine omnipotence, therefore, if it is to be a coherent notion, must be something less than the complete omnipotence which is the possession of all logically possible powers. It must be a narrower omnipotence, consisting in the possession of all logically possible powers which it is logically possible for a being with the attributes of God to possess. (If the definition is not to be empty 'attributes' must here be taken to mean those properties of Godhead which are not themselves powers: properties such as immutability and goodness.) This conception of divine omnipotence is close to traditional accounts of the doctrine while avoiding some of the incoherences we have found in them.

On this account, an omnipotent God will not have the power to make a table that God did not make. The power to make a table that one has not made is not a power that anyone can have; and the power to make a table that God did not make is not a power it is logically possible for someone to have who is identical with God. Any being with all the attributes of God will of course have, *inter alia*, the attribute of being identical with God.

What are we to say, on this account, in answer to the question whether an omnipotent God can make a being whom he cannot control? The power to create, while remaining omnipotent, a being that one cannot control is not a logically possible power, since the description of the power contains a hidden contradiction. The power to create a being that one cannot control and thereby give up one's omnipotence is not a power that could logically be possessed by a being who had the attributes of God including immutability. Consequently, the answer to the conundrum is in the negative: but this does not clash with the notion of divine omnipotence as we have now described it.

Powers such as the power to weaken, sicken, and die will not be parts of divine omnipotence since they clash with other divine attributes. What of the power to do evil? Clearly, the actual performance of an evil deed would be incompatible with divine goodness: but some theologians have thought that the mere power to do evil, voluntarily unexercised, is not only compatible with, but actually enhances the splendour of divine beneficence. If so, then the power to do evil, since it is clearly in itself a logically possible power, would be part of divine omnipotence.

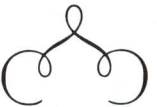

GOD'S OMNISCIENCE AND FREEWILL

ST. THOMAS AQUINAS

God's Eternal Knowledge

We proceed thus to the Thirteenth Article:—

Objection 1. It seems that the knowledge of God is not of future contingent things. For from a necessary cause proceeds a necessary effect. But the knowledge of God is the cause of things known, as was said above. Since therefore that knowledge is necessary, what He knows must also be necessary. Therefore the knowledge of God is not of contingent things.

Obj. 2. Further, every conditional proposition, of which the antecedent is absolutely necessary, must have an absolutely necessary consequent. For the antecedent is to the consequent as principles are to the conclusion: and from necessary principles only a necessary conclusion can follow, as is proved in *Poster.* i. But this is a true conditional proposition, *If God knew that this thing will be, it will be,* for the knowledge of God is only of true things. Now, the antecedent of this conditioned proposition is absolutely necessary, because it is eternal, and because it is signified as past. Therefore the consequent is also absolutely necessary. Therefore whatever God knows is necessary; and so the knowledge of God is not of contingent things.

Obj. 3. Further, everything known by God must necessarily be, because even what we ourselves know must necessarily be; and, of course, the knowledge of God is much more certain than ours. But no future contingent thing must necessarily be. Therefore no contingent future thing is known by God.

On the contrary, It is written (*Ps.* xxxii. 15), *He Who hath made the hearts of every one of them, Who understandeth all their works,* that is, of men. Now the works of men are contingent, being subject to free choice. Therefore God knows future contingent things.

From *Summa Theologica*, Part I. trans. Dominican Fathers of English Province (New York: Benziger Bros., Inc., 1947). Reprinted by permission of the publisher.

I answer that, Since, as was shown above, God knows all things, not only things actual but also things possible to Him and to the creature, and since some of these are future contingent to us, it follows that God knows future contingent things.

In evidence of this, we must observe that a contingent thing can be considered in two ways. First, in itself, in so far as it is already in act, and in this sense it is not considered as future, but as present; neither is it considered as contingent to one of two terms, but as determined to one; and because of this it can be infallibly the object of certain knowledge, for instance to the sense of sight, as when I see that Socrates is sitting down. In another way, a contingent thing can be considered as it is in its cause, and in this way it is considered as future, and as a contingent thing not yet determined to one; for a contingent cause has relation to opposite things: and in this sense a contingent thing is not subject to any certain knowledge. Hence, whoever knows a contingent effect in its cause only, has merely a conjectural knowledge of it. Now God knows all contingent things not only as they are in their causes, but also as each one of them is actually in itself. And although contingent things become actual successively, nevertheless God knows contingent things not successively, as they are in their own being, as we do, but simultaneously. The reason is because His knowledge is measured by eternity, as is also His being; and eternity, being simultaneously whole, comprises all time, as was said above. Hence, all things that are in time are present to God from eternity, not only because He has the essences of things present within Him, as some say, but because His glance is carried from eternity over all things as they are in their presentiality. Hence it is manifest that contingent things are infallibly known by God, inasmuch as they are subject to the divine sight in their presentiality; and yet they are future contingent things in relation to their own causes.

Reply Obj. 1. Although the supreme cause is necessary, the effect may be contingent by reason of the proximate contingent cause; just as the germination of a plant is contingent by reason of the proximate contingent cause, although the movement of the sun, which is the first cause, is necessary. So, likewise, things known by God are contingent because of their proximate causes, while the knowledge of God, which is the first cause, is necessary.

Reply Obj. 2. Some say that this antecedent, *God knew this contingent to be future,* is not necessary, but contingent; because, although it is past, still it imports a relation to the future. This, however, does not remove necessity from it, for whatever has had relation to the future, must have had it, even though the future sometimes is not realized. On the other hand, some say that this antecedent is contingent because it is a compound of the necessary and the contingent; as this saying is contingent, *Socrates is a white man.* But this also is to no purpose; for when we say, *God knew this contingent to be future,* contingent is used here only as the matter of the proposition, and not as its principal part. Hence its contingency or necessity has no reference to the necessity or contingency of the proposition, or to its being true or false. For it may be just as true that I said a man is an ass, as that I said Socrates runs, or God is: and the same applies to necessary and contingent.

Hence it must be said that this antecedent is absolutely necessary. Nor does it follow, as some say, that the consequent is absolutely necessary because the antecedent is the remote cause of the consequent, which is contingent by reason of the proximate cause. But this to no purpose. For the conditional would be false were its antecedent the remote necessary cause, and the consequent a contingent effect; as, for example, if I said, *if the sun moves, the grass will grow.*

Therefore we must reply otherwise: when the antecedent contains anything belonging to an act of the soul, the consequent must be taken, not as it is in itself, but as it is in the soul; for the being of a thing in itself is other than the being of a thing in the soul. For example, when I say, *What the soul understands is immaterial*, the meaning is that it is immaterial as it is in the intellect, not as it is in itself. Likewise if I say, *If God knew anything, it will be*, the consequent must be understood as it is subject to the divine knowledge, that is, as it is in its presentiality. And thus it is necessary, as is also the antecedent; *for everything that is, while it is, must necessarily be*, as the Philosopher says in *Periherm.* i.

Reply Obj. 3. Things reduced to actuality in time are known by us successively in time, but by God they are known in eternity, which is above time. Whence to us they cannot be certain, since we know future contingent things only as contingent futures; but they are certain to God alone, Whose understanding is in eternity above time. Just as he who goes along the road does not see those who come after him; whereas he who sees the whole road from a height sees at once all those traveling on it. Hence, what is known by us must be necessary, even as it is in itself; for what is in itself a future contingent cannot be known by us. But what is known by God must be necessary according to the mode in which it is subject to the divine knowledge, as we have already stated, but not absolutely as considered in its proper causes. Hence also this proposition, *Everything known by God must necessarily be*, is usually distinguished, for it may refer to the thing or to the saying. If it refers to the thing, it is divided and false; for the sense is, *Everything which God knows is necessary*. If understood of the saying, it is composite and true, for the sense is, *This proposition, 'that which is known by God is' is necessary*.

Now some urge an objection and say that this distinction holds good with regard to forms that are separable from a subject. Thus if I said, *It is possible for a white thing to be black*, it is false as applied to the saying, and true as applied to the thing: for a thing which is white can become black; whereas this saying, *a white thing is black*, can never be true. But in forms that are inseparable from a subject, this distinction does not hold: for instance, if I said, *A black crow can be white*; for in both senses it is false. Now to be known by God is inseparable from a thing; for what is known by God cannot be not known. This objection, however, would hold if these words *that which is known* implied any disposition inherent in the subject; but since they import an act of the knower, something can be attributed to the known thing in itself (even if it always be known) which is not attributed to it in so far as it falls under an act of knowledge. Thus, material being is attributed to a stone in itself, which is not attributed to it inasmuch as it is intelligible.

JONATHAN EDWARDS

Foreknowledge Inconsistent with Contingency

Having proved, that God has a certain and infallible prescience of the acts of the will of moral agents, I come now, in the *second* place, to shew the consequence; to shew how it follows from hence, that these events are *necessary*, with a necessity of connection or consequence.

The chief Arminian divines, so far as I have had opportunity to observe, deny this consequence; and affirm, that if such foreknowledge be allowed, 'tis no evidence of any necessity of the event foreknown. Now I desire, that this matter may be particularly and thoroughly enquired into. I cannot but think, that on particular and full consideration, it may be perfectly determined, whether it be indeed so, or not.

In order to ensure a proper consideration of this matter, I would observe the following things.

I. 'Tis very evident, with regard to a thing whose existence is infallibly and indissolubly connected with something which already hath, or has had existence, the existence of that thing is necessary. Here may be noted,

1. I observed before, in explaining the nature of necessity, that in things which are past, their past existence is now necessary: having already made sure of existence, 'tis too late for any possibility of alteration in that respect: 'tis now impossible, that it should be otherwise than true, that that thing has existed.

2. If there be any such thing as a divine foreknowledge of the volitions of free agents, that foreknowledge, by the supposition, is a thing which already *has*, and long ago *had* existence; and so, now its existence is necessary; it is now utterly impossible to be otherwise, than that this foreknowledge should be, or should have been.

From Jonathan Edwards, *Freedom of the Will* (1754), section 12.

3. 'Tis also very manifest, that those things which are indissolubly connected with other things that are necessary, are themselves necessary. As that proposition whose truth is necessarily connected with another proposition, which is necessarily true, is itself necessarily true. To say otherwise, would be a contradiction; it would be in effect to say, that the connection was indissoluble, and yet was not so, but might be broken. If that, whose existence is indissolubly connected with something whose existence is now necessary, is itself not necessary, then it may *possibly not exist,* notwithstanding that indissoluble connection of its existence.—Whether the absurdity ben't glaring, let the reader judge.

4. 'Tis no less evident, that if there be a full, certain and infallible foreknowledge of the future existence of the volitions of moral agents, then there is a certain infallible and indissoluble connection between those events and that foreknowledge; and that therefore, by the preceeding observations, those events are necessary events; being infallibly and indissoluby connected with that whose existence already is, and so is now necessary, and can't but have been.

To say, the foreknowledge is certain and infallible, and yet the connection of the event with that foreknowledge is not indissoluble, but dissoluble and fallible, is very absurd. To affirm it, would be the same thing as to affirm, that there is no necessary connection between a proposition being infallibly known to be true, and its being true indeed. So that it is perfectly demonstrable, that if there be any infallible knowledge of future volitions, the event is *necessary;* or, in other words, that it is *impossible* but the event should come to pass. For if it ben't impossible but that it may be otherwise, then it is not impossible but that the proposition which affirms its future coming to pass, may not now be true. But how absurd is that, on the supposition that there is now an infallible knowledge (i.e knowledge which it is impossible should fail) that it is true. There is this absurdity in it, that it is not impossible but that there now should be no truth in that proposition, which is now infallibly known to be true.

II. That no future event can be certainly foreknown, whose existence is contingent, and without all necessity, may be proved thus; 'tis impossible for a thing to be certainly known to any intellect without *evidence.* To suppose otherwise, implies a contradiction: because for a thing to be certainly known to any understanding, is for it to be *evident* to that understanding; and for a thing to be *evident* to any understanding, is the same thing, as for that understanding to *see evidence* of it: but no understanding, created or increated, can *see evidence* where there is none: for that is the same thing, as to see that to be, which is not. And therefore, if there be any truth which is absolutely without evidence, that truth is absolutely unknowable, insomuch that it implies a contradiction to suppose that it is known.

But if there be any future event, whose existence is contingent, without all necessity, the future existence of that event is absolutely *without evidence.* If there be any evidence of it, it must be one of these two sorts, either *self-evidence,* or *proof;* for there can be no other sort of evidence but one of *these two;* an evident thing must be either evident *in itself,* or evident in *something else;* that is, evident by connection with something else. But a future thing, whose existence is without all necessity, can have neither of these sorts of evidence. It can't be *self-evident:* for if it be, it may be now known by what is now to be seen in the thing itself; either its present existence, or the necessity of its nature: but both these are contrary to the supposition. It is supposed, both that the thing has no present existence to be seen; and also that it is not of such a nature as to be necessarily existent for the future: so that its future existence is not self-evident. And *secondly,* neither is there any *proof,* or evidence in *anything else,* or evidence of connection with some thing else that is evident; for this also is contrary to the supposition. 'Tis supposed, that there is now nothing existent, with which the future existence of the *contingent* event is connected. For such a connection destroys its *contingence,* and supposes necessity. Thus 'tis demonstrated, that there is in the nature of things absolutely no evidence at all of the future existence of that event, which is contingent, without all necessity (if any such event there be) neither self-evidence nor proof. And therefore the thing in reality is not evident; and so can't be seen to be evident, or, which is the same thing, can't be known.

Let us consider this in an example. Suppose that five thousand seven hundred and sixty years ago, there was no other being but the divine being; and then this world, or some particular body or spirit, all at once starts out of nothing into being, and takes on itself a particular nature and form; all in *absolute contingence,* without any concern of God, or any other cause, in the matter; without any manner of ground or reason of its existence; or any dependence upon, or connection at all with anything foregoing; I say, that if this be supposed, there was no evidence of that event before hand. There was no evidence of it to be seen *in the thing itself;* for the thing itself, as yet, was not. And there was no evidence of it to be seen *in any* thing else; for *evidence in something else, is connection with* something else; but such connection is contrary to the supposition. There was no evidence before, that this thing *would happen;* for by the supposition, there was no reason why it *should happen,* rather than something else, or rather than nothing. And if so, then all things before were exactly equal, and the same, with respect to that and other possible things; there was no preponderation, no superior weight or value; and therefore nothing that could be of any weight or value to determine any understanding. The thing was absolutely without evidence, and absolutely unknowable. An increase of understanding, or of the capacity of discerning, has no tendency, and makes no advance, to a discerning any signs or evidences of it, let it be increased never so much; yea, if it be increased infinitely. The increase of the strength of sight may have a tendency to enable to discern the evidence which is far off, and very much hid, and deeply involved in clouds and darkness; but it has no tendency to enable to discern evidence where there is none. If the sight be infinitely strong, and the capacity of discerning infinitely great, it will enable to see all that there is, and to see it perfectly, and with ease; yet it has no tendency at all to enable a being to discern that evidence which is not; but on the contrary, it has a tendency to enable to discern with great certainty that there is none.

III. To suppose the future volitions of moral agents not to be necessary events; or, which is the same thing, events which it is not impossible but that they may not come to pass; and yet to suppose that God certainly foreknows them, and knows all things; is to suppose God's knowledge to be inconsistent with itself. For to say, that God certainly, and without all conjecture, knows that a thing will infallibly be, which at the same time he knows to be so *contingent*, that it may possibly not be, is to suppose his knowledge inconsistent with itself; or that one thing that he knows is utterly inconsistent with another thing that he knows; 'tis the same thing as to say, He now knows a proposition to be of certain infallible truth, which he knows to be of contingent uncertain truth. If a future volition is so without all necessity, that there is nothing hinders but that it may not be, then the proposition which asserts its future existence, is so uncertain, that there is nothing hinders but that the truth of it may entirely fail. And if God knows all things, he knows this proposition to be thus uncertain. And that is inconsistent with his knowing that it is infallibly true; and so inconsistent with this infallibly knowing that it is true. If the thing be indeed contingent, God views it so, and judges it to be contingent, if he views things as they are. If the event be not necessary, then it is possible it may never be: and if it be possible it may never be, God knows it may possibly never be; and that is to know that the proposition which affirms its existence, may possibly not be true; and that is to know that the truth of it is uncertain; which surely is inconsistent with his knowing it as a certain truth. If volitions are in themselves contingent events, without all necessity, then 'tis no argument of perfection of knowledge in any being to determine preemptorily that they will be; but on the contrary an argument of ignorance and mistake: because it would argue, that he supposes that proposition to be certain, which in its own nature, and all things considered, is uncertain and contingent. To say in such a case, that God may have ways of knowing contingent events which we can't conceive of, is ridiculous; as much so, as to say, that God may know contradictions to be true, for ought we know, or that he may know a thing to be certain, and at the same time know it not to be certain, though we can't conceive how; because he has ways of knowing, which we can't comprehend.

Corol. 1. From what has been observed it is evident, that the absolute *decrees* of God are no more inconsistent with human liberty, on account of any necessity of the event which follows from such decrees, than the absolute *foreknowledge* of God. Because the connection between the event and certain foreknowledge, is as infallible and indissoluble, as between the event and an absolute decree. That is, 'tis no more impossible that the event and decree should not agree together, than that the event and absolute knowledge should disagree. The connection between the event and foreknowledge is absolutely perfect, by the supposition, because it is supposed, that the certainty and infallibility of the knowledge is absolutely perfect. And it being so, the certainty can't be increased; and therefore the connection between the knowledge and thing known, can't be increased; so that if a decree be added to the foreknowledge, it don't at all increase the connection, or make it more infallible and indissoluble. If it were not so, the certainty of knowledge might be increased by the addition of a decree; which is contrary to the supposition, which is, that the knowledge is absolutely perfect, or perfect to the highest possible degree.

There is as much of an impossibility but that the things which are infallibly foreknown, should be, or (which is the same thing) as great a necessity of their future existence, as if the event were already written down, and was known and ready by all mankind, through all preceeding ages, and there were the most indissoluble and perfect connection possible, between the writing, and the thing written. In such a case, it would be as impossible the event should fail of existence, as if it had existed already; and a decree can't make an event surer or more necessary than this.

And therefore, if there be any such foreknowledge, as it has been proved there is, then necessity of connection and consequence, is not at all *inconsistent* with any liberty which man, or any other creature enjoys. And from hence it may be inferred, that absolute decrees of God, which don't at all increase the necessity, are not at all inconsistent with the liberty which man enjoys, on any such account, as that they make the event decreed necessary, and render it utterly impossible but that it should come to pass. Therefore if absolute decrees are inconsistent with man's liberty as a moral agent, or his liberty in a state of probation, or any liberty whatsoever that he enjoys, it is not on account of any necessity which absolute decrees infer.

Corol. 2. Hence the doctrine of the Calvinists, concerning the absolute decrees of God, does not at all infer any more *fatality* in things, than will demonstrably follow from the doctrine of most Arminian divines, who acknowledge God's omniscience, and universal prescience. Therefore all objections they make against the doctrine of the Calvinists, as implying Hobbes's doctrine of necessity, or the stoical doctrine of fate, lie no more against the doctrine of Calvinists, than their own doctrine: and therefore it don't become those divines, to raise such an outcry against the Calvinists, on this account.

Corol. 3. Hence all arguing from necessity, against the doctrine of the inability of unregenerate men to perform the conditions of salvation, and the commands of God requiring spiritual duties, and against the Calvinistic doctrine of efficacious grace; I say, all arguings of Arminians (such of 'em as own God's omniscience) against these things, on this ground, that these doctrines, though they don't suppose men to be under any constraint or coaction, yet suppose 'em under necessity, with respect to their moral actions, and those things which are required of 'em in order to their acceptance with

God; and their arguing against the necessity of men's volitions, taken from the reasonableness of God's commands, promises, and threatenings, and the sincerity of his counsels and invitations; and all objections against any doctrines of the Calvinists as being inconsistent with human liberty, because they infer necessity; I say, all these arguments and objections must fall to the ground, and be justly esteemed vain and frivolous, as coming from them; being maintained in an inconsistence with themselves, and in like manner levelled against their own doctrine, as against the doctrine of the Calvinists.

NELSON PIKE

Divine Omniscience and Voluntary Action

In Book V, sec. 3 of his *Consolatio Philosophiae*, Boethius entertained (though he later rejected) the claim that if God is omniscient, no human action is voluntary. This claim seems intuitively false. Surely, given only a doctrine describing God's *knowledge*, nothing about the voluntary status of human actions will follow. Perhaps such a conclusion would follow from a doctrine of divine omnipotence or divine providence, but what connection could there be between the claim that God is *omniscient* and the claim that human actions are determined? Yet Boethius thought he saw a problem here. He thought that if one collected together just the right assumptions and principles regarding God's knowledge, one could derive the conclusion that if God exists, no human action is voluntary. Of course, Boethius did not think that all the assumptions and principles required to reach this conclusion are true (quite the contrary), but he thought it important to draw attention to them nonetheless. If a theologian is to construct a doctrine of God's knowledge which does not commit him to determinism, he must first understand that there is a way of thinking about God's knowledge which would so commit him.

In this paper, I shall argue that although his claim has a sharp counterintuitive ring, Boethius was right in thinking that there is a selection from among the various doctrines and principles clustering about the notions of knowledge, omniscience, and God which, when brought together, demand the conclusion that if God exists, no human action is voluntary. Boethius, I think, did not succeed in making explicit all of the ingredients in the problem. His suspicions were sound, but his discussion was incomplete. His

From *The Philosophical Review*, 74 (1965), pp. 27–46. Reprinted by permission of the author and *The Philosophical Review*.

argument needs to be developed. This is the task I shall undertake in the pages to follow. I should like to make clear at the outset that my purpose in rearguing this thesis is not to show that determinism is true, nor to show that God does not exist, nor to show that either determinism is true or God does not exist. Following Boethius, I shall not claim that the items needed to generate the problem are either philosophically or theologically adequate. I want to concentrate attention on the implications of a certain set of assumptions. Whether the assumptions are themselves acceptable is a question I shall not consider.

I.

A. Many philosophers have held that if a statement of the form "*A* knows *X*" is true, then "*A* believes *X*" is true and "*X*" is true. As a first assumption, I shall take this partial analysis of "*A* knows *X*" to be correct. And I shall suppose that since this analysis holds for all knowledge claims, it will hold when speaking of God's knowledge. "God knows *X*" entails "God believes *X*" and " '*X*' is true."

Secondly, Boethius said that with respect to the matter of knowledge, God "cannot in anything be mistaken."[1] I shall understand this doctrine as follows. Omniscient beings hold no false beliefs. Part of what is meant when we say that a person is omniscient is that the person in question believes nothing that is false. But, further, it is part of the "essence" of God to be omniscient. This is to say that any person who is not omniscient could not be the person we usually mean to be referring to when using the name "God." To put this last point a little differently: if the person we usually mean to be referring to when using the name "God" were suddenly to lose the quality of omniscience (suppose, for example, He came to believe something false), the resulting person would no longer be God. Although we might call this second person "God" (I might call my cat "God"), the absence of the quality of omniscience would be sufficient to guarantee that the person referred to was not the same as the person formerly called by that name. From this last doctrine it follows that the statement "If a given person is God, that person is omniscient" is an a priori truth. From this we may conclude that the statement "If a given person is God, that person holds no false beliefs" is also an a priori truth. It would be conceptually impossible for God to hold a false belief. " '*X*' is true" follows from "God believes *X*." These are all ways of expressing the same principle—the principle expressed by Boethius in the formula "God cannot in anything be mistaken."

A second principle usually associated with the notion of divine omniscience has to do with the scope or range of God's intellectual gaze. To say that a being is omniscient is to say that he knows everything. "Everything" in this statement is usually taken to cover future, as well as present and past,

---

[1]Boethius, *Consolatio Philosophiae*, Bk. V, sec. 3, par. 6.

events and circumstances. In fact, God is usually said to have had foreknowledge of everything that has ever happened. With respect to anything that was, is, or will be the case, God knew, *from eternity*, that it would be the case.

The doctrine of God's knowing everything from eternity is very obscure. One particularly difficult question concerning this doctrine is whether it entails that with respect to everything that was, is, or will be the case, God knew *in advance* that it would be the case. In some traditional theological texts, we are told that God is *eternal* in the sense that He exists "outside of time," that is, in the sense that He bears no temporal relations to the events or circumstances of the natural world.[2] In a theology of this sort, God could not be said to have known that a given natural event was going to happen before it happened. If God knew that a given natural event was going to occur *before* it occurred, at least one of God's cognitions would then have occurred before some natural event. This, surely, would violate the idea that God bears no temporal relations to natural events.[3] On the other hand, in a considerable number of theological sources, we are told that God *has always* existed—that He existed long *before* the occurrence of any natural event. In a theology of this sort, to say that God is eternal is not to say that God exists "outside of time" (bears no temporal relations to natural events); it is to say, instead, God has existed (and will continue to exist) at each moment.[4] The doctrine of omniscience which goes with this second understanding of the notion of eternity is one in which it is affirmed that God *has always* known what was going to happen in the natural world. John Calvin wrote as follows:

> When we attribute foreknowledge to God, we mean that all things have ever been and perpetually remain before, his eyes, so that to his knowledge nothing is future or past, but all things are present; and present in such manner, that he does not merely conceive of them from ideas formed in his mind, as things remembered by us appear to our minds, but really he holds and sees them as if (*tanquam*) actually placed before him.[5]

All things are "present" to God in the sense that He "sees" them as if (*tanquam*) they were actually before Him. Further, with respect to any given natural event, not only is that event "present" to God in the sense indicated, it has *ever been and has perpetually remained* "present" to Him in that sense. This latter is the point of special interest. Whatever one thinks of the idea that God "sees"

---

[2]This position is particularly well formulated in St. Anselm's *Proslogium*, ch. xix, and *Monologium*, chs. xxi–xxii; and in Frederich Schleiermacher's *The Christian Faith*, Pt. I, sec. 2, par. 51. It is also explicit in Boethius, *Consolatio*, secs. 4–6, and in St. Thomas Aquinas's *Summa Theologicae*, Pt. I, q. 10.

[3]This point is explicit in Boethius, *Consolatio*, secs. 4–6.

[4]This position is particularly well expressed in William Paley's *Natural Theology*, ch. xxiv. It is also involved in John Calvin's discussion of predestination, *Institutes of the Christian Religion*, Bk. III, ch. xxi; and in some formulations of the first cause argument for the existence of God, e.g., John Locke's *An Essay Concerning Human Understanding*, Bk. IV, ch. x.

[5]Calvin, *Institutes of the Christian Religion*, Bk. III, ch. xxi; this passage trans. by John Allen (Philadelphia, 1813), II, p. 145.

things as if "actually placed before him," Calvin would appear to be committed to the idea that God has *always known* what was going to happen in the natural world. Choose an event (E) and a time (t_2) at which E occurred. For any time (t_1) prior to t_2, (say, five thousand, six hundred, or eighty years prior to t_2), God knew at t_1 that E would occur at t_2. It will follow from this doctrine, of course, that with respect to any human action, God knew well in advance of its performance that the action would be performed. Calvin says, "when God created man, He foresaw what would happen concerning him." He adds, "little more than five thousand years have elapsed since the creation of the world."[6] Calvin seems to have thought that God foresaw the outcome of every human action well over five thousand years ago.

In the discussion to follow, I shall work only with this second interpretation of God's knowing everything *from eternity*. I shall assume that if a person is omniscient, that person has always known what was going to happen in the natural world—and, in particular, has always known what human actions were going to be performed. Thus, as above, assuming that the attribute of omniscience is part of the "essence" of God, the statement "For any natural event (including human actions), if a given person is God, that person would always have known that that event was going to occur at the time it occurred" must be treated as an a priori truth. This is just another way of stating a point admirably put by St. Augustine when he said: "For to confess that God exists and at the same time to deny that He has foreknowledge of future things is the most manifest folly.... One who is not prescient of all future things is not God."[7]

B. Last Saturday afternoon, Jones mowed his lawn. Assuming that God exists and is (essentially) omniscient in the sense outlined above, it follows that (let us say) eighty years prior to last Saturday afternoon, God knew (and thus believed) that Jones would mow his lawn at that time. But from this it follows, I think, that at the time of action (last Saturday afternoon) Jones was not *able*—that is, it was not *within Jones's power*—to refrain from mowing his lawn.[8] If at the time of action, Jones had been able to refrain from mowing

---

[6]Ibid., p. 144.

[7]Augustine, *City of God*, Bk. V, sec. 9.

[8]The notion of someone being *able* to do something and the notion of something being *within one's power* are essentially the same. Traditional formulations of the problem of divine foreknowledge (e.g., those of Boethius and Augustine) made use of the notion of what is (and what is not) *within one's power*. But the problem is the same when framed in terms of what one is (and one is not) *able* to do. Thus, I shall treat the statements "Jones was able to do X," "Jones had the ability to do X," and "It was within Jones's power to do X" as equivalent. Richard Taylor, in "I Can," *The Philosophical Review*, 69 (1960): 78–89, has argued that the notion of ability or power involved in these last three statements is incapable of philosophical analysis. Be this as it may, I shall not here attempt such an analysis. In what follows I shall, however, be careful to affirm only those statements about what is (or is not) within one's power that would have to be preserved on any analysis of this notion having even the most distant claim to adequacy.

his lawn, then (the most obvious conclusion would seem to be) at the time of action, Jones was able to do something which would have brought it about that God held a false belief eighty years earlier. But God cannot in anything be mistaken. It is not possible that some belief of His was false. Thus, last Saturday afternoon, Jones was not able to do something which would have brought it about that God held a false belief eighty years ago. To suppose that it was would be to suppose that, at the time of action, Jones was able to do something having a conceptually incoherent description, namely something that would have brought it about that one of God's beliefs was false. Hence, given that God believed eighty years ago that Jones would mow his lawn on Saturday, if we are to assign Jones the power on Saturday to refrain from mowing his lawn, this power must not be described as the power to do something that would have rendered one of God's beliefs false. How then should we describe it vis-à-vis God and His belief? So far as I can see, there are only two other alternatives. First, we might try describing it as the power to do something that would have brought it about that God believed otherwise than He did eighty years ago; or, secondly, we might try describing it as the power to do something that would have brought it about that God (Who, by hypothesis, existed eighty years earlier) did not exist eighty years earlier—that is, as the power to do something that would have brought it about that any person who believed eighty years ago that Jones would mow his lawn on Saturday (one of whom was, by hypothesis, God) held a false belief, and thus was not God. But again, neither of these latter can be accepted. Last Saturday afternoon, Jones was not able to do something that would have brought it about that God believed otherwise than He did eighty years ago. Even if we suppose (as was suggested by Calvin) that eighty years ago God knew Jones would mow his lawn on Saturday in the sense that He "saw" Jones mowing his lawn as if this action were occurring before Him, the fact remains that God knew (and thus believed) eighty years prior to Saturday that Jones would mow his lawn. And if God held such a belief eighty years prior to Saturday, Jones did not have the power on Saturday to do something that would have made it the case that God did not hold this belief eighty years earlier. No action performed at a given time can alter the fact that a given person held a certain belief at a time prior to the time in question. This last seems to be an a priori truth. For similar reasons, the last of the above alternatives must also be rejected. On the assumption that God existed eighty years prior to Saturday, Jones on Saturday was not able to do something that would have brought it about that God did not exist eighty years prior to that time. No action performed at a given time can alter the fact that a certain person existed at a time prior to the time in question. This, too, seems to me to be an a priori truth. But if these observations are correct, then, given that Jones mowed his lawn on Saturday, and given that God exists and is (essentially) omniscient, it seems to follow that at the time of action, Jones did not have the power to refrain from mowing his lawn. The upshot of these reflections would appear to be that Jones's mowing his lawn last Saturday cannot be counted as a voluntary action. Although I do not have an analysis of what it is for an action to be *voluntary*, it seems to me that a situation in which it would be wrong to assign Jones the *ability* or *power* to do *other* than he did would be a situation in which it would also be wrong to speak of his action as voluntary. As a general remark, if God exists and is (essentially) omniscient in the sense specified above, no human action is voluntary.[9]

As the argument just presented is somewhat complex, perhaps the following schematic representation of it will be of some use.

1. "God existed at t_1" entails "If Jones did X at t_2, God believed at t_1 that Jones would do X at t_2.

2. "God believes X" entails " 'X' is true."

3. It is not within one's power at a given time to do something having a description that is logically contradictory.

4. It is not within one's power at a given time to do something that would bring it about that someone who held a certain belief at a time prior to the time in question did not hold that belief at the time prior to the time in question.

5. It is not within one's power at a given time to do something that would bring it about that a person who existed at that earlier time did not exist at the earlier time.

6. If God existed at t_1 and if God believed at t_1 that Jones would do X at t_2, then if it was within Jones's power at t_2 to refrain from doing X, then (1) it was within Jones's power at t_2 to do something that would have brought it about that God held a false belief at t_1, or (2) it was within Jones's power at t_2 to do something which would have brought it about that God did not hold the belief He held at t_1, or (3) it was within Jones's power at t_2 to do something that would have brought it about that any person who believed at t_1 that Jones would do X at t_2 (one of whom was, by hypothesis, God) held a false belief and thus was not God—that is, that God (who by hypothesis existed at t_1) did not exist at t_1.

7. Alternative 1 in the consequent of item 6 is false. (from 2 and 3)

8. Alternative 2 in the consequent of item 6 is false. (from 4)

9. Alternative 3 in the consequent of item 6 is false. (from 5)

10. Therefore, if God existed at t_1 and if God believed at t_1 that Jones would do X at t_2, then it was not within Jones's power at t_2 to refrain from doing X. (from 6 through 9)

11. Therefore, if God existed at t_1, and if Jones did X at t_2, it was not within Jones's power at t_2 to refrain from doing X. (from 1 and 10)

---

[9]In Bk. II, ch. xxi, secs. 8–11 of *An Essay,* Locke says that an agent is not *free* with respect to a given action (i.e., that an action is done "under necessity") when it is not within the agent's power to do otherwise. Locke allows a special kind of case, however, in which an action may be *voluntary* though done under necessity. If a man chooses to do something without knowing that it is not within his power to do otherwise (e.g., if a man chooses to stay in a room without knowing that the room is locked), his action may be voluntary though he is not free to forbear it. If Locke is right in this (and I shall not argue the point one way or the other), replace "voluntary" with (let us say) "free" in the above paragraph and throughout the remainder of this paper.

In this argument, items 1 and 2 make explicit the doctrine of God's (essential) omniscience with which I am working. Items 3, 4, and 5 express what I take to be part of the logic of the concept of ability or power as it applies to human beings. Item 6 is offered as an analytic truth. If one assigns Jones the power to refrain from doing X at t_2 (given that God believed at t_1 that he would do X at t_2), so far as I can see, one would have to describe this power in one of the three ways listed in the consequent of item 6. I do not know how to argue that these are the only alternatives, but I have been unable to find another. Item 11, when generalized for all agents and actions, and when taken together with what seems to me to be a minimal condition for the application of "voluntary action," yields the conclusion that if God exists (and is essentially omniscient in the way I have described) no human action is voluntary.

C. It is important to notice that the argument given in the preceding paragraphs avoids use of two concepts that are often prominent in discussions of determinism.

In the first place, the argument makes no mention of the *causes* of Jones's action. Say (for example, with St. Thomas)[10] that God's foreknowledge of Jones's action was, itself, the cause of the action (though I am really not sure what this means). Say, instead, that natural events or circumstances caused Jones to act. Even say that Jones's action had no cause at all. The argument outlined above remains unaffected. If eighty years prior to Saturday, God believed that Jones would mow his lawn at that time, it was not within Jones's power at the time of action to refrain from mowing his lawn. The reasoning that justifies this assertion makes no mention of a causal series preceding Jones's action.

Secondly, consider the following line of thinking. Suppose Jones mowed his lawn last Saturday. It was then *true* eighty years ago that Jones would mow his lawn at that time. Hence, on Saturday, Jones was not able to refrain from mowing his lawn. To suppose that he was would be to suppose that he was able on Saturday to do something that would have made false a proposition that was *already true* eighty years earlier. This general kind of argument for determinism is usually associated with Leibniz, although it was anticipated in chapter ix of Aristotle's *De Interpretatione*. It has been used since, with some modification, in Richard Taylor's article, "Fatalism."[11] This argument, like the one I have offered above, makes no use of the notion of causation. It turns, instead, on the notion of its being *true eighty years ago* that Jones would mow his lawn on Saturday.

---

[10]Aquinas, *Summa Theologicae*, Pt. I, q. 14, a. 8.

[11]Richard Taylor, "Fatalism," *The Philosophical Review*, 71 (1962): 56–66. Taylor argues that if an event E fails to occur at t_2, then at t_1 it was true that E would fail to occur at t_2. Thus, at t_1 a necessary condition of anyone's performing an action sufficient for the occurrence of E at t_2 is missing. Thus at t_1, no one could have the power to perform an action that would be sufficient for the occurrence of E at t_2. Hence, no one has the power at t_1 to do something sufficient for the occurrence of an event at t_2 that is not going to happen. The parallel between this argument and the one recited above can be seen very clearly if one reformulates Taylor's argument, pushing back the time at which it was true that E would not occur at t_2.

I must confess that I share the misgivings of those contemporary philosophers who have wondered what (if any) sense can be attached to a statement of the form "It was true at t_1 that E would occur at t_2."[12] Does this statement mean that had someone believed, guessed, or asserted at t_1 that E would occur at t_2, he would have been right?[13] (I shall have something to say about this form of determinism later in this paper.) Perhaps it means that at t_1 there was sufficient evidence upon which to predict that E would occur at t_2[14]. Maybe it means neither of these. Maybe it means nothing at all.[15] The argument presented above presupposes that it makes straightforward sense to suppose that God (or just anyone) held a true belief eighty years prior to Saturday. But this is not to suppose that *what* God believed *was true eighty years prior to Saturday.* Whether (or in what sense) it was true eighty years ago that Jones would mow his lawn on Saturday is a question I shall not discuss. As far as I can see, the argument in which I am interested requires nothing in the way of a decision on this issue.

---

[12]For a helpful discussion of difficulties involved here, see Rogers Albritton's "Present Truth and Future Contingency," a reply to Richard Taylor's "The Problem of Future Contingency," both in *The Philosophical Review,* 66 (1957): 1–28.

[13]Gilbert Ryle interprets it this way. See "It Was to Be," in *Dilemmas* (Cambridge, Engl., 1954).

[14]Richard Gale suggests this interpretation in "Endorsing Predictions," *The Philosophical Review,* 70 (1961): 376–85.

[15]This view is held by John Turk Saunders in "Sea Fight Tomorrow?," *The Philosophical Review,* 67 (1958): 367–78.

MARILYN MCCORD ADAMS

Is the Existence of God a "Hard" Fact?[1]

Nelson Pike, in his article, "Divine Omniscience and Voluntary Action," argues that if an essentially omniscient and everlasting God exists, no human action is voluntary.[2] Pike's argument depends upon the following two claims:

4. It is not within one's power at a given time to do something that would bring it about that someone who held a certain belief at a time prior to the time in question did not hold that belief at the time prior to the time in question.

5. It is not within one's power at a given time to do something that would bring it about that a person who existed at an earlier time did not exist at an earlier time.[3]

In "Of God and Freedom,"[4] Professor Saunders evidently intends to discount these claims by arguing that the following statement

(A) One does not have the power (at a given time) so to act that the past (relative to that time) would be other than it was.

is false. Pike points out in the first part of his reply to Saunders that (A) has unrestricted application to all facts about the past.[5] He distinguishes "hard" from "soft" facts about the past (see Section I below) and claims that premises (4) and (5) are about restricted classes of "hard" facts: namely, facts about the beliefs and existence of persons respectively. But, Pike says, Saunders has argued only that (A) is false as applied to "soft" facts and has given no reason

From *The Philosophical Review*, 76 (1967), pp. 492–503. Reprinted by permission of the author and *The Philosophical Review*.

[1] I wish to thank Professor Nelson Pike for his encouragement and comments in the preparation of this paper. I am also indebted to my husband, Robert Merrihew Adams, and to Professor Keith Donnellan for helpful discussions and suggestions. Needless to say, however, none of these persons necessarily agrees with everything I say here.

[2] Nelson Pike, "Divine Omniscience and Voluntary Action," *The Philosophical Review*, LXXIV (1965), 27–46.

[3] *Ibid.*, p. 34.

[4] John Turk Saunders, "Of God and Freedom," *The Philosophical Review*, LXXV (1966), 219–25.

[5] Nelson Pike, "Of God and Freedom: A Rejoinder," *The Philosophical Review*, LXXV (1966), 369–79.

to think that (A) is false as applied to these restricted classes of "hard" facts as well. Elsewhere in his rejoinder, Pike indicates that in the original paper he had intended "belief" and "person" to occur in their ordinary senses in premises (4) and (5) respectively.[6] So understood, premises (4) and (5) seem to me to be true statements about "hard" facts. Pike seems also to concede that Saunders is right in claiming that (A) is false as applied to "soft" facts.

In this paper I shall assume that Saunders and Pike are correct at least in thinking that (A) is not generally true as applied to "soft" facts about the past. I shall argue, however, that the existence of an essentially omniscient and everlasting God is not a "hard" fact, and that as a consequence the argument of Pike's original paper fails. By arguing in this way, I shall be insisting on a position Pike considers in the second part of his reply to Saunders.

I.

It is useful before proceeding with the argument briefly to examine the distinction between "hard" and "soft" facts. Pike makes the distinction between "hard" and "soft" facts about the past by contrasting facts which were "fully accomplished" or "over-and-done-with" at a given past time with those which were not.[7] I think that the distinction Pike has in mind can also be drawn in terms of a statement's being about a given time. This alternative explanation is no less intuitive (it relies on an intuitive understanding of "happening" and "actual"), but it will be more convenient for my purposes.[8] Consider the following.

(B)	"Statement p is at least in part about a time t"	$= df.$	"The happening or not happening, actuality or nonactuality of something at t is a necessary condition of the truth of p."

Thus the statement "Caesar died 2009 years before Saunders wrote his paper" is at least in part about 44 B.C., since Caesar's death at that time is a necessary condition of the truth of that statement. It is also at least in part about 1965 A.D. since Saunders' writing his paper in 1965 A.D. is also a necessary condition of the truth of that statement. Given (B) the notion of a "hard" fact may be explained as follows.

(C)	"Statement p expresses a 'hard' fact about a time t"	$= df.$	"p is not at least in part about any time future relative to t."

[6]*Ibid.*, pp. 377–78.

[7]*Ibid.*, pp. 369–70.

[8]The following way of explaining the distinction was suggested to me by Robert Merrihew Adams.

Hence the statement "Caesar died in 44 B.C." expresses a "hard" fact about 44 B.C. But the statement "Caesar died 2009 years before Saunders wrote his paper" does not, since it is at least in part about 1965 A.D.

It should be clear from the above examples that the tense of the verb of the sentence used to express the statement in question is no indication of the times which the statement is in part about. A sentence with a past-tense verb may express a statement which is in part about the present and future; with a present-tense verb, the past and future; and with a future-tense verb, the present and past.

II.

The two features of the concept of God which are important for Pike's argument and with which I shall be concerned are *essential* everlastingness and *essential* omniscience.

The doctrine that God is everlasting can be summarized in two claims. The first is that God is the kind of thing to which temporal predicates apply—that is to say, God has time location. Thus according to this doctrine, it would not be a category mistake to say that God exists *now*, or that he existed *before* Saunders wrote his paper and *after* the death of Caesar. The second is that if God exists at any time, then He exists at all times.

To say that God is omniscient is also to make two claims about Him. The first is that God holds no false beliefs—that is, if God believes that p, then p. The second is that God's knowledge is complete; and therefore, if p, then God believes that p. Thus God is said to know everything that happens in the created world. Further, if God is said to be everlasting as well as omniscient, it is said that God has *always* known everything that happens, has happened, or will happen in the created world. Thus for everything that happens, has happened, or will happen, it is true to say that God knew it was going to happen *before* it happened.

What further is meant by saying not just that God is everlasting and omniscient, but also that He is *essentially* everlasting and *essentially* omniscient? I shall consider two answers to this question. The first is that the statements "God is everlasting" and "God is omniscient" are analytic (more formally, "x is God" entails "x is everlasting"; and "x is God" entails "x is omniscient"). The second (the answer which Pike gives) is to claim not just that the statements "God is everlasting" and "God is omniscient" are analytic, but in addition that the person x who is God would not be the individual person he is if he failed either to be everlasting or to be omniscient.

In what follows I shall begin by interpreting the doctrines of essential everlastingness and essential omniscience in the first way and argue from each of these doctrines in turn that the existence of an essentially omniscient and everlasting God is not a "hard" fact. In addition, I shall try to show how Pike's argument would fail if he had interpreted these doctrines in the first way. In the remainder of the paper, I shall maintain that these results are damaging to Pike's original argument even if one interprets the doctrines of essential everlastingness and essential omniscience as Pike does.

III.

Consider the doctrine of God according to which the statements "God is everlasting" and "God is omniscient" are analytic.

    1. The following is an argument from the doctrine of essential everlastingness alone that the existence of God is not a "hard" fact.

    (D) "God is everlasting" is analytic (that is, "x is God" entails "x is everlasting").

    (E) "x is everlasting" $= df.$ "If $(\exists t)$ (x exists at t), then (t) (x exists at t)."

∴ (F) "x is God" entails "If $(\exists t)$ (x exists at t), then (t) (x exists at t)."

∴ (G) "x is God and $(\exists t)$ (x exists at t)" entails "(t) (x exists at t)."

What (G) says is that it is a necessary condition of the truth of the claim that some extant individual x is God, that that individual exist at all times whatever. But the statement that an individual x exists at all times whatever is a statement which is in part about the future (future relative to any time t for which there is a t' later than t). Hence the statement that some extant individual x is God is a statement which is at least in part about the future. Therefore, the statement that some extant individual x (for whatever extant x you choose) is God does not state a "hard" fact about any time t for which there is a time t' later than t.

    Therefore, it follows merely from the claim that the statement "God is everlasting" is analytic that the existence of an essentially omniscient and everlasting God is not a "hard" fact about any time t for which there is a t' later than t. Hence, assuming that (A) is at least not generally true as applied to "soft" facts about the past, one cannot conclude by reference to (A) alone that it is not within someone's power at a time t' so to act that God would not have existed at an earlier time t even though He did exist at t. In particular, one cannot conclude by reference to (A) alone, that if an individual x is God at t (and hence in fact exists at all times whatever), no one can have the power at a time t' later than t so to act that x not exist at that *later* time (although if x is God at t, no one will in fact exercise such a power at t').

    I think the result just derived, if correct, indicates that Pike's argument would be invalid if he interpreted the doctrine of essential everlastingness in the first way. Pike claims to show that if an essentially omniscient and everlasting God exists, then Jones who mowed his lawn at t_2 did not have the power at t_2 to refrain from mowing his lawn. He proceeds by offering three (supposedly exhaustive) alternative descriptions of Jones's alleged power at t_2 to refrain from mowing his lawn—namely, "the power at t_2 to do something that would have brought it about that God held a false belief at t_1," "the power at t_2 to do something which would have brought it about that God did not hold the belief he held at t_1," and "the power at t_2 to bring it about that God did not exist at t_1"—and by eliminating each on the grounds that it is conceptually impossible that a human being have such a power (see steps 6–9 of Pike's original argument). Pike cites premise (5) as a warrant for step (9), the step in which he rejects the last of those descriptions. But if "person" occurs in its ordinary sense in premise (5), then premise (5) is a conceptual truth about what is within the power of human beings as regards a restricted class of "*hard*" facts. No reason has yet been given for supposing that it follows from the claim that it is conceptually impossible that a human being so act at t_2 that a certain "*hard*" fact—namely, the existence of a particular person—about t_1 would be other than it was, that it is conceptually impossible that a human being so act at t_2 that a certain "*soft*" fact—namely, the existence of God—about t_1 would be other than it was.

Therefore, if Pike had interpreted the doctrine of essential everlastingness in the first way, his inference of (9) from (5) would be invalid. Hence his argument would not provide sufficient reason for denying to Jones who mowed his lawn at t_2 the power at t_2 to refrain from mowing his lawn.

2. The following argument from the doctrine of essential omniscience may be used to establish the same conclusions.

(H) "x is God" entails "If p, then x believes p."
∴ (I) "p" entails "If x is God, then x believes p."
(J) "x is God" entails "If x believes p, then p."
∴ (K) "x believes p" entails "If x is God, then p."

Either the individual x holds beliefs about the future or x does not hold beliefs about the future. If x holds no beliefs about the future, then by (I) x is not God, since there are true statements about the future. But, applying (K), if x holds beliefs about the future, it is a necessary condition of individual x's being God that those beliefs about the future are true. Hence, that certain things happen (or do not happen) or obtain (or fail to obtain) in the future is a necessary condition of any individual x who holds beliefs about the future, being God. But since at any time t for which there is a t' later than t only individuals who hold beliefs about the future can be God, it is a necessary condition of any individual x's being God that certain things happen (or do not happen) or obtain (or fail to obtain) in the future. In that case, the statement that an individual x is God is a statement which does not express a "hard" fact about any time t for which there is a t' later than t.

Therefore, that the existence of God is not a "hard" fact about any time t for which there is a t' later than t follows also merely from the claim that "God is omniscient" is analytic. Since (A) is not generally true as regards "soft" facts about the past, one cannot conclude by reference to (A) alone that it is not within someone's power at t' so to act that the belief that p held at t by the individual x who is in fact God would be false.

In particular, one could not conclude by reference to (A) alone that Jones does not have the power at t_2 so to act that God would not have existed at t_1 in virtue of his having the power at t_2 to refrain from mowing his lawn. Consider the following. For any x whatever, the statement "x is God" does not express a "hard" fact about t_1 (since *ex hypothesi* there is a time t_2 later than t_1). Suppose an individual x believes at t_1 that Jones will mow his lawn at t_2. No reason has been given to suppose that Jones may not have the power at t_2 so to act that the belief of x at t_1 would be false even though the belief of x at t_1 was in fact true: namely, the power at t_2 to refrain from mowing his lawn. But by the argument from the doctrine of essential omniscience just presented, that power of Jones would be the power at t_2 so to act that an individual x who believed at t_1 that Jones would mow his lawn at t_2 was not God. If a certain individual x is God, then he must have believed at t_1 that Jones would mow his lawn at t_2 since Jones did mow his lawn at t_2. Further, assuming that x is the sole possessor of some of the other attributes of God,[9] no individual who did not believe at t_1 that Jones would mow his lawn at t_2 was God. Hence, assuming that x is the sole possessor of some of the other essential attributes of God, Jones's power at t_2 to refrain from mowing his lawn would be the power at t_2 so to act that God would not have existed at t_1 even though He did exist at t_1. Therefore, one could not conclude by reference to (A) alone that Jones does not have the power at t_2 so to act that God would not have existed at t_1 in virtue of his having the power at t_2 to refrain from mowing his lawn.

As discussed above in connection with the argument from essential everlastingness, Pike cites premise (5) as his warrant for denying to Jones the power at t_2 so to act that God would not have existed at t_1. But again, if "person" occurs in its ordinary sense in premise (5), then premise (5) is a conceptual truth about what is within the power of human beings as regards a restricted class of *"hard"* facts. No reason has yet been given for supposing that it follows from the claim that it is conceptually impossible that a human being so act at t_2 that a certain *"hard"* fact—namely, the existence of a

---

[9]This assumption is required to forestall the following objection. Suppose there are two individuals y and z who are alike in all respects except that y believed at t_1 that Jones would mow his lawn at t_2 and z believed at t_1 that Jones would refrain from mowing his lawn at t_2. Suppose further that the properties which y and z share include all the essential attributes of God except omniscience. Since Jones mowed his lawn at t_2, z was not God at t_1, though y may have been God at t_1 (if all the beliefs y and z share are true). Nevertheless, Jones's power at t_2 to refrain from mowing his lawn would not necessarily be the power at t_2 so to act that God would not have existed at t_1. For, if Jones had refrained from mowing his lawn at t_2, y would not have been God at t_1, but instead z might have been God at t_1 (if all the beliefs y and z share are true). (This objection was raised by Robert Merrihew Adams.)

I think it is logically impossible that more than one individual have all the essential properties of God except omniscience, but I shall not defend this claim here.

particular person—about t_1 would be other than it was, that it is conceptually impossible that a human being so act at t_2 that a certain *"soft"* fact—namely, the existence of God—about t_1 would be other than it was.

Therefore, if Pike had interpreted either the doctrine of essential everlastingness or the doctrine of essential omniscience in the first way, his inference of (9) from (5) would be invalid. Hence his argument would not provide a sufficient reason for denying to Jones who mowed his lawn at t_2 the power at t_2 to refrain from mowing his lawn.

IV.

The arguments in Section III explicitly presuppose analyses of essential everlastingness and essential omniscience different from those Pike employs in his argument. Pike agrees that the doctrines of essential everlastingness and essential omniscience imply that "God is everlasting" and "God is omniscient" are analytic. But he thinks that these doctrines also imply that everlastingness and omniscience are connected in a special way with the personal identity of the individual who is God: that is, if the individual x who is God failed either to be everlasting or to be omniscient, not only would x fail to be God but also x would fail to be the individual person x is.

I think, however, that this way of analyzing essential everlastingness and essential omniscience is in conflict with the criteria of identity for our ordinary concept "person." In the remainder of the paper I shall try to show that in view of this difficulty the reasoning offered in Section III above is telling against Pike's argument even if one interprets the doctrines of essential everlastingness and essential omniscience as Pike does.

As noted at the outset, Pike indicated in his original paper that he understood the concept "person" involved to be the ordinary concept "person." Further, it is clear that he thinks that an extant individual x's being a person and being the individual person he is are "hard" facts. For he seems to grant to Saunders that (A) is false as applied to "soft" facts, but denies that this concession damages premises (4) and (5).

If Pike were right in supposing that, say, omniscience can be tied to the conditions of personal identity (in the ordinary sense), it would be apparent why he thought he could infer from (5) that it was not within Jones's power at t_2 so to act that God would not have existed at t_1 even though He did exist at t_1 (step 9 of Pike's original argument). For on Pike's analysis, the individual x who is God must be such that if x failed to be omniscient and so failed to be God, x would be a different individual person from the person he in fact is. Therefore, if someone had the power at t_2 so to act that x would not have been omniscient at t_1 and hence not God at t_1 even though x was omniscient at t_1 and was God at t_1, he would have the power so to act that x would not have been the individual person he in fact was. But premise (5) says that it is impossible that any human being should have that power. Thus if omniscience could be tied to personal identity (in the ordinary sense) in the way Pike's analysis presupposes, it would be impossible that Jones should have the power at t_2 so to act that the person x who is God would not have been omniscient at t_1 and hence not God at t_1, so that his inference of (9) from (5) would be legitimate.

If, however, the ordinary concept of person is such that to be a person in the ordinary sense is a "hard" fact, and if the criteria of identity for the ordinary concept of person are such that to be the individual person one is is a "hard" fact, then being omniscient (or everlasting) can be a necessary condition neither of an individual x's being a person in the ordinary sense nor of x's being the individual person x is. For the arguments in Section III show that "x is everlasting" and "x is omniscient" express "soft" facts about any time t for which there is a time t' later than t. And if x's being a person in the ordinary sense, or x's being the individual person (in the ordinary sense) that x is, depended upon x's being omniscient or everlasting, then x's being a person in the ordinary sense, or being the individual person (in the ordinary sense) that x is, would be "soft" facts—which they are not. It seems, therefore, that Pike's analysis of essential omniscience cannot be correct if it is assumed that the concept involved is the ordinary concept of person.

It is possible, of course, to construct an extraordinary concept of person— "person$_2$"—such that an individual x would not be the individual person$_2$ x is if x failed to have any one of the attributes traditionally assigned to God. Might not Pike repair his inference of (9) from (5) by replacing "person" (in the ordinary sense) in (5) with "person$_2$"? I think not. For x's being the individual person$_2$ x is will not be a "hard" fact about any time t for which there is a t' later than t. Hence, since (A) is not generally true as applied to "soft" facts about the past, one cannot conclude from (A) alone that it is conceptually impossible that a human being have the power at t' so to act that a given person$_2$ would not have existed at an earlier time t even though that person$_2$ did exist at t. No reason has been given for supposing that the statement obtained by replacing "person" (in the ordinary sense) in (5) by "person$_2$" is true. Hence there is no reason to suppose that the inference of (9) from (5) (where "person" in 5 is replaced by "person$_2$") is sound.

Therefore, there is no adequate reason to suppose that Pike's inference of (9) from (5) holds good even if one employs a doctrine of God according to which "God is a person$_2$" is analytic.

V.

When considering objections similar to the ones I have raised in Section IV,[10] Pike expresses doubts as to whether or not they hold good but makes the following remarks as regards the consequences if they do hold good:

---

[10]Nelson Pike, "Of God and Freedom: A Rejoinder," *The Philosophical Review*, LXXV (1966), 378.

if the stipulation that God is essentially omniscient constitutes a modification of the ordinary concept of *person* and if this modification is sufficient to falsify principle 5, then we can no longer claim that God is a *person*. Again, what sense would it make to claim that God is a person and then to add that He is a person of such a sort that it would be within someone's power at a given time so to act that a person (of that sort) who existed at an earlier time would not have existed at an earlier time? This would simply be to say that the (so-called) person named "God" was not a *person* at all.

I think that Pike here misreads the upshot of the above objections to his argument. Neither the claim that the statement "x is God" does not express a "hard" fact about any time t for which there is a time t' later than t, nor the claim that the statement "God is a person$_2$" is analytic, is inconsistent with the claim that the statement "God is a person (in the ordinary sense)" is analytic. For to insist on all three of these claims is in effect to assert (*i*) that the individual x who is God falls under three concepts—"God," "person$_2$," and the ordinary concept "person"—the criteria of identity for each of which are different from the criteria of identity for each of the other two; and (*ii*) that it is a necessary condition for an individual x's falling under one of these concepts (that is, the concept "God") that that individual x fall under each of the other two concepts (that is, the concept "person$_2$" and the ordinary concept "person") where the criteria of identity for the concept "person$_2$" are different from the criteria of identity for the ordinary concept "person." But I can see no logical difficulty with (*i*), with (*ii*), or with their conjunction; and in any case no reason has been given by Pike to suppose that there is such a difficulty. Therefore, no reason has been given why one cannot say that it is a necessary condition of an individual x's being God that x be a person (in the ordinary sense), even if one admits that x would be the same individual person (in the ordinary sense) that x is even if x were not God, and claims that x would not be the same person$_2$ that x is if x were not God.

What is self-contradictory, assuming that my argument in Section IV is correct, is the claim that x's having any and/or all of the attributes traditionally assigned to God is a necessary condition of x's being the individual person (in the ordinary sense) that x is. But so far as I can see, one can still claim that God is a person in the ordinary sense and further that the statement "God is a person (in the ordinary sense)" is analytic. And this is true even if it be granted that "God is a person$_2$" is analytic.

VI.

In sum, I have argued that the existence of an essentially omniscient and everlasting God is not a "hard" fact and consequently that there is no adequate reason to suppose that Pike's inference of (9) from (5) in his original argument is legitimate. The claim that the existence of an essentially omniscient and everlasting God is inconsistent with the voluntary character of some human actions has yet to be made out.

JOHN MARTIN FISCHER

Freedom and Foreknowledge

A powerful argument can be made that God's omniscience is incompatible with human freedom.[1] If God is eternal and omniscient, then it might seem that my freedom now to do other than what I am doing must be the freedom so to act that a fact about the past (God's prior belief about my present activity) would not be a fact about the past. But since the past is "fixed," it seems that if God exists, then I am now not free to do other than what I am doing.

Many philosophers have been attracted to an Ockhamist response to this argument.[2] Both the Ockhamist and the incompatibilist can distinguish between "hard" and "soft" facts about the past; the hard facts are fixed while the soft facts need not be fixed. But the Ockhamist claims that God's prior

From *The Philosophical Review*, 92 (1983), pp. 67–79. Reprinted by permission of the author and *The Philosophical Review*.

I have benefited from comments by Carl Ginet, Norman Kretzmann, T. H. Irwin, and Judith Jarvis Thomson. I am especially indebted to Robert Stalnaker, many of whose suggestions have been incorporated in this paper.

[1]Nelson Pike, "Divine Omniscience and Voluntary Action" (pp. 429–36 in this volume); "Of God and Freedom: A Rejoinder," *The Philosophical Review*, 75 (July 1966): 369–79; and "Divine Foreknowledge, Human Freedom and Possible Worlds," *The Philosophical Review*, 86 (April 1977): 209–16. Pike also discusses the same basic argument in the fourth chapter of his book, *God and Timelessness* (New York, 1970).

[2]Some examples are: Marilyn Adams, "Is the Existence of God a 'Hard' Fact?" (pp. 437–45 in this volume), and William L. Rowe, *Philosophy of Religion* (Encino, Calif., 1978), pp. 154–69. The approach sketched below is called "Ockhamist" because William of Ockham distinguished between propositions about the past which are necessary and those which are not and argued that among those propositions about the past which are not now necessary are certain propositions about God. (Ockham, *Predestination, God's Foreknowledge and Future Contingents*, trans. Marilyn McCord Adams and Norman Kretzmann [New York, 1969], pp. 46–47, 92.) Roughly, Ockham claims that those propositions about the past which are true by virtue of contingent future events are not now necessary. Such propositions, it might be said, express "soft facts" about the past. A useful discussion of the Ockhamist approach can be found in Arthur Prior, *Past, Present and Future* (Oxford, 1967), pp. 121–27. John Turk Saunders agrees with the Ockhamist that certain propositions about God express soft facts (Saunders, "Of God and Freedom," *The Philosophical Review*, 75 [April 1966]: 219–25). Saunders holds a position which is even stronger than Ockhamism, since he believes that neither soft facts nor hard facts need be fixed (Saunders, "The Temptations of 'Powerlessness,'" *American Philosophical Quarterly*, 5 [April 1968]: 104–7).

belief about my present activity is a soft fact about the past and hence not fixed; my freedom is thus preserved. Some Ockhamists even claim that the very existence of God is also a soft fact about the past.

I shall argue that a very attractive presentation of the Ockhamist approach, one explicitly formulated by Marilyn Adams, is inadequate.[3] There are significant problems with Adams's attempt to characterize the hard fact/soft fact distinction. Further, I shall present a general challenge to *any* sort of Ockhamist attempt to explain this distinction.

I. PIKE'S ARGUMENT

Nelson Pike claims to exhibit the incompatibility of human freedom and divine foreknowledge, relative to certain plausible assumptions about God's nature.[4] These assumptions reflect central features of the standard Judeo-Christian conception of God. Pike explicitly adopts the assumption that if God exists, then God is essentially omniscient and God is eternal. On Pike's account, God is omniscient if and only if God believes all and only true propositions, and we might say that God is essentially omniscient if and only if God is omniscient in all possible worlds in which God exists. Pike says that God is eternal if and only if God has always existed and always will.[5]

Following Pike's presentation in a different article, I assume that the term "God" is a descriptive expression used to mark a certain *role*, rather than a proper name.[6] Whoever occupies the role of God is omniscient, omnipotent, eternal, etc. In contrast, the term "Yahweh" is a proper name; it refers to the person who actually occupies the role of God (if God exists). It is not necessarily true that Yahweh is omniscient, omnipotent, eternal, etc.; it is logically possible that some other person has been God.[7]

Since "God" is being used here as a non-rigid designator, there is some ambiguity in the assumptions about God's attributes. "God is essentially omniscient" does not mean that the person who is in fact God is essentially omniscient, but rather, that necessarily, whoever is God is omniscient. In terms of

---

[3] Adams, "Is the Existence of God a 'Hard' Fact?"

[4] Pike, "Divine Omniscience," pp. 429–36 in this volume.

[5] Thus Pike conceives of God's eternality as sempiternality—existence at all times. This conception is shared by the Ockhamist; it can be contrasted with the atemporal conception of eternality held by Boethius and Aquinas.

[6] Pike makes this assumption explicit in "Omnipotence and God's Ability to Sin," *American Philosophical Quarterly*, 6 (1969): 208–16, esp. 208–9.

[7] C. B. Martin argues for this approach in the fourth chapter of his *Religious Belief* (Ithaca, 1964).

possible worlds, God is essentially omniscient just in case for any possible world in which there is a person who is God, that person is omniscient. (One can assume that if God is eternal in a particular world, then it follows that there is one and the same person who is God at all times in that world. Pike need not accept this particular assumption, as it is not crucial to his argument.)

Though this is the approach to the term "God" that Pike appears to adopt, it might seem to be an unusual and unappealing position. I shall follow Pike in adopting this interpretation, but it is important to note that Pike could just as easily embrace the stronger interpretation according to which the person who is in fact God is essentially God. Nothing in Pike's proof, or in my criticism of Adams's Ockhamism, rests on adopting the weaker rather than the stronger interpretation of God's attributes.

In effect, Pike also appears to adopt what might be called the "fixed past" constraint on power attributions:

(FPC) It is never in any person's power at a time t so to act that the past (relative to t) would have been different from what it actually was.

Pike's view about the fixity of the past implies not only that one cannot causally influence the past; it implies that no person is free to do something which is such that, were he to do it, the past would have been different from what it actually was.

Pike's argument is essentially as follows. Suppose Jones did X at time t_2 and God exists. Since God exists, it follows from God's eternality that He existed at t_1 (a time prior to t_2). Let us call the person who was God at t_1, "Y." Since Jones did X at t_2, it follows from God's omniscience that He believed at t_1 that Jones would do X at t_2. Now if it was within Jones's power at t_2 to refrain from doing X, then (1) it was in Jones's power at t_2 to act in such a way that Y would have been God and would have held a false belief at t_1, or (2) it was in Jones's power at t_2 to act in such a way that Y would have been God but would not have held the belief He held at t_1, or (3) it was in Jones's power at t_2 to act in such a way that Y would not have been God at t_1.

But (1) is ruled out by God's essential omniscience, and (2) and (3) are ruled out by (FPC). Hence it was not in Jones's power at t_2 to refrain from doing X. If the argument is sound, it can easily be generalized to show that God's eternality and essential omniscience are incompatible with any human agent's being free at any time.

It should be pointed out that incompatibilism about divine foreknowledge and human freedom need not entail incompatibilism about human foreknowledge and human freedom. The problem is deeper with divine foreknowledge because of God's essential omniscience; perhaps it was in Jones's power at t_2 so to act that Smith (who actually held only correct beliefs) would have held a false belief at t_1. Pike wants to insist on an asymmetry between divine and human foreknowledge.[8]

II. HARD AND SOFT FACTS

It is sometimes in one's power so to act that facts about the past *would not* be facts. John Turk Saunders discusses such a fact:

> Although it is true that if I had refrained from writing this paper in 1965, Caesar's assassination would have been other than it is in that it would not have preceded by 2,009 years my writing this paper, it would be absurd to argue that I therefore did not have it in my power to refrain from writing this paper in 1965.[9]

It is obvious that the mere fact that if Saunders had refrained from writing his paper, then Caesar's assassination would not have preceded Saunders's writing his paper by 2,009 years did not render Saunders incapable of refraining; relative to 1965, "Caesar died 2,009 years prior to Saunders's writing his paper" expresses a soft fact about the past. Of course, it was not in Saunders's power so to act that Caesar would not have died on the steps of the Senate. Relative to Saunders's lifetime, the fact that Caesar died on the steps of the Senate is a hard fact about the past.

Pike agrees with the Ockhamist that there are both hard and soft facts about the past.[10] It is not easy to provide a precise characterization of the hard fact/soft fact distinction. Pike himself provides no such account, though he claims we can recognize clear examples of each sort.[11] The disagreement between Pike and the Ockhamist is about where to draw the line. Pike's position is that if the ordinary notions of belief and existence are applied to God, then God's belief at t_1 and God's existence at t_1 (including the fact that

---

[8]Pike says in his original paper: "The important thing to be learned from the study of Smith's foreknowledge of Jones's action is that the problem of divine foreknowledge has as one of its pillars the claim that truth is *analytically* connected with God's *beliefs*. No problem of determinism arises when dealing with human foreknowledge of future actions. This is because truth is not analytically connected with human belief even when (as in the case of human knowledge) truth is contingently conjoined to belief" (Pike, "Divine Omniscience). Thus it is clear that Pike as well as the Ockhamist *needs* the distinction between hard and soft facts.

[9]Saunders, "Of God and Freedom," p. 224. Unfortunately, Saunders's arithmetic is wrong since there is no 0 B.C. or A.D. 0. Hence, Caesar's death preceded Saunders's writing his paper by 2,008 years! For simplicity's sake, however, I shall ignore this and proceed with Saunders, Pike, and Adams in adding a year to history.

[10]Pike, "Of God and Freedom," pp. 369–70; Rowe makes a similar distinction between facts that are "simply about the past" and facts that are not (Rowe, *Philosophy of Religion*, pp. 162–65).

[11]Pike, "Of God and Freedom," pp. 369–70.

Y was God at t_1) are hard facts about the past relative to t_2. And if they were soft facts about the past relative to t_2, this would show that we were ascribing beliefs and existence to God in a special, nonstandard way.

Given the hard fact/soft fact distinction, the appropriate interpretation of Pike's claim about the fixity of the past should be made explicit:

(FPC*) It is never in any person's power at a time t so to act that any hard fact about the past (relative to t) would have been different from what it actually was.[12]

Marilyn Adams presents an account of the distinction which she believes supports compatibilism against Pike's attack. It will be useful to consider Adams's attempt at giving an account of the distinction:

(B) "Statement p is at least in part about a time t" $= df.$ "The happening or not happening, actuality or non-actuality of something at t is a necessary condition of the truth of p."

Thus the statement, "Caesar died 2,009 years before Saunders wrote his paper" is at least in part about 44 B.C., since Caesar's death at that time is a necessary condition of the truth of that statement. It is also at least in part about A.D. 1965 since Saunders's writing his paper in A.D. 1965 is also a necessary condition of the truth of that statement. Given (B) the notion of a "hard" fact may be explained as follows.

(C) "Statement p expresses a 'hard' fact about a time t" = df. "p is not at least in part about any time future relative to t."[13]

---

[12]Put in terms of possible worlds, the fixed past constraint is:

(FPC*) A possible world W^* (in which an agent does other than what he does in W at t) can establish that the agent had it in his power at t in W to do otherwise only if W and W^* have the same hard facts about the past relative to t.

In "Pike on Possible Worlds, Divine Foreknowledge, and Human Freedom," *The Philosophical Review*, 88 (July 1979): 441–42, Joshua Hoffman criticizes Pike's interpretation of the fixity of the past. Hoffman construes Pike as claiming that the possession of every power *entails* the occurrence or nonoccurrence of past circumstances. That is, Hoffman attributes to Pike the claim that the truth of a statement ascribing a particular power to an agent at a time in a world W *entails* that the past be as it is in W. Pike himself puts the constraint in a misleading way, saying: "If we assume that what is within my power at a given moment determines a set of possible worlds, all of the members of that set will have to be worlds in which what has happened in the past relative to the given moment is precisely what has happened in the past relative to that moment in the actual world" (Pike, "Divine Foreknowledge," p. 215). But nothing in Pike's position requires acceptance of the radical doctrine attributed to him by Hoffman. Pike's fixed past constraint commits him to the claim that if an agent performs an act in world W, then any possible world W^* in which he refrains from performing the act must have the same past as W, if W^* is to establish that the agent can in W refrain from performing the act. But there may be possible worlds (including W) in which the agent can perform the act (and *does* perform the act) in which the past histories (relative to the time of the act) are all different from one another; hence, the truth of a power-ascription need not *entail* the past history. Hoffman's criticism of Pike misses the mark and leaves the fixed past constraint unscathed.

[13]Adams, "Is the Existence of God a 'Hard' Fact?," p. 438 in this volume.

Adams uses this account to present an Ockhamist response to Pike's argument. On her account, God's belief at t_1 and the fact that Y was God at t_1 are deemed soft facts about t_1.

Adams claims that her account shows why "Caesar died 2,009 years before Saunders wrote his paper" does not express a hard fact about 44 B.C. But her account does *not* explain this unless it is interpreted to imply that *no* sentence expresses a hard fact. Adams says that "Caesar died 2,009 years before Saunders wrote his paper" is at least in part about 1965, since Saunders's writing his paper in 1965 is a necessary condition of the truth of that statement. But this seems plainly false; the statement entails that Caesar's death and Saunders's writing his paper be separated by 2,009 years, but it does not entail any two particular dates for the two events. The statement entails that the two events stand in a certain temporal *relation*, but it does not entail that they occur on any specific dates. Hence, Saunders's writing his paper in 1965 is *not* a necessary condition of Caesar's death being 2,009 years prior to Saunders's writing his paper, if we interpret "q is a necessary condition for p" as "p entails q."

One might reply that since it is true that Saunders wrote his paper in 1965, "Saunders wrote his paper in 1965" is *materially implied* by "Caesar died 2,009 years prior to Saunders's writing his paper." So if we interpret "q is a necessary condition for p" as "p materially implies q," Saunders's writing his paper in 1965 is a necessary condition of the truth of "Caesar died 2,009 years prior to Saunders's writing his paper." But it is obvious that if this sense of "necessary condition" is adopted, then *no* sentence will express a hard fact about 44 B.C. So Adams's account of Pike's intuitive distinction is inadequate as it stands. Adams gives no explication of the notion of a necessary condition by reference to which she can say that "Caesar died 2,009 years prior to Saunders's writing his paper" does not express a hard fact about 44 B.C.

Consider also the statement, "John F. Kennedy was assassinated." Given the entailment interpretation, this statement expresses a hard fact about 1961, since it does not *entail* the occurrence of anything subsequent to 1961. Of course, there are logically possible worlds in which Kennedy was assassinated in 1961. But we want to say that in 1962 (and in 1963, until November 22), it was within Oswald's power so to have acted that Kennedy would not have been assassinated. And again, it is obvious that the material implication interpretation of "necessary condition" is inadequate.

Complex statements further illustrate the inadequacy of the entailment account of "necessary condition." If Jones did not believe at t_1 that he would do X at t_2, then "Either Smith knew at t_1 that Jones would do X at t_2 or Jones believed at t_1 that Jones would do X at t_2," should *not* express a hard fact about t_1; the Ockhamist would say that Jones might have been able so to act at t_2 that this disjunctive statement would be false. Yet on Adams's account, the statement expresses a *hard* fact about t_1, since its truth does not entail that anything happens after t_1; the truth of the disjunction does not entail that anything happens (or fails to happen, etc.) after t_1.

In defense of Adams's approach, one might offer the following account of a necessary condition: q is a necessary condition for p if and only if p would not be true (or have been true) if q were not true (or had not been true). Let us call this interpretation the "counterfactual" account of a necessary condition. It *is* plausible to say that if Saunders had not written his paper in 1965, then it *would not* have been the case that Caesar died 2,009 years prior to Saunders's writing his paper. Thus, Adams could say, on the counterfactual account, that "Saunders wrote his paper in 1965" is a necessary condition of "Caesar died 2,009 years prior to Saunders's writing his paper." Also, it is perhaps reasonable to say (though I am not sure) that if Oswald had not shot Kennedy in 1963, then Kennedy would not have been assassinated. If this is so, then Adams could say that "Oswald shot Kennedy in 1963" is a necessary condition of "John F. Kennedy was assassinated." Similarly, if Jones had not done X at t_2, then it would have been false that either Smith knew at t_1 that Jones would do X at t_2 or Jones believed at t_1 that Jones would do X at t_2. Thus, Adams could say that "Jones did X at t_2" is a necessary condition of the disjunction.

But there is another sort of problem which afflicts both plausible accounts—both the counterfactual and entailment interpretations of "necessary condition." Suppose "Smith existed at t_1" is true. It is a necessary condition of the truth of this statement (on both the counterfactual and entailment accounts) that it is not the case that Smith existed for the first time at t_2. It is obvious that Smith's existing at t_1 entails that he does not exist for the first time at t_2. And if Smith had existed for the first time at t_2, then he would not have existed at t_1, so the counterfactual account fares no better than the entailment account. Thus, by (B), the statement "Smith existed at t_1" is at least in part about t_2; by (C) the statement *fails* to express a hard fact about t_1. But since Smith need not be eternal (or essentially omniscient), this is a disastrous result for Adams's account. The same sort of argument shows that Adams must say that "Jones believed at t_1 that Jones would do X at t_2" does not express a hard fact about t_1. This is because "It is not the case that Jones believed for the first time at t_2 that he would do X at t_2" is a necessary condition of "Jones believed at t_1 that he would do X at t_2."

Also, it is a necessary condition (on both interpretations) of the truth of the statement, "Piece of salt S dissolved at t_1," that S did not dissolve at t_2. One wants to say that this statement expresses a hard fact about t_1, but Adams's account does not capture this intuition (since the statement is at least in part about t_2).

It is not easy to see how Adams could provide an account of "necessary condition" which would avoid all the problems raised above. Without such an account, she has not presented an adequate explanation of the distinction between hard and soft facts.

III. THE INCOMPATIBILIST'S CONSTRAINT

Various contemporary Ockhamists have argued that on any acceptable account of the distinction between hard and soft facts, God's prior belief will be a soft fact about the past. I shall not here further discuss particular compatibilist accounts of the distinction; rather, I shall sketch a constraint on the account of the distinction which an incompatibilist might use to defeat *any* compatibilist characterization of the distinction. That is, I shall develop an explanation of the claim that God's prior belief is a hard fact about the past; this explanation will *not* imply that *human* foreknowledge is also a hard fact about the past. This might provide a way in which Pike could defend both his incompatibility claim and the asymmetry thesis—the thesis that God's foreknowledge undermines human freedom in a way in which human foreknowledge does not.

Consider the fact that Caesar died 2,009 years prior to Saunders's writing his paper. What lies behind our view that this fact is not a hard fact about 44 B.C.? We might say that it is a soft fact about 44 B.C. because one and the same physical process would have counted as Caesar's dying 2,009 years prior to Saunders's writing his paper, if Saunders wrote his paper in 1965, and would *not* have counted as Caesar's dying 2,009 years prior to Saunders's writing his paper, if Saunders had not written his paper in 1965. This captures the "future dependence" of soft facts; a soft fact is a fact *in virtue* of events which occur in the future.

Similarly, suppose that Smith knew at t_1 that Jones would do X at t_2. Smith's knowledge is a soft fact about t_1 because one and the same state of Smith's mind (at t_1) would count as knowledge if Jones did X at t_2, and would not count as knowledge if Jones did not do X at t_2. Exactly the same sort of future dependence explains why both facts—the fact about Caesar's death and the fact about Smith's knowledge—are soft facts.

Thus an incompatibilist might insist on the following sort of constraint on an account of the hard fact/soft fact distinction: the only way in which God's belief at t_1 about Jones at t_2 could be a soft fact about the past relative to t_2 would be if one and the same state of the mind of the person who was God at t_1 would count as one belief if Jones did X at t_2, but a different belief (or not a belief at all) if Jones did not do X at t_2. But it is implausible to suppose that one and the same state of the mind of the person who was God at t_1 would count as different beliefs given different behavior by Jones at t_2.

Suppose again that Jones did X at t_2. Y (being God) believed at t_1 that Jones would do X at t_2. Let us say that Y's mind was in state s at t_1; this constituted His believing that Jones would do X at t_2. Now if Y's mind were in state s and Jones did *not* do X, Y's mind being in s would still count as a belief that Jones would do X. (In this case, Y would not be God, since he would have a false belief.) Hence, Y's mind being in s at t_1 would *not* count as one belief if Jones did X at t_2 and another belief (or not a belief at all) if Jones did not do X at t_2.

Someone might agree that the incompatibilist's constraint is appropriate but disagree with what I have said about its application. That is, one might argue that if Jones had not done X at t_2, then the state of God's mind that actually constituted His believing that Jones would do X would not have constituted that belief. This position might be supported by extending

Putnam's point that meanings and beliefs ain't in the head.[14] According to Putnam, my belief that water is wet—the state of my mind that constitutes in fact, my believing that—would have been a different belief—the belief that XYZ is wet—if lakes and oceans on earth had been filled with XYZ rather than water. On this approach, the state of God's mind at t_1 that counts as His belief that Jones will do X at t_2 counts as that belief partly in virtue of the fact that Jones does in fact do X at t_2.

But this picture of God's omniscience is highly implausible. God's omniscience would be seriously attenuated if the same state of God's mind at t_1 would constitute different beliefs about Jones, depending on Jones's behavior at t_2. The following is a more appealing picture of God's omniscience. An Ockhamist might deny the appropriateness of the constraint, claiming that while it is not true that one and the same state of God's mind at t_1 would constitute different beliefs, depending on Jones's behavior at t_2, it is true that God's mind would have been in a *different* state at t_1 (from the one it was actually in), if Jones had not done X at t_2. Whereas Y's mind was actually in state s at t_1, it would not have been in s had Jones not done X at t_2.

If the Ockhamist makes this move, however, he weakens his argument to the conclusion that God's belief at t_1 is a soft fact about t_1. There is now an *asymmetry* between soft facts such as Caesar's dying 2,009 years prior to Saunders's writing his paper and Smith's knowing at t_1 that Jones will do X at t_2, on the one hand, and God's belief at t_1 that Jones will do X at t_2, on the other. But it was the assimilation of these sorts of facts that was the ground for claiming that God's belief at t_1 is a soft fact about t_1.

The incompatibilist can agree with the Ockhamist that the facts discussed above about Caesar's death and Smith's knowledge are "spurious" facts about the relevant times. They are temporal analogues of facts involving "mere Cambridge" spatial properties, such as the property of being ten miles south of a burning barn. But if the incompatibilist's constraint is rejected, then it is open to him to argue that God's prior belief is a *genuine* fact about the past.

The constraint I have proposed captures the incompatibilist's notion of the fixity of the past. If this constraint is acceptable, then Pike could defend both his incompatibility claim and the asymmetry thesis.

There is, however, one form of Ockhamism that is not defeated by the proposed constraint. Consider again, "If it was within Jones's power at t_2 to refrain from doing X, then (3) it was in Jones's power at t_2 to act in such a way that Y would not have been God at t_1." There are two ways in which it might be true that it was in Jones's power at t_2 so to act that Y would not have been God at t_1. First, Jones could have had it in his power at t_2 so to act that Y would

---

[14]Hilary Putnam, "The Meaning of 'Meaning,'" reprinted in Hilary Putnam, *Mind, Language, and Reality* (London, 1975), pp. 215–71, esp. pp. 223–27. Robert Stalnaker suggested to me the idea for the incompatibilist's constraint and pointed out the relevance of Putnam's point to it.

not have existed at t_1. Second, Jones could have been free at t_2 to act in such a way that Y (though existing) would not have filled the role of God at t_1. The Ockhamist might agree with Pike that the existence of a particular person is a hard fact about a time, but he might insist that the fact that the person is God is *not* a hard fact about a time.

Thus, the Ockhamist might claim (following Adams) that the fact that Y had the property of being God at t_1 is a soft fact about t_1. This is because the fact that Y was God at t_1 depends on the truth of Y's beliefs about future contingent events; indeed, since God is eternal, the fact that Y was God at t_1 depends on the fact that Y existed at t_2.

But the incompatibilist should point out that from the claim that Y's occupying the role of God at t_1 is a soft fact about t_1 it does *not* follow that Jones could have at t_2 so acted that Y would not have been God at t_1. There are soft facts about the past which are such that one cannot now so act that they would not have been facts. For instance, on Tuesday it was a soft fact about the past that on Monday it was the case that the sun would rise on Wednesday morning.[15] But on Tuesday, one could not have acted in such a way that it would not have been the case that on Monday it was true that the sun would rise on Wednesday.

Thus, even if the fact that Y was God at t_1 is a soft fact about t_1, this does not *suffice* to establish that Jones could have so acted at t_2 that Y would not have been God at t_1. Further, it is theologically implausible to suppose that any human agent is free so to act that the person who is actually God would not be God. This would make the identity of God dependent on human actions in an unacceptable way; such a God would hardly be worthy of worship. So, whereas the fact that Y was God at t_1 might be a soft fact about t_1, an Ockhamist who claims that one could have at t_2 so acted that Y would not have been God at t_1 would posit an unacceptable view of God. Incompatibilism can be defended even if Pike's claim that the fact that Y was God at t_1 is a hard fact about t_1 were false.

IV. CONCLUSION

Adams's formulation of Ockhamism is inadequate. I have not here argued that *no* account of the hard fact/soft fact distinction can be given which captures the Ockhamist intuition. Rather, I have posed a challenge to Adams's Ockhamism and have presented the incompatibilist's motivation for thinking that any Ockhamist account will be unacceptable. I have thus issued a twofold challenge to the Ockhamist: first, to formulate the hard fact/soft fact distinction in a way which yields Ockhamism, and second, to explain why the incompatibilist's constraint is inappropriate.

---

[15] I borrow this sort of example from Rowe, *Philosophy of Religion*, p. 165.

WILLIAM P. ALSTON

Divine Foreknowledge and Alternative Conceptions of Human Freedom

Nelson Pike's important 1965 paper, "Divine Omniscience and Voluntary Action"[1] presents an interestingly novel version of the old argument from divine foreknowledge to our inability to do (choose) other than what we in fact do.

1. "God existed at T_1" entails "If Jones did X at T_2, God believed at T_1 that Jones would do X at T_2.

2. "God believes X" entails " 'X' is true."

3. It is not within one's power at a given time to do something having a description that is logically contradictory.

4. It is not within one's power at a given time to do something that would bring it about that someone who held a certain belief at a time prior to the time in question did not hold that belief at the time prior to the time in question.

5. It is not within one's power at a given time to do something that would bring it about that a person who existed at an earlier time did not exist at that earlier time.

6. If God existed at T_1 and if God believed at T_1 that Jones would do X at T_2; then if it was within Jones's power at T_2 to refrain from doing X, then (1) it was within Jones's power at T_2 to do something that would have brought it about that God held a false belief at T_1, or (2) it was within Jones's power at T_2 to do something which would have brought it about that God did not hold the belief He held at T_1, or (3) it was within Jones's power at T_2 to do something that would have brought it about that any person who believed at T_1 that Jones would do X at T_2 (one of whom was, by hypothesis, God) held a false belief and thus was not God—that is, that God (who by hypothesis existed at T_1) did not exist at T_1.

7. Alternative 1 in the consequent of item 6 is false (from 2 and 3).

8. Alternative 2 in the consequent of item 6 is false (from 4).

9. Alternative 3 in the consequent of item 6 is false (from 5).

10. Therefore, if God existed at T_1 and if God believed at T_1 that Jones would do X at T_2, then it was not within Jones's power at T_2 to refrain from doing X (from 6 through 9).

11. Therefore, if God existed at T_1, and if Jones did X at T_2, it was not within Jones's power at T_2 to refrain from doing X from (1 and 10).[2]

From *The International Journal for the Philosophy of Religion* (1985), pp. 19–32. Reprinted by permission of Kluwer Academic Publishers, Holland.

[1]*The Philosophical Review* 74, No. 1 (January 1965), 27–46.

[2]pp. 33–34.

This argument has stimulated a flurry of discussion that shows no signs of abating.[3] But in this literature there is little attempt to spell out the intended sense of such crucial terms as 'power', 'ability', 'could have done otherwise', 'free', and 'voluntary'. And even where some attention is given to these terms there is no recognition that they might be used differently by different parties to the discussion. This is all the more surprising since, in another part of the forest, one finds elaborate analyses of competing sense of these terms. I refer, of course, to the extensive literature on free will. It is high time the fruits of this latter activity were brought to bear on Pike's argument, which, after all, is concerned to show that human actions are not free in some sense, that human beings lack the power, in some sense, to do other than what they do. I will be asking (1) what concepts of power, etc., Pike and other participants in the controversy mean to be using, and (2) how such concepts will have to be construed if their arguments are to be successful, or as successful as possible.

Rather than attempt to follow all the twists and turns in the free will literature, I will focus on the crucial distinction between a "libertarian" and a "compatibilist" understanding of terms like 'within one's power'. I will not attempt a full characterisation of either interpretation. Instead I will focus on one basic respect in which they differ, viz., on whether its being within one's power to do A at t requires that it be "really possible" that one do A at t. What is *really possible* at t is what is "left open" by what has happened up to t; it is that the non-occurence of which is not necessitated by what has happened up to t. Now there are various ways in which previous states of the world can necessitate, prevent, or leave open a state of affairs. It is the causal way that has dominated the free will discussion. A previous state of affairs, F, *causally* necessitates E at t if the necessitation is by virtue of causal laws.

> I. E is causally necessitated by a previous state of affairs, F = df. E is entailed by the conjunction of F and some causal laws, and E is not entailed by either conjunct alone.[4]

And to say that E is *causally possible* is to say that not-E is not causally necessitated by any previous states of affairs.

---

[3]In addition to the contributions that will be discussed in this paper, see Marilyn Adams, "Is The Existence of God A Hard Fact?", *The Philosophical Review* 76 (October, 1967), 209–16; Joshua Hoffman, "Pike on Possible Worlds, Divine Foreknowledge, and Human Freedom", *The Philosophical Review* 88 (1979), 433–42; and the latest entry, so far as I know, John Martin Fischer, "Freedom and Foreknowledge", *The Philosophical Review* 92 (1983), 67–79. At a recent Pacific Regional meeting of the Society of Christian Philosophers Pike presented a discussion of Fischer's paper, which was responded to by Marilyn Adams and Fischer, so that the conferees were treated to hearing Adams on Pike on Fischer on Adams on Pike, and Fischer on Pike on Fischer on Adams on Pike. "Enough!", you may well cry. And yet the beat goes on.

[4]This last requirement is designed to prevent causal necessitation from ranging over logical necessitation, in which a previous state of affairs alone entails E.

II. E is causally possible at t = df. There is no state of affairs prior to t, F, such that not-E is entailed by the conjunction of F and some causal laws without being entailed by either conjunct alone.

Being causally ruled out by the past is not the only threat to real possibility. Contemporary thinkers who suppose that God's foreknowledge rules out human free choice do not typically suppose that divine knowledge causes us to act as we do.[5] They think, rather, that since God is necessarily infallible the fact that God believes at t_1 that Jones will do X at t_2 *by itself* logically entails that Jones will do X at t_2, and hence is, by itself, logically incompatible with Jones' refraining from doing X at t_2. Let's say that a state of affairs is "situationally logically necessitated" when it is entailed by a previous state of affairs alone.

III. E is situationally logically necessitated by a previous state of affairs, F, = df. E is entailed by F alone.

And let's say that a state of affairs is "situationally logically possible" ('S-logically possible') when its nonoccurrence is not entailed by past facts alone.

IV. E is S-logically possible at t = df. There is no state of affairs prior to t, F, such that not-E is entailed by F.

We may think of an event as "really possible" when it is both causally and S-logically possible.

V. E is really possible at t = df. There is no state of affairs prior to t, F, such that either (a) not-E is entailed by the conjunction of F and some causal laws without being entailed by either conjunct alone, or (b) E is entailed by F alone.

This formulation can be simplified. Clearly if E is entailed by the conjunction of F and some causal laws, this covers both the case in which both conjuncts are needed for the entailment and the case in which E is entailed by F alone. Hence the following is logically equivalent to V.

VI. E is really possible at t = df. There is no state of affairs prior to t, F, such that E is entailed by the conjunction of F and some causal laws.

However IV, is more perspicuous in that it brings out the way in which a really possible event escapes being ruled out by the past in both of two ways.

---

[5]Some classical theologians, e.g., St. Thomas Aquinas (*Summa Theologiae*, I, Q. 14, a. 8) hold that divine knowledge causes what is known. But Aquinas never had the opportunity of discussing Pike's argument.

Since the basic claim of the libertarian is that I am not really free to do X at *t* if doing X is ruled out by what has already happened, she will want to use the broader notion of real possibility for a necessary condition of freedom. She will want to make it a necessary condition of being free to do E (having it within one's power to do E) that E is neither causally nor S-logically necessitated by past events.

Recently, under the influence of William of Ockham, a distinction between "hard" and "soft" facts has been injected into the discussion of these and related issues.[6] Roughly, a dated fact is a "hard" fact about the time in question if it is wholly about that time, if it is completely over and done with when that time is over. Otherwise it is a "soft" fact about that time. Thus the fact that I was offered the job at *t* is a hard fact about *t*; it embodies only what was going on then and is fully constituted by the state of the world at *t*. On the other hand, the fact that I was offered the job two weeks before declining it is not a hard fact about *t*, even if *t* is when I was offered the job. That fact is not fully constituted until two weeks past *t*. This distinction is relevant to our account of real possibility in the following way. A soft past fact can entail the occurrence of non-E without thereby preventing E from being really possible. The fact that I was offered the job two weeks before declining it at *t* entails that I did not accept it at *t*; but this obviously fails to show that it was not really possible for me to accept the job at *t*. Of course my not accepting the job at *t* is entailed by any fact that includes my declining it as a conjunct; but that has no bearing on whether accepting it was a real possibility for me at the moment of choice. Thus III.–VI. must be understood as restricted to states of affairs that have completely obtained before *t*, i.e., to *hard* facts about times prior to *t*.

Some recent thinkers, again following Ockham, have sought to draw the teeth of arguments like Pike's by claiming that a divine belief at *t* is not a hard fact about *t*; and hence that the fact that 'God believes at t_1 that Jones will do X at t_2' entails 'Jones will do X at t_2' does not show that Jones' refraining from doing X is not a real possibility for Jones at t_2.[7] If that contention is accepted, Pike's argument never gets out of the starting gate, and the question of the kind of freedom it shows to be impossible does not arise. Since the issue is controversial, I feel free to preserve my problem by simply assuming, for purposes of this discussion, that a divine belief at t_1 is a hard fact about t_1. Setting aside this additional complication will enable us to focus on the differential bearing of the argument on different conceptions of freedom.

---

[6]See, e.g., Marilyn Adams, "Is the Existence of God a Hard Fact?" loc. cit.; John Fischer, "Freedom and Foreknowledge", loc. cit.; Joshua Hoffman and Gary Rosenkrantz, "Hard and Soft Facts", *The Philosophical Review* 93 (July, 1984).

[7]Alfred J. Freddoso, "Accidental Necessity and Logical Determinism", *Journal of Philosophy* 80 (May, 1983), 257–78; Alvin Plantinga, "On Ockham's Way Out", *Faith and Philosophy* 2 (July, 1985).

The "compatibilist" interpretation of 'within one's power', by contrast, was specifically devised to insure a compatibility of free will and determinism. It does this by adopting the following account of what it is for something to be within an agent's power.

VII. It is within S's power at t to do A = df. If S were to will (choose, decide,...) at t to do A, S would do A.

In other words, its being within S's power to do A at t is simply a matter of S's being so constituted, and his situation's being such, that choosing to do A at t would have led to A's actually being done at t. As far as A is concerned, S's will would have been effective. To have been able to do other than what one actually did, in this sense, is obviously compatible with causal determinism. Even if my choice and action were causally necessitated by antecedent factors, it could still be the case that *if* I had chosen to do otherwise that choice would have been implemented. That counterfactual could be true even if it were causally impossible for me to choose or to do anything else. This is all quite analogous to the following physical analogue. Where only ball A hit ball C at t, it could still be true that *if* ball B had hit ball C at t instead, C would have moved differently from the way it in fact moved; and this can be true even if all these motions are causally determined.

Thus in the compatibilist's sense of 'A is within one's power' the causal possibility of A is not a necessary condition. And, by the same token, the S-logical possibility of A isn't either. Even if Jones's mowing his lawn logically follows from God's antecedent beliefs, that would seem to be compatible with the claim that *if* Jones *had* decided not to mow his lawn nothing would have prevented that decision from being implemented.[8] Hence we may say that neither form of real possibility is a necessary condition of A's being within one's power in a compatibilist sense of term.

II.

Turning now to the application of this distinction to the debate over foreknowledge and free will, I first want to ask what concept of 'within one's power' Pike was employing. He is not very forthcoming about this. In the original article his focal term was 'voluntary', and about this he says.

Although I do not have an analysis of what it is for an action to be *voluntary*, it seems to me that a situation in which it would be wrong to assign Jones the

---

[8]This may be contested. See the next section.

ability or *power* to do *other* than he did would be a situation in which it would also be wrong to speak of his action as voluntary.[9]

This makes 'voluntary' depend on 'within one's power', but it gives no hint as to the understanding of the latter. Nor does Pike offer any further clues in his responses to critics.

Faced with this situation we should perhaps follow Wittgenstein's dictum:

If you want to know *what* is proved, look at the proof.[10]

In that spirit, let's ask: in what sense of 'within one's power' does Pike's argument show that divine foreknowledge is incompatible with its being in anyone's power to do anything other than what one does? Or, not to take sides between Pike and his critics, in what sense of 'in one's power' is Pike's argument the strongest?

There would seem to be a clear answer to this question. We have distinguished the two concepts in terms of whether its being within one's power to do A requires that one's doing A is really possible. But Pike's argument is naturally read as being designed to show that, given God's forebelief that Jones mows his lawn at t_2, it is *not* really possible that Jones refrain from mowing his lawn at t_2. Underneath all its complexities Pike's argument essentially depends on the thesis that *God's believing at t_1 that Jones will do X at t_2* entails that *Jones will do X at t_2*, and hence that Jones not doing X at t_2 is not really possible. It is because of this entailment that in order for Jones to have the power at t_2 to refrain from doing X he would have to have the power to bring it about that the entailing fact did not occur, either because God did not exist at t_1 ((3) of Pike's step 6.), or did not believe at t_1 that Jones would do X at t_2 ((2) of step 6.), or would have to have the power to bring it about that the entailment does not hold, ((1) of step 6.). But if this entailment is the heart of the matter, the argument can be construed as an attempt to show that Jones' refraining at t_2 is not really possible, from which we conclude that it is not within his power to refrain. But we get this last conclusion only on a conception of *within one's power* that, like the libertarian conception, takes real possibility as a necessary condition. On the compatibilist conception the real impossibility of Jones' refraining cuts no ice. Thus it seems that Pike's argument shows, at most, that it is not within Jones' power to refrain from moving his lawn in a libertarian sense of that term.

---

[9]Op. cit., p. 33.

[10]Ludwig Wittgenstein, *Philosophical Grammar* (Berkeley: University of California Press, 1974), p. 369.

This may be contested. It may be claimed that the argument shows that Jones can't refrain even in a compatibilist sense. For if a necessarily infallible deity believes in advance that Jones mows his lawn at t_2, then Jones would do that even if he did decide to refrain. A mere momentary human decision surely wouldn't override eternal divine foreknowledge in the determination of what will happen. Hence if God believes in advance that Jones will do X at t_2, then even if Jones were to decide not to do X he would still do it. And so Pike's argument shows that it is not within Jones' power to refrain, even in a compatibilist sense.[11]

Thus we have plausible looking arguments on both sides. This is not an unusual situation with counterfactuals, which are notoriously slippery customers. If Jones had made a decision different from the one he in fact made, what would have ensued depends on what else would have been different from the actual world. It is clear that there can't be a world different from the actual world only in that Jones decided at t_2 to refrain from doing X. For the actual decision will have resulted from certain causes and will in turn contribute to the causation of subsequent events.[12] Hence if Jones had decided at t_2 to refrain from X the causal influences on his decision making would have been different; otherwise that decision to refrain would not have been forthcoming. And, in turn, the consequences of the decision to refrain from X will be different from the consequences of a decision to do X. The only alternative to this would be a change in causal laws that would permit this decision to refrain to be inserted into precisely the actual causal context. Hence a world in which Jones decides at t_2 to refrain from doing X will be different in *some* other respects from the actual world. And whether the counter-factual, 'If Jones had decided to refrain from X, he would have refrained from X' is true depends on just what additional differences from the actual world are being presupposed, implied, or allowed for. If we hang onto the actual causal laws and keep the causal context as similar as possible, then the decision to refrain would lead to refraining, and God's forebelief that Jones does X at t_2 would have to be different.[13] On the other hand, if we keep God's actual beliefs unaltered so far as possible then Jones will still do X at t_2, which implies that either some further causal influences on his behavior

---

[11] I am indebted to Pike for suggesting this line of argument, though he should not be taken as committed to it.

[12] Since the compatibilist typically assumes causal determinism, we are conducting this discussion on that assumption. If decisions, actions, and so on, are not strictly causally determined, similar points will hold, though the discussion would, perforce, be more complicated.

[13] I am assuming that the actual situation is such that there is nothing to prevent either a decision to do X or a decision to refrain from doing X from being carried out. This is a situation in which human beings often find themselves. If divine foreknowledge were to rule out the power to do other than what one in fact does, it would have to rule it out in this kind of situation.

are different, or that causal laws are not as they are in the actual world. So which is it to be?

I believe that it can be shown fairly easily that as the compatibilist understands his counterfactual, and as causal counterfactuals like this are commonly understood, the question of whether the proposition is true *is* the question of what would be the case if causal laws and causal factors were as much like the actual world as possible. When we wonder what Jones would have done had he decided differently, or whether that match would have lit if it had been struck, or whether Smith would have fallen from the ledge had the fireman not rescued him, we want to know what further difference this difference would have made, given our actual causal laws, and given the actual situation so far as it is logically compatible with this difference. If we are told that Jones still would have done X, despite the decision to refrain, if his behavior had been under radio control from Mars and the Martians in question had decided that Jones should do X, or if Jones' brain were organized in a quite different way, or if causal laws were quite different, that is all irrelevant to what we are asking. And it is equally clear that this is the way in which the compatibilist understands the counterfactual. For when the compatibilist maintains that, even given causal determinism, Jones *could* have refrained, in the sense that if he *had* decided to refrain he would have done so, what she is concerned to insist on is the point that the actual situation in which Jones found himself is such that a contrary decision, inserted into *that situation*, would give rise to a contrary action. Hence, as the compatibilist understands 'in one's power', divine forebelief that Jones does X at t_2 has no tendency to imply that it is not within Jones' power to refrain from doing X at t_2. The crucial counterfactual will still be true, even though in the counterfactual situation God's belief as to what Jones does at t_2, as well as God's belief as to what Jones decides at t_2, will be different.

It may be useful to look at the matter from another angle. It is often held that when we wonder whether Y would have happened if X had happened, what we want to know is whether Y happens in a situation in which X happens and which is otherwise as similar as possible to the actual situation. In a recently popular possible-worlds formulation, the question is as to whether Y is the case in all the X-worlds (worlds containing X) that are "closest" to the actual world. (For purposes of this highly compressed discussion let's understand 'closeness' as 'similarity'.) Now it may look as if there is a real contest on this point between those who think Pike's argument does apply to freedom in the compatibilist sense (extremists) and those who think that it does not (moderates). For the moderate will say that a Jones-decides-to-refrain world in which causal laws are the same and the causally relevant surroundings of Jones' decision are as much like the actual world as possible (but where God's belief about what Jones does at t_2 is different) is

closer to the actual world than a Jones-decides-to-refrain world in which
God's belief that Jones does X at t_2 is the same, but there are differences in
causal laws or causally relevant factors. And the extremist will make the
opposite judgement. This looks like a thorny issue as to which makes the
larger difference from the actual world: (a) differences in causal laws or causal
factors, or (b) differences in God's beliefs. And how do we decide a question
like that?

But this appearance of a deep impasse is deceptive. There is really no
contest. This can be seen once we set out the differences from the actual world
that obtain in the worlds claimed by each side to be closest. The worlds
favored by the extremist as closest we will call 'Set I' and the worlds favored
by the moderate as closest we will call 'Set II'. Let's begin by enumerating
the differences apart from God's beliefs.

Differences from the Actual World[14]

Set I	Both	Set II
Some additional causally relevant features of Jones's situation, or some causal laws, to block the implementation of the decision	Jones decision to refrain at t_2, together with whatever changes in the past are required to produce this decision, and some differences that result from the decision.	Jones refrains from doing X at t_2

Intuitively it looks as if Set I worlds are further from the actual world than
Set II worlds. But, says the extremist, it only looks that way until we realize
that Set II, but not Set I, worlds will also differ from the actual world by the
fact that God believes that Jones refrains from doing X at t_2. Hence, at the very
least, it is not clear that Set II worlds are closer to the actual world. However
a moment's reflection should assure us that this observation cuts no ice. Just
as we have to add to the differences specified above for Set II the additional
difference that God believes that Jones refrains from doing X at t_2, so we have
to add to the differences specified above for Set I the additional difference
that God believes that all these differences obtain. Thus bringing in differences in God's beliefs *could not* affect a previously existing difference in
closeness. If world A is closer to the actual world than world B on all counts
other than God's beliefs, then it can't be further away with God's beliefs taken
into account. For since the beliefs of an omniscient and infallible deity will

---

[14]This is oversimplified a bit. For example, there may well be other differences in Set II
that intervene between decision and execution. Moreover, each of the differences specified will
ramify causally both backwards and forwards in time.

exactly mirror what is the case, the differences introduced by God's beliefs will exactly mirror differences in other respects. And so if Set II worlds have the edge in closeness with God's beliefs left out, they will necessarily retain that edge with God's beliefs taken into account.

III.

On this basis of all this I will take it that Pike's argument is designed to show that it is not within anyone's power to do otherwise in a libertarian sense of that term. In what sense of the term are his critics contesting this?

The earliest published criticism of Pike's 1965 article was John Turk Saunders' "Of God and Freedom".[15] In considering the three alternatives embedded in step 6. of Pike's argument, Saunders concedes that Jones cannot have the first power, but he finds no bar to attributing the second or third. However he first reformulates these powers, since he takes Pike to have been construing them as powers to causally influence the past.

> ...it is contradictory to speak of a later situation causing an earlier situation, and consequently, it is contradictory to speak of its being in Jones's power to do something at t_2 which causes God not to exist, or not to have a certain belief, at t_1. But, while such powers are contradictory, there is no good reason to think that Jones must possess such powers if he has the power to refrain from X at t_2. The power to refrain from X at t_2 is, indeed, the power so to act at t_2 that either God does not exist at t_1 or else God does not at t_1 believe that Jones will do X at t_2. But Jones's so acting at t_2 would not bring it about that God does not exist at t_1, or that God does not hold a certain belief at t_1, any more than Jones's doing X at t_2 brings it about that God believes, at t_1, that Jones will do X at t_2. Jones's power so to act at t_2 is simply his power to perform an act such that if that act were performed, then certain earlier situations would be different from what in fact they are.[16]

Backwards causation turns out to be a non-issue however, since in his reply to Saunders Pike disavows any causal interpretation of 'bring it about' and acknowledges that Saunders' formulations might well do a better job of expressing his intent.[17]

Thus, it looks as if there is a head on confrontation between Pike and Saunders with respect to the possibility that Jones has the second and third powers mentioned in step 6. But this is so only if they are using 'within one's power' in the same sense. And this is definitely not the case, for it is clear from Saunder's article that he understands such terms in a compatibilist way.

---

[15]*The Philosophical Review* 75 (1966), 219–25.

[16]Ibid., p. 220.

[17]"Of God and Freedom: A Rejoinder", *The Philosophical Review* 75 (1966), p. 371.

...suppose that at t_1 I decide to skip at t_2 rather than run at t_2, that conditions are "normal" at t_1 and t_2 (I have not been hypnotized, drugged, threatened, manhandled, and so forth), and that I have the ability (knowhow) both to skip and to run. Suppose, too, that the world happens to be governed by empirical laws such that if ever a man in my particular circumstances were to make a decision of this kind, then he would not change his mind and do something else but would follow through upon his decision: suppose, that is, that, under the circumstances which prevail at t_1, my decision is empirically sufficient for my skipping at t_2. Clearly, it is in my power to run at t_2, since I know how to do so and the condition for the exercise of this ability are normal. If I were to exercise this power then I would not, at t_1, have decided to skip at t_2, or else the circumstances at t_1 would have been different.[18]

...although it (logically) cannot be both that my decision, under the circumstances, is empirically sufficient for my doing what I decide to do and also that I change my mind and do not do it, it does not follow that it is not in my power to change my mind and run instead. It follows only that I do not change my mind and run instead: for the fact that I know how to run, together with the fact that it is my own decision, under normal conditions, which leads me to persevere in my decision and to skip rather than to run, logically guarantees that I skip of my own free will and, accordingly, that it is in my power to change my mind and run. To maintain the contrary would be to suppose that some sort of indeterminism is essential to human freedom, on grounds that if ever, under normal conditions, my own decision is empirically sufficient for my doing what I do, then my own decision compels me to do what I do.[19]

Saunders plainly does not take the real possibility of S's doing A at t to be a necessary condition of its being within S's power to do A at t. He insists that even if antecedent events are causally sufficient for my doing B at t it could still be within my power to do A at t instead, and, indeed, that this will be within my power, provided I know how to do A, conditions are normal, and nothing is preventing whatever choice I make between A and B from issuing in action. This is obviously compatibilism; we even have the standard compatibilist line that to require indeterminism for freedom is to confuse causation with compulsion.

Thus Saunders and Pike are arguing past each other. The conclusion of Pike's argument is to be construed, as we have seen, as the claim that it is not within Jones's power at t_2 to refrain from doing X in a libertarian sense of 'within one's power'. Whereas Saunders holds that it is often within our power to do other than what we actually do in a compatibilist sense of 'within one's power'. They are simply not making incompatible claims.

---

[18]Op. cit., p. 221.

[19]Ibid., p. 222.

IV.

The other exchange I wish to examine is that between Pike and Alvin Plantinga. In *God, Freedom, and Evil*[20] Plantinga contends, like Saunders, that the powers Jones must have in order to be able to refrain are not, when properly understood, impossible at all. From now on let's concentrate on Pike's (2), the power, as Pike originally put it, to bring it about that God did not hold the belief He held at t_1.[21] In working toward his own version of this power Plantinga does not, like Saunders, first set aside a backwards causation interpretation. Instead he first considers the following version.

> It was within Jones' power, at T_2, to do something such that if he had done it, then at T_1 God would have held a certain belief and also *not* held that belief.[22]

Quite sensibly rejecting the supposition that Jones has any such power as this, Plantinga proposes instead the following as quite sufficient for Jones' having the power at t_2 to refrain from doing X.

> It was within Jones' power at T_2 to do something such that if he had done it, then God would not have held a belief that in fact he did hold.[23]

Let's call the power so specified, 'P'. The attribution of P, Plantinga says, would be "perfectly innocent". Note that this is substantially equivalent to Saunders' formulation.

We have seen that Saunders is a card-carrying compatibilist. This enables us to understand how he can regard P as "innocent". For, as we have seen, even if a necessarily infallible God believed at t_1 that Jones would do X at t_2, it could still be true that Jones could have refrained from doing X at t_2, in the sense that *if* he had decided to refrain nothing would have prevented the implementation of that decision. Hence in *that* sense he could, given God's antecedent infallible belief that he would do X, have the power so to act that one of God's antecedent beliefs would have been other than it was in fact. But how can Plantinga regard the attribution as innocent? It can't be for the same reason. Plantinga has made it abundantly clear that he takes what I have been calling the "real possibility" of S's doing A to be a necessary condition of its being within S's power to do A, and the real possibility of both doing A and refraining from doing A to be a necessary condition of S's freely doing A, or freely refraining from doing A.

---

[20]Grand Rapids, MI: William B. Eerdmans Pub. Co., 1974.

[21]I do so partly for the sake of greater focus in the discussion, and partly because more recent controversy over Pike's argument has centered around this part of the problem.

[22]p. 71.

[23]p. 71.

If a person is free with respect to a given action, then he is free to perform that action and free to refrain from performing it; no antecedent conditions and/or causal laws determine that he will perform the action, or that he won't. It is within his power, at the time in question, to take or perform the action and within his power to refrain from it.[24]

But if Jones' having a power to do A at t_2 requires that "no antecedent conditions and/or causal laws" determine that Jones does not do A at t_2, how can Jones have power P? For clearly *God believes that p at t_1 entails Jones does not do something at t_2 such that if he had done it God would not have believed that p at t_1.* And so if divine beliefs are "antecedent conditions" in the relevant sense, i.e., hard facts about the time at which a given such belief is held,[25] then Plantinga's condition for something's being within a person's power is not met by Jones and power P. Hence Plantinga, and anyone else who takes real possibility as a necessary condition for something's being within one's power, cannot regard the attribution of P to Jones as "innocent", at least not without denying that divine beliefs are "hard facts".

In support of this verdict look at the way Plantinga defends his "innocence" claim. As a preliminary, let's specify the proposition Plantinga numbers (51).

(51) God existed at t_1, and God believed at t_1 that Jones would do X at t_2, and it was within Jones' power to refrain from doing X at t_2.[26]

Now the defense:

For suppose again that (51) is true, and consider a world W in which Jones refrains from doing X. If God is essentially omniscient, then in this world W He is omniscient and hence does not believe at t_1 that Jones will do X at t_2. So what follows from (51) is the harmless assertion that it was within Jones' power to do something such that if he had done it, then God would not have held a belief that in fact (in the actual world) He did hold.[27]

We can see that there is something wrong with a libertarian's taking this line when we reflect that just the same case could be made for holding that its being within Jones' power to refrain from doing X at t_2 is compatible with

---

[24]*God, Freedom, and Evil*, p. 29.

[25]Plantinga does not question the "hardness" of divine beliefs in *God, Freedom, and Evil*.

[26]*God, Freedom, and Evil*, p. 69.

[27]Ibid., p. 71.

Jones' doing X at t_2 being causally determined. Here is that parallel case. Instead of (51) we will have its analogue for causal determinism.

> (51A) Causal factors obtained prior to t_2 that determined Jones to do X at t_2, and it was within Jones' power to refrain from doing X at t_2.

> Suppose that (51A) is true, and consider a world W in which Jones refrains from doing X. If causal determinism holds in this world W then either causal laws in W are different from what they are in the actual world or some of the causal factors that affect what Jones does at t_2 are different from what we have in the actual world. So what follows from (51A) is the harmless assertion that it was within Jones' power to do something such that if he had done it, then (assuming causal determinism still holds) either causal laws or causal factors would have been different from what they are in the actual world.

This is at least as strong as the case for the compatibility of divine foreknowledge of Jones' doing X, and Jones' power to refrain. If Jones can have it within his power to do something such that if he had done it then what God believed prior to that time would have been somewhat different, then surely Jones can have it within his power to do something such that if he had done it causal factors or causal laws would have been somewhat different.[28] Thus if Plantinga were in a position to argue as he does for the compatibility of *Jones' being able to do otherwise* with divine foreknowledge, he would equally be in a position to argue for the compatibility of *Jones' being able to do otherwise* with causal determinism. And that is just to say, once more, that Plantinga's argument goes through only on a compatibilist conception of 'within one's power'. It is not surprising, then, that in the forthcoming paper, "On Ockham's Way Out," Plantinga finds a different way to oppose Pike's argument—by arguing that the beliefs of a necessarily infallible being at *t* are not hard facts about *t*.

---

[28]There are two significant differences between the two cases. First Plantinga takes it that God necessarily exists; the non-existence of God in W does not constitute a possible difference between W and the actual world. Hence the non-existence of God is not one of the ways in which W could accommodate Jones' refraining from X at t_2. Whereas since causal determinism fails to hold in every possible world, its absence in W is one of the ways in which W could accommodate Jones' refraining from X at t_2. Second, even if determinism holds in W, the causal laws that hold there might be different in such a way as to permit Jones' refraining from X in the face of the same causal factors. But the theological analogue to the specific content of causal laws, viz., the infallibility of God, is taken to be necessary and so not to vary across possible worlds. Note that these two differences do nothing to shake the point that if Jones has the power to refrain from what is entailed by past facts he also has the power to refrain from what is causally necessitated by past facts. On the contrary, the two differences mean that there is even more room for variations across possible worlds in what *causally* determines what actually happens than there is with respect to what *theologically* determines what actually happens.

V.

The moral of all this is a simple but important one. If we are to consider attempts to show that it is within no one's power to do other than what one does, we had better attend to the variant possibilities for understanding 'within one's power', and we had better make explicit how it is being understood in a particular context. Else we run the risk of arguing to no purpose.[29]

---

[29]I have greatly profited from discussing the issues of this paper with Jonathan Bennett, Nelson Pike, Alvin Plantinga, and Peter van Inwagen.

PART FOUR

*RELIGIOUS
MORALITY
AND THE
MEANING OF LIFE*

PART INTRODUCTION
AND BIBLIOGRAPHICAL NOTES

The earlier parts of this book have explored the meaning and rational justification of religious belief. In this final part of the book, we will examine the implications of religious beliefs for human life, looking first at their implications for morality and then at their implications for our understanding of our own mortality.

The crucial question about religious morality can be stated very simply: Are moral codes mere reflections of the will of God (in which case it would seem that the actions in question are right or wrong only because God has willed us to do, or to refrain from doing, them) or are they reflections of God's knowledge that these actions really are right or wrong (in which case it would seem that they would be right or wrong independently of God)?

This issue was first raised by Plato in the *Euthyphro*. Euthyphro defines a holy action like the one he proposes doing as an action loved by the gods. Socrates tries to get Euthyphro to adopt the alternative view that the gods love certain actions because they are holy, that the moral value of the action, in other words, is independent of, and the cause of, the attitude of the gods to it. The argument presented by Socrates is a tricky one, and the reader will have to work very hard on it. A modernized version of an argument like it is found in the beginning of Baruch A. Brody's paper.

R. G. Swinburne begins his analysis by distinguishing certain moral truths, necessary moral truths, whose truth does not derive from any choice by God. He claims that this neither imposes inappropriate restrictions on God's power nor makes him less worth of worship. Swinburne goes on to argue that there are other moral truths, contingent moral truths, whose truth results from the ways in which God had structured the world. In either case, concludes Swinburne, God's commands are relevant either to creating the obligation or to strengthening it, not because God is powerful, but because he is our creator and because he is the owner of the world.

This last theme is developed extensively in the selection from Brody, who argues that God's ownership of the world, an ownership based upon his being its creator, has significant implications for our moral understanding of property rights, of suicide, and of euthanasia. In all these areas, the content of religious morality may be very different from the content of secular morality.

Both Swinburne and Brody are concerned with defending a form of religious morality in which the commands of God might make a difference to the actual content of morality. In this respect, their project differs from Robert Adams's project in the next selection. Adams is concerned to point out that religious people can say at the same time both that they follow certain moral principles because these principles are given by God whom they love and that these are the principles they would have adopted even if God had not commanded them to follow these principles. In this way, Adams argues, religious morality is compatible with human autonomy.

The final articles contain two very differing attitudes to these issue. Robert Young, in a careful critique both of Brody and Adams, concludes that it would be better theologically to adopt the view that the moral rightness of actions is independent of God's will. James Rachels, on the other hand, thinks that God, of necessity, should be worshipped, and worshiping involves following his commands regardless of their morality. Rachels actually uses this to argue that such a God cannot exist, for reasons that the reader should examine carefully.

We turn from an examination of the moral implications of religious belief to the implications of religion for beliefs about death and human survival. In the opening selection on that topic, Terence Penelhum identifies two different versions of belief in survival, the belief in the immortality of the soul and the belief in the resurrection of the body. After saying a bit about the history of those beliefs, he raises for discussion two difficulties for those beliefs. The first, which is a difficulty only for the belief in the immortality of a disembodied soul, is whether we can meaningfully ascribe to such disembodied souls any of the personal characteristics we assign to embodied human beings. The second, which is a difficulty faced in different ways by both of these beliefs, is whether we can meaningfully talk of these survivors as being identical with the embodied human being which existed before the death.

These challenges are picked up in the next two selections. In his essay, Anthony Quinton attempts to develop a theory of personal identity based on continuity of memory and character which would allow for personal identity even where there is no identity of body. Such a theory would, of course, meet one of Terence Penelhum's objections to the belief in the disembodied survival of the soul. At the end of the essay, however, he expressed some of Penelhum's qualms about ascribing personal characteristics to disembodied entities. George Mavrodes attempts to meet the personal identity challenge to the belief in the resurrection of the body in part by putting forward a Leibnizian believer theory of personal identity and in part by arguing that there is no problem about personal identity faced by the believer which isn't really faced by the nonbeliever as well.

The last two selections explore a rather different question, namely, whether human death, on the assumption that we do not survive, is actually a bad thing. Thomas Nagel argues that, at least from the perspective of the person whose life it is, death is a bad thing because death involves the cancellation of an indefinite number of possible goods which the person might have experienced. The mere fact that one dies at an age at which people normally die does not make one's death any less a bad thing. Bernard Williams sees it differently. He argues that death is a bad thing only if one has enough categorical desires to sustain the desire to live. When one no longer does, death might actually become a good thing. Immortality, from this perspective, would become a state of great tedium, and death, at least at the right time, a good thing. These readings usefully supplement our earlier selections, for there is no doubt that much of the religious belief in survival is connected to a belief that death is a bad thing, and these last readings force us to reconsider that belief.

There are three collections which contain much of the best recent material on the relation between religion and morality. They are Paul Helm's *Divine Commands and Morality* (Oxford University Press, 1979), Janine Idziak's *Divine Command Morality* (Edwin Mellen, 1979), and Gene Outka and John Reeder's *Religion and Morality* (Anchor, 1973). Other important recent books are Kai Nielsen's *Ethics Without God* (Pemberton, 1973) and Philip Quinn's *Divine Commands and Moral Requirements* (Oxford University Press, 1978).

Many important views about the issue of survival are collected in A. Flew's *Body, Mind and Death* (Macmillan, 1964). Good classical treatments include C. J. Ducasse's *A Critical Examination of the Belief in Life After Death* (Charles C. Thomas, 1961), J. Hick's *Death and Eternal Life* (Harper & Row, 1976), Corliss Lamont's *The Illusion of Immortality* (Philosophical Library, 1965), and H. H. Price's *Essays in the Philosophy of Religion* (Oxford University Press, 1972). Penelhum's views are presented more fully in his *Survival and Disembodied Existence* (Routledge & Kegan Paul, 1970), and another good recent treatment is J. Perry's *Personal Identity and Immortality* (Hackett, 1979).

RELIGIOUS MORALITY

PLATO

Why Are Holy Actions Holy

Socrates. But shall we...say that whatever all the gods hate is unholy, and whatever they all love is holy: while whatever some of them love, and others hate, is either both or neither? Do you wish us now to define holiness and unholiness in this manner?

Euthyphro. Why not, Socrates?

Socr. There is no reason why I should not, Euthyphro. It is for you to consider whether that definition will help you to instruct me as you promised.

Euth. Well, I should say that holiness is what all the gods love, and that unholiness is what they all hate.

Socr. Are we to examine this definition, Euthyphro, and see if it is a good one? or are we to be content to accept the bare assertions of other men, or of ourselves, without asking any questions? Or must we examine the assertions?

Euth. We must examine them. But for my part I think that the definition is right this time.

Socr. We shall know that better in a little while, my good friend. Now consider this question. Do the gods love holiness because it is holy, or is it holy because they love it?

Euth. I do not understand you, Socrates.

Socr. I will try to explain myself: we speak of a thing being carried and carrying, and being led and leading, and being seen and seeing; and you understand that all such expressions mean different things, and what the difference is.

Euth. Yes, I think I understand.

Socr. And we talk of a thing being loved, and, which is different, of a thing loving?

Euth. Of course.

From Plato's *Euthyphro.*

Socr. Now tell me: is a thing which is being carried in a state of being carried, because it is carried, or for some other reason?

Euth. No, because it is carried.

Socr. And a thing is in a state of being led, because it is led, and of being seen, because it is seen?

Euth. Certainly.

Soc. Then a thing is not seen because it is in a state of being seen; it is in a state of being seen because it is seen: and a thing is not led because it is in a state of being led; it is in a state of being led because it is led: and a thing is not carried because it is in a state of being carried; it is in a state of being carried because it is carried. Is my meaning clear now, Euthyphro? I mean this: if anything becomes, or is affected, it does not become because it is in a state of becoming; it is in a state of becoming because it becomes; and it is not affected because it is in a state of being affected: it is in a state of being affected because it is affected. Do you not agree?

Euth. I do.

Socr. Is not that which is being loved in a state, either of becoming, or of being affected in some way by something?

Euth. Certainly.

Socr. Then the same is true here as in the former cases. A thing is not loved by those who love it because it is in a state of being loved. It is in a state of being loved because they love it.

Euth. Necessarily.

Socr. Well, then, Euthyphro, what do we say about holiness? Is it not loved by all the gods, according to your definition?

Euth. Yes.

Socr. Because it is holy, or for some other reason?

Euth. No, because it is holy.

Socr. Then it is loved by the gods because it is holy: it is not holy because it is loved by them?

Euth. It seems so.

Socr. But then what is pleasing to the gods is pleasing to them, and is in a state of being loved by them, because they love it?

Euth. Of course.

Socr. Then holiness is not what is pleasing to the gods, and what is pleasing to the gods is not holy, as you say, Euthyphro. They are different things.

Euth. And why, Socrates?

Socr. Because we are agreed that the gods love holiness because it is holy: and that it is not holy because they love it. Is not this so?

Euth. Yes.

Socr. And that what is pleasing to the gods because they love it, is pleasing to them by reason of this same love: and that they do not love it because it is pleasing to them.

Euth. True.

Socr. Then, my dear Euthyphro, holiness, and what is pleasing to the gods, are different things. If the gods had loved holiness because it is holy, they would also have loved what is pleasing to them because it is pleasing to them; but if what is pleasing to them had been pleasing to them because they loved it, then holiness too would have been holiness, because they loved it. But now you see that they are opposite things, and wholly different from each other. For the one is of a sort to be loved because it is loved: while the other is loved, because it is of a sort to be loved. My question, Euthyphro, was, What is holiness? But it turns out that you have not explained to me the essence of holiness; you have been content to mention an attribute which belongs to it, namely, that all the gods love it. You have not yet told me what is its essence. Do not, if you please, keep from me what holiness is; begin again and tell me that. Never mind whether the gods love it, or whether it has other attributes: we shall not differ on that point. Do your best to make it clear to me what is holiness and what is unholiness.

R. G. SWINBURNE

Duty and the Will of God[1]

For a theist, a man's duty is to conform to the announced will of God. Yet a theist who makes this claim about duty is faced with a traditional dilemma first stated in Plato's *Euthyphro*[2]—are actions which are obligatory, obligatory because God makes them so (e.g. by commanding men to do them), or does God urge us to do them because they are obligatory anyway? To take the first horn of this dilemma is to claim that God can of his free choice make any action obligatory or non-obligatory (or make it obligatory not to do some action). The critic claims that the theist cannot take this horn, for God cannot make bad actions good. Nowell-Smith writes that 'an omnipotent, omniscient, creator of the Universe…might have evil intentions and might command me to do wrong; and if that were the case, though it would be imprudent to disobey, it would not be wrong.'[3] To take the second horn of

From *Canadian Journal of Philosophy*, vol. 4 (1974), pp. 213–27. Reprinted by permission of the author and the *Canadian Journal of Philosophy*.

[1] I am most grateful to Mr. D. A. McNaughton and other colleagues at Keele and to Dr. C. J. F. Williams for their helpful criticisms of an earlier version of this paper.

[2] *Euthyphro*, 9e.

[3] P. H. Nowell-Smith, 'Morality: Religious and Secular', in *Rationalist Annual* (1961); republished in Ian T. Ramsey (ed.), *Christian Ethics and Contemporary Philosophy* (London, 1966), pp. 93–112; see p. 97.

the dilemma is to claim that actions are good or bad in themselves and remain so whatever choices God makes. This horn looks very uncomfortable for the theist for two reasons; it suggests two separate limitations to God's power, two ways in which he is not omnipotent. First it suggests that God is limited in that if he is to urge men to do what is obligatory he has to urge them to do what is obligatory independently of any action of his. This suggestion, Hugo Meynell points out, 'may well seem to the theist to be blasphemous. It appears to imply that there is some objective standard of goodness and badness, prior to God's will and commandment, to which God's will and commandment are morally obliged to conform. But it is of the essence of "God", as most people understand the meaning of the term, that, if he exists at all, the moral law is dependent on his decrees and not *vice versa*.'[4] The second reason why grasping the second horn looks uncomfortable for the theist is that, since he must surely hold that it is no accident that God chooses to do what is good and so urges us to do what it is obligatory to do rather than what it is obligatory not to do, it would seem that he must hold that God is in some way necessitated to will what (independently of his will) is good. That again might seem a considerable restriction on his omnipotence. The purpose of this paper is to show that this dilemma for theism can be resolved, that it poses no threat to the coherence of theism, given a plausible assumption of metaethics.

I begin with a few terminological points. I understand by God the unconstrained, omnipotent, omniscient creator and sustainer of the Universe. I make the assumption that he exists and attempt to show that *Euthyphro* dilemma does not reveal an inner incoherence in that assumption.

I understand by "omniscient" "knowing everything which it is logically possible to know" and to begin with I understand by "omnipotent" "able to do anything logically possible". There are well known difficulties about these definitions but to deal with them would need separate papers.[5] These difficulties do not however, with an exception to be discussed, affect the issues

---

[4]Hugo Meynell, 'The Euthyphro Dilemma', *Proceedings of the Aristotelian Society*, Supplementary Volume (1972), pp. 223–34; see p. 224.

[5]I have attempted to provide a coherent account of the concept of omnipotence in my 'Omnipotence' (*American Philosophical Quarterly*, 10 (1973), 231–7). In his 'Omnipotence' (*Philosophy*, 48 (1973), 7–20) P. T. Geach claims (pp. 7 f.) that 'no graspable sense has ever been given to the sentence [*viz.*, "God can do everything", which he equates with "God is omnipotent"] that did not lead to self-contradiction or at least to conclusions manifestly untenable from a Christian point of view.' Geach sketches four accounts of omnipotence and brings objections against each of them. The objections to the first three accounts seem to tell against the coherence of the concept of omnipotence. I would claim in the cited article to have given an account of omnipotence immune from such objections. The objections to the fourth account seem to tell only against claiming that God is omnipotent. They suggest the need for modifying the claim that God is omnipotent in the way which I pursue in this paper. I must withdraw the claim of my earlier article to have given an account of omnipotence which allowed the theist to say that God is omnipotent, but continue to claim that I have given a coherent account of the concept of omnipotence such that it makes sense to say that there is an omnipotent being (although it is not coherent to say that that being is God).

discussed in this paper. By God being unconstrained I mean that his choices are not determined or influenced even in part by causes (as opposed to reasons) over which he has no control. Our choices are obviously influenced in part by many factors, psychological and physiological, over which we have no control, factors which act on us as it were from without, e.g. desires for food or sex or rest. Yet on our normal understanding of God, no factors over which he has no control act from without on God. His freedom is unimpaired by sensual desire or nervous impulses. Although our normal understanding of God involves thinking of him as unconstrained, this is a characteristic seldom mentioned explicitly in definitions of God, perhaps because it is felt that omnipotence entails being unconstrained. Omnipotence does not however entail being unconstrained. A being strongly influenced by sensual desires to do one action rather than another might still be *able* to do the latter action. Unconstrainedness needs explicit mention in a definition of God. I shall later argue that omniscience limits the omnipotence of an unconstrained agent, and so "omnipotent" in the definition of God will come to be understood not as just above but instead as 'able to do anything logically possible for an unconstrained and omniscient agent to do'.

I do not distinguish between an act being obligatory, being right, being a duty, and being an act which ought to be done. Unless otherwise stated I equate an obligatory action with a good action, and I equate a bad action with a wrong action and an action which ought not to be done. In these uses of moral terms I am riding rather roughshod over some subtleties of ordinary usage, but these subtleties do not affect the substance of my argument, and I make these equations to conform my terminology to that of others who have written on the subject.

I use all these terms—"obligatory", "duty", "good", etc. in moral senses, unless otherwise stated. In talking of duty, I am talking not of legal duty, but of moral duty—and so on. I understand "moral duty", "moral goodness" in a sense in which these are overriding. This means for example that if to do A rather than B would be to do the morally good action, while to do B rather than A would be to do an action which is good merely in some other respect (e.g. it is more pleasurable or aesthetically more satisfying) then to do A rather than B would be to do the action which is overall the better action. I use other moral terms, "duty", "right", etc. with similar entailments. We can of course use "moral" in a different sense, in a sense in which it makes sense to say that a man thinks that religion or art are more important than morality. But I am using "moral" and moral terms in what is, I suspect, the more usual sense, in which necessarily whatever a man thinks most important constitutes his morality.[6] The man who says 'Better to serve God than to do my duty' is a less usual and more paradoxical character than the man who says 'My duty is to serve God rather than do what others tell me is my duty'.

---

[6]For this distinction see Neil Cooper, 'Morality and Importance', in G. Wallace and A. D. M. Walker (eds.), *The Definition of Morality* (London, 1970).

I understand such moral terms as "right", "wrong" etc. in an objective sense, that is that sense in which actions are right or wrong quite independently of the agent's beliefs about whether or not he ought to do them. Brutus may have thought it right to kill Caesar, and for that reason we may judge him an honourable man who acted in accordance with the dictates of his conscience. In so far as this latter, that he followed his conscience, is the only criterion for the rightness of his action, you and I may agree that he did what he ought to have done. If we do say this, we are using "ought" in a subjective sense. We may however go on to discuss whether in fact, whatever Brutus' own view on the matter, he ought to have killed Caesar. You being a pacifist may say that he ought not to have done; I may say that he ought. Our disagreement is about whether he did what he ought to have done in an objective sense. It is in this sense that henceforward I will use the moral terms.

My assumption of metaethics is that expressions apparently attributing to things, goodness, obligatoriness etc. (e.g. 'capital punishment is always wrong') are statements which are true or false independently of human beliefs or attitudes towards those things; to call an action good is to attribute a property to it, not *merely* to express approval of it, commend it, or something similar. The status of ethical expressions is of course a very large philosophical issue on which it would be inappropriate to argue for a conclusion in an article devoted to another topic. Yet discussion of that topic is impossible without some view about the status of ethical expressions. In consequence I have to make an assumption about this and I shall make the one stated—that expressions apparently attributing to things goodness, obligatoriness, etc. are statements which are true or false independently of human beliefs or attitudes towards those things. I assume, in other words, that these are propositions of first-order ethics which have a truth-value, whether or not men recognize that truth-value, just as bodies are heavy or square or electrically charged whether or not men know this about them. The assumption does have a certain intrinsic plausibility. Torturing innocent children just for fun, one is inclined to say, is wicked whatever I or anyone else thinks about the matter—just as the Earth is a planet of the Sun, whether or not men recognize or approve this.

Given this assumption let us distinguish between contingent and necessary moral truths. A contingent moral truth is one which holds only because the world is as it is in some further contingent respect. A necessary moral truth is one which holds however the world is in contingent respects. Thus among contingent moral truths are such statements as 'I ought now to pay £10 to the bookshop' or 'I ought to give Smith a fail mark on his ethics paper'. These moral truths are contingent, because, although the cited actions are obligatory on me, they are obligatory only because of other contingent circumstances. Why I ought to pay the bookshop £10 is because I bought £10 of books from them and they have sent me a bill for the books. If such contingent circumstances did not hold, I would have no obligation to pay the bookshop £10. Contingent moral truths hold because the world is as it is in contingent respects. But that those moral truths hold under the contingent circumstances is itself a necessary moral truth. For if we state fully the contingent circumstances which make a contingent moral truth to hold, it cannot be a contingent matter that it does hold under those circumstances. Yet it is a moral truth that it does, and hence a necessary moral truth. It is a necessary moral truth that when I have bought £10 of books from the bookshop and they send me a bill for this, I ought to pay the bill. No doubt this moral truth holds because a much more general moral truth holds—that men ought to pay their debts—of which the specific truth is a consequence. Among the necessary moral truths one would expect to find general principles of conduct such as that one ought to care for one's children, not punish the innocent, not tell lies (together with whatever qualifications are needed). Nothing however for our purposes turns on which statements are necessary moral truths, or on the extent of the generality of those necessary moral truths. All that is important to see is that moral truths are either contingent or necessary in the stated senses; and that contingent moral truths hold because contingent circumstances are as they are and also because necessary moral truths hold.

My solution to the *Euthyphro* dilemma is in terms of this distinction. It is that the theist can happily take the first horn for actions which are contingently obligatory (i.e. for actions, the obligatoriness of which is a contingent moral truth), and the second horn for actions which are necessarily obligatory (i.e. for actions, the obligatoriness of which is a necessary moral truth). I proceed now to justify this solution.

To take the second horn for actions which are necessarily obligatory is to claim that their obligatoriness does not result from any free choice of God. Clearly that must be so. For a necessarily obligatory action is one which is obligatory however the world is in contingent respects, and a free choice of God is a contingent matter. This conclusion follows whatever the nature of those necessarily obligatory actions—it follows even if the only necessarily obligatory action were to do whatever God commands. That this was necessarily obligatory would be independent of the free choice of God. We have seen that if there is a contingent moral truth, then there is a necessary moral truth; from which it follows that if there is a contingently obligatory action, there is a necessarily obligatory action (*viz*. to do the former under the appropriate contingent circumstances). Hence if there are any obligatory actions at all (as we have been assuming), there is an obligatory action which is obligatory whatever the free choices of God. Does this mean that there cannot be an omnipotent God? We saw that grasping the second horn raised two separate difficulties for the theist in this respect. We must deal with each in turn.

First, there is the apparent limitation on God that if he is to urge men to do what is obligatory, he has to urge them to do what is obligatory independently of any action of his. Whether this is a limitation depends on whether the necessarily obligatory actions are obligatory from logical necessity or from some kind of factual necessity; that is whether the necessary moral truths that those actions are obligatory are analytic or synthetic. I understand "analytic" in a wide sense. I understand by a logically necessary or analytic statement a statement, the denial of which states nothing which it is coherent to suppose could be true. I understand by a synthetic statement a statement which is not analytic. If for any specified action which is obligatory (e.g. telling the truth) it is analytic that it is obligatory, then it is no restriction on God that if he is to urge men to do what is obligatory he must urge them to do those actions which of logical necessity are obligatory. In order to be omnipotent, as we have defined omnipotence, a being has only to be able to do the logically possible. We surely do not require that an omnipotent being be able to do the logically impossible for that requirement is not coherent. The traditional view that to be omnipotent a being does not have to be able to do the logically impossible seems correct.[7] The suggested restriction on God is no more a restriction than it is a restriction on God that if he is to keep Jones a bachelor he must keep him an unmarried man. If necessary moral truths are analytic, the first difficulty for the theist in grasping the second horn in respect of them disappears.

But if the necessity that if God is to urge men to do what is obligatory, he must urge them to do certain specifiable actions (e.g. truth telling) is a factual necessity, it does indeed involve a restriction on God's power. For it means that while it is coherent to suppose that God urge men to do what is obligatory without urging them to do these actions, there is nevertheless a natural necessity which prevents him from doing so. Yet the supposition that necessary moral truths are synthetic is indefensible, quite apart from any general difficulties in the idea of a synthetic necessary truth. Suppose that necessary moral truths are synthetic. Then take some necessary moral truth 'under circumstances C, A is obligatory'. This truth being synthetic, it is coherent to suppose that it does not hold. This could only be if there were a necessary moral truth of the form 'under circumstances C^1, A is not obligatory' (where C^1 is a subset of C). This latter would be a synthetic truth, though a necessary one. So our universe is one where 'under circumstances C, A is obligatory' is a necessary moral truth, yet it is coherent to suppose that there be a universe where it is not, and instead 'under circumstances C^1, A is not obligatory' is a necessary moral truth. Now necessary moral truths hold whatever the world is like in contingent respects. So the latter universe could be exactly the same as ours in all contingent respects. So if necessary moral truths were synthetic, it would be coherent to suppose that there is a universe which differs from ours in the respect that under circumstances C^1, A was not

---

[7]St. Thomas Aquinas, *Summa Theologiae*, 1a.25.3. See my 'Omnipotence', *American Philosophical Quarterly*, 10 (1973), 231–7.

obligatory, but in no contingent respect at all. Yet how could a world differ from ours solely in an ethical respect? What would it be like for a world to differ from our world solely in the respect that murder is not wrong in that world? What sense can be given to such a supposition? By the principle of supervenience[8] if one thing is good and another bad, they have to differ in some further respect, and if we understand by "further respect" "further contingent respect", it is hard to challenge that principle. I conclude that necessary moral truths are not synthetic. Hence they are analytic (in the stated sense) and so the first difficulty for a theist grasping the second horn for necessary moral truths disappears.

The second difficulty for a theist in grasping the second horn is that since presumably it is no accident that God chooses to do what is good, and so urges us to do what it is obligatory to do rather than what it is obligatory not to do, it would seem that he must be necessitated to choose to do what is, independently of his choice, good. I wish to show that if a being is unconstrained and omniscient, of logical necessity, he can choose only the good. This restriction on God is a restriction already imposed on his being omniscient and unconstrained. I shall however argue that it is one which makes him no less worthy of worship.

I begin with the point that actions, in the sense of things done intentionally, must have reasons, in the sense of reasons possessed by an agent for doing them. To do an action is to forward an end or goal, and the reason for doing the action is to forward the end. The doing of an action may be an end in itself or it may be the means to a further end. An action always has a reason, even if it is only the minimal reason that the agent wanted to do it. If a man says that he did something 'for no reason at all', the natural interpretation is that he did the action merely for the sake of doing it, not for any further reason. The suggestion that a man performed an action, that is did something intentionally, did something meaning to do it, without having a reason for doing it is incoherent. This can be seen by the fact that a crucial test for whether some movement of my body was an action of mine or merely something that happened to my body (e.g. a reflex movement) is whether I can give a reason for having done it, that is whether I can answer the question 'Why did you do it?' If I cannot answer the question, that shows that the movement is not properly described as an action which I did. Now having a reason for an action consists in regarding some state of affairs as a good thing and the doing of the action as a means to forwarding that state, and hence itself a good thing. If my reason for going to London is to meet Jones, I must regard it as in some way a good thing that I should meet Jones, and so in some way a good thing that I go to London. If I regard it as in no way a good thing that I should meet Jones, if I regard my meeting Jones as an event which would serve no useful function at all, meeting Jones cannot be my reason for

---

[8]See R. M. Hare, *The Language of Morals* (Oxford, 1952), pp.80 et seq.

going to London. The point that to do an action I must (of logical necessity) see my performance of it as in some way a good thing is a very old one due to Aristotle, emphasised by Aquinas, and re-emphasised in our day by, among others, Stuart Hampshire.[9]

What however are we to make of the suggestion that a man might see doing A as a good thing in one way (e.g. by its giving sensual pleasure to himself), doing B (an action doing which is incompatible with doing A) as a good thing in another way (e.g. by its contributing to the life-long peace of mind of someone else), see doing B as overall a better thing than doing A, but nevertheless do A rather than B? When it is suggested that a case is of this sort, we may well suspect that it is not, that the agent did not really see doing B as overall a better thing than doing A. Yet we are sometimes prepared to allow that the situation is as suggested. We do seem to allow the possibility that a man might do an action which he regarded as a good thing only in some respect but on balance a bad thing. But although we allow this possibility, we do feel that some further explanation is called for. If a man really does accept that to do B would be to do what is on balance the better action, he has adequate reason for doing B but totally inadequate reason for doing A. Rational considerations point clearly in one direction, yet the agent goes in the other direction. Yet to say that someone recognizes that he has adequate reason for doing B rather than A is to say that in so far as no factors other than reasons influence what he does, he will do B rather than A. For although a man's belief or recognition that something is so does not necessarily affect his behaviour, it can only fail to do so if some special explanation can be provided of what prevented it from affecting behaviour. If a philosopher denies this, he is committed to the connection between a man's beliefs and what he does being a merely contingent one—which allows as a logical possibility that none of a man's beliefs might make any difference to his actions—which is absurd! So if you said that you recognized that overall it would be better for you to go home rather than to go to the cinema, and then you went to the cinema, we should have to suppose either that you were lying or had changed your mind, or that factors other than reasons influenced what you did. An explanation of your behaviour is needed, not only in terms of what you believed about the relative merits of the actions, in terms that is of reasons; but also in terms of other factors such as sensual desires and neurological impulses which led you to do what you did not have adequate reason for doing. If a man has strong sensual desires, it makes sense to suppose that he recognizes B as the better action but nevertheless intentionally does A. Such non-rational factors over which the agent does not have control explain 'weakness of will', a man acting 'against his better judgement'. But the suggestion that a man might see B as the better action,

---

[9]'A man cannot be sincere in accepting the conclusion that some course of action is entirely mistaken, if he at the same time deliberately commits himself to this course of action' (Stuart Hampshire, *Freedom of the Individual* (London, 1965), p. 7.)

be subject to no non-rational forces 'pushing' him in the direction of doing A and nevertheless do A is incoherent.[10]

Moral considerations as we have understood them, are overriding. Why then does a man fail to do his duty? By my previous arguments either because he does not fully recognize his duty, or because he is influenced by forces not subject to his control. If the latter operate, the agent is in a situation of temptation, to which he may or may not yield.[11] Given all this, could God choose to do anything which was not morally good? Clearly not through ignorance, for he is omniscient. Both ordinary factual and moral truths are known to Him. While we have rather cloudy feelings that abortion and euthanasia are evils, he knows the truth about these matters (whatever it is!) with crystal clarity. God could not urge a man to murder his brother, through not knowing that murder was an evil. Nor could he choose to do something morally evil through being influenced by non-rational factors, through failing to resist temptation. By definition God is unconstrained and not subject to such factors. Of logical necessity a being unconstrained and omniscient does not choose the bad. This necessary restriction on God's omnipotence (to his not choosing to do an evil action) is a consequence of his being omniscient and unconstrained. The existence of this restriction means that we must understand the claim in our previous definition of God that he is omnipotent as saying that he is able to do anything logically possible for an unconstrained and omniscient agent to do.

God's omniscience (given that he is unconstrained) limits his omnipotence by limiting what he can set himself to do. If he chose to do an evil action he could do it. But being omniscient, he cannot choose to do it. This is because he will know that the action is an evil action, and so that he cannot by doing that action do an action which is better than any alternative (which is, by our previous argument, what every agent not influenced by non-rational forces seeks to do), and so he cannot do the action. It may at first seem surprising that knowledge can limit what we can set ourselves to do but a few mundane examples will easily show that it does. If I really know that I cannot jump to the moon, I cannot set myself or try to do it. No action of mine would properly be described as setting about jumping to the moon or trying to jump to the moon. I could only be said to be pretending to jump to the moon, or to be

---

[10]The extreme position on this issue of R. M. Hare as represented in Chapter 5 of *Freedom and Reason* seems to be that necessarily if a man believes that B is the better action, he will do B unless it is psychologically impossible for him to do B. Many writers have opposed this position. Steven Lukes has pointed out that ordinarily we describe men as tempted and yielding to temptation when there is no *irresistable* temptation for them to yield to. Irving Thalberg points out that 'ought implies might not'. In Hare's account of moral action it would never be appropriate to blame a man for not living up to his principles. See the contributions of Hare, Lukes, Thalberg and others published in Geoffrey Mortimore (ed.), *Weakness of Will* (London, 1971).

[11]Nothing which I have written implies that the outcome of a struggle with temptation is predetermined.

going through the motions which I would go through if I were trying to jump to the moon. If I really know that the bus has gone, I cannot try to catch it. My running to the bus-stop must be described in some other way.

My conclusion then is that God, being omniscient and unconstrained of logical necessity chooses only the good. Hence he will not urge us to do what it is obligatory not to do, but only what is obligatory to do.[12] Does this limitation on God's omnipotence make him less worthy of worship? Why should it? Being unconstrained hardly makes a being less worthy of worship. Although knowledge limits power of choice, by preventing us from trying to do what we cannot (e.g. change the past, or do good by murdering), quite clearly in general by allowing us to see what we can do and so allowing us to exercise our power effectively, it allows us to use the power of choice which we have much more effectively. That a being's power cannot be exercised in self-defeating ways surely does not detract from his dignity.

So much for necessarily obligatory actions. What now of contingently obligatory actions? Given that necessary moral truths which, as we have seen, are analytic truths are as they are, what makes a contingently obligatory action A obligatory in some contingent circumstance C? What makes it my duty to pay the bookshop is that I have bought books from them and they have sent me a bill. But if there is a God who is creator and sustainer of the Universe, any contingent circumstances C are either brought about directly or indirectly by God or brought about by the free choice of some other agent (e.g. a man) kept in existence by God and allowed by him to exercise his choice. In the former case God by bringing about C makes A obligatory. In the latter case God by keeping some other agent in existence and allowing him to bring about C has permitted some other agent to make A obligatory. Either way God's action makes A obligatory (though in the latter case he permits some other agent to share in making A obligatory). Why it is wrong for me to stick pins into you is that you are so made that sticking pins into you hurts terribly, and so is wrong, and it is God who has made you thus—given that God exists as defined—and so has made it obligatory on me not to stick pins into you. This point is well made by Meynell when he writes that 'what is good or right in human action and dispositions depends ultimately on the divine will, if God exists; since in that case the whole context

---

[12]This general view that necessarily God can only will the good, and that necessarily his freedom is only a freedom to choose between equally good alternatives, is that of Aquinas. Thus: 'The will never aims at evil without some error existing in the reason, at least with respect to a particular object of choice. For, since the object of the will is the apprehended good, the will cannot aim at evil unless in some way it is proposed to it as a good; and this cannot take place without error. But in the divine knowledge there cannot be error. God's will cannot, therefore, tend towards evil' (*Summa Contra Gentiles*, 1.95.3; translated by Anton C. Pegis under the title, *On the Truth of The Catholic Faith, Book I* (New York, 1955)).

of human life within which moral terms have their application, and from which they derive their significance depends on it.'[13]

So then the conclusion follows that if it is a necessary truth that under circumstances C, A is obligatory, then God as the author of circumstances C is responsible for the contingent truth that A is obligatory. This holds whatever the form of necessary moral truths. It is however pertinent to ask whether the circumstances C which make A obligatory are always, sometimes, or never the issue of an explicit command by God. The command would presumably become known through some vehicle of Revelation, e.g. Mahommet or the Bible or the Church, telling us on behalf of God that the command had been issued. Yet while this question is relevant, it is important to note that whatever answer we give to it, the basic solution to the dilemma outlined in the previous part of the paper remains.

My answer to the new question is that sometimes the command of God would make actions obligatory which would not otherwise be obligatory; and that always the command of God would make the strength of an obligation to do an action greater than it would otherwise be. Some actions however are obligatory whether or not God commands them; and so God cannot forbid them (since forbidding them would be evil, and it is not logically possible, as we have seen, for an omniscient and unconstrained being to do evil).

A powerful argument against this position is that we know perfectly well how to decide moral issues without bringing in the commands of God. Suppose we debate the rightness or wrongness of capital punishment. We know the kind of considerations which count for or against the wrongness of capital punishment as a penalty for murder. For is the consideration that if you find out that you have wrongly executed a man, you cannot remit any of his penalty or make amends. Against is the horror of murder and the need for an adequate punishment. Statistics of the deterrent effect of capital punishment or the lack of it are also relevant to one or other side of the controversy. We know how to settle the matter without bringing God in. Rightness or wrongness being established independently of God, his command cannot alter things.

This argument, though it seems initially powerful, is confused. Certainly we know how to decide moral issues if we ignore divine commands by supposing that there are none. But that does not mean that divine commands, if there are any, are irrelevant to moral issues, any more than the fact (if it is a fact) that we can show the wrongness of capital punishment, if we ignore any possible deterrent effect (i.e. suppose there to be none) means that deterrent effects if they exist, are irrelevant to its rightness or wrongness. Maybe divine commands, if they exist, are relevant, possibly decisively

---

[13]Meynell, *op. cit.*, p. 232.

relevant—even though we can settle moral issues on the assumption that divine commands do not exist. I shall now proceed to argue that if God has issued commands, they do have moral relevance.

Their relevance, contrary to what Geach seems[14] to claim, is nothing to do with the power of God. Power does not give the right to command, even if it is infinite power and even if it is benevolent power.

There are at least two different considerations which make the commands of God, if there are any such, impose moral obligations which did not exist before. The first is that, by definition, he is our creator and sustainer. We depend for our existence at each instant on his will. Now many would hold that men have an obligation to please their benefactors. A man who makes no effort to please those who have done much for him is generally felt to be behaving in an immoral way. A consequence of the general principle that men have an obligation to please their benefactors is that children have an obligation to please their parents, who brought them into the world and keep them alive, clothe, and feed them. The obligation to please parents would be fulfilled by conforming to the parents' wishes (which may be expressed by commands) e.g. that the child should do the shopping or the washing up, go to bed at a certain time or shut the door. There might be no special reason why the child ought or ought not to go to bed at the time in question other than that the parent has commanded it. But the parent's command makes what was otherwise not a duty a duty for the child. The child owes something to the parent in view of the parent's status. It is not that children have a duty to pay something back to the parent, but that because in an important respect the parent is the source of their being he is entitled to their consideration.

The moral views expressed in the last paragraph are by no means universal, but they are, I suspect, held by a considerable majority of the human race. A morality which did not think the worse of a man for making no effort to please those who had done him much good would seem a pretty poor morality. If the moral views of the last paragraph are correct then men are under a great obligation to obey the commands of God—a great obligation because, if theism is true, the dependence of the children of God on God is so much greater than the dependence of the children of men on men. We depend to a large extent on our parents for our initial existence and to some extent for our subsequent existence—they provide food, shelter, etc. But we depend on other persons too for our subsequent existence—the police, our parents' employers, the state's welfare officers etc. And our parents are only able to bring us into existence and sustain us because of the operation of various natural laws (e.g. the laws of genetics, and embryology), the opera-

---

[14]Peter Geach, *God and the Soul* (London, 1969), p. 127 [Reading XI]. For criticism of this see D. Z. Phillips, *Death and Immortality* (London, 1971), ch. 2.

tion of which, is, on the theistic hypothesis, due to God. However our dependence on God, the author of Nature, is, if he exists, total. He gave to our parents the power and inclination to bring us into being, and to them and to others the power to keep us alive. He keeps operative natural laws, as a result of which we have food and drink and health. Our obligation to God must be correspondingly very much greater than to our parents.

The other consideration which makes the commands of God impose moral obligations which did not exist before is that God is the creator of the inanimate world and, not being known to have ceded ownership of it, is properly adjudged its owner. What greater claim could one have to property than having created it *ex nihilo* unaided? The owner of property has the right to tell those to whom he has loaned it what they are allowed to do with it. Consequently God has a right to lay down how that property, the inanimate world, shall be used and by whom. If God has made the Earth, he can say which of his children can use which part. The Bible is full of claims that God has given to persons various possessions (and thereby commanded other persons to leave them alone). Thus the Lord is said to have declared to Joshua that he gave to the Israelites the land of Canaan (*Joshua* 1.2ff.). The right of God to dispose of the material objects of the world as he wishes is affirmed by Aquinas: 'What is taken by God's command, who is the owner of the Universe, is not against the owner's will, and this is the essence of theft.'[15] It follows from this that it is logically impossible for God to command a man to steal—for whatever God commands a man to take thereby becomes that man's and so his taking it is not stealing.

Again the moral principle about property to which I have appealed would not be universally accepted, but, possibly with qualifications, it would, I believe, be very generally accepted, and for those who do accept it the conclusion about God follows directly. So appealing to widely accepted moral principles, I have argued that God's commands can impose obligations which did not exist before. By parity of argument the commands of God can add to the obligation to do an action which is obligatory anyway. An action of a child which is wrong anyway becomes wrong in a new way if the parent forbids it.

Scotus claimed[16] that although acts were often good or bad in themselves apart from considerations about God, God's commands made it obligatory to do them. The same point is certainly involved in what Miss Anscombe claims in her article 'Modern Moral Philosophy'[17] when she claims that the concept of obligation only has a sense within a law concept of ethics,

---

[15]*Summa Theologiae*, 1a.2ae.94.5., ad. 2, New Blackfriars ed., trans. Thomas Gilby, O.P., Vol. XXVIII (London, 1966).

[16]See F. Copleston, *A History of Philosophy*, Vol. II (London, 1950), p. 547.

[17]*Philosophy*, 33 (1958), 1–19.

that is within a concept of ethics in which to be obliged is to be commanded. My argument suggests that commands sometimes make acts right or wrong and make acts which are right or wrong anyway right or wrong in a new respect. We could well reserve the word "obligation" to refer to an act which it would be wrong not to do, and which is made thus by a command. I have not myself used "obligation" in this way, because I do not think that normally its use is restricted in this way. But there would be a point in so restricting its use in order to give a name to a certain kind of act which otherwise does not have one.

Still, there are surely limits to the obligations which a divine command could create. Exactly where they are to be put men will differ. There are certainly limits to the obligations which a parent's command can create, and to the obligations to obey the owner of property in respect of its use. If a parent commands a child to kill his neighbour, the command imposes no obligation. Nor does the command of an owner of vast estates not to use some of his unwanted corn to feed the starving. At least, most people would accept these moral judgments. Some might urge that God is so much more truly the author of our being and the owner of the land than are human parents and property owners that there are no limits to the obligations which would be produced by his commands.[18] But most would surely judge that even God could not remove my obligation to keep a solemn promise when the keeping of it would cause pain to no one, or my obligation not to torture the innocent. But if for some action A if God commanded us to do A, it would still be our duty not to do A, God would not command us to do A. For then commanding us to do A would be inciting us to do evil. Since to incite to evil is evil, God who necessarily wills the good would not incite to evil.

However, wherever we draw the line, whether God could by commanding impose any obligation or none, makes no difference to the main argument of this paper. Whether or to whatever extent God can impose obligations by issuing commands, he can certainly, if he exists as defined, impose them by producing the circumstances which create them. And even if his commands would not impose obligations which did not exist before, it remains the case that if God urged us to do something, necessarily the doing of it would not be evil. For God who necessarily does not will evil will not urge men to do evil. I conclude that, given my metaethical assumption, whatever difficulties threaten the coherence of theism, the *Euthyphro* dilemma is not among them.

---

[18]As Ockham seems to have held. See F. Copleston, *A History of Philosophy*, Vol. III (London, 1953), pp. 104 f.

BARUCH A. BRODY

Morality and Religion Reconsidered[1]

There are many people who believe that, in one way or another, morality needs a religious backing. One of the many things that might be meant by this vague and ambiguous claim[2] is the following: there are certain moral truths that are true only because of the truth of certain religious truths. In particular, the truth of certain claims about the rightness (wrongness) of a given action is dependent upon the truth of certain religious claims to the effect that God wants us to do (refrain from doing) that action. This belief, in effect, bases certain parts of morality upon the will of God.

Philosophers have not commonly agreed with such claims. And there is an argument, whose ancestor is an argument in the *Euthyphro*,[3] that is supposed to show that such claims are false. It runs as follows: the proponents of the claim in question have reversed the order of things. Doing a given action *A* is not right (wrong) because God wants us to do (refrain from doing) *A*; rather, God wants us to do (refrain from doing) *A* because of some other reason which is the real reason why *A* is right (wrong) for us to do. For, if the situation were the way it is depicted by the proponents of the claim in question, we would have moral truths based upon the arbitrary desires of God as to what we should do (refrain from doing), and this is objectionable.

I would like to reexamine this issue and to show that the situation is far more complicated than philosophers normally imagine it to be. I should like to show (a) that the general argument suggested by the *Euthyphro* is not as persuasive as it is ordinarily thought to be, and (b) that it is even less persuasive when we see the religious claim applied to specific moral issues, and that this is so because the claims about the will of God can be supplemented by additional theological claims.

---

[1] I should like to thank David Rosenthal for his many insightful comments on an earlier version of this paper.

[2] Other things that might be meant are: (a) we know that certain moral truths are true because we know the truth of certain religious truths (perhaps, that God has revealed to us that the action is right), and (b) we have a reason to do what is right because of the truth of certain religious truths (perhaps, that God will reward us if we do). We will not discuss these claims in this paper.

[3] We leave aside, for this paper, the question as to exactly what was the argument in the *Euthyphro*. On that issue, see R. Sharvy's "Euthyphro 9d–11b", *NOÛS* (1972) which influenced the way I constructed the argument to be considered below.

1.

Let us begin by looking at the argument more carefully. We shall formulate it as follows:

(1) Let us suppose that it is the case that there is some action A that is right (wrong) only because God wants us to do (refrain from doing) it.

(2) There must be some reason for God's wanting us to do (refrain from doing) A, some reason that does not involve God's wanting us to do (refrain from doing) it.

(3) Therefore, that reason must also be a reason why A is right (wrong).

(4) So we have a contradiction, (1) is false, and either there are no actions that are right (wrong) because God wants us to do (refrain from doing) them or, if there are such actions, that is not the only reason why those actions are right (wrong).

What can be said by way of defense on (2)? The basic idea behind it seems to be the following: if God wanted us to do (refrain from doing) A, but he had no reason for that want that was independent of his act of wanting, then his act of wanting would be an arbitrary act, one that entails some imperfection in him. But God is a perfect being. Therefore, he must have some reason for wanting us to do (refrain from doing) A, some reason that is, of course, independent of that want of his. Now it is not entirely clear that this argument is sound, for it is not clear that the performance by an agent of an arbitrary act (even an arbitrary act of willing) entails some imperfection in the agent.[4] But we shall let that issue pass for now and focus, for the moment, on the crucial step (3).

It is clear that step (3) must rest upon some principle like the following:[5]

(Trans.) If p because of q and q because of r, then p because of r.

There are two things that should be noted about this principle. The first is that if we are to use it in our context we will have to take it as ranging over different types of cases in which we say "because." After all, there are significant differences between cases in which we make claims of the form

---

[4]This is a claim that would certainly be denied by writers in the Calvinist tradition. Thus, Jonathan Edwards, writes as follows in connection with the question of salvation and damnation:

> It is meet that God should order all these things according to his own pleasure. By reason of his greatness and glory, by which he is infinitely above all, he is worthy to be sovereign, and that his pleasure should in all things take place. [*Jonathan Edwards* (Hill and Wang: 1935) p. 119]

[5]It could, of course, rest upon the weaker principle, that only held in cases where q was some agent's wanting something. But all of the points we will make are equally applicable to this weaker principle.

"*A* is right (wrong) because God wants us to do (refrain from doing) *A*" and cases in which we make claims of the form "God wants us to do (refrain from doing) *A* because *r*," for it is only in the latter type of case that we have the reason-for-wanting, "because." The second point is that there are real problems with this principle. While Joe may go home because his wife wants him to do so, and she may want him to do so because she wants to have it out with him, it may well not be the case that he goes home because she wants to have it out with him. So the principle is going to need some modifying, and it is not clear how one is to do this while still preserving the inference from (1) and (2) to (3).

Still, let us suppose that this can be done. Our argument faces the following further objection: God's wanting us to do (refrain from doing) *A* is not the whole of the reason why the action is right (wrong); the additional part of the reason is that he is our creator to whom we owe obedience. And when we take into account the full reason, the argument collapses. After all, the *Euthyphro* argument would then run as follows:

(1') Let us suppose that there is some action *A* that is right (wrong) only because God wants us to do (refrain from doing) *A* and he is our creator to whom we owe obedience.

(2') There must be some reason for God's wanting us to do (refrain from doing) *A*, some reason that does not involve God's wanting us to do (refrain from doing) *A*.

(3') Therefore, that reason must also be a reason why *A* is right (wrong).

(4') So we have a contradiction, (1') is false, and either there are no actions that are right (wrong) because God, who is our creator and to whom we owe obedience, wants us to do (refrain from doing) them, or, if there are such actions, that is not the only reason why those actions are right (wrong).

And, even supposing that (Trans.) is true, (3') would not follow from (1') and (2').

It is clear that the proponents of the *Euthyphro* argument have got to block this move. How might they do so? The most straightforward move is to deny the moral relevance of the fact that God is our creator, to claim that even if he is, we have no obligation to obey his wishes and that, therefore, the reason advanced in (1') cannot be a reason why *A* is right (wrong).

Is this move acceptable? Consider, for a moment, our special obligation to obey the wishes of our parents.[6] Why do we have that obligation? Isn't it because they created us? And since this is so, we seem to have an obligation, in at least some cases, to follow their wishes. So, *x*'s being our creator can be part of a reason for doing (refraining from doing) an action *A* if the other part is that that is *x*'s wish. And if this is so in the case of our parents, why

---

[6]This analogy between our obeying the will of God and the will of our parents is based upon the Talmudic discussion (in *Tractate Kedushin*, 30[b]) of the obligation to honor one's parents.

shouldn't it also be so in the case of God? How then can the defendents of the *Euthyphro* argument say that the fact that God created us cannot, together with some facts about his wishes, be a reason for doing (refraining from doing) some action *A*?

The proponents of the *Euthyphro* argument have a variety of ways, of differing plausibilities, of objecting to this defense of (1'). They might claim: (a) that we have no special obligations at all to our parents; (b) that it is no part of the special obligations that we have to our parents to do (refrain from doing) what they want us to do (refrain from doing); (c) that our special obligations to our parents are due to something that they do other than merely creating us, something that God does not do, so the whole question of our special obligations to our parents has nothing to do with the truth of (1').[7]

But there is another move open to the proponents of the *Euthyphro* argument. Rather than attempting to object to (1'), they might construct the following alternative argument against it, one that has the additional merit of not depending upon (Trans.):

(1') Let us suppose that there is some action *A* that is right (wrong) only because God wants us to do (refrain from doing) *A* and he is our creator to whom we owe obedience.

(2'*) There must be some reason for God's wanting us to do (refrain from doing) *A*, some reason that does not involve God's wanting us to do (refrain from doing) *A*, and some reason that is, by itself, a reason why *A* is right (wrong).

(4') So we have a contradiction, (1') is false, and either there are no actions that are right (wrong) because God, who is our creator and to whom we owe obedience, wants us to do (refrain from doing) them, or, if there are such actions, that is not the only reason why those actions are right (wrong).

The trouble with this move, of course, is that it rests upon the extremely strong assumption (2'*), and even if, to avoid the problem with arbitrary acts of willing, we are prepared to grant (2'), there seems to be little reason to grant this stronger (2'*) with its extra assumption about what are the types of reasons that God has for his acts of willing.

In short, then, the traditional argument that the rightness or wrongness of an action cannot depend upon the will of God rests upon some dubious premises, and things get worse when we add the idea that we have an

---

[7]Of the three moves, the third seems most plausible. But religious people might well respond to it as follows: let us grant that our special obligations to our parents are due to additional facts about the parent-child relationship (e.g., the way parents raise and sustain their children, etc.). God has those additional relations to all of his creations, and they therefore still have to him the special obligation of obedience.

obligation to follow God's wishes because he is our creator. There is, however, more to say about this issue, for there are reasons to suppose that some particular moral truths may depend in a special way upon the idea that God is the creator. We turn, therefore, to a consideration of these special cases.

II.

Let us begin by considering a set of issues surrounding the idea of property rights. What is involved in one's owning a piece of property, in one's having a right to it? It seems to mean, in part, that while one may not use that property so as to infringe upon the rights of others, one may, if one wants, use it in such a way as to benefit while others lose. No doubt this distinction is unclear for there are cases in which it is difficult to say whether someone's rights have been infringed upon or whether he has simply lost out.[8] But the distinction is clear enough for our purposes.

How does one come to own a piece of property? One intuitively attractive picture runs as follows: if there is a physical object that belongs to no one, and if some person comes along and does something with it (mixes his labor with it), then the object in question belongs to that person.[9] He may then, in one way or another, transfer that property to someone else, who then has property rights in that object. Indeed, transference is now the most prevalent way of acquiring property. But all property rights are ultimately based, in this picture, upon these initial acts of acquisition through the mixing of one's labor with unowned objects. This picture certainly faces some familiar objections.[10] To begin with, what right does a person have to appropriate the ownerless piece of property for himself, thereby depriving all of us of the right to use it? And secondly, does the act of mixing his labor with it give him ownership rights over the initial, ownerless object or simply over the products (if any) of his interaction with it? But we shall leave aside these worries for now and suppose that something like this account is correct, for the question that we want to consider is whether or not it would have to be modified in light of any theological truths.

This picture clearly presupposes that, if there is such a thing as property owned by human beings, then there was, at least at one point in human history, such a thing as ownerless property, property that one could acquire if one mixed one's labor with it. But suppose that the universe was created by a personal God. Then, it might well be argued, he owns the whole

---

[8]Here is just one: let us suppose that I build a high wall at the back of my property, thereby depriving your yard of sunlight. There is no doubt that you have suffered a loss, but have I deprived you of any of your rights?

[9]See, for example, chapter 5 of Locke's *Second Treatise of Civil Government*.

[10]See, for example, chapter 3 of the First Memoir of Proudhon's *What is Property?*

universe, and there is not, and never has been, such a thing as ownerless property. Now suppose further that this creator allows men to use for their purposes the property that they mix their labor with, but he does so with the restriction that they must not use it in such a way as to cause a great loss to other people (even though the rights of these people are not infringed upon). That is to say, suppose that this creator allows people to take his property only if they follow certain of his wishes. Then, don't they have an obligation to do so, or, at least, an obligation to either return the property or to do so?[11] So, in short, if God, the creator, does wish us not to use the things of the world in certain ways, this will entail certain moral restrictions on property rights that might not be present otherwise.

Let us, at this point, introduce the idea of stewardship over property. We shall say that someone has stewardship over a piece of property just in case they own that piece of property subject to certain restrictions as to how they may use it and/or subject to certain requirements as to how they must use it, restrictions and/or requirements that were laid down by some previous owner of that piece of property. Now, what I have been arguing for is the idea that, if certain theological beliefs (that God created the universe but allows man to appropriate the property in it subject to certain restrictions and requirements that he lays down) are true, then men will have rights of stewardship, and not property rights, over the property that they possess. And if this is so, then there will be moral truths (about restrictions and requirements that property-possessors must follow)[12] that might not be true if these theological beliefs were false. So we have here a set of moral claims whose truth or falsehood might depend upon the truth or falsehood of certain theological claims.

The question that we must now consider is whether or not the *Euthyphro* argument, even if sound in general, could be used against the claim we are now considering. How would it run in this context? Presumably, it would run as follows:

(1′ ′) Let us suppose that there are certain restrictions on property rights and that they exist only because God, from whom we get our stewardship over the earth, has imposed them.

(2′ ′) There must be some reason why God has imposed these restrictions, a reason that does not involve his wanting us to follow them.

---

[11]If the individual was aware of what these wishes are before he takes the property, then it would seem that he has the obligation to follow them. But if he was not, and if they turn out to be strange and/or arbitrary, then perhaps he only has the weaker obligation, and then only from that time at which he becomes aware of what the wishes are.

[12]It goes without saying that what exactly these restrictions are will vary from one theological system to another. The cases that are of the most interest for current discussions of property rights have to do, of course, with those systems in which the restrictions require one, in effect, at least to take into account the interests of other people and not merely their rights.

(3′ ′) Therefore, that reason must also be a reason why we should follow those restrictions.

(4′ ′) So we have a contradiction, (1′ ′) is false, and either there are no such restrictions or there is some additional reason as to why they exist.

As we saw in the last section, when we considered (1′)–(4′), even if we grant (2′ ′) and (Trans.), (3′ ′) doesn't follow from (1′ ′) and (2′ ′). Now even if we grant what we are reluctant to grant in the last section, viz., that (1′) is objectionable because the mere fact that someone created us gives us no moral reason for following his wishes, we would still have no reason for independently objecting to (1′ ′). For if we have mere stewardship over the property we possess, then surely we do have an obligation to follow the wishes of him from whom we got our stewardship, and if God did create the world, then it certainly looks as though our property possession is a property stewardship gotten ultimately from God.

This point can also be put as follows. Neither (3′) nor (3′ ′) follows from the previous steps in their respective arguments, even if we grant the truth of (Trans.), because the reasons they provide for the moral claims in question involve some other theological facts besides God's willing certain things. Now the defenders of the *Euthyphro* argument may try to attack (1′ ′) on independent grounds, but it is difficult to see the grounds that they would have. So it looks then as though certain theological claims are relevant to certain moral truths having to do with the existence and extent of rights over property.

To be sure, the defenders of the *Euthyphro* argument might, in desperation, trot out the following argument:

(1′ ′) Let us suppose that there are certain restrictions on property rights and that they exist only because God, from whom we get our stewardship over the earth, has imposed them.

(2′ ′*) There must be some reason why God has imposed these restrictions, a reason that does not involve his wanting us to follow them, and one that is, by itself, a reason why we should follow these restrictions.

(4′ ′) So we have a contradiction, (1′ ′) is false, and either there are no such restrictions or there is some additional reason as to why they exist.

But like step (2′*) of the previous section, step (2′ ′*) has little to recommend it. Even if a perfect God has to have reasons for wanting us to behave in certain ways, and, a fortiori, for imposing restrictions on our behavior, it is unclear why they must meet the very strong final requirement laid down by (2′ ′*).

III.

In the previous section, we have discussed the implications of the theological idea that God, the creator, owns the universe for the issue of property rights. It is sometimes felt that this idea also has implications for the moral issue of the permissibility of suicide.[13] We will, in this section, explore that possibility.

The liberal argument for the permissibility of suicide is stated very clearly early on in the *Phaedo*:

> ...sometimes and for some people death is better than life. And it probably seems strange to you that it should not be right for those to whom death would be an advantage to benefit themselves, but that they should have to await the services of someone else. [62A]

It will do no good, of course, to object that the person might have some extremely important obligations that he would leave unfulfilled if he committed suicide, and this is why it is wrong for him to do so, because we could easily confine the discussions to cases in which he has no such obligations or to cases in which he could arrange for the executors of his estate to fulfill them. And moreover, such an argument would really only show that one should not be remiss in fulfilling one's obligations, it would not really show that there was something particularly wrong with the way the person who committed suicide did that.

Plato himself does not accept this argument for suicide (although he does think one can accede in being condemned to death), and he is opposed to suicide on the grounds that we are the possessions of the gods. His argument runs as follows:

> If one of your possessions were to destroy itself without intimation from you that you wanted it to die, wouldn't you be angry with it and punish it, if you had any means of doing so...so if you look at it this way, I suppose it is not unreasonable to say that we must not put an end to ourselves until God sends more compulsions like the one we are facing now. [62C]

Leaving aside the peculiarity of the idea that one ought, if one can, to punish those who succeed in destroying themselves—as opposed to the more reasonable idea that one ought to punish those who merely try,—the idea that Plato is advancing is that the gods' property rights extend to us, and that we therefore have no right to destroy ourselves unless they give their permission.[14]

---

[13]R. F. Holland, in "Suicide" in Rachels's *Moral Problems* (Harper and Row: 1971) discusses other ways in which the moral issues surrounding suicide are intertwined with theological questions.

[14]Plato here is assuming the overly strong thesis that we never have a right to destroy someone else's property without their permission. Whether and how he could get a weaker thesis that would still leave the argument intact is something that cannot be considered here.

There are cases in which many religious people want to allow that suicide is permissible. One such case[15] is that of the person who commits suicide rather than face being compelled to do some very evil act. Thus, in a great many religious traditions, it would even be thought to be a meritorious act to commit suicide rather than face being tortured into committing acts of apostasy. Another such case is that of the person who commits suicide rather than reveal under torture secrets that would lead to the destruction of many innocent people. Can these exceptions be reconciled with the argument against suicide that we have been considering? It seems to me that they can. After all, the crucial objection to our destroying ourselves is that we have no right to do so without the permission of our owner, God, and the religious person might well add the additional claim that God has (perhaps in a revelation) already given his permission in these cases.

Obviously, the *Euthyphro* argument cannot be raised against the claim that we are considering. After all, the crucial first premise[16] would be the claim that

(1′′′) Let us suppose that we cannot take our own lives only because we are the property of God, who created us, and he does not want us to destroy this piece of his property.

Then even if we add

(2′′′) There must be some reason why he doesn't want us to do so, some reason that does not involve this want of his.

we will not, even assuming (Trans.), get the crucial

(3′′′) Therefore, that reason must also be a reason why we should not take our own lives.

We can, no doubt, consider using

(2′′′*) There must be some reason why he doesn't want us to do so, some reason that does not involve this want of his, and which is, by itself, a reason why we should not take our own lives.

---

[15]For a discussion of such cases, see the opinion of Rabenu Tam mentioned in the Tosafot glosses to *Talmud, Tractate Avodat Zarah*, 18a.

[16]Notice that the obligation to listen to the wishes of the property owner is stronger here than in the previous case. Even if his wishes are strange and/or arbitrary, that does not give us a right to disregard them and destroy the property.

instead of (2′ ′), but it is no more plausible than (2′*) and (2′ ′ *). Nor can we easily object to (1′ ′ ′) in the way that we did to (1′). Even if we have no obligation to listen to the wishes of him who has created us, just because he has created us, we do have an obligation not to destroy someone else's property, and, if God created us, then perhaps we are God's property.

Having said this, we can now see that more is at stake here than a mere prohibition of suicide. For if we are the property of God, then perhaps we just have an obligation to do whatever he says, and then perhaps we can return to our initial general claims about morality and consider the possible claim that

(1′#) actions are right (wrong) for us to do just in case and only because God, who has created us and owns us and whom we therefore have an obligation to follow, wants us to do (refrain from doing) them.

So a great deal hinges on this point.

Despite all that we have seen, it is unclear that this argument against suicide (and, a fortiori, the more general claim just considered) will do. In the case of property rights, the crucial idea was that God, who created the world, owns all property, and this claim seemed a coherent one. But here, in (1′ ′ ′), the crucial idea is that God, because he created us, owns us. And perhaps one can object directly to (1′ ′ ′) that it is incoherent. Does it make sense, after all, to talk of an all-just being owning or possessing a human being? Isn't doing that an unjust act, one that cannot meaningfully be ascribed to an all-just being?

It is difficult to assess this objection. There is no doubt that the objection to the institution of slavery is exactly that we think it unjust for one human being to own another human being, to have another human being as his possession. But is it unjust for God, who is vastly superior to us and is our creator, to possess human beings? To put this question another way, is slavery unjust because it is wrong for one human being to possess another (in which case, both the argument against suicide and the general claim, with their supposition that we are the possessions of God, can stand) or because it is wrong that a human being be a possession, a piece of property (in which case, both collapse on the grounds of incoherence)? Religious people have, very often, opted for the former alternative,[17] and as it is difficult to see an argument to disprove their contentions; we have, probably, to conclude that theological claims might make a difference to the truth or falsity of moral claims concerning suicide, and perhaps to a great many other issues as well.

---

[17]This is evidenced in the Talmudic idea (*Kedushin*, 22[b]) that it is wrong for man to sell himself into slavery because God would object on the grounds that "they are my slaves, and not the slaves of slaves."

IV.

There is still one final issue about which it is often claimed that theological beliefs about the will of a God who created the world are relevant to the truth of moral beliefs about that issue. This is the moral issue raised by vegetarians. At least some vegetarians argue as follows: we normally suppose that it is wrong, except in certain very special cases, to take the life of an innocent human being. But we normally have no objections to taking the life of members of many other species to obtain from their bodies food, clothing, etc. Let us call these normal moral views the conventional consciousness. Now, argues the vegetarian, it is difficult to defend the conventional consciousness. What characteristics are possessed by all human beings, but by no members of any other species, and are such as to justify such a sharp moral distinction as the one drawn by the conventional consciousness?

I think that no one would deny that there is a gradation of development between different species, and most would concede that this gives rise to a gradation of rights. While few would object to killing a mosquito if it is being a minor nuisance, many would object to killing a dog on the same grounds. The interesting point, says the vegetarian, is that when we get to the case of human beings, the conventional consciousness accords to them many rights (including the strong right to life) even though there is not a sufficiently dramatic biological difference between these species to justify such a sharp moral difference. Therefore, concludes the vegetarian, we should reject the conventional consciousness and accord more of these rights (especially the right to life) to members of more species of animals.

This vegetarian argument draws further support from the fact that the intuitions embedded in the conventional consciousness are about species. After all, there are a variety of extreme cases (newly born infants, severely retarded individuals, people who are near death) in which many of the subtler features of human beings are not present but in which the conventional consciousness accords to the people in question far more rights than those normally accorded to animals. This makes it far more difficult to believe that there are some characteristics (a) possessed by all human beings, (b) not possessed by all animals, and (c) which justify the moral distinctions drawn by the conventional consciousness. So, the vegetarian concludes, we must reject the conventional consciousness.

There is a religious response to this vegetarian argument which runs as follows: when God created the world, he intended that man should use certain other species for food, clothing, etc. God did not, of course, give man complete freedom to do what he wants with these creatures. They are not, for example, to be treated cruelly. But, because that was God's intention, man can, and should use these creatures to provide him with food, clothing, etc. This view is embodied in the following Talmudic story:[18]

> A calf was being taken to the slaughter, when it broke away, hid his head under Rabbi's skirts, and lowed in terror. *Go, said he, for this wast thou created.* [B. Metzia, 85a]

It is pretty clear, once more, that the *Euthyphro* argument will not do against the claim we are considering. It is

(1′′′′) Man can take the lives of animals so that he can obtain from their bodies food, clothing, etc., only because God, who created the world and owns everything in it, intended that he do so.

and even if we grant

(2′′′′) There is some reason why he intended things that way, some reason that does not involve that intention.

and (Trans.), we do not get the crucial

(3′′′′) This must also be a reason why it is permissible for us to take the lives of animals for the sake of obtaining food, clothing, etc.

The crucial objection to this claim has to do with the coherency of (1′′′′). Let us suppose that we are not troubled by the religious claims discussed in the previous section; let us suppose that we find nothing objectionable with the idea that God owns us. Then, presumably, even if we are impressed with the vegetarian argument, we will still find nothing objectionable with the idea that God owns animals as well. But we may still find (1′′′′) objectionable. For it, in effect, supposes that God's property rights extend so far as to allow the life of the piece of property in question to be taken by others, indeed, to so order things that this is done. And is this compatible with the idea of an all-just being? After all, even enlightened systems of slavery did not allow the slave-owner to take (or to have taken) the life of his slave. Does God's majesty really mean then that he can do even this?

We are straining here with the limits of the idea that everything is God's property because he is the creator of everything. When we applied the idea to inanimate objects, we saw that it could have important implications for the question of property rights. If we didn't object to applying it to human beings, we saw that it could (at least) have important applications for the

---

[18]To be sure, Rabbi is punished for his answer, but only, as the text makes clear, because he fails to show compassion, not because his answer is unacceptable.

question of the permissibility of suicide. If we are now prepared to take it to further extremes, it could serve as a response to the vegetarian's argument about animals and their right to life.

V.

In a way, this essay can be seen as a gloss on the Psalmist's remarks that "the earth and all that fill it belong to God." We have tried to show that this idea may have important moral implications, and that it would therefore be wrong to suppose that there are no moral claims whose truth or falsehood may depend upon the truth or falsehood of theological claims. But it is, of course, clear that this is not the only theological belief that may have moral consequences. On other occasions, we shall look at other such theological beliefs.

ROBERT MERRIHEW ADAMS

Autonomy and Theological Ethics

Some theists believe that the moral rightness and wrongness of actions consists in agreement and disagreement, respectively, with God's commands. And even theists who do not hold this metaethical view do generally believe that all right action is commanded by God and should be done in obedience to him. I wish to respond here to one of the commonest objections to this belief: that it is incompatible with a proper regard for the virtue of autonomy.[1]

An earlier version of this paper formed part of a presentation at a meeting of the American Philosophical Association, at which Philip L. Quinn was my co-symposiast. For a different approach to these issues, see his interesting article on 'Religious Obedience and Moral Autonomy' in *Religious Studies*, 11 (1975), pp. 265–81.

From "Autonomy and Theological Ethics," *Religious Studies*, Vol. 15 (1979), pp. 191–94 by Robert Merrihew Adams. Reprinted by permission of the author and Cambridge University Press.

[1] I believe this constitutes the most important objection to divine command metaethics that I have not discussed in "A Modified Divine Command Theory of Ethical Wrongness," in Gene Outka and John P. Reeder, Jr., eds., *Religion and Morality* (Garden City, NJ: Doubleday, 1973), pp. 318–47.

It has become something of an axiom in modern ethical theory that we ought to be autonomous in our moral actions. The senses in which this axiom is understood are surprisingly varied; and the reasons for which it is accepted, when it is not part of a Kantian or noncognitivist metaethics, are often obscure. I will discuss two reasons that may be given for thinking that we ought to be autonomous in a sense that is incompatible with regarding all our moral action as obedience to any commander.

One reason has to do with *responsibility.* As a recent critic of divine command ethics puts it,

> There is no room in morality for commands, whether they are the father's, the schoolmaster's or the priest's. There is still no room for them when they are God's commands. A moral agent is only in very special circumstances permitted to shelter behind the excuse, 'I was ordered to do it'. In morality we are responsible even for those actions which are responses to commands. We are responsible for obeying a command. Some commands given by some people ought not to be obeyed. It would be wicked to obey them.[2]

The adherent of divine command ethics is sometimes compared to a soldier or official of the Nazi government of Germany in the Second World War who claims that he cannot be blamed for anything he did if he did it in obedience to orders. In both cases, it may be charged, there is an abdication of moral responsibility. The comparison is distasteful, but may be helpful in understanding the issues that are raised here.

Let us consider two hypothetical Nazi concentration camp guards who took part in the killing of hundreds of innocent and unresisting prisoners. We may call them the Conscientiously Obedient Nazi and the Cynical Nazi. The Conscientiously Obedient Nazi has always believed that he was doing the right thing, because he identifies his moral duty with his institutional duty to obey his superiors, and he killed in obedience to orders. It is somewhat misleading to say that he has abdicated his moral responsibility. He holds himself morally responsible to do his duty as he sees it, which is always to obey orders. We think he has an erroneous view of what his moral duty is. Indeed we think it is so horribly erroneous that we do not set much value on his conscientiousness. But it is as true of him as it is of anyone, that he holds himself responsible to do his moral duty.

The Cynical Nazi, on the other hand, has always thought that it was wrong for him to participate in killing the prisoners. But he thinks he ought to be excused for any serious blame, because his disobedience would have resulted in his own death and would not have saved any of the prisoners. He may be said to have abdicated his moral responsibility; he refuses to hold himself seriously responsible for what he did.

---

[2]Graeme de Graaff, "God and Morality," in Ian T. Ramsey, ed., *Christian Ethics and Contemporary Philosophy* (London: SCM Press, 1966), p. 34.

In so far as the conscientious adherent of divine command ethics is like either of these malefactors, he is clearly more like the Conscientiously Obedient Nazi than the Cynical Nazi. He holds himself responsible to do his ethical duty, which is to live in accordance with God's commands.

But perhaps what I have just said reflects a one-sided interpretation of the charge of abdicating responsibility. The Conscientiously Obedient Nazi does hold himself morally responsible for what he does, but he narrows the scope of his responsibility. He holds himself responsible only to obey orders. The first responsibility which a child receives from its parents is normally responsibility to follow very simple and direct instructions: for example, not to go in the street under any circumstances. As the child matures, it is ready to receive more responsibility. We speak of someone receiving or accepting *more* responsibility in proportion as fulfilling the responsibility involves making decisions that are more than just decisions to obey.

Of course divine command ethics can allow very large areas of discretion, and hence very large responsibility, if the divine commands are for the most part as general as 'Love your neighbor as yourself' and 'If possible, so far as it depends on you, live in peace with everyone'.[3] Still, it may be objected, in such an ethics there is a specific responsibility that is abdicated to the Divine Commander: namely, the responsibility of determining whether it is indeed right to love one's neighbor as oneself. This objection seems to me confused. What is it that we are told we ought to determine for ourselves? Whether God ought to have commanded neighbor-love? Surely that is his responsibility (so to speak) and not ours. Whether neighbor-love would have been right if God had not commanded it? That would seem to be a question of no immediate practical relevance for those who believe that God has commanded neighbor-love. Are we responsible, then, to determine whether neighbor-love is right, given that God commands it? But the adherent of divine command ethics does determine that for himself; he just does so on the basis of his belief that everything God commands is right. You may regard him as mistaken, but why irresponsible?

I suspect, however, that the discussion of responsibility does not get to the bottom of the matter. The second argument for autonomy has to do with *motives*. Let us compare the Conscientiously Obedient Nazi with three other characters: the Autonomous Nazi, the Conscientiously Obedient Relief Worker, and the Autonomous Relief Worker.

The Autonomous Nazi is a concentration camp guard who treats the prisoners just as the Conscientiously Obedient and Cynical Nazis treat them. But he kills prisoners, not merely from obedience or fear, as they do, but from a deep emotional and intellectual commitment to the aims and principles of Nazism. He would disobey orders if they seemed to him to betray the Nazi cause. Do we think better of him for his autonomy? I certainly don't. I would

---

[3]Leviticus 19:18 and Romans 12:18.

call him fanatical as well as autonomous, and think worse of him than of the Conscientiously Obedient Nazi.

Our relief workers are employed in a warehouse that handles shipments of food. Both of them try to ensure that the food actually goes to people who desperately need it, and does not end up in the hands of corrupt officials. The Conscientiously Obedient Relief Worker does this only because he has been instructed by his employers to do it, and believes unquestioningly that that morally obliges him to do it. The Autonomous Relief Worker directs the food to the poor, not just because he has been instructed to do so, but primarily because he cares about the needs of the poor. He would disobey instructions if they seemed to him to betray the humanitarian cause. I do think better of him than of the Conscientiously Obedient Relief Worker.

The chief difference between the autonomous and the conscientiously obedient person in these examples is that the latter does what he does just in order to be obedient, whereas the autonomous person does what he does at least partly for its own sake or for the sake of its consequences. Evildoing is worse, and well-doing is better, if done for its own sake and not just from obedience. This suggests another reason why one might think that divine command ethics leaves less room than it ought to for autonomy. It is presumably only in well-doing that it is morally good to obey God's commands. But in well-doing one will do even better if one acts out of love for the good to be accomplished, and not just for obedience' sake. It is better to avoid lies because one loves truthfulness, to deal fairly because one loves fairness, and to give to charity because one cares about people's needs, than to do those things just because one has been commanded, even by God, to do them. So perhaps the introduction of divine commands in ethics threatens to debase our motivation in well-doing.

Here it may be helpful to borrow the term 'theonomous' from Paul Tillich. According to Tillich,

> Autonomy asserts that man...is his own law. Heteronomy asserts that man...must be subjected to a law, strange and superior to him. Theonomy asserts that the superior law is at the same time, the innermost law of man himself, rooted in the divine ground which is man's own ground.[4]

Let us say that a person is *theonomous* to the extent that the following is true of him: He regards his moral principles as given him by God, and adheres to them partly out of love or loyalty to God, but he also prizes them for their own sakes, so that they are the principles he *would* give himself if he were giving himself a moral law. The theonomous agent, in so far as he is right,

---

[4]Paul Tillich, *The Protestant Era*, abridged edition, trans. J. L. Adams (Chicago: University of Chicago Press, 1960), p. 56f.

acts morally because he loves God, but also because he loves what God loves. He has the motivational goods both of obedience and of autonomy.

There is much in theological ethics that favors theonomy rather than pure heteronomy. We are told that God commands us to love our neighbors as ourselves. But we do not love them at all unless we care about them at least partly for their own sakes. The believer aspires to be filled with God's Spirit. But God presumably loves truthfulness, fairness, kindness, mercy, and other good qualities for their own sakes, and not just because he has commanded them. And one who is filled with God's Spirit ought to love them in some measure as God loves them. Suppose that God loves us and also loves those qualities. Should we expect him to want us to be truthful, fair, kind, merciful, and so forth heteronomously, solely because he has commanded us to behave that way? Should we not rather expect God to prefer us to be theonomous— loyal to him, but also acting out of love for the things that he loves?

Theonomy conforms with a normative principle of obedience to God. It is also compatible with some forms of divine command metaethics. For the theonomous person may love his moral principles for their own sake, but believe that they owe their status as moral principles wholly or partly to their divine sponsorship.

ROBERT YOUNG

Theism and Morality

In this paper I propose to give close attention to two recent discussions of the relation between theism and morality. It will be helpful first to sketch some of the considerations that have emerged from the many discussions of the relation between theism and morality and which form the background to the two recent contributions I shall discuss.

I.

In the *Euthyphro* Plato raises the issue of whether certain codes, principles and actions are morally right or wrong *only because God commands* them or of whether, alternatively, they are reflections of God's knowledge that these

From *Canadian Journal of Philosophy*, Vol. 7 (1977), pp. 341–51. Reprinted by permission of the author and the *Canadian Journal of Philosophy*.

codes, principles, actions really are morally right or wrong (in which case it would seem that they would be right or wrong independently of God). Euthyphro defines a holy or pious action as an action loved by the gods. Socrates tries to get Euthyphro to adopt the alternative view that the gods love certain actions because they are holy. In other words, he claims that the moral value of actions is independent of, and the cause of, the attitude of the gods to it.[1]

Of the various possible issues which people may have in mind when they speak of the relation between theism and morality, the issue discussed in the *Euthyphro* is the most significant philosophically. The others tend to centre around largely factual matters like: (i) Are certain of Yahweh's putative actions and commands in accordance with moral norms?—for instance, where he intervenes on behalf of Israel when she is not guiltless; in his savagery in the prosecution of war; in urging the theft of Egyptian property at the time of the escape from Egypt. (ii) Does acceptance of religious beliefs require concomitantly the acceptance of certain moral beliefs?

In general when the issue raised in the *Euthyphro* has been discussed by philosophers it has been concluded that Socrates was correct in defending the position he did. Doing a particular action, it has been argued, cannot be right *only because* God commands that it be right, since it is, first of all, perfectly conceivable that God could (according to Socrates and his supporters) have commanded that certain actions which are, in truth, wrong be right, but that this fact alone could surely not make the wrong action be right. Had God, for instance, willed that rape be morally right (or if God did will that Egyptian property be *stolen* by the fleeing followers of Moses—is expropriation of exploited wages theft?) his merely commanding it could surely not make it so. Since moral rightness is not (on an objectivist ethic) an arbitrary matter, if God is to command that some act be right, he cannot do so for no other reason than that he wants to, because this *would* render moral truth arbitrary.

Secondly, it has been argued that 'right' or 'ought' has a *meaning* which is independent of obeying God. For instance, William Frankena (in 'Is Morality Logically Dependent on Religion?') in G. Outka and J. Reeder (eds.), *Religion and Morality* (New York, 1973) argues in the following way to show there is no logical dependence of morality upon a Christian, or other theistic, view. He contends that it is to muddy the waters to define religion so broadly that all ultimate views or concerns about the universe—theistic, humanistic and atheistic—effectively fall under it. Yet if one doesn't, then it makes sense to talk about entailments which flow out

---

[1]Throughout I shall presume the truth of an objectivist metaethic because the problems to be discussed only get any real grip when this presumption is made, a presumption which historically has been common to the most significant discussions of these problems.

from some basic view of man which is not, however, theistic or Christian. To preclude such a possibility seems to be question-begging in favour of a logical dependence of morality on Christian, or other theistic, views.

There are two points which critics might make here to try to nullify Frankena's contention. First, it might be urged that Frankena's point is only about *meaning* and does not show that God's commands are not the *criterion* for moral rightness. If we waive any qualms occasioned by the introduction of the controversial meaning/criterion distinction the objector's point can be conceded. But it must be added that the initial point made above and much of my subsequent argument are directed specifically against claims about the criterion for moral rightness. Secondly, it has to be acknowledged that a theist might argue that while it *makes sense* to speak of entailments flowing out from some non-theistic view of man, it is only those which flow out of a theistic one that are *valid* (or, alternatively, supportable). And, of course, this may be so but, until we know whether it *is* God's commands that make actions and so on morally right, we cannot assess such a contention—the claims stand or fall together.

Against this background it may be wondered just why theists do object to the idea that such moral principles or codes as are supposed to be revealed by God are based upon his recognition of the independent rightness and wrongness of the actions referred to in the principles or codes. Basically it is, I suspect, because this would seem to entail that such codes or principles are not *essentially* theistic ones but merely ones supported by theists. Why this should be disturbing has not, I believe, ever convincingly been made out, though I would hazard that the heart of the worry is supposed to be that the attitude towards God's commands (displayed in accepting such a conclusion) is deficient. It may be clearer why believers wish to avoid subscribing to the alternative idea that such codes or principles merely reflect arbitrary commands on God's part as to how people should behave. This alternative must be rejected because the postulation of such arbitrary commands introduces an unreasoning, and hence imperfect, element into the conception of God.

II.

There are believers who, faced with these alternatives and finding neither acceptable, have tried to chart a third position which does not sever conceptually all connections between theism and morality. Two very recent papers by contemporary philosophers have attempted to show that God's commands are not arbitrary, that they are indeed reason-based, and yet that actions are right or wrong only because God has commanded that people do, or refrain from doing, them. Each is worth close study because the thesis common to them is not only arrestingly controversial but subtly argued for.

Baruch Brody in 'Morality and Religion Reconsidered' (pp. 491–503 in this volume) argues that once we take account of the fact that God is the creator and therefore has special rights *vis-à-vis* the world and everything in it, including human beings, then we can see why certain actions which would not otherwise be right or wrong are right or wrong just because God has willed that things be so in his creation. Brody's argument may best be taken in stages.

In the first stage he seeks to undermine the objection that his contentions rest on the mistaken assumption that there is moral relevance in the fact that God is our creator. He attempts to do this by drawing attention to the special obligations he claims we have to obey the wishes of our parents[2] and arguing that these special obligations provide an appropriate analogy for our obligations to our creator. One form of counter-argument to Brody here would be as follows: our special obligations to our parents are due to additional facts about the parent-child relationship (e.g. the way parents raise and sustain their children and so on). To this Brody replies that God also has these additional relations to all of his creatures, and, therefore, his creatures still have special obligations of obedience to him.

Brody also tries to anticipate a possible counter-argument which goes as follows:

(1) Let us suppose that there is some action, A, that is right (wrong) only because God wants us to do (refrain from doing) A and he is our creator to whom we owe obedience;

(2) There must be some reason for God's wanting us to do (refrain from doing) A, some reason that does not involve God's wanting us to do (refrain from doing) A, and some reason that is, by itself, a reason why A is right (wrong);

(3) So we have a contradiction, (1) is false, and *either* there are no actions that are right (wrong) because God, who is our creator and to whom we owe obedience, wants us to do (refrain from doing) them, *or*, if there are such actions, that is not the only reason why those actions are right (wrong).

Brody's objection is that (2) is extremely strong and that there is little reason to grant such a strong assumption which specifies the types of reason that God has for his acts of willing. It is, of course, only to be thought of as being extremely strong by those who deny that there could be any other right-making considerations than God's commands. There is no pressure on those who do not accept such a view to share Brody's intuitions about the strength of premise (2). So there seems to be no decisive barrier to someone's contending that even if there are special obligations owed to God because

---

[2]There are interesting connections here with remarks by B. Williams in *Morality* (Harmondsworth, 1973), ch. 8; R. Swinburne gives his backing to much the same point in 'Duty and the Will of God', *Canadian Journal of Philosophy*, 4 (1974), pp. 213–27 (especially pp. 224 f.).

he is our creator, these could not be such as to require our doing any action which was not judged on independent grounds to be morally right. As with the case of our parents, to which Brody appeals, if our genuine, special obligations to them were to come into conflict with a particular more stringent moral obligation, if we fulfilled our filial obligations this would not be to act morally rightly.

In the second stage of his argument, Brody considers three issues where he thinks theological beliefs are relevant to moral truths. First he considers the idea that if certain theological beliefs (e.g. that God created the universe but allows man to appropriate the property in it subject to certain restrictions and requirements that he lays down) are true, then men will have rights of stewardship, but not property rights, over the property they possess. And if this be so then there will be moral truths (about restrictions and requirements that property-possessors must follow) that might not be true if these theological beliefs were false. For if we have mere stewardship over the property we possess, then surely, urges Brody, we do have an obligation to follow the wishes of him from whom we got our stewardship, and if God did create the world, then it certainly looks (according to Brody) as though our possession of property is a property stewardship ultimately from God. The second issue Brody focuses on is the obligation we have not to suicide (except where God expressly permits this). He urges that we do have an obligation not to destroy without his permission someone else's property, and, if God created us, then being God's property we should not destroy ourselves except with his permission. Thirdly, if God owns all the animals in the world this may provide the basis, says Brody, for responding to the vegetarian's argument against the killing of animals for food, clothing etc., since God may have given express permission for their use for such purposes by others of his creatures.

It is worth remarking one rather odd consequence of this account, namely that moral truth assumes a special sort of conditional status. The moral truths will be such *if* God exists and is our creator. (I am tempted to add 'and only if' here, but Brody may not wish to deny that there could be a possible world in which God does not exist but yet these moral truths remain moral truths—for reasons not depending on God's determining will. Even so he does often talk as if he is committed to a form of the logical equivalence thesis.)

Much more importantly, though, anyone subscribing to a position like Brody's has to hold that even if a perfect God has reasons for wanting us to behave in certain ways, and, *a fortiori*, for imposing restrictions on our behaviour, that such reasons need not be independent of his merely wanting us to follow his restrictions. Perhaps Brody is right that it would be difficult to show that such a claim is unsupportable. Nevertheless, I remain unconvinced and want now to indicate why.

There do seem to be occasions where one would morally be justified in using some property, which one was stewarding, for purposes other than those decreed by the owner of the property. For example, where one could use the property to alleviate some serious human distress while not depriving the rightful owner of a significantly disproportionate share of his overall property holdings, so to act would surely be morally proper.

As for Brody's second example, it is instructive to notice that he appeals to the principle that we have an obligation not to destroy someone else's property which, as he states his position, seems to be a principle true *independently of whether we are God's property*. Now it may be that Brody wishes only to claim that there are *some* moral obligations whose basis is in theological truths, though *not* that *all* moral obligations are grounded in such considerations (see p. 141 above). If so then it would be necessary to consider a further point which he himself raises, namely the propriety of speaking of God possessing human beings. He suggests that there are two alternative reasons why one might object to such possession or enslavement. One could hold *either* that slavery is unjust because it is wrong for one human being to possess another (from which nothing would follow about the morality of a vastly superior being's having property rights over and hence possessing human beings), *or* that it is unjust because it is wrong that a human being be a possession, a piece of property (from which it would follow that even a vastly superior being like God morally could not claim property rights over human beings). Brody contends that religious believers have very often opted for the former alternative and that it is difficult to see how to disprove their contentions.

But whichever of these claims about injustice is accepted, one could ask 'Is the matter referred to unjust *because* God has decreed that it is?' The answer seems to be the same for either—'no'—and the reason is that it is certain features about what promotes human well-being which reveal the injustice of slavery and these would hold independently of God's being our creator. Furthermore, it does strike me as a dubious claim that theists as such should opt for the former of Brody's alternative possibilities. This for the reason that in e.g. the Judaeo-Christian tradition believers are said to be *sons and daughters* of God, not to stand in a relationship to him of master to slave or owner to chattel. Such believers, who would seem to be prime candidates for those accepting a theologically based morality, would not have the reason for espousing such a morality which is defended by Brody. Thirdly, if we take seriously Brody's reliance on the *absence* of strong reasons for rejecting his constructions of a theologically based morality (e.g. against suicide), it would seem that it would be entirely *optional* to view morality as theologically based. That is, it would be permissible but not obligatory to do so. This seems to be a highly restricted thesis. Indeed, the thesis thus construed would preclude our deriving most of the moral principles needed for an adequate moral conceptual scheme. Finally, it does appear that there could be circumstances under which suicide would at least be morally permissible even though God had not expressly revealed that such circumstances were morally proper ones within which suicide would not violate his property rights. And presumably such cases would be morally permissible because of considerations quite independent of God's determining, or even of his permissive, will. This, at the very least, would force the abandonment of any claim that a theologically based moral obligation was absolute. These third and fourth points do seem to rob the divine command theory of its natural interest.

Brody himself raises *one* serious worry about his third example, vegetarianism. His argument, as he acknowledges (p. 502), supposes that God's property rights extend so far as to allow the life of the piece of property in question to be taken by others. Even enlightened systems of slavery, as he points out, did not allow the slave-owner to take (or to have taken) the life of his slave. The trouble is that, having raised this objection, he fails to consider the further question of whether killing a sentient creature which was the property of another could ever be morally permissible even though the owner had not consented. Again, there surely are cases where, irrespective of considerations of God's will, this appears to be so.[3] (If this claim be thought question-begging against Brody, I could only say that I do not know how either side could hope to advance discussion of the issue any further because the counter-charge could equally well be brought against Brody.)

III.

The 'modified divine command theory' of ethical rightness and wrongness espoused by Robert Merrihew Adams ('A Modified Divine Command Theory of Ethical Wrongness', in Outka and Reeder (eds.), *op. cit.*) is a rather more subtle theory than Brody's, but I shall argue that it, too, is not finally acceptable.

Adams's starting point is that it is not logically impossible for God to command cruelty for its own sake. The central points of his thesis as he develops it are as follows: believers' claims that certain acts are wrong normally express certain attitudes toward those acts, whether or not that is part of the meaning of the claims;[4] that an act is wrong if, and only if, it is contrary to God's will or commands (assuming God loves us); that nonetheless, if God commanded cruelty for its own sake, neither obedience nor disobedience would be ethically wrong or ethically permitted; that if an act is contrary to God's will or commands that this is a non-natural objective fact about it; and that that is the only non-natural objective fact which obtains, if, and only if, the act is wrong.

---

[3]By focussing just on the notion of 'private property' (and, indeed, in taking it to be justifiable) Brody significantly narrows the range of questions about the obligatoriness of vegetarianism. He effectively sidesteps what may plausibly be regarded as more urgent questions about the justice of our treatment of non-humans as well as the possibility that meat-eating should be ruled out or reduced for consequentialist reasons.

[4]Adams's discussion of whether believers' claims are claims about the *meaning* of ethical terms is very good (see especially section VI). Even so, as he points out, his remarks on the meaning of such terms as believers use, are readily detachable from the rest of his theory. (Because the believer shares a common moral discourse with unbelievers, 'wrong' cannot just simply mean 'contrary to God's will or commands'. But this, as Adams recognizes, is a general difficulty that applies to much else than merely moral discourse.)

Adams's theory is legitimately a (modified) divine command theory because ethical facts are facts about the will and commands of God (hence their non-natural status). The crux of his theory is that since a modified divine command theorist *values* some things independently of God's commands (though not his conception of *ethical* right and wrong), such valuations will be necessary for, and be involved in, a divine command theorist's valuation of God and his commands. Where a favorable valuation of God seems to be precluded (because the believer considers God has commanded an unloving action) the believer's concept of right and wrong would collapse. I quote from Adams (p. 331):

> ...the modified divine command theorist also has reasons why he would not accept a divine command ethics in certain logically possible situations which he believes not to be actual. All of these reasons seem to me to involve valuations that are independent of divine command ethics. The person who has such reasons wants certain things—happiness, certain satisfactions—for himself and others; he hates cruelty and loves kindness; he has perhaps a certain unique and 'numinous' awe of God. And these are not attitudes which he has simply because of his beliefs about God's commands. They are not attitudes, however, which presuppose judgments of moral right and wrong.

One difficulty with this seems to be that if these *values* are, as Adams claims, not being *used* in the believer's concept of ethical wrongness, appeal could be made to them to override a moral judgment. Now Adams does claim to be explicating only the understanding of morality of one Judaeo-Christian believer (namely, himself). But it is also clear that he considers his explication catches the view of a wide cross-section of Judaeo-Christian believers. Typically, I would have thought, such believers share the conviction common among meta-ethical objectivists that moral values normally ought to be overriding. In certain circumstances it may be thought proper so to act that other values (e.g. prudential ones or aesthetic ones) are given precedence over moral values where the moral considerations are regarded as inconsequential. But it is usual to hold that *ceteris paribus* moral values ought to be overriding, unless their relative unimportance in the situation may be assumed. It seems pertinent to ask just what kind of values Adams takes his 'independent valuations' to be, given the possibility that they may be used to override moral judgments (even those believed to be commanded by God). Adams claims (p. 335) that

> ...(the believer's) positive valuation of (emotional/volitional pro-attitude toward) doing *whatever* God may command is not clearly greater than (his) independent negative valuation of cruelty.

Here a moral judgment is overridden by an independent value-judgment about the badness[5] of cruelty for its own sake. The suggestion seems to be, furthermore, that these 'valuations' are 'emotional/volitional pro-attitudes'. Underlying these pro-attitudes there presumably must be a reason why it is these rather than other pro-attitudes which the believer has. Adams does not seem to think the apparent irrationality of his valuations is important except in bringing to the surface problems of religious ethical motivation. But it surely is of consequence *why* he values kindness and the like. Perhaps (like Bishop Butler) he thinks we are just so constituted as to value kindness and be averse to cruelty. But if this is so we should, first, have been informed of this, and, second, have been given some reason for believing that the God who presumably constituted us thus would wish subsequently to command us to act against our inalienable preferences. This is, of course, purely a speculative remark. But it is, I think, worth repeating that Adams does owe us an account of why we do have the independent values he says we have.

As far as God's 'valuations' are concerned, Adams suggests (p. 340) that:

> It hardly makes sense to say that God does what He does *because* it is right. But it does not follow that God cannot have any reason for doing what He does. It does not even follow that He cannot have reasons of a type on which it would be morally virtuous for a man to act. For example, He might do something because He knew it would make His creatures happier.

There are two points worth considering here. To begin with, it just does make perfectly good sense to talk of God doing what he does because it is right. This holds even if we share Adams's view that truths about God's loving nature are only contingent truths. Adams's failure to do more than assert that a counter-position to his own 'hardly makes sense' is a serious flaw. Secondly, if God's reasons for doing what He does are not ones based on the moral rightness (and hence, other things being equal, the preferability) of certain courses of action, it would be helpful if we had some idea of what His motivations could possibly be. Adams's suggestion that it might be tied up with e.g. making his creatures happier seems to betray a misunderstanding of the point of morality. For many, including Judaeo-Christians, promoting the well-being of humans (and perhaps all sentient creatures) *is* the whole point, or a large part of the point, of having moral principles at all.

The final criticism I want to make concerns Adams's suggestion that the believer's moral concepts would break down if God commanded cruelty for its own sake. One would have thought that on Adams's theory a believer's judgments about the moral nature of God would be formed because of the

---

[5]It must be the 'badness' not the 'wrongness' to which Adams appeals.

obvious coincidence of God's actions with his commands (these latter being the measure of moral rightness). The proper response then for someone like Adams to God's commanding cruelty for its own sake (presuming that the evidence for the command actually having been given is incontrovertible) would be either that God had temporarily forsaken his other qualities (omniscience, etc.) *or* that he (the believer) had previously had a mistaken conception of the morally right as excluding cruelty for its own sake. The former presumably Adams would find unacceptable, yet it is hard to see how conceptual break-down could be confined to the believer's *moral* concepts. For given that the believer would, on Adams's construction, be forced to back his own independent valuations over and against the pro-cruelty pronouncement of a (contingently) wholly good but also all-knowing, etc., being, the believer would seem to be forced into a position where he gambles that his own independent valuations are more reliable than the deliberations of an all-knowing God[6] viewing things *sub specie aeternitatis*. A believer forced into such a position, and not regarding himself as duty-bound to endorse God's pronouncement, would surely end up having to jettison some others of his beliefs about God (whether or not the beliefs were about attributes supposed only to be contingently true of God).

The upshot of my consideration of the views of Brody and Adams is that their attempts to occupy the middle ground represent no gain for the Judaeo-Christian theist. The believer who accepts that God knows perfectly what is morally right and wrong (though not because it is his willing or commanding that makes actions morally right and wrong) does not appear to lose anything of theological consequence. Where there is evidence that God has willed something, it should be possible to establish the moral rightness of what he has willed by attending to those features which are right-making for actions. That God has willed such an action would provide a reason for doing it, but the reason would not have force independent of the pre-existing moral rightness of the action. There seems, then, to be theological *gain* in being free of the difficulties I have claimed beset even the most subtle versions of divine command theories. Furthermore, there seems to me to be no theological *loss* in endorsing the Socratic position on the relation between moral truth and the divine will. God's stature as wholly good is in no way diminished and the overridingness of moral truth is not called into question.[7]

---

[6]Even though I do not think his own position can be sustained, R. Swinburne does draw attention to the importance of God's omniscient nature in determining what God morally can will. See 'Duty and the Will of God', *op. cit.*, p. 481 f., above.

[7]I am grateful to John Kleinig, Bruce Langtry and Paul Helm for their vigorous but much appreciated criticism of a draft of this essay. I have continued to go my own way on some matters.

JAMES RACHELS

God and Human Attitudes

> Kneeling down or grovelling on the ground, even to express your reverence for heavenly things, is contrary to human dignity.
>
> *Kant*

I.

It is necessarily true that God (if He exists) is worthy of worship.[1] Any being who is not worthy of worship cannot be God, just as any being who is not omnipotent, or who is not perfectly good, cannot be God. This is reflected in the attitudes of religious believers who recognize that, whatever else God may be, He is a being before whom men should bow down. Moreover, He is unique in this; to worship anyone or anything else is blasphemy. In this paper I shall present an *a priori* argument against the existence of God which is based on the conception of God as a fitting object of worship. The argument is that God cannot exist, because no being could ever *be* a fitting object of worship.

However, before I can present this argument, there are several preliminary matters that require attention. The chief of these, which will hopefully have some independent interest of its own, is an examination of the concept of worship. In spite of its great importance this concept has received remarkably little attention from philosophers of religion; and when it has been treated, the usual approach is by way of referring to God's awesomeness or mysteriousness: to worship is to 'bow down in silent awe' when confronted with a being that is 'terrifyingly mysterious'.[2] But neither of these notions is of much help in understanding worship. Awe is certainly not the same thing

---

From *Religious Studies*, Vol 7 (1971), pp. 325–37. Reprinted by permission of Cambridge University Press and the author.

[1]Hartshorne and Pike suggest that the formula 'that than which none greater can be conceived' should be interpreted as 'that than which none more worthy of worship can be conceived'. Charles Hartshorne, *Anselm's Discovery* (LaSalle, Illinois, 1966), pp. 25–6; and Nelson Pike, *God and Timelessness* (London, 1970), pp. 149–60.

[2]These phrases are from John Hick, *Philosophy of Religion* (Englewood Cliffs, New Jersey, 1963), pp. 13–14.

as worship; one can be awed by a performance of *King Lear,* or by witnessing an eclipse of the sun or an earthquake, or by meeting one's favourite film-star, without worshipping any of these things. And a great many things are both terrifying and mysterious that we have not the slightest inclination to worship—I suppose the Black Plague fits that description for many people. The account of worship that I will give will be an alternative to those which rely on such notions as awesomeness and mysteriousness.

II.

Consider McBlank, who worked against his country's entry into the Second World War, refused induction into the army, and was sent to jail. He was active in the 'ban the bomb' movements of the fifties; he made speeches, wrote pamphlets, led demonstrations, and went back to jail. And finally, he has been active in opposing the war in Vietnam. In all of this he has acted out of principle; he thinks that all war is evil and that no war is ever justified. I want to make three observations about McBlank's pacifist commitments. (*a*) One thing that is involved is simply his recognition that certain facts are the case. History is full of wars; war causes the massive destruction of life and property; in war men suffer on a scale hardly matched in any other way; the large nations now have weapons which, if used, could destroy the human race; and so on. These are just facts which any normally informed man will admit without argument. (*b*) But of course they are not *merely* facts, which people recognise to be the case in some indifferent manner. They are facts that have special importance to human beings. They form an ominous and threatening backdrop to people's lives—even though for most people they are a backdrop only. But not so for McBlank. He sees the accumulation of these facts as having radical implications for his conduct; he behaves in a very different way from the way he would behave were it not for these facts. His whole style of life is different; his conduct is altered, not just in its details, but in its pattern. (*c*) Not only is his overt behaviour affected; so are his ways of thinking about the world and his place in it. His *self-image* is different. He sees himself as a member of a race with an insane history of self-destruction, and his self-image becomes that of an active opponent of the forces that lead to this self-destruction. He *is* an opponent of militarism just as he is a father or a musician. When some existentialists say that we 'create ourselves' by our choices, they may have something like this in mind.

Thus, there are at least three things that determine McBlank's role as an opponent of war: first, his recognition that certain facts are the case; second, his taking these facts as having important implications for his conduct; and third, his self-image as living his life (at least in part) in response to these facts. My first thesis about worship is that the worshipper has a set of beliefs about God[3] which function in the same way as McBlank's beliefs about war.

First, the worshipper believes that certain things are the case: that the world was created by an all-powerful, all-wise being who knows our every thought and action; that this being, called God, cares for us and regards us as his children; that we are made by him in order to return his love and live in accordance with his laws; and that, if we do not live in a way pleasing to him, we may be severely punished. Now these beliefs are certainly not shared by all reasonable people; on the contrary, many thoughtful persons regard them as nothing more than mere fantasy. But these beliefs are accepted by religious people, and that is what is important here. I do not say that this particular set of beliefs is definitive of religion in general, or of Judaism or Christianity in particular; it is meant only as a sample of the sorts of belief typically held by religious people in the West. They are, however, the sort of beliefs about God that are required for the business of worshipping God to make any sense.

Second, like the facts about warfare, these are not merely facts which one notes with an air of indifference; they have important implications for one's conduct. An effort must be made to discover God's will both for people generally and for oneself in particular; and to this end, the believer consults the church authorities and the theologians, reads the scripture, and prays. The degree to which this will alter his overt behaviour will depend, first, on exactly what he decides God would have him do, and second, on the extent to which his behaviour would have followed the prescribed pattern in any case.[4]

Finally, the believer's recognition of these 'facts' will influence his self-image and his way of thinking about the world and his place in it. The world will be regarded as made for the fulfilment of divine purposes; the hardships that befall men will be regarded either as 'tests' in some sense or as punishments for sin; and most important, the believer will think of himself as a 'Child of God' and of his conduct as reflecting either honour or dishonour upon his Heavenly Father.

What will be most controversial in what I have said so far (to some philosophers, though perhaps not to most religious believers) is the treatment of claims such as 'God regards us as his children' as in some sense factual. Wittgenstein[5] is reported to have thought this a total misunderstanding of

---

[3]In speaking of 'beliefs about God' I have in mind those typical of Western religions. I shall construct my account of worship in these terms, although the account will be adaptable to other forms of worship such as Satan-worship (see footnote 10, below).

[4]For example, one religious believer who thinks that his conduct must be very different on account of his belief is P. T. Geach: see his essay 'The Moral Law and the Law of God', in *God and the Soul* (London, 1969).

[5]Ludwig Wittgenstein, *Lectures and Conversations on Aesthetics, Psychology, and Religious Belief* (Berkeley, 1967). Edited by Cyril Barrett, from notes taken by Yorick Smythies, Rush Rhees, and James Taylor.

religious belief; and others have followed him in this.[6] Religious utterances, it is said, do not report putative facts; instead, we should understand such utterances as revealing the speaker's *form of life*. To have a form of life is to accept a language-game; the religious believer accepts a language-game in which there is talk of God, creation, Heaven and Hell, a Last Judgment, and so forth, which the sceptic does not accept. Such language-games can only be understood on their own terms; we must not try to assimilate them to other sorts of games. To see how this particular game works we need only to examine the way the language of religion is used by actual believers—in its proper habitat the language-game will be 'in order' as it is. We find that the religious believer uses such utterances for a number of purposes, e.g. to express reasons for action, to show the significance which he attaches to various things, to express his attitudes, etc.—but not to 'state facts' in the ordinary sense. So when the believer makes a typically religious assertion, and non-believer denies the same, *they are not contradicting one another;* rather, the non-believer is simply refusing to play the believer's (very serious) game. Wittgenstein (as recorded by his pupils) said:

> 'Suppose that someone believed in the Last Judgement, and I don't, does this mean that I believe the opposite to him, just that there won't be such a thing? I would say: "not at all, or not always."
>
> Suppose I say that the body will rot, and another says "No. Particles will rejoin in a thousand years, and there will be a Resurrection of you".
>
> If some said: "Wittgenstein, do you believe in this?" I'd say: "No." "Do you contradict the man?" I'd say: "No." '[7]

Wittgenstein goes on to say that the difference between the believer and the sceptic is not that one holds something to be true that the other thinks false, but that the believer takes certain things as 'guidance for life' that the sceptic does not, e.g. that there will be a Last Judgment. He illustrates this by reference to a person who 'thinks of retribution' when he plans his conduct or assesses his condition:

> 'Suppose you had two people, and one of them, when he had to decide which course to take, thought of retribution, and the other did not. One person might, for instance, be inclined to take everything that happened to him as a reward or punishment, and another person doesn't think of this at all.
>
> If he is ill, he may think: "What have I done to deserve this?" This is one way of thinking of retribution. Another way is, he thinks in a general way whenever he is ashamed of himself: "This will be punished."
>
> Take two people, one of whom talks of his behaviour and of what happens to him in terms of retribution, the other does not. These people think entirely differently. Yet, so far, you can't say they believe different things.

---

[6]For example, Rush Rhees, in *Without Answers* (London, 1969), ch. 13.

[7]Wittgenstein, p. 53.

Suppose someone is ill and he says: "This is punishment," and I say: "If I'm ill, I don't think of punishment at all." If you say: "Do you believe the opposite?"—you can call it believing the opposite, but it is entirely different from what we would normally call believing the opposite.

I think differently, in a different way. I say different things to myself. I have different pictures.'[8]

I will limit myself to three remarks about this very difficult view.[9] First it is not at all clear that this account is true to the intentions of those who actually engage in religious discourse. If a believer (at least, the great majority of those whom I have known or read about) says that there will be a Last Judgment, and a sceptic says that there will not, the believer certainly will think that he has been contradicted. Of course, the sceptic might not think of denying such a thing except for the fact that the believer asserts it; and in this trivial sense the sceptic might 'think differently' from the believer—but this is completely beside the point. Moreover, former believers who become sceptics frequently do so because they come to believe that religious assertions are *false;* and then, they consider themselves to be denying exactly what they previously asserted. Second, a belief does not lose its ordinary factual import simply because it occupies a central place in one's way of life. McBlank takes the facts about war as 'guidance for life' in a perfectly straightforward sense; but they remain facts. I take it that just as the man in Wittgenstein's example 'thinks of retribution' often, McBlank thinks of war often. So, we do not need to assign religious utterances a special status in order to explain their importance for one's way of life. Finally, while I realise that my account is very simple and mundane, whereas Wittgenstein's is 'deep' and difficult, nonetheless this may be an advantage, not a handicap, of my view. If the impact of religious belief on one's conduct and thinking can be explained by appeal to nothing more mysterious than putative facts and their impact on conduct and thinking, then the need for a more obscure theory will be obviated. And if a man believes that, *as a matter of fact,* his actions are subject to review by a just God who will mete out rewards and punishments on a day of final reckoning, that will explain very nicely why he 'thinks of retribution' when he reflects on his conduct.

III.

Worship is something that is *done;* but it is not clear just *what* is done when one worships. Other actions, such as throwing a ball or insulting one's neighbour, seem transparent enough. But not so with worship: when we

---

[8]Wittgenstein, pp. 54–5.

[9]The whole subject is explored in detail in Kai Nielsen, 'Wittgensteinian Fideism', *Philosophy,* 42 (1967), pp. 191–209.

celebrate Mass in the Roman Catholic Church, for example, what are we doing (apart from eating a wafer and drinking wine)? Or when we sing hymns in a Protestant church, what are we doing (other than merely singing songs)? What is it that makes these acts acts of *worship?* One obvious point is that these actions, and others like them, are ritualistic in character; so, before we can make any progress in understanding worship, perhaps it will help to ask about the nature of ritual.

First we need to distinguish the ceremonial form of a ritual from what is supposed to be accomplished by it. Consider, for example, the ritual of investiture for an English Prince. The Prince kneels; the Queen (or King) places a crown on his head; and he takes an oath: 'I do become your liege man of life and limb and of earthly worship, and faith and trust I will bear unto thee to live and die against all manner of folks.' By this ceremony the Prince is elevated to his new station; and by this oath he acknowledges the commitments which, as Prince, he will owe the Queen. In one sense the ceremonial form of the ritual is quite unimportant: it is possible that some other procedure might have been laid down, without the point of the ritual being affected in any way. Rather than placing a crown on his head, the Queen might break an egg into his palm (that could symbolise all sorts of things). Once this was established as the procedure to be followed, it would do as well as the other. It would still be the ritual of investiture, so long as it was understood that by the ceremony a Prince is created. The performance of a ritual, then, is in certain respects like the use of language: in speaking, sounds are uttered and, thanks to the conventions of the language, something is said, or affirmed, or done, etc.: and in a ritual performance, a ceremony is enacted and, thanks to the conventions associated with the ceremony, something is done, or affirmed, or celebrated, etc.

How are we to explain the point of the ritual of investiture? We might explain that certain parts of the ritual symbolise specific things, for example that the Prince kneeling before the Queen symbolises his subordination to her (it is not, for example, merely to make it easier for her to place the crown on his head). But it is essential that, in explaining the point of the ritual as a whole, we include that a Prince is being created, that he is henceforth to have certain rights in virtue of having been made a Prince, and that he is to have certain duties which he is now acknowledging, among which are complete loyalty and faithfulness to the Queen, and so on. If the listener already knows about the complex relations between Queens, Princes, and subjects, then all we need to tell him is that a Prince is being installed in office; but if he is unfamiliar with this social system, we must tell him a great deal if he is to understand what is going on.

So, once we understand the social system in which there are Queens, Princes, and subjects, and therefore understand the role assigned to each within that system, we can sum up what is happening in the ritual of investiture in this way: someone is being made a Prince, and he is accepting that role with all that it involves. (Exactly the same explanation could be given, *mutatis mutandis*, for the marriage ceremony.)

The question to be asked about the ritual of worship is what analogous explanation can be given of it. The ceremonial form of the ritual may vary according to the customs of the religious community; it may involve singing, drinking wine, counting beads, sitting with a solemn expression on one's face, dancing, making a sacrifice, or what-have-you. But what is the point of it?

As I have already said, the worshipper thinks of himself as inhabiting a world created by an infinitely wise, infinitely powerful, perfectly good God; and it is a world in which he, along with other men, occupies a special place in virtue of God's intentions. This gives him a certain role to play: the role of a 'Child of God'. My second thesis about worship is that in worshipping God one is acknowledging and accepting this role, and that this is the primary function of the ritual of worship. Just as the ritual of investiture derives its significance from its place within the social system of Queens, Princes, and subjects, the ritual of worship gets its significance from an assumed system of relationships between God and men. In the ceremony of investiture, the Prince assumes a role with respect to the Queen and the citizenry; and in worship, a man affirms his role with respect to God.

Worship presumes the superior status of the one worshipped. This is reflected in the logical point that there can be no such things as mutual or reciprocal worship, unless one or the other of the parties is mistaken as to his own status. We can very well comprehend people loving one another or respecting one another, but not (unless they are misled) worshipping one another. This is because the worshipper necessarily assumes his own inferiority; and since inferiority is an asymmetrical relation, so is worship. (The nature of the 'superiority' and 'inferiority' involved here is of course problematic; but on the account I am presenting it may be understood on the model of superior and inferior positions within a social system. More on this later.) This is also why *humility* is necessary on the part of the worshipper. The role to which he commits himself is that of the humble servant, 'not worthy to touch the hem of His garment'. Compared to God's gloriousness, 'all our righteousnesses are as filthy rags' (Isaiah 64:6). So, in committing oneself to this role, one is acknowledging God's greatness and one's own relative worthlessness. This humble attitude is not a mere embellishment of the ritual: on the contrary, worship, unlike love or respect, *requires* humility. Pride is a sin, and pride before God is incompatible with worshipping him.

On the view that I am suggesting, the function of worship as 'glorifying' or 'praising' God, which is usually taken to be its primary function, may be regarded as derivative from the more fundamental nature of worship as commitment to the role of God's Child. 'Praising' God is giving him the honour and respect due to one in his position of eminence, just as one shows respect and honour in giving fealty to a King.

In short, the worshipper is in this position: He believes that there is a being, God, who is the perfectly good, perfectly powerful, perfectly wise Creator of the Universe; and he views himself as the 'Child of God,' made for God's purposes and responsible to God for his conduct. And the ritual of worship, which may have any number of ceremonial forms according to the customs of the religious community, has as its point the acceptance of, and commitment to, one's role as God's Child, with all that this involves. If this account is accepted, then there is no mystery as to the relation between the act of worship and the worshipper's other activity. Worship will be regarded not as an isolated act taking place on Sunday morning, with no necessary connection to one's behaviour the rest of the week, but as a ritualistic expression of and commitment to a role which dominates one's whole way of life.[10]

IV.

An important feature of roles is that they can be violated; we can act and think consistently with a role, or we can act and think inconsistently with it. The Prince can, for example, act inconsistently with his role as Prince by giving greater importance to his own interests and welfare than to the Queen's; in this case, he is no longer her 'liege man'. And a father who does not attend to the welfare of his children is not acting consistently with his role as a father (at least as that role is defined in our society), and so on. The question that I want to raise now is, What would count as violating the role to which one is pledged in virtue of worshipping God?

In Genesis there are two familiar stories, both concerning Abraham, that are relevant here. The first is the story of the near-sacrifice of Isaac. We are told that Abraham was 'tempted' by God, who commanded him to offer Isaac as a human sacrifice. Abraham obeyed without hesitation: he prepared an altar, bound Isaac to it, and was about to kill him until God intervened at the last moment, saying 'Lay not thine hand upon the lad, neither do thou any thing unto him: for now I know that thou fearest God, seeing thou hast not withheld thy son, thine only son from me' (Genesis 22:12). So Abraham passed the test. But how could he have failed? What was his 'temptation'? Obviously, his temptation was to disobey God; God had ordered him to do something contrary to both his wishes and his sense of what would otherwise be right and wrong. He could have defied God; but he did not—he subordi-

---

[10]This account of worship, specified here in terms of what it means to worship God, may easily be adapted to the worship of other beings such as Satan. The only changes required are (*a*) that we substitute for beliefs about God analogous beliefs about Satan, and (*b*) that we understand the ritual of worship as committing the Satan-worshipper to a role as Satan's servant in the same way that worshipping God commits theists to the role of His servant.

nated himself, his own desires and judgments, to God's command, even when the temptation to do otherwise was strongest.

It is interesting that Abraham's record in this respect was not perfect. We also have the story of him bargaining with God over the conditions for saving Sodom and Gomorrah from destruction. God had said that he would destroy those cities because they were so wicked; but Abraham gets God to agree that if fifty righteous men can be found there, then the cities will be spared. Then he persuades God to lower the number to forty-five, then forty, then thirty, then twenty, and finally ten. Here we have a different Abraham, not servile and obedient, but willing to challenge God and bargain with him. However, even as he bargains with God, Abraham realises that there is something radically inappropriate about it: he says, 'Behold now, I have taken upon me to speak unto the Lord, which am but dust and ashes…Oh let not the Lord be angry…' (Genesis 18:27, 30).

The fact is that Abraham could not, consistently with his role as God's subject, set his own judgment and will against God's. The author of Genesis was certainly right about this. We cannot recognise any being *as God*, and at the same time set ourselves against him. The point is not merely that it would be imprudent to defy God, since we certainly can't get away with it; rather, there is a stronger, logical point involved—namely, that if we recognise any being *as God*, then we are committed, in virtue of that recognition, to obeying him.

To see why this is so, we must first notice that 'God' is not a proper name like 'Richard Nixon' but a title like 'President of the United States' or 'King'.[11] Thus, 'Jehovah is God' is a nontautological statement in which the title 'God' is assigned to Jehovah, a particular being—just as 'Richard Nixon is President of the United States' assigns the title 'President of the United States' to a particular man. This permits us to understand how statements like 'God is perfectly wise' can be logical truths, which is highly problematic if 'God' is regarded as a proper name. Although it is not a logical truth that any particular being is perfectly wise, it nevertheless is a logical truth that if any being is God (i.e. if any being properly holds that title) then that being is perfectly wise. This is exactly analogous to saying: although it is not a logical truth that Richard Nixon has the authority to veto congressional legislation, nevertheless it is a logical truth that if Richard Nixon is President of the United States then he has that authority.

To bear the title 'God', then, a being must have certain qualifications. He must, for example, be all-powerful and perfectly good in addition to being perfectly wise. And in the same vein, to apply the title 'God' to a being is to recognise him as one to be obeyed. The same is true, to a lesser extent, of 'King'—to recognise anyone as King is to acknowledge that he occupies a

[11]Cf. Nelson Pike, 'Omnipotence and God's Ability to Sin', *American Philosophical Quarterly*, (1969), pp. 208–9, and C. B. Martin, *Religious Belief* (Ithaca, 1964), ch. 4.

place of authority and has a claim on one's allegiance as his subject. And to recognise any being as God is to acknowledge that he has *unlimited* authority, and an unlimited claim on one's allegiance.[12] Thus, we might regard Abraham's reluctance to defy Jehovah as grounded not only in his fear of Jehovah's wrath, but as a logical consequence of his acceptance of Jehovah *as God*. Camus was right to think that 'From the moment that man submits God to moral judgment, he kills Him his own heart'.[13] What a man can 'kill' by defying or even questioning God is not the being that (supposedly) *is* God, but *his own conception of that being as God*. That God is not to be judged, challenged, defied, or disobeyed, is at bottom a truth of logic; to do any of these things is incompatible with taking him as One to be worshipped.

V.

So the idea that any being could be *worthy* of worship is much more problematical than we might have at first imagined. For in admitting that a being is worthy of worship we would be recognising him as having an unqualified claim on our obedience. The question, then, is whether there could be such an unqualified claim. It should be noted that the description of a being as all-powerful, all-wise, etc., would not automatically settle the issue; for even while admitting the existence of such an awesome being we might still question whether we should recognise him as having an unlimited claim on our obedience.

In fact, there is a long tradition in moral philosophy, from Plato to Kant, according to which such a recognition could never be made by a moral agent. According to this tradition, to be a moral agent is to be an autonomous or self-directed agent; unlike the precepts of law or social custom, moral precepts are imposed by the agent upon himself, and the penalty for their violation is, in Kant's words, 'self-contempt and inner abhorrence'.[14] The

---

[12]This suggestion might also throw some light on the much-discussed problem of how we could, even in principle, *verify* the existence of God. Sceptics have argued that, even though we might be able to confirm the existence of an all-powerful cosmic superbeing (if one existed), we still wouldn't know what it means to verify that this being is *divine*. And this, it is said, casts doubt on whether the notion of divinity, and related notions such as 'Christ' and 'God', are intelligible. (Cf. Kai Nielsen, 'Eschatological Verification', *The Canadian Journal of Theology*, 9, 1963.) Perhaps this is because, in designating a being as God, we are not only describing him as having certain factual properties (such as omnipotence), but also *ascribing* to him a certain place in our devotions, and taking him as one to be obeyed, worshipped, praised, etc. If this is part of the logic of 'God', then we shouldn't be surprised if God's existence, in so far as that includes the existence of divinity, is not entirely confirmable—for only the 'factual properties' such as omnipotence will be verifiable in the usual way. But once the reason for this is understood, it no longer seems such a serious matter.

[13]Albert Camus, *The Rebel*, translated by Anthony Bower (New York, 1956), p. 62.

[14]Immanuel Kant, *Foundations of the Metaphysics of Morals*, translated by Lewis White Beck (New York, 1959), p. 44.

virtuous man is therefore identified with the man of integrity, i.e. the man who acts according to precepts which he can, on reflection, conscientiously approve in his own heart. Although this is a highly individualistic approach to morals, it is not thought to invite anarchy because men are regarded as more or less reasonable and as desiring what we would normally think of as a decent life lived in the company of other men.

On this view, to deliver oneself over to a moral authority for directions about what to do is simply incompatible with being a moral agent. To say 'I will follow so-and-so's directions no matter what they are and no matter what my own conscience would otherwise direct me to do' is to opt out of moral thinking altogether; it is to abandon one's role as a moral agent. And it does not matter whether 'so-and-so' is the law, the customs of one's society, or God. This does not, of course, preclude one from seeking advice on moral matters, and even on occasion following that advice blindly, trusting in the good judgment of the adviser. But this is to be justified by the details of the particular case, e.g. that you cannot in that case form any reasonable judgment of your own due to ignorance or inexperience in dealing with the types of matters involved. What *is* precluded is that a man should, while in possession of his wits, adopt this style of decision-making (or perhaps we should say this style of *abdicating* decision-making) as a general strategy of living, or abandon his own best judgment in any case where he can form a judgment of which he is reasonably confident.

What we have, then, is a conflict between the role of worshipper, which by its very nature commits one to total subservience to God, and the role of moral agent, which necessarily involves autonomous decision-making. The point is that the role of worshipper takes precedence over every other role which the worshipper has—when there is any conflict, the worshipper's commitment to God has priority over any other commitments which he might have. But the first commitment of a moral agent is to do what in his own heart he thinks is right. Thus the following argument might be constructed:

(a) If any being is God, he must be a fitting object of worship.
(b) No being could possibly be a fitting object of worship, since worship requires the abandonment of one's role as an autonomous moral agent.
(c) Therefore, there cannot be any being who is God.

VI.

The concept of moral agency underlying this argument is complex and controversial; and, although I think it is sound, I cannot give it the detailed treatment here that it requires. Instead, I will conclude by answering some of the most obvious objections to the argument.

(1) What if God lets us go our own way, and issues no commands other than that we should live according to our own consciences? In that case there would be no incompatibility between our commitment to God and our commitments as moral agents, since God would leave us free to direct our own lives. The fact that this supposition is contrary to major religious traditions (such as the Christian tradition) doesn't matter, since these traditions could be mistaken. The answer here is that this is a mere contingency, and that even if God did not require obedience to detailed commands, the worshipper would still be committed to the abandonment of his role as a moral agent, *if* God required it.

(2) It has been admitted as a necessary truth that God is perfectly good; it follows as a corollary that He would never require us to do anything except what is right. Therefore in obeying God we would only be doing what we should do in any case. So there is no incompatibility between obeying him and carrying out our moral commitments. Our primary commitment as moral agents is to do right, and God's commands *are* right, so that's that.

This objection rests on a misunderstanding of the assertion that (necessarily) God is perfectly good. This can be intelligibly asserted only because of the principle that *No being who is not perfectly good may bear the title 'God'*.[15] We cannot determine whether some being is God without first checking on whether he is perfectly good;[16] and we cannot decide whether he is perfectly good without knowing (among other things) whether his commands to us are right. Thus our own judgment that some actions are right, and others wrong, is logically prior to our recognition of any being as God. The upshot of this is that we cannot justify the suspension of our own judgment on the grounds that we are deferring to God's command (which, as a matter of logic, *must* be right); for if, by our own best judgment, the command is wrong, this gives us good reason to withhold the title 'God' from the commander.

(3) The following expresses a view which has always had its advocates among theologians: 'Men are sinful; their very consciences are corrupt and unreliable guides. What is taken for conscientiousness among men is nothing more than self-aggrandisement and arrogance. Therefore, we cannot trust our own judgment; we must trust God and do what he wills. Only then can we be assured of doing right.'

---

[15]See above, section 4.

[16]Of course we cannot ever know that such a being is *perfectly* good, since this would require an examination of *all* his actions and commands, etc., which is impossible. However, if we observed many good things about him and no evil ones, we would be justified in putting forth the hypothesis that he is perfectly good and acting accordingly. The hypothesis would be confirmed or disconfirmed by future observations in the usual way.

This view suffers from a fundamental inconsistency. It is said that we cannot know for ourselves what is right and what is wrong; and this is because our judgment is corrupt. But how do we know that our judgment is corrupt? Presumably, in order to know that, we would have to know (*a*) that some actions are morally required of us, and (*b*) that our own judgment does not reveal that these actions are required. However, (*a*) is just the sort of thing that we can*not* know, according to this view. Now it may be suggested that while we cannot know (*a*) by our own judgment, we can know it as a result of God's revelation. But even setting aside the practical difficulties of distinguishing genuine from bogus revelation (a generous concession), there is still this problem: if we learn that God (i.e. some being that we take to be God) requires us to do a certain action, and we conclude on this account that the action is morally right, then we have *still* made at least one moral judgment of our own, namely that whatever this being requires is morally right. Therefore, it is impossible to maintain the view that we do have some moral knowledge, and that *all* of it comes from God's revelation.

(4) Many philosophers, including St. Thomas, have held that the voice of individual conscience *is* the voice of God speaking to the individual, whether he is a believer or not.[17] This would resolve the alleged conflict because in following one's conscience one would at the same time be discharging his obligation as a worshipper to obey God. However, this manoeuvre is unsatisfying, since if taken seriously it would lead to the conclusion that, in speaking to us through our 'consciences', God is merely tricking us: for he is giving us the illusion of self-governance while all the time he is manipulating our thoughts from without. Moreover, in acting from conscience we are acting under the view that our actions are right and not merely that they are decreed by a higher power. Plato's argument in the *Euthyphro* can be adapted to this point: If, in speaking to us through the voice of conscience, God is informing us of what is right, then there is no reason to think that we could not discover this for ourselves—the notion of 'God informing us' is eliminable. On the other hand, if God is only giving us arbitrary commands, which cannot be thought of as 'right' independently of his promulgating them, then the whole idea of 'conscience', as it is normally understood, is a sham.

(5) Finally, someone might object that the question of whether any being is *worthy* of worship is different from the question of whether we *should* worship him. In general, that X is worthy of our doing Y with respect to X does not entail that we should do Y with respect to X. For

---

[17]Cf. Geach: 'The rational recognition that a practice is generally undesirable and that it is best for people on the whole not even to think of resorting to it is thus *in fact* a promulgation to a man of the Divine law forbidding the practice, even if he does not realise that this is a promulgation of the Divine law, even if he does not believe there is a God.'

example, Mrs Brown, being a fine woman, may be worthy of a marriage proposal, but we ought not to propose to her since she is already married. Or, Seaman Jones may be worthy of a medal for heroism but perhaps there are reasons why we should not award it. Similarly, it may be that there is a being who is worthy of worship and yet we should not worship him since it would interfere with our lives as moral agents. Thus God, who is worthy of worship, may exist; and we should love, respect, and honour him, but not worship him in the full sense of the word. If this is correct, then the argument of section 5 is fallacious.

This rebuttal will not work because of an important disanalogy between the cases of proposing marriage and awarding the medal, on the one hand, and the case of worship on the other. It may be that Mrs Brown is worthy of a proposal, yet there are circumstances in which it would be wrong to propose to her. However, these circumstances are contrasted with others in which it would be perfectly all right. The same goes for Seaman Jones's medal: there are *some* circumstances in which awarding it would be proper. But in the case of worship—if the foregoing arguments have been sound—there are *no* circumstances under which anyone should worship God. And if one should *never* worship, then the concept of a fitting object of worship is an empty one.

The above argument will probably not persuade anyone to abandon belief in God—arguments rarely do—and there are certainly many more points which need to be worked out before it can be known whether this argument is even viable. Yet it does raise an issue which is clear enough. Theologians are already accustomed to speaking of theistic belief and commitment as taking the believer 'beyond morality', and I think they are right. The question is whether this should not be regarded as a severe embarrassment.[18]

---

[18]A number of people read earlier versions of this paper and made helpful comments. I have to thank especially Kai Nielsen, William Ruddick, Jack Glickman, and Steven Cahn.

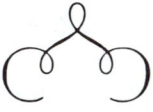

DEATH, SURVIVAL, AND THE MEANING OF LIFE

TERENCE PENELHUM

Life After Death

TWO CONCEPTS OF SURVIVAL

The doctrine of the immortality of the soul certainly predates Christianity. It finds its classic expression in Plato's dialogue, the *Phaedo*. This dialogue has as its dramatic setting the last day in the life of Socrates. Socrates has been condemned to death by the Athenians for allegedly corrupting the youth of the city with his philosophical questioning, and when the sun sets he must drink the cup of poison that will kill him. As Plato portrays his last day in prison before the carrying out of the sentence, Socrates devotes his final hours to discussion of whether the soul can survive the death of the body and whether death is to be feared. His conclusion is that the soul will survive and that the wise man need have no fear of death but should welcome it as a release of the soul from the bondage of the body. The arguments that Plato puts into the mouth of Socrates are based upon his belief that the human soul shows an awareness of a higher and nonmaterial realm of forms or ideas, of which it could not learn through the body and its sensory apparatus alone. The soul shows this awareness through its capacity to use general concepts and in particular through its powers of mathematical and moral reflection. It is thus identified primarily with the reason of man and is held to be alien to the body and essentially imprisoned within it. The philosopher is the man who is able to recognize the soul's higher kinship and attempts as far as he can to free the soul from the shackles of physical concerns. For him, at least, death will complete what he has partially succeeded in achieving during his

From *Religion and Rationality* by Terence Penelhum (New York: Random House, 1971), pp. 334–55. Reprinted by permission of the author.

lifetime. It is clear from the doctrine of the parts of the soul in the *Republic* that Plato recognizes the desires as parts of the soul also and not merely as functions of bodily states; but he thinks of the satisfaction of physical desires as alien to the natural concerns of the soul, which has its own, immaterial objects to seek after.

This doctrine has been enormously influential, and many have thought that it, or something like it, is also the Christian doctrine. Certain elements in the Platonic view (such as Plato's suggestion that the soul's higher aspirations reveal its preexistence and his belief that matter is a fundamentally negative, and even evil, principle) would have to be abandoned or amended for the two doctrines to be assimilated. But many Christians have thought that their belief is in essence the same as the doctrine we find in Plato. This obscures the fact that the doctrine of the resurrection of the body clearly seems to be a distinctively Christian contribution. When this fact is emphasized, it becomes important to decide how far the two beliefs are irreconcilable.

Some thinkers certainly hold that they are. Professor Oscar Cullmann, for example, has recently argued that there is a fundamental divergence between the Platonic and Christian doctrines and that this can be seen when we compare the serenity with which Socrates' doctrines enable him to face his approaching death in the *Phaedo*, with the agony that Jesus undergoes when faced with the approach of death in the Gospel narratives.[1] The primitive Christian tradition, he argues, does not present death as a welcome passage from one realm to another, but as the most elemental and horrifying reality that man confronts, because death is the destruction of the person, not his release. The distinctive Christian hope, expressed in the doctrines of the Resurrection of Christ and the final resurrection of men, is the hope that God will literally re-create what he has permitted death to destroy. This interpretation has been challenged by H. A. Wolfson, who has argued that the early Christian Church believed both in the survival of the soul and in the resurrection of the body, and that this combination of beliefs can readily accommodate all the original New Testament attitudes toward death.[2] The final doctrinal issue between them seems to be whether or not the soul continues in a disembodied state between death and resurrection. If so, then at the resurrection the person is made whole again by the soul's being reunited with the body (or, perhaps, by its being united with another body). If not, then the resurrection is indeed the reappearance of a person from annihilation.

I cannot comment profitably on the historical question that Cullmann and Wolfson debate; though some of the later discussion will bear on the logic of the two competing alternatives. There can be no doubt that the doctrine of the immortality of the soul, even though Greek in origin, has been held by

---

[1] Oscar Cullmann, *Immortality of the Soul or Resurrection of the Dead?* (London: Epworth, 1958).

[2] H. A. Wolfson, "Immortality and Resurrection in the Philosophy of the Church Fathers," in *Religious Philosophy* (Cambridge: Harvard University Press, 1961).

many members of the Christian tradition, whether it belonged originally to that tradition or not. The doctrine of the resurrection of the body, certainly authentically a part of the Christian tradition (since some form of it is clearly held by St. Paul),[3] is part of the most widely used creed of the Christian Church. Let us leave aside their historical relationship and look at the logical possibilities they present. I shall begin with the doctrine of the immortality of the soul, or, as I prefer to word it, the doctrine of disembodied survival. Before doing so, however, I shall attempt to clear the ground a little by indicating the major sources of difficulty that philosophers have discovered in these doctrines.

These difficulties divide themselves naturally into two groups. There are, first of all, difficulties about envisaging the kind of life that survivors of death in either sense could be said to lead. It is not enough to say that the nature of this life is totally unknown, for if this is taken seriously to the extent of our being unable to say that these beings will possess personal character-istics as we now understand these, it seems to leave the belief that they will survive without any content. If one wishes to avoid this pitfall, one has to ascribe to the survivors some characteristics that persons as we know them possess. This does not seem impossible in the case of the doctrine of the resurrection of the body; though it can be made impossible if unlimited stress is placed on the claim that the body of the survivor is transformed. Radical transformation is to be expected as part of such a doctrine, but total transfor-mation would rob the notion of survival of all clear meaning, for it is part of that notion that the *person* survives, and this seems to entail that the resulting being is a person also. But if the doctrine of the resurrection of the body is expressed in ways that avoids this danger, it is clearly possible for us to form a rough notion (which is all one can reasonably demand) of what such a future state would be like.

The difficulty seems much greater, however, when we consider the doctrine of disembodied survival. For it is not obviously intelligible to ascribe personal characteristics to a being that is denied to have any physical ones. The notion of human intelligence, for example, seems closely bound up with the things men can be seen to do and heard to say; the notion of human emotion seems closely bound up with the way men talk and behave; and the notion of human action seems closely bound up with that of physical move-ment. There is plenty of room for disagreement over the nature of these connections, but they cannot even exist in the case of an allegedly disembod-ied being. So can we understand what is meant by talk of disembodied intelligences, or disembodied sufferers of emotion, or disembodied agents? A natural answer to our present problem is: Disembodied survivors might have mental lives. They might, that is, think, imagine, dream, or have feelings. This looks coherent enough. On the other hand, for them to have

---

[3]See I Corinthians, Chapter 15.

anything to think *about* or have feelings *toward*, it might be necessary for them also to have that which supplies us with our objects of reflection or emotion, namely, perception. Some might also want to add the notion of agency (especially if they wish to use the doctrine of disembodied survival to offer explanations of the phenomena of psychical research). We must bear in mind, further, that disembodied persons could, of course, never perceive or meet each other, in any normal sense of these words. What we need to do, even at the risk of spinning fantasies, is to see how severely the belief in their disembodiment restricts the range of concepts that we can apply to them.

The second group of difficulties affects both doctrines, though in different ways. These are difficulties about the self-identity of the survivors. The belief that people survive is not merely the belief that after people's deaths there will be personal beings in existence. It is the belief that those beings will be the same ones that existed before death. One of the reasons for concern about the nature of the life a disembodied person might lead is that if this mode of life were *too* radically different from the sort of life we lead, those beings leading it could not be identified with us. This difficulty is critical, for even if we can readily understand what the future life that is spoken of would be like, its coming to pass would only be an interesting cosmic hypothesis, lacking any personal relevance, if the beings living that life were not ourselves.[4] This requirement connects with another. We have to be able to form some concept of what it is for the future, post-mortem being to remain the same through time in the future life, quite apart from his also being identifiable with some previous person who existed in *this* life. If, for instance, our being able to identify a person whom we meet now as some person we knew previously depends on our being able to discern some feature that he still possesses; and if that feature is something that a being in the future life could not possess, then it needs to be shown that there could be post-mortem persons who persist through time at all. There would have to be some substitute, in the case of post-mortem persons, for the feature that establishes identity for pre-mortem persons. If we are not able to indicate what this would be, we have no adequately clear concept of what talk of post-mortem persons means.

These problems about identity arise in quite different ways for the two doctrines of disembodied survival and bodily resurrection. A proponent of the doctrine of disembodied survival has to face the problem of the continuing identity of the disembodied person through time, by showing that what makes that person identical through time could be some wholly *mental* feature and that the absence of a body does not render the notion of a body inapplicable. (He may or may not do this by claiming that we use mental

---

[4]The emphasis on the importance of this is a most valuable feature of Antony Flew's contributions to this subject. See *A New Approach to Psychical Research* (London: Watts & Co., 1953) and his article "Immortality," in Paul Edwards (ed.), *Encyclopedia of Philosophy* (New York: Macmillan and Free Press, 1967), Vol. 4, pp. 139–50.

rather than physical features to identify pre-mortem beings through time.) This task may not be hopeless, though it looks as though we depend on the physical continuity of people for our ability to reidentify them. He must also succeed in showing that some purely mental feature will serve to identify the post-mortem person with his pre-mortem predecessor.

In the case of the doctrine of the resurrection of the body, the problem of how the post-mortem, resurrected person can remain identical through time in the future state does not look very difficult, since the sort of life envisaged for this being is an embodied one, similar in enough respects (one may suppose) to our own. So even if we decided that the continuity of the body is a necessary condition of the continuance of a person through time, this condition could easily be said to be satisfied in the case of a resurrected person. Yet we still have a difficulty: Could a post-mortem person, even in this embodied state, be identified with any pre-mortem person? For if the doctrine of resurrection is presented in a form that entails the annihilation of a person at death, it could reasonably be argued that what is predicted as happening at the resurrection is not, after all, the reappearance of the original person but the (first) appearance of a *duplicate* person—no doubt resembling the former one but not numerically identical with him. If this can be argued and cannot be refuted, we are in the odd position of being unsure whether or not to say that the future persons are the former ones. Philosophers have often noted the extent to which problems of identity seem to involve not discoveries but decisions—decisions on what to *call* a particular situation. The literature of personal identity is full of actual and imagined stories introduced to help us discover, by deciding how to talk of them, what the conditions of application of our concepts are. The doctrine of the resurrection of the body seems to present us with just such a matter of decision—namely, would this admittedly conceivable future state properly be described as the reappearance of a former person or as the first appearance of a duplicate of him?

DISEMBODIED PERSONALITY

Let us now look at the first group of difficulties, those connected with the possibility of applying our normal concepts of personal life to post-mortem beings. These seem to arise, as we have seen already, only in connection with the belief that men survive without their bodies, and I shall therefore only discuss them in this connection.

These difficulties raise the most fundamental issues in the philosophy of mind. There is no doubt that the belief that the soul continues after physical death is one of the major causes of the famous "Cartesian dualism" of mind and matter. The dualist position, formulated by Descartes in the seventeenth century, restated a metaphysical position very close in many ways to that of Plato. Descartes' position is, roughly, that the soul (or mind) and the body are two distinct substances that have no common properties and have a purely causal and contingent relationship with one another. The mind occupies no space, is free, and indivisible; whereas the body does occupy space, is incapable of spontaneous motion, and can be divided. Further, each person cannot fail to be aware of the contents of his own mind, whereas the possibility of knowledge of the external physical world needs philosophical demonstration in view of the fact that our senses sometimes deceive us.

In the *Meditations* Descartes argues for his metaphysical dualism on epistemological grounds like these. But whatever its surface and deep causes are, its strengths and weaknesses as a theory about the composition of the human person have dominated philosophical discussion for over two centuries. Only recently, through the work of Wittgenstein and Ryle, have philosophers freed themselves from this dominance.[5] It is not necessary to hold the dualistic view of the nature of embodied persons in order to maintain the post-mortem existence of *dis*embodied persons, but a combination of the two is natural and is very common on a popular level. If we can make sense of the view that the mind or soul is essentially independent of the body it is "in," then there would seem to be no real difficulty about understanding the belief that it can continue when its occupancy of that body ceases. It has become very clear, however, that the dualistic picture of the structure of a person forces its adherents into the view that a person's mental life and mental qualities are features of the history of his mind and have at best a causal relationship with what his body is seen to do. In fact the greater part of what we say about people commits us to certain expectations about their physical performances. This does not mean, as some overenthusiastic behaviorists seem at times to suggest, that people do not have private mental images, wishes, and thoughts. It means rather that their intelligence, will, and emotions do not consist only, or even mainly, in the occurrence of those private experiences. It is therefore very doubtful indeed that dualism could hope to do justice to the variety of people's mental lives; it is also doubtful that this mental life could continue without a body. The only way of seeing whether or not the latter can be made plausible seems to be the slow and tedious process of wondering, case by case, how much of what we now can ascribe to embodied persons could be ascribed to disembodied ones without absurdity. If little or nothing can be so ascribed, we cannot attach any content to the phrase "disembodied person." If some characteristics can be ascribed to such a person, we may be able to attach some content to this notion, although the concept of a person will be much attenuated in the process.

Disembodied persons can conduct no physical performances. They cannot walk or talk (or, therefore, converse), open and close their eyes or peer

---

[5]See Ludwig Wittgenstein, *Philosophical Investigations*, trans. by G. E. M. Anscombe (Oxford: Basil Blackwell, 1953); Gilbert Ryle, *The Concept of Mind* (London: Hutchinson, 1949).

(or, therefore, look), turn their heads and incline their ears (or, therefore, listen), raise their hands in anger or weep (or, therefore, give bodily expression to their emotions), or touch or feel physical objects. Hence they cannot perceive each other or be perceived by us. Can they, still, be said without absurdity to perceive physical things? Perhaps we could say so if we were prepared to allow that a being having a set of visual images corresponding to the actual disposition of some physical things was thereby *seeing* those things. We could say so if we were prepared to allow that a being having a sequence of auditory experiences that made him think correctly that a certain object was giving off a particular sound was thereby *hearing* that object. The notions of seeing and hearing would be attenuated, since they would not, if applied in such cases, entail that the person who saw was physically in front of the object he saw with his face turned toward it or that the person who heard was receiving sound waves from the object that was giving them off. On the other hand, many philosophers hold that such implications are at most informal ones that are not essential to the concepts in question. Perhaps we could also say even that disembodied percipients could *do* things to the objects (or persons) they see and hear. We might be able to say this if we imagined that sometimes these percipients had wishes that were immediately actualized in the world, without any natural explanation for the strange things that occurred; though obviously such fantasies would involve the ascription of occult powers to the spirits.[6] We might prefer to avoid all talk of interaction between the world of the spirits and ours, however, by denying that a disembodied being can see or hear or act in our world at all. Perhaps their lives consist exclusively of internal processes—acts of imagination and reflection. Such a life would be life in a dream world; and each person would have his own private dream. It might include dream images "of" others, though the accuracy of any reflections they occasioned would be purely coincidental.[7]

These informal suggestions indicate that it might be possible, given a good deal of conceptual elasticity, to accord to disembodied persons at least some of the forms of mental life with which we are familiar. It therefore seems overdoctrinaire to refuse to admit that such beings could be called persons. We must bear in mind, however, that they could hardly be said to have an *inter*personal existence. Not only would we be unable to perceive a disembodied person; but a disembodied person, being unable to perceive

---

[6]These suggestions and alternatives to some of them are discussed in Chapters 2, 3, and 4 of my book *Survival and Disembodied Existence* (London: Routledge & Kegan Paul, 1970).

[7]See H. H. Price, "Survival and the Idea of 'Another World,' " *Proceedings of the Society for Psychical Research*, 50 (1952); reprinted in J. R. Smythies (ed.), *Brain and Mind* (London: Routledge & Kegan Paul, 1965). For comments on Price see the Smythies volume and Penelhum, *Survival and Disembodied Existence*, Chapter 4.

another disembodied person, could have no more reason than we have to believe that others besides himself existed. Only if he can perceive embodied persons would he be in a position to know from anything other than memory that they exist or that they act in particular ways. The logic of the concept of disembodied persons clearly rules out the possibility of there being a community of such persons, even though by exercising conceptual care and tolerance we do seem able to ascribe some sort of life to disembodied individuals. In response to this, a verificationist might demand that before we can understand the ascriptions we have considered we should be able to say how we would *know* that a disembodied individual was having some experience or performing some act. But since we are dealing with a possible use of predicates that we have already learned, this verificationist demand seems too stringent.

We have also had to put aside another question whose bearing cannot be disputed, since it casts doubt on our ability to think of disembodied individuals. In asking whether some of the notions of a personal mental life can be applied, we have had to assume that there is a continuing, nonphysical subject to whom they can be applied, who has the experience or who does the action. This notion is essential to our understanding of the suggestion that there is a plurality of distinct individuals (whether they form a community or not), that on some occasion an experience is had by one of them rather than another, and that on another occasion a second experience is had by the same individual (or, indeed, a different individual) as had the first. In daily life the distinction between individuals and the continuing identity of individuals through time seems to depend upon the fact that each individual person has a distinguishable and persisting body. In the absence of a body are we able to form any notion of what has the experience or does the actions, has certain other experiences or actions in its past, and will have others in its future? In what follows, in order to retain some degree of clarity and simplicity in a philosophical area where obscurity is especially easy, I shall concentrate on trying to provide some account of what it might be for a disembodied person to retain identity through time. The philosophical theories we shall look at are usually also intended to offer some answer to the problem of distinguishing between two or more contemporaries—the problem, that is, of individuation. It is in any case hard to see how that question could have an answer if the problem of identity through time does not. I shall now turn, then, to the second, and more fundamental, of our two problems in the logic of the concept of survival.

THE PROBLEM OF IDENTITY: HUME'S SKEPTICISM

The logical problems one has to contend with when examining the concept of survival are to a large extent extensions of those that have puzzled philosophers when they have tried to analyze the notion of personal identity.[8] We all recognize one another; we are all familiar enough with the experience of wondering who someone is; and most of us know the embarrassment that follows when one makes a mistake about who someone is. Our day-to-day thinking about these matters suggests that we take it for granted that there are clearly understood factors that determine whether the man before us is Smith or not, or is who he says he is or not, even though we may be unable to decide sometimes, through lack of information, whether these factors obtain. Philosophers have been puzzled, however, when they have tried to say what these factors are. Skeptical philosophers have even wondered whether any such factors can be isolated; and if they cannot be, they have suggested, our assumption that people do retain their identities from one period of time to the next may be an illusion.

We do not need to spend much time here on this sort of skepticism. Its most famous exponent is Hume, who confessed himself unable to detect any stability in the mental life of men and therefore thought that the incessant changes that human minds undergo make it plainly false that they retain any identity at all.[9] Our belief that they do retain an identity is a convenient fiction but nothing better. This skepticism rests on an unstated assumption that there is some sort of logical conflict between the notions of sameness and change. If this were so, then in order to be sure that any type of being retained identity through time, we would have to be sure that it, or at least the essential part of it, remained unchanged through that time. If this is true, then of course Hume would be quite justified in relapsing into skepticism about personal identity. But once the assumption is exposed, its gratuitousness becomes apparent. Sameness or identity is an ambiguous notion; borrowing vocabulary found in Hume himself, we can distinguish between "numerical identity" and "specific identity." Two things are identical in the specific sense if they are exactly alike in some or all respects. This can only be true if they are, nevertheless, two distinct things—if, that is, they are *not* identical in the numerical sense. Two numerically different things may or may not be the same in the specific sense. One and the same thing (in the numerical sense) may be the same at one time as it was at an earlier time, or it may not. If it is not, it has changed. To say that just because it has changed it cannot be numerically the same is to confuse the two sorts of identity.

---

[8]For a general discussion of the problems of personal identity, see my article of that title in *Encyclopedia of Philosophy*, Vol. 6. This contains, besides a more rigorous treatment of issues raised briefly here, some extended discussion of the implications of the "puzzle cases," which I have had to omit from a short treatment of these topics. The latter part of my *Survival and Disembodied Existence* is intended to be a more thorough examination of the issues introduced in this chapter.

[9]See Hume's *Treatise of Human Nature*, Book I, Part 4, Section 6. The criticisms I make here are more informal versions of those I raised in "Hume on Personal Identity," *The Philosophical Review*, 44, No. 4 (1955), 571–89, reprinted in V. C. Chappell (ed.), *Hume* (New York: Doubleday, 1967), pp. 213–39.

Certain changes, however, may destroy a thing—that is, whatever remains of it is no longer sufficient to entitle us to say that that thing has continued in existence, and we are forced to say that something else is there, as when a house crumbles and a mere heap of stones remains. Even though Hume is wrong in thinking that the mere fact of change destroys numerical identity, it is still the case that for each *sort* of thing, certain changes will destroy that identity and certain others will not. Reducing all parts of a chair to ashes in a fire will destroy its identity, whereas changing the color of its surface by painting it will not. This suggests, once again, that the proper philosophical task is to discover, at least in the case of those classes of things that are of philosophical interest to us, what factors have to remain for a thing of that sort to continue in being and which ones do not. The problem of personal identity consists, in part, of trying to clarify this in the case of persons.

When we try to do this we are confronted with another oddity in a discussion like Hume's. He restricts himself, without any apparent recognition of the need to justify this restriction, to a consideration of only the mental factors that make up the being of a person and ignores the physical ones. If one makes this restriction, one is immediately confronted with the following facts that Hume stresses: first, he notes that the changes we can introspect within the mind succeed one another very rapidly; and second, he points out that one cannot detect any more stable element. Since we usually conceive of *things* as entities that change fairly slowly unless catastrophe strikes them and do not normally change nearly as rapidly as the contents of the mind seem to do, our ascription of identity to the person is apt to seem puzzling. But what needs to be questioned here is Hume's restriction. One of the major reasons for it is that Hume inherits the dualism that Descartes passed down from Plato into modern philosophy. It is a characteristic part of that tradition not merely to divide the human person into two parts but to identify the real person with the mind and assume that the body is merely a place that this person inhabits. If this identification is presupposed, then Hume's bewilderment in the face of the rapidity of mental change is understandable enough.

MENTAL AND BODILY CRITERIA OF IDENTITY

One way of trying to avoid this confusion is to resort to a doctrine that Hume recognizes to be without value: the doctrine of spiritual substance. This is the doctrine that in spite of the changingness of our mental lives, there is some hidden core to it that persists unchanged throughout, thus providing a backdrop against which the changes occur. This backdrop need not be *un*changing: It could be subject only to gradual change. The tacit assumption that it cannot change at all is only the result of assuming that identity and change are always inconsistent. But even if we allow that the spiritual substance to which the occurrences in our mental lives belong might itself be subject to gradual change, the doctrine is without value. For if the doctrine implies that we can find this relatively permanent core within by looking into ourselves, then it is false; for we cannot, as Hume emphasizes. If on the other hand, it is admitted that the doctrine postulates something that is not accessible to observation, there is another difficulty: It can at best be a matter of happy accident that when we judge someone before us to be the same person as someone we knew before, we are right. For the only thing that would make this judgment reliable is the knowledge that the features possessed by the present and the past person belonged to the same substance. Yet when the substance is inaccessible even to the person himself, how could we ever know that an identity judgment was true? It is obvious that our basis for such judgments must be something other than what the doctrine requires it to be, for how, otherwise, could we learn to make such judgments in the first place?

We base our identity judgments, at least of others, upon the observation of their physical appearance. This fact, plus the mysteriousness of the doctrine of spiritual substance, has made it very tempting for philosophers to say that what makes a person the same from one period to the next is the continuance of his body throughout the two periods. The human body has the relative stability that we associate with a great many observable material objects and is not usually subject to the rapid changes that go on in the human mind. The plausibility of the claim that bodily continuity is a necessary and sufficient condition of personal identity derives also from the fact that our judgments about the identity of persons are in the vast majority of cases based on our having looked at them, talked to them, and recognized them. This may be why even philosophers who have tacitly identified the person with his mind have assumed that a person cannot consist only of thoughts, feelings, images, and other fleeting and changing phenomena, but must consist, beneath this, of something more stable. For they have, perhaps, been looking within the mind itself for something that has the relative stability of the body, even though they have officially abandoned any belief that the body provides persons with their continuing identity.

Suppose, however, that they were to abandon body surrogates like spiritual substance. Suppose they were not to assume that the identity of a person consists in the persistence of some relatively stable element such as his body, but were to concentrate their attention solely upon what they consider to be the contents of his mental life. If they were to do this, it would seem that their only hope of giving an account of the self-identity of persons would be to suggest the existence of some relationship among the fleeting elements of which human mental life is composed. An appropriate relationship does seem available. Some of the later experiences in a man's life history are, the story might go, memories of the earlier ones. And only the same person who had the earlier experiences could have a memory of one of them among his later experiences. So we have here the possibility of a purely mental standard of identity: that person A at time T_2 is the same as person B

at some earlier time T_1 if and only if, among the experiences that person A has at T_2 there are memories of experiences that person B had at T_1. In the literature of the subject these two criteria of identity (bodily continuity and memory) have contended for priority.

The claim that personal identity can be understood solely in terms of memory can be accepted by someone who does not believe that a person can be identified with his mind or that anyone ever survives physical death. A philosopher who does not believe these things might still believe that the embodied person before him can be identified with Smith, whom he used to know, only if the person before him has the appropriate memories. But it is clear that someone who does believe those things must reject the thesis that only bodily continuity can be a criterion of personal identity. For if it is a necessary condition of a person's continuing that his body should continue, no one could survive in a disembodied form. Someone who accepts the doctrine of disembodied survival, therefore, will naturally incline toward the view that memory is the one necessary and sufficient condition of personal identity, since he must reject the traditional alternative position.

There is an artificiality about speaking, as I have, about two competing positions here. For in daily life it looks as though we use both standards of identity, resorting to one or the other depending on circumstances. Sometimes we decide who someone is by ascertaining facts about their physical appearance, height, weight, and the rest. Sometimes we decide who someone is by trying to determine whether or not they can remember certain past events that the person they claim to be could not fail, we think, to recall. Indeed, the barrier between these two methods becomes less clear than it first seems, when we reflect that we might try to reach our decision by seeing what skills a person has retained or what performances he can carry out. But although both standards are used, one might still have priority over the other. This would be the case if the other would not be available to us if the one were not or if the description of the one required some reference to the other.

It might look as though the use of the bodily criterion of identity presupposes that of memory in some way. For we cannot know, without resorting to our own or someone else's memory of the person in question, whether the body before us is the same one that the person we think he is had in the past. This is true, but it does not show that the man's own memories determine who he is. It only shows that other people could not determine the necessary physical facts about him unless they could rely on their own memories to do it, and this is not the same thing.

There are two arguments that tend to show, I think, that the bodily criterion has priority over the memory criterion. The first one, which is the less fundamental, rests on the fact that people forget things. We cannot say that the man before us is the man who performed some past action if and only if he remembers doing that action, for people forget actions they have done. But one might object on two counts that this need not refute the claim that his having the memory of that action is what makes that action his rather than someone else's. For, first, all we mean by this is that he *could* remember doing it, not that he *does* remember doing it; and, second, all we need is that he be able to remember doing some action or having some experience that the person who did the original action also did, or had.

Let us take these objections in order. The first will not do, for what do we mean when we say that he could remember doing the action in question? If we mean that it is in practice possible to get him to recall doing it, for instance, by psychoanalysis, then the retort is that all practicable methods might fail without thereby showing that the action was not done by him. If, on the other hand, we merely mean that it is in theory possible, then this requires further elucidation: Something that is possible in theory but not in practice is possible in virtue of some condition that in practice cannot bring it about. And this condition can only be the very fact that we are trying to elucidate, namely, the fact that the action was done by him and not by someone else. The other objection does not hold either, for a similar sort of reason. If we say that although the man before us cannot remember doing the action in question, he did do it because he can remember having some experience that the past person who did that action had, this presupposes that we understand what makes the past person who had that experience the same past person who did the original action. There must therefore be some standard of identity, actually satisfied, that we are appealing to in order to presuppose this. To say that this standard is itself that of memory is to raise our original question all over again.

The second and more fundamental argument rests on the fact that the notion of remembering is ambiguous. To say that someone remembers some action or event may mean merely that he believes he did it or witnessed it (without, at least consciously, basing this belief upon being told about it). It is possible, of course, for someone to remember something in this sense without what he remembers having happened at all and without its having happened to *him* even if it did occur. The more common use of the notion of remembering, however, concedes the truth of the man's belief, so that to say that the man remembers some action or event is to say that his claim to know about it is correct. Let us call these sense (i) and sense (ii) of "remember." Then we can say that to remember in sense (i) is to believe that one remembers in sense (ii).

It is apparent that memory in sense (i) cannot provide a criterion of personal identity. It is certainly not a sufficient condition of a man before us being the person that he claims to be that he remembers, in sense (i), doing or experiencing something done or experienced by the man he claims to be. For he could believe that he remembered doing something in this sense, even if nobody had done it. So we have to lean on sense (ii) of "remember." But this leads into a deeper problem. Let us simplify our discussion by concentrating solely upon a person's remembering doing an action or having an experience or witnessing an event and leave aside the complexities involved in someone's remembering some fact, such as that Caesar was murdered. To say that someone, in sense (ii), remembers, is not merely to report that he believes something, but to accept his belief to be true. But an integral part of his belief is not only that some action was done, some experience had, or some event witnessed, but that it was done or had or witnessed *by him*. In other words, to say that he remembers in sense (ii) is not just to say that he now has some mental image or some conviction, even though it is likely to include this; it is to say that the past action, experience, or event that he refers to is part of his own past. But it now becomes clear that we cannot even state the memory criterion of identity without having some prior (and therefore independent) notion of the identity of the person. So the identity of the person must in the end rest upon some other condition, and the claim that it could rest solely upon memory must be false. The bodily criterion of identity is the natural one to refer to here. If, because of some commitment to dualism, one refuses to resort to it, it becomes wholly mysterious what the criterion of personal identity can be.[10]

IDENTITY AND SURVIVAL

We can now return to the problem of survival. We were considering how far it is possible to make sense of the notion of the persistence of a disembodied person through time and of the claim that some particular future disembodied person will be identical with one of us in this world here and now. We can also ask how far the doctrine of the resurrection of the body frees us from the difficulties that the doctrine of disembodied survival encounters.

If bodily continuity is a necessary condition of the persistence of a person through time, then we cannot form any clear conception of the persistence of a person through time without a body nor of the identity of such a person with some previous embodied person. The previous reflections about the notion of personal identity leave us with two results: first, that to attempt to understand the self-identity of a person solely in terms of memory is impossible and, second, that when we are considering the case of flesh-and-blood persons there seems no alternative but to conclude that bodily continuity is a necessary condition of personal identity. These conclusions by themselves do not show that no substitute for bodily continuity could be invented when discussing the case of disembodied personality. But some substitute for it would have to be supplied by invention, and until it is, the notion of disembodied personal identity makes no sense.

---

[10]On this topic see Antony Flew, "Locke and the Problem of Personal Identity," *Philosophy*, 26 (1951), 53–68, and Sydney Shoemaker, "Personal Identity and Memory," *Journal of Philosophy*, 56 (1959), 868–882.

The main line of argument is now plain, but for greater completeness it may be desirable to apply it to the doctrine of disembodied survival in a little more detail. An adherent of this doctrine, anxious to avoid admitting the necessity of the bodily criterion of personal identity, might perhaps claim that a survivor of death would intelligibly be said to be identical with someone who had died, because he remembered the actions and experiences of that person. And he might be said intelligibly to persist through time in his disembodied state because later and earlier experiences in the afterlife could be similarly connected by memories.

Let us take the latter suggestion first. It is that the disembodied person who has some experience at some future time FT_2 will be identical with the disembodied person who will have had some experience at an earlier future time FT_1 if, along with the experience at FT_2, there is a memory of the one he had at FT_1. The difficulty is to make sense not only of a phrase like "along with the experience there is a memory," but also, of what it means to speak of a memory here at all. For it will have to be a memory in sense (ii). And to say that the disembodied person has a memory at FT_2 in sense (ii) of some experience had at FT_1 is to assume that the two experiences will have been had by the same person; and this time, since we have no bodily criterion of identity to fall back on, we have no way of interpreting this claim.

If we turn now to the problem of identifying the disembodied person with some person who has died, we find the same difficulty. To say that he can be so identified because he remembers the deeds or experiences of that person is once again to use the notion of remembering in sense (ii). But to do this is to presuppose that we understand what it is for the remembering to be identical with the person who did those deeds or had those experiences. And we do not actually understand this. For although the person who did those deeds had a body, the rememberer, by hypothesis, does not have one and therefore cannot have the same body. It does not seem possible, therefore, to find any answer to the problem of self-identity for disembodied persons.

What about the doctrine of the resurrection of the body? Given that we are talking of the future existence of persons with bodies, the notion of their lasting through time in their future state does not seem to present any logical difficulties. But what of their identity with ourselves? If we assume some one-to-one correspondence between the inhabitants of the next world and of this (that is, assume at least that the inhabitants of the next world each resemble, claim to be, and claim to remember the doings of inhabitants of this one), it might seem foolish to deny that they will be identical with ourselves. But foolishness is not logical absurdity. It is conceivable that there might be a future existence in which there were large numbers of persons each resembling one of us and having uncanny knowledge of our pasts. And if that world does come to be in the future, we shall not be in it. What would make it a world with us in it, rather than a world with duplicates of us in it and not ourselves? Unless we can give a clear answer to this, it seems, very paradoxically, to be a matter of arbitrary choice whether to say these future people are us or not.

Surely, the answer might run, they will have the same bodies that we now have. But this is precisely what is not obvious. Apart from questions about whether the future bodies are like ours in youth, maturity, or old age, the dissolution of the earthly body means that the future body will be in some sense new. To say that it is the old one re-created is merely to say it is the same one without giving any reason for saying it is identical with the original body rather than one very much like it. To answer this way, then, seems merely to face the same puzzle again. To say that the future beings will remember in sense (ii) our doings and feelings is to raise the same questions here as before. The only possible solution seems to be to insist that in spite of the time gap between the death of the old body and the appearance of the new one, something persists in between. But what? The person disembodied? If so, then the doctrine of the resurrection of the body does not avoid the difficulties that beset the doctrine of disembodied survival, for the simple reason that it falls back upon that very doctrine when its own implications are understood.

This argument does not show that the doctrine of the resurrection of the body is absurd in the way in which the doctrine of disembodied survival is. It shows rather that the doctrine of resurrection is merely one way, and a question-begging way, of describing a set of circumstances that can be described equally well in another fashion. Yet the difference between the two alternative descriptions is a vital one. For it comes to no less than the original question, namely, do we survive? It is a question that the doctrine provides an answer to but one that seems to have no conclusive grounds, even if the circumstances envisaged in the doctrine were admitted to be forthcoming.

The belief in survival, then, at least in this version, does not run into insuperable difficulties of logic. But it does not seem possible to describe a set of future circumstances that will unambiguously show it to be true. I have previously argued that if the doctrine is agreed to be coherent, it can offer a suitable answer to the difficulties about the verification of religious beliefs. I do not consider the present puzzle to show that it is not coherent. But it does show its status to be very baffling.

ANTHONY QUINTON

The Soul

1. THE SOUL AND SPIRITUAL SUBSTANCE

Philosophers in recent times have had very little to say about the soul. The word, perhaps, has uncomfortably ecclesiastical associations, and the idea seems to be bound up with a number of discredited or at any rate generally disregarded theories. In the history of philosophy the soul has been used for two distinct purposes: first, as an explanation of the vitality that distinguishes human beings, and also animals and plants, from the broad mass of material objects, and, secondly, as the seat of consciousness. The first of these, which sees the soul as an ethereal but nonetheless physical entity, a volatile collection of fire-atoms or a stream of animal spirits, on some views dissipated with the dissolution of the body, on others absorbed at death into the cosmic soul, and on others again as capable of independent existence, need not detain us. The second, however, the soul of Plato and Descartes, deserves a closer examination than it now usually receives. For it tends to be identified with the view that in each person there is to be found a spiritual substance which is the subject of his mental states and the bearer of his personal identity. But on its widest interpretation, as the nonphysical aspect of a person, its acceptance need not involve either the existence of a spiritual substance over and above the mental states that make up a person's inner, conscious life or the proposition that this spiritual substance is what ultimately determines a person's identity through time. When philosophers dismiss the soul it is usually because they reject one or both of these supposed consequences of belief in it.

It is worth insisting, furthermore, that the existence of a spiritual substance is logically distinct from its being the criterion of personal identity. So the strong, and indeed fatal, arguments against the substance theory of personal identity do not at the same time refute the proposition, self-evident to Berkeley and many others, that there can be no conscious state that is not the state of some subject.

As a criterion of identity spiritual substance has three main weaknesses. First, it is regressive in just the same way as is an account of the identity of a material object through time in terms of its physical components. No general

From *The Journal of Philosophy* 59 (1962): 393–409. Reprinted by permission of the author and *The Journal of Philosophy*.

account of the identity of a kind of individual thing can be given which finds that identity in the presence of another individual thing within it. For the question immediately arises, how is the identity through time of the supposed identifier to be established? It, like the thing it is supposed to identify, can present itself at any one time only as it is at that time. However alike its temporally separate phases may be, they still require to be identified as parts of the same, continuing thing. In practice we do identify some wholes through their parts, normally where the parts are more stable and persistent unities than the wholes they compose and where, in consequence, the parts are more readily identifiable, as, for example, when we pick out one person's bundle of laundry from the bundles of others after the labels have been lost. But this can be only a practical expedient, not a theoretical solution.

A second difficulty is to find any observable mental entity that can effectively serve as a criterion in this case. The only plausible candidate is that dim, inchoate background, largely composed of organic sensations, which envelops the mental states occupying the focus of attention. This organic background is a relatively unchanging environment for the more dramatic episodes of conscious life to stand out against. But both the fixity and the peripheral status of this background are only relative. It does change, and it, or its parts, can come or be brought into the focus of attention. Even if its comparatively undisturbed persistence of character suggests it as a criterion, its vagueness makes it even less accessible to public application than the general run of mental criteria and leaves it with little power to distinguish between one person and another. The organic background is, of course, as regressive a criterion as any other part of a person's mental life. Its only virtues are that it is observable and that it does seem to be a universal constituent of the momentary cross sections of a person's experience. In this last respect it is preferable to most distinguishable features of a person's mental life. For, generally speaking, the parts of a complex and enduring thing are not necessary to the identity of that thing. Just as a cathedral is still the same cathedral if a piece has been knocked off it, whatever the piece may be, so a person is the same person if he ceases to have a particular belief or emotion, whatever that belief or emotion may be.

Finally, if it is held that the spiritual substance is nevertheless a permanent and unaltering constituent of a person's conscious life, it follows that it must be unobservable and so useless for purposes of identification. Suppose that from its very first stirrings my consciousness has contained a continuous whistling sound of wholly unvarying character. I should clearly never notice it, for I can only notice what varies independently of my consciousness—the whistles that start and stop at times other than those at which I wake up and fall asleep. It is this fact that ensured from the outset that Hume's search for a self over and above his particular perceptions was bound to fail. The unobservability of spiritual substance, and its consequent inapplicability as a criterion, can also be held to follow directly from taking its status as substance seriously, as an uncharacterized substratum for qualities and relations to inhere in with no recognizable features of its own.

But to admit that spiritual substance cannot possibly be the criterion of a person's identity and that it cannot be identified with any straightforwardly observable part of a person's mental life does not mean that it does not exist. It has seemed self-evident to many philosophers that every mental state must have an owner. To believe this is not to commit oneself to the existence of something utterly unobservable. If it is true, although both subjects and mental states are unobservable in isolation, each can be observed in conjunction with the other. There is a comparison here with the relations and observability of the positions and qualities of material things. One cannot be aware of a color except as present at some place and at some time or of a position except as the place and time where some discernible characteristics are manifested. So it might be argued that one can be aware of a conscious subject only as in some mental state or other and of a mental state only as belonging to some subject or other. Critics of the Berkeleyan principle sometimes suggest that it is no more than a faulty inference from the subject-object structure of the sentences in which mental facts are reported. It would certainly be a mistake to infer that a conscious subject is something entirely distinct from all its states from the linguistic fact that we commonly assign mental states to owners. We say of a chair that it has a back, a seat, arms, and legs, but this should not and does not lead us to conclude that the chair is something over and above the parts that it has, appropriately arranged. A more usual argument for the principle starts from the premise that mental states are acts that cannot be conceived without an agent in the same way as there cannot be a blow without a striker or a journey without a traveler. The premise of this argument has been much criticized by recent philosophers. A feeling of depression or a belief in the trustworthiness of a friend is not a precisely datable occurrence but a more or less persisting dispositional state. Nor is it an instance of agency in the sense of being the intentional execution of a decision. But these mistaken implications do not affect the validity of the argument under consideration. A disposition requires a possessor as much as an act requires an agent, and the blow I get from a swinging door still presupposes the existence of the door even though it did not mean to hit me.

The strength of the argument lies in the fact that we can assert the existence of some mental state, a feeling of anger let us say, only when we are in a position to assert either that we ourselves are angry or that somebody else is. We have given no sense to the words "discovering the existence of a mental state that is not my own or anyone else's." The nearest we come to speaking in this way is when we say, for example, "there is a sadness about the place," when walking about some ruins in a contemplative frame of mind.

What we mean in this case is that the place inclines us to feel sad and might well give rise to the same inclination in others. And this capacity for producing sad feelings in myself and others, as a disposition, has its own substance, so to speak: the broken columns and collapsed walls with which it is bound up.

The subject in this rather thin and formal sense is not borne down in the ruin of that concept of spiritual substance in which it is proposed as the determinant of personal identity. It could be argued that it is a loose way of referring to the related series of other mental states or to the body or both with which any given mental state is universally associated by our manner of reporting such states. If it is something distinct from both of these, as it has traditionally been believed to be, it is not properly to be called the soul. It could not exist without any states at all, and even if it could it would be an emotionally useless form of survival of bodily death. Its existence, in fact, is irrelevant to the problem of the soul, which is that of whether a person is essentially mental in character and so distinct from his body, a connected sequence of mental states and not a physical object. It is irrelevant whether the sequence of mental states composing a person on this theory presupposes a distinguishable subject or not.

Spiritual substance cannot be the criterion of personal identity, and it may or may not be presupposed by the existence of conscious mental states. Whether as part or presupposition of our mental life, it should not be identified with the soul when this is conceived as the nonbodily aspect of a person. The well-founded conviction that there is no spiritual substance in the first sense and widespread doubts as to its existence in the second should not be allowed to obscure the issue of whether there is a unitary nonbodily aspect to a person and, if there is, whether it is the fundamental and more important aspect. Locke saw that spiritual substance could not account for personal identity and, although he believed in its existence, speculated whether it might not have been possible for God to endow a material substance with the power of thinking. Yet he clearly believed in the soul as the connected sequence of a person's conscious states, regarded this sequence as what a person essentially was, and held it to be capable of existing independently of the body. I want to consider whether an empirical concept of the soul, which, like Locke's, interprets it as a sequence of mental states logically distinct from the body and is neutral with regard to the problem of the subject, can be constructed.

2. THE EMPIRICAL CONCEPT OF THE SOUL

It will be admitted that among all the facts that involve a person there is a class that can be described as mental in some sense or other. Is it enough to define the soul as the temporally extended totality of mental states and events that belong to a person? It will not be enough to provide a concept of the soul as something logically distinct from the body if the idea of the series of a person's mental states involves some reference to the particular human body that he possesses. In the first place, therefore a nonbodily criterion of personal identity must be produced. For if the soul were the series of mental states associated with a given body, in the sense of being publicly reported by it and being manifested by its behavior, two temporally separate mental states could belong to the history of the same soul only if they were in fact associated with one and the same human body. This notion of the soul could have no application to mental states that were not associated with bodies. The soul must, then, be a series of mental states that is identified through time in virtue of the properties and relations of these mental states themselves. Both the elements of the complex and the relations that make an identifiable persisting thing out of them must be mental. To establish the possibility of such a mental criterion of identity will be the hardest part of the undertaking.

Locke's criterion of memory has been much criticized, and it is certainly untenable in some of the interpretations it has been given. It will not do to say that two mental states belong to the same soul if and only if whoever has the later one can recollect the earlier one if the possibility of recollection involved is factual and not formal. For people forget things, and the paradox of the gallant officer is generated in which he is revealed as identical with both his childish and his senile selves while these are not identical with each other. However, a more plausible criterion can be offered in terms of continuity of character and memory. Two soul-phases belong to the same soul, on this view, if they are connected by a continuous character and memory path. A soul-phase is a set of contemporaneous mental states belonging to the same momentary consciousness. Two soul-phases are directly continuous if they are temporally juxtaposed, if the character revealed by the constituents of each is closely similar, and if the later contains recollections of some elements of the earlier. Two soul-phases are indirectly continuous and connected by a continuous character and memory path if there is a series of soul-phases all of whose members are directly continuous with their immediate predecessors and successors in the series and if the original soul-phases are the two end points of the series. There is a clear analogy between this criterion and the one by means of which material objects, including human bodies, are identified. Two object-phases belong to the same object if they are connected by a continuous quality and position path. Direct continuity in this case obtains between two temporally juxtaposed object-phases which are closely similar in qualities and are in the same position or in closely neighboring positions. Indirect continuity is once again the ancestral of direct continuity. There is no limit to the amount of difference in position allowed by the criterion to two indirectly continuous object-phases, but in normal discourse a limit is set to the amount of qualitative difference allowed by the requirement that the two phases be of objects of the same kind. Character in the mental case corresponds to quality in the physical and memory to spatial position. The soul, then, can be defined empirically as a series of mental states connected by continuity of character and memory.

Now there is an objection to the idea that memory can be any sort of fundamental criterion of identity which rests on the view that a memory criterion presupposes a bodily criterion. I shall defer the consideration of this issue, however, until two less serious difficulties have been met. These are that the construction suggested requires an exploded Cartesian dualism about the nature of mental states and, arising out of this, that a person's character is not clearly distinguishable from his body. The former, Rylean, objection can be met without difficulty. Even if the most extreme and reductive version of logical behaviorism were correct, even if a person's mental states were simply and solely behavioral dispositions, actual or potential, his character a complex property of these dispositions, and his memory a particular disposition to make first-person statements in the past tense without inference or reliance on testimony, the empirical concept of the soul would still apply to something distinct from any particular human body, though some body or other, not necessarily human perhaps, would be required to manifest the appropriate dispositions in its behavior and speech. In other words, an extreme, reductive, logical behaviorism is perfectly compatible with reincarnation, with the manifestation by one body of the character and memories that were previously manifested by another body that no longer exists. The second objection is that the soul as here defined and the body cannot be clearly distinguished, since the possession of some sorts of character trait requires the possession of an appropriate sort of body. I do not see that there is much empirical foundation for this to start with. It would be odd for a six-year-old girl to display the character of Winston Churchill, odd indeed to the point of outrageousness, but it is not utterly inconceivable. At first, no doubt, the girl's display of dogged endurance, a world-historical comprehensiveness of outlook, and so forth, would strike one as distasteful and pretentious in so young a child. But if she kept it up the impression would wear off. We do not, after all, find the story of Christ disputing with the doctors in the temple literally unintelligible. And a very large number of character traits seem to presume nothing about the age, sex, build, and general physical condition of their host. However, even if this were an empirically well-founded point, it would not be a relevant one. It would merely show that the possession of a given trait of character required the possession of an appropriate *kind* of body, a large one or a male one or an old one, and not the possession of a *particular* body. As things are, characters can survive large and even emotionally disastrous alterations to the physical type of a person's body, and these changes may have the effect of making it hard to others to recognize the continuity of character that there is. But courage, for example, can perfectly well persist even though the bodily conditions for its more obvious manifestations do not.

3. MENTAL AND BODILY CRITERIA OF IDENTITY

In recent philosophy there have been two apparently independent aspects to the view that the mind is logically dependent on the body. On the one hand, there are the doctrines that hold mental states either to be or necessarily to involve bodily states, whether bodily movement and dispositions thereto or neural events and configurations. With these doctrines, I have argued, the empirical concept of the soul can be reconciled. On the other hand, many philosophers have insisted that the basic and indispensable criterion of personal identity is bodily. Even mind-body dualists like Ayer, who have accepted the existence of a categorically clear-cut class of mental events, have sometimes taken this position. In his first treatment of the problem he appears at first to give a mental account of the concept of a person as being a series of experiences. But the relation that connects them in his theory involves an indispensable reference to a particular persisting human body. A person is made up of those total mental states which contain organic sensations belonging to one particular human body, presumably to be identical itself in terms of continuity of qualities and spatial position. Ayer draws the conclusion that properly follows from this and from any other account of personal identity that involves reference to a particular human body, namely that the notion of a person's disembodied existence is a self-contradictory one and, further, that even the association of a personality with different bodies at different times is inconceivable. These conclusions may well seem to constitute a reductio ad absurdum of the bodily criterion of personal identity rather than a disproof of the possibility of a person's survival of death. To explore them a little further will help to present the claims of mental as against bodily criteria in a clearer light.

At the outset it must be admitted that the theory of a bodily criterion has a number of virtues. It has, first, the theoretical attraction of simplicity, in that it requires only one mode of treatment for the identification through time of all enduring things, treating human beings as just one variety of concrete objects. Second, it has a practical appeal, in that its application yields uncontentiously correct answers in the very great majority of the actual cases of personal identification with which we are called upon to deal. Finally, it has the merit of realism, for it is, in fact, the procedure of identification that we do most commonly apply. Even where, for lack of relevant evidence, it is inapplicable, as in the case of the Tichborne claimant, it would not be supposed that the result of applying other criteria such as memory would conflict with what the bodily evidence would have shown if it had been forthcoming. Is there anything better to set against these powerful recommendations in favor of a bodily criterion than that it entails that things many people have wanted very deeply to say about the survival of death are inconsistent? A supporter of the bodily criterion might argue that it was so much the worse for them, that their inconsistent assertions arose from attempting to assert and deny at the same time that a person no longer existed.

It does seem strange, all the same, to say that all statements about disembodied or reincarnated persons are self-contradictory. Is it really at all plausible to say this about such familiar things as the simpler type of classical ghost story? It may be argued that there are plenty of stories which are really self-contradictory and yet which can be, in a way, understood and enjoyed, stories about time machines, for example. To try to settle the case we had better consider some concrete instances. Suppose I am walking on the beach with my friend A. He walks off a fair distance, treads on a large mine that someone has forgotten to remove, and is physically demolished in front of my eyes. Others, attracted by the noise, draw near and help to collect the scattered remains of A for burial. That night, alone in my room, I hear A's voice and see a luminous but intangible object, of very much the shape and size of A, standing in the corner. The remarks that come from it are in A's characteristic style and refer to matters that only A could have known about. Suspecting a hallucination, I photograph it and call in witnesses who hear and see what I do. The apparition returns afterwards and tells of where it has been and what it has seen. It would be very peculiar to insist, in these circumstances, that A no longer existed, even though his body no longer exists except as stains on the rocks and in a small box in the mortuary. It is not essential for the argument that the luminous object look like A or that it speak in A's voice. If it were a featureless cylinder and spoke like a talking weighing machine we should simply take longer becoming convinced that it really was A. But if continuity of character and memory were manifested with normal amplitude, we surely should be convinced.

Consider a slightly different case. I know two men B and C. B is a dark, tall, thin, puritanical Scotsman of sardonic temperament with whom I have gone on bird-watching expeditions. C is a fair, short, plump, apolaustic Pole of indestructible enterprise and optimism with whom I have made a number of more urban outings. One day I come into a room where both appear to be, and the dark, tall, thin man suggests that he and I pursue tonight some acquaintances I made with C, though he says it was with him, a couple of nights ago. The short, fair, plump, cheerful-looking man reminds me in a strong Polish accent of a promise I had made to B, though he says it was to him, and which I had forgotten about, to go in search of owls on this very night. At first I suspect a conspiracy, but the thing continues far beyond any sort of joke, for good perhaps, and is accompanied by suitable amazement on their part at each other's appearance, their own reflections in the mirror, and so forth.

Now what would it be reasonable to say in these circumstances: that B and C have changed bodies (the consequence of a mental criterion), that they have switched character and memories (the consequence of a bodily criterion), or neither? It seems to me quite clear that we should not say that B and

C had switched characters and memories. And if this is correct, it follows that bodily identity is not a logically complete criterion of personal identity; at best it could be a necessary condition of personal identity. Of the other alternatives, that of refusing to identify either of the psychophysical hybrids before us with B or C may seem the most scrupulous and proper. But the refusal might take a number of different forms. It might be a categorical denial that either of the hybrids is B or C. It might, more sophisticatedly be an assertion that the concept of personal identity had broken down and that there was no correct answer, affirmative or negative, to the question: which of these two is B and which C? It might, uninterestingly, be a state of amazed and inarticulate confusion.

What support is there for the conclusion required by the empirical concept of the soul, that B and C have substituted bodies? First of all, the rather weak evidence of imaginative literature. In F. Anstey's story *Vice Versa* the corpulent and repressive Mr. Bultitude and his athletic and impulsive school-boy son are the victims of a similar rearrangement. The author shows not the smallest trace of hesitation in calling the thing with the father's character and memories the father and the thing with the father's body the son. (Cf. also Conan Doyle's *Keinplatz Experiment*.) A solider support is to be found by reflecting on the probable attitude after the switch of those who are most concerned with our original pair, B and C, as persons, those who have the greatest interest in answering the question of their personal identity: their parents, their wives, their children, their closest friends. Would they say that B and C had ceased to exist, that they had exchanged characters and memories or that they had exchanged bodies? It is surely plain that if the character and memories of B and C really survived intact in their new bodily surroundings those closely concerned with them would say that the two had exchanged bodies, that the original persons were where the characters and memories were. For why, after all, do we bother to identify people so carefully? What is unique about individual people that is important enough for us to call them by individual proper names? In our general relations with other human beings their bodies are for the most part intrinsically unimportant. We use them as convenient recognition devices enabling us to locate without difficulty the persisting character and memory complexes in which we are interested, which we love or like. It would be upsetting if a complex with which we were emotionally involved came to have a monstrous or repulsive physical appearance, it would be socially embarrassing if it kept shifting from body to body while most such complexes stayed put, and it would be confusing and tiresome if such shifting around were generally widespread, for it would be a laborious business finding out where one's friends and family were. But that our concern and affection would follow the character and memory complex and not its original bodily associate is surely clear. In the case of general shifting about we should be in the position of people trying to find their intimates in the dark. If the shifts were both frequent and spatially radical we should no doubt give up the attempt to identify individual people, the whole character of relations between people would change, and human life would be like an unending sequence of shortish ocean trips. But, as long as the transfers did not involve large movements in space, the character and memory complexes we are concerned with could be kept track of through their audible identification of themselves. And there is no reason to doubt that the victim of such a bodily transfer would regard himself as the person whom he seems to remember himself as being. I conclude, then, that although, as things stand, our concept of a person is not called upon to withstand these strains and, therefore, that in the face of a psychophysical transfer we might at first not know what to say, we should not identify the people in question as those who now have the bodies they used to have and that it would be the natural thing to extend our concept of a person, given the purposes for which it has been constructed, so as to identify anyone present to us now with whoever it was who used to have the same character and memories as he has. In other words the soul, defined as a series of mental states connected by continuity of character and memory, is the essential constituent of personality. The soul, therefore, is not only logically distinct from any particular human body with which it is associated; it is also what a person fundamentally is.

It may be objected to the extension of the concept of personal identity that I have argued for that it rests on an incorrect and even sentimental view of the nature of personal relations. There are, it may be said, personal relationships which are of an exclusively bodily character and which would not survive a change of body but which would perfectly well survive a change of soul. Relations of a rather unmitigatedly sexual type might be instanced and also those where the first party to the relationship has violent racial feelings. It can easily be shown that these objections are without substance. In the first place, even the most tired of entrepreneurs is going to take some note of the character and memories of the companion of his later nights at work. He will want her to be docile and quiet, perhaps, and to remember that he takes two parts of water to one of scotch, and no ice. If she ceases to be plump and red-headed and vigorous he may lose interest in and abandon her, but he would have done so anyway in response to the analogous effects of the aging process. If he has any idea of her as a person at all, it will be as a unique cluster of character traits and recollections. As a body, she is simply an instrument of a particular type, no more or no less interesting to him than a physically identical twin. In the case of a purely sexual relationship no particular human body is required, only one of a more or less precisely demarcated kind. Where concern with the soul is wholly absent there is no interest in individual identity at all, only in identity of type. It may be said that this argument cuts both ways: that parents and children are concerned only that they should have round them children and parents with the same sort of character and memories as the children and parents they were with yesterday. But this is doubly incorrect. First, the memories of individual persons cannot be exactly similar, since even the closest of identical twins must see things from slightly different angles; they cannot be in the same place at the same time. More seriously, if more contingently, individual memories, even of identical twins, are seldom, if ever, closely similar. To put the point crudely, the people I want to be with are the people who remember me and the experiences we have shared, not those who remember someone more or less like me with whom they have shared more or less similar experiences. The relevant complexity of the memories of an individual person is of an altogether different order of magnitude from that of the bodily properties of an entrepreneur's lady friend. The lady friend's bodily type is simply enough defined for it to have a large number of instances. It is barely conceivable that two individual memories should be similar enough to be emotionally adequate substitutes for each other. There is the case of the absolutely identical twins who go everywhere together, side by side, and always have done so. Our tendency here would be to treat the pair as a physically dual single person. There would be no point in distinguishing one from the other. As soon as their ways parted sufficiently for the question of which was which to arise, the condition of different memories required for individuation would be satisfied.

It may be felt that the absolutely identical twins present a certain difficulty for the empirical concept of the soul. For suppose their characters and memories to be totally indistinguishable and their thoughts and feelings to have been precisely the same since the first dawning of consciousness in them. Won't the later phases of one of the twins be as continuous in respect of character and memory with the earlier phases of the other as they are with his own earlier phases? Should we even say that there are two persons there at all? The positional difference of the two bodies provides an answer to the second question. Although they are always excited and gloomy together, the thrills and pangs are manifested in distinct bodies and are conceivable as existing separately. We might ignore the duality of their mental states, but we should be able in principle to assert it. As to the matter of continuity, the environment of the two will be inevitably asymmetrical, each will at various times be nearer something than the other, each will block some things from the other's field of vision or touch; so there will always be some, perhaps trivial, difference in the memories of the two. But even if trivial, the difference will be enough to allow the application in this special case of a criterion that normally relies on radical and serious differences. However alike the character and memories of twin no. 1 on Tuesday and twin no. 2 on Wednesday, they will inevitably be less continuous than those of twin no. 2 on the two days.

4. MEMORY AND BODILY IDENTITY

I must now return to the serious objection to the use of memory as a criterion of personal identity whose consideration was postponed earlier. This has been advanced in an original and interesting article on personal identity recently published by Sydney S. Shoemaker in *The Journal of Philosophy*.[1] He argues that memory could not be the sole or fundamental criterion for the identity of other people, because in order to establish what the memories of other people are I have to be able to identify them in a bodily way. I cannot accept sentences offered by other people beginning with the words "I remember" quite uncritically. I must be assured, first, that these utterances really are memory claims, that the speaker understands the meaning of the sentences he is using, and, secondly, that his memory claims are reliable. Mr. Shoemaker contends that it is essential, if either of these requirements is to be satisfied, for me to be able to identify the maker of the apparent memory claims in an independent, bodily way. In order to be sure that his remarks really are intended as memory claims, I have to see that he generally uses the form of words in question in connection with antecedent states of affairs of which he has been a witness. And to do this I must be assured that he is at one time uttering a memory sentence and at another, earlier, time is a witness of the event he purports to describe; in other words I must be able to identify him at different times without taking his apparent memories into account. The point is enforced by the second requirement about the conditions under which I can take his memory claims as trustworthy. To do this I must be able to establish at least that he was physically present at and, thus, in a position to observe the state of affairs he now claims to recollect.

There is a good deal of force in these arguments, but I do not think they are sufficient to prove that the soul is not logically distinct from the particular body with which it happens to be associated at any given time. In the first place, the doubt about the significance of someone's current memory claims is not one that I must positively have laid to rest before taking these claims as evidence of his identity. The doubt could seriously arise only in very special and singular circumstances. If someone now says to me, "I remember the battle of Hastings," I will presume him to be slightly misusing the words, since I have good reasons for thinking that no one now alive was present at that remote event. I shall probably take him to be saying that he remembers that there was such a thing as the battle of Hastings, having learnt of it at school, or that it took place in 1066, that Harold was killed at it, that it was the crucial military factor in the Norman conquest, and so forth. But if, on being questioned, he says that these reinterpretations distort the meaning he intended, that he remembers the battle of Hastings in the same way as he remembers having breakfast this morning, if perhaps a little more dimly, then

---

[1] "Personal Identity and Memory." 56, 22 (Oct. 22, 1959): 868.

I cannot reasonably suppose that he doesn't understand the meaning of his remark though I may well think that it is false, whether deliberately or not. Mr. Shoemaker admits that in a case of apparent bodily transfer the significance of a person's memory claims could be established by considering the way in which he used memory sentences after the transfer had taken place. So at best this part of his argument could prove that in order to identify people we need to be able to make at least local applications of the criterion of bodily identity. They must be continuous in a bodily way for a period of time sufficient to enable us to establish that they are using memory sentences correctly. But in view of the somewhat strained and artificial character of the doubt in question, I am inclined to reject even this modest conclusion. At best it is a practical requirement: people must be sufficiently stable in a bodily way for me to be able to accumulate a large enough mass of apparent memory claims that are prima facie there to infer from the coherence of these apparent claims that they really are memory claims and not senseless noises.

The reliability of the memory claims of others is a more substantial issue. For, unlike significance, it is a feature of apparent memory claims that we commonly do have serious reason to doubt. It must be admitted, further, that if I have independent reasons for believing that Jones's body was physically present at an event that Jones now claims to remember, I have a piece of strong evidence in support of the correctness of his claim. It is not, of course, conclusive. Even if he were looking in the direction at the time, he might have been in a condition of day-dreaming inattentiveness. The question is, however: is it in any sense a necessary condition for the correctness of my acceptance of a man's present memory claim that I should be able, in principle, to discover that the very same body from which the claim under examination now emerges was actually present at the event now purportedly remembered? I cannot see that it is. To revert to the example of a radical psychophysical exchange between B and C. Suppose that from B's body memory claims emerge about a lot of what I have hitherto confidently taken to be C's experiences. I may have good reason to believe that C's body was present at the events apparently recalled. If the claims are very numerous and detailed, if they involve the recollection of things I didn't know B had seen although I can now establish that they were really present for C to observe, and if the emission of apparent C memories from B's body and vice versa keeps up for a fair period, it would be unreasonable not to conclude that the memory claims emerging from B's body were in fact correct, that they were the memory claims of C not of B, and that therefore the person with B's body was in fact not now B but C. Here again a measure of local bodily continuity seems required. I shall not say that C inhabits B's body at all unless he seems to do so in a fairly substantial way and over a fair period of time. But as long as the possibility of psychophysical exchange is established by some salient cases in which the requirement of local bodily continuity is satisfied I can reasonably conjecture that such exchange has taken place in other cases where the translocation of memory claims is pretty shortlived. At any rate it is only the necessity of local bodily continuity that is established, not the necessary association of a person with one particular body for the whole duration of either. Bodily continuity with a witness is a test of the reliability of someone's memory claims, and it is an important one, but it is not a logically indispensable one.

5. THE PROBLEM OF DISEMBODIMENT

Nothing that I have said so far has any direct bearing on the question whether the soul can exist in an entirely disembodied state. All I have tried to show is that there is no necessary connection between the soul as a series of mental states linked by character and memory and any particular continuing human body. The question now arises: must the soul be associated with some human body? The apparent intelligibility of my crude ghost story might seem to suggest that not even a body is required, let alone a human one. And the same point appears to be made by the intelligibility of stories in which trees, toadstools, pieces of furniture, and so on are endowed with personal characteristics. But a good deal of caution is needed here. In the first place, even where these personal characteristics are not associated with any sort of body in the physiological sense, they are associated with a body in the epistemological sense; in other words, it is an essential part of the story that the soul in question have physical manifestations. Only in our own case does it seem that strictly disembodied existence is conceivable, in the sense that we can conceive circumstances in which there would be some good reason to claim that a soul existed in a disembodied state. Now how tenuous and nonhuman could these physical manifestations be? To take a fairly mild example, discussed by Professor Malcolm, could we regard a tree as another person? He maintains with great firmness that we could not, on the rather flimsy ground that trees haven't got mouths and, therefore, could not be said to speak or communicate with us or make memory claims. But if a knothole in a tree trunk physically emitted sounds in the form of speech, why should we not call it a mouth? We may presume that ventriloquism, hidden record-players and microphones, dwarfs concealed in the foliage, and so forth have all been ruled out. If the remarks of the tree were coherent and appropriate to its situation and exhibited the type of continuity that the remarks of persons normally do exhibit, why shouldn't we regard the tree as a person? The point is that we might, by a serious conceptual effort, allow this in the case of one tree or even several trees or even a great many nonhuman physical things. But the sense of our attribution of personality to them would be logically parasitic on our attributions of personality to ordinary human bodies. It is from their utterances and behavior that we derive our concept of personality, and this concept would be applicable to nonhuman things only by more or less far-fetched analogy. That trees should be personal presupposes, then, the personality of human beings. The same considerations hold in the extreme case of absolutely minimal embodiment, as when a recurrent and localized voice of a recognizable tone is heard to make publicly audible remarks. The voice might give evidence of qualitative and positional continuity sufficient to treat it as an identifiable body, even if of an excessively diaphanous kind. The possibility of this procedure, however, is contingent on there being persons in the standard, humanly embodied sense to provide a clear basis for the acquisition of the concept that is being more or less speculatively applied to the voice.

Whatever the logic of the matter, it might be argued, the causal facts of the situation make the whole inquiry into the possibility of a soul's humanly or totally disembodied existence an entirely fantastic one. That people have the memories and characters that they do, that they have memories and characters at all, has as its causally necessary condition the relatively undisturbed persistence of a particular bit of physiological apparatus. One can admit this without concluding that the inquiry is altogether without practical point. For the bit of physiological apparatus in question is not the human body as a whole, but the brain. Certainly lavish changes in the noncerebral parts of the human body often affect the character and perhaps even to some extent the memories of the person whose body it is. But there is no strict relationship here. Now it is sometimes said that the last bit of the body to wear out is the brain, that the brain takes the first and lion's share of the body's nourishment, and that the brains of people who have starved to death are often found in perfectly good structural order. It is already possible to graft bits of one human body on to another, corneas, fingers, and even, I believe, legs. Might it not be possible to remove the brain from an otherwise worn-out human body and replace it either in a manufactured human body or in a cerebrally untenanted one? In this case we should have a causally conceivable analogue of reincarnation. If this were to become possible and if the resultant creatures appeared in a coherent way to exhibit the character and memories previously associated with the brain that had been fitted into them, we could say that the original person was still in existence even though only a relatively minute part of its original mass and volume was present in the new physical whole. Yet if strict bodily identity is a necessary condition of personal identity, such a description of the outcome would be ruled out as self-contradictory. I conclude, therefore, not only that a logically adequate concept of the soul is constructible but that the construction has some possible utility even in the light of our knowledge of the causal conditions of human life.

GEORGE I. MAVRODES

The Life Everlasting and the Bodily Criterion of Identity

"I believe in...the resurrection of the body and the life everlasting. Amen." With these words the Apostle's Creed comes to a close, and with them also it expresses, I think, an important element in the orthodox Christian faith. As a very minimum this element involves the claim that the lives of at least some human beings do not come to a permanent end with their bodily deaths here, but that these individuals will either continue their lives beyond the incident of death or else that they will resume their lives at some point in the future, and that this continued or resumed life will be everlasting. An additional element seems to be the claim that this continued or resumed life will be a bodily life, and that it involves the resurrection—presumably somehow or other a reconstitution—of the body which died here.

Naturally, one might think of critical questions to ask about this belief, such as that of what reason or justification might be given in favor of supposing that it is true, or that of how such an apparently difficult operation might be accomplished. I think that Christians have usually been inclined to answer the former of these questions by saying that one knows of such things primarily by the revelation of God. And they usually have not thought of much of interest to say about the second question beyond saying that the resurrection of the body and the life everlasting are gifts of God, who is presumably able to do such things. In this paper I do not intend to pursue these questions at all, and so I will say nothing either in support or in criticism of such answers.

I turn, instead, to a somewhat different question, one which some philosophers apparently think is somehow prior to the questions I have just mentioned. This is the question of what, if any, sense can be made out of the identification of the persons who live the life everlasting with persons who began their careers in this world and died here. Some philosophers not only think that this question is prior to the others I have just mentioned—they apparently think it is the only philosophical question about immortality and similar topics. John Passmore, for example, writes, "As for immortality, there have often been doubts about whether this is really a question for philosophy.

Reprinted by permission of the author and of the editor of NOÛS from Vol. XI, No. 1, (March 1977), pp. 27–39.

But insofar as it is, the question is whether it is possible to identify the being who is said to live after death with the living being by any of the ordinary means used in identification—that is, the means by which we determine whether we are both talking about the same person."[1]

Antony Flew asserts both the priority and the enormity of the difficulty involved in this question. He writes, "Any reconstitution doctrine is confronted with the question 'How is the reconstituted person on the last day to be identified as the original me, as opposed to a mere replica, an appropriately brilliant forgery?' There seems to be no satisfactory answer to this question, at least for a pure reconstitution theory. This question is, however, logically prior to all questions about the reasons, if any, that might be brought forward in support of such a doctrine.

"This decisive objection seems rarely to have been raised, and when it has been, its force has not usually been felt.... Notwithstanding the form of the original question, the difficulty is not one of 'How do you know?' but of 'What do you know?' The objection is that the reconstituted people could only be mere replicas of and surrogates for their earthly predecessors. Neither the appeal to the cognitive and executive resources of Omnipotence nor the appeal to the supposed special status of the person in question does anything at all to meet this contention."[2]

In a somewhat similar spirit, but with a different twist, Terence Penelhum argues that if there is a temporal gap between the death of a person and the appearance of an apparently resurrected person much like him, then it is open to us to *decide*, whichever way we want, whether to consider these to be just one person or two distinct persons. If I understand him correctly, he means to claim that, since ordinary bodily continuity has been broken, the claim that the new person is identical with the old one is neither true nor false *prior to our decision about how to speak of it*. And after our decision it will have whatever value our decision has ascribed to it. So he writes that in ordinary, this-worldly, cases of the identification of persons, even after comas, failures of memory, etc., "there are bodily facts which establish who it is. The absence of those facts, though perhaps...not a fatal barrier to identification on memory-claims alone, certainly renders it optional. With the gap between the death of the one body and the appearance of the resurrection-body all necessity for saying Smith's successor is Smith disappears, however possible it is. And it does not seem that Smith *need* concern himself with being his own successor unless that successor *has* to be identified with Smith. And without the continuity of the body, the identification does not *have* to be performed. The critical difference between a person's looking forward to his own resurrected future and his predicting the future existence of a being like himself

---

[1] John Passmore, "Philosophy," in *The Encyclopedia of Philosophy*, edited by Paul Edwards (New York: Macmillan Publishing Co. & The Free Press), Vol. 6, p. 223.

[2] Antony Flew, "Immortality," in *The Encyclopedia of Philosophy*, Vol. 4, p. 140.

seems to depend on a decision which can, in default of bodily continuance, be taken equally well one way or the other."[3]

If we were to put the objection we are here considering in its bluntest form it would come to something like this: We can know from the outset, and before we get into questions and claims about revelation, omnipotence, and the like, that the beliefs to which I referred in the first paragraph of this paper are false. Not even the omnipotence of God can bring about the state of affairs envisioned in those beliefs. For that state of affairs is conceptually impossible. That is a blunt statement of the position but it is perhaps not exactly accurate. More accurately, this position holds that there is a conceptual incompatibility between the state of affairs envisioned in his belief and some empirical facts about this world, facts which we know to be plainly true. While therefore it is abstractly possible that an omnipotent God could actualize the state of affairs in question, it is not possible for him to do so *given what actually happens in the world*. And it may also be held that it is now too late for God to alter the course of this world in such a way as to make possible the life of the world to come, at least in a way which would be importantly relevant to these Christian beliefs.

The conceptual incompatibility alleged here is supposed to be generated by a criterion of personal identity. As I understand it, the person who urges such an incompatibility need not deny that there may be a "world to come," perhaps a better world than this one, nor that there may be human beings in it living an everlasting life. What he denies is that any of those fortunate people could be identical with any person who has lived and died in this world, or at least with any person who has died in this world some considerable time ago. This sort of objector—I will call him the Criterial Sceptic—holds that in order for the person in the world to come to be identical with a person who has died in this world they, or he, would have to satisfy a criterion of identity. They, or he, would have to have the very same body. But we know perfectly well that the bodies of many of those to whom this doctrine is supposed to apply have already decayed and passed out of existence. So no person in the world to come could have *that* body. And so no person in the world to come could be identical with that long-dead resident of this world.

At this juncture we might formulate the relevant aspect of the bodily criterion of identity as follows:

(1) For any x and y, x is the same person (human being) as y only if x has the same body as y.

More accurately, we should say that either (1) is the bodily criterion, or that it is a (conjunctive) part of that criterion, or that the criterion entails (1). The

---

[3]Terence Penelhum, *Survival and Disembodied Existence* (New York: Humanities Press, 1970), pp. 96–7.

latter claim is the minimum which is acceptable for this position. For unless the criterion at least entails (1) it will not serve to rule out the possibility that some person who lived and died in this world is identical with a person who will live again in the world to come.

The objection which is based on this criterion, if it holds good, cuts to the heart of the beliefs in question. For the Christian does not merely hold that there shall be people living a blessed life in the world to come, nor even that such people will in some way or other be very much like some people who have lived here. He believes that it is these very people themselves, the people who have begun their careers in this world and here suffered the agony of death, who will share that blessed life. And when he believes in or hopes for that destiny for himself it is indeed *for himself*. He hopes that it shall be *he*, and not another, who will "attain unto the resurrection of the dead." If, therefore, the Criterial Sceptic should be right, then a major element in what the last sentence of the creed expresses will be false, and the Christian faith will be severely impoverished. In this paper I want to examine some aspects of the position which the Criterial Sceptic holds.

Let us begin by considering a state of affairs which only partially represents what the Christian believes, and which seems to differ from that belief in one, perhaps important, respect. This state of affairs is described as

(2) At a certain time there exists in this world a person, x, who has a body, A, and the life of this person extends through time t_1. At some future time, perhaps in the world to come, there exists a person, y, with a body, B, and the life of this person extends through t_2. *And A is in no sense the same body as B.*

And suppose too that

(3) It is claimed that x is the same person as y.

Now, the claim referred to in (3) may be puzzling to some of us. Perhaps this puzzlement will be expressed in questions to the one who makes the claim, questions such as "What do you mean by claiming that y is the same person as x?" or "What is it that makes y the same person as x?" But the import of such questions may also be unclear and puzzling. The one who hears them may be at a loss to understand just what it is the questioner wants. And for that reason, or perhaps for some other, he may be at a loss as to just how to respond. So he may reply essentially by repeating the original claim, perhaps with extra emphasis. "They just *are* the same person, that's all! Or to put it another way, you've been calling that person in the world to come by the name 'y.' But it's old x, after all, and you shouldn't let the new name confuse you." Such a reply may seem singularly unilluminating, simply restating, as it does, the original claim. Perhaps we shall nevertheless have to make do with some such reply in the end. But at any rate we are not at that end yet.

A person, I said, might be at a loss as to how to explain his identity claim in this case. But perhaps not everyone will be at such a loss. Someone with philosophical inclinations might, for example, think of replying something like this. "When I say that y is identical with x I mean something which in conjunction with any true statement which predicates a given property of x will entail a true statement predicating that property of y. So, for example, if it is true that x was born in Biloxi, Mississippi, then my claim, in conjunction with that fact, entails that y was born in Biloxi, Mississippi." And perhaps this reply goes further than the previous one.

This reply probably reminds us of what is sometimes called "Leibniz' Law," and it is intended to do so. A first stab at formulating that law might go like this:

(4) For any entities x and y, x is identical with y IFF x has every property which y has, and vice versa.

As it stands, this has some difficulties. First, it may suggest, in conjunction with certain empirical facts, that I had no youth. For one of my properties is that of being gray-haired. But the only plausible candidate for Mavrodes-as-youth did not have gray hair. So perhaps this formulation entails that I am not identical with that candidate. This difficulty can be remedied. While it is true of me now that I have gray hair it is also true of me now that in 1950 I had brown hair. It is also true of the candidate for Mavrodes-as-youth that he had brown hair in 1950, and there is no empirical reason to think that it is not true of him that he has gray hair now. Probably if we want a version of Leibniz' Law which applies to diachronic, as well as synchronic, identity then we need to formulate it in terms of properties such as these.

Some properties are such that even if a given thing has them at some time it need not have them at every time at which it has any property at all (i.e., at any time at which it exists). Having brown hair is apparently such a property. Let us call these the "time-variable properties." There are other properties such that if an entity has one of them at some time then it has that property at all times that it has any properties at all. Call these the "time-stable properties." Now we can propound the thesis that to every property which a thing has at an arbitrarily chosen time, t, there corresponds a time-stable property which it has at all times. For take any arbitrarily chosen property, P, which the thing has at t. If P is time-stable then it is itself the corresponding property, and the thing will have P whenever it exists. If P is time-variable, then *having P at t* is the corresponding time-stable property which the thing will have as long as it exists. And if we want a version of Leibniz' Law which will apply to diachronic identity then we should formulate it in terms of time-stable properties only.

A second difficulty is that Leibniz' Law may not apply to what we may call "intensional" properties. Consider, for example, the property of *being thought by Porphyry to be a different heavenly body from the Morning Star.* Now, it seems possible that Porphyry thought that the Evening Star was a different heavenly body from the Morning Star. But it seems very unlikely that he thought that the Morning Star was a different heavenly body from the Morning Star. In conjunction with the stated version of Leibniz' Law this may suggest that the Morning Star is not identical with the Evening Star. I am not sure how this should be handled. Perhaps there is some correct analysis of intensional predicates which will show that the two statements about Porphyry's beliefs do necessarily have the same truth value after all. If so, well and good. If not, then I suppose that Leibniz' Law should be restricted to cover non-intensional predicates only. Since only non-intensional predicates function in the remainder of my discussion that is the procedure I adopt here.

The third difficulty grows out of a suggestion by Peter Geach.[4] He holds, if I understand him correctly, that expressions of the form "x and y are the same entity," "x is the same thing as y," etc., are ill-formed. The corresponding well-formed expression would be "x is the same s as y," where "s" is a variable ranging over sorts or kinds. So we should say that Samuel Clemens is the same *person* as Mark Twain, that the Evening Star is the same *planet* as the Morning Star, and so on. I do not know whether Geach's view of this matter is correct, or, if it is, just how Leibniz' Law might be amended to take it into account. Assuming that his view is correct, however, the following conjecture seems to me to have a good bit of plausibility. We begin by observing that to any property which a thing has, and for any sort to which that thing belongs, there corresponds a property which that thing has and which can be possessed only by a thing of that sort. For consider any arbitrarily chosen property, P, which a certain thing has, and any arbitrarily chosen sort, S, to which that thing belongs. Then that thing will have the property of *being an S which has P*, and this is a property which only S can have. Call such properties in general "sort-bound properties," and call properties which are bound to a given sort, S, "S-bound properties." Then Leibniz' Law can be reformulated in terms of being the same thing-of-a-sort and in terms of sort-bound properties.

Taking these difficulties and possible difficulties into account, a more cautious formulation of Leibniz' Law might be

(5) For any x, y, and z, where x and y are individuals and z is a sort or kind, x is the same z as y IFF x has every time-stable, non-intensional, z-bound property which y has, and vice versa.

And now a person who is inclined to accept the claim in (3) may say that x and y satisfy the right hand part of (5) (where the sort in question is

---

[4]Peter Geach, "Identity," *The Review of Metaphysics* 21 (1967): 3–12.

that of human being), and that is the explanation which he can give of the claim that they are the same person. I will call a person who responds in this way a "Leibnizian Believer."

The Criterial Sceptic, however, will deny that x and y can be the same person, and so he will deny the claim in (3). He denies this because he holds that the criterion for any x and y being the same human person is that they have the same body. But in description (2) it is stipulated that the bodies A and B, which belong to x and y, are in no sense the same body. (This, of course, is the respect in which this situation differs from the one which the Christian expects to be actualized.) Because their bodies are not identical, says the Criterial Sceptic, the x and y referred to in (2) cannot be the same person.

It may be important to notice here that the Leibnizian Believer can maintain that in a certain sense x and y do have the same body after all, despite the explicit disclaimer in (2). In fact, his Leibnizian position requires him to claim that x and y have the same *two* bodies. He must hold that since it is true of x that he has body A at t_1 then it must also be true of y that he has body A at t_1. And in the same way it must be true of both x and y that he has body B at t_2. What the Leibnizian Believer does here, of course, is to admit—indeed, to insist—that x and y have the same body at *any given time*. This is just one of the many time-stable properties which they share. The Criterial Sceptic must also insist that if x and y are to be identical then they must have the same body at any given time. But he cannot be satisfied to leave it at that, for, if he were so satisfied, he would have no reason to reject the claim put forward in (3). He must insist that if x and y are to be identical then if x has a certain body at some time then y has that very same body at every time at which y exists. And that is a requirement which the situation described in (2) does not satisfy.

What options do these disputants have? Assuming that they restrict themselves to the situation envisioned in (2), the Leibnizian Believer who accepts the claim in (3) seems compelled to reject the bodily Criterion of identity. The Criterial Sceptic, on the other hand, seems to have two options as he rejects the claim in (3). He might just reject Leibniz' Law and be done with it. But he could also do something else. He could accept Leibniz' Law and then go on to point out that, on his view, the property of *having body* α is a time-stable property (or, at least, that *being a human being who has body* α is a time-stable property). For if this is so then it is not hard to show that there is a time-stable property which either x or y must have if they are to be identical but which they cannot both have if the description in (2) is to be satisfied. So, on this interpretation, even Leibniz' Law will show that x and y are not identical. So perhaps the Criterial Sceptic has the more flexible position.

But perhaps, too, we were too hasty in thinking that the Leibnizian Believer has only one option. Inspired by the versatility of his opponent why should he not say that he, in his turn, can accept the bodily criterion of identity. Only, he will insist, the phrase "has the same body" must be interpreted to mean "has the same body at any particular time t." Interpreted in that way the bodily criterion of identity is perfectly compatible with the x and y described in (2) being the same person. If the Criterial Sceptic is to reject the claim in (3) then he must reject this interpretation of his criterion. He must insist that (1) be read as

(6) For any x and y, x is the same person as y only if x has, at every time at which x exists, the same body which y has at any time at which y exists.

And so the Criterial Sceptic needs a sense of "same" (in the phrase "same body") which is diachronic.

So much, then, for the discussion of the situation envisioned in (2). Many Christians, at least, will think that it is not a crucial case nor the strongest case. For they profess to believe in the resurrection of the body, the body which ran through its career in this world and then died, and not merely in the production of a new body for the world to come. So they believe that if y, in the world to come, is identical with some this-worldly x, then the body which y has in that world to come *is*, in some sense, the same body which x had in this world. Does this improve their position vis à vis the Criterial Sceptic?

Such a sceptic, I think, is likely to say that the believer's position is not thereby strengthened, at least not with respect to many of those who are supposed to share in the life everlasting. For as a matter of fact they have already died, long ago, and their bodies have already decayed and totally ceased from existing. And so it is not possible that there should be a body, now or in the future, which is identical with the one they had during their earthly career. But why should this last consequence be thought to follow upon the former undisputed facts? Why should it be impossible that a certain body should perish, decay, and cease from existing, and then that later on that same body should be resurrected and take its place again in the realm of existing things?

The Sceptic will not be embarrassed by these questions, and will take them as a welcome opportunity to clarify further his sense of the diachronic identity of bodies. He has a criterion for such identity. The relevant part of it is as follows:

(7) For any x and y, x is the same body as y only if x is spatio-temporally continuous with y.

But if a body has decayed and ceased to exist by t_1 then there is a time immediately after t_1 during which it does not exist. If it were to be resurrected and brought again into existence at some later time, t_2, then it would suffer from a temporal gap between t_1 and t_2. The body which existed at t_2 would not be spatio-temporally continuous with the body which existed before t_1. And so, according to (7), they could not be identical.

Now, a Leibnizian Believer who accepts the resurrection of the body might simply challenge (7) at this point. And perhaps that is what he should do in the end. At this point, however, it might be useful to accept (7) provisionally, and to request some further account of it. After all, if there are criteria for identity for persons and for bodies, should there not also be a criterion for spatio-temporal continuity? And what is spatio-temporal continuity anyway? Is not this a technical notion much less familiar to us than the notions of person and body? If, as the sceptic seems to suggest, a whole host of believers have been mistaken and confused over what these familiar notions allow as possible should we not be even more wary of supposing that we can handle correctly this technical and unfamiliar notion? What more can be said to guide us?

Here again the sceptic will probably not be embarrassed. Whether it is a criterion or not, he will offer us a further explanation of what he is getting at. Informally, the idea seems to be something like this: Body x occupies some set of spatio-temporal points, and body y similarly occupies a set of points. These sets of points may be isolated from each other in the following sense. It may be that every continuous path through space and time from any point in the first set to any point in the second set passes through some spatio-temporal location in which there is no body at all. And if the locations of x and y are isolated from each other in that way then x and y are not spatio-temporally continuous. I put this here as only a necessary condition for spatio-temporal continuity, and not a sufficient condition. For there may possibly be other necessary conditions. It may, for example, be necessary that the bodies which "bridge the gap" between x and y be of a certain sort if x and y are to be continuous. But those further conditions, if there are any, are irrelevant to my argument here.

Perhaps we could state this necessary condition more formally as follows:

(8) For any x and y, if x and y are bodies, then x is spatio-temporally continuous with y if and only if there is a spatio-temporal point, ST_1, at which x is located, and a point, ST_2, at which y is located, and there is a compact series of points including ST_1 and ST_2 such that there is a body located at every point in this series.

Well, perhaps so. This explanation does not seem to have escaped from technicality, but maybe if we work through it carefully it will be clear enough. Except for one point. Or perhaps even that is clear enough. At any rate it is this. The expression "ST_1" appears twice in the formula above. What is the relation between the point referred to in its first occurrence and that referred to in its second occurrence?

But of course the answer is obvious, isn't it? These two uses of "ST_1" refer to the same point. Of course they do. But this answer, though obvious, is crucial. For if we allow these two uses to refer to two different points then

(8) will not rule out the claim that the resurrection body is spatio-temporally continuous with some long perished earthly body. So it would seem that the sceptic cannot afford to abandon this answer. And this reply invites us to ask about the criterion of identity for spatio-temporal points. This question bodes more embarrassment for the sceptic than did the earlier ones.

It may be important to notice here that we cannot avoid this question merely by stylistic changes which eliminate the word "same" from the answer, or which eliminate the double use of "ST_1" in (8). I suppose that we can make such changes. (We can, for that matter, restate the Christian hope of enjoying the life everlasting so that it does not require the word "same.") These words are not crucial, but the fact which lies behind them is. If (8) is to be applicable to the diachronic identity of bodies then we must say two things about a single point. We must state its relation to the body in question and we must state its relation to another point. And in doing this we must understand that we are saying these two things about the very same point. And so, it would seem, we must understand what it is for something to be "the very same point."

Here, I think, the line of inquiry which we have been following begins to draw to a close. For it is hard to think of a criterion of identity for spatio-temporal points which will be attractive to the Criterial Sceptic. What seem to be the options? Well, I suppose that a feeble step forward might be taken by saying that x and y are the same point if and only if they have the same spatio-temporal coordinates. But of course the question will be asked again, and the sceptic will be wedged even more tightly in the constricting corner. Or the sceptic may simply opt for a Leibnizian account of sameness here. But surely the believer will seize on this to justify his reliance on Leibniz' Law from the beginning. If, after all, even the sceptic comes to nothing better than this is in the end....

On the other hand, the sceptic may here formulate a criterion which does not depend on bodies, times and spaces, but which makes use of some other notions. I do not know what such a criterion might be. But any such attempt seems likely to give aid and comfort to the believer. For if there is such a criterion for points, and if the identity of bodies depends in the end upon such a criterion, then why should there not also be a non-spatio-temporal, non-physical criterion for persons too, thus avoiding all the difficulties which the Criterial Sceptic has raised? Or, finally, the sceptic may simply say that no criterion is available here, nor is any needed. Spatio-temporal points, he might say, are "criterially primitive." We understand what is meant by "same" here without the use of criteria. Point x just is the same as y, and there is no more to be said about it. I suspect that this is correct. But correct or not, will it not almost surely incite the believer to reply that we understand "same person" at least as well as "same spatio-temporal point"? And if we understand the one without criteria then why should we not also understand the other in the same way? It looks suddenly as though whatever the sceptic says opens up a plausible position for the believer to occupy.

This concludes the body of my argument. In some sense, I have not solved the problem posed by people such as Flew, Passmore, and Penelhum. I have not shown that the resurrection body satisfies the continuity criterion for identity with the this-worldly body, and hence I have not shown that the resurrected person satisfies the bodily identity criterion for identity with some pre-mortem person. What I have argued, essentially, is that the problem cannot have the gravity which philosophers such as these are inclined to assign to it. Either it must be much more serious, infecting all of our ordinary judgments about the identity of this-worldly persons with the incoherence or arbitrariness which they ascribe to resurrection judgments, or it is less serious, having, in all likelihood, the same sort of solution which validates our ordinary judgments. In the first case the Christian's faith, though perhaps rather bad off, would not be worse off than the more prosaic faith of his non-religious colleagues, and he and they could survey the dismal logical prospects together. In the second case, too, the Christian's faith would seem to be no worse off than that of his secular counterparts. But in the second case the prospects, or some of them at least, are more cheerful. The believer might even invite his counterpart to consider some of them with him. But who knows whether that is philosophy?

THOMAS NAGEL

Death

If death is the unequivocal and permanent end of our existence, the question arises whether it is a bad thing to die.

There is conspicuous disagreement about the matter: some people think death is dreadful; others have no objection to death *per se*, though they hope their own will be neither premature nor painful. Those in the former category tend to think those in the latter are blind to the obvious, while the latter suppose the former to be prey to some sort of confusion. On the one hand it can be said that life is all we have and the loss of it is the greatest loss we can sustain. On the other hand it may be objected that death deprives this supposed loss of its subject, and that if we realize that death is not an unimaginable condition of the persisting person, but a mere blank, we will see that it can have no value whatever, positive or negative.

Reprinted by permission of the author and the editor of NOÛS, from Vol. IV, No. 1, (February 1970), pp. 73–80.

Since I want to leave aside the question whether we are, or might be, immortal in some form, I shall simply use the word 'death' and its cognates in this discussion to mean *permanent* death, unsupplemented by any form of conscious survival. I want to ask whether death is in itself an evil; and how great an evil, and of what kind, it might be. The question should be of interest even to those who believe in some form of immortality, for one's attitude toward immortality must depend in part on one's attitude toward death.

If death is an evil at all, it cannot be because of its positive features, but only because of what it deprives us of. I shall try to deal with the difficulties surrounding the natural view that death is an evil because it brings to an end all the goods that life contains. We need not give an account of these goods here, except to observe that some of them, like perception, desire, activity, and thought, are so general as to be constitutive of human life. They are widely regarded as formidable benefits in themselves, despite the fact that they are conditions of misery as well as of happiness, and that a sufficient quantity of more particular evils can perhaps outweigh them. That is what is meant, I think, by the allegation that it is good simply to be alive, even if one is undergoing terrible experiences. The situation is roughly this: There are elements which, if added to one's experience, make life better; there are other elements which, if added to one's experience, make life worse. But what remains when these are set aside is not merely *neutral:* it is emphatically positive. Therefore life is worth living even when the bad elements of experience are plentiful, and the good ones too meager to outweigh the bad ones on their own. The additional positive weight is supplied by experience itself, rather than by any of its contents.

I shall not discuss the value that one person's life or death may have for others, or its objective value, but only the value it has for the person who is its subject. That seems to me the primary case, and the case which presents the greatest difficulties. Let me add only two observations. First, the value of life and its contents does not attach to mere organic survival: almost everyone would be indifferent (other things equal) between immediate death and immediate coma followed by death twenty years later without reawakening. And second, like most goods, this can be multiplied by time: more is better than less. The added quantities need not be temporally continuous (though continuity has its social advantages). People are attracted to the possibility of long-term suspended animation or freezing, followed by the resumption of conscious life, because they can regard it from within simply as a *continuation* of their present life. If these techniques are ever perfected, what from outside appeared as a dormant interval of three hundred years could be experienced by the subject as nothing more than a sharp discontinuity in the character of his experiences. I do not deny, of course, that this has its own disadvantages. Family and friends may have died in the meantime; the language may have changed; the comforts of social, geographical, and cultural familiarity would be lacking. Nevertheless these inconveniences would not obliterate the basic advantage of continued, though discontinuous, existence.

If we turn from what is good about life to what is bad about death, the case is completely different. Essentially, though there may be problems about their specification, what we find desirable in life are certain states, conditions, or types of activity. It is *being* alive, *doing* certain things, having certain experiences, that we consider good. But if death is an evil, it is the *loss of life*, rather than the state of being dead, or nonexistent, or unconscious, that is objectionable.[1] This asymmetry is important. If it is good to be alive, that advantage can be attributed to a person at each point of his life. It is a good of which Bach had more than Schubert, simply because he lived longer. Death, however, is not an evil of which Shakespeare has so far received a larger portion than Proust. If death is a disadvantage, it is not easy to say when a man suffers it.

There are two other indications that we do not object to death merely because it involves long periods of nonexistence. First, as has been mentioned, most of us would not regard the *temporary* suspension of life, even for substantial intervals, as in itself a misfortune. If it ever happens that people can be frozen without reduction of the conscious lifespan, it will be inappropriate to pity those who are temporarily out of circulation. Second, none of us existed before we were born (or conceived), but few regard that as a misfortune. I shall have more to say about this later.

The point that death is not regarded as an unfortunate *state* enables us to refute a curious but very common suggestion about the origin of the fear of death. It is often said that those who object to death have made the mistake of trying to imagine what it is like to *be* dead. It is alleged that the failure to realize that this task is logically impossible (for the banal reason that there is nothing to imagine) leads to the conviction that death is a mysterious and therefore terrifying prospective *state*. But this diagnosis is evidently false, for it is just as impossible to imagine being totally unconscious as to imagine being dead (though it is easy enough to imagine oneself, from the outside, in either of those conditions). Yet people who are averse to death are not usually averse to unconsciousness (so long as it does not entail a substantial cut in the total duration of waking life).

If we are to make sense of the view that to die is bad, it must be on the ground that life is a good and death is the corresponding deprivation or loss, bad not because of any positive features but because of the desirability of what it removes. We must now turn to the serious difficulties which this hypothesis raises, difficulties about loss and privation in general, and about death in particular.

---

[1]It is sometimes suggested that what we really mind is the process of *dying*. But I should not really object to dying if it were not followed by death.

Essentially, there are three types of problem. First, doubt may be raised whether *anything* can be bad for a man without being positively unpleasant to him: specifically, it may be doubted that there are any evils which consist merely in the deprivation or absence of possible goods, and which do not depend on someone's *minding* that deprivation. Second, there are special difficulties, in the case of death, about how the supposed misfortune is to be assigned to a subject at all. There is doubt both as to *who* its subject is, and as to *when* he undergoes it. So long as a person exists, he has not yet died, and once he has died, he no longer exists; so there seems to be no time when death, if it is a misfortune, can be ascribed to its unfortunate subject. The third type of difficulty concerns the asymmetry, mentioned above, between our attitudes to posthumous and prenatal nonexistence. How can the former be bad if the latter is not?

It should be recognized that if these are valid objections to counting death as an evil, they will apply to many other supposed evils as well. The first type of objection is expressed in general form by the common remark that what you don't know can't hurt you. It means that even if a man is betrayed by his friends, ridiculed behind his back, and despised by people who treat him politely to his face, none of it can be counted as a misfortune for him so long as he does not suffer as a result. It means that a man is not injured if his wishes are ignored by the executor of his will, or if, after his death, the belief becomes current that all the literary works on which his fame rests were really written by his brother, who died in Mexico at the age of 28. It seems to me worth asking what assumptions about good and evil lead to these drastic restrictions.

All the questions have something to do with time. There certainly are goods and evils of a simple kind (including some pleasures and pains) which a person possesses at a given time simply in virtue of his condition at that time. But this is not true of all the things we regard as good or bad for a man. Often we need to know his history to tell whether something is a misfortune or not; this applies to ills like deterioration, deprivation, and damage. Sometimes his experiential *state* is relatively unimportant—as in the case of a man who wastes his life in the cheerful pursuit of a method of communicating with asparagus plants. Someone who holds that all goods and evils must be temporally assignable states of the person may of course try to bring difficult cases into line by pointing to the pleasure or pain that more complicated goods and evils cause. Loss, betrayal, deception, and ridicule are on this view bad because people suffer when they learn of them. But it should be asked how our ideas of human value would have to be constituted to accommodate these cases directly instead. One advantage of such an account might be that it would enable us to explain *why* the discovery of these misfortunes causes suffering—in a way that makes it reasonable. For the natural view is that the discovery of betrayal makes us unhappy because it is bad to be betrayed—not that betrayal is bad because its discovery makes us unhappy.

It therefore seems to me worth exploring the position that most good and ill fortune has as its subject a person identified by his history and his possibilities, rather than merely by his categorical state of the moment—and that while this subject can be exactly located in a sequence of places and times, the same is not necessarily true of the goods and ills that befall him.[2]

These ideas can be illustrated by an example of deprivation whose severity approaches that of death. Suppose an intelligent person receives a brain injury that reduces him to the mental condition of a contented infant, and that such desires as remain to him can be satisfied by a custodian, so that he is free from care. Such a development would be widely regarded as a severe misfortune, not only for his friends and relations, or for society, but also, and primarily, for the person himself. This does not mean that a contented infant is unfortunate. The intelligent adult who has been *reduced* to this condition is the subject of the misfortune. He is the one we pity, though of course he does not mind his condition—there is some doubt, in fact, whether he can be said to exist any longer.

The view that such a man has suffered a misfortune is open to the same objections which have been raised in regard to death. He does not mind his condition. It is in fact the same condition he was in at the age of three months, except that he is bigger. If we did not pity him then, why pity him now; in any case, who is there to pity? The intelligent adult has disappeared, and for a creature like the one before us, happiness consists in a full stomach and a dry diaper.

If these objections are invalid, it must be because they rest on a mistaken assumption about the temporal relation between the subject of a misfortune and the circumstances which constitute it. If, instead of concentrating exclusively on the oversized baby before us, we consider the person he was, and the person he *could* be now, then his reduction to this state and the cancellation of his natural adult development constitute a perfectly intelligible catastrophe.

This case should convince us that it is arbitrary to restrict the goods and evils that can befall a man to nonrelational properties ascribable to him at particular times. As it stands, that restriction excludes not only such cases of gross degeneration, but also a good deal of what is important about success and failure, and other features of a life that have the character of processes. I believe we can go further, however. There are goods and evils which are irreducibly relational; they are features of the relations between a person, with spatial and temporal boundaries of the usual sort, and circumstances which may not coincide with him either in space or in time. A man's life includes much that does not take place within the boundaries of his body

---

[2]It is certainly not true in general of the things that can be said of him. For example, Abraham Lincoln was taller than Louis XIV. But when?

and his mind, and what happens to him can include much that does not take place within the boundaries of his life. These boundaries are commonly crossed by the misfortunes of being deceived, or despised, or betrayed. (If this is correct, there is a simple account of what is wrong with breaking a deathbed promise. It is an injury to the dead man. For certain purposes it is possible to regard time as just another type of distance.) The case of mental degeneration shows us an evil that depends on a contrast between the reality and the possible alternatives. A man is the subject of good and evil as much because he has hopes which may or may not be fulfilled, or possibilities which may or may not be realized, as because of his capacity to suffer and enjoy. If death is an evil, it must be accounted for in these terms, and the impossibility of locating it within life should not trouble us.

When a man dies we are left with his corpse, and while a corpse can suffer the kind of mishap that may occur to an article of furniture, it is not a suitable object for pity. The man, however, is. He has lost his life, and if he had not died, he would have continued to live it, and to possess whatever good there is in living. If we apply to death the account suggested for the case of dementia, we shall say that although the spatial and temporal locations of the individual who suffered the loss are clear enough, the misfortune itself cannot be so easily located. One must be content just to state that his life is over and there will never be any more of it. That *fact*, rather than his past or present condition, constitutes his misfortune, if it is one. Nevertheless if there is a loss, someone must suffer it, and *he* must have existence and specific spatial and temporal location even if the loss itself does not. The fact that Beethoven had no children may have been a cause of regret to him, or a sad thing for the world, but it cannot be described as a misfortune for the children that he never had. All of us, I believe, are fortunate to have been born. But unless good and ill can be assigned to an embryo, or even to an unconnected pair of gametes, it cannot be said that not to be born is a misfortune. (That is a factor to be considered in deciding whether abortion and contraception are akin to murder.)

This approach also provides a solution to the problem of temporal asymmetry, pointed out by Lucretius. He observed that no one finds it disturbing to contemplate the eternity preceding his own birth, and he took this to show that it must be irrational to fear death, since death is simply the mirror image of the prior abyss. That is not true, however, and the difference between the two explains why it is reasonable to regard them differently. It is true that both the time before a man's birth and the time after his death are times when he does not exist. But the time after his death is time of which his death deprives him. It is time in which, had he not died then, he would be alive. Therefore any death entails the loss of *some* life that its victim would have led had he not died at that or any earlier point. We know perfectly well what it would be for him to have had it instead of losing it, and there is no difficulty in identifying the loser.

But we cannot say that the time prior to a man's birth is time in which he would have lived had he been born not then but earlier. For aside from the brief margin permitted by premature labor, he *could* not have been born earlier: anyone born substantially earlier than he was would have been someone else. Therefore the time prior to his birth is not time in which his subsequent birth prevents him from living. His birth, when it occurs, does not entail the loss to him of any life whatever.

The direction of time is crucial in assigning possibilities to people or other individuals. Distinct possible lives of a single person can diverge from a common beginning, but they cannot converge to a common conclusion from diverse beginnings. (The latter would represent not a set of different possible lives of one individual, but a set of distinct possible individuals, whose lives have identical conclusions.) Given an identifiable individual, countless possibilities for his continued existence are imaginable, and we can clearly conceive of what it would be for him to go on existing indefinitely. However inevitable it is that this will not come about, its possibility is still that of the continuation of a good for him, if life is the good we take it to be.[3]

We are left, therefore, with the question whether the nonrealization of this possibility is in every case a misfortune, or whether it depends on what can naturally be hoped for. This seems to me the most serious difficulty with the view that death is always an evil. Even if we can dispose of the objections against admitting misfortune that is not experienced, or cannot be assigned to a definite time in the person's life, we still have to set some limits on *how* possible a possibility must be for its nonrealization to be a misfortune (or

---

[3] I confess to being troubled by the above argument, on the ground that it is too sophisticated to explain the simple difference between our attitudes to prenatal and posthumous nonexistence. For this reason I suspect that something essential is omitted from the account of the badness of death by an analysis which treats it as a deprivation of possibilities. My suspicion is supported by the following suggestion of Robert Nozick. We could imagine discovering that people developed from individual spores that had existed indefinitely far in advance of their birth. In this fantasy, birth never occurs naturally more than a hundred years before the permanent end of the spore's existence. But then we discover a way to trigger the premature hatching of these spores, and people are born who have thousands of years of active life before them. Given such a situation, it would be possible to imagine *oneself* having come into existence thousands of years previously. If we put aside the question whether this would really be the same person, even given the identity of the spore, then the consequence appears to be that a person's birth at a given time *could* deprive him of many earlier years of possible life. Now while it would be cause for regret that one had been deprived of all those possible years of life by being born too late, the feeling would differ from that which many people have about death. I conclude that something about the future *prospect* of permanent nothingness is not captured by the analysis in terms of denied possibilities. If so, then Lucretius' argument still awaits an answer. I suspect that it requires a general treatment of the difference between past and future in our attitudes toward our own lives. Our attitudes toward past and future pain are very different, for example. Derek Parfit's unpublished writings on this topic have revealed its difficulty to me.

good fortune, should the possibility be a bad one). The death of Keats at 24 is generally regarded as tragic; that of Tolstoy at 82 is not. Although they will both be dead for ever, Keats' death deprived him of many years of life which were allowed to Tolstoy; so in a clear sense Keats' loss was greater (though not in the sense standardly employed in mathematical comparison between infinite quantities). However, this does not prove that Tolstoy's loss was insignificant. Perhaps we record an objection only to evils which are gratuitously added to the inevitable; the fact that it is worse to die at 24 than at 82 does not imply that it is not a terrible thing to die at 82, or even at 806. The question is whether we can regard as a misfortune any limitation, like mortality, that is normal to the species. Blindness or near-blindness is not a misfortune for a mole, nor would it be for a man, if that were the natural condition of the human race.

The trouble is that life familiarizes us with the goods of which death deprives us. We are already able to appreciate them, as a mole is not able to appreciate vision. If we put aside doubts about their status as goods and grant that their quantity is in part a function of their duration, the question remains whether death, no matter when it occurs, can be said to deprive its victim of what is in the relevant sense a possible continuation of life.

The situation is an ambiguous one. Observed from without, human beings obviously have a natural lifespan and cannot live much longer than a hundred years. A man's sense of his own experience, on the other hand, does not embody this idea of a natural limit. His existence defines for him an essentially open-ended possible future, containing the usual mixture of goods and evils that he has found so tolerable in the past. Having been gratuitously introduced to the world by a collection of natural, historical, and social accidents, he finds himself the subject of a *life*, with an indeterminate and not essentially limited future. Viewed in this way, death, no matter how inevitable, is an abrupt cancellation of indefinitely extensive possible goods. Normality seems to have nothing to do with it, for the fact that we will all inevitably die in a few score years cannot by itself imply that it would not be good to live longer. Suppose that we were all inevitably going to die in *agony*—physical agony lasting six months. Would inevitability make *that* prospect any less unpleasant? And why should it be different for a deprivation? If the normal lifespan were a thousand years, death at 80 would be a tragedy. As things are, it may just be a more widespread tragedy. If there is no limit to the amount of life that it would be good to have, then it may be that a bad end is in store for us all.

BERNARD WILLIAMS

The Makropulos Case: Reflections on the Tedium of Immortality

This essay started life as a lecture in a series 'on the immortality of the soul or kindred spiritual subject'.[1] My kindred spiritual subject is, one might say, the mortality of the soul. Those among previous lecturers who were philosophers tended, I think, to discuss the question whether we are immortal; that is not my subject, but rather what a good thing it is that we are not. Immortality, or a state without death, would be meaningless, I shall suggest; so, in a sense, death gives the meaning of life. That does not mean that we should not fear death (whatever force that injunction might be taken to have, anyway). Indeed, there are several very different ways in which it could be true at once that death gave the meaning to life and that death was, other things being equal, something to be feared. Some existentialists, for instance, seem to have said that death was what gave meaning to life, if anything did, just because it was the fear of death that gave meaning to life; I shall not follow them. I shall rather pursue the idea that from facts about human desire and happiness and what a human life is, it follows both that immortality would be, where conceivable at all, intolerable, and that (other things being equal) death is reasonably regarded as an evil. Considering whether death can reasonably be regarded as an evil is in fact as near as I shall get to considering whether it should be feared: they are not quite the same question.

My title is that, as it is usually translated into English, of a play by Karel Čapek which was made into an opera by Janaček and which tells of a woman called Elina Makropulos, *alias* Emilia Marty, *alias* Ellian Macgregor, alias a number of other things with the initials 'EM', on whom her father, the Court physician to a sixteenth-century Emperor, tried out an elixir of life. At the time of the action she is aged 342. Her unending life has come to a state of

---

From "The Makropulos Case: Reflections on the Tedium of Immortality," in *Problems of the Self*, pp. 82–100 by Bernard Williams. Reprinted by permission of Cambridge University Press.

[1] At the University of California, Berkeley, under a benefaction in the names of Agnes and Constantine Foerster. I am grateful to the Committee for inviting me to give the 1972 lecture in this series.

boredom, indifference and coldness. Everything is joyless: 'in the end it is the same', she says, 'singing and silence'. She refuses to take the elixir again; she dies; and the formula is deliberately destroyed by a young woman among the protests of some older men.

EM's state suggests at least this, that death is not necessarily an evil, and not just in the sense in which almost everybody would agree to that, where death provides an end to great suffering, but in the more intimate sense that it can be a good thing not to live too long. It suggests more than that, for it suggests that it was not a peculiarity of EM's that an endless life was meaningless. That is something I shall follow out later. First, though, we should put together the suggestion of EM's case, that death is not necessarily an evil, with the claim of some philosophies and religions that death is necessarily not an evil. Notoriously, there have been found two contrary bases on which that claim can be mounted: death is said by some not to be an evil because it is not the end, and by others, because it is. There is perhaps some profound temperamental difference between those who find consolation for the fact of death in the hope that it is only the start of another life, and those who equally find comfort in the conviction that it is the end of the only life there is. That both such temperaments exist means that those who find a diagnosis of the belief in immortality, and indeed a reproach to it, in the idea that it constitutes a consolation, have at best only a statistical fact to support them. While that may be just about enough for the diagnosis, it is not enough for the reproach.

Most famous, perhaps, among those who have found comfort in the second option, the prospect of annihilation, was Lucretius, who, in the steps of Epicurus, and probably from a personal fear of death which in some of his pages seems almost tangible, addresses himself to proving that death is never an evil. Lucretius has two basic arguments for this conclusion, and it is an important feature of them both that the conclusion they offer has the very strong consequence—and seems clearly intended to have the consequence— that, for oneself at least, it is all the same whenever one dies, that a long life is no better than a short one. That is to say, death is never an evil in the sense not merely that there is no-one for whom dying is an evil, but that there is no time at which dying is an evil—sooner or later, it is all the same.

The first argument[2] seeks to interpret the fear of death as a confusion, based on the idea that we shall be there after death to repine our loss of the *praemia vitae,* the rewards and delights of life, and to be upset at the spectacle of our bodies burned, and so forth. The fear of death, it is suggested, must necessarily be the fear of some experiences had when one is dead. But if death is annihilation, then there are no such experiences: in the Epicurean phrase, when death is there, we are not, and when we are there, death is not. So, death

---

[2] *de Rerum Natura* III, 870 *seq*, 898 *seq*.

being annihilation, there is nothing to fear. The second argument[3] addresses itself directly to the question of whether one dies earlier or later, and says that one will be the same time dead however early or late one dies, and therefore one might as well die earlier as later. And from both arguments we can conclude *nil igitur mors est ad nos, neque pertinet hilum*—death is nothing to us, and does not matter at all.[4]

The second of these arguments seems even on the face of things to contradict the first. For it must imply that if there *were* a finite period of death, such that if you died later you would be dead for less time, then there *would* be some point in wanting to die later rather than earlier. But that implication makes sense, surely, only on the supposition that what is wrong with dying consists in something undesirable about the condition of being dead. And that is what is denied by the first argument.

More important than this, the oddness of the second argument can help to focus a difficulty already implicit in the first. The first argument, in locating the objection to dying in a confused objection to being dead, and exposing that in terms of a confusion with being alive, takes it as genuinely true of life that the satisfaction of desire, and possession of the *praemia vitae*, are good things. It is not irrational to be upset by the loss of home, children, possessions—what is irrational is to think of death as, in the relevant sense, *losing* anything. But now if we consider two lives, one very short and cut off before the *praemia* have been acquired, the other fully provided with the *praemia* and containing their enjoyment to a ripe age, it is very difficult to see why the second life, by these standards alone, is not to be thought better than the first. But if it is, then there must be something wrong with the argument which tries to show that there is nothing worse about a short life than a long one. The argument locates the mistake about dying in a mistake about consciousness, it being assumed that what commonsense thinks about the worth of the *praemia vitae* and the sadness of their (conscious) loss is sound enough. But if the *praemia vitae* are valuable; even if we include as necessary to that value consciousness that one possesses them; then surely getting to the point of possessing them is better than not getting to that point, longer enjoyment of them is better than shorter, and more of them, other things being equal, is better than less of them. But if so, then it just will not be true that to die earlier is all the same as to die later, nor that death is never an evil—and the thought that to die later is better than to die earlier will not be dependent on some muddle about thinking that the dead person will be alive to lament his loss. It will depend only on the idea, apparently sound, that if the *praemia vitae* and consciousness of them are good things, then longer consciousness of more *praemia* is better than shorter consciousness of fewer *praemia*.

---

[3]*Ibid*, 1091.

[4]*Ibid*, 830.

Is the idea sound? A decent argument, surely, can be marshalled to support it. If I desire something, then, other things being equal, I prefer a state of affairs in which I get it from one in which I do not get it, and (again, other things being equal) plan for a future in which I get it rather than not. But one future, for sure, in which I would not get it would be one in which I was dead. To want something, we may also say, is to that extent to have reason for resisting what excludes having that thing: and death certainly does that, for a very large range of things that one wants.[5] If that is right, then for any of those things, wanting something itself gives one a reason for avoiding death. Even though if I do not succeed, I will not know that, nor what I am missing, from the perspective of the wanting agent it is rational to aim for states of affairs in which his want is satisfied, and hence to regard death as something to be avoided; that is, to regard it as an evil.

It is admittedly true that many of the things I want, I want only on the assumption that I am going to be alive; and some people, for instance some of the old, desperately want certain things when nevertheless they would much rather that they and their wants were dead. It might be suggested that not just these special cases, but really all wants, were conditional on being alive; a situation in which one has ceased to exist is not to be compared with others with respect to desire-satisfaction—rather, if one dies, all bets are off. But surely the claim that all desires are in this sense conditional must be wrong. For consider the idea of a rational forward-looking calculation of suicide: there can be such a thing, even if many suicides are not rational, and even though with some that are, it may be unclear to what extent they are forward-looking (the obscurity of this with regard to suicides of honour is an obscurity in the notion of shame). In such a calculation, a man might consider what lay before him, and decide whether he did or did not want to undergo it. If he does decide to undergo it, then some desire propels him on into the future, and *that* desire at least is not one that operates conditionally on his being alive, since it itself resolves the question of whether he is going to be alive. He has an unconditional, or (as I shall say) a *categorical* desire.

The man who seriously calculates about suicide and rejects it, only just has such a desire, perhaps. But if one is in a state in which the question of suicide does not occur, or occurs only as total fantasy—if, to take just one example, one is happy—one has many such desires, which do not hang from the assumption of one's existence. If they did hang from that assumption, then they would be quite powerless to rule out that assumption's being questioned, or to answer the question if it is raised; but clearly they are not

---

[5]Obviously the principle is not exceptionless. For one thing, one can want to be dead: the content of that desire may be obscure, but whatever it is, a man presumably cannot be *prevented* from getting it by dying. More generally, the principle does not apply to what I elsewhere call *non-I desire*: for an account of these, see 'Egoism and Altruism', pp. 260 *seq*. They do not affect the present discussion, which is within the limits of egoistic rationality.

powerless in those directions—on the contrary they are some of the few things, perhaps the only things, that have power in that direction. Some ascetics have supposed that happiness required reducing one's desires to those necessary for one's existence, that is, to those that one has to have granted that one exists at all; rather, it requires that some of one's desires should be fully categorical, and one's existence itself wanted as something necessary to them.

To suppose that one can in this way categorically want things implies a number of things about the nature of desire. It implies, for one thing, that the reason I have for bringing it about that I get what I want is not merely that of avoiding the unpleasantness of not getting what I want. But that must in any case be right—otherwise we should have to represent every desire as the desire to avoid its own frustration, which is absurd.

About what those categorical desires must be, there is not much of great generality to be said, if one is looking at the happy state of things: except, once more against the ascetic, that there should be not just enough, but more than enough. But the question might be raised, at the impoverished end of things, as to what the minimum categorical desire might be. Could it be *just* the desire to remain alive? The answer is perhaps 'no'. In saying that, I do not want to deny the existence, the value, or the basic necessity of a sheer reactive drive to self-preservation: humanity would certainly wither if the drive to keep alive were not stronger than any perceived reasons for keeping alive. But if the question is asked, and it is going to be answered calculatively, then the bare categorical desire to stay alive will not sustain the calculation— that desire itself, when things have got that far, has to be sustained or filled out by some desire for something else, even if it is only, at the margin, the desire that future desires of mine will be born and satisfied. But the best insight into the effect of categorical desire is not gained at the impoverished end of things, and hence in situations where the question has actually come up. The question of life being desirable is certainly transcendental in the most modest sense, in that it gets by far its best answer in never being asked at all.

None of this—including the thoughts of the calculative suicide—requires my reflection on a world in which I never occur at all. In the terms of 'possible worlds' (which can admittedly be misleading), a man could, on the present account, have a reason from his own point of view to prefer a possible world in which he went on longer to one in which he went on for less long, or—like the suicide—the opposite; but he would have no reason of this kind to prefer a world in which he did not occur at all. Thoughts about his total absence from the world would have to be of a different kind, impersonal reflections on the value *for the world* of his presence or absence: of the same kind, essentially, as he could conduct (or, more probably, not manage to conduct) with regard to anyone else. While he can think egoistically of what it would be for him to live longer or less long, he cannot think egoistically of what it would be for him never to have existed at all. Hence the sombre words of Sophocles[6] 'Never to have been born counts highest of all…' are well met by the old Jewish reply—'how many are so lucky? Not one in ten thousand'.

Lucretius' first argument has been interestingly criticised by Thomas Nagel,[7] on lines different from those that I have been following. Nagel claims that what is wrong with Lucretius' argument is that it rests on the assumption that nothing can be a misfortune for a man unless he knows about it, and that misfortunes must consist in something nasty *for* him. Against this assumption, Nagel cites a number of plausible counter-instances, of circumstances which would normally be thought to constitute a misfortune, though those to whom they happen are and remain ignorant of them (as, for instance, certain situations of betrayal). The difference between Nagel's approach and mine does not, of course, lie in the mere point of whether one admits misfortunes which do not consist of or involve nasty experiences: anyone who rejects Lucretius' argument must admit them. The difference is that the reasons which a man would have for avoiding death are, on the present account, grounded in desires—categorical desires—which he has; he, on the basis of these, has reason to regard possible death as a misfortune to be avoided, and we, looking at things from his point of view, would have reason to regard his actual death as his misfortune. Nagel, however, if I understand him, does not see the misfortune that befalls a man who dies as necessarily grounded in the issue of what desires or sorts of desires he had; just as in the betrayal case, it could be a misfortune for a man to be betrayed, even though he did not have any desire not to be betrayed. If this is a correct account, Nagel's reasoning is one step further away from Utilitarianism on this matter than mine,[8] and rests on an independent kind of value which a sufficiently Utilitarian person might just reject; while my argument cannot merely be rejected by a Utilitarian person, it seems to me, since he must if he is to be consistent, and other things being equal, attach disutility to any situation which he has good reason to prevent, and he certainly has good reason to prevent a situation which involves the non-satisfaction of his desires. Thus, granted categorical desires, death has a disutility for an agent, although that disutility does not, of course, consist in unsatisfactory experiences involved in its occurrence.

The question would remain, of course, with regard to any given agent, whether he had categorical desires. For the present argument, it will do to leave it as a contingent fact that most people do: for they will have a reason, and a perfectly coherent reason, to regard death as a misfortune, while it was Lucretius' claim that no-one could have a coherent reason for so regarding it.

---

[6] *Oedipus at Colonus* 1224 *seq.*

[7] 'Death', *NOÛS* IV.1 (1970), pp. 73 *seq.* Reprinted with some alterations in Rachels ed., *Moral Problems*.

[8] Though my argument does not in any sense imply Utilitarianism; for some further considerations on this, see the final paragraphs of this paper.

There may well be other reasons as well; thus Nagel's reasoning, though different from the more Utilitarian type of reason I have used against Lucretius, seems compatible with it and there are strong reasons to adopt his kind of consideration as well. In fact, further and deeper thought about this question seems likely to fill up the apparent gap between the two sorts of argument; it is hard to believe, for one thing, that the supposed contingent fact that people have categorical desires can really be as contingent as all that. One last point about the two arguments is that they coincide in not offering— as I mentioned earlier—any considerations about worlds in which one does not occur at all; but there is perhaps an additional reason why this should be so in the Utilitarian-type argument, over and above the one it shares with Nagel's. The reason it shares with Nagel's is that the type of misfortune we are concerned with in thinking about X's death is X's misfortune (as opposed to the misfortunes of the state or whatever); and whatever sort of misfortune it may be in a given possible world that X does not occur in it, it is not X's misfortune. They share the feature, then, that for anything to be X's misfortune in a given world, then X must occur in that world. But the Utilitarian-type argument further grounds the misfortune, if there is one, in certain features of X, namely his desires; and if there is no X in a given world, then *a fortiori* there are no such grounds.

But now—if death, other things being equal, is a misfortune; and a longer life is better than a shorter life; and we reject the Lucretian argument that it does not matter when one dies; then it looks as though—other things always being equal—death is at any time an evil, and it is always better to live than die. Nagel indeed, from his point of view, does seem to permit that conclusion, even though he admits some remarks about the natural term of life and the greater misfortune of dying in one's prime. But wider consequences follow. For if all that is true, then it looks as though it would be not only always better to live, but better to live always, that is, never to die. If Lucretius is wrong, we seem committed to wanting to be immortal.

That would be, as has been repeatedly said, with other things equal. No-one need deny that since, for instance, we grow old and our powers decline, much may happen to increase the reasons for thinking death a good thing. But these are contingencies. We might not age; perhaps, one day, it will be possible for some of us not to age. If that were so, would it not follow then that, more life being *per se* better than less life, we should have reason so far as that went (but not necessarily in terms of other inhabitants) to live for ever? EM indeed bears strong, if fictional, witness against the desirability of that; but perhaps she still laboured under some contingent limitations, social or psychological, which might once more be eliminated to bring it about that really other things were equal. Against this, I am going to suggest that the supposed contingencies are not really contingencies; that an endless life would be a meaningless one; and that we could have no reason for living eternally a human life. There is no desirable or significant property which life would have more of, or have more unqualifiedly, if we lasted for ever. In some part, we can apply to life Aristotle's marvellous remark about Plato's Form of the Good:[9] 'nor will it be any the more good for being eternal: that which lasts long is no whiter than that which perishes in a day'. But only in part; for, rejecting Lucretius, we have already admitted that more days may give us more than one day can.

If one pictures living for ever as living as an embodied person in the world rather as it is, it will be a question, and not so trivial as may seem, of what age one eternally is. EM was 342; because for 300 years she had been 42. This choice (if it was a choice) I am personally, and at present, well disposed to salute—if one had to spend eternity at any age, that seems an admirable age to spend it at. Nor would it necessarily be a less good age for a woman: that at least was not EM's problem, that she was too old at the age she continued to be at. Her problem lay in having been at it for too long. Her trouble was it seems, boredom: a boredom connected with the fact that everything that could happen and make sense to one particular human being of 42 had already happened to her. Or, rather, all the sorts of things that could make sense to one woman of a certain character; for EM has a certain character, and indeed, except for her accumulating memories of earlier times, and no doubt some changes of style to suit the passing centuries, seems always to have been much the same sort of person.

There are difficult questions, if one presses the issue, about this constancy of character. How is this accumulation of memories related to this character which she eternally has, and to the character of her existence? Are they much the same kind of events repeated? Then it is itself strange that she allows them to be repeated, accepting the same repetitions, the same limitations—indeed, *accepting* is what it later becomes, when earlier it would not, or even could not, have been that. The repeated patterns of personal relations, for instance, must take on a character of being inescapable. Or is the pattern of her experiences not repetitious in this way, but varied? Then the problem shifts, to the relation between these varied experiences, and the fixed character: how can it remain fixed, through an endless series of very various experiences? The experiences must surely happen to her without really affecting her; she must be, as EM is, detached and withdrawn.

EM, of course, is in a world of people who do not share her condition, and that determines certain features of the life she has to lead, as that any personal relationship requires peculiar kinds of concealment. That, at least, is a form of isolation which would disappear if her condition were generalised. But to suppose more generally that boredom and inner death would be eliminated if everyone were similarly becalmed, is an empty hope: it would be a world of Bourbons, learning nothing and forgetting nothing, and it is unclear how much could even happen.

---

[9]*Ethica Nicomachea* 1096^b 4.

The more one reflects to any realistic degree on the conditions of EM's unending life, the less it seems a mere contingency that it froze up as it did. That it is not a contingency, is suggested also by the fact that the reflections can sustain themselves independently of any question of the particular character that EM had; it is enough, almost, that she has a human character at all. Perhaps not quite. One sort of character for which the difficulties of unending life would have less significance than they proved to have for EM might be one who at the beginning was more like what she is at the end: cold, withdrawn, already frozen. For him, the prospect of unending cold is presumably less bleak in that he is used to it. But with him, the question can shift to a different place, as to why he wants the unending life at all; for, the more he is at the beginning like EM is at the end, the less place there is for categorical desire to keep him going, and to resist the desire for death. In EM's case, her boredom and distance from life both kill desire and consist in the death of it; one who is already enough like that to sustain life in those conditions may well be one who had nothing to make him want to do so. But even if he has, and we conceive of a person who is stonily resolved to sustain for ever an already stony existence, his possibility will be of no comfort to those, one hopes a larger party, who want to live longer because they want to live more.

To meet the basic anti-Lucretian hope for continuing life which is grounded in categorical desire, EM's unending life in this world is inadequate, and necessarily so relative to just those desires and conceptions of character which go into the hope. That is very important, since it is the most direct response, that which should have been adequate if the hope is both coherent and what it initially seemed to be. It also satisfied one of two important conditions which must be satisfied by anything which is to be adequate as a fulfilment of my anti-Lucretian hope, namely that it should clearly be *me* who lives for ever. The second important condition is that the state in which I survive should be one which, to me looking forward, will be adequately related, in the life it presents, to those aims which I now have in wanting to survive at all. That is a vague formula, and necessarily so, for what exactly that relation will be must depend to some extent on what kind of aims and (as one might say) prospects for myself I now have. What we can say is that since I am propelled forward into longer life by categorical desires, what is promised must hold out some hopes for those desires. The limiting case of this might be that the promised life held out some hope just to that desire mentioned before, that future desires of mine will be born and satisfied; but if that were the only categorical desire that carried me forward into it, at least this seems demanded, that any image I have of those future desires should make it comprehensible to me how in terms of my character they could be my desires.

This second condition, the EM kind of survival failed, on reflection, to satisfy; but at least it is clear why, before reflection, it looked as though it might satisfy the condition—it consists, after all, in just going on in ways in which we are quite used to going on. If we turn away from EM to more remote kinds of survival, the problems of those two conditions press more heavily right from the beginning. Since the major problems of the EM situation lay in the indefinite extension of one life, a tempting alternative is survival by means of an indefinite series of lives. Most, perhaps all, versions of this belief which have actually existed have immediately failed the first condition: they get nowhere near providing any consideration to mark the difference between rebirth and new birth. But let us suppose the problem, in some way or another, removed; some conditions of bodily continuity, minimally sufficient for personal identity, may be supposed satisfied. (Anyone who thinks that no such conditions could be sufficient, and requires, for instance, conditions of memory, may well find it correspondingly difficult to find an alternative for survival in this direction which both satisfies the first requirement, of identity, and also adequately avoids the difficulties of the EM alternative.) The problem remains of whether this series of psychologically disjoint lives could be an object of hope to one who did not want to die. That is, in my view, a different question from the question of whether it will be him—which is why I distinguished originally two different requirements to be satisfied. But it is a question; and even if the first requirement be supposed satisfied, it is exceedingly unclear that the second can be. This will be so, even if one were to accept the idea, itself problematical, that one could have reason to fear the future pain of someone who was merely bodily continuous with one as one now is.[10]

There are in the first place certain difficulties about how much a man could consistently be allowed to know about the series of his lives, if we are to preserve the psychological disjointness which is the feature of this model. It might be that each would in fact have to seem to him as though it were his only life, and that he could not have grounds for being sure what, or even that, later lives were to come. If so, then no comfort or hope will be forthcoming in this model to those who want to go on living. More interesting questions, however, concern the man's relation to a future life of which he did get some advance idea. If we could allow the idea that he could fear pain which was going to occur in that life, then we have at least provided him with one kind of reason which might move him to opt out of that life, and destroy himself (being recurrent, under conditions of bodily continuity, would not make one indestructible). But physical pain and its nastiness are to the maximum degree independent of what one's desires and character are, and the degree of identification needed with the later life to reject that aspect of it is absolutely minimal. Beyond that point, however, it is unclear how he is

---

[10]One possible conclusion from the dilemma discussed in 'The Self and the Future'. For the point, mentioned below, of the independence of physical pain from psychological change, see p. 54.

to bring this later character and its desires into a relation to his present ones, so as to be satisfied or the reverse with this marginal promise of continued existence. If he can regard this future life as an object of hope, then equally it must be possible for him to regard it with alarm, or depression, and—as in the simple pain case—opt out of it. If we cannot make sense of his entertaining that choice, then we have not made sense of this future life being adequately related to his present life, so that it could, alternatively, be something he might want in wanting not to die. But can we clearly make sense of that choice? For if we—or he—merely wipe out his present character and desires, there is nothing left by which he can judge it at all, at least as something *for him;* while if we leave them in, we—and he—apply something irrelevant to that future life, since (to adapt the Epicurean phrase), when they are there, it is not, and when it is there, they are not. We might imagine him considering the future prospects, and agreeing to go on if he found them congenial. But that is a muddled picture. For whether they are congenial to him as he is now must be beside the point, and the idea that it is not beside the point depends on carrying over into the case features that do not belong to it, as (perhaps) that he will remember later what he wanted in the earlier life. And when we admit that it is beside the point whether the prospects are congenial, then the force of the idea that the future life could be something that he *now* wanted to go on to, fades.

There are important and still obscure issues here,[11] but perhaps enough has been said to cast doubt on this option as coherently satisfying the desire to stay alive. While few will be disposed to think that much can be made of it, I must confess that out of the alternatives it is the only one that for me would, if it made sense, have any attraction—no doubt because it is the only one which has the feature that what one is living at any given point is actually *a life.* It is singular that those systems of belief that get closest to actually accepting recurrence of this sort seem, almost without exception, to look forward to the point when one will be released from it. Such systems seem less interested in continuing one's life than in earning one the right to a superior sort of death.

The serial and disjoint lives are at least more attractive than the attempt which some have made, to combine the best of continuous and of serial existence in a fantasy of very varied lives which are nevertheless cumulatively effective in memory. This might be called the *Teiresias* model. As that case singularly demonstrates, it has the quality of a fantasy, of emotional pressure trying to combine the uncombinable. One thing that the fantasy has to ignore is the connexion, both as cause and as consequence, between having one range of experiences rather than another, wishing to engage in one sort

---

[11]For a detailed discussion of closely related questions, though in a different framework, see Derek Parfit, 'Personal Identity', *The Philosophical Review*, LXXX (1971), pp. 3–27.

of thing rather than another, and having a character. Teiresias cannot have a character, either continuously through these proceedings, or cumulatively at the end (if there were to be an end) of them: he is not, eventually, a person but a phenomenon.

In discussing the last models, we have moved a little away from the very direct response which EM's case seemed to provide to the hope that one would never die. But perhaps we have moved not nearly far enough. Nothing of this, and nothing much like this, was in the minds of many who have hoped for immortality; for it was not in this world that they hoped to live for ever. As one might say, their hope was not so much that they would never die as that they would live after their death, and while that in its turn can be represented as the hope that one would not really die, or, again, that it was not really oneself that would die, the change of formulation could point to an after-life sufficiently unlike this life, perhaps, to earth the current of doubt that flows from EM's frozen boredom.

But in fact this hope has been and could only be modelled on some image of a more familiar untiring or unresting or unflagging activity or satisfaction; and what is essentially EM's problem, one way or another, remains. In general we can ask, what it is about the imaged activities of an eternal life which would stave off the principle hazard to which EM succumbed, boredom. The Don Juan in Hell joke, that heaven's prospects are tedious and the devil has the best tunes, though a tired fancy in itself, at least serves to show up a real and (I suspect) a profound difficulty, of providing any model of an unending, supposedly satisfying, state or activity which would not rightly prove boring to anyone who remained conscious of himself and who had acquired a character, interests, tastes and impatiences in the course of living, already, a finite life. The point is not that for such a man boredom would be a tiresome consequence of the supposed states or activities, and that they would be objectionable just on the utilitarian or hedonistic ground that they had this disagreeable feature. If that were all there was to it, we could imagine the feature away, along no doubt with other disagreeable features of human life in its present imperfection. The point is rather that boredom, as sometimes in more ordinary circumstances, would be not just a tiresome effect, but a reaction almost perceptual in character to the poverty of one's relation to the environment. Nothing less will do for eternity than something that makes boredom *unthinkable*. What could that be? Something that could be guaranteed to be at every moment utterly absorbing? But if a man has and retains a character, there is no reason to suppose that there is anything that could be that. If, lacking a conception of the guaranteedly absorbing activity, one tries merely to think away the reaction of boredom, one is no longer supposing an improvement in the circumstances, but merely an impoverishment in his consciousness of them. Just as being bored can be a sign of not noticing, understanding or appreciating enough, so equally not being bored can be a sign of not noticing, or not reflecting, enough. One might make the immortal man content at every moment, by just stripping off from him consciousness which would have brought discontent by reminding him of other times, other interests, other possibilities. Perhaps, indeed, that is what we have already done, in a more tempting way, by picturing him just now as at every moment totally absorbed—but that is something we shall come back to.

Of course there is in actual life such a thing as justified but necessary boredom. Thus—to take a not entirely typical example—someone who was, or who thought himself, devoted to the radical cause might eventually admit to himself that he found a lot of its rhetoric excruciatingly boring. He might think that he ought not to feel that, that the reaction was wrong, and merely represented an unworthiness of his, an unregenerate remnant of intellectual superiority. However, he might rather feel that it would not necessarily be a better world in which no-one was bored by such rhetoric and that boredom was, indeed, a perfectly worthy reaction to this rhetoric after all this time; but for all that, the rhetoric might be necessary. A man at arms can get cramp from standing too long at his post, but sentry-duty can after all be necessary. But the threat of monotony in eternal activities could not be dealt with in that way, by regarding immortal boredom as an unavoidable ache derived from standing ceaselessly at one's post. (This is one reason why I said that boredom in eternity would have to be *unthinkable*.) For the question would be unavoidable, in what campaign one was supposed to be serving, what one's ceaseless sentry-watch was for.

Some philosophers have pictured an eternal existence as occupied in something like intense intellectual enquiry. Why that might seem to solve the problem, at least for them, is obvious. The activity is engrossing, self-justifying, affords, as it may appear, endless new perspectives, and by being engrossing enables one to lose oneself. It is that last feature that supposedly makes boredom unthinkable, by providing something that is, in that earlier phrase, at every moment totally absorbing. But if one is totally and perpetually absorbed in such an activity, and loses oneself in it, then as those words suggest, we come back to the problem of satisfying the conditions that it should be me who lives for ever, and that the eternal life should be in prospect of some interest. Let us leave aside the question of people whose characteristic and most personal interests are remote from such pursuits, and for whom, correspondingly, an immortality promised in terms of intellectual activity is going to make heavy demands on some theory of a 'real self' which will have to emerge at death. More interesting is the content and value of the promise for a person who is, in this life, disposed to those activities. For looking at such a person as he now is, it seems quite unreasonable to suppose that those activities would have the fulfilling or liberating character that they do have for him, if they were in fact all he could do or conceive of doing. If they are genuinely fulfilling, and do not operate (as they can) merely as a compulsive diversion, then the ground and shape of the satisfactions that the intellectual enquiry offers him, will relate to *him*, and not just to the enquiry. The *Platonic introjection*, seeing the satisfactions of studying what is timeless and impersonal as being themselves timeless and impersonal, may be a deep illusion, but it is certainly an illusion.

We can see better into that illusion by considering Spinoza's thought, that intellectual activity was the most active and free state that a man could be in, and that a man who had risen to such activity was in some sense most fully individual, most fully himself. This conclusion has been sympathetically expounded by Stuart Hampshire, who finds on this point a similar doctrine in Spinoza and in Freud:[12] in particular, he writes '[one's] only means of achieving this distinctness as an individual, this freedom in relation to the common order of nature, is the power of the mind freely to follow in its thought an intellectual order'. The contrast to this free intellectual activity is 'the common condition of men that their conduct and their judgements of value, their desires and aversions, are in each individual determined by unconscious memories'—a process which the same writer has elsewhere associated with our having any character at all as individuals.[13]

Hampshire claims that in pure intellectual activity the mind is most free because it is then least determined by causes outside its immediate states. I take him to mean that rational activity is that in which the occurrence of an earlier thought maximally explains the occurrence of a later thought, because it is the rational relation between their contents which, granted the occurrence of the first, explains the occurrence of the second. But even the maximal explanatory power, in these terms, of the earlier thought does not extend to total explanation: for it will still require explanation why this thinker on this occasion continued on this rational path of thought at all. Thus I am not sure that the Spinozist consideration which Hampshire advances even gives a very satisfactory sense to the *activity* of the mind. It leaves out, as the last point shows, the driving power which is needed to sustain one even in the most narrowly rational thought. It is still further remote from any notion of creativity, since that, even within a theoretical context, and certainly in an artistic one, precisely implies the origination of ideas which are not fully predictable in terms of the content of existing ideas. But even if it could yield one sense for 'activity', it would still offer very little, despite Spinoza's heroic defence of the notion, for *freedom*. Or—to put it another way—even if it offered something for freedom of the intellect, it offers nothing for freedom of the individual. For when freedom is initially understood as the absence of 'outside' determination, and in particular understood in those terms as an unquestionable *value*, my freedom is reasonably not taken to include freedom

---

[12] *Spinoza and the Idea of Freedom*, reprinted in *Freedom of Mind* (Oxford: Clarendon Press, 1972), pp. 183 *seq*; the two quotations are from pp. 206–7.

[13] *Disposition and Memory, Freedom of Mind*, pp. 160 *seq*; see especially pp. 176–7.

from my past, my character and my desires. To suppose that those are, in the relevant sense, 'outside' determinations, is merely to beg the vital question about the boundaries of the self, and not to prove from premises acceptable to any clear-headed man who desires freedom that the boundaries of the self should be drawn round the intellect. On the contrary, the desire for freedom can, and should, be seen as the desire to be free in the exercise and development of character, not as the desire to be free of it. And if Hampshire and others are right in claiming that an individual character springs from and gets its energies from unconscious memories and unclear desires, then the individual must see them too as within the boundaries of the self, and themselves involved in the drive to persist in life and activity.

With this loss, under the Spinozist conception, of the individual's character, there is, contrary to Hampshire's claim, a loss of individuality itself, and certainly of anything that could make an eternity of intellectual activity, so construed, a reasonable object of interest to one concerned with individual immortality. As those who totally wish to lose themselves in the movement can consistently only hope that the movement will go on, so the consistent Spinozist—at least on this account of Spinozism—can only hope that the intellectual activity goes on, something which could be as well realised in the existence of Aristotle's prime mover, perhaps, as in anything to do with Spinoza or any other particular man.

Stepping back now from the extremes of Spinozist abstraction, I shall end by returning to a point from which we set out, the sheer desire to go on living, and shall mention a writer on this subject, Unamuno, whose work *The Tragic Sense of Life*[14] gives perhaps more extreme expression than anyone else has done to that most basic form of the desire to be immortal, the desire not to die.

> I do not want to die—no, I neither want to die nor do I want to want to die; I want to live for ever and ever and ever. I want this 'I' to live—this poor 'I' that I am and that I feel myself to be here and now, and therefore the problem of the duration of my soul, of my own soul, tortures me.'[15]

Although Unamuno frequently refers to Spinoza, the spirit of this is certainly far removed from that of the 'sorrowful Jew of Amsterdam'. Furthermore, in his clear insistence that what he desperately wants is this life, the life of this self, not to end, Unamuno reveals himself at equal removes from Manicheanism and from Utilitarianism; and that is correct, for the one is only the one-legged descendant of the other. That tradition—Manichean, Orphic, Platonic, Augustinian—which contrasts the spirit and the body in

---

[14]*Del sentimiento trágico de la vida*, translated by J. E. Crawford Flitch (London: 1921). Page references are to the Fontana Library edition, 1962.

[15]*Ibid.*, p. 60.

such a sense that the spiritual aims at eternity, truth and salvation, while the body is adjusted to pleasure, the temporary, and eventual dissolution, is still represented, as to fifty per cent, by secular Utilitarianism: it is just one of the original pair of boots left by itself and better regarded now that the other has fallen into disrepair. Bodies are all that we have or are: hence for Utilitarianism it *follows* that the only focus of our arrangements can be the efficient organisation of happiness. Immortality, certainly, is out, and so life here should last as long as we determine—or eventually, one may suspect, others will determine—that it is pleasant for us to be around.

Unamuno's outlook is at the opposite pole to this and whatever else may be wrong with it, it salutes the true idea that the meaning of life does not consist either in the management of satisfactions in a body or in an abstract immortality without one. On the one hand he had no time for Manicheanism, and admired the rather brutal Catholic faith which could express its hopes for a future life in the words which he knew on a tombstone in Bilbao:[16]

> Aunque estamos in polvo convertidos
> en Ti, Señor, nuestra esperanza fía,
> que tornaremos a vivir vestidos
> con la carne y la piel que nos cubria.

At the same time, his desire to remain alive extends an almost incomprehensible distance beyond any desire to continue agreeable experiences:

> For myself I can say that as a youth and even as a child I remained unmoved when shown the most moving pictures of hell, for even then nothing appeared quite so horrible to me as nothingness itself.[17]

The most that I have claimed earlier against Lucretius is not enough to make that preference intelligible to me. The fear of sheer nothingness is certainly part of what Lucretius rightly, if too lightly, hoped to exorcise; and the *mere* desire to stay alive, which is here stretched to its limit, is not enough (I suggested before) to answer the question, once the question has come up and requires an answer in rational terms. Yet Unamuno's affirmation of existence even through limitless suffering[18] brings out something which is implicit in the claim against Lucretius. It is not necessarily the prospect of pleasant times

---

[16]*Ibid.*, p. 79.

[17]*Ibid.*, p. 28.

[18]An affirmation which takes on a special dignity retrospectively in the light of his own death shortly after his courageous speech against Millán Astray and the obscene slogan '¡Viva la Muerte!' See Hugh Thomas, *The Spanish Civil War* (Harmondsworth: Pelican, 1961), pp. 442–4.

that creates the motive against dying, but the existence of categorical desire, and categorical desire can drive through both the existence and the prospect of unpleasant times.

Suppose, then, that categorical desire does sustain the desire to live. So long as it remains so, I shall want not to die. Yet I also know, if what has gone before is right, that an eternal life would be unliveable. In part, as EM's case originally suggested, that is because categorical desire will go away from it: in those versions, such as hers, in which I am recognisably myself, I would eventually have had altogether too much of myself. There are good reasons, surely, for dying before that happens. But equally, at times earlier than that moment, there is reason for not dying. Necessarily, it tends to be either too early or too late. EM reminds us that it can be too late, and many, as against Lucretius, need no reminding that it can be too early. If that is any sort of dilemma, it can, as things still are and if one is exceptionally lucky, be resolved, not by doing anything, but just by dying shortly before the horrors of not doing so become evident. Technical progress may, in more than one direction, make that piece of luck rarer. But as things are, it is possible to be, in contrast to EM, *felix opportunitate mortis*—as it can be appropriately mistranslated, lucky in having the chance to die.